THE CAMBRIDGE
COMPANION TO

THE LITERATURE OF
THE FIRST WORLD WAR

EDITED BY
VINCENT SHERRY

CAMBRIDGE
UNIVERSITY PRESS

CAMBRIDGE UNIVERSITY PRESS
Cambridge, New York, Melbourne, Madrid, Cape Town, Singapore, São Paulo

Cambridge University Press
The Edinburgh Building, Cambridge CB2 8RU, UK

Published in the United States of America by Cambridge University Press, New York

www.cambridge.org
Information on this title: www.cambridge.org/9780521821452

First published 2005

A catalogue record for this publication is available from the British Library

Library of Congress Cataloguing in Publication data
The Cambridge companion to the literature of the First World War / edited by Vincent Sherry.
p.   cm. – (Cambridge companions to literature)
Includes bibliographical references and index.
ISBN 0 521 82145 2 (alk. paper) – ISBN 0 521 52897 6 (pbk. : alk. paper)
1. Literature, Modern – 20th century – History and criticism.   2. World War, 1914–1918 –
Literature and the war.   I. Sherry, Vincent B.   II. Series.
PN771.C27   2004
809′.93358 – dc22   2004054230

ISBN 978-0-521-82145-2 hardback
ISBN 978-0-521-52897-9 paperback

Transferred to digital printing 2008

The Cambridge Companion to the Literature of the First World War

The Great War of 1914–18 marks a turning point in modern history and culture. This *Companion* offers critical overviews of the major literary genres and social contexts that define the study of the writings produced by the First World War. The volume comprises original essays by distinguished scholars of international reputation, who examine the impact of the war on the major national literatures, principally those of Great Britain, Germany, France, and the United States. Additional consideration is given to the way the war affected modernism, the European avant-garde, film, and women's writing. A final section of essays addresses the legacy of the war in subsequent literary and popular culture. The *Companion* offers readers a chronology of key events and publication dates leading up through and following the war, and it provides a current bibliography of further reading organized by major scholarly topics.

Stanley Spencer, *The Resurrection of Soldiers*, in Sandham Memorial Chapel, Burghclere,
1928–29 (detail). © Estate of Stanley Spencer 2005. All rights reserved, DACS.
Photo © National Trust Photographic Library / A. C. Cooper

CONTENTS

ILLUSTRATIONS

NOTES ON CONTRIBUTORS

CATHARINE SAVAGE BROSMAN is Professor Emerita of French at Tulane University and Honorary Research Professor at the University of Sheffield. Her publications include *Malraux, Sartre, and Aragon as Political Novelists* (1964); *Art as Testimony: The Work of Jules Roy* (1989); *Visions of War in France: Fiction, Art, Ideology* (1999), as well as books on Gide, Martin du Gard, Sartre, Beauvoir, and Camus, various edited volumes, and many essays and articles.

CLAIRE BUCK teaches English at Wheaton College in Massachusetts. Her publications include *H. D. and Freud: Bisexuality and a Feminine Discourse* (1991); *The Bloomsbury Guide to Women's Literature* (1992); and many articles on women's writing. She is currently writing a study of English nationalism, dissident sexualities, and First World War writing.

JAMES CAMPBELL is Associate Professor and Coordinator of Graduate Studies in English at the University of Central Florida. His articles on First World War literature have appeared in *ELH* and *NLH*, and he is currently completing a book on sexuality, gnosis, and the literature of the war.

STANLEY CORNGOLD is Professor of German and Comparative Literature at Princeton University. He is presently completing a Norton Critical Edition of *Kafka's Selected Stories*. Other recent publications include *Lambent Traces: Franz Kafka* (2004); *Complex Pleasure: Forms of Feeling in German Literature* (1998); and *The Fate of the Self* (1994).

PAUL EDWARDS is Professor of English and History of Art at Bath Spa University College. He is the author of *Wyndham Lewis: Art and War* (1992) and *Wyndham Lewis: Painter and Writer* (2000). He has edited books on Vorticism and modernist London, as well as producing critical editions of several of Wyndham Lewis's books.

EDNA LONGLEY is Professor Emerita in the School of English, Queen's University, Belfast. Her books include *The Living Stream: Literature and*

Revisionism in Ireland (1994) and *Poetry & Posterity* (2000), and she has edited *The Bloodaxe Book of Twentieth-Century British and Irish Poetry* (2000).

LAURA MARCUS is Reader in English at the University of Sussex. Her publications include *Auto/biographical Discourses: Theory, Criticism, Practice* (1994); *Virginia Woolf: Writers and their Work* (1997); and *Freud's "The Interpretation of Dreams": New Interdisciplinary Essays* (1999). She has co-edited, with Peter Nicholls, *The Cambridge History of Twentieth-Century English Literature* (2004), and is currently working on a book on cinema, literature, and modernity.

JOHN T. MATTHEWS is Professor of English at Boston University. His books include *The Play of Faulkner's Language* (1982) and *"The Sound and the Fury": Faulkner and the Lost Cause* (1990). He has received an NEH fellowship for his current book-length study, *Raising the South: Southern Fictions and the Birth of a Modern Nation*. He is editing the *Blackwell Companion to the Modern American Novel* and *Faulkner, A Short Introduction: Seeing Through the South*.

SHARON OUDITT is Reader in Modern Literary Studies at Nottingham Trent University. She is author of *Fighting Forces, Writing Women: Identity and Ideology in the First World War* (1994); *Women Writers of the First World War: An Annotated Bibliography* (2000); and other publications on gender, literature, and European culture.

MARJORIE PERLOFF is Professor Emerita of English and Comparative Literature at Stanford University. Her most recent books are *21st Century Modernism* (2002) and *The Vienna Paradox* (2004). Her study of the avant-garde, *The Futurist Moment* (1986), has recently been reissued with a new introduction.

VINCENT SHERRY is Pierce Butler Professor of English at Tulane University. His books include *The Great War and the Language of Modernism* (2003); *James Joyce: Ulysses* (1994; 2004); *Ezra Pound, Wyndham Lewis, and Radical Modernism* (1993); and *The Uncommon Tongue: The Poetry and Criticism of Geoffrey Hill* (1987). He is currently writing a book on pan-European decadence and literary modernism in English.

DAVID TROTTER is King Edward VII Professor of English Literature at the University of Cambridge. His most recent books are *Cooking with Mud: The Idea of Mess in Nineteenth-Century Art and Fiction* (2000) and *Paranoid Modernism* (2001). He currently works on the history of early cinema.

CHRONOLOGY

1895: Crane, *The Red Badge of Courage*
1896: First modern Olympiad, Athens
1898: Zeppelin builds airship
1899: Anglo-Boer War (1899–1902)
1900: International Socialist Congress in Paris
First radio transmission of human voice
Freud, *Interpretation of Dreams*
1901: Death of Queen Victoria, Edward VII king
First Nobel Prizes awarded
1902: Stieglitz, *Camera Work*
1903: First airborne flight by Wright brothers
Emmeline Pankhurst founds Women's Social and Political Union in
Britain
Shaw, *Man and Superman*
1904: Russo-Japanese War (1904–5)
Anglo-French *entente*
Chekhov, *The Cherry Orchard*
Hardy, *The Dynasts* I (II, 1906; III, 1908)
1905: Isadora Duncan establishes first school of "modern dance," Berlin
Einstein publishes on Special Theory of Relativity
1906: Liberal party wins in British parliamentary elections
Doughty, *The Dawn in Britain*
Sinclair, *The Jungle*
Sorel, *Réflexions sur la violence*
1907: Anglo-Russian *entente*
First exhibit of "Cubism" in Paris
Conrad, *The Secret Agent*
1908: Gertrude Stein, *Three Lives*
1909: North Pole reached by Perry
Kandinsky's first abstract paintings

Diaghilev, Ballets Russes in Paris

Marinetti, *Futurist Manifesto*

Pound, *Personae*

Schönberg, *Five Orchestral Pieces*

1910: Death of Edward VII, George V king

Post-Impressionist exhibit in London

1911: Barrie, *Peter Pan*

Emma Goldman, *Anarchism and Other Essays*

1912: Social Democratic Party wins 110 seats in German Reichstag

Titanic sinks

Captain Scott's (lost) expedition to South Pole

Wars of Balkan States (1912–13)

Duchamp, *Nude Descending a Staircase*

Georgian Poetry 1911–12, ed. Sir Edward Marsh

1913: Stravinsky, *Le Sacre du printemps*

Einstein, *Theory of Relativity*

Proust, *Du côté de chez Swann*

Thomas Mann, *Tod in Venedig*

Blaise Cendrars, *La Prose du Transsibérien*

1914: Joyce, *Dubliners*

Frost, *North of Boston*

Burroughs, *Tarzan of the Apes*

Hardy, *Satires of Circumstance*

Des Imagistes: An Anthology, ed. Pound

Yeats, *Responsibilities*

Wyndham Lewis founds *Blast* as journal of Vorticism

Assassination of Jean Jaurès in Paris

28 June: Assassination of Archduke Franz Ferdinand, heir to throne of Austria-Hungary, in Sarajevo, Bosnia

28 July: Austria-Hungary declares war on Serbia

1 August: Germany declares war on Russia

3 August: Germany declares war on France

4 August: German troops enter Belgium

4 August: Great Britain declares war on Germany

4 August: United States President Wilson declares neutrality

11–12 August: Austro-Hungarian troops invade Serbia

22 August: Battle of Mons begins

26–29 August: Germans defeat Russians at Battle of Tannenberg

2 September: Writers convened for Government War Propaganda, London

6 September: Battle of the Marne begins

14 September: First Battle of Aisne begins

13 October–15 November: First Battle of Ypres

28 October: Turkey enters war on side of Central Powers

21 December: First German air raid on Britain

25 December: Christmas truce (unofficial), Western Front

Deaths in war: Charles Péguy, Alfred Lichtenstein, Georg Trakel

1915: 18 January: First German Zeppelin attacks on England

4 February: German U-boat attacks on Allied and neutral shipping; Germany declares blockade of Britain

18–19 March: Allied naval attack on Dardanelles

28 March: Sinking of first passenger ship, the British liner *Falaba*

April–June: German concentration on Eastern Front, driving Russians out of Poland

22 April: First gas attack, by Germans, at Ypres

25 April–10 August: Allied landings at Gallipoli

7 May: Sinking of the *Lusitania* causes diplomatic crisis between Germany and United States

23 May: Italy declares war on Austria-Hungary

25 May: British Liberal Prime Minister Asquith forms coalition government

31 May: First Zeppelin raid on London

6 August: Suvla Bay attack at Gallipoli begins

19 December: Sir Douglas Haig named BEF Commander in France

28 December: Allied withdrawal from Gallipoli begins

Deaths in war: Rupert Brooke, Julian Grenfell, Charles Hamilton Sorley, August Stramm, Henri Gaudier-Brzeska

Romain Rolland, *Au-dessus de la mêlée*

Rolland wins Nobel Prize for Literature

Rilke, "Fünf Gesänge, August 1914"

Stramm, "Wunde"

René Benjamin, *Gaspard*

Buchan, *The Thirty-Nine Steps*

Lawrence, *The Rainbow* (banned in Britain)

Edith Wharton, *Fighting France*

May Sinclair, *Journal of Impressions in Belgium*

Brooke, *1914 & Other Poems*

Griffith's film, *Birth of a Nation*

1916: February: Great Britain introduces conscription

21 February–18 December: German attack at Verdun in longest battle of war, ultimately won by French

24–30 April: Easter Rising in Ireland

31 May: Battle of Jutland, major naval engagement of war

5 June: Sinking of *HMS Hampshire*, death of Lord Kitchener

1 July: Anglo-French offensive at Somme begins; nearly 60,000 British casualties in first assaults

28 August: Hindenburg appointed German Chief of Staff

15 September: British tanks first used, at Flers-Courcelette, Somme front

6 December: David Lloyd George becomes British Prime Minister

18 December: President Wilson requests statements of aims from warring nations

Deaths in war: Alan Seeger, Umberto Boccioni, Antonio Sant'Elia

Saussure, *Cours de linguistique générale*

Barbusse, *Le Feu: journal d'une escouade*

Kafka, *Metamorphoses*

1914–1916: Eine Anthologie (verse) published by anti-war *Die Aktion*

Sorley, *Marlborough and Other Poems*

H. D., *Sea Garden*

H. G. Wells, *Mr. Britling Sees It Through*

Dada in Zurich

1917:   1 February: Germany resumes unrestricted submarine warfare (after respite)

3 February: United States breaks diplomatic relations with Germany

11 March: British capture Baghdad

15 March: Tsar Nicholas II abdicates as result of Russian Revolution

6 April: United States declares war on Germany

9 April: Start of Arras offensive

29 April–10 June: Mutiny in French army

18 May: John Pershing given command of AEF

25 June: First United States troops arrive in France

31 July: Third Battle of Ypres (Passchendaele) begins

October–November: Bolshevik Revolution in Russia, Communist government under Lenin

7 December: United States declares war on Austria-Hungary

9 December: Jerusalem taken by British

22 December: Russia engages in separate peace negotiations with Germany at Brest-Litovsk

Deaths in war: T. E. Hulme, Francis Ledwidge, John McCrae,
    Edward Thomas
Freud, *Introduction to Psychoanalysis*
Eliot, *Prufrock and Other Observations*
Edward Thomas, *Poems*
Sassoon, *The Old Huntsman*
Dos Passos, *One Man's Initiation*
Léon Werth, *Clavel soldat*
Stefan Georg, "Der Krieg"

1918:   8 January: President Wilson announces 14 Points Peace Programme
    3 March: Soviet Russia finalizes peace negotiations in
        Brest-Litovsk treaty, freeing German troops for final campaign
        on Western Front
    21 March: Start of German major spring offensive, in Battle of
        Picardy
    9 April: Second German spring offensive launched, Battle of Lys
    25 May: German U-boats appear in United States waters
    27 May–5 June: Third German spring offensive, Third Battle of
        Aisne
    15 July: Second Battle of the Marne, final effort of German spring
        offensive
    16–17 July: Former Tsar Nicholas and family murdered by
        Bolsheviks
    18 July–7 August: German retreat at the Marne
    22 August: Allied breakthrough at Albert
    3 October: Germany and Austria communicate peace initiatives to
        United States
    5 October: Allied forces capture Hindenburg Line
    17 October–24 October: British advance to Sambre and Schledt
        rivers; Germans surrender in large numbers
    21 October: Germany stops unrestricted submarine warfare
    30 October: Turkey arranges armistice with Allies
    3 November: German fleet mutinies at Kiel
    9 November: Kaiser Wilhelm II of Germany abdicates
    11 November: Armistice
    14 December: Lloyd George wins British General Election
    Deaths in war: Joyce Kilmer, Isaac Rosenberg, Wilfred Owen,
        Guillaume Apollinaire
    Votes for women in Britain over 30, men over 21
    World-wide influenza epidemic
    Rebecca West, *Return of the Soldier*

Edith Wharton, *The Marne*
Georges Duhamel, *Civilisation, 1914–1917*
Gerard Manley Hopkins, *Poems*, ed. Robert Bridges
Sassoon, *Counter-Attack*
Edward Thomas, *Last Poems*
Spengler, *Der Untergang des Abendlandes* (trans., 1922, *The Decline of the West*)
Chaplin, in *Shoulder Arms*

1919: 10–15 January: Communist revolts in Berlin
18 January: Paris Peace Conference begins
25 January: League of Nations accepted in principle at Peace Conference
6 February: Meeting of German National Assembly in Weimar
14 February: Completion of draft covenant for League of Nations
7 May–28 June: Drafting and signing of Treaty of Versailles
Pound, *Quia Pauper Amavi*
Eliot, *Poems*
Keynes, *The Economic Consequences of the Peace*
Sassoon, *War Poems*
McCrae, *In Flanders Fields and Other Poems*

1920: First meeting of the League of Nations
Eliot, *The Sacred Wood: Essays on Poetry and Criticism*
Pound, *Hugh Selwyn Mauberley*
Lawrence, *Women in Love*
Vernon Lee (Violet Paget), *Satan the Waster*
Ernst Jünger, *In Stahlgewittern*

1921: Formation of Irish Free State, partition of Northern Ireland
Owen, *Poems*, intro. Sassoon
Dos Passos, *Three Soldiers*
Chaplin, in *The Kid*
Pirandello, *Six Characters in Search of an Author*

1922: Lloyd George coalition falls
BBC established, begins transmissions
Mussolini, March on Rome
Montague, *Disenchantment*
Willa Cather, *One of Ours*
Joyce, *Ulysses*
Eliot, *The Waste Land*
Woolf, *Jacob's Room*
E. E. Cummings, *The Enormous Room*

1923: Collapse of German currency

Wharton, *A Son at the Front* (written 1919)
Wallace Stevens, *Harmonium*
Freud, *The Ego and the Id*
Roland Dorgelès, *Le Réveil des morts*

1924: Breton, *Manifeste du surréalisme*
Mann, *Der Zauberberg*
Death of Lenin, succeeded by Stalin

1925: Hitler, *Mein Kampf*
Fitzgerald, *The Great Gatsby*
Yeats, *A Vision*
Hemingway, *In Our Time*
Kafka, *The Trial*
Woolf, *Mrs. Dalloway*
Eisenstein, *Battleship Potemkin*

1926: General Strike in Britain, 26 April–12 May (mine workers for six
months more)
Faulkner, *Soldier's Pay*
Hemingway, *The Sun Also Rises*
T. E. Lawrence, *The Seven Pillars of Wisdom*
Mottram, *The Spanish Farm Trilogy* (1924–26)

1927: Lindbergh, solo transatlantic flight
Heidegger, *Being and Time*
Proust, *Le Temps retrouvé*
Zweig, *Der Streit um den Sergeanten Grischa*
Faulkner, *Sartoris* (*Flags in the Dust*)
First "talkie" film (*The Jazz Singer*)

1928: Radclyffe Hall, *The Well of Loneliness*
Lawrence, *Lady Chatterley's Lover*
Weill and Brecht, *Die Dreigroschenoper*
Blunden, *Undertones of War*
Ford, *Parade's End* (tetralogy completed)
Erich Maria Remarque, *Im Westen nichts Neues*
Ludwig Renn (Arnold Friedrich Vieth von Golßenau), *Krieg*

1929: Wall Street crash
Aldington, *Death of a Hero*
Hemingway, *A Farewell to Arms*
Graves, *Good-bye to All That*
Jünger, *Das Wäldchen 125, eine Chronik aus den Grabenkämpfen
1918*
English translations of Jünger, *The Storm of Steel*, and Remarque,
All Quiet on the Western Front

1930: Nazis elected to German Reichstag
Film of *All Quiet on the Western Front* wins Oscar
"Private 19022" (Frederic Manning), *The Middle Parts of Fortune*
    (also known as *Her Privates We*)
Sassoon, *Memoirs of an Infantry Officer*
Williamson, *The Patriot's Progress*
English translation of Jünger, *Copse 125*

1933: Hitler becomes Chancellor of Germany
Roosevelt, "New Deal"
Vera Brittain, *Testament of Youth*

1934: Fitzgerald, *Tender is the Night*

1935: Italy invades Abyssinia

1936: Death of George V, Edward VIII king (abdicates to marry
    Mrs. Simpson), George VI king
Spanish Civil War begins
Mussolini and Hitler form Rome–Berlin Axis
Chaplin, in *Modern Times*

1937: Chamberlain becomes Prime Minister
German planes bomb Guernica in Spain
Picasso, *Guernica*
David Jones, *In Parenthesis*
Rosenberg, *Collected Works*
Death of Ivor Gurney

1938: Germany invades and annexes Austria
Chamberlain's policy of appeasement with Hitler, "Munich
    Agreement"

1939: Germany invades Poland; Second World War begins

VINCENT SHERRY

Introduction

"The *Great* War," yes, of 1914–18: the adjective the contemporary record applied to the event emphasizes still some monumental, colossal quality in it. For reasons that were unclear, or that changed and became even more unclear, there were 10 million dead in less than half a decade, as the major nation states of Europe and North America aligned and engaged in a conflict that mobilized, galvanized, and exhausted their resources of human, financial, intellectual, and spiritual capital. On the landscape of modern time this war stands accordingly as a landmark, a milestone or turning point. Yet the differences it supposedly locates between centuries new and old blur now as history mixes three – the twenty-first, the twentieth, the nineteenth – into the line of sight. If it is famed as a "watershed event," that is, the horizon it defines keeps disappearing, but not into unfamiliar distances, rather into recognizable similarities. The cinema that depicts the massive battles of this first mass war presents the vistas in which we see, as it were, miniature or toy versions of ourselves: the stick-figure militia in epic perspectives, a soldiery jerking forward toward certain death with the odd bravado of mechanical dolls – the dream of the machine, the whole romance of industrial technology that enchanted the cultural imagination of the nineteenth century, all of this was concluded and grimly disproved in the awful outcomes of mass mechanized warfare. A cynicism particular to the twentieth century looks back to this Great War as its major, shaping occasion.

In its geo-political outlines, too, subsequent history has followed the model of the specific military configuration of the conflict. The face-off situation of the two major armies on the Western Front provided the initial image, the most vividly material form, for those rival alliances that underlay the Second World War and that continued (with changes of side) through the Cold War. The many dreads of the twentieth century find their prime type and defining instance in the four years (and more) of stalemated trench warfare: the inevitable menace of that second war, approaching through the 1920s and 1930s, and then the threats of nuclear conflagration over the next fifty years. Another legacy lies in the distortions that total war enforced on the discourses of a culture, in the totalizations of view – the exaggerations that stimulated the required popular involvement, the hate campaigns, the cartoon enmities, all in all, the mechanism of oppositional thinking and the bogus extremities it effected. Gigantism is a feature equally of the political and military dimensions of mass warfare, and it scales much of the subsequent experience of the century to its intimidations, at once intimate and immense. The figure on the poster commanding recruits for the new mass armies of 1914 is the image within the image of Big Brother, insignia of a totalitarian dictatorship that represents just one later state and stage of (this first) total war.

As the First World War, then, this Great War tends to be represented by political historians as one in a series reiterating a type. No less correctly, however, and perhaps more tellingly, historians of literature tend to find a record of the novelty it constituted to contemporary sensibilities and, so, of the shock it goes on reporting. Its singularity, the difference it made, is preserved as a presentiment by British poets and novelists in particular, and even through the second half of its embattled century. Philip Larkin, one of the most representative voices in the literary culture of post-World War II England, expresses this attitude in 1960 in "MCMXIV," which proclaims

> Never such innocence,
> Never before or since,
> As changed itself to past
> Without a word –

Larkin images this "innocence" in a poetic transcription of a familiar photograph, where a crowd of young men in London on the first Monday of August 1914 peers into a camera that stands, in effect, as ourselves – into a future whose terrible truths we know far better, or worse, than they:

> These long uneven lines
> Standing as patiently
> As if they were stretched outside
> The Oval or Villa Park,
> The crowns of hats, the sun
> On moustached archaic faces
> Grinning as if it were all
> An August bank holiday lark . . .[1]

Those "archaic faces" image their own (last) prewar moment on the far side of a divide that we project from our own point in historical time. This is a division which Larkin reiterates through an allusion later in the poem

1 Central London Recruiting Depot, August 1914

to the "Domesday lines," a reference to the first land survey of Britain, drawn up in 1085–86, and an image here of some ancient or residual form of order for the British landscape of early 1914. This configuration of distant antiquity represents a location Larkin establishes from the outset of the poem by inscribing his title in Roman numerals, which present that 1914 date, it seems, in some remote sign system, some alternative calendar, an unpronounceable chronology, like some ur-*zeit* toward which, in effect, the numbers count backwards. Larkin applies these touches, not just to set that older moment in the gloaming of a romantic nostalgia, but to magnify the feeling of disparity between Then and Now, Before and After.

While later writers see the war as a boundary marker in the history of values and attitudes, this tendency is evident especially and first of all in the writing of that moment. Already in *1914*, the book of sonnets by Rupert Brooke that was published in 1915, that title date is mythopoeically inscribed. Now, Brooke's sonnets exemplify the decorous measures of the "Georgian" style in verse writing, which had been in vogue since 1911; this was a poetics of elegant simplicity, where a classical transparency in literary vocabulary combined with a steady grace of verbal music and the deep appeal of pastoral's imaginative prospects:

> There are waters blown by changing winds to laughter
> And lit by the rich skies, all day. And after,
>   Frost, with a gesture, stays the waves that dance
> And wandering loveliness. He leaves a white
>   Unbroken glory, a gathered radiance,
> A width, a shining peace, under the light.[2]

In late summer 1914, this poetic sensibility turns to accept and even celebrate the emergent event. But this is a rhythmical diction which, even as it rises to idealize the advent of war, outdates itself in doing so. Sestet to "The Dead," these six lines offer an elegy for soldiers dying already in numbers that multiply Brooke's cherished "he" into *anomie*. And the "radiance" on the Western Front "gathered" no benign prospects "under the light" of its flares, it revealed a bone-yard of astonished horror at the atrocities technological weapons had effected on the dead. Brooke's sumptuous testament is most moving in its irrelevance. A first year forgone as soon as the second, "1914" is already commemorated and raised and framed from this far side of time in a legend of precious loss, one that feels as though it were made real by Brooke's own death in the second year of war.

But the image in which Brooke greeted the bracing claims of the new martial experience – "as swimmers into cleanness leaping"[3] – remains vivid in cultural memory, among other reasons, for the profound irony it affords in historical retrospect. It is the same reason that returns Larkin, forty-five years later, to the moment it holds in freeze frame. Like the figures in the early-August 1914 photograph, the bodies of Brooke's fabled army float for ever in a sort of mid-air sempiternity, suspended between the ideal England from which they have taken their leap and . . . well, the rest of the century, which is no cleansing pleasance of late summer. "Never such innocence again." Whether or not this "innocence" is invented in historical retrospect, whether or not it functions just as a way of reckoning a not so wonderful present in relation to an ever better past, the map of cultural history offers no site for this act of imaginative psychology so inviting as the moment of the Great War.

Yet the nostalgia can be upheld, it may be supported by the sturdier material of standard intellectual and social histories. The Europe of 1914 was politically and ethnically variegated but it was also, to some considerable degree, culturally unified, and it was held together under a standard of values whose collapse may count as a more than abstract tragedy. Liberalism is a term whose significance is always relative to a particular instant in cultural time, insofar as the liberation it pronounces as its namesake value will be gauged in relation to the constraints of contemporary convention, while the freedoms it wins will evolve into subsequent expectations. Nonetheless, the dominant concepts of this intellectual tradition – the value of rationalism, a faith in Progress, the code of reasonable freedom – enjoyed a particular dominance in the public culture of turn-of-the-century Europe. And the influence of this body of philosophical attitude was being proven in a number of actual political situations: with the power of the Social Democratic Party in Germany, in the ongoing mandate the Liberal government in Britain enjoyed since its landslide victory in the elections of 1906, and in the continued optimism of *la belle époque* in France. It is the force of contrast between the establishing premises of those cultural values – rational gradualism, technological progress, scientific meliorism – and the hitherto unimaginable atrocity of mass mechanical conflict that makes this Great War stand out as the sizeable event it really was. Indeed, it stands on the seismic line of divide between centuries, or, as we perceive it, between Then and Now, Better and Worse.

Granted, this majority consciousness of liberal values and practices was being contested by increasingly powerful oppositional minorities. On the political spectrum, these ranged (by conventional measures) from right to left: from the exertions of neo-monarchial interests such as *Action française* to the threats of working-class insurgency and underclass revolution, not only in Germany and Russia but also in France and Great Britain. The English version of this pan-European phenomenon is recounted memorably by George Dangerfield, in *The Strange Death of Liberal England* (1935).

Dangerfield argues that a broad if loosely strung coalition of interests from the workers' and women's movements combined with the constant volatility of Ireland to threaten the center of Liberal political power in Britain. In this reading, the war does not undermine the existing structures of British society, as it does in most popular understandings. It serves instead to absorb the forces of internal dissent, to project these outward toward a shared enemy and, so, to deflect the energies of incipient revolt. As engagingly anecdotal as it is boldly proposed, Dangerfield's version of history continues to exert an appeal to readers for reasons that may include also the validity of its sometimes daring argument.

What *would have occurred*, however, remains a possibility unproven in time. And the cultural authority of intellectual and political Liberalism was sufficiently strong to withstand those apparent challenges – the resistance it generated, indeed, by virtue of the hegemony it enjoyed. A sensible outlook on this complex situation is to see the Europe of 1914 balanced on an increasingly precarious platform of old codes, enfeebled beliefs. This system may have been ready to fall, even fated to fall, but the fact that its framework of ideals collapsed manifestly in the conflagration of war makes this the marking event for the time's turn. And the main literature of major record seems to attain this status by witnessing, in fact insisting on, this sense of difference.

It is this sense of difference that is scored into the signal phenomenon of this moment in cultural and literary history: "modern*ism*." As a comprehensive term, modernism includes in that emphatic suffix an understanding that it is not just modernity as a chronological condition that is being referenced: the word invokes a self-conscious awareness and assertion of this modernity, all in all, some enabling claim of difference to precedent convention, to the way things *were*. Of course the movement or energy that we label "modernism" was forming already and even altering itself in the years before the war, when the turn of the century had stirred a sense of passage between Old and New. Developments in material science and technological production also provided powerful coadjutors to aesthetic invention of comparable kind. Yet the most profoundly modernist writing is not marked by a simple optimistic confidence in progress or novelty (even its own). This literature has in its imaginative content some record of disruption in the conventional expectations of liberal modernity, some experience of the absconding or compromise of those promises. These intimations are enjoined on an alert awareness most forcibly in the circumstances of this Great War. And so the literature of properly modernist record testifies in its various ways to the provocative possibilities of this moment. To take the major names of London modernism in the war years: Ezra Pound, T. S. Eliot, and Virginia Woolf all work in ways that echo and answer to the crisis they have registered in the mainstay frameworks of intellectual and political Liberalism. The unmaking of its once established language compels these literary inventors to remake it, and this novel imaginative idiolect can be heard as the inner record of this change-over moment in cultural time.

In literary bibliographies outside the modernist canon, too, the war marks the occasion to which any number of substantial transformations, all manner of significant initiatives, can be attributed. These far-reaching, influential developments can be followed by various registers in the several national traditions of pan-European and transatlantic literary cultures. In Britain, for vivid instance, the Georgian sensibility of the prewar years was not only challenged, it was ultimately transformed by the dire realities of the martial experience it was called upon to witness. The high-gloss, arcadian surface of Brooke and his companion talents lost its sheen, its credibility. A new convention formed around the strong models of (the later) Siegfried Sassoon and Wilfred Owen, which featured in their discordant tones a lyric of often fierce realism. In French writing of the war, it is the novel that provides the genre of most significant and conspicuous invention. A newly daring naturalism came into the representation of protagonist-narrators' martial experience, originally and most influentially Henri Barbusse's *Le Feu* (1916). In Germany, too, the precedent conventions of fiction writing were staggered by accounts like Ernst Jünger's *In Stahlgewittern* (1920), whose title (*Storm of Steel*) fairly augurs the foreign objects raining tempestuously, invasively, into the statelier cadences of German prose in the prewar years. Even the international "avant-garde," a label that indicates the militarization of literary and artistic activities that this "advanced guard" proclaimed in the years leading up to war, was compelled to reconceive such orientations, when, like Keats's poet, they awoke and found that their dreams had come true. American writers were catapulted into a frame of international reference to which only the most urbane and privileged of their compatriots had acceded in the prewar decades. Participation in the war strongly altered the ways in which the new nation could imagine itself, and the intensity and extent of that experience may be measured, inversely, by the relative brevity of the country's actual involvement in the military action of the war.

The literary history of this tumultuous moment is represented in a comprehensive account in the essays gathered here. As a glance at the table of contents may indicate, the three-part organization implements a two-fold system of division: in time and space, by historical phase and national geography. Thus the literature of (roughly) contemporary record is examined in Parts I and II, whose division accommodates the several major sources of its production: the extensive preserves in the British tradition in Part I, the work done from the Continent and by Americans in II. Part III then follows the legacy of the war as a subject in the subsequent record of the century, variously, in British fiction, in transatlantic literary criticism, and in visual media.

The apparently unequal portions afforded the material of Britain (Part I) and the European Continent and America (Part II) reflect the fact that, for a number of reasons in cultural history, the literature written in English retains the largest readership. Within these conditions, the specifically British record of the war remains the most popular, the most powerful and affective. So intense is the imaginative register in British literary history, indeed, that the import of the event can be followed in the difference it made genre by genre, in writing done by women in particular, and in view of the special grouping "modernism" confers as a term on a sensibility distinctive to this moment in modern English cultural time – these are the several categories of classification and analysis in the five chapters of this first part. The same conditions have nonetheless generated a somewhat insular scheme of literary history for many readers, a sort of English version of the New Yorker's map of the universe. From this outlook, the diverse work of other national literatures shifts into distances or peripheries in which it shrinks in significance – or, when it offers its monuments, like Remarque's *All Quiet on the Western Front*, these tend to stand isolated, contextless, like the end points of processes whose histories, whose other cultural productions, have gone missing. If, then, in contrast to Part I, Part II appears heterogeneous in content, it represents nonetheless a dedicated attempt to redress English near-sightedness. It indicates the variety and particularity of other, non-British traditions and representations.

Where, in those several national legacies, the war varies as a subject of imaginative construction, it also moves through time and changes as a function of the developing memory of the twentieth century. How it is reconstituted in subsequent literary fiction, and how critical scholarship continues to negotiate the terms in which the significance of the original literature is understood: these are the coverage areas of the first two chapters of Part III. They are complemented in the third, the last chapter of the book, with a view to the ongoing, changing representation of the war in twentieth-century film and video. The war coincided with the coming of "the movies" as a form of popular entertainment, and the conventions of this emergent medium were shaped to some significant degree by current political conditions, most notably, by the new demand for national propaganda, which various governments implemented through the movie-houses. The historically informed understanding which Laura Marcus offers in this last chapter complements and extends the sort of carefully contextualized assessments which the other chapters, dedicated to the several literary legacies, also present.

In the section on the writing of British provenance, Paul Edwards demonstrates how the memoir, a genre invested with specific expectations about class and masculinity, even natural landscape, certainly writing style, was challenged and changed by the unprecedented event of the war. The stability of English social structures, which find their microcosm in the country's military hierarchy and their imaginative representation in the framework of the novel, is the issue addressed centrally by David Trotter; he follows the response of the "combat novel" in particular to the extraordinary pressures being exerted on existing class systems by trench warfare. A similarly targeted report on the impact of these conditions on lyric poetry shows in Edna Longley's account of the transformation this subgenre underwent during the war. Accordingly, she presents this event as the main context and provocation for the sort of innovation literary historians have formerly found mainly in "modernism." The particularly liberating effect the war extended to women is recovered by Claire Buck as the circumstance in which we may understand their new depth and exceptional breadth of literary activity. Self-representation in writing is a process that complements and extends a developmental gender history that features, not just new opportunities for work but, ultimately, consequentially, the acquisition of women's long-sought right of suffrage and, in the franchise, the capacity of potentially meaningful social representation. As an event in political and intellectual history, of course, the war provides the defining crisis of mainstream European liberalism, nowhere more than in Britain. Here the majority Liberal government was required to rationalize involvement in a conflict in a way that defied the major, sustaining precedents of its partisan traditions, its standards of moral rationalism as well as its logic of international policy. How this breakdown in the public language of English Liberalism is assimilated as the condition of major literary innovation by London modernists is the critical story I tell in the last chapter of this first section.

Liberal models of culture and history had been contested as well by the energies of a Continental avant-garde. Its militarization of the arts is studied comprehensively, in the first essay of Part II, by Marjorie Perloff, who follows the complications of prewar motive through postwar consequences. The wide range of international reference here also stakes out the larger area of coverage in this second section of the book. Catharine Brosman's chapter on the French writing of the war situates the event within an extended record of national memory. She shows how the conflict is appropriated and reacted to by separate interest groups in French culture in 1914 and then replayed variously, changeably, in the subsequent decades. For quite specific reasons, as Stanley Corngold proposes in the next chapter, the earliest moment of the war seems to be localized and preserved in German cultural memory. At the outset, the event effects the sort of unifying experience a new nation takes as an exhilarating affirmation; not surprisingly, wide-eyed zealotry combines with incipient dismay. This range of feelings plays in varying combinations through the major works of record and culminates in the consciousness of that most complex monument of the early postwar age, Thomas Mann's *The Magic Mountain*. In America, the relatively lengthy period of "latency" between the outbreak of war and national involvement encloses a moment in which the writers of this country can project its role in a kind of ideal, imaginary time, some prospective myth of American destiny in world history. John Matthews's chapter captures the sensibility special to this early phase and, in telling contrast, sets out the record of reversal and recognition in the hallmark novels of the next two decades, in effect, in the canon of modern American fiction.

The later phases of this ongoing engagement are surveyed and mapped in the specific locale of post-Second World War British fiction in the first essay of Part III, where Sharon Ouditt shows how the original literature of the Great War is consistently rewritten over successive decades. What this tradition witnesses in the constant process of reimagining the war is the great capacity of its initial literary record, not just to be recycled, but to be rediscovered, and to be found anew because the recognitions it registers are instinct, it seems, with the presumptions, the underlying character, of our own developing modernity. Understandably, then, the historical content and depth of its original literature represents a virtually inexhaustible resource for scholars. The internal logic of a forty year process of critical reconnaissance, here as the chronology of its major phases and dominant topics, is set out as an intellectual history-in-miniature in the chapter by James Campbell. This is a tradition whose frame of reference has expanded gradually over four decades, beginning with a virtual immersion in the canon of British war writing but extending at length to an international and transhistorical outlook and interdisciplinary set of attentions. The present volume takes its place in this evolving series.

Conventional gender identities are reinvented. The narratives of rationalism, those models of logical progress now forgone as a promise for history, are recast. The avant-garde is turned forward through the war into a retrograde state, a neoclassicism as guarded and fragile as the postwar calm of the early 1920s. The stories which literary historians propose as the plot or consequence of the war are as various as this multifarious event. Each of these meanings appears as a mostly local truth, a glyph dispatched as it were from just one of those multiple fronts. Thus the use and value of a volume such as this may be the gesture it makes toward the composite quality of the bigger picture – and toward representing a necessary plurality of views, not just a variegated range of subject. Even so, there are topic areas for which I wish there were room to provide coverage: the writing of the war from colonial perspectives (Canada, Ireland, Australia and New Zealand as well as India and Africa), for instance, and from the Russian experience, which is a record relatively undeveloped in the awareness of Continental and Anglo-American readers. Also important is the vantage of pan-European and transatlantic economics, where the recasting of the older Gold Standard in the task of financing the war impacts powerfully on the work of verbal currency, too, on the establishment of meaning and value for counters in the linguistic system. In ways little and large, with long recognized facts and still emerging bodies of knowledge (and knowledge of bodies), this Great War of 1914–18 affords one of the most powerful resources in our developing memory – our deepening identity – as modern persons. The ever wider horizons in which we understand the import and consequences of the war measure the immense prepotency of this event in the cultural history of centuries past, and passing, and to come.

NOTES

1. Philip Larkin, "MCMXIV," in *Collected Poems* (1988; rpt. London: Faber, 1990), 127.
2. Rupert Brooke, "The Dead," in *The Collected Poems of Rupert Brooke* (1915; rpt. New York: Dodd, Mead, and Company, 1925), 110.
3. Brooke, "Peace," in *ibid.*, 107.

I

THE GREAT WAR IN BRITISH
LITERARY CULTURE

I

PAUL EDWARDS

British war memoirs

The genre, "memoir," is an odd one, encompassing simple chronicles and more elaborate, analytic or poetically structured accounts. Those First World War memoirs that have become canonical in literary studies have, not surprisingly, been the more structured work of poets. These are the main focus of the present chapter, but other, less-known work will be touched on. As with the poetry of these memoirists, one of the chief literary interests of their work is the way traditional generic or formal literary features (corresponding broadly with a set of received values about masculinity, heroism, the countryside, and so on) are twisted into something different by the necessity of representing experience that compels a revaluation of all such values. These memoirs are the work, mainly, of writers who do not otherwise conspicuously engage with modernity, perhaps because they were too young to have reached any sort of maturity as writers before their war experience. And after the war that experience remained as their most intense reality – despite the efforts of Robert Graves, for example, to say *good-bye to all that*." The stress that traditional forms undergo in these memoirs (as in the war poetry of the same and other poets) is sufficient to turn the writers into something very close to modernists, almost against their will, and in relation to the war only. Still, they form a kind of "alternative current" of modernism in England by virtue of which the movement is sometimes seen as largely a response to the upheaval of the war. The prototype of such understanding is the public response to the official exhibitions of war paintings held in London in 1919.[1] "Cubism" could now be "understood," even if it was not liked.

Literature moves at a different pace from painting, and "literature," unlike "art," was not commissioned by the authorities. Herbert Read found, besides, that publishers were not interested in "anything bleak" in 1919, when he tried to publish his short memoir of the retreat of the British Fifth Army from St. Quentin in the face of the final, apparently overwhelming attacks by German forces in March 1918. It remained unpublished until

1925. *In Retreat* is an early example of the "bare unvarnished truth" school of memoirists: "One thing I wished to avoid, and that was any personal interpretation of the events – any expatiation, that is to say, whether of the imagination or of the intellect. I wanted the events to speak for themselves unaided by any art."[2] It required considerable skill – a kind of art – to achieve such an effect, and in attempting it Read was following imagist precepts. He was already in the modernist current, predisposed by his reading of Nietzsche to a "revaluation of values," and an admirer of T. E. Hulme (whose essays he later edited). Some of the ingredients of Read's memoir would become standard (though this does not dull the hallucinatory clarity of Read's own work): the chaos of battle, with pointless or mistaken orders arriving from the staff, advantageous military positions wasted, men killed by their own side's artillery, instances of comradeship and instances of selfish indifference.

Read makes the constant concern with food and sleep a prominent theme, and (particularly through food) establishes one of the contrasts that will pervade later memoirs – here, that between the comradeship of the men at the Front and the selfish, pampered complacency of those (staff, politicians, profiteers, and journalists) who grow fat on the spoils of war. At one point the starving and exhausted Read and the men under his command are refused food and shelter by a couple of sedentary soldiers in a hut equipped with a blazing stove, on which coffee simmers, and a table "laden with bread, tinned foods, butter; food, food, food." One of the occupants is "fat, very fat, with a tight, glossy skin."[3] Contrast this with an earlier passage, where Read's men have established defensive positions round a small village. Read's servant has brought wine and cider from a cellar, but is sent off again with others for food. They return "with bottles of red wine and a large tin of army biscuits," which Read is reluctant to distribute for fear of the effect of alcohol on empty stomachs:

> So S. and I each took a wine glass, and starting at different points, we began to go a round of the men. Each man lay curled up in his shallow pit, resting. To each we gave a glass of wine and a few biscuits. They took it thankfully. There was a lull in the distant fighting: I don't remember any noise of fire during that hour. The sun was warm and seemed to cast a golden peace on the scene. A feeling of unity with the men about me suddenly suffused my mind.[4]

The symbolism of this communion requires no comment. *In Retreat* looks a lot more "literary" now than it could have done when it was published, but that is the fate of all realism, and of imagism, too, despite its "direct treatment of the 'thing,' whether subjective or objective."[5]

Another early memoir of the war, C. E. Montague's *Disenchantment*, first published in February 1922, exemplifies the other end of the genre's spectrum. Far more consciously literary than Read's – teeming with allusions and quotations from Shakespeare, Wordsworth, Arnold, and others – it is organized analytically. It is not an account of personal experience (though it certainly draws on and conveys such experience) but an argument about what the war has done to England and Englishness: military incompetence, lying politicians and journalists, a church that has betrayed its mission, bureaucratic obsession with image rather than reality (what Montague calls "whiting the sepulchre"), the degeneration of England's stock by slums and industrialization, the broken promises of "a land fit for heroes," a generation of workers grown cynical about the competence and motives of their supposed superiors. All that is implicit in Read and later memoirists is here, stated explicitly and fully, with war-weary stoicism. It is a rich, grim, and impressive accumulation of symptoms of the cultural malaise that, though Montague could not know it, would accompany Britain's imperial decline over the twentieth century and even survive to color the public reaction to Tony Blair's idealistic participation in the invasion of Iraq in the twenty-first.

Disenchantment is as much symptom as diagnosis, for it is itself disenchanted and resorts a little desperately to the values and culture Montague seems to know cannot be resurrected. Its range of reference, connecting particular concrete war experience back to a known England, remains impressive:

Perhaps the undersized boys from our slums and the underwitted boys from the "agricultural, residential, and sporting estates" of our auctioneers' advertisements would get to their goal, the spirit wresting prodigies of valour out of the wronged flesh, hold on there for an hour or two with the shells splashing earth up about them . . . when great rain-drops make its surface jump, and then fall back under orders, without any need, the brain of our army failing to know what its muscle had won. Then, while you saw the triumphant Australians throw back a protective flank from the left of their newly-won front to the English right, far in their rear, you knew bitterly what the Australians were saying once more: "They've let us down again!" "Another Tommy officer who didn't know he'd won!" As if it were the fault, that day, of anyone there! Our men could only draw on such funds of nerve and physique, knowledge and skill, as we had put in the bank for them. Not they, but their rulers and "betters," had lost their heads in the joy of making money fast out of steam, and so made half of our nation slum-dwellers. It was not they who had moulded English rustic life to keep up the complacency of sentimental modern imitators of feudal barons . . . Like the syphilitic children of some jolly Victorian rake, they could only bring to this harsh examination such health and sanity as all the pleasant vices of Victorian and Edwardian England had left them.[6]

"The Gods are just, and of our pleasant vices / Make instruments to plague us."[7] Montague's memoir represents the culture of English liberalism at the end of its tether, anticipating Siegfried Sassoon's later exploration of an individual mind at the end of its tether. *Disenchantment* is prophetic of the desperate over-insistence on an "organic" national culture by F. R. Leavis and *Scrutiny*, which also had its roots in the war. The "cure" Montague offers is, on the one hand, a rhetorical renewal of Boy Scout resolutions ("To get down to work, whoever else idles; to tell no lies, whoever else may thrive on their use; to keep fit, and the beast in you down"), on the other an equally rhetorical appeal to war veterans to insist on peace: "Let them clap the only darbies they have – the Covenant of the League of Nations – on to the wrists of all future poets, romancers, and sages."[8] But disenchantment had gone too deep for these remedies, and it was to remain an undertone of other war memoirs yet to be written – as Montague himself predicted: "We seem to be in for a goodly literature of disappointment."[9]

Turning to canonical works, Edmund Blunden's *Undertones of War* (1928) belongs to that wave of memoirs written from sufficient temporal distance – and in Blunden's case geographical distance, for it was written in Japan – to need to take account of a possible audience not entangled in some way with the war itself. It addresses not only other combatants and civilians duped by wartime propaganda, but also a generation still in their early childhood during the war. Blunden draws attention to the problem of voice in his "Preliminary," and mentions his dissatisfaction with the tone of an earlier attempt at recording his experiences.[10] Tone and persona are vital, for the process of approaching the truth of the war – that is, "such mysteries as Mr. Hardy forthshadowed in *The Dynasts*" – is itself the projection of a persona. His war poems, he explains, entailed "some other personations."[11]

Here the "personation" will be of his own earlier self, a "harmless young shepherd in a soldier's coat," still unpoisoned by the war's worst horrors as the memoir closes.[12] It is an act of Romantic recollection of an "unfallen" state: "that coincidence of nature without and nature within which I long to remember." Shepherds are conventionally assumed to exemplify such a natural condition, but literary shepherds – writers of pastoral – are more aware than most of the artifice involved in their claims to simplicity. Blunden's return to an earlier self will be an act of literary revivalism, addressed to those who have "gone the same journey." As for other readers: "*Neither will they understand*" (Blunden's italics).[13] But how many who have been through trench warfare will also be in tune with Hardy's *The Dynasts*? Despite staking a claim on Romantic ground Blunden is really occupying modernist territory: an unseizable truth conveyed by an unknowable person to a various audience that must select itself.

2 Rough pastoral: German and British troops, Christmas truce, 1914

In a chapter entitled "Domesticities," Blunden self-consciously returns to the literary problems sketched in his preface, for they are central to an understanding of what his wartime experience comprised. It is a long passage – too long to quote in full – that now disclaims the "high exaltation" of *The Dynasts* (and the sumptuous rhetoric of *Othello*) in favor of an egalitarian openness to the chance of memory: "Each circumstance of the British experience that is still with me has ceased for me to be big or little, and now appeals to me more even than the highest exaltation of pain or scene in the 'Dynasts' . . ."[14] The openness may be egalitarian, but the memory is trusted to collect details that will take the narrative closest to "the soul of war" – again a Romantic (Wordsworthian) faith. There remains the problem of structuring the narrative when a traditional hierarchy of "big or little" no longer applies and memory is crowded. Blunden's comment on this problem is frequently quoted by critics, but not the sentence that precedes it and is connected to it by "So that . . ." I shall not elide "irrelevant" details, since it is precisely criteria of relevance that are in question here:

> Towards Hooge one brazen morning, running in a shower of shells along "The Great Wall of China" (one dull shell struck within a rifle's length of us, and exploded something else), Kenward the corporal and I saw a sentry crouching and peering one way and another like a birdboy in an October storm. He spoke, grinned and shivered; we passed; and duly the sentry was hit by a shell. So that in this vicinity a peculiar difficulty would exist for the artist to select the sights, faces, words, incidents, which characterized the time. The art is rather to collect them, in the original form of incoherence.[15]

The apparent reduction of the death of the "birdboy" (another shepherd in a soldier's coat) to an instance of an aesthetic dilemma is so quietly done that it is easily overlooked in the momentum of reading. But the death of the sentry should be worth more than such a detached "so that." This is Blunden's implicit point, however: the "soul of war" is precisely in the slighting of the death of such innocents by the grander strategic aims of those charged with directing the war (mentioned on the previous page as "adjust[ing] armies in coloured inks on vast maps at Montreuil or Whitehall"). By enacting in miniature its own slighting, Blunden's "argument" quietly draws attention to the fact that there is actually no larger argument (or "grand narrative," in today's terminology) in which the boy's death makes sense. Yet despite his "misuse" of it as a mere illustration, he trusts "those whom I foresee as readers"[16] to register the death as what it is, unique, but representative of the war's cruel "incoherence."

Although, at such a moment of destabilizing narrative self-reflection, Blunden's is virtually a "modernist" stance, his modernism is, like that of other Georgian poets compelled to represent war and destruction, adopted through force of circumstance rather than aesthetic predilection. It doesn't come naturally to him, so that on a level of form the book obeys the unwelcome imperatives of the experience it records. Romance is forced to accommodate a grim realism, just as the idyllic pastoral arcadia of France and Flanders is knocked to pieces by high explosives. Time and again the memoir returns to the beauty of the French landscape, villages, farms, and churches, and as the war proceeds (culminating in Blunden's experience at the Third Battle of Ypres – Passchendaele, in 1917) the violence and destruction become more terrible.

According to Paul Fussell, Blunden's continued ability in the face of such knocks to recuperate his literary forces and renew the stylistic antiquarianism of his narrative shows his continuing resistance to the war. Fussell allows that Blunden's literary refinement can lead to the "archness of the confirmed schoolmaster," but is more tolerant of this than many modern readers will be. For him, Blunden is not escaping into the past but "engaging the war by selecting from the armoury of the past weapons against it which seem to have the greatest chance of withstanding time."[17] Time will tell. It seems to me that Blunden's Romanticism – with all the literary prototypes it provides him – makes for something more complex and interesting than resistance. The most haunting moments of memory in the book are those conspicuously "Gothick" occasions where Blunden contemplates ruins, wayside shrines, and broken tombs:

> I recall the singular, phantasmal appearance of another wealthy house in Mailly. The Engineers used it as a headquarters. Its large drawing-room was furnished in delicate Arcadian style, the suite and the curtains being of a silver-grey silk, the piano of a light volatile design and clear tinge answering it; the tall windows were blocked with sandbags thoughtfully painted white, as though they, too, would harmonize! Perhaps the hues of dust and dimness helped them somewhat in this impossibility. The room was unreal and supernatural . . .[18]

Such self-consciously "literary" memories draw the memoirist back into the experience at least as much as they resist it, and in this they parallel Blunden's reluctance at the time (reported several times in the memoir) to leave the Front and his companions to take on safer postings in the rear. Neither Blunden nor his memoir quite emerge from the confines of Romanticism or the confines of the war. The prose section of the book finishes with the characteristic trajectory of the narrative throughout recapitulated in miniature: Buire-sur-Ancre where "the willows and waters in the hollow make up a picture so silvery and insubstantial that one would spend a lifetime to paint it" followed by a vision of its future destruction in the German advances of spring 1918 – unsuspected at the time, so that "No destined anguish lifted its snaky head to poison a harmless young shepherd in a soldier's coat." The (Romantically) sublime horror of the destruction, which will apparently change Blunden from what he has been throughout his experience, is deferred, beyond possible narration, by the "shepherd" he then was.[19]

A work in some ways comparable to Blunden's, Guy Chapman's *A Passionate Prodigality* has remained outside the literary canon, but is remarkably accomplished and powerful; like Blunden's its power is not immediately revealed but accumulates until it climaxes in a terrible account of the Third Battle of Ypres. Chapman's memoir was published four years after Blunden's, and on the first page the author signals his indebtedness to his predecessor. "I was loath to go," he tells the reader, echoing Blunden's opening sentence, "I was not anxious to go."[20] Blunden even makes a physical appearance in the memoir, inspecting Chapman's position on Observatory Ridge before his own battalion moves in to take over: "a very young, very fair and very shy subaltern from the Royal Sussex." He gives Chapman a small book: *The Harbingers: Poems by E. C. Blunden*. Chapman puts it in his knapsack along with Shakespeare, Sir Thomas Browne, and Meredith's *Evan Harrington* (Blunden was reading Young's *Night Thoughts*).[21] Chapman was in some ways as literary a soldier as Blunden (he was later to write a biography of William Beckford) and his memoir is allusive and adorned with recondite epigraphs.

While Chapman's homage suggests that Blunden's example provided a necessary template for his own expression of fascinated horror at the war – for, loath as he may have been to go, like Blunden, he becomes loath also to leave his comrades at the Front – his account of Ypres moves explicitly into areas of horror that Blunden is content merely to hint at. Chapman walks along a trench crowded with dead: "As I walked along the edge with Smith, my eye caught something white and shining. I stooped. It was the last five joints of a spine. There was nothing else, no body, no flesh. This apparition overcame me." "I could not abide bare fresh bones," he writes at another point, explaining why he excused himself when his colonel "tried vainly to interest me in a complete jaw without skull or cervicle, and with the teeth still flecked with blood."[22]

Like Blunden's, Chapman's memoir does not extend beyond the boundaries of his war experience, though Chapman *was* there till the end. *A Passionate Prodigality* closes with him on a troop train: "We passed over into Germany. No trumpets sounded."[23] For Blunden the war itself seems to have been a "literary" experience, since it came to him directly through an inherited, primarily pastoral, mode of perception. In comparison, Chapman could be said instead to use a voice he has learned from Blunden to represent an experience that was not directly literary to anything like the same extent. This makes Blunden's, for a student of literature, the richer work; in other respects, however, the advantage may well be with Chapman. In passing over into Germany he at least intimates a future, but Blunden seems never to have come to terms with the modern world. His revulsion from it is signaled with typical obliquity early in *Undertones* when he mentions the theft of his grandfather's ebony walking stick (brought with him to serve as his "pilgrim's staff") on his arrival at Etaples from England. "I was away from it only a few minutes – it went. But this was before the war was officially certified to be making the world safe for democracy."[24] Democracy, for Blunden, is theft.

Siegfried Sassoon's trilogy, *The Complete Memoirs of George Sherston* (1928, 1930, and 1936) is a generic oddity, its "fictional" mask gradually slipping until (in the final part) the persona of Sherston becomes virtually an irrelevance. The persona is, of course, a distancing device, and it became less necessary as the experience the trilogy recounts became more distant in time. Giving that experience a narrative form no doubt had a purgative function. Paul Fussell believes the *Memoirs* should be treated as fiction, especially since they leave out the whole dimension of Sassoon's identity as a poet. He has a point, but if the work is still read it is because it provides an account of Sassoon's own experience: it is read as a record of truth – a shaped record, but not a novel – and as such it is included in the present discussion.

The Sherston–Sassoon doubling (or substitution – the first editions were published anonymously) mirrors Sassoon's representation of his identity as fractured: one of the mysteries Sherston notices about himself:

> First the newly-gazetted young officer . . . anxious only to become passably efficient for service at the front . . . Next came the survivor of nine months in France . . . less diffident, and inclined, in a confused way, to ask the reason why everyone was doing and dying under such soul-destroying conditions. Thirdly arrived that somewhat incredible mutineer who had made up his mind that if a single human could help stop the War by making a fuss, he was that man.[25]

There are even more "Sherstons" than this, however; he has already enumerated another set of different selves presented to different categories of visitor while convalescing.[26] And later on in Ireland the "mutineer" will revert to the fox-hunting man of the first volume, only to be succeeded once again by the brave, aggressive officer at the Front. At the conclusion of the final volume (which precedes the actual start of writing the trilogy), Sherston, wounded and in hospital in England, is completely riven by the conflict among the various impulses he feels, each corresponding to a different personality. He is angry at not having been killed; he regards the war as a "dirty trick which had been played on me and my generation," but the "one thing" he has learned is that the "Prussian system is the best" and that children should be "taught to offer their finest instincts for exploitation by the unpitying machinery of scientific warfare."[27] Unable to reconcile these conflicts himself, he welcomes as a "benediction" the unexpected visit of W. H. R. Rivers, the psychiatric specialist who treated him at Slateford (as Sassoon calls Craiglockhart hospital).

Rivers is the last in a line of men whom Sherston has taken as authorities whose endorsement he apparently requires to certify his own identity. His arrival is a "benediction" because he has accepted what Sherston has become without pressing a role onto him; the truth is enough. The trilogy is a continuation of the talking cure with the (now deceased) Rivers, and Sassoon attempts to meet standards that would have satisfied him: "What exactitude would he find in such a representation of psychological experience as this, and how far would he approve my attempt to describe him?"[28] The *Memoirs*, whatever they imply about the war, are not an anti-war polemic; Sassoon had made his case against the war in his poems, and Sherston makes his protest when he issues his (actually Sassoon's) statement of "wilful defiance of military authority" at the close of *Memoirs of an Infantry Officer*. The protest made political points about the war, which had become a war of "aggression and conquest"; the suffering of combatants was being "deliberately prolonged" for "evil and unjust" ends.[29] Sherston (like Sassoon) invited court martial by such "wilful defiance." Instead, through various maneuverings by the authorities and his friend David Cromlech (modeled on Robert Graves, who gives his own account in *Good-bye to All That*), his defiance is defused into a medical problem, conveniently summed up as "shell shock." The narrator neither repudiates the political assertions in the protest nor justifies them. In a way that could be seen as endorsing the authorities' treatment of his actions as a medical problem, the narrative is only concerned with their psychological significance in "Sherston's Progress."

So the *Memoirs* have psychology at their center, but the psychology of Sherston is ultimately only of importance to us because of the war experience that tests it, almost to destruction. This makes the trilogy a kind of travesty of a "novel of education," tracking its hero from infancy to manhood: his early "education" consists solely in the outdoor sports of fox-hunting and cricket, with "manhood" represented by the helpless and tormented figure in hospital at the end. The 200-page long prelude detailing Sherston's apprenticeship as a sportsman might seem disproportionate, but an undercurrent of prospective irony pervades these pages: Sherston's sympathy with the fox he hunts, his purchase of costume and accouterments, the description of the sweating, nervous exhaustion of a hunted stag, barbed wire as the chief danger to huntsmen, the squalid dwellings of the poor from which Sherston averts his gaze, the mention of "socialist" opposition to the sport and war. The war has been so powerful as to seep back into, and color, Sherston's innocent youth.

The prelude is essential to our understanding of Sherston's reactions to the war. It shows us a privileged boy whose public identity is virtually entirely formed by others' expectations. It is a surprisingly attractive portrait because of the openness with which the narrative admits the gap between external image and internal reality. The progress of the unconfident little boy toward prize-winning success in outdoor pursuits is shadowed by a continual consciousness, not so much of his being a fraud, as of possessing a self not really defined by this progress. During a visit to Stephen Colwood (a race-winning contemporary to emulate), at Sunday service Sherston characteristically worries that he might stand or kneel conspicuously at the wrong moment. The feeling of displacement increases: "But who was I, and what on earth had I been doing? My very name suddenly seemed as though it scarcely belonged to me." Beside him is the reliable Stephen, and "there was no doubt about his identity."[30] The moment is proleptic of the conclusion, when the authentically named Rivers will secure Sherston at a far more acute crisis. Rivers is the only character Sassoon presents undisguised by a pseudonym.[31]

We can understand the wartime Sherston as still split, and continuing to behave as expected. He likens his eagerness to raid enemy trenches and gain a Military Cross to his previous eagerness to win horse races "because that had seemed a significant way of demonstrating my equality with my contemporaries. And now I wanted to make the World War serve a similar purpose." The medal (whose ribbon he throws into the Mersey in disgust) means "much the same" as his point-to-point cups.[32]

One aspect of Sassoon's "psychology" that is omitted (though with knowledge of his biography it may perhaps be inferred) is his homosexuality. In the legal and cultural climate of the time it was politic to conceal this, and we might speculate on its biographical importance in the process of partitioning of identity that Sassoon records. Even without this element, however, the Memoirs exemplify the thesis of Ford Madox Ford's Parade's End that a great part of the stress of war is manifested in the intensification of factors already present in peacetime life. It is easy to trace this intensification on a purely personal level through Sherston's experience; his dependency on a succession of traditional (though varying) masculine figures that the war removes from him one by one, is clear: Dixon, the groom who initiated him to hunting, Stephen Colwood and, most decisively, Dick Tiltwood, "the bright countenance of truth; ignorant and undoubting; incapable of concealment but strong in reticence and modesty." Dick, like Stephen, has been a reassuring presence in church ("I glanced at Dick and thought what a young Galahad he looked"), and it is an angry desire to avenge his death that powers Sherston's bravery ("I went up to the trenches with the intention of trying to kill someone.")[33]

So at the climax of Memoirs of an Infantry Officer, before the Battle of Arras, Sherston has nothing left but "the Battalion spirit" – esprit de corps – to sustain him, but the human beings who embody that spirit rapidly become casualties and are replaced. A theatrical "heroism" is the only option, as he sees it: "I must play at being a hero in shining armour, as I'd done last year [when he won his MC]; if I didn't, I might crumple up altogether."[34] But with the rapid turnover of "humanity," such an option is less realistic than becoming an insect while chance decides if you survive or are crushed "like a beetle."[35]

Any attempt to find a cultural or historical significance in this beyond the personal effect of war must be tentative. The trilogy seems to record a social transformation, leaving behind the bucolic idyll of rural sports chronicled in the novels of R. S. Surtees and *The Pickwick Papers*. There is even a Dickensian Trustee in London in charge of the young Sherston's allowance, duly sending prudent letters of advice that the young wastrel ignores. All this is rendered pointless by the war and the new world that succeeds it. Even an apparent return to that bucolic world, when Sherston goes hunting with "the Mister" around Limerick, only confirms the point: "'There'll be houses burnt and lives lost before the year's ended . . . and you officers, friends of Mr Blarnett's though you be, had better be out of Ireland than in, if you set value on your skins.'"[36]

But the world of Dickens and Surtees is that of the early nineteenth century, not the late nineteenth, and the feudal society of Sherston's youth is not the real thing, despite the presence of "squires" (or serfs) and Arthurian Galahads. It is a Victorian revival. Fox-hunting, here, is a semi-ritualistic activity that serves an ideological function of maintaining the illusion of a set of social relations that are in reality quite different, as the "Mister's" warning to Sherston about unrest in Ireland confirms. We may recall C. E. Montague's gibe against those "who had moulded English rustic life to keep up the complacency of sentimental modern imitators of feudal barons." Sherston's experience of disintegration takes on a historical significance, then, as the war removes those ideological façades that had sustained him. The battalion spirit (the military equivalent of the feudal spirit) cannot survive the mechanized, production-line replacement of casualties, and the role of "hero in shining armour" is revealed as no more than a role, while the reality is closer to that most mechanical form of life, the scuttling beetle.

The account of the Battle of Arras is rendered nightmarish by refraction through this personal and cultural consciousness at the end of its tether. Particularly horrifying is the description of the Tunnel, where Sherston tries to wake a figure under a blanket with a kick and a curse, only to discover that the man is a dead German soldier, hand still clasped to the blackened wound on his neck. Equally vivid is the image that concludes the preceding section: "Floating on the surface of the flooded trench was the mask of a human face which had detached itself from the skull."[37] The images are horrifying in their physical reality, but gain an additional power through their subliminal evocation of the war's destruction of delusive identities and intolerable revelation of the ultimate fact of death behind them.

Sassoon has Sherston give intimations of what, politically, might lie this break-up of identities that has been so personally harrowing for him, "in 1917 I was only beginning to learn that life, for the majority of the population, is an unlovely struggle against unfair odds, culminating in a cheap funeral."[38] His growing awareness that for the poor as well the war simply renders more intense what is already there in civilian life is taken no further in the narrative, but it may be significant that after the war Sassoon became the literary editor of the socialist newspaper, the *Daily Herald*.

Given Sassoon's need for searching self-analysis, it is not surprising that he fell out with Robert Graves over Graves's autobiography, *Good-bye to All That*. He and Edmund Blunden put their heads together and filled a copy of the book with denunciatory annotation, which they intended to donate to the British Museum.[39] They saw it as a money-making venture, not recognizing, or not liking, its *reductio ad absurdum* of the Bairnsfather spirit.[40] As savage farce, the book shares a tone with a certain strain in modernism; its jests are "too deep for laughter," in Wyndham Lewis's phrase. Not surprisingly, Lewis appreciated the book, which in his own autobiography he called a "masterly winding-up of a bankrupt concern."[41] But many readers will be as irritated as Sassoon and Blunden. The first edition is much more definitely a "good-bye" than the revised version Graves issued in 1957. Writing it was "an opportunity for a formal good-bye to you and to you and to you and to me and to all that; forgetfulness, because once all this has been settled in my mind and written down and published it need never be thought about again; money."[42] The 1957 revision removes this explanation and is prefaced instead by a prologue effectively distancing the author from the "me" he said good-bye to in 1929.

Like Sassoon, Graves begins with the prewar period, and this section of the book, detailing his family background, seems intended to serve a similar structural function of delineating a world that the war put an end to. Like Sassoon's work, it is marked by dramatic irony – the fact that Graves's mother's family was German, for instance, or that he did not fit in at school. Theoretically the callow public school priggishness[43] and know-all superiority that the young Graves exhibits should be what he says "good-bye" to, but in fact the narrating Graves of the final chapters is little changed from the opening chapters. It is as if his war experience prevents him from maturing beyond that younger self. "Robert, you have the finest natural balance that I have ever seen in a climber," says Geoffrey Young, the author of "the only satisfactory text-book on rock-climbing" before the war, and the older Graves feels compelled to publish the remark. And the postwar Graves finds it necessary to report the number of times he revised his poems: "I have never written a poem in less than three drafts; the greatest number I recall is thirty-five . . . The average at this time was eight; it is now six or seven."[44] He boasts of getting Walter De la Mare to "admit" that he had been forced to leave the assonance of "roves" and "rose" in his famous lines,

> Ah, no man knows
> Through what wild centuries
> Roves back the rose;

because no other word but "roves" was strong enough. Graves must have known perfectly well that De la Mare chose the word precisely because of the assonance: the point of the anecdote is a childish need to demonstrate his own superior poetic taste.[45]

Graves seems as split as Sassoon, though not painfully so. He shows a contradictory desire to perform well in a publicly validated role and simultaneously debunk the project in which he has achieved excellence. This tendency (following the rule enunciated by Ford) is intensified in wartime; Graves takes tremendous pride in the traditions of his historic regiment (as well as exhibiting only questionable modesty about his own soldierly prowess) yet simultaneously mocks and rejects these traditions when manifested (largely as "bull") at the Front. These contradictions are not resolved in the narrative; Graves simply says good-bye to them.

A telling passage about Edmund Blunden is omitted from the 1957 revision. Both Blunden and Graves were studying at Oxford after the war, and living at Boar's Hill: "Edmund had war-shock as badly as myself, and we would talk each other into an almost hysterical state about the trenches. We agreed that we would not be right until we got all that talk on paper. He was first with *Undertones of War*."[46] Here is a key to understanding *Good-bye to All That* (if not Blunden's memoir). Its grim humor – in the absurdist account of the Battle of Loos, for example – has a hysterical edge to it, and that hysteria (or "neurasthenia") is a defense against an unbearable reality. If Graves's personality is exasperating (to some readers, at least), *Good-bye to All That* remains vivid and accessible; many who have been deterred by the length of *The Complete Memoirs of George Sherston* or the artifice of *Undertones of War* are likely to have read Graves's memoir eagerly from start to finish.

Graves's "good-bye" to English culture has left him difficult to classify as a writer: not really a Georgian poet, yet not a modernist, either. His later quasi-modernist obsession with Celtic myth is certainly related to the archaizing tendency of one strand of modernism, yet in Graves it remains purely personal, instead of becoming what T. S. Eliot called "a way of controlling, of ordering, of giving a shape and significance to the immense panorama of futility and anarchy which is contemporary history."[47]

Eliot was a great admirer of *In Parenthesis* by David Jones, welcomed it as a publisher and wrote an enthusiastic introduction to it in 1961. First published in 1937, *In Parenthesis* is not strictly a memoir, but neither can it be confined by any other generic description, and it avowedly concerns "some things I saw, felt, & was part of" during the war.[48] Far more even than Blunden's or Sassoon's work, it longs to accommodate the modern soldier's experience to a sacral, timeless history that stretches back to Celtic Arthurian legend and beyond. At the same time it is devoted to the most "trivial" of detail, such as tinned butter: "Watcyn had already opened the *Dairymaid* canned butter, it was just light enough to know the green and gilt of the enamelled tin. It was an extremely good brand."[49] The narrative, part verse, part a mannered quasi-Joycean prose, moves abruptly between myth and modernity (not always without strain), here bringing suddenly to sharp focus the precise sensation of, say, stumbling along a waterlogged trench in the dark, there seeing through the figures of sleeping soldiers to their primordial archetypes, the "armed sleepers under the mounds" of Celtic myth.[50] What enables the work to accommodate, side by side, such disparate vocabularies as military jargon, music-hall song, jingoistic newspaper talk, soldiers' profane slang, and the heroic phraseology of *chansons de geste*, is Jones's all-comprehending love, sustained by religious faith. But the accommodation is not easily achieved, and, as Jones admits in his preface, beyond a certain point in the war (July 1916 is the date given – that is, the commencement of the Battle of the Somme) it cannot be sustained: "The wholesale slaughter of the later years, the conscripted levies filling the gaps in every file of four, knocked the bottom out of the intimate, continuing, domestic life of small contingents of men, within whose structure Roland could find, and, for a reasonable while, enjoy, his Oliver."[51] For this reason *In Parenthesis* is an elegiac work, consciously cut off from a large area of war experience, and not allowed to reach that point of disintegration recorded by Sassoon, when Arthurian chivalry could only manifest itself as a desperate pretense.

When Edmund Blunden was shyly presenting his slim volume of verse to Guy Chapman at Observatory Ridge near Ypres, Wyndham Lewis was a few hundred yards to their rear serving as a second-lieutenant in charge of six-inch howitzers. His reading-matter was quite different: Proudhon, Marx, and *The Charterhouse of Parma*. This very deliberate choice signals a quite different – "un-English" – approach to the war. Lewis's autobiography, *Blasting and Bombardiering*, was not written until 1937, when the fashion for war books had passed.[52] Lewis had spent much energy in the thirties promoting appeasement of Germany, in the hope of avoiding another war. *Blasting and Bombardiering* is as he says, a *"good-bye to all that,"* but "that" in this case includes the whole cultural complex of war, modernism and what Lewis regarded as the postwar "saturnalia" of the twenties. Apart from David Jones (a postwar latecomer to modernism), Lewis was the only major modernist to have survived significant experience on the Western Front. He was not made into a modernist by the war, but had already produced a great deal of the writing and painting on which his reputation still rests. His memoir begins with a scene that illustrates the point: he is interrupted by the camp adjutant while drilling his squad in training and, standing to attention, is interrogated by him about the meaning of a Vorticist painting of his (Lewis gives it the significantly evocative title, *Break of Day – Marengo*) illustrated in that morning's *Daily Sketch*.[53]

Blasting and Bombardiering is as much about Lewis's fellow-modernists, Pound, Joyce, and Eliot, as it is about the war, and its statement about these "Men of 1914" that *"We are the first men of a Future that has not materialized"* has entered the mythology of modernism.[54] The varieties of cultural arrest that the present chapter has identified in the memoirs discussed were felt by Lewis as a more general British postwar resistance to any modernist art and writing that attempted a positive revaluation of the modernity that had as its negative face the inhumanity of mechanized war. Modernization proceeded, but a "shell-shocked" English culture averted its gaze. Lewis's most intense and complex explorations of the experience of the war and of its significance are not in *Blasting and Bombardiering*, however, but in his war art – particularly the large *A Battery Shelled* (1919, Imperial War Museum) – and, peculiarly transformed, in his fantasy novel of posthumous existence "outside Heaven," *The Childermass* (1928), a comprehensive anatomy of the trauma caused by the war in postwar culture. Nevertheless, Lewis's account of the war of the heavy-gunner in *Blasting and Bombardiering* is vivid, evocative, and readable.

New war memoirs continued to appear into the 1960s and beyond.[55] It is curious to read E. J. Campbell's comment on how little he saw of the 1918 retreat (in which he served as a field gunner): "It's much better on TV or at the cinema, the battles there look far more realistic."[56] TV! Of course, war veterans survived into the television era, but the remark still brings one up with a jolt. For Campbell writes about his experiences with as vivid an immediacy as Herbert Read had done fifty years earlier. Sent to reconnoiter some river crossings on the Somme for the retreating battalion, he was filled with wonder at the apparent irreconcilability of the peaceful scene before him with the likelihood of imminent attack by an unseen enemy. Beside a "clear running stream with tall poplars above our heads and spring flowers at our feet" he sees a "distraught-looking" infantry officer from whom he thinks he may get information:

> "It's a funny war," I said. I thought he would know what I meant.
>
> But he did not know. He looked at me, he saw my artillery badges, he was on foot, I was riding; he may have been the only survivor from his company. "It may be for you," he said, and the sound of his voice still hurts after more than fifty years, I hated his thinking that it had all been easy for us.[57]

It is a vital function of literature to keep that hurt and voice alive, for it is now only in literature that they live with their original immediacy. As I conclude this chapter, an obituary in the day's newspaper announces the death of the last surviving officer who served with the British army on the Western Front.

NOTES

1. "Canadian War Memorials," Royal Academy (Jan.–Feb. 1919), "The Nation's War Paintings and other Records," Royal Academy (Dec. 1919–Jan. 1920). C. R. W. Nevinson's pre-1917 "Cubist" war paintings had already established the connection.
2. Herbert Read, "Introduction," *In Retreat* (1925; rpt. London: Imperial War Museum, 1991), 7. This facsimile has an excellent Introduction by John Onions.
3. *Ibid.*, 37–38.
4. *Ibid.*, 29.
5. Ezra Pound, "A Retrospect," in *Literary Essays of Ezra Pound*, ed. T. S. Eliot (1918; rpt. London: Faber and Faber, 1954), 3.
6. C. E. Montague, *Disenchantment* (1922; rpt. London: Chatto & Windus, 1924), 159–60.
7. William Shakespeare, *King Lear*, ed. Kenneth Muir (London: Methuen, 1964), v, iii, 170.
8. Montague, *Disenchantment*, 211, 228.
9. *Ibid.*, 1.
10. This fragment, "De Bello Germanico" (1918), was published in 1930, reprinted Edmund Blunden, *Undertones of War* (London: Folio Society, 1989).
11. Edmund Blunden, *Undertones of War* (Harmondsworth: Penguin, 1982), 7, 8.
12. *Ibid.*, 242.
13. *Ibid.*, 7.
14. *Ibid.*, 181.
15. *Ibid.*, 182.
16. *Ibid.*, 181.
17. Paul Fussell, *The Great War and Modern Memory* (1975; rpt. with new afterword, New York and Oxford: Oxford University Press, 2000), 268–69.
18. Blunden, *Undertones*, 111.
19. *Ibid.*, 242. In fact Blunden spent the remainder of the war in England, so did not witness the intimated future horrors.

20. Guy Chapman, *A Passionate Prodigality: Fragments of Autobiography* (1935; rpt. Leatherhead: Ashford Buchan and Enright, 1985), 13. *Undertones*, 15.
21. Chapman, *Passionate Prodigality*, 207.
22. *Ibid.*, 188, 217–18.
23. *Ibid.*, 281.
24. Blunden, *Undertones*, 17.
25. Siegfried Sassoon, *The Complete Memoirs of George Sherston* (London: Faber, 1972), 558.
26. *Ibid.*, 450–51.
27. *Ibid.*, 654–55.
28. *Ibid.*, 534.
29. *Ibid.*, 496.
30. *Ibid.*, 124.
31. Sassoon writes that if Rivers were still alive (he had died in 1922), he might have been "obliged to call him by some made-up name, which would seem absurd" (*Ibid.*, 534).
32. *Ibid.*, 296, 509.
33. *Ibid.*, 241, 258, 274–75.
34. *Ibid.*, 421.
35. *Ibid.*, 431, 437.
36. *Ibid.*, 580.
37. *Ibid.*, 437, 435.
38. *Ibid.*, 425.
39. See Martin Seymour-Smith, *Robert Graves: His Life and Work*, revised edn. (London: Bloomsbury, 1995), 197–99.
40. Bruce Bairnsfather's humorous drawings of life in the trenches featured the long-suffering "Old Bill."
41. Wyndham Lewis, *Blasting and Bombardiering* (London: Eyre and Spottiswoode, 1937), 6.
42. Robert Graves, *Good-bye to All That*, 2nd edn. (London: Jonathan Cape, 1929), 13.
43. "Public" schools in England are fee-paying schools.
44. *Good-bye*, 391. In the 1957 revision the numbers are omitted; see *Good-bye to All That* (Harmondsworth: Penguin, 1973), 256.
45. *Good-bye*, 397. In the revised version, Graves is less pushy, asking instead of telling De la Mare (262). But an anecdote about W. H. Davies's high opinion of Graves as a poet is strengthened.
46. *Ibid.*, 360–61.
47. T. S. Eliot, "*Ulysses*, Order and Myth" (1923), in *James Joyce: The Critical Heritage*, ed. R. H. Deming, vol. 1 (London: Routledge and Kegan Paul, 1970), 268.
48. David Jones, *In Parenthesis* (1937; revised edn., London: Faber and Faber, 1978), ix.
49. *Ibid.*, 97
50. *Ibid.*, 45, 51, 198–99 (note 36).
51. *Ibid.*, ix.

52. Wyndham Lewis, *Blasting and Bombardiering* (London: Eyre and Spottiswoode, 1937). The 1967 Calder and Boyars edition was expanded and revised by Lewis's widow.
53. *Ibid.*, 23–25.
54. *Ibid.*, 258 (Lewis's italics).
55. For example, R. J. Campbell, *The Ebb and Flow of Battle* (1977; rpt. Oxford: Oxford University Press, 1979); M. L. Walkington, *Twice in a Lifetime* (London: Samson Books, 1980).
56. Campbell, *Ebb and Flow*, 78.
57. *Ibid.*, 48.

2

DAVID TROTTER

The British novel and the war

In James Hanley's *The German Prisoner* (1930), two defiantly proletarian British soldiers, O'Garra and Elston, lose contact with their unit during an assault on the German lines. The "fog of war" has had the effect, it seems, of putting them once and for all beyond authority's reach. They capture a young German soldier called Otto Reiburg whose fair hair and fine clear eyes represent to them a provocatively bourgeois "grace of body." The buried "rottenness" in O'Garra shoots up like filth from a sewer in a deathly premature ejaculation. O'Garra and Elston begin to beat Reiburg unconscious. Elston urinates on him. O'Garra drives a bayonet into his anus. "Elston laughed and said: 'I'd like to back-scuttle the bugger.'" And that appears to be that. The worst obscenity, in a performance obscene from beginning to end, is that Reiburg remains unraped. The Sadean utopia O'Garra and Elston have built for themselves inside war's thickening excremental fog is dedicated to the pursuit of death alone. A shell duly puts an end to them both.[1]

Gunn, the veteran protagonist of Liam O'Flaherty's *Return of the Brute* (1929), is another man subject to deathly ejaculations. The object of Gunn's desire is a raw recruit feminized by cowardice, whose timidity becomes to him a "seductive temptation." He at once gives in to and overcomes temptation by murdering a sadistic corporal, as it were on his friend's behalf, while they are out on a raid. "Now he was really an animal, brutish, with dilated eyes, with his face bloody."[2] Gunn has joined O'Garra and Elston inside the fog of war.

Such brutishness is not absolutely unprecedented in fiction. One thinks of Zola's Rougon-Macquart novels, or of D. H. Lawrence's "The Prussian Officer" (1914), in which a young recruit murders the officer who has persecuted him sexually. But there is nothing else quite like it in British First World War fiction. Indeed, it is from the scarcity of such scenes that an account of the British war novel must begin. The most obvious explanation for that scarcity turns on class.

Hanley and O'Flaherty were of proletarian origin; both served in the ranks during the war, and both fully intended to do justice to the brute's point of view.[3] Most British war novels were written by middle-class writers who fully intended to do justice to the point of view either of the officer and gentleman, or of the gentleman-ranker (that is, the un-brutish private soldier whose superior education made him worthy of, though not necessarily ambitious for, a commission). The implicit investment these novels all make, with or without enthusiasm, is in the durability of the class-system. The class-system goes to war, and survives, even if its individual representatives do not (they often do not). What gets lost in the excremental fog conjured up by Hanley and O'Flaherty is not just desire, but the class-system.

Not having to worry about the class-system's survival enables Hanley and O'Flaherty to conceive protagonists whose existence is in action. O'Garra, Elston, and Gunn act on their impulses. They get to do things they might not otherwise have done. They kill people intentionally. Middle-class writers, by contrast, seem to have convinced themselves that the price of collective durability was the individual's painful and sometimes profoundly damaging adaptation to a new and hostile environment. Adaptation is in essence reactive. It often entails, or is realized by, suffering; at the very least, it requires one not to do things one might otherwise have done. On the whole, British war novels, like British war memoirs, have a lot to say about physical and mental suffering. Reading these novels and memoirs, one wonders why the Germans ever lost the war, since little meaningful action is taken against them. What requires explanation, in the paradigmatic British war novel, is the belief it articulates that a maximum of individual adaptability will ensure a minimum of collective change.

I have spoken of the paradigmatic British war novel. I should perhaps have spoken more narrowly of the paradigmatic British combat novel, since I have in mind writing which derives the entirety of its substance and shape from the unique event, or series of events, known as the First World War. The British combat novel relies on familiarity with a form of warfare which, although not altogether unprecedented, had never before taken place on such a scale, and to such devastating effect, and did not take place again. Such books would be inconceivable without that form of warfare. In them, existence before the war and existence after the war has a meaning only in relation to what happened in between: the microcosm of the trenches. The shape of the story told about what happened in between is the shape of existence within the microcosm.

This is not to argue that trench experience should be regarded as the sole criterion of authenticity, and therefore, by some accounts, of literary value. I am very much in sympathy with critics who believe that, whether or not we regard them as combatants, the women who served as nurses or ambulance-drivers during the war made a significant contribution to its literature.[4] How better to grasp the nature of the physical and mental damage done by a particular form of combat than through the eyes of the women whose task was to help repair it? Furthermore, if we are to understand the social as well as the military dimension of combat, we surely cannot afford to ignore the testimony of refugees, cabinet ministers, munitions workers, pacifists, and bereaved parents. On the whole, however, the novels written by and about noncombatants have as their topic the consequences of war in general. Thus, Mr. Britling's response to his son's death in the trenches, in Wells's *Mr. Britling Sees It Through* (1916), is not at all unlike Mr. Osborne's response to *his* son's death at Waterloo, in Thackeray's *Vanity Fair* (1848).

By contrast, the novels written by and about combatants have as their topic the unique flavor of this war to end all wars, its difference from other wars. When Wells came to describe a futile attack, in *Mr. Blettsworthy on Rampole Island* (1928), he found the flavor he needed in a novel written by a combatant about combatants, A. D. Gristwood's *The Somme* (1927).[5] My concentration on the combat novel is in the name of the historical specificity it arose out of and sought to commemorate.

A great deal of admirable work has already been done to identify and contextualize examples of the British First World War combat novel.[6] The need, now, I think, is to define the belief which animates it, the belief that the maximum of individual adaptability will ensure a minimum of collective change. The first section of this chapter will argue, by reference to specific examples, that we can indeed speak of a paradigmatic British First World War combat novel. The second section will investigate the positioning of the combat novel's protagonist – a positioning at once loose and absolutely unbreakable – within a class-system built to last. The third section will assess the cost to the individual of the demand that she or he should adapt to a new and extremely hostile environment, but adapt without changing. The war defined that unbreakable looseness as trauma. If the combat novel was conservative in its advocacy of a renewed commitment to the British class-system, it was radical in its insistence on the damage done in the renewing.

The nature of damage

According to Samuel Hynes, the figure of the "damaged man" began to receive sympathetic attention during the middle years of the war. Hynes has shown that after the war this figure became a "dominant character" in literature, radically altering the "whole idea of literary war."[7] Hynes's prime example of the figure of the damaged man is Harry Penrose, the protagonist of A. P. Herbert's *The Secret Battle* (1919), a sensitive and idealistic young man who endures the ordeal of Gallipoli – an ordeal to which the laziness and spite of some of his fellow-officers is a major contributing factor – and is then sent to France. In France, his superiors start, at first with little justification, to doubt his courage. Obliged to undertake ever more dangerous tasks in order to prove himself, Penrose is wounded, and evacuated to England. His nerve has gone. However, he insists on returning to the Front, where he breaks down under fire, and turns tail. He is court-martialled, and shot.

In his vivid fantasy of participation in a "Greeklike struggle," as in his susceptibility to the macabre tales savoringly told by veterans, Harry Penrose greatly resembles Henry Fleming, the protagonist of Stephen Crane's *The Red Badge of Courage* (1895), who also turns tail, but gets his red badge anyway, from a random blow to the head, and honorably resumes combat.[8] *The Red Badge of Courage* is the archetypal "secret battle" novel, the first modern war book. In September 1916, somewhere in the Ypres salient, Ford Madox Ford found that Crane's "visualization" of an army encampment had "superimposed" itself on the "concrete objects" in the world around him.[9] He was, for a moment, living the book.

There is, however, a crucial difference between Crane's version of the secret battle and Herbert's. Penrose, unlike Fleming, but like the vast majority of the protagonists of British First World War fiction, including those who serve in the ranks, is middle-class, and conscious of it. He is every inch – in his basic decency, in his Oxford education, in the crush he develops on a "young Apollo" among his fellow-officers – the English gentleman. The performance at issue in this fantasy of status (this classed and gendered fantasy) constitutes the British combat novel. The protagonist must perform, or be branded a coward; so must the novel. If one fails, the other may yet succeed, by readjusting expectations. Such, at least, is the stated aim of the narrator of *The Secret Battle*.

The readjustment involves, above all, a description of the battlefield: the environment in which the protagonist has been required to perform. The plain-speaking narrator of *The Secret Battle*, a fellow-officer (Herbert had served at Gallipoli and in France) insists that the explanation for Penrose's conduct is to be found among the "dreary commonplaces of all war-chronicles."[10] These commonplaces might be thought dreary because they turn neither on exhilaration nor on terror, but on disgust. There is no escaping disgust, in First World War narratives. Disgust might be thought the inevitable (that is, "natural") response to many of the scenes witnessed during battle and its long-drawn-out aftermath. But it is more than that. It is the feeling above (or below) all others which these war chronicles intend to provoke in their readers. Oddly, given its pervasiveness, little account has been taken of the nature and uses of this feeling.[11] Here, I shall concentrate on disgust's relation to fear.

As a response, disgust lies somewhere between fight and flight. The nineteenth-century French psychiatrist Théodule Ribot concluded that disgust takes over when flight is impossible: "the organism cannot escape by movement in space from the repugnant body which it has taken into itself, and goes through a movement of expulsion instead."[12] In the trenches, of course, flight was, indeed, impossible. Precisely because it sets in when one is immobile, however, disgust can sometimes produce a phenomenology: a description of being-in-the-world, of what existence still means, if anything, once the customary methods of conceiving it (political, moral, theological) have been suspended. British combat novels and memoirs achieve a quite astonishing purchase on the texture of event.

Trench warfare instigated a carnival of all the faculties. "Everything visible or audible or tangible to the sense – to touch, smell and perception – is ugly beyond imagination," wrote W. Beach Thomas, who had witnessed five months of fighting on the Somme in 1916.[13] Returning from leave, in May 1916, Lieutenant Wyn Griffith realized that he now had more to lose, "for the deadening power of months of trench habit had been lifted from my mind leaving my fibre bare to the weakest blast of war." The medium of war's weakest (but still toxic) blast was disgust. "Sound, sight and smell were all challenged at once, and they must in concert submit to the degrading slavery of war."[14] The ugliness, then, was complex. But the complexity, as articulated by the novels and memoirs, reveals a high degree of organization, a *history*.

Steven Connor has argued that modernity should be understood not in terms of the subordination of the proximity senses, as typified by the ear, to the hegemony of the eye, but rather in terms of a fraught and continually renewed argument between the powers of ear and eye. Ear and eye offer different versions of what being-in-the-world is like. Sight has often been understood as a principle of integration, sound as disintegrative. Although we can only see one thing at a time, we can hear several sounds simultaneously. Furthermore, sound often carries menace unless we can trace it back to a specific source, or visualize its origin. Noise, especially loud noise, is always "agonistic": it involves the maximum at once of arousal and of passivity.[15] The sound of the guns, composite and sourceless, was a primary terror for the soldier in the trenches. And not just enemy guns. Chronicle after chronicle describes a journey to or from the Front line during which concealed British artillery suddenly and shockingly looses off.

In the hierarchy of the senses, sight belongs at the top, largely because the distance at which it acts makes possible an array of measures of precaution and control. The proximity senses traditionally rank lower. Lowest of all is smell. That there are bad sounds need not diminish the glory of hearing. That there are delightful fragrances has done little to elevate smell: traditionally, the best odor is not a good odor, but no odor at all.[16] The combat novels and memoirs describe smell as the most disintegrative principle of all, the most damaging to moral and perceptual fibre. Everywhere it undermines vision. The eyes can usually be averted from a bad sight (though it may well return as a mental image). But a bad smell is inside you before you can do anything about it. It takes possession.

The difference is semantic as well as cognitive. Smells are hard to define. "Even though the human sense of smell can distinguish hundreds of thousands of smells and in this regard is comparable to sight or hearing," Dan Sperber has observed, "in none of the world's languages does there seem to be a classification of smells comparable, for example, to colour classification." There is no taxonomy of smells, no semantic field. When we define smells, we do so in terms either of their causes (the smell of incense, the smell of excrement) or of their effects (a heady perfume, an appetising smell). In the domain of smell, "metonymy remains active and infallibly evokes cause or effect."[17] Whereas the unpleasantly tactile possesses its own rich and versatile idiom (oozy, squishy, gummy, dank, and so on), an idiom richly at work in combat novels and combat memoirs, the unpleasantly odorous does not. The tactile is a stimulus to literary invention.[18] By contrast, it is the *lack* of an appropriate semantic field which renders the mere allusion to a bad smell in narrative profoundly unsettling. It produces either a helpless metonymic proliferation, or an abrupt halt, a lapse into no-meaning. A bad smell always returns from elsewhere, from beyond conscious recollection.

The Secret Battle chronicles Harry Penrose's education in disgust, which connects with, but is not quite the same thing as, his education in fear. On his way to war, Penrose amply betrays his infatuation with an heroic ideal, as Stephen Fleming had done before him. On their first night in the front line, the narrator introduces Penrose to reality in the shape of the stench emanating from a dead Turk. For the narrator, it is enough to know that the stench exists. Penrose needs to define it minutely by tracing it back to a source. "Forthwith he swarmed over the parapet, full of life again, nosed about till he found the reeking thing, and gazed on it with undisguised interest." He shows, as yet, no sign of horror or disgust. War will destroy that immunity. It will train him in horror and disgust. A "complex irritation" made of sounds, smells, animosities, slights, and the "disgustful torment" of disease corrodes his "young system."[19] The enemy plays a part in all this, but only a small part. The final stage in the destruction of Penrose's young system occurs when the company takes over a trench seized from the

Turks. Surveying the corpses sprawled in the "corrupt aftermath" of battle, the narrator adopts the position of a generalized observer. Such corrupt aftermaths, we are to understand, were drearily commonplace.

> But there was a hideous fascination about the things, so that after a few hours a man came to know the bodies in his bay with a sickening intimacy, and could have told you many details about each of them – their regiment, and how they lay, and how they had died, and little things about their uniforms, a missing button, or some papers, or an old photograph sticking out of a pocket . . . All of them were alive with flies, and at noon when we took out our bread and began to eat, these flies rose in a great black swarm and fell upon the food in our hands. After that no-one could eat. All day men were being sent away by the doctor, stricken with sheer nausea by the flies and the stench and the things they saw, and went retching down the trench.

The phenomenology is in the enforced intimate attention, in the nausea. The narrator remembers that first evening when Penrose had jumped over the parapet to look at the dead Turk. "He had seen enough now."[20]

The best solution to nausea was to remain uneducated in it; or, more precisely, to fall back on a different kind of training, a training in ignorance of the body. Fortunately for the British army such training had been amply provided by the public schools. Penrose knows, and is able convincingly to enact, paternalism. He is a good officer because he performs concern for his men, and nonchalance. He cheerfully undertakes the "melancholy rite" of demonstrating to a reluctant sentry how safe it is to raise one's head above the parapet by doing so himself, without fuss. "He had a keen dramatic instinct, and I think in these little scenes rather enjoyed the part of the unperturbed hero calming the timorous herd."[21] It is no coincidence that the scene involves a reassertion of the ascendancy of sight. When he volunteers to act as scouting officer, Penrose makes himself into the very epitome of the powers of the eye. His task is not just to see, but to see without being seen. The scout performs invisibility. If a flare goes up, he freezes, because "to keep still in any posture is better than to move." Penrose's performance of seeing-without-being-seen is a way to exorcize the body on all other occasions in the trenches brought so fully into play, by sound, smell, touch, and taste. When one of his men panics, and the scouting party is caught out in the open, the exposure destroys his ability to perform in general.[22] Thereafter, he has no defense against disgust and the phenomenology it generates.

It may be that the British public was not ready, in 1919, for Herbert's account of the incapacitating effects of an education in disgust. The book did not sell. It was reissued, however, in 1924, with an admiring preface by

Winston Churchill; and then again in 1928, as the demand for chronicles of damaged men and women took off, ten years after the end of the war which had done the damage. Britain in the late 1920s was of course not quite the same place. Much has been made, for example, of the fact that the "classic" memoirs and novels were written in the aftermath not of the war itself, but of the General Strike, "war's echo in society," which began on 4 May 1926.[23] Eric Leed even suggests that it was not until the Depression had "closed the gap" between civilian and ex-soldier, by reducing both to powerlessness, that the combat novels and memoirs began to appear in substantial numbers.[24] Another significant difference, and one to which I shall return, lay in the development in the early 1920s of a particular psychiatric vocabulary; in their depiction of mental suffering, the memoirs and novels were to some extent the product of a new traumatology, a "culture of trauma."[25] Broadly speaking, however, there was a fair amount of consistency between the war literature published before traumatology and the Strike and the war literature published after it. With some notable exceptions, as we have seen, they had the same story to tell: the story of damage, of middle-class suffering.

The power of the paradigm is evident even, or especially, in those novels which sought to modify it from within. John Hardcastle, the hero of James Lansdale Hodson's *Grey Dawn – Red Night* (1929), is of working-class origin. Like Paul Morel, in Lawrence's *Sons and Lovers* (1913), whom he closely resembles, Hardcastle has raised himself above both physical labor and a drunken father by employment in white-collar jobs, first as a solicitor's clerk, then as a journalist. On the boat to France, he reads two stories about running away, Crane's *The Red Badge of Courage* and Conrad's *Lord Jim*.[26] He could become Stephen Fleming, the canny proletarian survivor; or Lord Jim, who owns up, like the gentleman he is, and takes his punishment.

Work matters, in this novel: it is one of the few to describe in detail the working practices, as the British army conceived them, of warfare. Hardcastle, a lance-corporal in the Twentieth Royal Fusiliers, believes that he will win his secret battle against fear and disgust by a commitment to work. For him, as for the gentlemanly Harry Penrose, the real test lies in the corrupt aftermath of ground taken from the enemy. "It affected him more than all else, and now that they had passed through the dread spot, from time to time the stench again came and dwelt in his nostrils."[27] He escapes the stench, as before the war he had escaped his drunken father, by employment in a "white-collar" job: as an orderly at company headquarters. He might have been an upwardly mobile Henry Fleming. But Hodson cannot leave it there. He seems to have felt that his novel had to be a story about middle-class suffering, even though the hero is not (or not yet) middle class. Conrad eclipses both Crane and Lawrence. Hardcastle is killed while on his way back from company headquarters to take up the offer of a commission. The novel itself has left him out in the open. It does not know how to tell a story about combat which would include social mobility (or a story about social mobility which would include combat).

If the prospect of social mobility sets one limit to the story of middle-class suffering, then the prospect of cowardice unpunished, or punished lightly, sets another: we need to ask (the combat novel needs to ask) how far adaptation can go. A. D. Gristwood's *The Somme* (1927), a story of middle-class suffering, begins with a description of ground just taken from the enemy. As in *The Secret Battle*, the flies settling on bloated corpses form the *pièce de résistance*, the ultimate provocation to nausea. In his preface, H. G. Wells characterized *The Somme* as an antidote to the "high enthusiastic survey" of the war which had been undertaken by Herbert's admirer, Winston Churchill. Low, and unenthusiastic, it certainly is. Gristwood seems to want to ask how low and unenthusiastic one can get, as a combatant and a writer, without ceasing to be a gentleman.

Everitt, Gristwood's protagonist, doesn't run away. But he doesn't *not* run away, either. *The Somme* is the story of his survival, after being wounded in a futile "advance," and of the long journey back from no-man's-land to No. 5 General Hospital at Rouen. Everitt fails to perform. He abandons his part in the assault on the enemy trenches and flops into a shell-hole. "Perhaps after all they could *not* see him. Above all he must lie still, for it seemed that shots answered his slightest movement."[28] But he cannot perform immobility, either. He is hit in the leg and the arm. Everitt is a bit of a brute. Like Hanley's O'Garra and Elston, like O'Flaherty's Gunn, he comes into his own in no-man's-land, in war's excremental fog. Unlike them, he will not act, but suffer. What he suffers is an immobilization in and by disgust more complete than that suffered by any other protagonist in British combat fiction. The novel's concluding section describes his near-entombment in a hammock slung two feet from the roof of a carriage on a hospital train full of the dead and dying. He realizes that his wounds have gone septic. "The stench seemed more offensive whenever in his twistings and turnings he raised the folds of the blanket on his cot. The sickening sweetish odour filled him with a shuddering disgust, and appetite fled."[29] Everitt's shuddering disgust is an adaptation of a kind; but a great deal too close to brutishness for comfort.

Soldiering as philanthropy

There are no British war novels about colonels (let alone brigadiers or field-marshals). As far as literature is concerned, this was indeed, as the title of

Charles Carrington's memoir has it, *A Subaltern's War*.[30] The novels, like most of the memoirs, have a lot to say about the trials and tribulations of leadership, and of being led: but not much about the enemy, who are a nuisance, and frequently the cause of spectacular random destruction, but do not figure in the defining psychomachia. The term "strafe," ubiquitous in both, has reference rather more often to reprimands delivered by unsympathetic senior officers than it does to incoming artillery fire. The class-position specific to a subaltern in the Kitchener battalions raised at the beginning of war was an ambiguous one. The power of the novels and memoirs some of them subsequently wrote stems from that ambiguity.

John Keegan has described the difficulties an embryonic officer in this largely non-professional army might expect to face in "adopting a personal style to match the rank which chance had thrust upon him." The difficulties were eased somewhat by the army's decision to recruit the first temporary officers as far as possible from the public schools. Keegan points out that the eighteen-year-old who went on to the Royal Military College could be treated on arrival as someone "already formed" in character and attitude, someone whose only deficiency was in tactical training.[31] These eighteen-year-olds achieved a certain style merely by being themselves. Like the relationship between classes in civilian society, the relationship between officers and men in the British army was based on the exchange of deference for paternalism. Junior officers enjoyed all the privileges of rank: on condition that they did not shirk the dangers and hardships to which the men under their command were exposed, and made a genuine effort to protect them from the excesses of military discipline.[32] A single maxim, Ford Madox Ford wrote, was drummed into the junior officer: "The comfort and equanimity of the Men come before every exigency save those of actual warfare!" One consequence of this obligatory paternalism was "a knowledge of the lives, the aspirations, the sexual necessities even, of a large crowd."[33] The apology made to a staff officer who has been kept waiting by Christopher Tietjens, the protagonist of Ford's *Parade's End* (1924–28), is a declaration of pride. There were, Tietjens explains, some men to see to. "And, you know ... 'The comfort and – what is it? – of the men comes before every – is it "consideration"? – except the exigencies of actual warfare'."[34]

Most combat novels include at least one officer like Tietjens, or like Captain Mottram, in Hodson's *Grey Dawn – Red Night*, the epitome of new army paternalism. "He was gentle, almost womanly, with wounded or exhausted men, and would walk behind you and offer to share your load of rations."[35] The generalizing "you" and "your" indicate that such officers, although exceptional, were by no means a rarity. Even O'Flaherty's brutes speak fondly of an officer who looks after them "with the same enthusiasm that a man would show towards expensive and cherished horses on hunting days."[36]

The enthusiastic or almost womanly concern, the pride taken in service: that was what being oneself meant. There was, of course, an abundant moral earnestness in the subaltern's paternalism. But it also had a psychological or even psychiatric dimension. Paternalism entailed, inexorably, a literal and figurative *self-lowering*. The subaltern knelt at his men's feet. "Their feet were the most important part of them, I thought, as I made my sympathetic inspection of sores and blisters."[37] Christopher Tietjens would have understood. Equally assiduous in inspecting and attending to what had previously been beneath their notice were the self-consciously middle-class women recruited into the Voluntary Aid Detachments (VADs). "Every task, from the dressing of a dangerous wound to the scrubbing of a bed mackintosh, had for us in those early days a sacred glamour which redeemed it equally from tedium and disgust."[38]

There was psychological damage, as well as sacred glamor, in such self-lowering. The descent did not always bottom out. Sometimes it took the middle-class woman or man down into irredeemable tedium and disgust. Helen Smith, the ambulance-driving protagonist of Evadne Price's *Not So Quiet . . .: Stepdaughters of War* (1930), believes that it has become VAD policy to subject its middle-class recruits to the utmost degradation. Smith finds no glamor at all in the task of cleaning out the cook's room, which is full of rubbish, and reeks of sweat. Worse is to follow. "How we dread the morning clean-out of the insides of our cars, we gently-bred, educated women they insist on so rigidly for this work that apparently cannot be done by women incapable of speaking English with a public-school accent!"[39] Smith sees politics, rather than moralism, in the sacrifice demanded of middle-class volunteers.

If there was a precedent for self-lowering in British middle-class culture, it is to be found in that combination of evangelical or reforming fervor with an insatiable curiosity about how the other half lives which constituted the philanthropic movement. The figure of the philanthropist, male or female, was crucial both to the understanding and to the management of class-relations in the period leading up to the First World War.[40] During that period, a significant number of men and women found a kind of redemption by renouncing the privileges of birth and making a life for themselves in the slum or among factory-workers. There was sacred glamor to be won by such renunciations. On the whole, however, the privileges of birth survived intact. The philanthropist did not, for example, marry into or encourage political organization within the working class. He or she remained recognizably middle class, and proud of it, whatever the environment. Philanthropy combined a maximum of individual adaptability with a minimum of collective change.

Some of the best-known war writers were brought up to think and behave philanthropically. Robert Graves's mother, for example, had wanted to go to India, after training as a medical missionary; but marriage to a widower with five children suggested to her that she "could do as good work on the home-mission field."[41] Others, like Siegfried Sassoon, developed an interest in social reform as a result of what they had seen during the war.[42] The combat novel also witnessed one or two such transformations. Peter Currage, the protagonist of Christopher Stone's *The Valley of Indecision* (1920), falls under the sway of a visionary general who believes that the war has reinvigorated the "officer class" by obliging its members to attend, for the first time, to the needs of those over whom they exercise authority. Here Currage, like the hero of a nineteenth-century Condition of England novel, resolves to lead a crusade against materialism and complacency.[43] The general's political prescription (strong leaders, discipline, comradeship) sounds a lot like fascism, and it would be possible to think of one or two British combat novels in those terms.[44] On the whole, however, the subaltern philanthropists did not do fascism. Stone's later novel, *Flying Buttresses* (1927), is an account of Currage's emergence from this "religious phase, or craze," to play a more productive role as a traditional village squire.[45] The belief that the war had created a classless brotherhood of suffering and sacrifice was by no means widespread, but it found an echo in some rather unexpected places. In *The Well of Loneliness* (1928), for example, Radclyffe Hall allows Stephen Gordon to convince herself that the service she and other "inverts" have given during the war will be the means of their subsequent integration into society.[46]

The part played in nineteenth-century philanthropy and social reform by the slum was taken over, in the British combat novel and memoir, by the labyrinthine trench-system. Graves spent much of his first spell as officer of the watch in the trenches acquainting himself with their deceptive "geography": he repeatedly got lost a lot among "culs-de-sacs and disused alleys."[47] The war correspondent Philip Gibbs, whose work took him backwards and forwards between GHQ and the trenches, reported that the former had indeed heard of the latter, but only in the way that the fashionable West End of London had heard of the sordid East End, as a "nasty place" full of "common people."[48] Edmund Blunden remembered a stint as field works officer during which the trenches in his sector "began to look extremely neat." An itinerant general with a mania for chloride of lime complimented the field works officer on his achievement of a truly dazzling level of whiteness; "but actually it was powdered chalk that had enabled us to satisfy his sanitary imagination."[49] Here, as so often in the combat novels and memoirs, the subaltern acts as the West End's representative in the East. Sharing the condition of his men – mud, vermin, shell-fire, exhaustion – he looks after them, and polices them, in the name of a distant authority. Trench warfare, one might say, was Victorian philanthropy's last hurrah (or last gasp).

One novelist who experienced the war as Philip Gibbs had was R. H. Mottram. Mottram saw combat, but his fluency in French got him transferred to the claims commission, whose task it was to settle disputes between the British army and its civilian hosts and suppliers. Although not a staff officer, he was attached to divisional headquarters, and thus saw life, as he put it, from a level slightly above the trenches, but below officialdom.[50]

Mottram's admirable *The Spanish Farm Trilogy* (1924–26) is a sequence of novels much concerned with point of view. It adapts from Arnold Bennett's Clayhanger tetralogy the device of describing the same event from different points of view in successive volumes. In the first volume, *The Spanish Farm*, Madeleine Vanderlynden, who manages the farm on her father's behalf, and who has been seduced by the son of a local landowner, has a brief affair with a British architect-turned-officer, Geoffrey Skene. The second volume, *Sixty-Four, Ninety-Four!*, describes the affair from Skene's point of view. In the third, *The Crime at Vanderlynden's* (1926), a staff officer, the methodical Dormer, a bank clerk in civilian life, is given the job of identifying the man responsible for the damage done to a shrine on the Spanish Farm; he fails.

Like Gibbs, Mottram was in no doubt about the rigidity of the class-system which regulated life in the army. "If the trenches were the slums of that great city of two million English-speaking men, stretching across 80 miles of France," the narrator observes, then the roads traveled by a liaison officer like Skene were a "residential suburb," while corps headquarters had "the atmosphere of a London Club": "tea, cigarettes, conversation all belonged to people used to the very best, who were not going to alter their habits for a mere war." Skene and Dormer inhabit this terrain, without being defined by it. They have the philanthropist's talent for self-revision. The "endless adaptability" required of the new army officer encourages Skene to put his skills as an architect to use, not because he has been told to, but because it interests him. It is grimly appropriate that he should finish the war conducting sanitary inspections from a base in the cellar of a model house destroyed by shell-fire: "social reform murdered."[51] Mottram's development of a narrative method attuned to the intensities and limitations of point of view enables him to render effectively the fluidity of the subaltern–philanthropist's positioning at or just above the level of the slum.

The adjustment downwards undertaken by philanthropist and subaltern alike was at once a de-classing (a willful abandonment of the privileges of birth) and a de-classifying: the loss of the set of distinctions (between inside and outside, self and world) which had hitherto made identity conceivable. Disgust, which is the ultimate act of de-classifying, the body's acknowledgment that the distinction between self and world has collapsed (that the bad sound or bad smell is already inside), configures the philanthropic encounter. That is what the slum feels like, or the trenches, to those who cannot altogether forget the bourgeois drawing-room they chose honorably to abandon. Disgust brings one down to the level of things which have been brought down by an exposure of their materiality, their formlessness: the pile of excrement in the centre of a courtyard, the rotting corpse on the parapet. The rhetorical function this disgust serves, in the slum or trench chronicle, is to establish a certain singularity. The nausea felt by the philanthropist sets him or her apart both from the lower-class men and women whose behavior or circumstances have induced it, and from the upper-class men and women who have never known anything like it. From Edwin Chadwick's *Report on the Sanitary Condition of the Labouring Population of Great Britain* (1842) onward, reforming narratives vigorously performed an exemplary disgust.[52]

Even more comprehensively brought down by nausea than the subalterns were the gentleman-rankers who had honorably abandoned the privileges of birth in order to serve as private soldiers. In Hodson's *Grey Dawn – Red Night*, John Hardcastle, who is working class, but a journalist by profession, enlists as a private. So evident are the marks of a superior education (the marks which will eventually single him out for middle-class suffering) that he is immediately put in charge of "four or five youths and men, who were without collars, who smelt, and who were more or less tipsy." These he conducts to a training-camp near Liverpool. The camp, and the other men in it, make him ill. "Hardcastle lay there feeling as if he had been dropped from the sky into a filthy slum from which there was no escape."[53] Procuring a pass, he catches the train to Liverpool, and gratefully blends into a crowd of staff officers drinking whisky and soda at the Midland Adelphi Hotel. The Lawrence Hodson seems closest to here is the Lawrence whose disgust at the spectacle of mass conscription was to form the basis of the "Nightmare" chapter of *Kangaroo* (1923).[54]

The most celebrated gentleman-rankers in British First World War fiction are Bourne, in Frederic Manning's *The Middle Parts of Fortune* (1929), and Winterbourne, in Richard Aldington's *Death of a Hero* (1929): the coincidence in naming indicates that both these men are at a social and psychic limit, a "bourne" of some kind. Winterbourne is bullied by the NCOs of his training battalion, who are all old army regulars. Like Helen Smith's persecutors, in *Not So Quiet . . .* , they take revenge on what remains of his gentility by forcing him to remove the accumulated filth from the officers' mess kitchen. The memory of this degradation haunts him nauseously; he attributes to it the anxiety and depression he feels in combat. The élan of his former life dissolves. "He suffered at feeling that his body had become worthless, condemned to a sort of kept tramp's standard of living." But, ever the philanthropist, indeed, all the more the philanthropist after his reduction to kept tramp, he remains unwilling to apply for a commission: "it was contrary to his notion that he ought to stay in the ranks and in the line, take the worst and humblest jobs, share the common fate of the common men."[55] Staying in the ranks costs him his life.

At one point in *The Middle Parts of Fortune* an officer called Mr. Rhys tries to "get into touch" with the men, and to learn their thoughts, "without putting aside anything of his prestige and authority over them." "Only a great man," the narrator concludes, as the narrators of so many Condition of England novels had concluded before him, "can talk on equal terms with those in the lower ranks of life." Mr. Rhys, it seems, is "neither sufficiently imaginative, nor sufficiently flexible in character, to succeed."[56] Much the same could be said of someone like Walter Egremont, in George Gissing's *Thyrza* (1887), who tries to bring "spiritual education" to the "upper artisan and mechanic classes" (there is no point, he reckons, in disturbing the "mud" at the bottom of the social order).[57] Bourne, by contrast, does possess flexibility of character.

Bourne is, as far as I know, the only fictional trench-philanthropist who succeeds in developing, as a way not to be himself, an effective working-class style. Bourne improvises brilliantly. He can conjure a meal, or a bottle of whisky, or some sympathetic advice, out of nothing. His abilities as a scrounger earn him a kind of celebrity. These exploits establish *bricolage* as the working-class alternative to the middle-class show put on by Captain Malet, who likes to anticipate the launch of an attack by climbing out of the trench and strolling up and down on the parapet.[58] Malet performs nonchalance. Bourne puts things (anything and everything) to use. Bourne's style seems to work as well, in its way, as Malet's. But it is only a style. For all his scrounging, Bourne remains indisputably a gentleman in the eyes both of his companions and of his superiors. Acknowledging this – acknowledging the falseness of his hesitation between styles – he decides, reluctantly, to apply for a commission. Like Gissing's Walter Egremont, he will retreat from his slum. He is killed, like Hodson's John Hardcastle, on the point of setting off to train as an officer. Manning, like Hodson and Aldington, can see no way out for the gentleman-ranker. The gentleman-ranker cannot be allowed to cross that threshold within the class-system whose preservation is the only reason for his existence.

Trauma (or the uses of nausea)

In H. M. Tomlinson's *All Our Yesterdays* (1930), the narrator, an intelligence officer, visits a frontline unit in trenches somewhere beyond Ypres. "I was led through roofless houses and by broken walls, traversed a back-kitchen and yard were there was nothing but old bottles and a perambulator without wheels, passed a dead horse, and then met an aerial torpedo." Aerial torpedo apart, this could be a passage taken from any number of nineteenth-century accounts of the social reformer's or sensation-seeking journalist's entry into an urban slum. As, indeed, could the description which follows it of the descent into a damp, cluttered, foul-smelling dugout (for dugout, read slum-cellar). The occupants regale their visitor with the story of a fellow-officer who has been blown up by a shell, but will not get a wound stripe, because he was "only" driven head-first into the belly of a corpse. "And after that Mac never sang. He wouldn't eat. He only wanted to wash out his mouth with neat whisky." Disgust not only marks those who have been lowered, perhaps beyond redemption; it has become their uniform, their style, their element. After hearing about Mac, the visitor sets off to find a friend who is serving in the ranks, whom he thinks should apply for a commission. But this gentleman-ranker has gone lower than most, lower even than Hardcastle or Bourne. "He was going to put up with it. He would not allow me to try to change his fate."[59]

It is quite likely that the story of the man driven head-first into a corpse derives from the psychiatric literature on "shell shock." In "Repression of War Experience," printed in the *Lancet* on 2 February 1918, and then in *Instinct and the Unconscious* (1920), W. H. R. Rivers had written about an officer "flung down" by an explosion in such a way that his face struck and penetrated the belly of a German soldier several days dead. "Before he lost consciousness the patient had clearly realised his situation, and knew that the substance which filled his mouth and produced the most horrible sensations of taste and smell was derived from the decomposed entrails of an enemy." Haunted thereafter by "persistent images of taste and smell," like Mac in *All Our Yesterdays*, the man had to leave the army.[60]

The First World War was a psychiatric as well as a literary war, and after it there may have been some collusion between these two ways of thinking about distress of mind. Septimus Smith, in Virginia Woolf's *Mrs. Dalloway* (1925), haunted by memories of a friend blown to bits in front of his eyes, seems to belong to both. In Aldington's *Death of a Hero*, combat reduces

Winterbourne to an "anxiety complex" or "'worry' neurosis":[61] the fear of fear itself. Like *Death of a Hero*, Ford's *Parade's End* is in some measure a meditation on the theory as well as the practice of fear. "It seemed to me," Ford explained, "that, if I could present, not merely fear, not merely horror, not merely death, not merely even self-sacrifice . . . but just worry; that might strike a note of which the world would not so readily tire."[62] He could strike that note in part because he had read *Instinct and the Unconscious*.[63]

One point which Rivers tactfully does not make about his traumatized patient is that for him nausea evidently had its uses: it got him honorably out of the war, wound stripe or no. Rivers seems to have thought that so intense a disgust had left no room for fear. In another context, he described more explicitly the way in which horror and disgust sometimes took the place of fear in war neurosis.

> In those who suffer thus from the effect of war-experience, one party in the original conflict is usually the re-awakened danger-instinct in some form or other with its accompanying affect of fear, but this is often wholly displaced by the affect of horror associated with some peculiarly painful incident of war, or by the affect of shame following some situation which the sufferer fears that he has failed to meet in a proper manner.[64]

What traumatology seems to be saying, in this instance, is that war experience, which we might consider absolute in its extremity, is in fact relative. The feelings which constitute it derive their force not only from the horrific event which first provoked them, but also from their relation to each other. Experience at the human limit is thus not something one has, or succumbs to, but something one tries, often unsuccessfully, to put to use. Being disgusted is better than being afraid. It serves that purpose, at least. To grasp the relativity of traumatic experience is to create some space beyond it, so that one is no longer right up against the void. Adaptability, in short, had its psychiatric as well as its social dimension.

The narrator of *The Secret Battle* develops a "theory of the favourite fear." The favorite fear both disables and enables. It disables because it identifies a particular situation as intolerable. It enables because the panic induced by that situation in particular makes the panic induced by other situations seem trivial by comparison. "One man feels safe in the open, but in the strongest dug-out has a horror that it may be blown in upon him."[65] In *Instinct and the Unconscious*, Rivers returned frequently to the case of an officer in the Royal Army Medical Corp who suffered acutely from claustrophobia.[66] A phobia is always a "favorite" (that is, highly specific) fear. The enclosed spaces intolerable to the claustrophobe are a haven to the agoraphobe, who fears open terrain above all; and vice versa. On 9 January 1918, James

Dunn, a medical officer in the Royal Welch Fusiliers, noted in his diary that he had always found confinement in an enclosed space "hateful." He was subsequently awarded the MC and Bar and the DSO for his exploits in attending to the wounded in the open under heavy fire.[67]

Was it possible to nurture favorite disgusts, as well as favorite fears? I have already described the revulsion provoked in Harry Penrose and John Hardcastle by a highly specific battlefield horror: the "corrupt aftermath" of ground taken from the enemy (above, 40, 41). Edmund Blunden's "unwelcome but persistent retrospect" of a place called Stuff Trench was of a shellhole which had been put to use as a latrine, "with those two flattened German bodies in it, tallow-faced and dirty-stubbled."[68] It is the first time we've met the bodies, in *Undertones of War*; no story attaches to them. But to Blunden they are none the less utterly specific ("those two flattened German bodies"). The act of specification, performed at the time or in retrospect, seems to have been a way to consolidate a favorite disgust. Robert Graves devoted a poem and a vivid passage in *Good-bye to All That* to an "unforgettable" corpse he had come across in Mametz Wood.[69] Specification puts these corpses to use. It converts them from something to be frightened by, as evidence of death's near-certainty, into an object of disgust: an object of disgust like no other. So acute was the disgust provoked in him by one corpse in particular that Edwin Vaughan, returning to headquarters for instructions, felt unable to pass by it, and chose instead the shell-swept road. He took back with him to the front line an old oilsheet, which he spread over the offending corpse. It was from this point, with its horror outshining all other horrors, that he next led his platoon into action. It may be that he could not have done so from any other point.[70]

A combat novel does not have to be psychiatric to be effective. But the most effective First World War combat novels, I would suggest, are those which recognize that, for many of those who served in it, fear and disgust were a resource (adaptability's resource) rather than an affliction. In *The Middle Parts of Fortune*, Bourne devises for himself a kind of battlefield phenomenology. He begins with the thought that "it is infinitely more horrible and revolting to see a man shattered and eviscerated, than to see him shot." But such burdens fall on the eye, whose distance from the horrible and revolting sight is also a guarantee of safety. "The mind is averted as well as the eyes . . . And one moves on, leaving the mauled and bloody thing behind." The favorite disgust – a disgust powerful enough to supervene on all other disgusts – may require a further self-lowering, from sight to touch, or smell. Suddenly he remembers the "festering, fly-blown corruption" of the intermingled British and German dead in Trones Wood. "Out of one bloody misery into another, until we break. One must not break." The sheer relativity of horror is its saving grace. Later in the novel, Bourne, knowing that his nerve has almost gone, uses his awareness of the location of a particularly loathsome corpse to force himself out into and through an artillery barrage. Manning, however, has set a limit to Bourne's phenomenology, and to his bricolage: he is shot while returning from a raid designed to exploit and develop powers of improvisation.[71]

Christopher Tietjens, in *Parade's End*, sees active service both as the superintendent of a vast base camp from which drafts are despatched to the front line, in *No More Parades*, and as the officer temporarily in command of a battalion during the German offensive of March 1918, in *A Man Could Stand Up –*. Ford had believed that "being out in France" would at least cut him off from "private troubles." Far from it. "I have gone down to the Front line at night, worried, worried, worried beyond belief about happenings at home in a Blighty that I did not much expect to see again – so worried that all sense of personal danger disappeared and I forgot to duck when shells went close overhead."[72] So it is with Tietjens. *Parade's End* can be distinguished from all other British combat novels by the extent to which it relativizes anxiety. The favorite fears and disgusts which occupy its protagonist's head in rapid and colorful succession derive in equal measure from private and from public trouble. In *A Man Could Stand Up –*, a *coup de théâtre* has Tietjens, muddied and bloodied from the aftermath of an artillery barrage, brought face to face with the spruce inspecting general who has persecuted him relentlessly since before the war, because he wants to marry his wife.[73] But the novel does not rely on *coups de théâtre*. Its entire method inscribes, or brings about, relativity. The first part of *A Man Could Stand Up –* is told from the point of view of Valentine Wannop, Tietjens's (eventual) lover, as she takes a class in physical education on the morning of the Armistice. The third part, told partly from her point of view and partly from his, is set later that day. Folded into this account of the war's ending is the description of Tietjens's experiences in the trenches during its final months. Narrative method thus intricately aligns hero and heroine, public trouble and private trouble. "Both are in claustrophobic circumstances (girls' school, trenches); both are temporarily in command (of a class of agitated girls, of a regiment of anxious men); and both are waiting for a crisis."[74] Ford's achievement in *A Man Could Stand Up –* is to have relativized the combat novel itself, as a literary form dedicated to stories of adaptability without change in the new and hostile environment of trench warfare. The combat novel in *A Man Could Stand Up –* exists only in relation to the war novel which frames it, and whose meaning (that there are other environments requiring adaptability, and perhaps change) it in turn produces.

NOTES

1. James Hanley, *The German Prisoner* (London: privately printed, 1930), 25, 32–33, 35–36.
2. Liam O'Flaherty, *The Return of the Brute* (London: Mandrake Press, 1929), 186.
3. On Hanley, see Anne Rice, "'A Peculiar Power about Rottenness': Annihilating Desire in James Hanley's 'The German Prisoner,'" *Modernism/Modernity*, 9 (2002): 75–89; and, more generally, John Fordham, *James Hanley: Modernism and the Working Class* (Cardiff: University of Wales Press, 2002). O'Flaherty, Hanley's equally interesting precursor, does not appear to have received as much attention.
4. Ariela Freedman, "Mary Borden's *Forbidden Zone*: Women's Writing from no man's land," *Modernism/Modernity*, 9 (2002): 109–24; Margaret R. Higonnet, "Authenticity and Art in Trauma Narratives of World War I," *ibid.*, 91–107; Sharon Ouditt, *Fighting Forces, Writing Women: Identity and Ideology in the First World War* (London: Routledge, 1994).
5. The point is made by Hugh Cecil, *The Flower of Battle: British Fiction Writers of the First World War* (London: Secker & Warburg, 1995), 86.
6. Most notably by Cecil, in *ibid.*, which has chapters on Richard Aldington, V. M. Yeates, Wilfrid Ewart, Robert Keable, Ronald Gurner, Herbert Read, Oliver Onions, Peter Deane (Pamela Hinkson), and Richard Blaker. See also: Bernard Bergonzi, *Heroes' Twilight: A Study of the Literature of the Great War*, 2nd edn. (Basingstoke: Macmillan, 1980); Philip Hager and Desmond Taylor, *The Novel of World War I* (New York: Garland, 1981); Eric J. Leed, *No Man's Land: Combat and Identity in World War I* (Cambridge: Cambridge University Press, 1981); George Parfitt, *Fiction of the First World War* (London: Faber & Faber, 1988); Modris Eksteins, *Rites of Spring: The Great World War and the Birth of the Modern Age* (London: Bantam, 1989); Samuel Hynes, *A War Imagined: The First World War and English Culture* (London: Bodley Head, 1990); John Onions, *English Fiction and Drama of the Great War, 1918–39* (Basingstoke: Macmillan, 1990); Harold Orel, *Popular Fiction in England, 1914–1918* (Hemel Hempstead: Harvester Wheatsheaf, 1992).
7. Hynes, *War Imagined*, 304.
8. Stephen Crane, *The Red Badge of Courage*, ed. Pascal Covici (Harmondsworth: Penguin, 1983), 46.
9. Max Saunders, *Ford Madox Ford: A Dual Life*, 2 vols. (Oxford: Oxford University Press, 1996), II, 21.
10. A. P. Herbert, *The Secret Battle*, 4th edn. (London: Methuen, 1929), 1.
11. Trudi Tate has used Julia Kristeva's idea of the "abject" to explore the presence of corpses in combat narratives: *Modernism, History and the First World War* (Manchester: Manchester University Press, 1998), 68–69.
12. Théodule Ribot, *The Psychology of the Emotions* (London: Walter Scott, 1897), 213–14.
13. W. Beach Thomas, *With the British on the Somme* (London: Methuen, 1917), 275.
14. Wyn Griffith, *Up to Mametz* (London: Severn House, 1981), 111–13. First published in 1931.

15. Steven Connor, "The Modern Auditory I," in *Rewriting the Self: Histories from the Renaissance to the Present*, ed. Roy Porter (London: Routledge, 1997), 203–23; "Feel the Noise: Excess, Affect and the Acoustic," in *Emotion in Postmodernism*, ed. Gerhard Hoffmann and Alfred Hornung (Heidelberg: Universitätsverlag Carl Winter, 1997), 146–72.

16. William Miller, *The Anatomy of Disgust* (Cambridge, Mass.: Harvard University Press, 1997), 75.

17. *Rethinking Symbolism*, trans. Alice L. Morton (Cambridge: Cambridge University Press, 1975), 115–16.

18. Santanu Das, "'Kiss Me, Hardy': Intimacy, Gender, and Gesture in World War I Trench Literature," *Modernism/Modernity*, 9 (2002): 51–74.

19. Herbert, *Secret Battle*, 40, 89.

20. *Ibid.*, 104–06.

21. *Ibid.*, 51.

22. *Ibid.*, 123–24.

23. Hynes, *War Imagined*, 420.

24. Leed, *No Man's Land*, 191–92.

25. Ben Shephard, *A War of Nerves: Soldiers and Psychiatrists, 1914–1994* (London: Pimlico, 2002).

26. James Hodson, *Grey Dawn – Red Night* (London: Victor Gollancz, 1929), 151.

27. *Ibid.*, 248.

28. A. D. Gristwood, *The Somme* (London: Jonathan Cape, 1927), 57.

29. *Ibid.*, 112.

30. Charles Carrington, *A Subaltern's War* (London: Peter Davies, 1929).

31. John Keegan, *The Face of Battle* (Harmondsworth: Penguin, 1978), 278–80.

32. G. D. Sheffield, *Leadership in the Trenches: Officer–Man Relations, Morale and Discipline in the British Army in the Era of the First World War* (Basingstoke: Macmillan, 2000), 72.

33. Ford Madox Ford, "Chroniques i: Editorial," *Transatlantic Review* 2 (1924): 94–98, 96–97.

34. Ford Madox Ford, *Parade's End* (Harmonsworth: Penguin, 1982), 296, 340.

35. Hodson, *Grey Dawn*, 204.

36. O'Flaherty, *Return of the Brute*, 38.

37. Siegfried Sassoon, *Memoirs of an Infantry Officer* (London: Faber and Faber, 1997), 130.

38. Vera Brittain, *Testament of Youth* (London: Virago, 1979), 210. On the social basis of the VAD organization, see Ouditt, *Fighting Forces*, ch. 1.

39. Evadne Price, *Not So Quiet . . . : Stepdaughters of War* (London: A. E. Marriott, 1930), 59–60. One of Smith's colleagues remarks that if she were choosing women to drive ambulances she would not worry too much about their moral qualities. "It would be 'Are you a first-class driver?' not 'Are you a first-class virgin?'" (126).

40. Frank Prochaska, *The Voluntary Impulse: Philanthropy in Modern Britain* (London: Faber and Faber, 1988); and "Philanthropy," in *The Cambridge Social History of Britain 1750–1950*, ed. F. M. L. Thompson, III (Cambridge: Cambridge University Press, 1990), 357–93.

41. Robert Graves, *Good-bye to All That* (Harmonsworth: Penguin, 1960), 13.

42. Siegfried Sassoon, *Siegfried's Journey 1916–1920* (London: Faber and Faber, 1945), 114–15. Wilfred Owen visited an Edinburgh slum while at Craiglockhart: Dominic Hibberd, *Wilfred Owen: The Last Year 1917–1918* (London: Constable, 1992), 35. Charles Carrington was one of the very few who exceeded the philanthropic model altogether. So alienated did he feel from his middle-class family that he spent his leave in the East End of London with friends of men in his platoon: *Soldier from the War Returning* (London: Hutchinson, 1965), 178–88, 280–81.

43. Christopher Stone, *The Valley of Indecision* (London: Collins, 1920), 189–90.

44. See David Ayers, *English Literature of the 1920s* (Edinburgh: Edinburgh University Press, 1999), 19–29, on Richard Aldington's *Death of a Hero*.

45. Christopher Stone, *Flying Buttresses* (London: A. M. Philpot, 1927), 27.

46. Claire Buck, "'Still Some Obstinate Emotion Remains': Radclyffe Hall and the Meanings of Service," in *Women's Fiction and the Great War*, ed. Suzanne Raitt and Trudi Tate (Oxford: Oxford University Press, 1997), 174–96.

47. Graves, *Good-bye to All That*, 88.

48. Philip Gibbs, *Now It Can Be Told* (1920), quoted by Paul Fussell, *The Great War and Modern Memory* (Oxford: Oxford University Press, 1975), 83. Published in Britain as *Realities of War* (London: Heinemann, 1920). In the 1929 edition, Gibbs apologized for the vehemence of his criticism of the General Staff.

49. Edmund Blunden, *Undertones of War* (Oxford: Oxford University Press, 1956), 90, 128–29, 132.

50. R. H. Mottram, "A Personal Record," in R. H. Mottram, John Easton, and Eric Partridge, *Three Personal Records of the War* (London: Scholartis Press, 1929), 4–5.

51. R. H. Mottram, *The Spanish Farm Trilogy* (London: Chatto & Windus, 1927), 376–77, 465.

52. David Trotter, "The New Historicism and the Psychopathology of Everyday Modern Life," *Critical Quarterly*, 42 (2000) 36–58.

53. Hodson, *Grey Dawn*, 97.

54. Mark Kinkead-Weekes, *D. H. Lawrence: Triumph to Exile* (Cambridge: Cambridge University Press, 1996), 332, 382–84.

55. Richard Aldington, *Death of a Hero* (London: Chatto & Windus, 1929), 273–74, 276, 333–38, 388.

56. Frederic Manning, *The Middle Parts of Fortune* (Harmondsworth: Penguin, 1990), 149.

57. George Gissing, *Thyrza*, ed. Jacob Korg (Hassocks: Harvester, 1974), 14.

58. Manning, *Middle Parts*, 22.

59. H. M. Tomlinson, *All Our Yesterdays* (London: Heinemann, 1930), 412–13, 416, 423–36.

60. W. H. R. Rivers, "Repression of War Experience," in *Instinct and the Unconscious: A Contribution to a Biological Theory of the Psycho-Neuroses*, 2nd edn. (Cambridge: Cambridge University Press, 1922), 185–204, 192. "It was peculiarly horrible," Gristwood observed in *The Somme*, "to fall face downwards on a dead man" (37).

61. Aldington, *Death of a Hero*, 376, 428.

62. Ford Madox Ford, *It Was the Nightingale* (London: Heinemann, 1934), 174–80, 206.

63. I cannot prove this. My hypothesis is based on what I take to be an allusion to Rivers's theory of the "suppression" of instinct in *Parade's End*, 80.
64. Rivers, *Instinct and the Unconscious*, 123.
65. Herbert, *Secret Battle*, 132–33.
66. Rivers, *Instinct and the Unconscious*, e.g. 170–84. In Erich Maria Remarque's *All Quiet on the Western Front* (1928), a young recruit goes mad from enclosure during heavy shelling. "It is a case of claustrophobia," says the narrator: "he feels as though he is suffocating here and wants to get out at any price." The colleagues who try to restrain him feel that they too are sitting in their own graves, "waiting to be closed in." *All Quiet on the Western Front*, trans. Brian Murdoch (London: Jonathan Cape, 1994), 75–76.
67. Keith Simpson, "Dr. James Dunn and Shell-shock," in *Facing Armageddon: The First World War Experienced*, ed. Peter Liddle and Hugh Cecil (London: Leo Cooper, 1996), 502–19, 512.
68. Blunden, *Undertones*, 157.
69. Graves, *Good-bye to All That*, 175.
70. Edwin Vaughan, *Some Desperate Glory* (Basingstoke: Macmillan, 1994), 218–21.
71. Manning, *Middle Parts*, II, 173–76, 235.
72. Ford, "A Day of Battle," essay not published in Ford's lifetime, dated 15 September 1916; quoted by Saunders, *Ford Madox Ford*, II, 197.
73. Ford, *Parade's End*, 637–44.
74. Saunders, *Ford Madox Ford*, 215.

3

EDNA LONGLEY

The Great War, history, and the English lyric

Arms and the muse

In the BBC TV series *Blackadder Goes Forth* the flying-ace Lord Flasheart says: "I'm sick of this damn war – the blood, the noise, the endless poetry." This echoes satire during the Great War itself, as when the *Wipers Times* "regrett[ed] to announce that an insidious disease is affecting the Division, and the result is a hurricane of poetry."[1] Since a "strange *scabies scribendi*" also afflicted "civilian verse-makers,"[2] and newspapers printed poems, poetry virtually became a mass medium in Britain – a phenomenon unmatched in other combatant countries. Catherine Reilly's bibliography lists 2,225 published poets and (1914–22) about 50 anthologies with titles like *Soldier Songs, The Muse in Arms, From the Front: Trench Poetry*.[3] While most of this outpouring has been remaindered by history, it set the scene for poetry conditioned by the war, poetry that internalized the war, poetry that remains a model for public poetry. Great War poetry is read, imitated, and quoted in shifting contexts. Before the Iraq War, the anthology *101 Poems Against War* appeared. Its cover quotes Wilfred Owen ("All a poet can do today is warn"), as does an afterword by the Poet Laureate, Andrew Motion: "Towards the end of the First World War, amidst the squalor and tragedy of the Western Front, something fundamental changed . . . The patriotic imperative 'Dulce et Decorum Est' became 'that [*sic*] old lie,' and . . . our sense of 'a war poet' was transformed."[4]

However, the view that the Battle of the Somme caused a poetic paradigm-shift has given way to a less linear picture: a complex of literary, historical, and ideological variables stretching back into the nineteenth century.[5] It's true that *101 Poems* neatly counterpoints *The Spirit of Man* (1915), a best-selling anthology edited by the then Poet Laureate, Robert Bridges. Bridges draws on classical and French texts, the Bible, and English poetry up to Rupert Brooke's *1914* sonnets whose vogue helped to launch the poetic war effort. Sub-headings like "Christian Virtue," "The Happy Warrior," and "Life in Death" reinforce the message that "our beloved who fall in the fight . . . die nobly, as heroes and saints die."[6] Such easy recruitment of the western and Christian canons explains why Siegfried Sassoon should write, after visiting Thomas Hardy: "What a contrast to arrogant old Bridges with his reactionary war-talk."[7] Yet Sassoon himself reworks heroic-saintly motifs; few poems are anti-war in a universal, contextless sense; and Homer's *Iliad* appears on both sides of the question. There may be little difference between bad poems glorifying the Great War and bad poems deploring the Iraq war.

But if war serves to distinguish poetry from verse, it also edges poetry into the background. The thematic bias of the category "war poetry" often homogenizes or ghettoizes poets discussed in this chapter. Conversely, when critics construe the Great War in the aesthetic terms of "modernism," or modernism is itself at issue, these poets' structures seldom enter the equation. I will argue that the years 1914–18 "transformed" the English lyric more generally. Here I will highlight Wilfred Owen and Edward Thomas, whose complementary reworking of the lyric has been obscured because Thomas's poems are not trench poems (he was killed soon after reaching the Front) but "of the war" in a holistic sense that reflects back on trench poetry too. To quote his poem "Roads": "Now all roads lead to France." For Julian Symons, "'war poets,' as such, do not exist."[8] War poetry, then, may be less a category than a multi-generic special case – even the quintessential case – of the encounter between form and history. The fact that the army (in contrast to the other services and to French and German military practice) relied so heavily on new recruits peculiarly entangled the Western Front with British intellectual life. This accelerated the war's epistemological shock to what W. B. Yeats calls "established things": to metaphysical systems, ideas of history, assumptions about poetic means and ends.[9]

Anthologies constitute a rough guide to the thematic bias, and to how it changes its theme. Wartime anthologies unsurprisingly put patriotism first, although they become more eclectic. E. B. Osborn, editor *of The Muse in Arms* (1917), admires the "British warrior's . . . capacity for remembering the splendour and forgetting the squalor" of war, and two of his sub-headings are "Chivalry of Sport" and "The Christian Soldier." But he makes contradictory room for "voices" (Sassoon, Charles Hamilton Sorley, Ivor Gurney, Robert Graves) that "cry aloud from the 'battered trenches' against the established order of things."[10] In fact, during the war "soldier poet" was a tautology – "almost as familiar as a ration-card," says Edmund Blunden)[11] – rather than a problematic critical category. Later, with Owen's *Poems* (1920) finally in print, critics like John Middleton Murry sought to conceptualize Great War poetry: "Wilfred Owen was the greatest poet of the war [because he] bowed himself to the horror of war until his soul was penetrated by it."[12] The "spirit of man" was gradually reread in Owen's and Sassoon's terms: protest, pity, responsibility, sensibility. As for poets themselves: during the 1930s and 1940s they looked to Great War poetry for its moral vision, political thrust, and renewed topicality. But it also influenced their broader concern with how the forms of lyric poetry might negotiate historical crisis.[13]

In 1964 I. M. Parsons's *Men Who March Away* and Brian Gardner's *Up the Line to Death* inaugurated a second cluster of anthologies which, together with new editions of the poets, helped to give Great War poetry its current presence as a distinct but fuzzy category hovering somewhere between aesthetics and politics. While Parsons claims to base his selection on literary "value," Gardner's "book about war" lets the reader decide which poems "are great poetry in any company [and which] are valid in the context of the war." But both titles invoke the trench poem, and sub-headings (an ideological graph since *The Spirit of Man*) inscribe the narrative – from "Visions of Glory" to "The Bitter Truth" – lately recycled by Andrew Motion.[14] Jon Silkin resisted the thematic tide by flagging up a "concern with excellence" as the first principle of his *Penguin Book of First World War Poetry* (1979), an anthology organized by poet (Owen and Isaac Rosenberg get most space), not theme. Himself a poet, Silkin speaks for the post-1960 surge of interest from poets in which aesthetics played a more various part. Latterly, Silkin's canon has been democratized by an anthological third wave that subordinates aesthetics to social history rather than to either patriotism or protest. This trend, which also re-admits patriotic poetry, consciously opposes earlier constructions. For instance, Martin Stephen's *Poems of the First World War* (1988) rejects the idea that the poetry "of an educated class with an awareness of literature" is "typical or representative."[15] Simon Featherstone's *Introductory Reader* (1995) explains this kind of revisionism by noting how the Thatcher years "caused a revaluation and revival of nationalist feelings and rhetorics in England." Yet if Stephen recasts the war poetry anthology as cultural history, Featherstone recasts it as cultural studies. His "Discussion" headings include "Popular Culture," "Gender," and "British Cultures." Featherstone rightly says that war poetry cannot be "separated from the literary and intellectual cultures of the society that produced it."[16] But one way to think more integrally is to think aesthetically. When anthologists have scoured all the margins and revisited the imperial center, there remains poetry which, by changing poetry itself, situates the Great War in more complex configurations. Here the conscripted Muse in Arms gives way to the Great War as primary muse.

This is not to retread the view that the only Great War poet is a trench poet. Virtually every poet of the period wrote war poems in some sense. Yet certain patterns – a matter of timing, of psycho-imaginative receptivity – link those soldier poets for whom the Great War was an aesthetically defining moment. Equally, the war may have exhausted some talents that survived: Sassoon found a never-repeated vocation as well as a flair for "satirical epigram."[17] In autumn 1916 Rosenberg proposed to "saturate myself with the strange and extraordinary new conditions of this life [which] will all refine itself into poetry later on" ("later on" ended in April 1918).[18] Owen, killed in November 1918, had a little longer to frame his poetic mission in terms of war: "I came out in order to help these boys – directly by leading them as well as an officer can; indirectly, by watching their sufferings that I may speak of them as well as a pleader can."[19] Three survivors, Graves, Gurney, and Edmund Blunden, took longer still. Graves, who did not reprint his (rather weak) trench poems, sublimated psychic wounds in his later muse of the White Goddess. Gurney's and Blunden's most immediate war poetry is retrospective. Gurney's postwar poems, written in an asylum, replay the war on an obsessive loop-tape.

These poets were born between 1886 (Sassoon) and 1896 (Blunden). Edward Thomas (b. 1878) was a late developer. For Thomas, the war coalesced with a receptivity prepared by many psychological and literary factors, including the influence of his friend Robert Frost. A self-styled "hurried and harried prose man," Thomas began writing poetry in December 1914. In July 1915, after "a long series of moods & thoughts," he enlisted.[20] In April 1917 he was killed at Arras. Another time-factor, of course, was the fact that time might run out. War poetry can be prospective and prophetic too: "Sharp on their souls hung the imminent ridge of grass" (Owen, "Spring Offensive"). The Great War sharpened the lyric encounter with death as well as history. Sorley (killed at Loos in 1915) was only twenty when, in "Two Sonnets," he brooded on immortality: "And your bright Promise, withered long and sped / . . . blossoms and is you, when you are dead."[21] Given this deadline, some "bright Promise" quickened its life-work. Owen's "*annus mirabilis*" telescoped years. In two years Thomas wrote 144 poems.

Tradition: worn out or worn new?

Why poetry? In theory, it takes less time to write and read. Diaries and letters contain war impressions that become poems before (if poets survive) they become memoirs. Poetry allows for improvisation, rapid response. And, as it proved from Brooke to Owen, poetry's symbolic and mnemonic force reaches where prose cannot touch.

Brooke's death in April 1915 en route for Gallipoli added iconic potency to the resonant soundbites of his sonnets: "Now, God be thanked Who has matched us with His hour" ("I. Peace"); "If I should die, think only this of me: / That there's some corner of a foreign field / That is for ever England" ("v. The Soldier"). Effectively, Brooke had scripted his own hagiography: "Frost . . . leaves a white / Unbroken glory, a gathered radiance, / A width, a shining peace, under the night" ("IV. The Dead"). Brooke hit the spot not only because his death was exploited by church and state, but because his sonnets work at such a high symbolic pitch. The implicitly resurrected body folds into the soul and both into "the eternal mind" ("The Soldier"): a consolatory trope, programmed for rhythmic resolution, which Owen's cosmology would invert by orbiting around the dying or dead body. Brooke blends "Chivalry of Sport" and "Christian Soldier" with Romantic poetry. His sonnets seem mesmerized by "the white radiance of eternity" in Shelley's "Adonais," a template for self-elegiac portraits of the artist. Brooke's "unbroken glory" might reflexively span the post-Romantic lyric, symbolic transcendence, and the English poet turned soldier poet-hero, martyr, savior. Brooke's elegists, eulogists, and plagiarists disseminated this poeticized national mystique (ironically akin to Irish martyrology of the poets executed after the Easter Rising). Especially influential was "Into Battle" by Julian Grenfell, an aristocrat, professional soldier, and amateur poet killed in May 1915: "The thundering line of battle stands, / And in the air Death moans and sings; / But Day shall clasp him with strong hands / And Night shall fold him in soft wings." Here the underlying image is of a child being put to bed by his mother. Individual immaturity, with wider cultural and psycho-sexual contexts in the upbringing of upper-class young men, helped to produce such sublimations of love and death: a patriotic *Liebestod*.[22] The mystique's compensatory aspect may also reflect imperial anxiety after near-defeat by the Boers. The editor of *Songs and Sonnets for England in War Time* (1914) already follows Brooke in therapeutically mixing chivalry with Shelley: "In the stress of a nation's peril the poet at last comes into his own again . . . Prophet he is, champion and consoler."[23]

Brooke's vogue prompted ideologues to enlist English poetry for their own *Kulturkampf* against Germany's boasted *Kultur*. For Osborn, German poets are "moved more by hatred for other people's countries than by love of their own, and, as munitions of spirituality, their poems are of less value than Zulu war-chants."[24] Poets who were not Brooke-clones had to react. Perhaps, to adapt a saying of Yeats's, out of the quarrel with Brooke they made war poetry. And in combating "munitions of spirituality" they defined their own aesthetics. When Owen read Brooke (in 1916), he drafted "An Imperial Elegy," which opens up Brooke's cosy-corner grave, collapses his Anglocentrism into European catastrophe, and redirects his mystification:

> Not one corner of a foreign field
> But a span as wide as Europe;
> An appearance of a titan's grave,
> And the length thereof a thousand miles,
> It crossed all Europe like a mystic road,
> Or as the Spirits' pathway lieth on the night . . .

Thomas's "Bugle Call," which also subverts another Brooke sonnet ("Blow out, you bugles, over the rich Dead!"), has the poet-speaker "making words" in ironic counterpoint to a "call" from the ambiguous muse of war:

> "No one cares less than I,
> Nobody knows but God
> Whether I am destined to lie
> Under a foreign clod"
> Were the words I made to the bugle call in the morning . . .

Thomas called Brooke's sonnets "a nervous attempt to connect with himself the very widespread idea that self sacrifice is the highest self indulgence." Sorley, too, saw Brooke as a self-publicist: "far too obsessed with his own sacrifice regarding the going to war of himself (and others) as a highly intense, remarkable and sacrificial exploit, whereas it is merely the conduct demanded . . . by the turn of circumstances." Rosenberg came to dislike "Brooke's begloried sonnets" because "the war should be approached in a colder way, more abstract, with less of the million feelings everybody feels."[25]

The Great War inspired not just "endless poetry" but endless sonnets. The sonnet is often a touchstone or synecdoche for English poetry – hence *Songs and Sonnets for England*. Thomas and Sassoon took Shakespeare's *Sonnets* to war, and they were Owen's model for homoerotic sonnets. War sonnets condense larger dialectics. In February 1917 Gurney conceived a set of "Sonnets 1917" as "a counterblast against 'Sonnetts [*sic*] 1914,' which were written before the grind of war . . . They are the protest of the physical against the exalted spiritual; of the cumulative weight of small facts against the one large. Of informed opinion against uninformed (to put it coarsely and unfairly)."[26] Sorley had already deconstructed Brooke, sonnet to sonnet, word to word:

> When you see millions of the mouthless dead
> Across your dreams in pale battalions go,
> Say not soft things as other men have said,
> That you'll remember. For you need not so.
> Give them not praise. For, deaf, how should they know
> It is not curses heaped on each gashed head?

Nor tears. Their blind eyes see not your tears flow.
Nor honour. It is easy to be dead.
Say only this, "They are dead."

On one level, this celebrated sonnet addresses a mass-audience, present and future, in a strike against the consolatory commemoration blueprinted by Brooke and by Laurence Binyon's "For the Fallen": "They shall not grow old, as we that are left grow old." But Sorley's "you" also implies an *ars poetica*. The sonnet's falsely resolving rhythms (it ends "Great death has made all his for evermore") undermine Brooke's unities.

No sonnet or anti-sonnet has ever had more effect. Sorley proved a powerful antidote to Brooke in quarters that mattered. Graves introduced Sorley's posthumous *Marlborough and Other Poems* (1916) to Sassoon, who introduced the book to Owen. Sorley helped Sassoon, initially a Brooke-clone, to say hard things – some of them in sonnets. Sassoon exploits the sonnet's potential for "satirical epigram" and for juxtaposing evocation and comment: "Our chaps were sticking 'em like pigs . . . 'O hell!' / He thought – 'there's things in war one dare not tell / Poor father sitting safe at home, who reads / Of dying heroes and their deathless deeds'" ("Remorse"). Sassoon's sonnets often consist of couplets, long geared to epigram, and he introduces mixed speakers or mixed speech-registers into a mainly monologic mode. It is by cross-fertilizing the sonnet with Hardy's *Satires of Circumstance* that Sassoon arrives at his "device of composing two or three harsh, peremptory, and colloquial stanzas with a knock-out blow in the last line."[27] Owen absorbed these technical shock-tactics. His "Parable of the Old Man and the Young" treats the story of Abraham and Isaac as an irregularly rhymed "found" sonnet, in which "son" is rhymed with itself. Then a further, fully rhymed couplet changes the biblical ending: "But the old man would not so, but slew his son, / And half the seed of Europe, one by one." Owen's "Dulce et Decorum Est" is a transgressive double sonnet whose structural deviations set up the famous climax with its brilliant dissyllabic rhyme and short last line: "My friend, you would not tell with such high zest / To children ardent for some desperate glory, / The old Lie: Dulce et decorum est / Pro patria mori."

The "counterblasting" war sonnet inwardly complicates (or complicates by inwardness) the construction of memory, whether historical or individual. Brooke renders event and commemoration – like past and future, life and death, peace and war, war and poetry – a single condition: "And we have come into our heritage" ("III. The Dead"). Gurney's postwar "Riez Bailleul" begins with the speaker "Behind the line there mending reserve posts, looking / On the cabbage fields with other men carefully tending cooking; /

Hearing the boiling; and being sick of body and heart," and hence dreaming of England. But this scene is ironically a "glimpse most strangely / Forced from the past" to hide present-day "pain" experienced back in England. Gurney then opens up the full war context, projecting what might have occurred beyond the frozen glimpse: "a farmer's treasure perhaps soon a wilderness." The participial phrases, the octet's lack of a main verb, the double-rhymed couplets all reinforce a sense of consciousness trapped in a circle of historical and psychological pain.

Thomas's sonnet "A Dream," dated just before he enlisted, turns on the strangeness of wartime, of time in war:

> Over known fields with an old friend in dream
> I walked, but came sudden to a strange stream.
> Its dark waters were bursting out most bright
> From a great mountain's heart into the light.
> They ran a short course under the sun, then back
> Into a pit they plunged, once more as black
> As at their birth: and I stood thinking there
> How white, had the day shone on them, they were,
> Heaving and coiling. So by the roar and hiss
> And by the mighty motion of the abyss
> I was bemused, that I forgot my friend . . .

Thomas's syntax, which always plays with sequence, moves from the security of "known" and "old" to "dream." Proverbial rather than epigrammatic, his couplets are ruffled by mimesis of the waters whose "Heaving and coiling" bursts into the sestet. At the sonnet's heart stands the self-dreaming poet "thinking there" in a subjunctive way which produces a poem within a poem. "Bemused" puns on morbid fascination with the muse of war. The sonnet's syntactical coils, replicating the waters' "mighty motion," place the speaker at a symbolic hiatus between daylight and underworld. It ends with him reflexively "Saying: 'I shall be here some day again.'" Like Gurney, Thomas portrays consciousness trapped in time, unable to bring it under conceptual control, subject to apocalyptic repetition. Another sonnet, "February Afternoon," ends: "And God still sits aloft in the array / That we have wrought him, stone-deaf and stone-blind." Here Thomas challenges the millenarian synchronicity of Brooke's "Now, God be thanked Who has matched us with His hour." The struggle of Great War poetry to comprehend its locus in time and space changes the metaphysical bearings of the lyric poem. Sorley calls the war "a chasm in time."[28]

If the sonnet could survive the war (and worse sonneteers than Brooke), so might the English lyric which it figures, and which itself figures English literature. The subverted sonnet epitomizes this poetry's critical dimension, its own anthological and canonical bent. Poets' war letters and diaries abound in incidental canon-making. Thus Gurney in 1917: "The best way to learn to write is to read classics like Milton, Keats and Shakespeare, and the Georgian poets . . . One learns form and the true use of language from those, and flexibility and the modern touch from these."[29] A later section of this chapter will insert "war poetry" into arguments about "the modern touch." But poetic tradition since "Spring had bloomed in early Greece," to quote Owen's sonnet-lament "1914," was on the line. Poets not only sift war-poem models (as when Thomas praises Coleridge's "Fears in Solitude" because "a large part of it is humble" or Rosenberg says "The Homer for this war has yet to be found – Whitman got very near the mark 50 years ago with 'Drum Taps'")[30] they also spin a larger intertextual web, at once horizontal and vertical. Thus Owen connects tunneled dugouts to the under-worlds of Homer, Virgil, Dante, Milton, and Keats; quotes Yeats in ironical epigraph; quarrels with Tennysonian elegy; and (in "Insensibility") revises Shelley's *Defence of Poetry*.

Why were Romantic poets so revisited? There was again the need to counter Brooke. Owen's "A Terre," spoken by a soldier "blind, and three parts shell," also quotes "Adonais": "'I shall be one with nature, herb, and stone,' / Shelley would tell me." Romantic words and images presented an open goal for irony. In Rosenberg's "Returning, We Hear the Larks," "joy" and the bird-icon of Romantic transcendence hover above the trenches:

> But hark! joy – joy – strange joy.
> Lo! heights of night ringing with unseen larks,
> Music showering our upturned list'ning faces.
> Death could drop from the dark
> As easily as song –
> But song only dropped,
> Like a blind man's dreams on the sand
> By dangerous tides,
> Like a girl's dark hair for she dreams no ruin lies there,
> Or her kisses where a serpent hides.

Yet irony is not the whole story. The oxymoron "strange joy" covers the trenches too, as Rosenberg adapts several Romantic tropes to war's ambiguous muse. In Great War poetry, literary allusion becomes at once ironical, interrogative, and revisionary. If the war exposed the emptiness of post-Romantic poeticalities, it also reactivated the conceptual and linguistic radicalism of Romanticism itself, and impelled a chastened Romantic idealism into new manifestos.

Poets did this in distinctive ways. For example, Keats goes as deep for Thomas as for Owen (Thomas's book on Keats [1916] was read by Owen and Gurney) but, up to a point, they develop different Keatsian structures. The sensory Keats and prophetic Keats steer Owen's effort to fuse evocation, empathy, and warning. "Exposure," whose "merciless iced east winds" make "La Belle Dame sans Merci" a war muse, redeploys Keats's poetry of sensations:

> Sudden successive flights of bullets streak the silence.
> Less deathly than the air that shudders black with snow,
> With sidelong flowing flakes that flock, pause, and renew;
> We watch them wandering up and down the wind's nonchalance,
> But nothing happens.

Owen plays rich assonance, dramatizing a "deathly" seduction, against a plain refrain. Thomas's "Rain" (set in an army camp) also internalizes chilly weather while revising the Keatsian death-wish and the patriotic *Liebestod*. But this psychodrama is more consistently interior and symbolic. Another soliloquy of trapped consciousness, "Rain" interweaves a downpour, the war dead ("myriads"), and the temptations of nihilism:

> Rain, midnight rain, nothing but the wild rain
> On this bleak hut, and solitude, and me
> Remembering again that I shall die
> And neither hear the rain nor give it thanks
> For washing me cleaner than I have been
> Since I was born into this solitude.
> Blessed are the dead that the rain rains upon:
> But here I pray that none whom once I loved
> Is dying tonight or lying still awake
> Solitary, listening to the rain,
> Either in pain or thus in sympathy
> Helpless among the living and the dead,
> Like a cold water among broken reeds,
> Myriads of broken reeds all still and stiff,
> Like me who have no love which this wild rain
> Has not dissolved, except the love of death,
> If love it be for what is perfect and
> Cannot, the tempest tells me, disappoint.

War infiltrates and tests all poetry's mechanisms of tradition. Great War poetry can resemble a computer checking itself for viruses. And if poetry improvises, it also trawls. A more-or-less finished poem by Owen exists in a complex relation to his Keatsian *juvenilia*, his reading, "bouts of horrible danger" in January–February 1917,[31] his drafts, his remarkable letters, the impact of Sassoon when the shell-shocked or war-shocked poets met at Craiglockhart Hospital in Edinburgh (September 1917). (The gestation of "Exposure" is a case in point.) Owen and Thomas served a more intensive aesthetic apprenticeship than the other soldier poets discussed here. This included work on the fictive "self", the lyric "I." But Owen needed time to integrate his sense of tradition not only with war experience but with his sense of the contemporary: a process active in his dense intertextual critique. Thomas – a poetry critic, writer of "country books," and analyst of English culture – was, he discovered, strangely prepared. All Thomas's prose, creative and critical, feeds his poetry, and allusions to the lyric corpus are deeply embedded in image, word, or rhythm (the resonances of "rain"). Some resources on which he draws surface in his anthology *This England* (1915) and his poem "Lob" (1915): resources seen not as timeless "heritage" but as subject to history and metamorphosis. Similarly, "Words" celebrates the English language as "Worn new / Again and again."

Thomas's review article "War Poetry" (1914) rebukes poems and anthologies that meet the demand "for the crude, for what everybody is saying or thinking, or is ready to begin saying or thinking."[32] Hence his own historical "anthology from the work of English writers rather strictly so called [built] round a few most English poems like 'When icicles hang by the wall' – excluding professedly patriotic writing because it is generally bad."[33] Thomas weaves the same song into "Lob" – which anthologizes his anthology. This 150-line poem, written in vigorous couplets and full of intertextual liaisons, features an elusive protagonist who personifies tradition (poetic tradition being its epitome) as the human mind inhabiting and constructing the natural world, locality, culture, language, literature: "This is tall Tom that bore / The logs in, and with Shakespeare in the hall / Once talked." In proposing some connective tissues that might enable English poetry to survive the war, "Lob" strangely preempts *The Waste Land*.

Politics, poetics

Perhaps the deepest politics of Great War poetry concern literary positioning. But this informs its other political functions: as direct intervention in the propaganda field; as less conscious ideology; as structures that reimagine politics.

Thomas illustrates the point that poets' attitudes do not fall into a simple pro-war/anti-war polarity. T. E. Hulme (killed in 1917), the originator of Imagism, could write articles that criticized both pacifists and the General Staff. For Hulme, Germany's hegemonic ambition made the war "a necessary stupidity, but still a stupidity."[34] And Siegfried Sassoon would return to action despite his "Soldier's Declaration" (July 1917):

> I believe that this War, upon which I entered as a war of defence and liberation, has now become a war of aggression and conquest . . . I am not protesting against the military conduct of the War, but against the political errors and insincerities for which the fighting men are being sacrificed . . . Also I believe that [this protest] may help to destroy the callous complacence with which the majority of those at home regard the continuance of agonies which they do not share and which they have not sufficient imagination to realise.[35]

Nor is the famous Declaration itself strictly pacifist, although sponsored by Bloomsbury pacifism.[36] Sassoon was also obeying the logic of his poetic campaign against complacent authority, and discharging personal anger, grief, and guilt. Adrian Caesar argues that emotional turmoil drove him to seek an alternative form of martyrdom by risking court-martial and opprobrium. In fact, Graves (who disapproved of his actions) ensured that Sassoon was sent to Craiglockhart as a supposed victim of shell-shock. Caesar finds troubling the failure of Sasssoon and Owen to be consistent pacifists. He notices ambivalent attitudes to violence; voyeuristic, sado-masochistic, and misogynistic overtones; fascination with war as poetic material; élitist pride in the poet's special ability to suffer; equation of the poet (not just the common soldier) with Christ: overall, a transposition rather than exorcism of Brooke's sacrificial tropes.[37] But poetic motives are usually mixed. And perhaps poets must pitch their whole artistic psychology into the historical gyres if they are to resist the murkier political unconscious behind "munitions of spirituality." This is what Owen means by calling himself "a conscientious objector with a very seared conscience"; or by saying (however self-dramatizingly) that to describe "an incomprehensible look, which a man will never see in England . . . I think I must go back and be with them."[38]

"Protest" has many shades. "But nothing happens" might make something happen. Sassoon's directly polemical poems expose the gap between the language of politicians, generals, bishops, armchair patriots, "Yellow-Pressmen" ("Fight to a Finish") etc., and the experience of soldiers who "blunder through the splashing mirk," "crawl on their bellies through the wire" ("Trench Duty"), or end up as "riddled corpses round Bapaume" ("Blighters"). Of Sassoon's three main modes – satirical epigram, narrative-documentary, and case-history – the latter two are most variable in quality. Lacking Owen's rhythmical and textural depth, he blurs impressions with overrepeated verbs ("blunder," "grope") or overdetermined adjectives: in "Prelude: The Troops," "Disconsolate men . . . stamp their sodden boots / And turn dulled, sunken faces to the sky / Haggard and hopeless." After meeting and reading Sassoon, Owen told his sister: "you will find nothing so perfectly truthfully descriptive of war"; and began writing poems "in Sassoon's manner."[39] One such was "The Next War," a sonnet satirizing Brooke's "Peace" which ends: "And the worst friend and enemy is but Death." Owen's sestet begins: "Oh, Death was never enemy of ours! / We laughed at him, we leagued with him, old chum." Here colloquialism goes further than in Sassoon. By inserting the voice of fighting men into an old sonnet trope, Owen is able to conceive "greater wars: when every fighter brags / He fights on Death, for lives; not men, for flags."

Owen's long perspective raises the political as well as aesthetic stakes. "Next" reappears in his draft-Preface: "these elegies are to this generation in no sense consolatory. They may be to the next."[40] "Strange Meeting," which places dead friend-enemies in a European inferno (another historical chasm or repetition), also looks ahead: "Now men will go content with what we spoiled, / Or, discontent, boil bloody, and be spilled . . . None will break ranks, though nations trek from progress." A fundamental difference between Owen and Sassoon – between Preface and Declaration – is the religious concept of history, and hence of politics, which Owen takes from his evangelical Anglican background. The evangelical tradition stresses bible-reading, salvation through Christ's sacrifice, emotional commitment, spreading the gospel in direct language, practical ethics.[41] And, to quote Dominic Hibberd: Owen remained "attuned to the music, stories and splendid language that had helped to shape his imagination since childhood."[42] He says himself apropos "the big number of texts which jogged up in my mind in half-an-hour": "I am more and more Christian as I walk the unchristian ways of Christendom." For Owen, "Armageddon" was no cliché. Although he had rejected Christianity ("murdered my false creed"), his war poems take place on a cosmic stage between earth and heaven, heaven and hell, body and soul, death and life.[43] What afflicts human beings matters in large metaphysical terms: "By his dead smile I knew we stood in Hell" ("Strange Meeting"). Besides its intertextuality with the Bible, Owen's poetry adapts the structures of sermon, prayer, litany, parable, psalm, sacrament, prophecy – partly in order to blaspheme against the established church as against Brooke, the established war poet. Caesar finds that Owen's "political position was never very lucidly articulated." Featherstone, however, contrasts Sassoon's "outraged statement against the way that civic and political responsibilities were unfulfilled during the war" with Owen's more radical enquiry into "the failure of the philosophy of progress and social betterment."[44] Owen's anatomy of "futility," with its theological and prophetic dimension, secretes an alternative politics. His vision resembles the Messianic thinking of Walter Benjamin two decades later.

Forms of mourning, personal and national

3 British soldier, battlefield rites

4 The Great Silence, 11 a.m., 11 November 1920

Owen's poetry and prose define "war poetry" in aesthetic-ethical language. "Insensibility" builds on Shelley's *Defence* by associating imagination with "compassion," and by distinguishing between enforced and inveterate moral "dullness":

> Happy are these who lose imagination:
> They have enough to carry with ammunition . . .
> Having seen all things red,
> Their eyes are rid
> Of the hurt of the colour of blood for ever . . .
> But cursed are dullards whom no cannon stuns,
> That they should be as stones.
> Wretched are they, and mean
> With paucity that never was simplicity.
> By choice they made themselves immune
> To pity and whatever moans in man
> Before the last sea and the hapless stars;
> Whatever mourns when many leave these shores . . .

In his study of *Modern Elegy* Jahan Ramazani says: "The guilty self-divisions in many of [Owen's] poems suggest a delight in self-torment, the poet occupying a dual position as both victimised soldier and performer of the victimisation. The reader's position is similarly dual."[45] Yet this is no position of paralysis. Owen's dialectical "pity," his doubling of victim and oppressor, friend and enemy, speaker and implied audience, belongs to the sphere of Marx as well as Freud. He exacts from himself and his readers an empathy tantamount to evangelical conversion and hence productive of action. The pronouns of "Apologia pro Poemate Meo" dramatize how and why "I," the mediating poet, seeks to put "you" in "their" shoes: "except you share / With them in hell the sorrowful dark of hell . . . You shall not come to think them well content / By any jest of mine." By thus fusing aesthetics with ethics, poetry with pity, Owen ultimately figures political agency: "Above all I am not concerned with Poetry. My subject is War and the pity of War. The Poetry is in the pity."[46] Owen's "pleading" has had its political influence, and still makes its political demand. His humanized Christ is finally neither crucified soldier nor self-crucifying poet but the actively redemptive spirit, posited in "Strange Meeting," that "would wash" the wounds of history "from sweet wells." Owen not only indicts the politics of Old Testament patriarchy; he rewrites the New Testament.

He does so partly by manipulating focus and angle. As a generic contributor to war poetry, this (untitled) homoerotic love poem highlights the individual victim:

I saw his round mouth's crimson deepen as it fell,
  Like a sun, in his last deep hour;
Watched the magnificent recession of farewell,
  Clouding, half-gleam, half-glower,
And a last splendour burn the heavens of his cheek.
  And in his eyes
The cold stars lighting very old and bleak,
  In different skies.

This poem begins with dark voyeurism, a dying fall, and ends with cosmic alienation. Great War poetry reimagines politics through its own power dynamics. It alters perspectives or pronouns, redistributes stress, plays with scale. Owen, who so magnifies one face, notes the irony that "[I] who write so big am so minuscule."[47] In contrast, Rosenberg, Gurney, and Thomas often write small. Rosenberg's "Break of Day in the Trenches" gives structural and perceptual precedence to a "queer sardonic rat." This transfer of authority is both an eloquent displacement activity and a critique of the war's absurdity. The rat, credited with "cosmopolitan sympathies" as he crosses the lines, is told: "It seems you inwardly grin as you pass . . . haughty athletes, / Less chanced than you for life." Gurney's aesthetic indeed proves "the cumulative weight of small facts." The democracy of his trench retrospects – like Rosenberg, he was not an officer – mingles people and things: banter, frizzling bacon, gramophone music, death. The mix seems at once egalitarian, metonymic (as compared with allegory or symbol elsewhere), and incommensurable. "The Silent One" begins:

Who died on the wires, and hung there, one of two –
Who for his hours of life had chattered through
Infinite lovely chatter of Bucks accent:
Yet faced unbroken wires; stepped over, and went
A noble fool, faithful to his stripes, and ended.

To discuss Great War poetry is always to discuss the politics and metaphysics of memory. This applies not only to its status as elegy but to its status as historiography. The poetry encodes all later modes of record and remembrance, including revisionist twists and deconstructionist self-doubt: "Say only this, 'They are dead.'" Sorley's instruction about writing the war also covers narratives of the "nation": the European crux on which the war's own politics depended. (Sorley hoped, indeed, that after the war "all brave men [would] renounce their country and confess that they are strangers and pilgrims on the earth."[48]) One of Thomas's first poems, "Old Man" (December 1914), problematizes the construction of memory and the ability of "word" to represent "thing." The poem starts from a plant's ambiguous

names which "Half decorate, half perplex, the thing it is," and ends by
opening up another cognitive abyss: "Only an avenue, dark, nameless, without end." Yet Thomas does not give up on history but writes alternative
narratives. His prewar prose reads landscape in environmental and micro-
historical ways which his poetry concentrates.[49] If Owen's poetry-as-history
is anthropocentric, Thomas's is ecocentric, ecological. Thomas, too, rejected
Christianity but humanity ("a parochial species") became less, not more,
central to his vision.[50] His poem "The Word" scrambles mnemonic priorities in that the speaker has forgotten "so many things," including "names
of the mighty men / That fought and lost or won in the old wars," but can
remember "a pure thrush word."

Nonetheless this – a poetic manifesto – is strategic, too. Thomas wanted
to reconceive rather than "renounce" his country. The poet who (he was
over-age) enlisted for the most considered patriotic motives[51] must have
resented Brooke's appropriation of "England." "This Is No Case of Petty
Right or Wrong" insists: "I hate not Germans, nor grow hot / With love
of Englishmen, to please newspapers." But, loving English landscape and
culture, Thomas accepts the logic of putting his life where his poetry is. This
resembles Owen's thought: "Do you know what would hold me together on
a battlefield?: the sense that I was defending the language in which Keats
and the rest of them wrote!"[52] In "Smile, Smile, Smile," another poem that
attacks newspaper jingoism, Owen puts a question mark after "Nation?,"
here seen through the eyes of "half-limbed readers" for whom "England one
by one had fled to France." True to his religious conception of history, Owen
distinguishes the worthy nation, the Platonic nation-in-exile, the nation of
the dead, from the unworthy nation that swallows propaganda like "Peace
would do wrong to our undying dead." Meanwhile, Thomas rethinks an
England where "the dead / Returning lightly dance" ("Roads") in terms
opposed to imperialism and aggressive nationalism.

The national, regional, and ethnic bearings of Great War poets are as significant as their class.[53] Rosenberg's and Sassoon's Jewishness (at opposite
ends of the class-spectrum) should be reckoned with, as should Sorley's Scottish, Graves's German-Irish, and Thomas's Welsh parentage. Thomas's redef-
initions of England draw on Yeats's literary nationalism as well as on the element in Welsh tradition that makes "Land of my Fathers," he says, "exulting
without self-glorification or any other form of brutality."[54] He praises Irish
poets for speaking of Ireland "with intimate reality," whereas "Britannia is
a frigid personification."[55] *This England* tries to find England by breaking
up Britannia, by "never aiming at what a committee from Great Britain and
Ireland would call complete."[56] In poetically implementing "Home Rule all
round," Thomas anticipates the politics of UK devolution.

Moreover, Thomas's "England," with its trace-elements of Yeats's Ireland, Frost's New England, and bardic Wales, is dialectical rather than unitary. He breaks nationality down further into "a system of vast circumferences circling about the minute neighbouring points of home."[57] This makes poetry's own local specifics the model for a refigured England. "Home," a positive microcosm, dramatizes a return "from somewhere far" to a locus where "one nationality / We had, I and the birds that sang, / One memory." Thomas's dialectic moves between the possibility that a more complex story of nationality and its metaphysical shadow "home" might be read from "English words" "worn new"; and the possibility that war has caused or disclosed an abyss, a nothingness, an *unheimlich* perplexity of language and vision, which bars access to the future *via* the past. "The Combe," in contrast to "Lob," symbolizes an England self-violated, self-estranged from its own traditions. The combe's "mouth is stopped with bramble, thorn, and briar," and it looks "far more ancient and dark . . . since they killed the badger there / Dug him out and gave him to the hounds, / That most ancient Briton of English beasts." Thomas's dialectic about England, his paradox of the "Home Front," passed to Ivor Gurney, for whom he became a muse. In "The Mangel-Bury," which conflates Thomas's death, his poem "Swedes," the trenches, and Gurney's own Gloucestershire localism: "the long house / Straw-thatched of the mangels stretched two wide wings; / And looked as part of the earth heaped up by dead soldiers."

"What 'modern'"

All these poets, of course, were "concerned with poetry." The war Muse entered the matrix of modern poetry: the coteries, manifestos, anthologies, arguments. Nor was Great War poetry a vulgarly thematic digression between prewar avant-garde enterprises and *The Waste Land*. Some American critics overstate the extent to which the Great War can be configured with literary modernism – an emphasis that recalls the tendency of American troops to arrive late and claim the credit. Jay Winter's objections to reading "the cultural history of the Great War as a phase in the onward ascent of modernism" and his corrective stress on "the persistence of tradition" have particular implications for how we read modern poetry.[58] Again, not only Rosenberg's rat had "cosmopolitan sympathies." Owen *et al.* were no less internationally minded than poets later called "modernist." Seven months in Germany educated Sorley in German literature as well as in the dangers of nationalism. Two years in France led Owen to French symbolism through his friendship with the gay French poet, Laurent Tailhade.[59] Thomas's reviews had picked up everything that happened in poetry after 1890, including the Irish Revival, while his alliance with Frost placed him on one side of an enduring Anglo-American debate about poetry and modernity. Rosenberg's training at the Slade and Gurney's at the Royal College of Music linked them with wider movements in the arts.

As for coterie, war itself grouped poets: Graves and Sassoon met in the Royal Welch Fusiliers, Sassoon and Owen at Craiglockhart. But poets also belonged eclectically to such formations as Edward Marsh's "Georgian" stable and Harold Monro's Poetry Bookshop. In March 1916 Monro, who published *Des Imagistes* (1912) as well as the Georgian anthologies (1912–22), went through Owen's poems, indicating "what was fresh and clever, and what was second-hand and banal; and what Keatsian, and what 'modern'" (Owen's report).[60] In 1914 the poetic field was dialectically constituted by reactions to the aestheticism of the 1890s. Thomas and Frost shared ideas about "speech and literature" that stressed the interplay of "sentence-sounds" with line or stanza. They questioned Pound's *vers libre* tenets and Imagism's appeal to the eye.[61] Thomas was seeking an elusive balance when he attacked Walter Pater's handling of language as if it were "marble," Swinburne's "musical jargon that . . . is not and never could be speech,"[62] Here he was partly quarrelling with his own youthful tastes; whereas Owen (as in "I saw his round mouth's crimson") synthesized Keats, *fin de siècle* "beauty," and war. He took Swinburne as well as Shakespeare to the Front. As Hibberd says: "a language of Romantic Agony" continued "into Owen's later work: femmes fatales sending men to death, the 'pallor of girls's brows,' bleeding mouths, mass sacrifice."[63]

Hardy and Yeats were at once precursors and players. Paul Fussell rather likes the idea that Hardy, "the master of situational irony," wrote the war.[64] Most poets were hugely conscious of Hardy: not only his satires but his Boer War poems, new war poems, and epic *The Dynasts* (1903–08) which sets the "vast international tragedy" (Preface) of the Napoleonic wars in a cosmic context where personifications like the Spirit Ironic and Spirit of the Pities debate its meaning. Thomas had long advocated Hardy's poetry but his own poetry (although in some ways more pessimistic) tends to question its determinism. Thus Thomas's "As the Team's Head Brass" rewrites Hardy's "In Time of 'The Breaking of Nations'" (1915) in which "a man harrowing clods" and "a maid and her wight" are said to outlast "War's annals." Thomas conceives the historical moment in both more radical and more dialectical terms. "As the Team's Head Brass," spoken by a presumed soldier who converses with a ploughman, is framed by lovers "disappearing into" and emerging from a wood. This, however, does not guarantee a postwar restoration of epistemological security. Here "War's annals" include the ploughman saying, "One of my mates is dead. The second day / In France they killed him," and macabre speculation:

> "Have you been out?" "No." "And don't want to, perhaps?"
> "If I could only come back again, I should.
> I could spare an arm. I shouldn't want to lose
> A leg. If I should lose my head, why, so,
> I should want nothing more . . . "

Owen's aestheticism left him unmoved by Hardy, whose poetry he found "potatoey."[65] His epigraphs from Yeats, if ironical, suggest their similar path from beauty and dream to history's "blood-dimmed tide" (Yeats, "The Second Coming"). "The Show" is prefaced by a quotation from Yeats's *The Shadowy Waters*: "the dreams the ever-living / Breathe on the burnished [misquoted as 'tarnished'] mirror of the world." The poem itself turns out to be an apocalyptic nightmare, which ends:

> And Death fell with me, like a deepening moan.
> And He, picking a manner of worm, which half had hid
> Its bruises in the earth, but crawled no further,
> Showed me its feet, the feet of many men,
> And the fresh-severed head of it, my head.

Yeats, too, was given to war-inflected apocalypse, as at the end of "Nineteen Hundred and Nineteen." This sequence's other parallels with Owen include the poet-speaker's lament for lost belief in progress; his guilty sense of complicity in violence; and an image of "the mother" left "murdered at her door, / To crawl in her own blood" – which refers to a Black and Tan atrocity. A related image is at the core of Yeats's "Meditations in Time of Civil War": "Last night they trundled down the road / That dead young soldier in his blood." These images are marked by trench poetry, as are both sequences by the war in general. Thus Yeats's notorious omission of Owen from his *Oxford Book of Modern Verse* (1936) suggests complex denials. His "distaste" for "certain poems written in the midst of the Great War" can be explained politically, as Yeats keeping his Irish nationalist distance; or aesthetically, as his current doctrine of "tragic joy" causing him to misread Owen: "passive suffering is not a theme for poetry." Or it can be explained by aesthetic politics: Great War poetry competed with Yeats's as a model for the young, underwriting (he thought) the committed, social-realist poetry of the 1930s.[66]

Yet Owen and Thomas (like the 1930s poets) are broadly on Yeats's formal wavelength. Free-verse Great War poetry ranges from post-Imagist trench poems by Richard Aldington, F. S. Flint, and Hulme himself, to David Jones's Eliot-influenced multimedia montage *In Parenthesis* (1937).[67] But in effect, whatever happened next (although Rosenberg may be a part-exception), the story of form at the wartime moment is the story of how traditional forms internalize history as new complications of voice, syntax, diction, image, stanza, line, rhyme, assonance – ultimately, rhythm. Part of the effect is the poetry's often unsettling air of work in progress or draft.

Thomas activates the widest stanzaic range – perhaps testing tradition. He also intensifies Frost's free blank verse, as when war-talk roughs up the line of "As the Team's Head Brass." "Insensibility" suggests how Owen can exploit irregular line- or stanza-length. Briefer lines set up the painfully prolonged "Of the hurt of the colour of blood for ever." Yet such effects combine with Owen's seemingly most formalist innovation: consonantal or assonantal rhyme. This repetition-device is the opposite of enjambment and elision. It holds the note to make the rhetorical point. Nor does it just affect line-endings but clinches Owen's tendency to slow things up, to create gaps between words ("Of the hurt of the colour of blood"). Consonantal clashes make "his round mouth's crimson'" a long five syllables. At the end of "The Show" the shock of "head" is paced by internal self-rhyme as well as by "hid." Owen and Thomas at once destabilize and stabilize form, as if the breaking of nations and remaking of form were coterminous. Thomas's typical structure catches poet and reader in syntactical mazes where assonance often serves elision. Owen's typical structure is a mode of rhyme that displays individual words in a heightened physicality which also heightens difference or oxymoron: "imagination" / "ammunition." That Thomas quarrels with aestheticism, whereas Owen transforms its "shows" by giving them political force, underlies their complementarity.

Rosenberg, too, upsets the retrospective binary model of how "modern poetry" came about. "Returning, We Hear the Larks" and "Break of Day in the Trenches" distinctively blend Imagist freeze-frames, irregular line-length, and discursive comment. Sassoon calls his poetry "scriptural and sculptural"[68] – a phrase that points to affinities with Owen. Rosenberg's masterpiece "Dead Man's Dump" is written in uneven verse-paragraphs, occasionally rhymed:

> None saw their spirits' shadow shake the grass,
> Or stood aside for the half used life to pass
> Out of those doomed nostrils and the doomed mouth,
> When the swift iron burning bee
> Drained the wild honey of their youth . . .
> Will they come? Will they ever come?

> Even as the mixed hoofs of the mules,
> The quivering-bellied mules,
> And the rushing wheels all mixed
> With his tortured upturned sight,
> So we crashed round the bend,
> We heard his weak scream,
> We heard his very last sound,
> And our wheels grazed his dead face.

In "Dead Man's Dump" intense metaphor and powerful detail add up to a global symbol. Great War poetry aspires to the condition of symbol. In 1919 T. S. Eliot could see only two kinds of war poetry: "Romance" and "Reporting."[69] But the clash between the mystique and its critics is often a clash of symbols. Owen's aesthetic-political scope is greater than Sassoon's because he realized the symbolic potential latent in Sassoon's structures of protest. Gurney's "physical against the . . . spiritual" is not just description versus abstraction but the symbolic battleground where more complex "truth" wins. Owen, Thomas, and Rosenberg also belong in a stricter sense (as does Yeats) to the mutations of French Symbolism in Britain and Ireland. The cosmos or natural world still supplies symbols but with receding or compromised back-up systems. Onto the post-Christian and post-Romantic symbolic repertoire, the Great War grafts its own blood-dimmed iconography: the trenches, no man's land, bugle-calls, bullets, gas, flares, wire, poppies, dead men's dumps. Yet the poetry can create tragic or elegiac shape around fractured consciousness, dismembered bodies, and lost heads. Unlike Imagism, it reorients rather than discards the transcendental dimension of Symbolism. As in Yeats, this religious residue becomes a way of conferring meaning (however terrible) or of seeking meaning. Symbolism now acts in and on the history that has complicated it along with the other constituents of lyric form. In Owen's "The Send-Off" rhythm is crucial to the symbolic translation whereby one troop-departure implies them all: "Down the close darkening lanes they sang their way / To the siding-shed, / And lined the train with faces grimly gay . . ."

As with symbolism, so with genre. Owen calls his war poems "elegies," and the first line of "The Send-Off" might also symbolize Great War poetry as a collective elegiac enterprise. Owen's and Thomas's landscapes meet in "darkening lanes." Elegy is arguably both a genre and the over-arching genre of war poetry. Indeed, the Great War may have made all lyric poetry more consciously elegiac and self-elegiac. Thomas's poetry often represents itself as a journey into the dark, into obsolescence or dissolution. In "Aspens" he identifies his art with the tree that "ceaselessly, unreasonably grieves."

This fits with Ramazani finding "elegy for elegy" in the "melancholic . . . unresolved, violent, and ambivalent" character of modern mourning.[70] Yet generic hybridity and elegy's intersection with other genres are also part of the picture. This chapter has noted the roles of love poem and interior soliloquy – the latter now dramatizing shell shock, neurasthenia, depression. Poets switch between writing *about* "Mental Cases" (the title of a poem by Owen) and writing *as* them. Freudian-Apocalyptic nightmares are one zone where the lyric "I" meets history, where generic hybridity mutually complicates personal and public responses to war. "Dulce et Decorum Est" mixes dream-trauma, reportage, *j'accuse*, elegy. The term "protest-elegy," itself a hybridization or oxymoron, suggests that personal and public elegy also complicate one other. At the personal level, modern "immersion" in loss (Ramazani), stripped of consolatory ritual, problematizes mourning, and may reduce poetic elegy to a textual sign of fading traces.[71] At the public level, anti-consolatory elegy politicizes mourning and keeps it alive. Perhaps Owen's "Futility" blends the two by inventing its own tender ritual ("Move him into the sun") while posing its more than rhetorical question: "O what made fatuous sunbeams toil / To break earth's sleep at all?"

When Owen and Thomas mix genres, such as elegy and pastoral, they create meanings that illuminate "what 'modern.'" The issue of pastoral and war is not confined to whether invocations of rural landscape figure naively as nostalgia or knowingly as irony. What matters is the ability to hold pastoral (the sum of literary negotiations with Nature) and war in the same frame. Here Blunden may not do quite enough, as when in "The Guard's Mistake," after "Surrounding pastoral urged them to forget," a company is surprised by enemy fire. Nonetheless, Blunden's retrospects belong to the transference whereby the "torn fields of France" (Rosenberg, "Break of Day") also signify a violated England and violated English pastoral, while the trenches haunt English landscape. The "war pastoral" (another oxymoron) of Gurney, Rosenberg, Thomas, and Owen effects this transference most disturbingly. The simplistic title of Gurney's first collection, *Severn and Somme* (1917), strangely forebodes the inability of his later poetry to disentangle either French/trench and English landscape, or peace and war. Rosenberg's "August 1914," which symbolizes the war as "A burnt space through ripe fields," and his "swift iron burning bee" imply an unprecedented crisis for pastoral. Yet since "torn fields" are at the nub of the whole crisis, Rosenberg's images equally query modernity in its guise as machinery of war. A similar crux shapes Thomas's dialectics. Stan Smith notes that his landscapes are full of ghosts: not just the "missing" of rural England but its earlier depopulation by economic modernity.[72] Marks on landscape attach these absences to longer vistas of human obsolescence, prospective as well as retrospective. In the dialectical "Two Houses" a "smiling" farmhouse faces ground where "the turf heaves" (a trench-image) over a ruin, and "the hollow past / Half yields the dead that never / More than half hidden lie." Set "among the living and the dead" ("Rain"), between tradition and dissolution, Thomas's poetry peculiarly suggests the ethos of war.

War pastoral blocks the consolation with which pastoral has (on the whole) traditionally supplied elegy. War reinforced Thomas's ecocentric view that human beings were risking their status as "citizens of the earth."[73] The "grief" of "Aspens" encompasses war, losses produced by modernity, the dark avenue or cognitive abyss ahead. Up to a point, Thomas writes elegies for pastoral. This is his mode of "warning." The origins of Owen's poetry in aestheticism and Christianity mean that he rarely concedes independence to natural systems. Sunbeams "break earth's sleep" only to create human beings. Thus Nature cannot console or even (as in Thomas) correct, because it is always subject to human constructions. Owen's war pastoral remains anthropocentric, but turned inside out by the assault on his Keatsian perception of Nature as a positive medium or metaphor for the body's sensory life. In "Spring Offensive" (oxymoron again) a French hillside changes its benign aspect, its pathetic fallacy, to stage Armageddon: "earth set sudden cups / In thousands for their blood." This is a parodic communion too. Both poets focus on "earth," which Thomas tends to set in avenues of time, Owen in arenas of space. For the ecocentric Thomas, earth is our violated habitat. For the anthropocentric Owen, earth has become a planetary theatre of war – literally, world war. He fuses a sterile earth with the devastated body and deformed soul, as in the exterior vista of "The Show," "pitted with great pocks and scabs of plagues," or the interior of "Strange Meeting": "granites which titanic wars had groined." Owen's fascination with the earthbound Titans, who challenged Zeus, is itself expressive. The complementary scope of the poets' different metaphysics, different forms, different warnings, suggests that we might see Great War poetry as the point where poetry first takes the full shock of the new.

NOTES

For sources of quotations from poetry, see bibliography below.

1. Patrick Beaver, ed., *The Wipers Times* (London: Macmillan, 1973), 45.
2. E. B. Osborn, ed., *The Muse in Arms* (London: John Murray, 1917), xiv.
3. See Catherine W. Reilly, *English Poetry of the First World War: A Bibliography* (London: George Prior, 1978).

4. Paul Keegan and Matthew Hollis, eds., *101 Poems Against War* (London: Faber, 2003), 135–36.
5. See Malvern Van Wyk Smith, *Drummer Hodge: The Poetry of the Anglo-Boer War* (Oxford: Clarendon Press, 1978).
6. Robert Bridges, *The Spirit of Man: An Anthology in English & French From the Philosophers and Poets* (London: Longman's, Green & Co., 1915), Preface.
7. Rupert Hart-Davis, ed., *Siegfried Sassoon: Diaries 1915–1918* (London: Faber, 1983), 282.
8. Julian Symons, ed., *An Anthology of War Poetry* (London: Penguin, 1942), viii.
9. W. B. Yeats, *Essays and Introductions* (London: Macmillan, 1961), 499.
10. Osborn, *Muse in Arms*, vii, xxii.
11. Frederick Brereton, ed., *An Anthology of War Poems* (London: Collins, 1930), 13.
12. John Middleton Murry, "The Poet of the War," *Nation and Athanaeum* 19: February 1921.
13. See, for instance, Louis MacNeice's statement in 1936: "The nineteen-thirty school of English poets ... derives largely from Owen," *Selected Literary Criticism of Louis MacNeice*, ed. Alan Heuser (Oxford: Clarendon Press 1987), 63.
14. I. M. Parsons, ed., *Men Who March Away: Poems of the First World War* (London: Chatto and Windus, 1964), 13; Brian Gardner, ed., *Up the Line to Death: The War Poets 1914–1918* (London: Methuen, 1964), xxv, xx. The subheadings are Parsons's.
15. Martin Stephen, ed., *Poems of the First World War* (London: Routledge, 1988; J. M. Dent, 1991), xiv.
16. Simon Featherstone, ed., *War Poetry: An Introductory Reader* (London: Routledge, 1995), 11, 1.
17. Siegfried Sassoon, *Siegfried's Journey 1916–1920* (London: Faber, 1945), 29.
18. Ian Parsons, ed., *The Collected Works of Isaac Rosenberg* (London: Chatto & Windus, 1979), 248.
19. John Bell, ed., *Wilfred Owen: Selected Letters* (Oxford: Oxford University Press 1985), 351.
20. R. George Thomas, ed., *Letters from Edward Thomas to Gordon Bottomley* (London: Oxford University Press, 1968), 203, 253.
21. For Sorley, see Jean Moorcroft Wilson, *Charles Hamilton Sorley: A Biography* (London: Cecil Woolf, 1985).
22. For Grenfell, see Nicholas Mosley, *Julian Grenfell* (1976; rpt. London: Persephone Books, 1999).
23. See extract from introduction to this (the earliest) anthology in Dominic Hibberd, ed., *Poetry of the First World War: A Casebook* (London: Macmillan, 1981).
24. Osborn, *Muse in Arms*, xvii.
25. R. George Thomas, ed., *Edward Thomas: Selected Letters* (Oxford: Oxford University Press, 1995), 111; Wilson, *Sorley*, 175; Parsons, *Collected Rosenberg*, 237.
26. R. K. R. Thornton, ed., *Ivor Gurney: War Letters* (London: Hogarth Press, 1984), 130.
27. Sassoon, *Siegfried's Journey*, 29.
28. See Wilson, *Sorley*, 167.
29. Thornton, *Gurney: War Letters*, 196.

30. See Edna Longley, ed., *A Language not to be Betrayed: Selected Prose of Edward Thomas* (Manchester: Carcanet, 1981), 131; Parsons, *Collected Rosenberg*, 250.
31. Bell, *Owen: Selected Letters*, 306.
32. Edward Thomas, "War Poetry," *Poetry and Drama* 2 (December 1914), reprinted in Longley, *Selected Prose of Thomas*, 131–35 (132).
33. Edward Thomas, ed., *This England: An Anthology from her Writers* (Oxford: Oxford University Press, 1915), Prefatory Note.
34. See Robert Ferguson, *The Short Sharp Life of T. E. Hulme* (London: Allen Lane, 2003), 235–42.
35. See Jean Moorcroft Wilson, *Siegfried Sassoon: The Making of a War Poet 1886–1918* (London: Duckworth, 1998), 373–74.
36. Sassoon had read Bertrand Russell's *Justice in War-Time* (which he later introduced to Owen). For Russell's "impresario" role, see Wilson, *Sassoon*, 373.
37. See Adrian Caesar, *Taking It Like a Man: Suffering, Sexuality and the War Poets* (Manchester: Manchester University Press, 1993).
38. Bell, *Owen: Selected Letters*, 247, 306.
39. *Ibid.*, 273–74.
40. For Owen's drafting of the Preface, see Dominic Hibberd, *Wilfred Owen: A New Biography* (London: Weidenfeld and Nicolson, 2002), 317.
41. For the roots of evangelical Anglicanism, see Elisabeth Jay, *The Religion of the Heart: Anglican Evangelicalism and the Nineteenth-Century Novel* (Oxford: Oxford University Press, 1979).
42. Hibberd, *Wilfred Owen*, 97.
43. Bell, *Owen: Selected Letters*, 246, 68.
44. Caesar, *Taking it like a Man*, 167; Featherstone, *Introductory Reader*, 62.
45. Jahan Ramazani, *Poetry of Mourning: The Modern Elegy from Hardy to Heaney* (Chicago and London: University of Chicago Press, 1994), 86.
46. See the discussion of Owen's draft Preface in Hibberd, *Wilfred Owen*, 317.
47. Bell, *Owen: Selected Letters*, 297.
48. Letter, 15 January 1915, quoted in *A Deep Cry: A Literary Pilgrimage to the Battlefields and Cemeteries*, ed. Anne Powell (Aberforth: Palladour Books, 1993), 30.
49. See Edna Longley, "'The Business of the Earth': Edward Thomas and Ecocentrism," in *Poetry & Posterity* (Tarset: Bloodaxe Books, 2000), 23–51.
50. Writing on George Meredith, Thomas refers to "the desire of a man to make himself, not a transitory member of a parochial species, but a citizen of the earth." See Longley, *Selected Prose of Thomas*, 37.
51. The public schoolboys Sassoon, Graves, and Sorley joined up at once: "the conduct demanded . . . by the turn of circumstances" (Wilson, *Sorley*, 175). Gurney was moved partly by patriotism, partly by hope of curing the instability that already troubled him. Rosenberg (who hated war) joined up mainly because he had no job and his family needed money. For Owen's thought-processes, see *Selected Letters*. For Thomas's, see *Selected Letters*.
52. Bell, *Owen: Selected Letters*, 130.
53. None of the poets discussed can strictly be called "working-class." Owen's father was a railway official; Gurney's a tailor; Rosenberg's an impoverished but educated Jewish immigrant.

54. For Thomas's Welshness, see his *Beautiful Wales* (1905) and a novel, *The Happy-Go-Lucky Morgans* (1913). The quotation is from the latter: see Longley, *Selected Prose of Thomas*, 221.

55. Review of John Cooke, ed., *The Dublin Book of Irish Verse, Morning Post*, 6 January 1910.

56. Thomas, Prefatory Note to *This England*.

57. Last sentence of "England," *The Last Sheaf* (London: Jonathan Cape, 1928), 91–111, reprinted in Longley, *Selected Prose of Thomas*, 222–31.

58. Jay Winter, *Sites of Memory, Sites of Mourning: The Great War in European Cultural History* (Cambridge: Cambridge University Press, 1995), 223, 3.

59. See Hibberd, *Wilfred Owen*, 132–40.

60. Bell, *Owen: Selected Letters*, 181.

61. Thomas wrote to Frost in May 1914: "you really should start doing a book on speech and literature, or you will find me mistaking your ideas for mine and doing it myself . . . However, my Pater would show you I had got on to the scent already." *Selected Letters*, 93.

62. Thomas wrote full-length studies of *Walter Pater* (1913) and *Algernon Charles Swinburne* (1912). For the quotations, see Longley, *Selected Prose of Thomas*, 152, 47.

63. Hibberd, *Wilfred Owen*, 146.

64. Paul Fussell, *The Great War and Modern Memory* (Oxford: Oxford University Press, 1975, 2000), 6.

65. Bell, *Owen: Selected Letters*, 272.

66. W. B. Yeats, ed., *The Oxford Book of Modern Verse* (Oxford: Clarendon Press, 1936), xxxiv.

67. For war poems by Flint and Aldington, see Peter Jones, ed., *Imagist Poetry* (London: Penguin, 1972). Hulme wrote one war poem, "Trenches: St. Eloi," which he dictated to Pound when Pound visited him in hospital.

68. Foreword, *Collected Works of Rosenberg*, ix.

69. T. S. Eliot, "Reflections on Contemporary Poetry," *Egoist*, 6 July 1919: 39.

70. Ramazani, *Poetry of Mourning*, 4, 8.

71. *Ibid.*, 4; and see William Watkin, "Poppypetal: Thanatropism, Pathos and Pathology in Contemporary Elegy Theory," in *Last before America: Irish and American Writing*, eds. Fran Brearton and Eamonn Hughes (Belfast: Blackstaff, 2001), 36–53.

72. See Stan Smith, *Edward Thomas* (London: Faber, 1986), 66 ff.

73. See n. 50.

POETRY BIBLIOGRAPHY

Blunden, Edmund. *Undertones of War*. London: Penguin, 1982.

Brooke, Rupert. *The Complete Poems*. London: Faber, 1932.

Gurney, Ivor. *Collected Poems*, ed. P. J. Kavanagh. Oxford: Oxford University Press, 1984.

Hardy, Thomas. *Selected Poems*, ed. Robert Mezey. London: Penguin, 1998.

Owen, Wilfred. *Complete Poems and Fragments*, ed. Jon Stallworthy. London: Oxford University Press, 1983.

Rosenberg, Isaac. *Collected Works*, ed. Ian Parsons. London: Chatto & Windus, 1979.
   Selected Poems. London: Enitharmon, 2003.
Sassoon, Siegfried. *Collected Poems 1908–1956*. London: Faber, 1961.
Sorley, Charles Hamilton. *Collected Poems*, ed. Jean Moorcroft Wilson. London: Cecil Woolf, 1985.
Thomas, Edward. *Collected Poems*, ed. R. George Thomas. Oxford: Clarendon, 1978.
Yeats, W. B. *Selected Poems*, ed. Timothy Webb. London: Penguin, 2000.

4

CLAIRE BUCK

British women's writing of the Great War

"The time has come," the Foreman said
   "To talk of many things,
Of Screws and Shells and Overalls
   Of clocking on, and Kings
And why the shaft gets boiling hot
And should the mandrels sing?"[1]

This short extract from E. S. Caley's "The Foreman and the Manager," a parody of Lewis Carroll's "The Walrus and the Carpenter," raises many issues central to women's war writing and the feminist scholarship that has brought both women's experience of the war years and their considerable body of writings on the war to public attention since the 1980s. Published in a munitions factory newspaper, the poem is about male responses to the huge impact of the war on gender roles. The Foreman, according to Claire A. Culleton, who discusses this poem in her rich account of women and working-class culture, has recognized the need for women's labor and is lecturing the manager of a munitions factory on the need to begin instructing the new female workforce. Culleton tells us that munitions workers numbered 900,000 of the nearly 3,000,000 women employed in British factories by the end of the war. Another 2,000,000 "worked in the First Aid Nursing Yeomanry, the Women's Land Army, the Volunteer Aid Detachment, and other paramilitary organizations,"[2] working both at home and in the war zone, albeit not as combatants. Women's mass entry into previously male jobs fundamentally challenged the period's dominant assumptions about women's capacities and proper role in the home. Even though women were forced out of these jobs at the end of the war, their experience of "Screws and Shells and Overalls" marked British twentieth-century society and contributed to women's economic, social, and sexual emancipation.

In the same way that women workers, both middle and working class, were pushed out of their wartime jobs after 1918, women's contribution to war

5 "Screws and Shells and Overalls": women munitions workers, Britain

writing was until the 1980s largely invisible. Women wrote and published extensively about the war; for example, between 1914 and 1918 women's poetry was published in single-author collections, anthologies, and the leading newspapers and periodicals of the day, as well as factory newspapers, women's magazines, and local newspapers. Of the more than 2,000 poets publishing during these years a quarter were women. By contrast soldiers on active service wrote less than a fifth of the total output.[3] This widespread circulation of women's poetry during the war years is not recorded in later-century anthologies or criticism. For example, Jon Silkin's 1979 *Penguin Book of First World War Poetry* included only Anna Akhmatova and Marina Tsvetayeva, and Brian Gardner's *Up the Line to Death: The War Poets 1914–1918* (1964) contained no women.[4]

Combatant experience, particularly trench experience on the Western Front, swiftly became a guarantee of the authenticity of war writing. The privileging of soldiers' first-hand accounts began during the war, in, for example, discussions of war poetry in the pages of the *Times Literary Supplement*. Not only was it presumed that the soldiers' first-hand experience of the horrors of trench warfare protected them from the naïve jingoism of the civilian, but women all too soon came to represent the culpable war enthusiasm of the home front. As symbols of nation and home, women were memorably addressed by Siegfried Sassoon in his sonnet "Glory of Women": "You love us when we're heroes, home on leave, / Or wounded in a mentionable place."[5] He links women to a failure to imagine the conditions of war, and conflates the middle-class norms of sexual propriety over which women had little or no control with a willful silence about the true nature of war. The equation of women with a civilian home front that could never successfully comprehend the war experience of the soldier set up a significant obstacle for feminist critics attempting to restore women's writing to visibility and to explain its value.

The crucial retrieval work done since 1980 by critics such as Margaret Higonnet, Catherine Reilly, Jane Marcus, Claire Tylee, and Agnes Cardinal, had to be done in tandem with a wider feminist reconceptualization of the relationship between war and gender, most memorably in Sara Ruddick, *Maternal Thinking: Toward a Politics of Peace* (1989) and Helen M. Cooper *et al.*, *Arms and the Woman* (1989).[6] Critics, such as Nosheen Khan in *Women's Poetry of the First World War* (1988), Claire Tylee in *The Great War and Women's Consciousness* (1990), and Sandra Gilbert and Susan Gubar in *No Man's Land* (1987)[7] among many others, have relocated women's writing against the assumption that war is an exclusively male experience. Women's writing gives us, they argue, much needed access to women's different historical experience of war and tells us about women's relationship to militarism. It has not always been easy, however, to escape the assumptions of traditional literary criticism on the war. The near exclusive focus on the work of a few soldiers who wrote about the war's horror has encouraged a series of myths about war writing that do not stand up to closer inspection.[8] Most pervasive is the belief in a standard trajectory from naïve enthusiasm to ironic disillusion, despite contrary evidence that both criticism of and support for war coexisted from 1914 onwards. Recent feminist scholars have their own version of this myth of disillusion. Women writers who diagnose or subvert the conjunction of masculinity, militarism, and English nationalism have proved much easier to write about than those for whom Britain's part in the war seemed just or simply inevitable.

The privileging of experience as a criterion of value in Great War criticism, albeit limited to male combatant experience, has also sat well with early second wave feminist criticism's emphasis on women's experience. Thus, critics often look at the writing, particularly the major war genres of memoirs, autobiography, letters, and diaries, for evidence about women's experience of war. This work is welcome for the new insights it has generated about how war affects women in specific ways. Unfortunately, it has also trapped feminist critics, often against their stated intentions, into comparisons between men's and women's writing, on such varied grounds as the claims to suffering and sacrifice in the war effort, and on aesthetic grounds. Women almost always lose since combatant realism, deriving its authority from the eyewitness, so often sets the standard for aesthetics.

Feminist criticism has only recently begun to analyze how aesthetics shapes the gendered meanings of war. In order to understand the historical place of women's war writing more clearly we still need to name the ways women were forced to negotiate the relationship between gender, nationalism, and war in their choices of genre and means of publication and circulation of their texts. Women's writing helped produce and reproduce the meaning of the war in Britain, both during and afterwards, so that we can learn much from such an analysis about all First World War writing. It makes sense to begin with poetry since the genre's privileged relationship to aesthetics has made women's poetry of the 1914–18 period the clearest challenge to critics.

Poetry

In *Mr. Punch's History of the Great War* (August 1918), *Punch* comments on how the "[w]ar has not only stimulated the composition, but the perusal of poetry, especially among women," and although women's memoirs and fiction are now much better remembered, poetry was the preeminent genre for women writers between 1914 and 1918.[9] Reilly's bibliographic research revealed 532 women poets writing about the war, both during and after, although few are remembered outside of the specialist work of feminist scholarship.[10] Some were already established writers before the war, as for example, Alice Meynell, Charlotte Mew, Edith Nesbit, May Sinclair, Cicely Hamilton, an important suffrage writer, and Katharine Tynan, a recognized *fin-de-siècle* poet of the Celtic Revival. Tynan is singled out in an early *Times Literary Supplement* assessment of *Poems in War Time* from 1915 as remarkable for her "simplicity and poignancy, pity, and tenderness . . . a woman's tender, all-hospitable heart."[11] The reviewer offers a conventional picture of Tynan's feminine virtues as a poetess, but talks knowledgeably and intelligently about her reworking of ballads and carols, contrasting her with a range of male poets who sacrifice poetry to public rhetoric. Some women such as Enid Bagnold, Elizabeth Daryush, Mary Webb, and Edith Sitwell were beginning to establish themselves as writers when the war broke out, while yet others, Margaret Postgate Cole, Vera Brittain, Eleanor Farjeon, Nancy Cunard, and Rose Macaulay, only became famous after the war, sometimes because of the war, as in the case of Brittain, whose *Testament of Youth* (1933) epitomizes the war memoir for many readers.

Even while poetry is arguably the most central of women's wartime genres, readers have often found it disappointingly backward-looking in both style and subject matter, many poems reiterating a version of femininity rooted in home front experiences of waiting and mourning. This may say more about readers and critics than about the poetry itself. The outbreak of the war coincided with hot debate about the proper form, language, and sensibility of modern poetry. The first Georgian anthology of 1912 had declared a modern English poetics that combined established verse forms with naturalism. Imagists and Vorticists, like H.D., Richard Aldington, and Ezra Pound were by 1914 announcing the poetic revolution of modernism, as they introduced the experimental rhythms of free verse, and caricatured Victorian poetics as linguistically florid and emotionally mawkish. Most poets, whether male or female, combatant or civilian, still espoused formal meter, stanzaic forms, and familiar genres such as the short lyric, sonnet, elegy, and ballad. To later twentieth-century critics, trained to associate poetic and political innovation with a modernist aesthetics, the wide variety of formal choices and their specific period implications are often invisible. Because modernism has so fundamentally altered our understanding of Victorian and Edwardian poetry, aesthetic value may not be a useful framework for understanding women's war poetry.

Aesthetics remains important, however, insofar as the meaning of particular stylistic choices is necessarily linked for women poets to patriotism as a discourse structured by gender difference. The same is true for male poets, but the gendering of patriotism makes the use of particular verse forms different for men and women. First World War poets of both gender frequently couple so-called "traditional" verse forms with a patriotic-heroic rhetoric linking war and love and defining each soldier's death through a discourse of national honor. Later readers, themselves conditioned by the victory of modernist aesthetics in the twentieth century, the devastation of two world wars, and the anti-war rhetoric of the Vietnam era, are understandably alienated. Yet a return to the pre-modernist context in which the women war poets wrote reveals both a subtle use of Victorian and Edwardian forms to situate discourses of militarism and patriotism, and the intense pressures on women poets as women to publicly represent national honor.

Women's importance to the war effort was acknowledged by the government and by the wider culture in many ways. The recruitment campaign that led to slogans such as "Women of England Say 'Go'" not only spoke for women, but also directly addressed them. Women were asked to put pressure on the men in their lives to enlist. Even the infamous white feather campaign was part of a government-orchestrated effort to mobilize women to recruit male soldiers, resulting also in the unreflective jingoism of poems such as Louisa Prior's "To a Hesitant Briton," Marjorie Pratt's "To a 'Shirker,'" and Jessie Pope's infamous "The Call," in which the speaker asks:

> Who's for the trench –
> Are you, my laddie? . . .
> Who's fretting to begin,
> Who's going out to win?
> And who wants to save his skin –
> Do you, my laddie?[12]

The speaker's peculiar authority to shame the reluctant young man derives from women's special place in the home, that metonymy for the nation, with moral and spiritual influence on men. This role was easily adapted to wartime propaganda. Patriotic poems by women appeared not only in publications like *The Times* and the *Spectator* but were quoted in sermons and reprinted in leaflet form for the troops, as in the case of Lucy Whitmell's "Christ in Flanders," or, like Tynan's "Greeting: From the Women at Home," published in the 1917 Christmas issue of *Blighty*, a newspaper distributed to the frontline troops.[13]

Women's poetry was actively used to promote and give definition to women's relationship to nationalism at the time, particularly in their role as mothers. G. W. Clarke's *A Treasury of War Poetry, 1914–1917* (1917), which appeared in both Britain and the United States, includes a final section titled "Women and the War"; it groups all but a couple of the poems by women, with subjects such as a mother's pride in her soldier son and her anguish at his death. A woman's words end the anthology, with Sara Teasdale's poem "Spring in War-Time" protesting the coming of spring with its suggestions of hope and regeneration. Each stanza places the conventional imagery of spring, "bud and leaf," lengthening daylight hours, and apple blossom, against a final couplet that registers the effects of war, for example: "How can it [spring] have the heart to sway / Over the graves, / New graves?"[14] Placed at the end of the volume, Teasdale's poem acquires an additional resonance, asked to conjure another spring, that of postwar regeneration. The poem itself refuses renewal and regeneration whilst painfully acknowledging its inevitability, but in Clarke's anthology Teasdale finds herself acting the role of earth mother, mourning like Circe for Proserpine but ultimately doomed to unwilling fertility. Clarke thus recruits women, as female poets and subjects, to their place as ideological supports for the nation, representing its organic continuity with nature, and the country's natal link to its soldiers through the mother poet.

Critics have noted the explicit challenge pro-war suffragists mounted against the limiting of women to traditional feminine war work. Cicely Hamilton, an important pre- and postwar feminist playwright who worked in a British army hospital in France, wrote in 1916 of the misery of passivity in the "Non-Combatant." The speaker, whose gender remains unspecified, suffers the wound of redundancy: "With life and heart afire to give and give / I take and eat the bread of charity. / In all the length of this eager land, / No man has need of me." More outspoken in her 1918 protest, "Drafts," Nora Bomford demanded the right to fight and die alongside men: "Why should men face the dark while women stay / To live and laugh and meet the sun each day."[15] Thus, resistance to women's ideological work representing hearth and nation for the male soldier was not limited to pacifist and anti-war poets. However, British women were prominent in feminist anti-war work.

Despite considerable obstacles from the government, English suffragists attended The Hague Women's International Peace Conference in 1915, insisting that militarism was antithetical to women's interests and even her very nature. In verse we find outspoken criticism of the war linked to feminist politics in S. Gertrude Ford's 1917 poem, "'A Fight to the Finish'":

> 'Fight the year out!' the War-lords said:
> What said the dying among the dead?
> 'To the last man!' cried the profiteers:
> What said the poor in the starveling years?[16]

Ford gives her concise analysis of the war's economic and ideological roots a feminist cast, "Nobody asked what the women thought," echoing the speeches of suffragists like Helena Swanwick and Sylvia Pankhurst.[17]

Critique was quite politically and stylistically various. We have Ford's diagnosis of the interconnections between militarism, patriarchy, and capitalism written in the cadence of another war skeptic, Thomas Hardy. Different is the apocalyptic seer of Cunard's "Zeppelins" with its resonance of both Blake and Revelations: "I saw the people climbing up the street / Maddened with war . . . /And after followed Death, who held with skill / His torn rags royally, and stamped his feet." Like Cunard, Edith Sitwell in "The Dancers" turns to a mythic register as commensurate with the horror of battle: "The floors are slippery with blood: / The world gyrates too . . ." In this poem, perhaps influenced by Vernon Lee's "Ballet of the Nations" (discussed below), she takes a trope familiar in Great War writing, that of the civilian population dancing while soldiers died, and turns it into the dance of death: "We are the dull blind carrion-fly / That dance and batten / . . . We dance, we dance, each night."[18] Although Sitwell, like many combatant poets, casts the civilian population as criminally naïve parasites, "blind carrion-fly" feeding on the rotting bodies of the soldiers, she detaches this rhetoric from that of the heroic, suffering soldier, and redirects it toward a universalizing anti-war discourse, signaled in the poem's opening, where "the world gyrates too."

Margaret Sackville, a prominent Scottish activist in peace organizations and outspoken anti-war poet, skillfully represents the losses inflicted by war on civilians and soldiers alike without recourse to the language of national sacrifice. "A Memory," for example, ends: "Not by the battle fires, the shrapnel are we haunted; / Who shall deliver us from the memory of these dead?" These dead are the civilians in a village devastated by an attack, where they "lie unburied" in the street and "a bayoneted woman stares in the marketplace." Sackville self-consciously protests the idealization of a male soldier's heroism and valor, by focusing on a woman's body, and "the low sobbing of women / The creaking of a door, a lost dog – nothing else." Here there is "no pride of conquest" and neither is there any reflection on the soldiers who did this. They are left out of the picture altogether, not even named as Germans or English. Where she invokes the terms of sacrifice, as in "Sacrament," she holds it resolutely to a Christian pacifist agenda in which the blood of the dead is "this wine of awful sacrifice outpoured." But the blood pollutes and destroys: "These stricken lands! The green time of the year / Has found them wasted by a purple flood . . . / Not all our tears may cleanse them from that blood."[19] Sackville detaches the symbolism of blood and sacrifice from its Christian support, implicitly refusing the use of Christiantity as support for a militaristic nationalism.

Other anti-war poets assume a working-class perspective, like that of the mother in May Herschel-Clarke's "For Valour," for whom the bronze posthumous medal is inadequate payment for the "golden hair, / And firm young flesh as white as snow." In a quintessential dramatic monologue, Herschel-Clarke uses the working-class mother to question the patriotic rhetoric of the soldier whose "valour" in dying for his country is worth more than his life. Simultaneously, she questions the woman's patriotic duty in bearing children for her country, "[s]ay, don't you think I've done my bit? . . . / Jest bronze . . . *Gawd! What a price to pay!*" Emily Orr's "A Recruit From the Slums" mounts a savage attack on the rhetoric of recruitment, following Kipling's example in taking the working-class soldier's part against a government that embodies middle-class interests. Each stanza turns on the famous Kitchener slogan: "what have you done for your country?", as, for example, "What has your country done for you, / Child of city slum," and "What can your country ask from you, / Dregs of the British race?"[20] But despite her recognition of the cynical betrayal represented by this call to national service, registered too in the title of her postwar volume of poems, *A Harvester of Dreams* (1922), the poem ends by contrasting the hypocrisy of the government with an endorsement of the soldiers' heroic sacrifice.[21]

Orr's ambivalence reveals the degree to which both pro- and anti-war poetry shared the same cultural framework. She evidently intends to correct the dominant eugenicist portrait of the working-class poor as symbolizing national decline, a condition which includes a perceived confluence of moral and physical degeneration. The poem transforms urban slum-dweller into hero through the experience of battle: "And why we were born we could hardly guess / Till we felt the surge of battle press / And looked the foe in the face."[22] However, the effect of this transformation is to initiate the slum-dwellers into the proper English manliness, which is the other pole to the eugenicist slur. According to the last stanza, they learn the value of comradeship based on sacrifice. Unlike the preceding three stanzas, the last opens with a popular biblical tag instead of a question: "Greater love hath no man than this / That a man should die for his friend." The slum recruit responds with the recognition that "our bones were made from the English mould." The rhetoric of a brotherhood of soldiers dying for their country could be used to support nationalism, to intensify the tragedy of the war by marking the nobility of young men who remained loyal to each other even while betrayed by their country, and in Orr's example to show the true value of the so-called "dregs of the British race." Elisabeth A. Marsland has commented on this potential ambiguity in protest poetry.[23] The representation of the soldier as noble victim of government policy brings protest and patriotism dangerously close together because of the integral role that stories of male comradeship and courage in battle play in building national unity and pride.

By far the majority of women poets, however, reiterate the nobleness of the soldier whose sacrifice buys England security and peace, and more disturbingly provides the blood that ensures national unity. Eva Dobell's "Pluck" depicts a seventeen-year-old soldier, now wounded in hospital, who has told a "gallant" lie in order to join up "[w]hile other boys are still at play." Although "he shrinks in dread / To see the 'dresser' drawing near," the boy ultimately displays true stoic courage to "face us all, a soldier yet, / Watch his bared wounds with unmoved air."[24] Dobell seeks to pay tribute to the young man's courage in the face of tragedy, but in doing so she turns his literal status as a soldier into militaristic metaphor, by measuring his courage by his soldierliness. Brittain, famous now as both feminist and pacifist, eulogized her fiancé: "Of heart without reproach or hint of fear, / Who walks unscathed amid War's sordid ways / . . . Roland of Roncesvalles in modern days."[25] The language of medieval chivalry displaces the politics and day-to-day actualities of modern warfare with a literary fantasy of pure and honorable knights. And the speaker turns into a passive feminine figure, whose role is confined by the chivalric romance model Brittain borrows, that is, to remain faithful to the memory of her knight and thereby guarantee his purity.

More self-consciously than Brittain, May Wedderburn Cannan writes in 1916 of the soldiers who have "died to give us gentleness." Responding to poems such as Brooke's "The Dead," she seems to imitate his diction and pathos with a view to giving the civilian's answer: "I have thought, some day they may lie sleeping / Forgetting all the weariness and pain, / And smile to think their world is in our keeping, / And laughter come back to the earth again."[26] She echoes and is echoed by many others who write of the dead as having "made it possible and sure / For other lives to have, to be,"[27] or who serve their country in dying "to serve a friend," as Alice Meynell writes in "Summer in England, 1914."[28] Meynell's poem displays a painful awareness of the devastation of the battlefield by dwelling on the pastoral abundance of England in the later summer and fall of 1914. Although many surviving combatants also wrote elegies for the men who had died, women's elegies enact the classic female task of mourning the dead soldier. It may be more comfortable for critics today to concentrate on the poems that simultaneously protest the war and subvert its supporting discourses of nationalism and militarism, but the overwhelming pervasiveness of patriotic, elegiac work in women's First World War poetry demands a reading that attends fully to the gendered nature of citizenship.

Drama

If women's poetry has been a problem for later critics, women's drama has, until very recently, been all but invisible. The prewar years saw the emergence of a new women's theatre that challenged the "masculinist managerial and organizational structures of Edwardian theatre" that had "offered little, if any support for the woman playwright."[29] The Actresses' Franchise League had played a significant role after its formation in 1908 in training suffragists in public speaking and in organizing women's theatre in a wide spectrum of settings, ranging from Elizabeth Robins's well-known *Votes for Women* (1913) to the "spectacles" of suffrage political demonstrations. The League also established a play department run by Inez Bensusan to support dramatic writing by women.

The war interrupted this new promotion of women as actors, directors, and playwrights, and the war years figure as an ellipsis in critical histories of women and the theatre that is only now being filled. Additionally, women's largest contribution was probably in the area of amateur theatricals, and "the very nature of amateur theatricals indicates that scripts, published or in manuscript form, are more likely to be found outside larger institutions and libraries."[30] Birmingham Reference Library War Poetry Collection, for example, lists over twenty plays as poetry rather than drama, of which only a quarter are to be found in larger research libraries. While a richer body of work is being uncovered, the plays that are presently available need to be understood in a context of the war's negative effects on women's drama.

The declaration of war in August 1914 was accompanied by the immediate but temporary closure of London theatres. When they reopened managers largely turned to the entertainment of both troops on leave and the new female workforce, who saw a sudden increase in money and independence. Indeed, commentators in the postwar period saw the theatre as deleteriously feminized thanks to a growing female audience.[31] The licensing of plays by the Lord Chancellor combined with the censoring effects of the Defence of the Realm Act of 1915 and its later amendments to restrict possibilities of wartime drama, particularly if it criticized the war or took the Front as its subject. By comparison, women's plays in the United States were published and performed considerably more frequently up until the country's entry into the war, when the Espionage and Subversion Acts of 1917 and 1918 changed the climate. For example, Marion Craig Wentworth's strongly feminist and pacifist play, *War Brides* (1914), was produced in New York in 1915 and made into a film, but "never licensed for performance in Britain."[32]

Commercial London theatre was not, of course, the only venue for dramatic production and it remains to be seen what kinds of women-authored or -directed theatre was active in the regional repertory theatre, independent theatre, subscription theatre, Sunday theatre, or other types of dramatic performance. For example, with Annie Horniman's financial backing the Gaiety Theatre in Manchester performed new works by both women and men between 1907 and 1917. From its formation in 1911 until the early 1920s, The Pioneer Players, Edy Craig's subscription theatre society, performed weekly at small London theatres and public halls. The Pioneer Players staged Gwen John's one-act play *Luck of War* in May 1917.[33] This play examines the effects of the war on working-class women and their families by staging a scenario like Tennyson's "Enoch Arden" (1864), in which a soldier, missing and presumed dead, returns home to find that his wife has remarried. The story is told from the woman's perspective, with the brutal and unsympathetic husband telling his wife that: "I left you t' country, Ann, as a soldier 'as to do. But if you'd been one o' them blatant brassy-haired hussies I shouldn't 'a done it."[34] John, not to be confused with the painter of the same name, allows George to express the brutalities of his experience at the Front and engages with Ann's emotional and financial difficulties at home. For example, the government reduces Ann's income by cutting off her separation allowance and putting her on a pension after George has been presumed dead. However, the play ends with Ann reunited with George, having abandoned Amos, a significantly better husband and father. Thus the play is typical of the Pioneer Players' wartime productions in explicitly addressing the problems that the war posed but avoiding "clear solutions."[35]

John's play shows us that despite the inhospitable climate of the theatre profession and war conditions, women were active in a number of ways, especially if we look beyond commercial London theatre and the narrower definition of the well-made stage play. The broader category of performance is also helpful here, allowing us to see the role of women as actors who, as early as October 1914, had begun to work as entertainers for the troops, at the instigation of Lena Ashwell, manager of the Kingsway Theatre in London and a leading member of the AFL. Much of this entertainment took the form of scenes from Shakespeare, Sheridan, Shaw, and Barrie, but Gertrude Jennings wrote comic sketches, such as *Poached Eggs and Pearls: A Canteen Comedy in 2 Scenes* (1916) and *Allotments* (1917), for Ashwell's companies, while Cicely Hamilton wrote and produced *The Child in Flanders* for Christmas 1917.[36] By 1917, twenty-five companies were performing over 1,400 shows a month in France alone. Most of the women were members of the AFL.[37]

As writers, directors, and actors women also contributed to amateur theatrical productions aimed at supporting the war effort. The magazines and newspapers of women's organizations such as the Women's Volunteer

Reserve and Munitions Factories provide a record of amateur performance as a significant recreational activity for women war workers. Jane Potter discusses a three-scene play, "Discipline," that was included in the *Women's Volunteer Reserve Magazine*, July 1916, which shows two women, the middle-class Miss Earle and the working-class Emma Jones, united in their common bond as service women. The play concludes with a tableau in which the entire WVR Company stands to attention while the National Anthem is played. "Discipline" evidently served a number of purposes to do with morale and the building of unity in both the WVR and a nation faced with class divisions that threatened to fracture the imagined cohesiveness of patriotism. In the context of women's war work, drama seems to have had much to do with middle-class concerns about working-class morals. Theatre took its place in an array of "wholesome recreational pursuits," and other more coercive methods such as women police, designed to control newly independent working women.[38]

The tableau that ends "Discipline" refers back to a long tradition of nineteenth-century theatrical spectacle representing war. Pageants and tableaux were effective forms for the many women who used amateur dramatic performances for propaganda, recruitment, and fund-raising, all forms of war service seen as appropriate to women. Pageants "placed contemporary events in the setting of a heroic past,"[39] offering continuity and order to a population confronting the disturbances of war. Typically, pageants such as Gladys Davidson's *Brittania's Revue* (*c.*1914) and May Bell's *Brittania Goes to War*, which was published in 1919 but almost certainly performed much earlier, provide a spectrum of allegorical characters. These represent the nations and countries fighting the war, types such as Tommy Atkins, the Red Cross Nurse, the Land Girl, and Virtues such as Honour and Chivalry. In *Brittania's Revue* Brittania summons these characters on stage to express loyalty through patriotic songs and verse-speeches. National and imperial unity are performed through the martialing of Scotland and Wales, and colonies such as Ireland, Canada, South Africa, and India, all of whom are heralded with national songs or dances. Ireland, for example, sings "In Erin's Isle there beats one heart, one mind; / Although we oft have squabbled, now you'll find / United we stand." Despite, or more likely because of, the British government's constant anxiety through the war about Irish resistance to English colonial domination, Davidson represents the Anglo-Irish conflict as a trivial "squabble" that can be set aside in the interests of national and imperial unity.[40]

Although these pageants reflect a longer history of British national and imperial propaganda, and were primarily associated with support for the war, the pageant was also available to more politically dissident perspectives, having for example been used to effect by the prewar suffrage movement, in, for example, Cicely Hamilton's famous *A Pageant of Great Women* (1911). In the immediate war context, Vernon Lee's savagely anti-war drama, *Ballet of the Nations* (1915), although conventionally read as a masque or a reworking of a medieval morality play, derives some of its satiric force from imperial pageants like *Brittania Rules*. Set in a London square, the play includes a dance orchestrated by Death and performed by the nations and other allegorical figures. Satan and Clio, the muse of history, whose job is to narrate the scene under Satan's direction, form an audience. The ballet is described as increasingly grotesque with the dancers "chopping and slashing, blinding each other with squirts of blood and pellets of human flesh,"[41] although the dancers are not directly visible to the audience. Neither is the accompanying Orchestra of Patriotism, composed of Passions such as Heroism, Pity, Love of Adventure, Idealism, Science, and Organization, entirely audible. Unlike the patriotic pageant or tableau, *Ballet of the Nations* presents the war as violent and grotesque waste, a perspective amplified through the inclusion of an introduction and lengthy notes in Lee's 1920 version, *Satan the Waster*.[42]

Lee's complex Brechtian text emphasizes Satan's staging of the war as spectacle and was ill received on its first publication.[43] George Bernard Shaw reviewed the 1920 version enthusiastically in the *Nation*, praising Lee as an Englishwoman who "by sheer intellectual force, training, knowledge, and character, kept her head when Europe was a mere lunatic asylum." Other writers of the inter-war years seem to have seen it as a prescient model of pacifist writing, as for example Margaret Skelton, who acknowledged Lee's text as a source for her own anti-war novel *Below the Watchtowers* (1926).[44] In addition to Skelton, Gillian Beer finds Lee's influence in Miss la Trobe's pageant in Virginia Woolf's *Between the Acts* (1941).[45] These traces are important to a picture of women's resistance to the war, at the time and in the years following, as coherent and collaborative.

The 1929 production of R. C. Sherriff's *Journey's End*, which represented trench experience on the West End stage for the first time, is usually understood by critics to have initiated the difficult process of coming to terms with the war in British theatre. Although Sheriff's play was undoubtedly significant (Brittain describes it as a spur to her own "women's" memoir *Testament of Youth*), a critical focus on mainstream London theatre once again obscures women's theatre.[46] As early as 1924, Hamilton's *The Old Adam: A Fantastic Comedy* was played at the Birmingham Repertory Theatre, coming to Ashwell's Kingsway Theatre the following year.[47] *The Old Adam* is a remarkable satire on British militarism set in the imaginary country of Paphalagonia, much like Britain. In this three-act play, the government is offered a weapon that will end war by disabling all modern weapons. Instead of negotiating a peace the Paphalagonians go off to war with pikes, horses, and handcarts. The play ends with government ministers and a bishop cheering the departure of the first regiment of volunteers. The curtain falls to the sound of "It's a long way to Tipperary," leaving a 1924 audience to ponder its own patriotic enthusiasm for the war that had just ended, and the myths of heroism and righteousness that fueled it.

During the 1920s and 1930s, women dramatists frequently used the war to explore changes in women's relationship to the family and to their traditional domestic roles, as in G. B. Stern's plays *The Matriarch* (1931) and *The Man Who Pays the Piper* (1931).[48] M. E. Atkinson's *The Chimney Corner* (1934), a one-act play evidently influenced by Susan Glaspell's *Trifles*, shows a community of Belgian women during the war.[49] The women work for the Germans, as nurses and domestic servants, but all the time their subservience masks their participation in a resistance network signaled by codes such as the wearing of a safety pin on the underside of a skirt. The obvious patriotism of Atkinson's subject may obscure the play's implication; it was not only the Germans who underestimated and undervalued women's service work during the war.

Muriel Box, a prolific dramatist, screenwriter, and film director, is another example of a writer who used the stage to dramatize women's war work. Published in a collection of new plays for all-women casts in 1935, *Angels of War* does not seem to have been performed until 1981, when Mrs. Worthington's Daughters, a British feminist theatre group, took it on tour.[50] The play takes place in the months before the Armistice and portrays a women's ambulance unit from the arrival of a new and idealistic young recruit, through her disillusionment and "hardening" to the unit's demobilization. Although the play is set just behind the British front lines, and centered on the women who were most involved in frontline experience, all three acts of *Angels of War* take place in one claustrophobic room where the women are billeted. This quasi-domestic setting, motivated in a practical sense by the limited resources of the amateur players for whom the play was originally designed, intensifies the play's thematic preoccupation both with women's new wartime opportunities and freedoms, and with the idea of all-female communities. Box's complex use of theatrical space to represent the way men's and women's different relationships to the war were enacted through the management of space is but one example of how drama offers a specific dimension to women's representation of the war. Until we have available the full range of plays, venues, and performance genres in which women participated as writers, actors, performers, managers, and directors, any account of drama and gender in First World War writing will be provisional.

Prose

"War," complained the *Times Literary Supplement*, perhaps with Angela Brazil's schoolgirl stories about German spies in mind, "has become as much the stock-in-trade of the novelist as are treasure islands, pirate schooners or the Great North road."[51] The division into culturally sanctioned war stories and those seen as unpatriotic or trivializing is useful for thinking about the wealth of wartime and postwar prose, from novels and short stories to memoirs, diaries, and journalism, and is intimately linked to the question of who has the license to comment on the war.

Much wartime prose by both genders was written directly in support of the war, including works of propaganda commissioned by the War Propaganda Bureau. First-person accounts of nursing in the war zone, such as Millicent Sutherland's *Six Weeks at the War*, published by the London *Times* in 1914, and Phyllis Campbell's *Back of the Front: Experiences of a Nurse* (1915), ghost-written to help substantiate the *Bryce Report on German Atrocities*, appeared from as early as 1914.[52] The well-known novelist Mary Ward (Mrs. Humphrey Ward) was recruited to the propaganda effort in 1915, leading to *England's Effort* (1916), *Towards the Goal* (1917), and *Fields of Victory* (1919), all based on government-authorized tours of military sites in England and France.[53] These reports on the war effort were both aimed at building US support for the war and maintaining civilian patriotism at home.

As a leading member of the prewar Anti-Suffrage League and government propagandist, Ward has "low standing" in the canon of First World War women's writing.[54] Her war work as a government propagandist is nonetheless significant for its contradictions, with Ward propelled into a prominent position as a spokeswoman on what she saw as a man's issue. Relentless detailing of facts is mingled with the claim to have seen for herself, testifying to an anxiety to measure her authority to report on the war by her truthfulness, despite her willing subjection to the government censor. The difficulties of her position and her anxieties about the relationship between literature and propaganda are obliquely addressed in novels such as *Missing* (1917) and *Harvest*, published in 1920 but written in 1918.[55] These novels often "interrogate the terms in which they choose to support the war"[56] by organizing the action around secrets about the war. The preoccupation with truths concealed or withheld reflects on Ward's own position as a government propagandist committed to telling the truth about war under strict censorship.

Other eyewitness accounts such as Mildred Aldrich's impressions of life in France during the war, or the many memoirs of war-zone nursing, such as Violetta Thurstan's *Field Hospital and Flying Column* (1915), Kate Finzi's

Eighteen Months in the War Zone (1916), Olive Dent's *A V.A.D. in France* (1917), and G. M. McDougall's *A Nurse at War* (1917), implicitly ask how they can represent the war adequately.[57] Tylee points out that Aldrich, an American whose journalistic impressions in *A Hilltop on the Marne* (1915) and *On the Edge of the War Zone* (1917) were published in England, commits herself to a distanced and neutral stance at the cost of representing the war as a spectacle.[58] Writers like Finzi and Dent, by contrast, speak from a position of engagement as nurses and VADs, but are authorized at the time by the values they share with national culture as much as by their position as women war workers. Thus, they portray the war as a special initiation and adventure, made the more so by its horrors, which are thus accommodated rather than minimized. For Finzi the war is full of horror, "arms rotting off . . . half heads," but it is also "something one would not have missed," while Dent describes it as "a great purifier" that has "brought out valour indescribable, self-sacrifice unforgettable . . . It has made better women of us all."[59] Not surprisingly, the *Daily Mail* serialized excerpts from Dent's memoir, while a major-general endorsed Finzi's book by writing an introduction praising both the book and the work of women nurses.

The works of these and other pro-war women, like Flora Sandes, whose *An English-Woman Sergeant in the Serbian Army* (1916) turns her life as a combatant soldier in the Serbian army into an adventure story, cast an interesting light on Gilbert and Gubar's much contested argument about women's experience of the war as a form of highly sexualized liberation.[60] These writers do give evidence of such liberation, but their capacity to see the war as heroic adventure is evidently deeply rooted in more conservative forms of patriotism and militarism. The contradictoriness of women's position, which has been the focus of most critics since Gilbert and Gubar, is clearly evident in May Sinclair's eyewitness account of seventeen days spent in Belgium with an ambulance unit in 1914.

Sinclair, who published parts of her *Journal of Impressions in Belgium* early in 1915 in the *English Review* and in complete form that September, focuses on the psychology of war, and on "how femininity is constituted in relation to the war."[61] An important progenitor of early modernism with a particular interest in psychoanalysis, Sinclair risks the charge of being "too personal," as one reviewer defined it, by examining her own responses, whether "black funk . . . shameful and appalling terror" or a highly sexualized excitement, "a little thrill . . . growing till it becomes ecstasy."[62] Her embrace of these abject feelings produced highly ambivalent responses in reviewers and later critics; Tylee, for example, calls her both sentimentalizing and self-indulgent.[63] But Sinclair's fascination with the war, albeit uncomfortable, allowed her to explore the interconnections between sex, love, and aggression, a focus central to twentieth-century psychoanalysis and to her many novels and short stories about the war such as *Tasker Jeevons* (1916), *The Tree of Heaven* (1917), *The Romantic* (1920), and *Anne Severn and the Fieldings* (1922).[64] Sinclair, as an enthusiastic supporter of the war, does not belong in a feminist canon of self-conscious female resisters, but her scrutiny of war perversions, ranging from its thrills and ecstasies to the unheroic cowardice that Sinclair discovers in herself and some of her characters, denaturalizes the experiences that underwrite other eyewitness accounts.

On the other side of the spectrum from these pro-war texts, we have Mary Agnes Hamilton's *Dead Yesterday* and Rose Macaulay's *Non-Combatants and Others*. They appeared within a few months of each other in 1916, the former rooted in international socialism and the latter in Christian pacifism, while Rebecca West published her famous novella *Return of the Soldier* in June 1918.[65] None of these novels was exclusively read as anti-war at the time of their publication, and West's subtle and sympathetic examination of the costs of a militarized English masculinity for men and women has also met with a surprisingly critical reception from some recent feminist critics.[66] Macaulay also published a series of postwar satires on government bureaucracy and the propaganda machine, including *What Not: A Prophetic Comedy* (1919), only published after the war, and *Potterism* (1917), an attack on the Northcliffe press.[67]

Although critical of the war, none of these works fell foul of the Defence of the Realm Act (DORA), unlike Rose Allatini's now-forgotten novel *Despised and Rejected*, which was banned soon after publication in 1918, presumably because of the strength with which it linked pacifism to sexuality.[68] Allatini uses the romance genre as vehicle for her portrait of an aggressively militaristic society that rejects pacifists, artists, and homosexuals with similar brutality. Her anti-war message operates therefore within the context of the many romance novels, both popular and middlebrow of the period, that represent the war as a purifying force. Berta Ruck and Ruby M. Ayres, two popular romance writers, promoted the idea of the Great War as having given men back their manliness and restored women to admiring subservience.[69] The suffrage movement and artistic movements such as aestheticism, with their associated images of overly masculine women and effete men, were alike blamed for the degeneration of prewar society.[70]

Allatini reconfigures the manly soldier hero of these popular women's romances through her high-minded and courageous hero Dennis, who is homosexual, pacifist, and an artist. Dennis at first denies his homosexuality and tries to repress his passionate love for Alan, a socialist conscientious objector. It is only when Alan is on the verge of imprisonment that he is willing to consummate the relationship sexually. Dennis then himself awaits arrest, able to compose music for the first time since the outbreak of the war, so that homosexuality, art, and pacifism are linked both thematically and narratively. During the trial, the book's moral agenda was discussed at length, making it clear that although banned as "likely to prejudice the recruiting, training and discipline of persons in his Majesty's forces," its linking of sexuality and pacifism was the source of its threat. As Tylee explains it, "belligerence had been bound into the very definition of masculinity, and . . . homosexuality and the refusal to kill were intimately related in their defiance of the established notions of manhood."[71]

Allatini's novel loses clarity when it comes to Dennis's female counterpart, Antoinette, whose inversion is revealed to her by Dennis: "there's a certain amount of the masculine element in you, and of the feminine element in me, we both have to suffer in the same way."[72] Gay Wachman analyzes in detail the reasons why, at the end, Allatini strands Antoinette in a position of frustrated desire for Dennis, despite her clear homosexuality.[73] Allatini's interest in the politics of conscientious objection as a response to militarized masculinity is incompatible with an exploration of lesbianism, which inversion theorics associate with a belligerent manliness. The same connection between female inversion and masculinity made possible Radclyffe Hall's extensive use of the Great War to represent the lesbian in both "Miss Ogilvy Finds Herself" (1934) and *Well of Loneliness* (1928), her famous postwar lesbian romance that was banned on publication.[74] Unlike Allatini, Hall was happy to associate lesbianism with masculine heroism and militarism in the interests of making the invert an acceptable figure within English culture.

The link between war, gender, and sexuality that is so central to Allatini and Hall also motivates the war narratives of English modernists. The much neglected writer Mary Butts subverts the ideal of a biological, aggressive masculinity in her story about a male costumier turned soldier, "Speed the Plough" (1923), while her novel *Ashe of Rings* (1925) connects the repressions of family life to the cruelty and violence of war. Other better-known women modernists also make femininity central to their representation of war, for example, West, in *Return of the Soldier* (1918), where the soldier's story is narrated by his female cousin; Woolf, most famously in *Jacob's Room* (1922) and *Mrs. Dalloway* (1926); and Katherine Mansfield, in her remarkable 1915 short story "An Indiscreet Journey,"[75] based on her own "indiscreet" trip to the war zone to spend a weekend with her lover Francis Carco. So too, of course, do their American counterparts Stein, Willa Cather, H.D., and Mary Borden. Allyson Booth has argued that the formal markers of modernism have a close relationship to "the perceptual habits appropriate" to the Great War, for example "the dissolution of borders around the self, the mistrust of factuality, the fascination with multiple points of view."[76]

For these women modernists the reinvention of fictional forms is often in the service of analyzing those aspects of English culture that made the war possible.

Woolf's first war novel, *Jacob's Room* (1922), begun only two years after the Armistice, takes on the astonishingly bold task of unpacking England's national imaginary at the very moment it is being constructed. The life-story of Jacob Flanders, the novel examines and dismantles the iconic figure of the young Englishman of officer class who came to symbolize England's lost generation. While West's novella generates considerable sympathy for her male protagonist, Woolf is relentless in locating Jacob as the unselfconscious beneficiary of masculine middle-class privilege. Her portrait of the young man at Cambridge, a world in which women are merely intruders, is nearly identical to that in her feminist ur-text *A Room of One's Own*,[77] published only seven years later. The novel is also the first in which Woolf fully realizes her aim to represent character as ultimately unknowable. Jacob's character is mediated through a series of viewpoints, and even the narrator is refused omniscience, being specified as older and female, creating "deliberate boundaries between herself and her central character."[78] When Jacob dies in Flanders at the end of the novel the reader is left to ask whether he is the victim of his society or the embodiment of the values of an England that supported the war.

The British government decided early in the war that soldiers' bodies should not be returned to England despite the proximity of the Western Front, an understandable decision when one considers that the death toll on the first day of the Battle of the Somme in July 1916 was 20,000 men. Woolf's novel, as Booth argues, registers this double absence, of both the dead man and his corpse, through its insistence on absence more than loss as the central definer of Jacob's death.[79] Although the novel has been described as an elegy, it might be more accurate to see it as replacing elegy with a necessary investigation of the mechanisms by which a culture will begin to fill the space of that loss with its own myths. Woolf, for example, regularly refers to gravestones and their memorializing function, as when the anonymous narrator observes a mason's van carrying tombstones "recording how someone loves someone who is buried at Putney." Not only are the tombstones weirdly mobile instead of reassuringly and monumentally fixed, but they "pass too quickly for you to read more."[80] As an allegory for both the novel itself as Jacob's memorial and for England's wider efforts to claim the meanings of the soldiers' deaths for national history, Woolf's traveling tombstones refuse the consolations of Brooke's "corner of a foreign field / That is forever England."

Skepticism about elegy also informs Katherine Mansfield's famous short story "The Fly" (1923), in which the pleasures of sadism replace the indulgence of a good cry for a middle-aged man, the boss, who has died in the war. The boss slowly tortures a fly until it finally d sted by the struggle to live, leaving the man with "a grinding feelin hed-ness" so frightening to him that he must repress it.[81] The na k of mourning is given a nasty and significant twist in that the sto s the reader in the survivor's pleasure at "the spectacle of sufferir the anxiety of guilt."[82] As with *Jacob's Room* the apparent simplicity of grief is refused along with the genre of elegy.

Although traces of the war are visible in most writing in the postwar period, for women as well as men the late twenties and early thirties mark a watershed for memoirs and fiction. Notable examples include the English-American writer Mary Borden's *The Forbidden Zone* (1929), which was first published in England, Evadne Price's *Not So Quiet . . . : Stepdaughters of War* (1930), written under the pseudonym Helen Zenna Smith, Irene Rathbone's *We That Were Young* (1932), Sylvia Pankhurst's *The Home Front* (1932), Storm Jameson's *No Time Like the Present* (1933), and Vera Brittain's *Testament of Youth* (1933).[83] These works responded to the deluge of personal accounts and memoirs published by male combatants, most famously by Sassoon, Blunden, Aldington, and Graves. Like the men, women wrote both autobiography and fictionalized war memoir, using the authority of personal experience to present the bleak horror of the Great War. Women writers faced the additional task of inserting the woman's story into an increasingly uniform story of war experience as combatant experience. Consequently, these works, by contrast with either Woolf or Mansfield, focus almost exclusively on the female war worker, whether VAD, nurse, munitions worker, or WAAC. The only exception here is Sylvia Pankhurst, whose radical and distinctive mix of Communism, pacifism, and Suffragism produces a quite different style of memoir dedicated to exposing the violently repressive militarism of the British state during the Great War and the working-class woman's acute suffering under that state. Pankhurst's emphases are reflected in later twentieth-century writers such as Sheila Rowbotham and Chris Hannan, who both write plays about women's working-class resistance during the war, and in Pat Barker's *Regeneration* trilogy, which locates the combatant's experience in the context of British wartime culture.[84]

Most women writers, however, were locked into a direct response to the male war story, although their strategies varied considerably. Borden uses a spare modernist hyper-realism similar to Stein and Hemingway in her collection of short sketches, stories, and poems about nursing in a military hospital in France. Published the following year, in 1930, Price's fictional memoir, which was based on the unpublished diaries of a real ambulance driver, Winifred Young, is described by Jane Marcus as an extreme form of socialist realism in which she "reproduces the minefield of the forbidden zone as a dotted landscape on the body of the text, setting up disquieting relations between text and white space on the book's pages."[85] By contrast Brittain chose to write a formally conventional memoir appropriate to her intense desire to convey the historical experience of her youth in *Testament*.

Each of these texts wrestles with the logic of the war zone as a preeminently masculine space, searching for ways to redefine that space to accommodate femininity. Borden addresses this problem directly and memorably in a much-quoted passage about the desexualization of both men and women in the army hospitals: "It is impossible to be a woman here. One must be dead . . . There are no men here, so why should I be a woman? There are heads and knees and mangled testicles. . . .but no men." To be a woman here means to be sexualized and to have feelings, and Borden's sketches adopt a flat narrative voice intentionally divested of affect. Possibly the only sexual being in *The Forbidden Zone* is the urban criminal turned soldier in "Enfant de malheur." This man coalesces in one wounded body the marks of a highly sexualized Parisian underworld literalized in his many obscene tattoos and an uncanny classical beauty which leads the narrator to describe him as "fashioned by Praxiteles."[86] At the same time, his penal service in the French *Bataillons d'Afrique* and the narrator's description of him as "apache" invest him with a racialized exoticism. The source of the apache's fascination in Borden's text seems to lie in the challenge his impurity poses for various representatives of European civilization, including an English nurse who is the type of asexual virtuous femininity. Borden's text focuses here a more pervasive tendency of writers to renegotiate femininity through class and racial difference, particularly that of male soldiers. Enid Bagnold, for example, in her memoir *Diary Without Dates* (1918), uses her VAD narrator's encounter with a black African soldier to mediate her own class relations with the working-class Tommies she nurses.[87]

Changing definitions of femininity are also explored through the figure of the masculine woman, as in the case of Tosh, the glamorous, aristocratic driver from *Not So Quiet* who cuts her glorious red hair, happy to "unsex" herself because so obviously a mix of tomboy and mother. Tosh stands for an acceptable cross-dressing still anchored in conventions specific to her class and to the genre of the girl's school story. Price reflects here the difficult negotiation of the "masculinity" of war work by women, faced with a series of regulations aimed to reinstate the codes of proper femininity even as women moved beyond traditional female roles. Tosh is foil to the cartoon-like Mrs. Bitch, the Unit Commander, who has inappropriately embraced masculine power, becoming petty-minded and sadistic as a result. In one sense femininity does not survive the war. *Not So Quiet* ends with an apocalyptic scene in which the heroine's fellow-workers lie dead and dying around her, a mass of mangled and dismembered female bodies. Her heroine survives, but Price marks this survival by shifting from first- to third-person narration, leaving her protagonist without emotion or "soul," no longer human or feminine. Even Brittain's representation of the women's war in *Testament of Youth* charts the death of the feminine heart, although the conclusion emphasizes resurrection through Brittain's postwar commitment to anti-war internationalist politics and her 1924 engagement to G. E. G. Catlin. Ultimately, however, *Testament* is motivated by Brittain's insistence on mourning as the true anti-war work, and hence seals the relationship between femininity and emotion, as she channels both into the peace agenda of the early League of Nations.

As a survivor of the Great War Brittain believed herself, with others of the interwar years, responsible for preventing a future war. The men and women who reinterpreted English and European history in fiction, memoir, and political history during the 1930s, did so under the growing certainty that another war impended. Storm Jameson, in addition to her Great War memoir, published a trilogy of novels between 1934 and 1936, *Mirror in Darkness*, charting the political history of postwar England.[88] West's travelogue about Yugoslavia, *Black Lamb and Grey Falcon* (1941), reframes English history within the apparently marginal history of the Balkans, deliberately stitching together individual and collective memory.[89] In a different register, part realist, part spy story, and part fantasy, Stevie Smith's *Over the Frontier* (1938) represents her character traveling across "the familiar nightmare landscape of the Western Front" even though the novel's overt subject is 1930s Germany.[90] The urgency these writers all share about the future has its roots in the Great War. As Jameson wrote so memorably in her 1969 autobiography: "In 1934 an American reviewer, a woman, complained that 'like so many English writers, Storm Jameson seems unable to outgrow the war'. I retorted that the war we could not outgrow was not the one we had survived but the one we were expecting."[91] Jameson's gloomy insight here, that our preoccupation with past wars is always a response to the war that has not yet happened, tells us something of why later twentieth-century writers, critics, and readers still return to the Great War as a subject. And, thanks largely to the efforts of feminist critics, women writers are now central to that return.

NOTES

1. E. S. Caley, "The Foreman and the Manager," *Shell Chippings*, 1.1 (September 1916), 5: Cited in Claire A. Culleton, *Working Class Culture, Women, and Britain, 1914–1921* (New York: St. Martin's Press, 1999), 115–16.

2. Culleton, *Working Class Culture*, 1–3.
3. Catherine Reilly, *English Poetry of the First World War: A Bibliography* (London: George Prior, 1978).
4. Jon Silkin, ed., *The Penguin Book of First World War Poetry* (London: Penguin, 1979); Brian Gardiner, ed., *Up the Line to Death: The War Poets 1914–1918* (London: Methuen & Co., 1964).
5. Silkin, ed., *First World War Poetry*, 132.
6. Sara Ruddick, *Maternal Thinking: Toward a Politics of Peace* (Boston: Beacon Press, 1989); Helen M. Cooper, Adrienne Auslander Munich, and Susan Merrill Squier, eds., *Arms and the Woman* (Chapel Hill: University of North Carolina Press, 1989).
7. Nosheen Khan, *Women's Poetry of the First World War* (Lexington: University of Kentucky Press, 1988); Claire Tylee, *The Great War and Women's Consciousness: Images of Militarism and Womanhood in Women's Writings, 1914–1964* (Iowa City: University of Iowa, 1990); Sandra Gilbert and Susan Gubar, *No Man's Land: The Place of the Woman Writer in the Twentieth Century* (New Haven: Yale University Press, 1989).
8. Elisabeth A. Marsland, *The Nation's Cause: French, English and German Poetry of the First World War* (London: Routledge, 1991), 14–28.
9. *Mr. Punch's History of the Great War* (London: Cassell & Co. Ltd, 1919), 247–48.
10. Catherine Reilly, *Scars Upon My Heart: Women's Poetry and Verse of the First World War* (London: Virago, 1981), xxxiv.
11. *Times Literary Supplement*, 1 July 1915, 217.
12. Reilly, *Scars*, 88.
13. Khan, *Women's Poetry*, 42; *Blighty Christmas Number*, 1917, reprinted by Department of Printed Books, Imperial War Museum, London.
14. G. W. Clarke, ed., *A Treasury of War Poetry, 1914–1917: British and American Poems of the World War 1914–1917* (Boston and New York: Houghton Mifflin Co. and Cambridge: The Riverside Press, 1917), 251.
15. Reilly, *Scars*, 46, 12.
16. *Ibid.*, 38.
17. Joan Montgomery Byles, *War, Women, and Poetry, 1914–1945: British and German Writers and Activists* (Newark: University of Delaware Press, 1995), 17–32.
18. Reilly, *Scars*, 26, 100.
19. *Ibid.*, 95.
20. *Ibid.*, 55, 87.
21. Emily Orr, *A Harvester of Dreams* (London: Burns, Oates & Washbourne Ltd., 1922).
22. Reilly, *Scars*, 87.
23. Marsland, *Nation's Cause*, 157.
24. Reilly, *Scars*, 31.
25. Vera Brittain, "To Monseigneur," in *Poems of the War and After* (New York: Macmillan, 1934), 13.
26. Reilly, *Scars*, 19.
27. Murial Stuart, "Forgotten Dead, I Salute You," in Reilly, *Scars*, 104–5.

28. Reilly, *Scars*, 73–74.
29. Elaine Aston and Janelle Reinelt, eds., *Cambridge Companion to Modern British Women Playwrights* (Cambridge: Cambridge University Press, 2000), 4.
30. Jane Potter, "Hidden Drama by British Women: Pageants and Sketches from the Great War," in *Women, The First World War, and the Dramatic Imagination: International Essays (1914–1999)*, ed. Claire Tylee (London: Edwin Mellen Press, 2000), 119.
31. Maggie B. Gale, *West End Women: Women and the London Stage 1918–1962* (London: Routledge, 1996), 14.
32. Claire Tylee, with Elaine Turner and Agnes Cardinal, eds., *War Plays By Women: An International Anthology* (London: Routledge, 1999), 13.
33. Gwen John, *Luck of War* (London: Benn, 1917).
34. Cited in Julie Holledge, *Innocent Flowers: Women in the Edwardian Theatre* (London: Virago, 1981), 138.
35. Katharine Cockin, *Women and Theatre in the Age of Suffrage: The Pioneer Players, 1911–1925* (New York: Palgrave, 2001), 156.
36. Cicely Hamilton, *The Child in Flanders* (London: French, 1922); Gertrude Jennings, *Poached Eggs and Pearls: A Canteen Comedy* (London: French, 1917), *Allotments* (London: French, 1917).
37. Potter, "Hidden Drama," in *Women, The First World War*, ed. Tylee, 116–17.
38. *Ibid.*, 118.
39. *Ibid.*, 119.
40. Quoted in *ibid.*, 119. See Christina Reid, *My Name, Shall I Tell You My Name*, in *War Plays*, ed. Tylee, 210–23, for a contemporary play that reevaluates the role of the First World War in Protestant Ulster political memory.
41. Vernon Lee (pseudonym of Violet Paget), *Ballet of the Nations: A Present Day Morality* (London: Chatto, 1915).
42. Vernon Lee, *Satan the Waster: A Philosophic War Trilogy* (London: Jonathan Cape, 1920).
43. Gillian Beer, "The Dissidence of Vernon Lee: *Satan the Waster* and the Will to Believe," in *Women's Fiction and the Great War*, ed. Suzanne Raitt and Trudi Tate (Oxford: Oxford University Press, 1997), 107–31.
44. Shaw is quoted in *ibid.*, 109; see also *ibid.*, 124.
45. *Ibid.*, 128.
46. R. C. Sherriff, *Journey's End: A Play in Three Acts* (New York: Brentano's, 1929). See Paul Berry and Mark Bostridge, *Vera Brittain: A Life* (London: Chatto & Windus, 1995), 239.
47. Cicely Hamilton, *The Old Adam: A Fantastic Comedy* (New York: Brentano's, 1927).
48. Gladys Bertha Stern, *The Matriarch* (London: Samuel French, 1931); *The Man Who Pays the Piper* (London: Samuel French, 1931). Stern was also the author of *Children of No Man's Land* (London: Duckworth & Co., 1919), a novel about the war from the perspective of a Jewish family and published in the United States as *Debatable Ground* (New York: Knopf, 1921). See also Clemence Dane, *Bill of Divorcement* (London: Heineman, 1922), Joan Temple, *The Widow's Cruise* (London: Ernest Benn, 1926), Henrietta Leslie, *Mrs. Fischer's War* (London: Jerrolds, 1931) for other examples.

49. M. E. Atkinson, *The Chimney Corner: A Play for Women in One Act* (London: H. F. W. Deane & Sons Ltd, 1934).

50. Muriel Box, "Angels of War," in *War Plays*, ed. Tylee, 115–39.

51. *Times Literary Supplement* (1916): 416. Cited in Tylee, *The Great War*, 107. Angela Brazil, *The Luckiest Girl in the School* (London: Blackie, 1916).

52. Millicent Sutherland, *Six Weeks at the War* (London: The Times, 1914); Phyllis Campbell, *Back of the Front: Experiences of a Nurse* (London: Newnes, 1915).

53. Mary Ward (Mrs. Humphrey Ward), *England's Effort: Six Letters to an American Friend* (London: Smith Elder, 1916), *Towards the Goal: Letters on Great Britain's Behalf in the War* (London: Murray, 1917), and *Fields of Victory* (London: Hutchinson, 1919).

54. Helen Small, "Mrs. Humphrey Ward and the First Casualty of War," in *Women's Fiction and the Great War*, ed. Raitt and Tate, 26.

55. Mary Augusta Arnold Ward, *Missing* (New York: Collins, 1917); *Harvest* (London: Collins, 1920).

56. Small, "Mrs. Humphrey Ward," 18.

57. Violetta Thurstan, *Field Hospital and Flying Column: Being the Journal of an English Nursing Sister in Belgium and Russia* (London: Putnam, 1915); Kate Finzi, *Eighteen Months in the War Zone: The Record of a Woman's Work on the Western Front* (London: Cassell, 1916); Olive Dent, *A V.A.D. in France* (London: Grant Richards, 1917); G. M. McDougall, *A Nurse at War: Nursing Adventures in Belgium and France* (New York: McBride, 1917).

58. Mildred Aldrich, *A Hilltop on the Marne* (London: Constable, 1915); *On the Edge of the War Zone* (London: Constable, 1917).

59. Finzi, *Eighteen Months*, 227; Dent, *A V.A.D.*, 337.

60. Flora Sandes, *An English-Woman Sergeant in the Serbian Army* (London: Hodder & Stoughton, 1916); See Gilbert and Gubar, *No Man's Land*.

61. Suzanne Raitt and Trudi Tate, "Introduction," *Women's Fiction and the Great War*, 1–17. May Sinclair, *A Journal of Impressions in Belgium* (London: Hutchinson, 1955); extracts published in the *English Review*, 20 (1915): 166–83, 313–14, 468–76.

62. Sinclair, *Journal*, 8, 14.

63. Tylee, *The Great War*, 30–31.

64. May Sinclair, *Tasker Jeevons: The Real Story* (London: Hutchinson, 1916); *The Tree of Heaven* (London: Cassell, 1917); *The Romantic* (London, Collins, 1920); and *Anne Severn and the Fieldings* (London: Hutchinson, 1922).

65. Mary Agnes Hamilton, *Dead Yesterday* (London: Duckworth, 1916); Rose Macaulay, *Non-Combatants and Others* (London: H & S, 1916); Rebecca West, *Return of the Soldier* (London: Nisbet, 1918).

66. Tylee, *The Great War*, 144; Gay Wachman, *Lesbian Empire: Radical Cross-writing in the Twenties* (New Brunswick N. J.: Rutgers University Press, 2001), 120–22.

67. Rose Macaulay, *What Not: A Prophetic Comedy* (London: Constable, 1919); *Potterism: A Tragic-comic Farce* (London: Constable, 1920).

68. Rose Allatini (pseudonym A. T. Fitzroy), *Despised and Rejected* (1918; rpt. New York: Arno, 1975).

69. See Enid Bagnold, *The Happy Foreigner* (1920; rpt. London: Virago, 1987); Berta Ruck (later pseud. Amy Roberta Onions), *Khaki Kisses* (London: Hutchinson,

1915); Ruby M. Ayres, *Richard Chatterton, V. C.* (London: Hodder & Stoughton, 1915). See Potter, "'A Great Purifier': The Great War in Women's Romances and Memoirs 1914–1918," in *Women's Fiction and the Great War*, ed. Raitt and Tate, 85–106.

70. See also the suffrage writer Cicely Hamilton's novel *William – An Englishman* (London: Skeffington, 1919), which turns its pacifist hero into a pro-war soldier.

71. "A Pernicious Book," *The Times* (London), 28 September 1918; Tylee, *The Great War*, 123.

72. Allatini, *Despised and Rejected*, 220.

73. Wachman, *Lesbian Empire*, 103–20.

74. Radclyffe Hall, *The Well of Loneliness* (London: Jonathan Cape, 1928); *Miss Ogilvy Finds Herself* (London: Heineman, 1934).

75. Mary Butts, "Speed the Plough," in *Speed the Plough* (London: Chapman & Hall, 1923), *Ashe of Rings* (Paris: Three Mountains Press, 1925); Virginia Woolf, *Jacob's Room* (London: Hogarth, 1922), *Mrs. Dalloway* (London: Hogarth, 1926); and Katherine Mansfield, "An Indiscreet Journey," in *Something Childish and Other Stories* (London: Constable, 1924).

76. Allyson Booth, *Postcards from the Trenches: Negotiating the Spaces Between Modernism and the First World War* (New York: Oxford University Press, 1996), 4.

77. Virginia Woolf, *A Room of One's Own* (London: Hogarth, 1929).

78. Kate Flint, "Introduction" to Virginia Woolf, *Jacob's Room* (Oxford: Oxford University Press, 1992), xvii.

79. Booth, *Postcards*, 44–49.

80. Woolf, *Jacob's Room*, 154.

81. Katherine Mansfield, "The Fly," *Women, Men, and the Great War: An Anthology of Stories*, ed. Trudi Tate (Manchester: Manchester University Press, 1995), 72.

82. Con Coroneos, "Flies and Violets in Katherine Mansfield," in *Women's Fiction and the Great War*, ed. Raitt and Tate, 216.

83. Mary Borden, *The Forbidden Zone* (London: Heinemann, 1929); Evadne Price (Helen Zenna Smith), *Not So Quiet . . .: Stepdaughters of War* (London: Marriott, 1930); Irene Rathbone, *We That Were Young* (London: Chatto, 1932); E. Sylvia Pankhurst, *The Home Front* (London: Hutchinson, 1932); Margaret Storm Jameson, *No Time Like the Present* (London: Cassell, 1933); Vera Brittain, *Testament of Youth* (London: Gollancz, 1933).

84. Sheila Rowbotham, *Friends of Alice Wheeldon* (London: Pluto, 1986); Chris Hannan, "Elizabeth Gordon Quinne," in *Scot-Free: New Scottish Plays* (London: Nick Hearn, 1990); Pat Barker, *Regeneration* (London: Penguin, 1992), *The Eye in the Door* (London: Penguin, 1993), *The Ghost Road* (London: Penguin, 1995).

85. Jane Marcus, "Corpus/Corps/Corpse: Writing the Body of War," in *Arms and the Woman*, ed. Cooper, Munich, and Squier, 146.

86. Borden, *The Forbidden Zone*, 60, 99.

87. Enid Bagnold, *Diary Without Dates* (1918; rpt. London: Virago, 1988).

88. Storm Jameson, *The Mirror in Darkness*, comprising *Company Parade* (London: Cassell & Co., 1934), *Love in Winter* (London: Cassell & Co., 1935), and *None Turn Back* (London: Cassell & Co., 1936).

89. Rebecca West, *Black Lamb and Grey Falcon: A Journey Through Yugoslavia in 1937*, 2 vols. (New York, Viking, 1941; Macmillan, 1942).

90. Stevie Smith, *Over the Frontier* (London: Cape, 1938); Janet Montefiore, *Men and Women Writers of the 1930s: The Dangerous Flood of History* (London: Routledge, 1996), 70.
91. Storm Jameson, *Journey From the North*, vol. 1 (London: Harvill Collins, 1969), 306.

5

VINCENT SHERRY

The Great War and literary modernism in England

A consensus understanding continues to represent the Great War of 1914–18 as the signal event of artistic modernism. In this account, the war stands as a watershed episode: it draws a line through time, dividing the nineteenth from the twentieth centuries; thus it provides the shaping occasion for artists who take novelty, invention, and precedent-dismaying energy as their establishing aim and motive. The readiness of this connection does not discredit it. Global in scope, shattering in its impact on national traditions as well as class structures and gender identities, this first world war scored a profound disruption into prevailing standards of value and so opened the space in cultural time in which radical artistic experimentation would be fostered. Yet the self-evident element in this reckoning has allowed literary historians to be content with the generalized formulation, taken at somewhat distant retrospect. The relative dearth of work in a historically informed understanding of the "modernist war" has been furthered by the fact that much of this modernist writing came out of a civilian circumstance, whereas readers' attention has been drawn understandably to the dramas attending the production of combat narratives (novels and memoirs) and trench poetry. No less compelling, however, are the conditions impinging on the modernist literature of the war.

Political London presents one of the liveliest sites in the global picture of this world war. A crisis internal to the governing party of Britain defined this moment in local political time. English Liberals had to maintain support for a war which, by precedent and convention, by partisan tradition and policy principle, they ought to have opposed. This contradiction entered the language through which the rationale of the war was constructed, generating inconsistencies, hypocrisies, and increasingly evident untruths as the verbal record of the event. The compromised logic of party-line thinking shaped the experience of the ideological war for the more alert members of the urban civilian population, including the major writers of Anglo-American modernism, Ezra Pound, T. S. Eliot, and Virginia Woolf, all of whom resided in London through the war years.

What did the Liberal argument sound like? How were the syntax and vocabulary of the party's intellectual conventions and ethical principles manipulated in service to the war aims? What values were dominant in partisan tradition, that is, and how were these risked and lost in the greater game of seeking support for the war? A summary review of the attitudes and practices of Liberal political culture may lead to a reading of the work the London modernists evolved out of the war years. For it is the special distinction of these modernists to register the crisis in that majority dialect and take it as the opportunity of a new literary idiom, one whose import may be equal to that of the tradition whose breakdown enables these innovations.

Rival factions within the Liberal party were already formed before 1914 on the issue – in principle – of war. To one side, the memory of the great Victorian Prime Minister W. E. Gladstone preserved the ethic and method of moral rationalism. This Liberal tradition maintained that armed force required an informed act of logical conscience, a choice reasoned freely and in public and in accord with the loftiest moral values. To the other side, Liberal imperialists proceeded under the operative standards of realpolitik. In this way of thinking, the British military served as an instrument of security: its power could be parleyed through agreements with other European nations; these alliances might require involvement in hostilities, but these engagements might hardly be appealed to the codes of Gladstonian probity – the imperialists tended to negotiate English interests within a frame of global reference that put practical or local advantage and commercial concerns first.[1] Since 1906, the most powerful positions within the majority government were held by Liberal imperialists – Prime Minister H. H. Asquith and his Foreign Secretary Sir Edward Grey – but the logic of foreign policy was still controlled in its public discussions by Gladstonian protocols. In this situation, Asquith and Grey needed to keep private their alliance-building with France and Russia. Officially, they continued to deny the existence of these "secret agreements" (dubbed as such by an already suspicious public), at least until early August 1914, when the network of European connections was activated.[2] At this moment, as Britain paused before the awful prospect of a Continental war, those rival traditions within Liberalism were evidenced in tensions that anticipated, in substantial detail, the major crisis this developing event would present to dominant values of partisan – and national – life.

The Foreign Secretary's speech before Parliament on 3 August provided the loftiest expression of the partisan rationale for war, arguing the moral cause of a righteous defense of France in view of the imminent German incursion into neutral Belgium.[3] But other pressures – the commitments hidden in the "secret agreements" – were also coming to bear on the Liberal government. The tension between these rival frames of partisan reference is reflected in the editorial reports on Grey's address in the two leading Liberal dailies on 4 August.

The *Manchester Guardian* holds true to the standard of reason at liberty, which, in this instance, the writer depicts as a compromised principle. This report protests that citizens and Parliament have not been given information sufficient to "form a reasoned judgment on the current of our policy." In Grey's conclusion that Britain must go to France's aid, even when Germany has vowed not to move on any undefended areas, the writer accurately intuits that the Secretary is being compelled by forces that exceed those of the moral rationale he has claimed. "His reasons are extraordinary," the editorial demurs. "Is it rational? Can it be deduced, we will not say from the terms of the Entente, but from the account of secret conversations which was given yesterday? Can it be reconciled with any reasonable view of British policy? It cannot."[4]

The especially strenuous effort of "reconcile[ing]" these eventualities with a "reasonable view of British policy" may be evidenced in the language of the news leader in the *Westminster Gazettte*, which offers this narrative – and argumentative – paraphrase of Grey's speech:

> Sir Edward Grey passed to the consideration of the present position of the French fleet in the Mediterranean which *evidently* sprang out of the plans for co-operation. The French fleet was in the Mediterranean *because of the feeling of confidence* between the two countries. *Hence it followed* that if a foreign fleet came down the channel we could not stand aside and see it attack the defenceless coast of France. *The House was brought to the conclusion* that we had a definite obligation to defend the coast of France from attack, and, generally speaking, it showed that it was prepared to support the government in taking action. France was *therefore* entitled to know and know at once that she could depend on British support . . .[5]

Tellingly, this report of "The House and Sir Edward Grey's Statement" bears the subtitle: "Logic of Events." Complying entirely with Grey's own rationalistic stratagems, the report pays special attention to insert those conjunctions that establish cause and reasoned transition in the argument. This language of analytical and ethical reasoning is obviously imposed on a resistant circumstance, however. The second-thought, second-hand, overlaid nature of this rhetoric of ethical reasoning is the one conclusion that may be safely drawn from this passage.

Another representative instance of Liberal compromise and partisan doubletalk comes in two accounts in the *Westminster Gazette* a week before the outbreak of war. The timely issue goes to the question of Liberal participation on the side of the party's inveterate enemies, those benighted powers of *Mitteleuropa*, Serbia first of all but behind it Csarist Russia. On 28 July the main editorial finds "The Serv . . . a man of primitive emotions and tastes, for whom town life seems to have little or no attraction . . . There are few towns in the country worthy of the name." In a land in which the light of "civilisation" is eclipsed, the commentator continues, "the staple industries" are those benighted activities of "pig-rearing" and elementary "husbandry."[6] Four days later, however, acting on the kind of information this unofficial yet privileged organ of the Liberal party was often able to obtain, the paper redraws the portrait of the Serbian national character in a piece of ethnographic conversion as stunning as it is unacknowledged. "Posed gracefully before me," this writer opens, "stands a typical Servian: the lines of Apollo flow easily and naturally round his robust figure. It is a good, honest, sun-scorched face." If "the majority are illiterate," as this writer concedes strategically, so too, the immediate appeal goes, "they are quite intelligent," etc. etc.[7] God of logic (as well as music and poetry), Apollo has cast out Caliban, but he presides over the poetry of the Liberal case as its dubious muse.

One of the incidental values of these several pieces, played in advance of the event, is the readiness they demonstrate in the Liberal idiom. "Reason in all things" is a poetics, ethically addressed but aesthetically prepared, and the fact that it springs into service already and beforehand witnesses quite evidently its established, well-endowed power. Even its compensatory measures reveal strength. The moral cause of the war may be doubted, indeed profoundly doubted, but the rationale of the partisan case will be asserted in a rationalistic language all the more strenuously and, apparently, unabashedly.

Critical witness against this consensus understanding was left initially to sensibilities not invested in the political establishments and cultural institutions of the majority party. Women, disfranchised for most of the war (the several stages of enfranchisement began in 1918), offered some of the most cogent critiques. Irene Cooper Willis, for instance, brought out *How We Went into the War: A Study of Liberal Idealism* in November 1918 from the National Labour Press, whose affiliation with the more radical or non-conformist side of the Labour party (its leadership had entered into political coalition with the Liberal government by early 1916) reinforces her own angle of critical view. The major contribution that Willis makes to an

MILITARY SERVICE ACT
1916

EVERY UNMARRIED MAN
of
MILITARY AGE
Not excepted or exempted under this Act
CAN CHOOSE
ONE OF TWO COURSES:

(1) He can **ENLIST AT ONCE** and join the Colours without delay;

(2) He can **ATTEST AT ONCE UNDER THE GROUP SYSTEM** and be called up in due course with his Group.

If he does neither, a third course awaits him:
HE WILL BE DEEMED TO HAVE ENLISTED
under the Military Service Act
ON THURSDAY, MARCH 2nd 1916.

HE WILL BE PLACED IN THE RESERVE. AND BE CALLED UP IN HIS CLASS.
as the Military Authorities may determine.

Published by THE PARLIAMENTARY RECRUITING COMMITTEE, LONDON . POSTER No. 154.   Printed by DAVID ALLEN & SONS, L? Harrow, MDX.

6 Liberal reason conscripts free choice: British conscription/recruiting poster

understanding of the public construction of the war is her alertness to its verbal surfaces. Again and again she exposes the hollowness of Liberal logic behind the holiness of avowed cause.[8] Her skeptical temper is shared, but also prepared long in advance, by Dora Marsden, who is positioned within the political culture of Britain at the extremity of her work as founding editor of the *Freewoman* (1911), later the *New Freewoman* (1913), subsequently the *Egoist* (1914), where she continued as chief contributing editor. Already by 15 September 1914 Marsden can attitudinize the moral rationalism of the partisan case. Rehearsing the now-established ethic of the Liberal cause, she repeats the response to the question "Why We English Fight?" by Lord Rosebery: "To maintain," he proposed, "the sanctity of international law in Europe." She then rephrases this Liberal imperialist in a clarifying parody: "'Mumbo-jumbo, Law and Mesopotamia' can always be relied on to work all the tricks, and cloak all the spoof."[9]

This mimic wit instances at once an intellectual critique of the current Word and an imaginative kindling of linguistic possibility. This double measure of informed invention is the manifold capacity she shares with the company she keeps in the *Egoist*, the journal of Anglo-American literary modernism in its nascent day. Pound and Eliot will generate and inflect their own versions of the Liberal idiom, a heckling echo heard again and again through several decades in Woolf's work. The poets' American background grants them some vantage for critical review over British usage, and Woolf's position as a woman fixes her at a congruent angle of remove from the political linguistic of a machismo Liberalism. If Anglo-American literary modernists write their English, as Hugh Kenner has quipped, like a foreign language, handling it with the care of relative aliens, the status these three writers share as familiar outsiders in wartime London may account in some substantial part for their ability to reiterate the Liberal idiom, but with a difference, the import and value of which may be assessed in due course.

In "Studies in Contemporary Mentality," a twenty-part series published through 1917 in the *New Age*, Pound conducted a review of literary and political journalism in wartime Britain. The dominant quality in this verbal culture proves to be an indomitable "reasonableness," a trait that appears nonetheless, in its service to the current war effort, in heavy duress. While this sensibility works with the force of a national or ethnic character, it finds its chief exemplar and reference point in the hallmark venues of intellectual Liberalism. This partisan tradition sets the tone of national war discourse. Pound pronounces this consolidating insight when he finds a defining standard for British political idiom in Liberalism's most distinguished literary weekly, the *New Statesman*:

I knew that if I searched long enough I should come upon some clue to this mystery. The magnetism of this stupendous vacuity! The sweet reasonableness, the measured tone, the really utter undeniability of so much that one might read in this paper!... The *New Statesman* is a prime exemplar of the species, leading the sheltered life behind a phalanx of immobile ideas; leading the sheltered thought behind a phalanx of immobile phrases. This sort of thing cannot fail. Such a mass of printed statements in every issue to which no "normal, right-minded" man could possibly take exception![10]

A "reasonableness" that consists of "measured tone" only, and so coalesces into the merest feeling of rationality; a logic as hollow as it is polished in presentation, well-managed indeed in all its impressive "vacuity," its "stupendous" emptiness: these are the sounds of contemporary Liberalism at war, a linkage Pound clinches with the metaphors of mobilization and images of military formation. This sensibility stands exposed at the extremity of his ridicule in its vapid sagacity and absurd sententiousness. "That is really all there is to it," he summarizes, but tauntingly: "One might really learn to do it oneself."[11]

How might Pound do it himself? How to parley the rational inanities of official war discourse into new words, in verse? Pound's boast locates the main project and major dare of his emergent enterprise. But his mimic initiative proves a good deal more difficult – and so, potentially, more significant – than his vaunt might concede. The challenge entails a shift at first to a completely new register for him.

"Jodindranath Mawhwor's Occupation," "An Anachronism at Chinon," "Aux Etuves de Weisbaden [*sic*]," and "Our Tetrarchal Précieuse: A Divagation from Jules Laforgue":[12] the prose fables Pound composed in 1916–17 represent at once a new genre of literary fiction and a novel practice with imaginative language. The verbal texture of these pieces is sampled fairly by the otherwise odd combinations in those titles. Where the exotic denominations jostle his simple English words, Pound anticipates the way in which the common prosaic sense of his English sentences will be obtruded upon by obscure, even incomprehensible reference. Mock-logical, his capricious reasonableness or parody rationality rhymes with the sound of the British times, as recorded by the student of contemporary mentality. And a number of references to the current war – some explicit, others cryptic (reflecting the coded language of contemporary censorship) – establish the local provocation and timely urge for this new usage.

The often bizarre vocabulary in these prose pieces suggests the peculiar suitability, for Pound's emergent purpose, of the work of translation (the last and best of these performances is a highly worked rendition of Jules Laforgue's "Salome"). In the rhetorical fiction of presenting the text of a foreign language, he can sound out regions of feeling that appear strange indeed to the rational grammar of a standard English. The advantages of composition out of – and into – other tongues will be evident again and again in this local and topical project of modernism, whose writers will be estranging their English, straining it against its own native "sense." These opportunities locate the motive for the otherwise idiosyncratic labor of *Homage to Sextus Propertius* (1919), the (highly) creative translation Pound undertook as his main poetic endeavor through the second half of the war.[13]

This Roman poet was chosen also for reasons beyond Pound's imaginative interests in linguistic difference. In his *Elegiae*, Propertius presents himself as a poet desiring to write of love when conventional expectation pressures him to proclaim a martial-minded verse. A poet of this moment is supposed to celebrate the imperial aims and military campaigns of the Augustan dynasty. His crafty engagement with those rules shows his persona making his evident requests for permission to sing about "Cynthia" but addressing instead, more interestingly and slyly, quietly and indeed devastatingly, the attitudes and practices of an imperial poetics.[14] The mock-heroic diction of his *Elegiae*, his parodic Virgilisms, the hollow triumphalism and empty finishes of those all too heavily labored martial cadences, which turn Augustan verse convention into august inanities: Propertius provides Pound a model for echoing the times against the times. This is a pattern the modern poet adapts to the syntax and vocabulary of his own political present.

The opening verse paragraph of Pound's poem recasts its Latin original in an extensive interpolation, which, in the guise of a poet's invocation of his Roman muse, acknowledges the deity reigning over the discourses of the current war:

> Out-weariers of Apollo will, as we know, continue their Martian generalities,
>   We have kept our erasers in order.[15]

Liberal divinity, god of logic as well as music and poetry, Apollo has been suborned to the work of current verse, worn out not by generals but by the "generalities" of war, by political abstraction, by ideological argument. The *Westminster Gazette* editorial of 31 July 1914 sampled in advance the obverse turn the spirit of seemly reason would take over the course of the war, and the result is summed up thus by Pound as work done, an embodied consequence. How, Propertius-like, might he play along with and pull against this existing linguistic condition?

The verbal art special to *Propertius* features an interplay between an archly rationalist syntax and a wittily impenetrable vocabulary. On one side, the persona of the classics translator demonstrates a declarative knowiness about the materia poetica, here the site of ancient history and myth.

Moving easily through this range of reference, Pound's speaker builds a progression of apparently factual statements as logical, common-sensible propositions of obvious knowledge. On the other side, however, Pound's reader frequently experiences allusions to chronicle legend and literary fable that are fetched from the depths of Mediterranean antiquity and featured, it seems, for their very unfathomability. Consider, in this representative catalogue, the interaction between the cozily local knowiness of Pound's persona and the discomfitingly distant incomprehensibility of these citations, which, one by one, and with the help of a classics manual, might be identified, but which, as substantial parts of a single imaginative narrative, challenge almost any reader's grasp of what the story is, of what is actually going on here:

> For Orpheus tamed the wild beasts-and held up the Threician river;
> And Cithaeron shook up the rocks by Thebes
>   and danced them into a bulwark at his pleasure,
> And you, O Polyphemus? Did harsh Galatea almost
> Turn to your dripping horses, because of a tune, under Aetna?
> We must look into the matter.[16]

Who, most of us must ask, was Galatea? And how close did she get when she *"almost"* turned to the horses of Polyphemus? That specifying adverb is Pound's interpolation,[17] whose blank space in the Latin original reveals the hollowness of his own (carefully) concocted knowledgeability. There is a particularly *pseudo*logical quality to this tone, as indicated by another interpolated word, the first: "For." This conjunction establishes the expectation of cause-and-effect sequence, the impression that some logical proposition is in process. It builds some presentiment of common-sense meanings, one that Pound complements with those reassuring words of common speech. He steadily undercuts this promise, however, by enforcing the awareness that we do not know these mythological personages very well, if at all. "We must," the next interpolation goes, "look into the matter," but when we do we see through the easy loquacity, the familiarizing fiction of inserted words like these, and find reason-seemingness as the aim and intended effect. Pound's new conceit echoes to the background sound of these times, and the immense pressure this moment exerts on his verse is shared as the working conditions of his co-national and modernist accomplice.

Eliot's arrival in London in early August 1914 (having fled from Germany, where, at Marburg, in early summer, he had begun a year of study abroad) coincides with the beginning of an identifiably dry time in his young poetic life. A number of personal causes may be called upon to account for his difficulty, including his already troubled marriage, but forces external to his private situation also contribute to the writer's impasse. The public Word has been taken over, in the extremity of current circumstance, by the majority power. And where Liberalism is inimical, even hateful, to Eliot,[18] the (virtually) total control it exerts over public language establishes a force field of immensely negative effect. He goes silent.

This spell can be broken, however, through his cultivation of a substitute tongue. Eliot can write in French. The freeing effect does not represent escape but, like humor, works through a sort of transforming exaggeration, which amplifies the bizarre capacities the language of the English political moment is demonstrating, where a native sense has become a stranger indeed to its own verbal reason. As in Pound's foreign language exercises, Eliot's syntax is apparently rational, while the content – the words, the references – can appear odd, illogical, incomprehensible. And it is a mark of the one modernist project the two poets comprise that Eliot's French direction is taken up initially at the behest of Pound. Understanding the impasse his friend had reached by mid-1916, he put Eliot to the task of translation – orienting him specifically toward the collection from which Pound would select the text of his own (1917) rendition, Laforgue's *Moralités légendaires*:

> To the shrill piping of the quowhombom and the muffled rattle of the bass trpaxli mingled with the plaintive wail of the thirty captive kings, they circled thrice forwards and thrice backwards, clockwise and counterclockwise, according to the sacred ritual of the rpat, and finally when the signal was given by the pswhadi or high priest, they turned a flip flop somersault and disappeared down their own throats, leaving the assembly in darkness.[19]

This excerpt, which Eliot includes in a letter to Conrad Aiken of 21 August 1916, sounds notes wholly consonant with Pound's prose fables, featuring neologisms in a sort of nonce logic, using these non-words to turn the rationalistic syntax of an otherwise "sensible" narrative prose into a meaninglessness as capricious as the final image here. The piece strikes the first note of the rationalist travesty Eliot will put on in French in the next literary season.

"Petit Epître" is the first of Eliot's spring 1917 efforts:

> Ce n'est pas pour quo'on se dégoute
> Ou gout d'égout de mon Ego
> Qu'ai fait des vers de faits divers
> Qui sentent un peu trop la choucroute.
> Mais qu'est ce que j'ai fait, nom d'un nom,
> Pour faire ressortir les chacals?[20]

Eliot encloses echoes of whole words within others – "gout" in "dégoute," "d'égout" – and reiterates similar phonetic formations across differing phrases – "fait des vers" in "faits divers" – to emphasize and consolidate the material sound of these words. He arranges the physical body of the language, however, inside a highly elaborate apparatus of syntactical ratiocination – that very French array of rhetorical negatives, antithetical conjunctions, subordinate and relative clauses. The discriminating thinking that this rationalistic syntax fosters in standard French, however, has turned into a sheer mouthful of Gallic bread and cheese. And the sauerkraut – "choucroute" – to which Eliot's speaker refers worriedly gestures toward the local prompt for this new conceit of reason-seeming nonsense – in the civilian culture of the war, which proscribed this stereotypically German food. Further evidence of this political pressure comes in the next stanzas, where he adapts the format of the "questionnaire," in which "rédacteurs" or newspaper editors aim inquiries at a civilian populace as menacing as the answers provided are nonsensical, contradicting any question–response logic but echoing all too audibly to the dominant quality of rationalistic inanity in the political journalism of the war.

This initiative extends into English literary idiom for Eliot in a poetic form which his French interlude has also drawn to his attention: the quatrain stanza, modeled for him (as for Pound) preeminently by Théophile Gautier. In late spring 1917, Eliot composed at least five poems in this new measure.[21] This considerable surplus of productivity witnesses the release of energies pent up for several years, but it also registers the stimulus of his discovering a shape most particularly cadenced, a rhythm quickening to presentiments that have been forming in his verbal imagination over several years of this ongoing war. Within its tightly maintained structure of alternately rhyming lines, a regimen that translates into a stiffly disciplined metric, Eliot's stanzas develop a semi-discursive syntax and vocabulary to convey an impression of well-regulated thought that dissolves constantly, however, into preposterousness. This prosody reembodies the sort of logical nonsense that dominates the public discourses of the Liberal war. And so it is no accident that one of Eliot's earliest efforts in the quatrain measure, "Airs of Palestine, No. 2," takes as its target and point of critical mimicry Sir John Spender, editor of the Liberal *Westminster Gazette*:

> God from a Cloud to Spender spoke
> And breathed command: "Take thou this Rod,
> And smite therewith the living Rock";
> And Spender hearkened unto God . . .

And such as have the skill to swim
Attain at length the farther shore
Cleansed and rejoiced in every limb,
And hate the Germans more and more.

They are redeemed from heresies
And all their frowardness forget;
And scales are fallen from their eyes
Thanks to the Westminster Gazette.[22]

The odd tonality, where scriptural references and religious diction mingle with the lower bawdry of a barracks-room ballad-rhythm, serves at once to echo and characterize the moral rationales for the war, that doggerel logic, which Spender's paper and its partisan likes have tirelessly offered. This tone also offers a rough-but-ready replica of the mock-sententiousness and pseudo-reasonableness that the later, more polished quatrains will smooth out.

The conceit of Eliot's quatrain art finds its signature piece in one of its last performances, "Sweeney among the Nightingales," which, in keeping with the counter-rhythm of his new poetics, works equally to invite and defy an impression of considered or even consistent significance. On (most of) its surface, the piece presents a topical satiric caricature, featuring the habitués of a seedy London bistro as a contemporary bestiary, a virtual zoology of pseudohuman types: there is "ape-neck Sweeney," there is "the silent vertebrate in brown," while another personage "tears at the grapes with murderous paws." This little misanthropic comedy can be scripted readily to a master narrative of cultural history, a dominant mythology, one in which Eliot is usually assigned a primary part: the "Lost Generation" of the first postwar moment. This rootless, pan-European and transatlantic vagabondage finds its dramatis personae in the poem's international cast of characters: the Irish "Sweeney," the Slavic Jew "Rachel née Rabinovitch," etc. The establishing circumstance of the recent war is also imaged cryptically but vividly in the visage of Sweeney himself. The "zebra stripes along his jaw" reflect the creases cut into his neck by the stiff collar of the dress uniform worn by military personnel in the Great War – Sweeney is the soldier, returned to London from the Front. Just so, however, the poem opens onto another level of potential significance, which its imaginative apparatus makes every pretence of claiming. The majestic cadenza of the final quatrains –

The host with someone indistinct
Converses at the door apart,
The nightingales are singing near
The convent of the Sacred Heart,

> And sang within the bloody wood
> When Agamemnon cried aloud
> And let their liquid siftings fall
> To stain the stiff dishonoured shroud[23]

– includes, in the reference to Agamemnon, a closural event prepared in advance by the Greek epigraph, which Eliot has taken from Aeschylus' tragedy *Agamemnon*. There the soldier returning from the Trojan war cries out as he is stabbed by his scheming wife Clytemnestra – a feminine menace Eliot also reflects in his poem in the threat these various "nightingales" (the word, in French, is slang for prostitutes) present to the male protagonist. Could Agamemnon really be the heroic prototype of Sweeney?[24] His "ape-neck" might equip him with a gift for simian mimicry, but it hardly enables him to resemble the Hellenic hero credibly. Why devise this parallel *manqué*? The meaning of Eliot's framing action may lie not in the content it organizes but in the gesture it represents – specifically, in the empty gesture it presents, where the epigraph and last stanza join to promise a formal logic that goes unembodied in the poem's central *mise-en-scène*. This failure is amplified through the rhythm particular to the quatrain, which appears driven, inexorably as ever, but by a premise as contradictory as Sweeney's claim to heroic fame. Yet the home front to which this soldier has returned also preserves a memory of equally compromised rationales for the nobility of that military enterprise, a failure Eliot echoes and answers through the ramifying irony of the poem's structural conception.

The culmination of Eliot's engagement with the historical and political event of the war comes in the poem he composes at the moment of its official conclusion. "Gerontion" takes shape through July 1919.[25] This is the month during which the "peace" treaty is being finalized at Versailles, an event to which the poem makes several decisive references.

In the closing moment of the poem, Eliot's speaker represents the substance of the monologue-disquisition that has just occurred as "small deliberations" – small, presumably, because "Gerontion" means, most specifically, a little old man. Where he expands these "small deliberations," in his mind's eye, to "multiply variety / In a wilderness of mirrors,"[26] however, Eliot is conveying a larger circumstance as the coincident occasion of the poem's event. He is imaging the scene in which the "deliberations" of (supposedly) "great men" will have recently taken place – in the Great Hall of Mirrors of the Trianon Palace at Versailles. If the "wilderness of mirrors" secures this allusion, an irony special to the history being inscribed at Versailles lies in that otherwise mysterious apprehension of "wilderness." This royal estate stood originally as a monument to Enlightenment civilization, since its demesne mapped the rationalist's universe to the scheme of metered and reasoned degree, which its reflecting halls and formal gardens comprised. The emblematic edifice of this first Age of Reason is overshadowed now by the consummation of the second, in the rituals of savage, retributive justice just conducted at Versailles.

Other references to this event provide the orienting points for the speaker's long, central meditation on "History," which, in this representation, "has many cunning passages, contrived corridors / And issues."[27] As in the Great Hall of Mirrors in Versailles, the image of "History" repeats in a receding frame, playing a trick of substance and multiple reflections. This mirage-like prospect seems especially and even willfully deceptive, however, the illusion peculiarly shrewd, insofar as these "passages" are "cunning," the "corridors" being "contrived" – presumably, around the "issues" being argued, which include the guilt the Allied powers officially imposed on Germany and the war reparations plan this maneuver authorized. Eliot's current work in the Colonial and Foreign Department at Lloyd's Bank certainly alerted him to the worst consequences of this economic punishment. The critical emphasis in his representation falls on the insidiousness of the case-making, moreover, a stress that echoes back to the sort of devious reasoning all too familiar to him from the discourses of the Liberal war. And it is this specifically English sensibility that Eliot puts on the rhetorical line in the poem's character-in-voice.

Eliot's aged speaker belongs to the senescence of contemporary British Liberalism, a generation that has authored in words a war its old men have not fought in body. Gerontion makes this admission in the opening moment of the poem, establishing his membership in that particular generation and partisan class. He also performs that identity, orienting himself toward the reality of the war in a verbalist rite that is well rehearsed if badly managed:

> I was neither at the hot gates
> Nor fought in the warm rain
> Nor knee deep in the salt marsh, heaving a cutlass,
> Bitten by flies, fought.[28]

Within the ceremonial antiquity of the old man's diction, the clausal construction projects the progressive discriminations of verbal reason – "neither / Nor / Nor" – as its stipulative spirit, its motivating action. The ambitious program and plan of a thrice-suspended period turns into the wreckage its phrasal sequence actually makes of it, however. This masterfully awkward contortion of rationalist syntax resonates against the background sound of English Liberalism at war. And Eliot extends the sensibility of his speaking character to its revealing extreme in the central meditation on "History."

"Think now," his speaker proposes to open this deliberation, whose rhetorical contours require a representation at length:

> History has many cunning passages, contrived corridors
> And issues; deceives with whispering ambitions,
> Guides us with vanities. Think now
> She gives when our attention is distracted,
> And what she gives, gives with such supple confusions
> That the giving famishes the craving. Gives too late
> What's not believed in, or if still believed,
> In memory only, reconsidered passion. Gives too soon
> Into weak hands, what's thought can be dispensed with
> Till the refusal propagates a fear. Think
> Neither fear nor courage saves us. Unnatural vices
> Are fathered by our heroism. Virtues
> Are forced upon us by our impudent crimes.
> These tears are shaken from the wrath-bearing tree.
> The tiger springs in the new year. Us he devours. Think at last
> We have not reached conclusion, when I
> Stiffen in a rented house. Think at last
> I have not made this show purposelessly . . .[29]

The repetitive insistence on some deliberated significance – "Think now," "Think now," "Think / Neither," "Think at last," "Think at last" – proceeds to the "conclusion," however, which "we have not reached." The logic is hortative only. Where a sequence of appeals goes unembodied in any solid consequence, Eliot seizes this conceit of reason-seeming nonsense as an animating force, as witnessed especially near the end of the main passage, where he turns the words of progressive and logical proposition into a composite of contradictions. How is it, after all, that an "unnatural vice" can be biologically "fathered," and a vile unreal thing begotten from a natural good? Whose "impudent crimes" are capable of generating "virtues"? These disparities, however, seem unapparent to the speaker, who talks through them with every seemliness of reasonable and coherent meaning. The inverse ratio and particular power of this verse show in its capacity to outsize its own rationalist measures, reaching through the sense it feigns to the illogic it really means, where the emotion that is released grows in ratio to its overwhelming of an older Reason. This complex effect is the meaning recent "History" has revealed to the critical imagination of the modernist, who, like Pound, distinguishes his art by the special faculty he manifests for tapping this awareness and providing the extraordinary moment of history the answering echo of a new imaginative language.

If their American background affords Eliot and Pound some working externality of perspective on the words of British Liberalism, Virginia Woolf enjoys a special intimacy with the idiom of the party's intellectual command – a conversancy she assumes, however, with the critical difference her gender confers. She knows the philosophical conventions underlying the language of partisan authority from the source and model of her father, Sir Leslie Stephen, a dean in the clerisy of cultural liberalism, who put its core values of "reason in all things" into the extreme form of his own intellectual personality. A strongly logical agnosticism combined with a scholarly passion for the eighteenth century, that first Age of Reason, to form the main determination of his long career: to establish the basis of morality, not in theology, but in right reason.[30] If this irascible rationalist has dropped out of most accounts of his daughter's intellectual makeup, the genuine legacy he left her needs to be reckoned, for her intensely contested relation with him as patriarch serves as prelude and pattern for her subsequent engagements with liberal cultural power. It was Leslie's junior contemporaries who authored and prosecuted the Liberal war, and Woolf's critical audition on those performances has been fostered as the complex benefice of his paternity. To those provocations she responds with full cognizance and, as a consequence, develops a novel language of fictional prose – an accomplishment paramount even among the modernists, for Woolf's inwardness with the tradition at stake makes its crisis her lasting, substantial opportunity.

The earliest record of this engagement comes in the first literary effort Woolf undertakes since her breakdown in January 1915, in April 1917 (the miraculous season of modernism in wartime London), in "The Mark on the Wall." The story features the narrator-protagonist's play of consciousness in identifying the title-subject. While this "inside" action anticipates the sort of imaginative self-absorption that Woolf's later modernist writing will typically offer, it also includes a number of references to the "external" circumstance of the war – as in the striking finale, which records strongly the background sound of the journalistic war:

> Someone is standing over me and saying –
> "I'm going out to buy a newspaper."
> "Yes?"
> "Though it's no good buying newspapers . . . Nothing ever happens. Curse this war; God damn this war! . . . All the same, I don't see why we should have a snail on our wall."
> Ah, the mark on the wall! It was a snail.[31]

Less volubly, more intricately and ingeniously, Woolf recalls the discourses of the war government in particular, indicating in the verbal play in this passage her own prepossessing engagement with that partisan dialect, as her narrator interrupts herself thus:

> – but these generalisations are very worthless. The military sound of the word is enough. It recalls leading articles, cabinet ministers – a whole class of things indeed which as a child one thought the thing itself, the standard thing, the real thing, from which one could not depart save at the risk of nameless damnation. Generalisations bring back somehow Sunday in London, Sunday afternoon walks, Sunday luncheons, and also ways of speaking of the dead . . .[32]

Woolf's words play through the *"military sound"* of *"general*isations" to the target and point, not of army generals but of this war's ideological language, to the policy documents and partisan briefs of those "leading articles" by "cabinet ministers." These martial-minded generalisations recall the "Martian generalities" Pound's "out-weariers of Apollo" pronounce, in the same season, in the critical figure he fashioned to invoke the same political culture and practice as Woolf. Where Pound listens to public speakers wearied with their eager but specious appeals to the god of Reason, Woolf hears an equally meaningless – "worthless" – language in official rationales. She represents the Word and clerisy of a political and intellectual Liberalism with an intimacy and familiarity, however, that signal her main point of difference to Pound's jocoserious plaint. The official idiom is, for her, the verbal substance of closely acquainted customs – it was spoken on those "Sunday afternoon walks, Sunday luncheons." Her closeness with the tradition at risk gives the turn it is taking in the public sphere the force and import, in her own writing, of a revolution from within. And so the "inside" language of "The Mark" registers the crisis of reasonable speech "outside" the room, which Woolf echoes and amplifies in her own transfiguring idiom in her mature modernist prose. Indeed, the instigation of this new verbal practice carries the nerve and courage of one willing to dare "nameless damnation," which is, for one raised to the absolute standards of rationalist language, the damnation of namelessness.

The risk initially brings exhilaration, some feeling of release from Reason's seemly forms. High verbal spirits carry Woolf's first response to the collapse of rationalist language – right (wrong) into the echoing differential of her own sentences. Mock-logical, quasi-propositional, her new prosody already moves the syntax into novel sequences and permutations in the early paragraphs of "The Mark," beginning with her opening deliberations on the identity of the title subject. "If that mark was made by a nail," the narrator proposes, it can't have been for a picture, it must have been for a miniature – the miniature of a lady with white powdered curls, powder-dusted cheeks, and lips like red carnations. A fraud of course, for the people who had this house before us would have chosen pictures in that way – an old picture for an old room. That is the sort of people they were – very interesting people, and I think of them so often . . .[33]

The cautious hypothesis of the initial conditional clause loses its head as a surplus of verbal energy runs an abundance of words over the ratios that the specifically rationalist grammar prescribes. This insurgent force is concurrent with fantasy, but the wholly imaginary character of the lady's face in the conjectured portrait carries also a tone of prudent surmise: "a fraud *of course.*" This emphatic phrase assumes for the deliberation it concludes some process of (logical) course, through which, of course, we have not followed. This discrepancy between the forms of verbal reason and a sublogical or pararational content locates a comic moment for Woolf that is also the growing point of her mature, modernist oeuvre. The freedom it bespeaks is instinct with a tremendous creative potential.

For the pseudological comedy in "The Mark" is streaked with intimations of the history that has allowed it to be staged. An event of terrible consequence – the "god-damned" war of those newspapers – unmakes the father's language, and the disintegration of this system is at once the stimulus to extraordinary verbal invention on Woolf's part and an occasion of really shaking recognitions. These may be rehearsed to frame the graver implications of the modernist project her writing will bring into its consummate form.

The formidable import of this failure of rationalist language is augured in the Liberal journalism in the days immediately preceding the outbreak of hostilities. The notion that the speech of Reason could not only articulate the logic of proper action but direct the development of events was the great casualty. The language of proper, rational morality was collapsing, in the terrified presentiment of one journalist, into "the logic of events beyond our control."[34] This was the auto-logic of the alliance system, which, at this moment, instanced a kind of diabolical parody of deliberative, ethical reasoning. Liberal freethinkers had always resisted this system (and so drove partisan alliance-building into secrecy), since it preempted the liberty of ethical decision. Now, however, day by day, country by country in the alliance system succumbed, in the shaken impression of another reporter, "to the spell of an ironic fate."[35] There was an insistent, irresistible recognition that events were being compelled by forces outside Liberal control and, indeed, beyond language itself.

Woolf reclaims this intimation as the condition of the language the war left her – most urgently in her representation of the onset of that event in *Jacob's Room* (1922). In the two decades of family history in the novel that precede the outbreak of war, which will claim the life of the eponymous Jacob, there is a series of advance, premonitory signals, the most representative of which comes in the account of Jacob's Continental tour, undertaken early in the summer of 1914. "And then, here is Versailles,"[36] goes the whole of a one-sentence paragraph. The import of this allusion lies in a future this instant in narrative-historical time cannot comprise: the war that will be officially concluded in the Great Hall of Mirrors at Versailles has not even begun. As a name and place, nonetheless, "Versailles" cannot help but stir an immense range of associations for the reader, in 1922 and after. As a nominal monument to the first Age of Reason, "Versailles" also stands as an emblematic site, one which recalls in particular the fate a rationalistic language will have suffered in prosecuting the war that is (only) formally concluded there. Measured and reasoned speech cannot comprehend the range of meanings and feelings its words have picked up from the history they have failed to regulate. The unspokenness of those meanings – indeed, their unspeakability – is the most expressive dimension in this allusion. For a sensibility formed in accordance with the Liberal belief in the speakable reason of things, the most expressive record of the meaning of the war lies in this failure of language. This new poetics, whereby the expressive potential of words grows in inverse proportion to how much they withhold from disclosure, acknowledges at once its own novel power and a content as somber as the history it cannot name.

Thus the historical narrative of later summer edges its references to the imminent event with a reticence that speaks the Liberal's unspeakable distress:

> Now the agitation of the air uncovered a racing star. Now it was dark. Now one after another lights were extinguished. Now great towns – Paris – Constantinople – London were black as strewn rocks . . . The salt gale blew in at Betty Flanders's bedroom window, and the widow lady, raising herself slightly on her elbow, sighed like one who realizes, but would fain ward off a little longer – oh, a little longer! – the oppression of eternity.[37]

The breeze blowing into Betty Flanders's bedroom from the east is salted with the menace of events developing in England's direction from the Continent. The "extinguish[ing]" of the "light" coincides with the onset of war, imaging in particular the slippage of those powers of "civilization" for which the Liberal campaign would be nominally fought. Betty Flanders's family name also calls up the site of the conflict's most famous battlefield and mass grave. Yet Woolf never claims that association overtly. And the tropes that invoke the emergent conflict all turn away from any direct reference to the terrible event they portend (a conceit Woolf repeats in representing the distant eventuality of the war in "Time Passes," the central section of *To the Lighthouse*).[38] This passage quickens with the terror of the original wordlessness. The trepidation Betty Flanders feels about some impending but unnamed fate comes from the same place. Woolf draws from this resource a manifold of unforetold power.

The historical basis for this linguistic sensibility is clarified and claimed in its signal episode in *Jacob's Room*. In the chronicle fiction of the novel's last part, Woolf restages the events of early August 1914. She moves the international story to a focal point at Whitehall, center of the British foreign and diplomatic services and site of that institution's "inexorable gravity," where

> sixteen gentlemen, lifting their pens or turning perhaps rather wearily in their chairs, decreed that the course of history should shape itself this way or that way, being manfully determined, as their faces showed, to impose some coherency upon Rajahs and Kaisers and the mutterings in bazaars, the secret gatherings, plainly visible in Whitehall, of kilted peasants in Albanian uplands; to control the course of events.[39]

Here Leslie Stephen's younger colleagues in the diplomatic corps suffer the particular crisis of their patrician Liberalism, attempting to implement into history the "coherency," the clarifying moral rationalism of its Victorian (Gladstonian) gnosis. Woolf makes evident the conflict between its faith in the ethical reasonableness of policy, bespoken with the "inexorable gravity" of its old mens' efforts "to control the course of events," and the imminent riot of *Mitteleuropa*, configured as the incomprehensibility of those barbarous tongues. This is the dissonance that provides the instigating, substantiating occasion of Woolf's major work.

The centering of critical attention on the political culture of the English war helps literary history to recover the importance of a figure who usually goes unremarked in commentary on *Mrs. Dalloway*, the novel which affords the war such an extensive remembrance. Not the unfortunate Doris Kilman, that Anglo-German relict of pan-European conflict, nor Septimus Warren Smith, the psychologically tortured veteran, who have dominated scholarly response. The neglected personage is one of sizeable – and, now, identifiable – importance in the cultural economy of the Liberal war: Dr. (Sir) William Bradshaw. A knighted man of science, a figure laying claim to high and representative importance in the broadest compass of cultural politics, a spiritual colleague of Leslie Stephen, Bradshaw aims his professional attention, in the early postwar moment of the novel's historical fiction, at rehabilitating veterans with combat trauma. His success in this effort relies on the efficacy of a one-word cure, a particularly Liberal motto and refrain: "Proportion," where the sense of balance, or, more exactly, scale or *ratio*, goes to the root meaning of *ratio*nality. Woolf's narrator echoes Bradshaw in free indirect speech, a liberal mimicry which takes proportion beyond all measure:

> Proportion, divine proportion, Sir William's goddess, was acquired by Sir William walking hospitals, catching salmon, begetting one son in Harley Street by Lady Bradshaw, who caught salmon herself and took photographs scarcely to be distinguished from the work of professionals. Worshiping proportion, Sir William not only prospered himself but made England prosper, secluded her lunatics, forbade childbirth, penalised despair, made it impossible for the unfit to propagate their views until they, too, shared his sense of proportion – his, if they were men, Lady Bradshaw's, if they were women (she embroidered, knitted, spent four nights out of seven at home with her son), so that not only did his colleagues respect him, his subordinates fear him, but the friends and relations of his patients felt for him the keenest gratitude for insisting that these prophetic Christs and Christesses, who prophesied the end of the world, or the advent of God, should drink milk in bed, as Sir William ordered; Sir William with his thirty years' experience of these kinds of cases, and his infallible instinct, this is madness, this sense; in fact, his sense of proportion.[40]

A rationalistic attitude and practice are manifest everywhere in the language of this passage – in the structure of graded relation, the hierarchical order of main and subordinate clauses, the bracketing action of the parentheses. The rationalist of language is the rationer of status. Bradshaw measures out the relative values of autonomy and dependence – physician and patient, health and sickness, freedom and confinement – with an authority he deploys through syntax, with the force of the habit that assumes his advantage. The formidable endowment of this culturally conferred power, however, will have failed to cure the veteran of the Liberal war, Warren Smith, who takes his life at the end of the novel. And Bradshaw has manifestly lost his own sense of balance, a root meaning gone radically wrong, as Woolf travesties the very notion of measure or restraint in this antic refrain.

With this tradition in ruins by the end of the war, Woolf directs her inventive power to its once presumptive authority: to Bradshaw's hierarchically rationed sentence. *Mrs. Dalloway* finds its most expressive syntax in the insubordinate clause. Woolf sets up periodic sequences whose conclusions she refuses to reach, whose subordinations she refuses to obey. And a direct testament to the presence of the war in this development comes in a sentence fully representative of her new direction. It features Clarissa early in the novel, sorting, shopping:

> And as she began to go with Miss Pym from jar to jar, choosing, nonsense, nonsense, she said to herself, more and more gently, as if this beauty, this scent, this colour, and Miss Pym liking her, trusting her, were a wave which she let flow over her and surmount that hatred, that monster, surmount it all; and it lifted her up and up when – oh! a pistol shot in the street outside![41]

The veteran Septimus, it turns out, registers simultaneously the motor car explosion this closing phrase invokes. For him, the noise echoes to the background sound of his trench experience. The holocaust Smith's response embodies as a physical memory consummates the logic of Liberal Reason in history. The sentence presents the disheveled remnant of that degraded, disproved, inconclusive rationalism. Into this intensive manifold Woolf has concentrated a representative instance of her new usage. The specifically modernist idiom that she typifies thus recovers a resonant memory of the history occasioning it.

Modern*ism*: to the experience of being chronologically modern the suffix adds a sense of self-consciousness about the meaning of "modern." Most accurately, then, the word conveys a feeling of belonging to a particular moment of history, a specified Now, a *special* present, which is made more intense by virtue of some self-conscious difference to what went before. The 1914 war locates a moment of major breakage within the mainstream tradition of liberal modernity, which features Public Reason as its premier value and practice.[42] The London modernists will take the fracture in those established attitudes as the enabling, signifying condition of their exceptional art. And in this signal respect the three modernists featured here really earn the term posterity has conferred on them.

Within a larger configuration of London modernism, of course, the response was composite, various. As Vorticist and editor of *Blast*, Wyndham Lewis was perhaps the premier representative of the English avant-garde. Like many artists in the European avant-garde, Lewis drew an energy of self-presentation from the resources of cultural and political nationalism, and, like many Futurists, he compounded this persona with masculinist values. In his specifically British instance, this gendered identity spoke through the language and attitudes of rationalism, Liberal or not. Those "sixteen gentlemen . . . being manfully determined" to "impose some coherency" on "the course of events" represent, not just the prepossessing gender in the cultural construction of English Reason, but, as a hazarded class, the critical opportunity of the major modernist enterprise, Woolf's most notably. Lewis

declines the opportunity, resisting in particular Eliot's practice of poetic pseu-
dologic, which he cartoons indeed as an emasculated condition.[43] In this
crucial respect, he chooses the value of continuity in the mainstream British
tradition.

David Jones, whose *In Parenthesis* (1937) models itself on the already
accomplished modernism of Eliot, presents a rich and dense evocation of the
author's service on the Western Front.[44] Jones's verse-with-prose experiment
hardly seems secondhand, but this neo-modernist work witnesses no evident
attention to Liberal England's disability – as an instigating condition of new
writing.

The novel quality in modernist response to this extraordinary moment in
history is fostered by a sense of *difference*, an awareness in particular of the
disabled claims of the formerly majority values of Liberal rationalism. Pound
and Eliot and Woolf give an exceptional, clarifying, expansive witness to this
disintegrating tradition, in whose ruins they recompose a new literary order.
This responsiveness provides their writing a historical content and depth
and, in that highly timely quality, its lasting memory and significance as well
as its original energy.

NOTES

1. A good contemporary reference on the ideas and values of political and intellectual Liberalism comes from L. T. Hobhouse, *Liberalism* (London: Williams and
Norgate, 1910), a volume aimed at the broad-based readership of the series in
which it appeared, the Home University Library of Modern Knowledge. The rival
values and practice of Gladstonian and imperial Liberalism may be found on 104,
221.
2. The existence of these "secret agreements" and the influence they exert on British
policy and action constitute the subject of the major exposé by the founding
director of the Union of Democratic Control (of foreign policy), E. D. Morel,
Truth and the War (London: National Labour Press, 1916), esp. 35–41, 273–300.
3. The text of the speech was printed in all the major dailies on 4 August, e.g., "Sir
E. Grey's Speech," *Manchester Guardian*, 7–8.
4. "Peace or War," *Manchester Guardian*, 4 August 1914, 6.
5. "A Dramatic Scene: The House and Sir Edward Grey's Statement: Logic of
Events," *Westminster Gazette*, 4 August 1914, 10.
6. "The Peasant Nation," *Westminster Gazette*, 28 July 1914, 4.
7. Seppings Wright, "What Can Servia Do?," *Westminster Gazette*, 31 July 1914,
1–2.
8. Irene Cooper Willis, *How We Went into the War: A Study of Liberal Idealism*
(Manchester: National Labour Press, 1918), esp. "The Holy War," 86–141. Willis's
attention concentrates on the salient articles from the early months of the war in
the dailies most obviously aligned with the Liberal party, the *Manchester Guardian*
and the *Daily News and Leader*, and on the partisan literary weeklies, the *New
Statesman* and the *Nation*, where the tone of the intellectual campaign was struck.

9. Dora Marsden, "Views and Comments," *Egoist*, 15 September 1914, 344. See also the commentary on "cant," "Views and Comments," *Egoist*, 1 September 1914, 323–25, and "Quid Pro Quo," *Egoist*, 15 August 1914, 301.

10. Pound, "Studies in Contemporary Mentality," IV, "The 'Spectator,'" *New Age*, 6 September 1917, 407.

11. *Ibid.*, 407.

12. In the same sequence, all of these prose pieces were published in the *Little Review*: May 1917, 12–18; June 1917, 14–21; July 1917, 12–16; July 1918, 3–12.

13. In a letter to Iris Barry on 27 July 1916, in *Selected Letters of Ezra Pound, 1907–41*, ed. D. D. Paige (1950; rpt. New York: New Directions, 1971), 90, Pound refers to a project of translating Propertius as a Roman poet of especially timely interest and relevance; Humphrey Carpenter, in *A Serious Character: The Life of Ezra Pound* (Boston: Houghton Mifflin, 1988), 324, quotes an unpublished letter by Pound to his father, of 3 November 1918, as likely evidence that the poem has been recently completed.

14. An account of Propertius' address to contemporary verse conventions is provided by J. P. Sullivan, *Ezra Pound and Sextus Propertius: A Study in Creative Translation* (Austin: University of Texas Press, 1964), 58–64, 75–76.

15. "Homage to Sextus Propertius," in *Personae: Collected Shorter Poems of Ezra Pound* (1926; rev. edn., ed. Lea Baechler and A. Walton Litz [New York: New Directions, 1990]), 205.

16. *Ibid.*, 206.

17. The relevant texts of Propertius' Latin and a standard prose translation are provided helpfully by K. K. Ruthven, *A Guide to Ezra Pound's "Personae" 1926* (Berkeley: University of California Press, 1969); the Guide is arranged by the alphabetized sequence of Pound's poems' titles.

18. An account of Eliot's complex interaction with the political and intellectual culture of Liberalism, including the strongly negative attitude he expresses toward the premises of pan-European liberalism, is provided by Vincent Sherry, *The Great War and the Language of Modernism* (New York: Oxford University Press, 2003), esp. 157, 162–63, 171, 351 n. 13.

19. This text and the information regarding Pound's counsel are provided in the letter of 21 August 1916 to Conrad Aiken, in *The Letters of T. S. Eliot*, vol. I, *1898–1922*, ed. Valerie Eliot (London: Faber, 1988), 145–46.

20. Eliot, *Inventions of the March Hare: Poems 1909–1917*, ed. Christopher Ricks (New York: Harcourt Brace, 1996), 86. Much of the poetry Eliot wrote between 1917 and 1919 is also included in this volume. The various drafts, with Ricks's extensive critical commentary, give the best picture of Eliot's development in this crucial interim.

21. A good record of Eliot's extraordinary productivity at this time comes in a letter of 30 April 1917 to his mother by Vivien Eliot, in *The Letters of T. S. Eliot*, vol. I, 178.

22. In *Inventions of the March Hare*, 84–85.

23. *Ibid.*, 380–81.

24. The late addition of the Greek epigraph – it is not included in the penultimate draft of the poem – suggests that the heroic parallel comes to Eliot as a second thought, which he includes to complicate the hermeneutic of Sweeney; see the

summary of the manuscript evidence by Ricks, *Inventions of the March Hare*, 381.

25. Eliot mentions the poem as "this new one, 'Gerontion,'" on 9 July 1919 in a letter to John Rodker, in *The Letters of T. S. Eliot*, vol. I, 312.

26. In *Inventions of the March Hare*, 350–51.

27. *Ibid.*, 350.

28. *Ibid.*, 349.

29. *Ibid.*, 350.

30. A concise but comprehensive portrait of Woolf's father's intellectual character is drawn by Hermione Lee, *Virginia Woolf* (London: Chatto & Windus, 1996), 69–71. The most detailed account of her father's position in British intellectual culture comes from Noel Annan, *Leslie Stephen: The Godless Victorian* (Chicago: University of Chicago Press, 1984), esp. "British Rationalism," 165–91, "The Revelation of the Eighteenth Century," 221–33, and "The Moral Society," 267–99.

31. "The Mark on the Wall" appeared in July 1917, along with Leonard Woolf's "Three Jews," as the first publication of the Woolfs' newly founded Hogarth Press. It was reprinted, with minor variations, in *Monday or Tuesday* (London: Hogarth, 1921), which provides the basis for the text in *The Complete Shorter Fiction of Virginia Woolf*, 2d edn., ed. Susan Dick (San Diego: Harcourt Brace Jovanovitch, 1989), 89.

32. In *The Complete Shorter Fiction*, 86.

33. *Ibid.*, 83.

34. "A Dramatic Scene: The House and Sir Edward Grey's Statement: Logic of Events," *Westminster Gazette*, 4 August 1914, 10.

35. "Comments," *New Statesman*, 1 August 1914, 513.

36. Virginia Woolf, *Jacob's Room* (1922; rpt. San Diego: Harcourt Brace Jovanovitch, 1990), 128.

37. *Ibid.*, 160.

38. Virginia Woolf, *To the Lighthouse* (1927; rpt. San Diego: Harcourt Brace Jovanovitch, 1990), 125–43.

39. Woolf, *Jacob's Room*, 171–72.

40. Woolf, *Mrs. Dalloway* (1925; rpt. San Diego: Harcourt Brace Jovanovitch, 1990), 99–100.

41. *Ibid.*, 13.

42. The best representation of this salient value and its comprehensive practice in western political tradition comes from John Rawls, *Political Liberalism* (1993; rpt. New York: Columbia University Press, 1996), esp. xxiv, xxvi–xxviii, xxx, 47–59, 212–27.

43. Wyndham Lewis, *Men without Art* (London: Cassell, 1934), "T. S. Eliot: The Pseudo-Believer," 65–100, esp. 88.

44. David Jones, *In Parenthesis* (London: Faber, 1937).

II

THE WORLD WAR: PAN-EUROPEAN VIEWS, TRANSATLANTIC PROSPECTS

6

MARJORIE PERLOFF

The Great War and the European avant-garde

In 1915, the French poet Guillaume Apollinaire, who had enlisted in the cavalry in late 1914, wrote a poem called "Guerre" ("War"), which begins:

> Rameau central de combat
>   Contact par l'écoute
> On tire dans la direction "des bruits entendus"
> Les jeunes de la classe 1915
> Et ces fils de fer électrisés
> Ne pleurez donc pas sur les horreurs de la guerre
> Avant elle nous n'avions que la surface
> De la terre et des mers
> Apres elle nous aurons les abîmes
> Le sous-sol et l'espace aviatique . . .

> Central combat sector
>   Contact by sound
> We're firing toward "noises that were heard"
> The young men of the class of 1915
> And those electrified wires
> Then don't weep for the horrors of war
> Before the war we had only the surface
> Of the earth and the seas
> After it we'll have the depths
> Subterranean and aerial space . . .[1]

To Anglophone readers, whose touchstone for the poetry of the Great War is the lyric of Rupert Brooke, Wilfred Owen, or Siegfried Sassoon, the apocalyptic sentiments expressed in Apollinaire's "War" must seem all but incomprehensible. Did *les jeunes de la classe 1915* really believe that the war would provide entrance to a Brave New World in which the heights of the heavens and depths of the earth would be sounded?

The answer, surprisingly, is yes. Or perhaps not so surprisingly given that *avant-garde* was originally a military term: it referred to the front flank of the army, to the advance guard that prepared the way for the rest of the troops. The avant-garde is by definition *embattled*, and for the European avant-garde of the early century war signified, at least at the outset of the conflict, both revolution and liberation. It was not until 1916, when the realities of trench warfare could no longer be ignored, that the avant-garde changed its mind about war. But by then, many of its finest artists – the Italian Futurist painter Umberto Boccioni (1880–1916) and architect Antonio Sant'Elia (1888–1916), both serving on the Italian Front, the French sculptor Henri Gaudier-Brzeska (1891–1915), serving at Neuville St. Vaast, and the German Expressionist painter Franz Marc (1880–1916), who fought in the Battle of Verdun – had been killed. Others were severely wounded: in 1916 Apollinaire himself received a head wound from which he never fully recovered (he died of influenza in 1918), while his friend and fellow poet Blaise Cendrars lost his right arm in combat. In Russia, the man considered by Roman Jakobson as the greatest poet of the century, Velimir Khlebnikov, was a victim, first of the war, then of the October Revolution and the Civil Wars. He died of gangrene poisoning resulting from starvation in 1922 at the age of thirty-seven.

But in the first years of the war, Cendrars and Khlebnikov were caught up in a war fever that may have been most intense in Germany, which had become, by 1914, the most powerful country in the world. After centuries as a loosely integrated set of autonomous principalities, the new unified Germany created by Bismarck in 1870 had modernized itself with a vengeance. Industrialization moved with amazing speed: the production of steel, for example, which was only a quarter of Britain's in the early 1870s, had caught up by 1914 and equaled that of Britain, France, and Russia combined. Mass education had produced an astonishingly high rate of literacy. And, as Modris Eksteins explains in his *Rites of Spring*, the watchword, especially in Berlin, became *Die Flucht nach Vorne*, the flight forward.[2] Novelty was prized for its own sake and inner freedom considered much more important than liberty or equality. The Nietzschean command, *Du sollst werden, der du bist* ("You shall become what you really are"), gave rise to the restless search for new forms, new modes of being.

The enemy of this *Flucht nach Vorne* was Britain, which represented, in German eyes, the Old Order, the land of bourgeois comfort, complacency, arrogance, and the status quo. Britain, writes Ecksteins, was "the symbol of an ethic of enterprise and progress based on parliament and law"; it stood for a way of life inimical to the "thrusting energy and instability Germany was seen to typify." For the "new Germans," Britain's pretensions as to free trade, the open market, and a liberal ethic, masked its real purpose, which was to retain its international position as the great imperial power. War, in this scheme of things, meant, as Magnus Hirschfeld, the leader of Berlin's homosexual movement put it, the fight for "honesty" and "sincerity" against the "smoking jacket culture of Britain and France." War, wrote Hermann Hesse to a friend in 1914, was a matter of art: "To be torn out of a dull capitalistic peace was good for many Germans and it seems to me that a genuine artist would find greater value in a nation of men who have faced death and who know the immediacy and freshness of camp life."[3] And Franz Marc, whose *Red Horses* and *Tiger* of 1912–13 represented primitivist forms in intense expressionist colors, wrote in his prospectus for the *Blaue Reiter Almanac* (1912):

> Today art is moving in a direction toward which our fathers never even have dreamed. One stands before the new works as in a dream and hears the horsemen of the Apocalypse in the air. An artistic tension is felt all over Europe . . . Everywhere in Europe new forms are sprouting like a beautiful anomalous seed, and all the places where new things are occurring must be pointed out.[4]

Then, when war broke out, Marc wrote from the Front, "Let us remain soldiers even after the war . . . for this is not a war against an eternal enemy . . . it is a European civil war, a war against the inner invisible enemy of the European spirit."[5]

Even Dada, or, more accurately, pre-Dada, was not immune to this view of war as apocalyptic purge. "For a while," recalls Richard Huelsenbeck in *Memoirs of a Dada Drummer*, "my dream had been to make literature with a gun in my pocket."[6] In Berlin in 1914, he met Hugo Ball, who had been co-founder of the Munich magazine *Revolution*:

> I had been seeing a good deal of Hugo Ball, but one day he vanished. Although a civilian, he had hopped on an army train, and the soldiers had cheerfully let him ride along. In Liège, he was taken out and arrested, but when they realized that he was an idealist and not a spy, they sent him back home. He returned to Berlin and worked for various magazines.[7]

Ball soon left Germany behind and settled with his wife, the *chanteuse* Emmy Hennings, in Zurich, where they founded the Cabaret Voltaire, which soon attracted such other avant-gardists in exile as the Romanian Tristan Tzara (born Sammy Rosenstock), and the Alsatian Hans (or Jean) Arp. Exile, as we shall see later, was often a precondition of avant-garde activity. More important: the prewar and war avant-garde was most prominent, not in the great urban centers like Berlin or Paris, but on the periphery, especially in those still backward but rapidly industrializing nations, Italy and Russia. "The closer to Paris, which was the centre," explains Pontus Hulten, "and the more established the bourgeois culture, the stronger was the resistance to the new ideas . . . The more peripheral countries moved directly into a new, constructive phase, as there was less to be destroyed."[8]

Take the famous *Futurist Manifesto* of 1909. Its author, the Italian F. T. Marinetti, shrewdly published his piece on the front page of the Paris newspaper *Le Figaro* (February 20), so as to put the art world, whose center was certainly Paris, on notice that a new Italian art and poetry had arrived. Never mind that at the time the manifesto was published, not a single Futurist painting or sculpture had yet been produced. The power and shock value of the Manifesto was to change all that: by 1910, the Futurists artists themselves had moved to center stage.

The outrageous content of the 1909 Manifesto, especially its advocacy of war, must be understood in this context. The Manifesto has often been reviled for its ninth proposition, "We will glorify war – the world's only hygiene – militarism, patriotism, the destructive gesture of freedom-bringers, beautiful ideas worth dying for, and scorn for woman."[9] What do these pugnacious and offensive words really mean? The Manifesto begins with a narrative:

> We had stayed up all night, my friends and I, under hanging mosque lamps with domes of filigreed brass, domes starred like our spirits, shining like them with the prisoned radiance of electric hearts. For hours we had trampled our atavistic ennui into rich oriental rugs, arguing up to the last confines of logic and blackening many reams of paper with our frenzied scribbling.
>
> An immense pride was buoying us up, because we felt ourselves alone at that hour, alone, awake, and on our feet, like proud beacons or forward sentries against an army of hostile stars glaring down at us from their celestial encampments. Alone with stokers feeding the hellish fires of great ships, alone with black specters who grope in the red-hot bellies of locomotives . . .[10]

Like much of Marinetti's writing, this passage is oddly contradictory. The drive to break with the past, to Make It New, and especially to celebrate the new working classes is ironically offset by the luxury and exoticism of the poet's salon, with its hanging mosque lamps, its domes of filigreed brass, and its rich oriental rugs. Marinetti had been brought up in wealthy surroundings in Egypt – later in the Manifesto, he refers to the ditch in which his car overturns as resembling "the blessed black breast of my Sudanese nurse"[11] – and his own rebellion is still couched in the language of Decadence he had inherited. Making it new became, for him as for other avant-gardists, inseparable from Primitivism and Orientalism: in Futurist painting, stokers and railroad workers are depicted, not as ordinary men, but as part of an exotic and colorful landscape. The enemy, in this context, was the status quo: the timid and provincial nineteenth-century culture that had turned

Italy into no more than a vast museum, where the locals acted as *cicerones* for British and American tourists, an Italy feeding on its glorious Renaissance past with no confidence in its own ability to produce great art. Indeed, so hopeless was the backward Italy of the papacy and the monarchy, of the traditional family in which the wife/mother was wholly subservient to her husband, that it must be exploded from within. Hence Marinetti's manifestos boast titles like "Against Past-Loving Venice" and "Down with Tango and Parsifal." Tango was what high society types were dancing and hence execrable; *Parsifal* (Wagner) symbolized the power and would-be domination of Germany.

The Manifesto thus becomes a celebration of "the love of danger, the habit of energy and fearlessness" (Proposition no. 1). The formula for poetry is not "emotion recollected in tranquility" (Wordsworth) or negative capability (Keats) but "Courage, audacity, and revolt" (no. 2). No more is literature "a pensive immobility, ecstasy, and sleep"; rather, "We intend to exalt aggressive action, a feverish insomnia, the racer's stride, the mortal leap, the punch and the slap" (no. 3). And the New Beauty, which can only be born out of struggle (no. 7), is the "beauty of speed" (no. 4), so that "A roaring car that seems to ride on grapeshot is more beautiful than the *Victory of Samothrace*" (no. 4).

"VORTEX," as Ezra Pound was to put it just a few years later, "is ENERGY." And again, "The image is not an idea. It is a radiant node or cluster . . . a VORTEX, from which, and through which, and into which, ideas are constantly rushing."[12] Only energy, Marinetti believed, could transform an Italy that had "for too long" served as "a dealer in secondhand clothes." "We mean to free her from the numberless museums that cover her like so many graveyards." In this scheme of things, war is equated with revolution; war is what will destroy the old world and allow the new to be born. Marinetti's eleventh and final proposition is worth citing in full because it set the stage for so much brilliant painting by Marinetti's Futurist followers:

> 11. We will sing of great crowds excited by work, by pleasure, and by riot; we will sing of the multicolored, polyphonic tides of revolution in the modern capitals; we will sing of the vibrant nightly fervor of arsenals and shipyards blazing with violent electric moons; greedy railway stations that devour smoke-plumed serpents; factories hung on clouds by the crooked lines of their smoke; bridges that stride the rivers like giant gymnasts, flashing in the sun with a glitter of knives; adventurous steamers that sniff the horizon; deep-chested locomotives whose wheels paw the tracks like the hooves of enormous steel horses bridled by tubing; and the sleek flight of planes whose propellers chatter in the wind like banners and seem to cheer like an enthusiastic crowd.[13]

If this hyperbolic homage to technology now strikes us as curiously naïve, we must remember that the romance with the machine and especially the airplane was ubiquitous for the artists coming of age during the *avant-guerre*. Even Franz Kafka, in the subtle and ironic depiction of aviation found in his youthful newspaper article "Die Aeroplane in Brescia" (1909), describes himself as mesmerized, at the Brescia Air Show, by the image of the aviator Louis Blériot (who was soon to be celebrated as the first aviator to cross the English Channel), so seemingly relaxed, even bored, before take-off, so disciplined once up in the air. "One can see," writes Kafka, "his erect upper body above the wings; his legs extend deep down into the machine of which they have become a part. The setting sun . . . shines on the floating wings." Hesitating in midair for a moment, the plane suddenly lifts. "What is happening?" Kafka asks. "Up there, 20 metres above the earth, a man is imprisoned in a wooden cage and defends himself against a freely chosen invisible danger. We, however, stand below, wholly caught up in a trance and watch this man."[14]

Neither Marinetti nor Kafka nor Robert Delaunay, whose 1914 Synchronist painting *Homage to Blériot*, with its colorful biplanes circling a diminutive Eiffel Tower and its abstracted images of propellers, had any idea that the airplane, designed as it seemed to be for transportation and sport, would soon be used to drop bombs on one's enemy. War, in these heady years of the *avant-guerre*, was conceived as a kind of noisy purge – bang bang bang! – as in Marinetti's long onomatopoeic performance piece *Zang Tuum Tuumb*. Its consequences were simply not understood. The most recent European war, after all – the Franco-Prussian War – had taken place in 1870, before any of the Futurists were so much as born.

Accordingly, when the Futurists painters – Umberto Boccioni and Giacomo Balla, Carlo Carrà and Gino Severini, all of them from lower-middle class provincial backgrounds – took up Marinetti's call, they interpreted his prescriptions as aesthetic rather than political. Boccioni's *The City Rises* of 1910 (figure 7) can be seen as an almost textbook illustration of Marinetti's "We will sing of great crowds . . ." In *Futurist Painting: The Technical Manifesto* (1910), Boccioni made the case for a simultaneism as the new space–time of modernity: "How often have we not seen upon the cheek of the person with whom we are talking the horse which passes at the end of the street. Our bodies penetrate the sofas upon which we sit, and the sofas penetrate our bodies."[15] And his great bronze sculpture of 1913, *Unique Forms of Continuity in Space* (figure 8) fuses human, animal, and machine parts to create a monstrous helmeted, faceless and armless figure (with protruding swelled chest, narrow waist, and winged legs), striding the universe like a colossus.

7 Umberto Boccioni, *The City Rises*, 1910–11

In a similar vein, the Futurist architect Sant'Elia complained, in his *Manifesto of Futurist Architecture*, of the "supreme imbecility of modern architecture, perpetuated by the verbal complicity of the academies, the internment camps of the intelligentsia, where the young are forced into the onanistic recopying of classical models instead of throwing their minds open in the search for new frontiers."[16] But despite this violent language, Sant'Elia was essentially a visionary: his ink and colored pencil drawings for *La Città nuova* typically have airplane hangars on the roof even as trains and motorways pass through the buildings' underground chambers with a metal footway at street levels (see figure 9). Sant'Elia's buildings were inspired, at least in part, by the American skyscraper, but the Italian architect wanted a "tower" that would stand, not in isolation, but as part of a larger community structure. Accordingly, the geometric grid with its standard rectangular windows is everywhere embedded in the variegated rounded, elliptical, and conical masses that make the resulting structure look curiously weightless, permeable, and interpenetrating. Right angles intersect oblique surfaces in a structure notable for its decenteredness: the expected front entrance, for example, is replaced by a number of openings at unexpected sites. The tubular external elevator shafts (since imitated in dozens of skyscraper hotels) arise from a mysterious place below ground, whose location is not visible to the eye of the viewer. Indeed, the variety of levels and bridges, of ramps and tunnels, of metal filigree and solid concrete, and the differentiation of tower

8 Umberto Boccioni, *Unique Forms of Continuity in Space*, 1913

and balcony shapes, makes the whole structure seem to be floating. Such design, suggests Sanford Kwinter, sets the stage for the "truly polymorphous, procedural – action – or information-based-archictectures that began to emerge in the late '50s and '60s." Sant'Elia's New City "is a system . . . with no inside or outside, no center and no periphery, merely one virtual circulating substance – force – and its variety of actualized modes – linear, rotating, ascending, combining, transecting."[17]

9 Antonio Sant'Elia, *La Città nuova*

How to reconcile this visionary utopianism with the cult of war? In 1915, when Boccioni and Sant'Elia joined the Batallion of Cyclist Volunteers, they shared the patriotic fervor of their fellow-interventionists: war, for the moment, seemed like the next adventure in making oneself over. Disillusion rapidly set in. Shortly before he was killed in a fall from his horse in August 1916, Boccioni wrote in his diary:

I shall leave this existence with a contempt for all that is not art. There is nothing more terrible than art. Everything I see now is on the levels of games compared to a good brushstroke, a harmonious verse or a sound musical chord. By comparison everything else is a matter of mechanics, habit, patience of memory. Only art exists."[18]

As such poignant remarks reveal, the Futurists could never quite reconcile their aesthetics to their actual political situation. Energy, violent transformation, vision, technoculture, rejection of the past: these qualities animated the striking variety of Futurist experiments, from the performance art of the *serrate futuriste* (Futurist evenings), to cinema, radio, and the decorative arts. What the Italian movement lacked, however, was a built-in critique that would have made poets, artists, and architects understand the downside of novelty and ceaseless change. Marinetti's *Technical Manifesto of Futurist Literature* (1912) is a case in point. The manifesto makes the case for *parole in libertà*, words set free from the "straightjacket" of normal syntax. Poetry, Marinetti argued, could get rid of most parts of speech, especially the decorative adjective along with the adverb, that "old belt buckle that holds two words together." Punctuation was also to be eliminated so that poetry might be "an uninterrupted sequence of new images" – the "imagination without strings." Ezra Pound's Imagism comes directly out of this doctrine. And further: Marinetti advocated the destruction of "the *I* in literature; that is, all psychology"[19] – an idea that appealed enormously to D. H. Lawrence.[20] "To substitute for human psychology, now exhausted, the lyric obsession with matter": this seemed, on the face of it, a useful antidote to bourgeois individualism.[21] And this new materialist poetics would use, not free verse, but free words, scattered across the page.

Marinetti's own *parole in libertà* are, as Johanna Drucker points out in her book *The Visible Word*, among the finest early exemplars of visual poetics.[22] Certainly, these "poems" are more interesting than most of the normative Italian lyrics of the day, including Marinetti's own. But the endless cataloguing of "analogous" nouns, as in "noise + weight of the sun + orange odor of the sky + 20000 right angles," and onomatopoeic typographic units, capturing the sound and look of battle, as in *Karazouc-zouc-zouc/Karazouc-zouc-zouc/nadI-nadI AAAΛaaaaa*, is also tiresome in its simplification and reduction of experience. Marinetti's technical inventiveness far outstripped his powers of analysis and left him vulnerable to charges of mere bombast. For a more profound relation of avant-garde to the Great War, we must turn to the Russian variant of Futurism.

The Word as Such

In his memoir *My Futurist Years*, Roman Jakobson, himself once a Futurist poet under the pseudonym Aljagrov, describes the wild poetry evenings in

Moscow cafés in 1914, when he himself was still a teenage Gymnasium student and Vladimir Mayakovsky a mere twenty-one. When Marinetti, "the caffeine of Europe," as he was called, arrived in town, the poets were ready to challenge his ideas, "if not to 'throw rotten eggs,' as [Mikhail] Larionov proposed, then in any event to greet him with open hostility."[23] Still, Marinetti exerted his personal charm on the group:

> The atmosphere in the Alpine Rose was very friendly. When we were getting ready to leave there was a parting toast, and someone asked: "Will you come to visit us again soon?" Marinetti answered: "No, there will be a great war," and said that "we will be together with you against the Germans." I recall how Goncharova, quite strikingly, raised her hand and said: "To our meeting in Berlin!"[24]

Natalya Goncharova and her companion Mikhail Larionov were among the most radical and outspoken of the Russian Futurist artists; like Marinetti, they celebrated "the whole brilliant style of modern times – our trousers, jackets, shoes, trolleys, cars, airplanes, railways, grandiose steamships," and declared that "ours is a great epoch, one that has known no equal in the entire history of the world."[25] Performance artists, they painted their faces and ran through the Moscow streets in costume. At the same time – and here is where the paradox of the avant-garde comes in – Goncharova insisted on promoting an exclusively Russian art – especially icons and *lubki*, the peasant woodblocks which influenced such of her artist's books as *A Game in Hell*. "I shake the dust from my feet and leave the West," she declared in 1913, "considering its vulgarizing significance trivial and insignificant . . . my path is toward the source of all arts, the East." And in the Rayonist Manifesto of that year, she and Larionov declared, "Long live nationality!", setting the stage for Goncharova's pugnacious toast "to our meeting in Berlin."[26]

The sometimes bellicose nationalism of the Russian avant-garde no doubt reflected its provincial origins: most of the leading artists and poets who converged in Moscow and Petersburg came from the distant provinces: Mayakovsky from the Caucasus, Khlebnikov from the Caspian Sea, Kruchonykh from the southern Ukraine, and Malevich from a village near Kiev where his father worked in a sugar factory. In his autobiography, Malevich gives a moving account of his first contact, at age twelve, with professional artists – three painters sent down from Petersburg to paint icons in the village church – and how their example revolutionized his thinking.[27]

Rapidly urbanized and often living in poverty, the avant-garde embraced the cause of revolution. In their 1912 *A Slap in the Face of Public Taste* (1912), printed demotically on gray and brown wrapping paper with a sackcloth cover (the color, one reviewer wrote maliciously, is that of "a fainted louse"), the poets produced a manifesto that resembles Marinetti's in calling for the "overthrow" of the Academy and urging its reader to "Throw Pushkin, Dostoyevsky, Tolstoy, *et al.*, overboard from the Ship of Modernity."[28] The manifesto further called for a new language and descried all attempts at showing "good taste." *A Slap* was followed in 1913 by Khlebnikov and Kruchenykh's pamphlet *Slovo kak takovoe* ("The Word as Such"), which made the case for *zaum* or transrational poetry and declared that "New verbal form creates a new content, and not vice-versa."[29] The terms *sdvig* (shift, dislocation) and *faktura* (texture), so important to Russian Formalist theory a few years later, were put forward here, the general view being that "new poetry" requires an entirely new language. Even the letter, as the manifesto *The Letter as Such* put it, has magic properties.

The linguistic revolution not only preached but practiced by the Russian avant-garde was much more far-reaching than that of its Italian counterpart. Indeed, it remains central to poetics today: witness the so-called Language movement that came into being in the US in the mid-1970s – a movement that has strenuously made the case for the primacy of the signifier rather than its referent. At the same time, on the threshold of the 1914 war, Marinettian jingoism was echoed by poets like Mayakovsky. The latter had joined the Social Democratic party as early as 1908 when he was fourteen, and he was soon arrested and jailed for printing and distributing illegal literature. From then on, his spirit was resolutely agonistic – *contra*. The outbreak of war seemed to spell the overthrow of the hated autocratic regime. As his American biographer Edward J. Brown tells us:

> [Mayakovsky] was caught up in the mighty wave of patriotic and anti-German fever that infected all levels of Russian society in that year . . . Patriotic jingles to accompany propaganda posters occupied the poet from August to October 1914, and he even produced a number of drawings, an enterprise in which he was joined by many artists of the Russian avant garde . . . The posters, called *lubki*, were primitive in content, and aimed at a wide and tasteless audience. The verses were on the same level: Austrians and Germans figure as repellent cartoon characters impaled on the bayonets or pitchforks of brave Russian soldiers, defending the Slavic lands.[30]

Again, in "Civilian Shrapnel," a series of articles for the liberal magazine *Virgin Soil*, Mayakovsky declares that war is "magnificent" because it threatens to dislodge the philistines who have dominated poetry and replace them with a poetic muse who "wants to ride the gun-carriage wearing a hat of fiery orange feathers."[31]

The war, so it seemed at first, was merely the transition to the longed-for 1917 Revolution. "Cubism and Futurism," Malevich declared in 1919, "were revolutionary movements in art, anticipating the revolution in economic and political life of 1917."[32] But of course it didn't work out that way. The Russian Futurists assumed naïvely that being avant-garde was preparation enough for the construction of the new proletarian state. But, as Leon Trotsky wrote in *Literature and Revolution* (1922):

> To say that Futurism has freed art of its thousand-year-old bonds of Bourgeoisdom is to estimate thousands of years very cheaply. The call of The Futurists to break with the past, to do away with Pushkin, to liquidate tradition, etc., has a meaning insofar as it is addressed . . . to the closed-in circle of the Intelligentsia. In other words, it has meaning only insofar as the Futurists are busy cutting the cord which binds them to the priests of bourgeois literary tradition. But the meaninglessness of this call becomes evident as soon as it is addressed to the proletariat. The working class does not have to, and cannot know the old literature, it still has to commune with it, it still has to master Pushkin, to absorb him, and so overcome him.[33]

The argument that aesthetic change by no means guarantees meaningful political change has been made throughout the twentieth century. It is an argument that, like its opposite, is always simplified. In the case of the Russian avant-garde, the most interesting case (and one that goes against the common wisdom of Mayakovsky or even Malevich) is that of Khlebnikov.

An ardent Germanophobe, before the war, Khlebnikov was given to declaring that he eagerly awaited the moment when "the Russian steeds" would "trample the streets of Berlin." But when he was drafted on 8 April 1916, he seems to have had a wholesale conversion. As an enlisted man in the 2nd company of the 93rd Reserve Infantry Regiment, Khlebnikov felt totally lost. He wrote his friend Nikolai Kulbin that "he could not remain a soldier because he had already sworn an oath to poetry."[34] On 8 April 1916, he wrote the following poem, this one down-to-earth and realistic unlike his earlier avant-garde experiments:

> Me too? You mean I'll have to grab a gun
> (a dumb thing, heavier
> than handwriting)
> and go marching down some highway,
> beating out 365 × 317 regular heartbeats a day?
> Knock my head to fragments and forget
> the government of twenty-two-year olds,
> that attack the madness of elder statesmen?

Another gnomic little poem reads:

> The King is out of luck:
> The King is under lock
>   And key
> Infantry Regiment Ninety-three
> Will be the death of the child in me.

And a lyric called "Palm Sunday" contains the lines:

> From the pen of war comes one full stop after another,
> graveyards grow suburbs like capital cities –
> different people, different dispositions.
> The whole wide world has bandaged its feet
> in ragged strips of young men's bodies . . .[35]

The outbreak of the Revolution freed Khlebnikov, at least for the moment: he left his regiment, wandered from place to place, sometimes falling into the hands of the Reds, sometimes the Whites. By 1920, he was living near Baku on the Caspian sea, working feverishly on his mathematical theory of history, to be published as *The Tables of Destiny*. In 1921, he was briefly back in Moscow, preparing his writings for publication; then he left again, hoping to return to his family home in Astrakhan, but died before he could get there.

In a statement about his work (1919), Khlebnikov declared, "I swore to discover the Laws of Time and carved that promise on a birch tree (in the village of Burmakino, Yaroslavl) when I heard about the battle of Tsushima."[36] The reference is to the Russo–Japanese War of 1904–5, but it might have been about World War I and the Civil Wars as well. To explain to himself the horrors of death in battle, Khlebnikov had to invent a series of complex mathematical formulae, based on the algorithms of 2 and 3. *The Tables of Destiny* seems almost perverse in its elaborate numerology, but the fantastical and gnomic book provides us with what Yeats called, with reference to *A Vision*, "metaphors for poetry." The prophetic books present, for example, new theories of space/time in exceptionally rich metaphoric language, in keeping with Khlebnikov's earlier *Zaum* poetry.[37]

In February 1921, Khlebnikov, then living on the Russian/Persian border, wrote sadly to Mayakovsky, "The writer's inkwell is dry, and the fly was *not* amused when it dove in for a swim." And he adds, "I have studied much and become a master of numbers. I could create a springtime of numbers, if only the presses were working. But instead of a heart I seem to have something resembling a chunk of wood or a kippered herring."[38] But in these years he wrote a series called "Hunger," which gives one of the most vivid pictures we have of the famine of the Civil War years. Here is a lyric from the "In the Village" section:

> In the hut next door with the board roof
> a grim-faced father
> broke up the bread into breadcrumbs
> with hardened fingers.
> only to look at.
> It wouldn't fill a sparrow, the one
> that chirped just now.
> You eat with your eyes nowadays.
> "Times aren't right," the father muttered.
> The black bread looked like topsoil
> With bits of ground-up pine cone.
> At least their eyes can eat.
> Mother stood by the stove,
> white with pain.
> Black coals of hunger
> burn in the pits of her eyes.
> The thin slice of a white mouth.[39]

The matter-of-factness of this little poem is astonishing. The contrast of black and white – the "black coals of hunger" versus the "thin slice of a white mouth" – the notion of eating only with one's *eyes*, the transferred epithet in the last line, in which slice refers not to the bread but to the mother's mouth, and the suggestion that soon the family may well be eating topsoil filled with ground-up pine cones – these stark images are presented without comment; there is no moralizing about war and its sufferings, no generalization of any sort. Although Paul Schmidt's colloquial translation cannot capture the sound structure of this poem, its pain comes through.

The sequence continues in this vein:

> Roast mouse.
> Their son fixed it, went and
> Caught them in the field.
> They lie stretched out on the table,
> Their long dark tails.
> Today it's a decent dinner,
> A real good meal!
> Just a while back the housewife would shudder
> and holler, smash the pitcher to smithereens
> if she found a mouse drowned in the cream.
> But now, how silent and peaceful.

Dead mice for dinner
stretched out on the table,
dangling dark tails . . .⁴⁰

Again, the lyric is depersonalized, documentary, imagistic, almost casual. Ironically, in ways Marinetti did not anticipate, war did turn out to be "the hygiene of the people," in that it eliminated so many of them from the earth. The death motif dominates Khlebnikov's later work as it does Mayakovsky's in the years preceding his suicide.

The Great Wheel and the Tower

The Russian situation is thus particularly dark but it was also the situation that produced what were perhaps the greatest avant-garde works. Now let us go back to the more equivocal situation in the France of the early war years, when Apollinaire so romantically celebrated "les jeunes de la classe 1915."

Here the key figure is the poet, novelist, travel-writer, journalist Blaise Cendrars, whose *La Prose du Transsibérien et de la petite Jeanne de France* (1913) anticipates the Great War in uncanny ways. John Dos Passos, who translated and illustrated this and other Cendrars poems in a beautiful edition of 1931, has this to say in his Foreword:

> The poetry of Blaise Cendrars was part of the creative tidal wave that spread over the world from the Paris of before the last European war. Under various tags, futurism, vorticism, modernism, most of the best work in the arts of our time has been the direct product of this explosion, that had an influence in its sphere comparable with that of the October revolution in social organization and politics and the Einstein formula in physics.

Dos Passos cites Joyce and Stein, the early Eliot and Wyndham Lewis, Stravinsky and the Diaghilev ballet, and concludes sadly:

> Meanwhile, in America at least, poetry (or verse, or little patches of prose cut into inevitable lengths on the page, or whatever you want to call it) has, after Masters, Sandburg and the Imagists, subsided again into parlor entertainment for highschool English Classes.
>
> The stuffed shirts have come out of their libraries everywhere and rule literary taste . . . A young man just starting to read verse in the year 1930 would have a hard time finding out that this method of putting words together had only recently passed through a period of virility, intense experimentation and meaning in everyday life.⁴¹

In Cendrars's case, the "intense experimentation" involved verbal–visual collaboration. As published by the radical press *Les Hommes nouveaux*, *La Prose du Transsibérien* bore the subtitle, "poems, simultaneous colors, in an edition attaining the height of the Eiffel Tower." The "first simultaneous book," as it was advertised, was made up of a single sheet of paper, divided down the center, which unfolded like an accordion, through twenty-two panels to a length of almost seven feet. The height of the Eiffel Tower was to be attained by lining up the 150 copies of the text vertically. The book was the collaboration of Cendrars and the painter Sonia Delaunay (see figure 10). The left half contains Delaunay's painted semi-abstract forms in bright primary colors, culminating at the bottom in a small Eiffel Tower, like an innocent red phallus, penetrating an orange Great Wheel with a green center. On the right, the text, prefaced by a Michelin railway map of the Trans-Siberian journey from Moscow to the Sea of Japan, similarly moves down the page.[42]

But Delaunay's visual images by no means "illustrate" Cendrars's poem. On the contrary, the visual and verbal seem to be intentionally at odds. There is nothing in Sonia Delaunay's warm, colorful biomorphic forms that matches the violence and anxiety of Cendrars's poem. But the mood of "La Prose" was itself deeply ambivalent as even Cendrars's letters testify. "This war," Cendrars wrote to a friend in September 1914 on his way to the Front (as a Swiss national, whose real name was Freddy Sauser, he had enlisted in the French Foreign Legion), "is a painful delivery, needed to give birth to liberty. It fits me like a glove. Reaction or Revolution – man must become more human. I will return. There can be no doubt." And a little later, "The war has saved my life. This sounds like a paradox, but a hundred times I have told myself that if I had continued to live with those people [the bohemian artists of Montparnasse], I would have croaked."[43]

Like the Futurists, Cendrars was yearning for some sort of apocalypse. But the long poem he had written a year earlier – he called it "La Prose" because "Poem seems too pretentious, too closed. Prose is more open, popular"[44] – is full of violent imagery that moves from the exuberance of the opening to the horror and bloodshed of its later sections. In the Dos Passos translation, *The Prose of the Transsiberian* begins:

> I was a youngster in those days,
> Hardly sixteen and already I couldn't remember my childhood.
> I was sixteen thousand leagues away from the place I was born,
> I was in Moscow, the city of a thousand and three belfries and
>   seven railroadstations,
> And the seven railroadstations and the thousand and three
>   belfries weren't enough for me

10 Blaise Cendrars and Sonia Delaunay, *La Prose du Transsibérien et de la petite Jeanne de France*, 1913

For youth was so burning and so mad
That my heart smoldered like the temple of Ephesus or
    flared like the Red Square in Moscow
At sundown.
And my eyes were headlights on the old roads.
I was already such a poor poet
That I never knew how to get to the end of things . . .[45]

VORTEX IS ENERGY! In the opening strophes of Cendrars's poem, violence is a form of sexual exuberance and adolescent excitement, but even in the early Moscow scenes, this exuberance is tinged with pain. The sun, for example, is seen as a "festering wound," a "crumbling ember." And in the fourth strophe, we read:

There wasn't enough in the towers and the terminals that
    filled my eyes with stars
Guns thundered war in Siberia
Hunger cold plague cholera
Millions of corpses rolled over and over in the silty stream
    of the Amur.[46]

The reference here, as in Khlebnikov, is to the Russo-Japanese War of 1904–05, specifically to the Battle of Port Arthur in Manchuria, but Cendrars's account of being "swallowed into the war like into a tunnel" eerily anticipates the Great War and his own role in it. For a time, as the poet journeys eastward, he is thrilled with his adventure and distracts his companion "little Jeanne," whose homesick refrain, "Say, Blaise, are we very far from Montmartre?", punctuates the poem with fantastic science-fiction stories about the Fiji islands, where "Couples faint with love in the long grass," and the "high plateaus" of Mexico where "the tulip trees grow tall" and "the tousled lianas are the sun's hair." Speed and flight, so ubiquitous in the literature of the *avant-guerre*, are central to these surreal fantasies:

If you want we'll take an airplane and fly over the country
of a thousand lakes,
Where the nights are unreasonably long;
The prehistoric ancestor'll be scared of my motor
I'll make a landing
And build a hangar for my airplane out of fossil bones of
mammoths.[47]

But the clowning can't be sustained. Jeanne falls asleep (and later unaccountably disappears from the scene), and as the train draws nearer Mongolia, the poet's vision, rather like Rimbaud's in *Le Bateau ivre*, darkens:

I've seen
I've seen the silent trains the black trains coming back from
the Far East that passed like haunts
And my eye like the red light on the rear car still speeds
behind those trains.
At Talga 100,000 wounded dying for lack of care;
I went through all the hospitals of Krasnoyarsk
And at Khilok we passed a long hospital train full of soldiers
that had gone mad;
I saw the dressing stations the widening gashes of wounds,
bleeding at full throb
And amputated limbs dance or fly off into the shrieking wind.
Conflagration flared in every face in every heart . . .[48]

And after further hallucinatory visions, the poet gets off the train at the "last station": "When I got off at Harbin they'd just set fire to the offices of the Red Cross."[49]

For the reader who knows that Cendrars was to lose his right forearm in 1916, the reference to "amputated limbs" dancing or flying off "into the shrieking wind" is quite surreal. In 1913, after all, Europe was at peace and no one could have known what would happen within the year. Yet here in Cendrars's hallucinatory war dispatch, we have "100,000 wounded dying for lack of care," soldiers "gone mad," and the "widening gashes of wounds, bleeding at full throb" – exactly as those wounds would bleed in the war to come. Indeed, Cendrars's imagery prefigures the poet's own exclamation in *Au coeur du monde* (1917), written not long after his arm had been amputated, *Ma main coupée brille au ciel dans la constellation d'Orion* ("My cut-off hand shines in the sky in the constellation of Orion").[50] And further: *main coupée* reminds us of the famous last line of Apollinaire's "Zone" (1913), in which the rising sun is paradoxically seen as a broken neck: "Soleil cou coupé."

Yet it is important to note that neither Cendrars nor Apollinaire ever turned to pacifist poetry. Violence, energy, *Die Flucht nach Vorne* – these were judged to be the very spark of life. As the poet of *Au coeur du monde* puts it, "I am the man who no longer has a past."[51] And so, in the last section of *The Prose of the Transsiberian*, the "last station," with its image of burning offices of the Red Cross, suddenly vanishes and, as in film montage, Paris reappears – a Paris the poet seems never to have left. Paris is now invoked as that "great warm hearth with the crisscrossed brands of your streets and the old houses leaning over them and warming themselves." And if Paris is the center of the universe, its own center is the *gare centrale*, that "Central terminal, transfer station of the will, crossroad of unrest."[52] In the spirit of

Futurism, Cendrars calls the *gare centrale* "the finest church in the world." But the past is not so easily occluded: notice the lassitude, the *tristesse* of the poem's conclusion, in which an ordinary Blaise, no longer the charming adolescent who doesn't know where to stop or the imaginative adventurer conjuring up scenes of tropical island magic, goes to the Lapin Agile to have a few drinks. And *The Prose* concludes with the invocation:

> Paris
> Ville de la Tour unique du grand Gibet et de la Roue.
>
> Paris
> City of the only Tower and the great Scaffold and the Wheel.[53]

No longer is the Eiffel Tower the charming and colorful icon of Apollinaire and the Delaunays. For Paris is also the city of the great Scaffold or Guillotine, and although the Wheel is literally the great ferris wheel erected next to the Eiffel Tower for the Paris Exposition of 1900, it is also the wheel of life and, given its juxtaposition to the scaffold, of death.

In this sense, Cendrars's poem captures, as well as any poem or fiction I can think of, the promise of the *avant-guerre* and its impending destruction by the Great War. Interestingly, even the absurdly grandiose daydreams with which Blaise entertains Jeanne contain negative images. In the Fiji Islands, where "Couples faint with love in the long grass," "syphilis stalks where it's warm under the banana trees."[54] So much for tropical paradise. But for Cendrars, such contradictions are never the occasion for moralizing or meditation; rather, he wants to convey, as fully as possible, what the actual mechanized landscape – a landscape into which war will inevitably erupt – is like.

For the contemporary reader, accustomed to equating "war poetry" with "anti-war poetry," the response of the avant-garde to World War I must seem problematic, if not reprehensible. How can we read a poet who declares that "War is the hygiene of the people"? And how could such writers as Cendrars and Khlebnikov not have undertaken a strenuous critique of the ideology of war or have worked to prevent future wars? There are, I think, two answers. First, as I have argued throughout this chapter, the word "war" carried very different meanings in 1914 from those it carries today. But second – and more important – it is only when poetry plays a minor role in society, when, as is the case today, it tends to be equated with elevated thought and vague moral uplift and is obviously not designed to *change* anything, that the public expects the poet to be a "nice" person, a spokesman for justice, freedom, and "right thinking." But history teaches us that the ethical and the aesthetic have rarely been equivalent, as Plato, who banished the poets from the republic, was the first to know.

A case in point is the artist who was perhaps the greatest avant-gardist of the war era – Marcel Duchamp. When war was declared in August 1914, Duchamp was twenty-five years old. Both his brothers were called up within the first few weeks, but Duchamp, having completed his one year of military service, was temporarily exempt. He was working on the *Nine Malic Molds* and did not wish to be distracted. By October, many of his fellow-artists – Picabia, Léger, Braque, Gleizes, Metzinger – had been called up and his sister had joined the nursing corps. As Calvin Tomkins tells it:

> As the fighting intensified and the German troops overran Belgium, deferments were canceled. Duchamp was summoned before a draft board in January 1915. In the course of his physical exam however, it was discovered that he had a slight rheumatic heart murmur – nothing serious, but enough to keep him out of the army. "I have been condemned to remain a civilian for the entire duration of the war," he wrote to [his patron, Walter] Pach who was back in New York by this time. "They found me too *sick* to be a soldier. I am not too sad about this decision: you know it well."[55]

Despite the taunts of friends and relatives, Duchamp had only one plan: to leave Paris and go to New York. He arrived in June 1915, and the war years proved to be his most productive: it was in this period that he made his most famous readymades and completed most of the work on the *Large Glass*.

When the US entered the war in April 1917, Duchamp was soon looking for a way to escape yet again. This time he chose Buenos Aires, a city as far removed from the action as possible, a city where there were no recruiting posters or wartime restrictions and he knew no one. Having made elaborate arrangements for the storage of his art works in the interim, Duchamp sailed for Buenos Aires in September 1918. German submarines were said to be a threat, but the voyage turned out to be quite calm. "Delightful voyage," Duchamp wrote to his young friends Florine and Ettie Stettheimer, "The boat is slow and gentle."[56] He had been in Buenos Aires only three weeks when he received the news that his brother Raymond Duchamp-Villon, who had been wounded at the Front near Champagne, had died of typhoid fever. It was a great personal tragedy – the brothers were very close – but it did nothing to change Duchamp's aloofness from the war. On the contrary, after the Armistice was signed in November, he stayed on in Argentina, returning to France only in June 1919, and then only for four months since, by this time, he recognized that his artistic life was in America. And art was what this ostensible anti-artist lived for.

In his own day, Duchamp was judged harshly by French artists (and some American ones) for his apolitical stance, his indifference to the fate of his country. But today we tend to judge such matters differently: Duchamp, we posit, did what he felt had to do, and the great art works are there to support his decision. Who, in any case, was right? Duchamp or his alter ego Ludwig Wittgenstein, who left Cambridge to enlist in the Austrian army as soon as war was declared, believing that the war (of which he wholly disapproved) was a testing ground, a trial that would "turn [him] into a different person."[57] The war, he told a nephew many years later, "saved my life; I don't know what I'd have done without it."[58] Here Wittgenstein is referring to the personal crisis, triggered by the war, that made him rethink the propositions and mode of the *Tractatus*.

Yet just a few months into the war, the same Wittgenstein wrote in his secret journal:

> I feel . . . more than ever the tragedy of our – the German race's – situation! For that we cannot defeat England seems to me as good as certain. The English – the best race in the world – *cannot* lose! We, however, can lose and will lose, if not this year then the next. The thought that our race will be defeated depresses me terribly because I am German through and through![59]

On the face of it, this remark is oddly irrational. Neither England nor Germany represented a "race," and even if a given nation were "the best race in the world," victory in war was hardly guaranteed. Still, Wittgenstein's remark is as poignant as it is endearing, largely because he takes the whole matter so seriously, assuming that it is up to *him* – to the *individual* – to *understand* what is happening. It is this complexity and unexpectedness of response that makes the writing and art-making of World War I so fascinating. Nothing is taken for granted: the Great War, viewed positively or negatively, is simply *there* as a terrifying fact of life – the decisive event of modernism.

NOTES

1. Guillaume Apollinaire, *Calligrammes*, trans. Anne Hyde Greet (Berkeley: University of California Press, 1980), 160–61.
2. Modris Eksteins, *Rites of Spring: The Great War and the Birth of the Modern Age* (Boston: Houghton Mifflin, 1989), 73.
3. *Ibid.*, xv, 92, 94.
4. Rose-Carol Washton Long, ed., *German Expressionism, Documents from the End of the Wilhelmine Empire to the Rise of National Socialism* (Berkeley: University of California Press, 1993), 47.
5. Eksteins, *Rites of Spring*, 94.

6. Richard Huelsenbeck, *Memoirs of a Dada Drummer*, ed. Hans. J. Kleinschmidt, trans. Joachim Neugroschel (New York: Viking, 1974), xiii.

7. *Ibid.*, 2.

8. Pontus Hulten, ed., *Futurism & Futurisms* (New York: Abbeville Press, 1986), 17.

9. F. T. Marinetti, *Selected Writings*, ed. and trans. R. W. Flint (New York: Farrar, Straus and Giroux, 1972), 42.

10. *Ibid.*, 39.

11. *Ibid.*, 40.

12. Ezra Pound, *Gaudier-Brzeska* (1916; New York: New Directions, 1970), 22, 92.

13. Marinetti, *Selected Writings*, 42.

14. Franz Kafka, "Die Aeroplane in Brescia," *Bohemia* 82 (no. 269), 29 September 1909, 1–3, 3. My translation. The German text is available at www/unimarburg.de/~naeser/brescia/htm.

15. Umbrio Apollonio, ed., *Futurist Manifestos* (Boston: MFA Art Works, 2001), 28.

16. *Ibid.*, 169.

17. Sanford Kwinter, *Architectures of Time: Toward a Theory of the Event in Modernist Culture* (Cambridge, Mass.: MIT Press, 2001), 65.

18. Caroline Tisdall and Angelo Bozzolla, *Futurism* (New York: Oxford University Press, 1978), 181.

19. Marinetti, *Selected Writings*, 84, 87.

20. See D. H. Lawrence, letter to Arthur MacLeod, 2 June 1914, and letter to Edward Garnett, 5 June 1914, in *The Cambridge Edition of the Letters of D. H. Lawrence*, vol. II, 1913–16, ed. George J. Zytaruk and James T. Boulton (Cambridge: Cambridge University Press, 1981), 180–87.

21. Marinetti, *Selected Writings*, 87.

22. Johanna Drucker, *The Visible Word: Experimental Typography and Modern Art, 1909–1923* (Chicago: University of Chicago Press, 1994), 105–40.

23. Roman Jakobson, *My Futurist Years*, ed. Bengt Nagfeldt, trans. Stephen Rudy (New York: Marsilio, 1992), 20.

24. *Ibid.*, 22.

25. See John Bowlt, ed., *Russian Art of the Avant-Garde: Theory and Criticism 1902–1934* (New York: Viking, 1976), 89.

26. *Ibid.*, 55, 90.

27. Kasimir Malevich, "Chapters from an Artist's Autobiography," trans. Alan Upchurch, *October*, 34 (1985): 25–44; see 31–32.

28. Vladimir Markov, *Russian Futurism: A History* (Berkeley: University of California Press, 1968), 46.

29. *Ibid.*, 131.

30. Edward J. Brown, *Mayakovsky, A Poet in the Revolution* (Princeton: Princeton University Press, 1973), 109–10.

31. See *ibid.*, 111.

32. Kasimir Malevich, *Essays on Art, 1915–1933*, 2 vols., ed. Troels Andersen, trans. Xenia Glowacki-Prus and Arnold McMillin, 2nd edn. (London: Rapp and Whiting, 1968), I, 94.

33. Leon Trotsky, *Literature and Revolution* (1922; New York: Russell and Russell, 1957), 130.

34. Markov, *Russian Futurism*, 298, 299.

35. Velimir Khlebnikov, *Collected Writings*, vol. III: *Selected Poems*, trans. Paul Schmidt (Cambridge, Mass.: Harvard University Press, 1997), 51, 51–52, 52–53.
36. Khlebnikov, *Collected Writings*, vol. I: *Letters and Theoretical Writings*, trans. Paul Schmidt (Cambridge, Mass.: Harvard University Press, 1987), 148.
37. See Marjorie Perloff, *Twenty-First Century Modernism: The "New" Poetics* (Cambridge: Blackwell, 2002), 121–54.
38. Khlebnikov, *Collected Writings*, I, 128.
39. Khlebnikov, *Collected Writings*, III, 106.
40. *Ibid.*
41. John Dos Passos, Foreword to Blaise Cendrars, *Panama or the Adventures of My Seven Uncles and Other Poems*, trans. and illustrated by John Dos Passos, bilingual edn. (1931; Paris: Denoël, 1994), 31–32.
42. See Marjorie Perloff, *The Futurist Moment: Avant-Garde, Avant-Guerre, and the Language of Rupture* (1986; Chicago: University of Chicago Press, 2003), 3–13.
43. See Blaise Cendrars, *Oeuvres complètes* (Paris: Le Club français du livre, 1969), vol. XVI: *Inédits secrets*, ed. Miriam Cendrars, 398, my translation; cf. Jay Bochner, *Blaise Cendrars: Discovery and Re-Creation* (Toronto: University of Toronto Press, 1978), 56–59.
44. Cendrars, *Inédits secrets*, 371.
45. Dos Passos, trans. Cendrars, *Panama*, 37–38.
46. *Ibid.*, 40.
47. *Ibid.*, 64, 66.
48. *Ibid.*, 75–76.
49. *Ibid.*, 80.
50. Blaise Cendrars, *Oeuvres complètes*, vol. I: *Poésies complètes* (Paris: Denoël, 1946), 196.
51. *Ibid.*, 197.
52. Dos Passos, trans. Cendrars, *Panama*, 80, 82.
53. *Ibid.*,
54. *Ibid.*, 64.
55. Calvin Tomkins, *Duchamp* (New York: Henry Holt, 1996), 140.
56. *Ibid.*, 207.
57. Ray Monk, *Ludwig Wittgenstein: The Duty of Genius* (New York: The Free Press, 1990), 111–16.
58. Brian McGuiness, *Wittgenstein: A Life*, vol. I: *Young Ludwig 1889–1921* (Berkeley: University of California Press, 1988), 204.
59. Monk, *Ludwig Wittgenstein*, 113–14.

7

CATHARINE SAVAGE BROSMAN

French writing of the Great War

The fifty-month-long Great War affected France as no other country. With dozens of major battles on its territory, greater losses per capita than any other nation in men wounded and killed (some 1,385,000 dead out of 39 million in 1914), countless villages destroyed or disfigured and woods, fields, orchards ruined, France, the chief prize, was also the chief casualty of the war, both physically and emotionally. The effects persisted for decades and indeed last until this day. The scars left on the countryside and the national consciousness were deep, and few aspects of French life were left untouched. No town or village is without its memorial, prominently located. Some areas were permanently depopulated: twelve villages destroyed around Verdun, the site of the bloodiest battle, which France fought alone for over 300 days, have never been rebuilt, although a chapel has been erected on each site, and thousands of acres there remain off-limits because of live shells. The number of deaths and mutilations contributed to a serious decrease in the birthrate, already much lower than Germany's before 1914, and to national obsession with natality. Maurice Barrès, a militant nationalist from Lorraine, whose wartime journalism fills fourteen volumes, wondered whether France could recover from the bleeding. The French recoiled from the idea of further fighting on their territory; the rapid collapse of 1940 is not unrelated to awful memories of the previous war. Early in World War II, for instance, peasants removed army mines strategically placed to help protect against invasion.

That, despite the ultimate victory of the Allies over German *Kultur*, what was called "civilization" likewise was a casualty has been widely acknowledged. To many French, around 1900, the word *civilisation* had designated a society built on premises – or national myths – developed from the Revolution of 1789 onward, especially during the Third Republic, established after the Franco-Prussian War (1870–71). Among these was the doctrine of progress. Victor Hugo stated it clearly: "Le progrès est le mode de l'homme. La vie générale du genre humain s'appelle le Progrès; le pas collectif du genre humain s'appelle le Progrès" (Progress is the mode of mankind.

Human life in general is called Progress; the collective step of human beings is called Progress).[1] The same vision of improvement inspired Emile Zola's novel of the Franco-Prussian War, *La Débâcle* (1892), in which he imagined a greater, purer France arising ultimately from the ashes of defeat.

The prewar period, or *belle époque*, seemed to justify this vision. France had recovered its position as a great power and prospered, notwithstanding huge indemnities paid earlier to Germany and the loss of Alsace and part of industrial Lorraine. Economic stability appeared assured. National security was reinforced by laws requiring two years of military service (1905), then three (1913). Despite national rivalries, European balance of power was maintained, and revolutionary agitation checked. Foreign musicians and painters flocked to the French capital, joining a dynamic Parisian avant-garde. New literary stars shone; in 1913 alone there appeared a half-dozen brilliant and highly original works.

French society was not, however, monolithic: class structure bred unrest, many Catholics had never accepted the republic, and France had been shaken in the 1890s by the drawn-out, divisive Dreyfus Affair, which pitted the army, church, monarchists, and other conservatives against republican liberals – socialists, anti-clericals, Jews. Xenophobia grew; anti-republicanism was rampant; acts of anarchy threatened stability. The 1905 law separating church and state polarized still further conservatives and republicans. Papal reaction was vehement: earlier calls for "rallying" to the republic, largely unheeded anyway, were dropped. Membership in the Socialist party increased dramatically; anti-patriotic and anti-militarist sentiments became more pronounced. Georges Sorel's *Réflexions sur la violence* (1906), advocating the General Strike, preceded a wave of labor unrest.

To these disorders were added international disputes arising from colonial competition, first with England, then, more seriously, with Germany, whose sabre-rattling led to grave incidents, especially in 1911 at Agadir (Morocco). The novelist Roger Martin du Gard wrote, "Cette crise démolit tous mes espoirs intellectuels, toutes mes convictions, toute ma foi dans le progrès . . . Je pense que rien de tout cela n'en sortira indemne" (This crisis demolishes all my intellectual hopes, all my convictions, all my faith in progress. I believe that none of that will come out of this unscathed).[2] Other intimations of disorder followed, confirmed by events in summer 1914. Many thoughtful observers were dismayed.

Yet upon declaration of war by France, "an outpouring of patriotic fervour affected all classes . . . the humiliations of 1870 and 1871 would be reversed."[3] (The frenzy was international; in Russia, the czar's cousin, Nicholas Mikhailovich, wrote on 30 July 1914: "Everyone is for the war and not one discordant note has been sounded to date."[4]) The *union sacrée*, or national agreement to prosecute the war, appeared broadly based. Although many disagreed with the policy, which violated their party traditions, the Socialists joined in the hope that war would bring about an international society eschewing national and class interests. Patriotic rhetoric was accepted widely by writers, painters, thinkers. "C'est la guerre de la civilisation . . . La guerre à la guerre" (It's the war of civilization . . . War against war).[5]

Shortly, however, preconceptions about the conflict – its duration, its modes of prosecution – were challenged, and the unprecedented destructiveness, German entrenchment, and a near-stalemate forced attitudes to change. Though Marcel Proust, in *Le Temps retrouvé* (*Time Regained*), gently mocks the cliché about the prewar – a time "dont il est convenu de dire que nous sommes séparés par des siècles . . . tout lien est rompu avec le passé" (from which it is conventional to say we are separated by centuries . . . every tie is broken with the past) – French war fiction both reflected and accentuated awareness that France was irrevocably changed.[6] The supposedly humane foundations of Europe appeared undermined. Georges Duhamel, a physician who served four years and performed 2,000 operations, intended his title *Civilisation* (a collection of war sketches) as ironic and antiphrastic. Paul Valéry wrote that the Great War "n'a fait qu'accuser et précipiter le mouvement de décadence de l'Europe" (only made clearer and hastened the movement of European decadence). The result: "Nous autres civilisations, nous savons maintenant que nous sommes mortelles" (We civilizations now know that we are mortal).[7] Later, the outbreak of the second world conflict scarcely more than twenty years after the first ended brought corroboration to such pessimism. Although some viewed the Great War dialectically, in Zola's manner, as the evil that would restore a compromised national community, by 1940 visions of a new society to rise from the ashes were either dead or transposed to still another postwar.

Among prewar writings that shaped the national mood and promoted enthusiasm for war are novels connected to the French Nationalist Revival, calling for recovery of the lost territories and revenge, in contrast to the rapprochement with Germany favored by some.[8] The argument was that Germans and French were of different races, unalterably opposed and irreconcilable. (By "race" was meant national stock, not a broader anthropological category.) In *Colette Baudoche* (1909), by Barrès, the heroine rejects the suit of a German who boards in her mother's house in occupied Metz; he is a foreigner. The implication is clear: what is desirable is not cooperation across the Rhine, but affirmation of national identity and recovery of integral portions of France amputated through German aggression. This attitude assumed what Marshal Philippe Pétain would later call Eternal France, deterministically rooted in the past, the people, the territory.[9] That in fact there was no *single* ethos in the politically and culturally divided nation was unimportant.

Essays by Ernest Psichari – *L'Appel des armes* (1913) (The Call to Arms) and *Le Voyage du centurion* (1915) (The Centurion's Journey) – developed the theme of French renewal through devotion to nation and God. A grandson of the positivist historian Ernest Renan, Psichari denounced the doctrine of progress, attempted to rehabilitate the military's image (tarnished in the Dreyfus Affair), and proclaimed an ethic of purity and abnegation, borne out by his death in battle, 1914. Unlike writings by Charles Maurras of *L'Action française* (the newspaper, a daily from 1908, of the monarchist movement by the same name), Psichari's are not polemics, but a philosophical attempt to ground patriotic service.

More widely read was journalist Charles Péguy, an unorthodox, non-Marxist socialist, defender of Dreyfus, and eloquent nationalist whose death at the Marne added authority to his voice. Although he dedicated his *Jeanne d'Arc* (1897) in part to martyrs for the future Universal Socialist Republic, his anti-intellectualism, Catholicism (sentimental and heterodox), and nostalgic attachment to an essential France, especially medieval France, precluded his being a true internationalist; he was, in fact, the antithesis of the modern. In the climate of increasing Franco-German rivalry, his 1905 essay *Notre patrie* (*Our Fatherland*) challenged socialist pacifism and celebrated patriotism. This patriotism grew more militant and magnetized his literary energies in dramas and poetry. He was, as one historian writes, "happily resigned to war."[10] "Heureux ceux qui sont morts pour la terre charnelle / Mais pourvu que ce fût dans une juste guerre" (Happy are those who have died for the carnal earth / But provided that it were in a just war).[11]

The literary effects of the Great War were enormous; for many writers, it was the defining moment of their lives, as the Dreyfus Affair had been for their elders. These effects included the death of promising young writers and of established authors (Péguy, Alain-Fournier) who otherwise would have continued brilliant careers, presumably; imprisonment of some (Jacques Rivière, for instance); injury or mental trauma to others, resulting in an interrupted career or changed outlook, often pacifism or profound alienation. Guillaume Apollinaire's injury probably made him vulnerable to influenza, which killed him; Pierre Drieu La Rochelle's frontline experiences and hospitalizations seem to have shaken all his moorings, leading to wavering politics, hatred of "soft" France, self-destructive behavior, admiration for Germans, and collaboration during the second war, finally suicide; Louis-Ferdinand Céline's misanthropy and pessimism – even his profound anti-Semitism – were not unrelated to near-loss of his arm; Blaise Cendrars *did* lose an arm; Joë Bousquet, paralyzed by battle injury, took many years to find his literary voice. Various cultural undertakings, such as the monthly *La Nouvelle Revue française* and Jacques Copeau's Théâtre du Vieux-Colombier, were suspended.

The war produced also more felicitous literary results. Publication of his innovative seven-part novel, which began with *Du côté de chez Swann* (*Swann's Way*) (1913), having been suspended, Proust rewrote it from the galley proofs, expanding it immensely. Although André Gide ceased publishing for five years, the somber atmosphere of Verdun and the Somme is reflected in his moving notebook of 1916, *Numquid et tu . . .?* (first trade edition 1926). Valéry, having begun before 1914 what was to be a short poem, had composed only fragments. "Vint la guerre" (War came).[12] Under its shadow, he developed them into a 512-line poem, *La Jeune Parque*, 1917 (*The Young Fate*), whose verbal beauty, illustrating brilliantly the poetic resources of French and thus glorifying his nation, masked his anguish.

Literary continuity was, furthermore, not entirely broken by the unprecedented conflict. Zola's naturalistic "slice of life," cut from raw experience, featuring often-common characters in sordid circumstances and the triumph of nature over culture, thus tending toward pessimism, proved itself in day-to-day recording and historical reconstruction of trench warfare, where technology magnified nature's destructiveness. Henri Barbusse, sometimes called the Zola of the trenches, echoed his great predecessor's descriptions of the mines in *Germinal*. But the war, more violent, ghastly, and immense than even Zola's floods, mines, and Paris Commune, required pushing the boundaries of naturalism even further.

In this connection the general question of literary renewal in France arises. Conscious innovation is a nearly permanent feature of the French literary landscape; throughout the 1800s, Paris had been a *locus amoenus* of innovation, and many writers felt it incumbent upon them to cultivate novelty, as a gesture of social rebellion or mark of individuality. Before 1914, striking new departures, now considered modern, were visible. Gide had led the way in 1895 with *Paludes* (*Marshlands*), an early meta-fiction, which challenges its plot and fictional status and invites readers' contribution. Alfred Jarry's *Ubu roi*, an iconoclastic drama, dates from 1896. Apollinaire experimented with collage-like juxtapositions, abrupt transitions, and esoteric allusions, and eliminated all punctuation at proof stage in his 1913 collection *Alcools* – the same year Proust dazzled the percipient. Whatever the connections to the general cultural landscape and Zeitgeist, none of these innovative works owed its subject matter or shape to the war. Rather, their new techniques, especially formal departures, turned out to suit, indeed foreshadow aspects of the cultural catastrophe – art preceding intuitively its subject matter.

The chief genre of Great War writing in France is the novel – whether fully fictionalized or closer to notebook or memoir; secondary are poetry and the essay. Some war authors wrote little else, or at least their reputations depend on their war books; some distinguished themselves otherwise. They range from right-wing (conservative, nationalist, occasionally Catholic) through centrist to left-wing, with a few political hybrids. All war books were subject to judgment on ideological grounds (politics within the novels, authors' statements), particularly as opinions and parties polarized.

French literature of the war, nearly all concerned with the Western Front although French forces were in the Balkans also, falls conveniently into periods. The first consists of works contemporaneous with the conflict. If immediacy and directness signify authenticity, they are the truest products of the war, close to the trenches and untouched by postwar perspective. Their documentary value is thus high, although even apparently spontaneous texts underwent artistic arrangement. A second period runs from the Armistice through the 1920s. The 1930s constitute a third period, during which the Great War appears in a new light – that of failed peace-making, economic crisis, and fascism.

Albert Thibaudet, writing in 1922, observed that the hundreds of war accounts, often very similar, published by then were important by quantity more than quality; if Barbusse's *Le Feu* (*Under Fire*), 1916 – to many, combatants and noncombatants alike, the quintessential literary expression of trench warfare – had not been published, its place would have been taken by a similar work.[13] Such reductionism, if ever pertinent, is no longer so, since in fact, by sales, historical importance, and perceived literary value, it and other narratives stood out as exceptional. A brief survey can begin with René Benjamin's *Gaspard* (*Gaspard the Poilu*). Published early in the war (1915) and frequently reprinted, it was well received, no doubt because of its humorous and rather tender portrait of *poilus* and their heroism and popular language.[14] Not anti-patriotic – Benjamin was a conservative, even reactionary – *Gaspard* nevertheless depicts the disorder and incomprehensibility marking the conflict from its early stages. "Je m'figurais pas la guerre comme ça" (I didn't imagine war like this), says a soldier, his ungrammatical speech suggesting vulnerability, thus victimization. The title character "ne comprenait rien à cette bataille cruelle, où on ne voyait toujours aucun ennemi et où son régiment fondait sous un feu d'enfer" (didn't understand anything in that cruel battle, where one never saw the enemy and his regiment melted away under a hellish fire).[15]

Barbusse's *Le Feu*, the most famous French demythification of the war, took a different position. Pursuing the topos of incomprehensibility, it also condemns the conflict as criminal and denounces militarism. "Honte à la gloire militaire! Honte aux armées!" (Shame on military glory! Shame on armies!).[16] Barbusse, who served as an infantryman and then stretcher-bearer, was willing to fight, though fundamentally opposed to war; he blamed German imperialism and hoped, like many other Socialists, that a new social organization and permanent peace would result from the final, horrible spasm of competitive nationalism. *Le Feu*, awarded the 1917 Goncourt Prize, went through numerous reprintings and sold nearly a quarter-million copies by the end of 1919. It was banned in Germany – a tacit acknowledgment by a fearful and bellicose government that literary products do affect readers and may bring about change – but French authorities dared not censor it because of its immediate and widespread popularity (which revealed the depth of anti-war feeling). Among its readers were Wilfred Owen, Siegfried Sassoon, and Nikolai Lenin.

The book, drawn in part from Barbusse's notebooks, is episodic and uses first-person narration, favored previously by psychological novelists more than naturalists but fitting here: this was, after all, *Barbusse's* experience, barely transposed, not an invention. The reduced fictitiousness not only suits the author's documentary purpose but conveys the feel of war – the repetitious, senseless days, the absence of progress, the feeling of being mired. More than Benjamin, Barbusse incorporates military slang and coarse colloquialisms, though he explicitly recognizes problems of recreating authentic speech. The style helped break down canons of language, thus, like the war itself, changing standards. Well-known motifs, some inherited from nineteenth-century war fiction, receive new formulation, beginning with the trench itself, its mud, filth, stench – and the soldiers, "des espèces d'ours qui pataugent et grognent" (sorts of bears which flounder and grunt).[17] More bodies suffer, and more continually and horribly, than in previous French war fiction; the suffering body, in its generality, not particularity, *is* the burden of the book. The motif of incomprehensibility is paralleled by that of *unsayability*, the unspeakable horror of the trenches defying description. Where optimism persists, it is a progressivist vision of a world without class and national conflict.

Fears of German barbarism thus turn into resentment against the power structure: politicians, industrialists, and "*château*-generals" (comfortably settled in country houses) who send the *poilus* into the trenches and over the top. Soldiers who earlier marched off to glory with banners flying, flowers tossed, and bands playing are actually but sheep sent to slaughter by an uncaring nation. Similarities of combatants on both sides and social differences between men and officers are emphasized, so that class seems more important than nation. "Ah! mon vieux . . . on parle de la sale race boche.

Ideal and actual images of French soldiery

11 French funding poster

12 Infantrymen: *les poilus* or the hairy ones

Les hommes de troupe, j'sais pas si c'est vrai ou si on nous monte le coup là-dessus aussi, et si, au fond ce ne sont pas des hommes à peu près comme nous" (Ah! old chap . . . people talk about the filthy race of Huns. Common soldiers – I don't know if it's true or if we're being lied to about that also, and if at bottom they aren't men about like us).[18] Group cohesion illustrated by the *escouade* (squad) of the subtitle – the only thing that can offset the dehumanizing experience – depends on working-class fraternity, depicted also in the frontline truces of 1914–15.

Werth's *Clavel soldat* was composed 1916–17 during the author's convalescence after action at the Front.[19] Though faithful to its autobiographical foundation, it is less a chronicle than a meditation on war. The reference point is anti-nationalist and Socialist (Karl Liebknecht is mentioned): "La patrie n'est qu'une forme mystique de l'administration" (The nation is only a mystical form of administration). Yet Clavel volunteers for service, to avoid being a "dilettante of peace"; he accepts, reluctantly, the doctrine that war can further peace. He becomes thoroughly disabused: "Chaque jour de guerre auquel les peuples consentent les accoutume à la guerre, prépare une guerre nouvelle dans l'avenir" (Each day of war to which nations consent accustoms them to war, prepares a new war in the future). Like *Le Feu*, the book piles horrors on horrors: a mendacious press, brutal officers, filth and mud, acute suffering, dehumanization. Difference of caste between men and officers is emphasized, and fraternity between French and Germans, as when Clavel gives his water-bottle to a wounded man and hears "Danke."[20] Especial attention is paid to the moral abyss separating combatants in the trenches from politicians, *embusqués* (those with cushy posts), and those at home; truths must not be told or would not be believed.

Duhamel's *Vie des martyrs, 1914–1916* (*Lives of the Martyrs*), 1917, and *Civilisation*, 1918, are accounts in various narrative voices, most of them wounded men. It appalled Duhamel that *Civilisation*, awarded the Goncourt Prize, was viewed by authorities as a contribution to the war effort; he had wanted instead to inspire revulsion for war. Patriotic rhetoric and official reports are compared to battlefield realities – the enormous, senseless sufferings of the dying and mutilated. Broad strokes of irony subvert patriotic orthodoxy: "L'ardeur enthousiaste du combat! L'angoisse exquise de bondir en avant, baïonnette luisante au soleil; la volupté de plonger un fer vengeur dans le flanc saignant de l'ennemi, et puis la souffrance, divine" (The enthusiastic ardor of combat! The exquisite anxiety of leaping forward, with one's bayonet shining in the sun; the delight at plunging an avenging blade into the enemy's bleeding flank, and then pain, divine).[21] The immense evil (as Duhamel terms it) engendered by the machine age and "rotten Europe" are castigated; the conflict has no redeeming value.

Entirely new to French war fiction, the Franco-British alliance occasioned works portraying the former enemies as valued friends. In 1918 Benjamin published *Le Major Pipe et son père* (*Major Pipe and His Father*), a charming Anglophilic portrait of the English behind their lines and at home. Drawing contrasts with the French, Benjamin praises British self-control, preparedness, and fair play. The Germans, however, are depicted as unfeeling brutes. André Maurois, known for his biographies of British figures, made his literary début that same year with *Les Silences du Colonel Bramble* (*The Silence of Colonel Bramble*), based on his experience as a liaison officer assigned to the British Expeditionary Force. Through his autobiographical character, and often by means of contrast with the French, he depicts, wittily and tolerantly, British officers. He notes their peculiar habits and attitudes – stoicism, laconism, humor, irony – and their tendency to compare war and sport – not as a moral perversion, but as a manner of dealing with adversity and adversaries. Conversations carry the narrative weight, since the raw truths of the trenches count less than attitudes toward them. Human beings appear incorrigible in their taste for blood. "C'est une loi à peu près constante de l'humanité . . . que les hommes passent à faire la guerre à peu près la moitié de leur temps" (It is a nearly constant law of humanity that men spend about half their time making war).[22] The conclusion is resigned irony and appreciation for the enduring qualities of England and France.

The books just discussed are generally episodic, weakly plotted, sometimes diary-like, often in the present tense. Action comes from occasional military engagements and the unexpressed general plot of war, which originally is the *point*, battles, even pauses between them, being stages toward its end, victory the ostensible goal. But where participants do not adopt its stated rationale, action often seems undirected, pointless, except in an immediate, narrow context (saving a friend, trying to sleep). Character is similarly sketchy, with many fleeting presences, though ultimately certain voices and personalities do dominate. Offsetting fragmented or indecisive actions and incomplete characterization are agglutinated groups (for example, Barbusse's squad). Collectivities have begun to replace those individuals that dominated the nineteenth-century French novel, at least until Zola introduced the crowd as an actor, parallel to its modern role as an historical agent. The various voices in *Le Feu* constitute a collective presence, threatened, even dissolved by a historical action that surpasses comprehension and seems to exist without human consent; yet this presence, in its individual expressions, is cohesive enough to appear, retrospectively, as itself an agent of change, foreshadowing future waves of insurgents, strikers, fascist enthusiasts, and colonial rebels from the 1920s to the century's end.

The most impressive French war poetry is Apollinaire's *Calligrammes* (1918). His status as a foreigner until French citizenship was granted in 1916 did not prevent his volunteering for the French army in 1914; it may, however, explain his intense patriotism. An artilleryman (later an infantry officer), he composed while in combat scores of poems, marked by spontaneity and imagination, and produced twenty-five mimeographed copies of a small collection (1915).

Apollinaire's prewar poetry and art criticism had already emphasized the "merveilleux" (marvelous) of modernity. Using free verse, loosely organized into stanzas, he easily transferred this painterly vision of juxtaposed machines (airplanes, tramways) and other urban elements to the "Merveille de la guerre" ("Wonder of War") – the unprecedented spectacle of a modern battlefield, with shells flowering or bursting like stars, cannons thundering in waves, and fountains of blood. "Notre armée invisible est une belle nuit constellée / Et chacun de nos hommes est un astre merveilleux / O nuit ô nuit éblouissante" (Our invisible army is a beautiful starry night / And each of our men is a marvelous star / Oh night oh dazzling night). Visions are often simultaneous, multi-profiled, shattering and exploding like bombs and blown-up bodies; and yet these juxtaposed, analytic images tend toward synthesis. Meanwhile, the poet's predilection for medieval motifs and tones sanitizes the battle, connecting it to chivalry (sometimes in regular verse), as in "L'Adieu du cavalier" ("The Cavalier's Farewell"): "Ah Dieu! que la guerre est jolie / Avec ses chants ses longs loisirs" (Oh Lord! how lovely is war / with its songs its long idleness). Destruction and death are expressed now with detachment (in the lyric just quoted, the cavalryman simply "mourut là-bas" [died over there]), now in a personal, melancholic mode: "Les obus miaulaient un amour à mourir / . . . / Ton souffle nage au fleuve où le sang va tarir" (Shells mewed a love to die for / Your breath swims in the river where the blood will dry up).[23]

Cendrars, born Frédéric Sauser in Switzerland, naturalized in 1916, was co-author of a late July 1914 appeal, republished widely and considered enormously successful, to non-citizens to join up.[24] He joined a regiment of foreigners, thereafter incorporated into the Foreign Legion, and participated in intense fighting until badly wounded in 1915 (his arm was amputated). Before 1914, he had published long, idiosyncratic travel poems, cultivating modernity, in which he had abandoned punctuation and traditional verse and relied on juxtaposition. (He may have influenced Apollinaire; he claimed to have created the first "simultaneist" book.)

His short free-verse poem "Shrapnells," dated October 1914, begins: "Dans le brouillard la fusillade crépite et la voix du canon vient jusqu'à nous" (In the fog the gunfire crackles and the canon's voice reaches us).[25]

The longer *La Guerre au Luxembourg* (*The War in the Luxembourg*), dated 1916, published 1917, contrasts, yet identifies, civilian life with the Front by deft use of detail and multiple voices evoking children's games in the Luxembourg Gardens in Paris: "Pâle automne fin d'été / On ne peut rien oublier / Il n'y a que les petits enfants qui jouent à la guerre / La Somme Verdun / Mon grand frère est aux Dardanelles / Comme c'est beau / Un fusil" (Pale autumn end of summer / One can't forget anything / Only little children play at war / The Somme Verdun / My big brother is in the Dardanelles / How fine a rifle is).[26] A sort of prose poem, *J'ai tué* (*I Have Killed*), first published in 1918, begins by evoking objectively a military campaign – bits of debris indicating a village demolished and lives destroyed, the experience of bombardment – before turning personal: "J'ai tué. Comme celui qui veut vivre" (I have killed. Like one who wants to live).[27] Hating and condemning war, Cendrars nevertheless recognized that his service had furnished him with the conditions for achieving manhood and heightened experience. Explosions, bombings, and mutilation – not treated as *merveilleux* but rather as profoundly unsettling and destructive, with bodies hurled through the air, screaming, vaporized – haunt much of his subsequent writing.

Paul Claudel's *Poèmes de guerre* and its sequel (1915, 1916, reprinted 1922) deserve consideration because of his literary stature. After being illumined by faith as a young man, he adopted a militant Catholic outlook that permeates his writing and could accommodate no other views, including science. Politically, he was conservative, though as a career diplomat he served under governments of all stripes. Composed in variable free-verse lines, his poems display unapologetic and vigorous patriotism, founded on an essentialist view of nationhood (Germany is compared to Cain, for instance). This essentialism is not, however, historically or pseudo-scientifically grounded, as for Barrès, but determined irrationally.

"Tant que vous voudrez, mon général" (As long as you wish, General) (1915) begins as a soldier drinks with comrades before the next attack. All are equal, their various civilian callings subsumed into the condition of *troops*. The initial familiar tone is then replaced by typical Claudelian bombast, with litany-like repetitions suggesting a sacred cause: "Tant qu'il y aura ceux d'en face pour tenir ce qui est à nous sous la semelle de leurs bottes / . . . / Tant qu'il y aura de la viande vivante de Français pour marcher à travers vos sacrés fils de fer / Tant qu'il y aura un enfant de femme pour marcher à travers votre science et votre chimie" (As long as there are those facing us who hold what is ours under their boot soles / . . . / As long as there is Frenchmen's living flesh to march through your confounded wire / As long as there is a child of woman to march across your science and your chemistry). To mock such chauvinism mixed with Christian motifs ("Livraison de mon corps et de mon sang"

[Delivery of my body and blood]) and clothed in bad poetry is tempting, especially when one reflects that Claudel was never at the Front.[28] However, in 1915 millions of French shared that patriotism and the conviction that God was on their side, and Claudel's many admirers doubtless were moved.

To these wartime texts should be added Romain Rolland's *Au-dessus de la mêlée* (*Above the Battle*), an article first published in Geneva, then collected with others under the same title (Paris, 1915). Although Rolland, living in Switzerland when war began, initially shared the enthusiasm of most French, he soon was disenchanted. He imagined that the principal belligerents could be led to renunciation of nationalism in favor of social justice. The volume was officially denounced and, for a while, its circulation was prohibited and its author ostracized, though his international reputation was very high as he became the torch-bearer for pacifism. His positions were expressed subsequently in *Salut à la révolution russe* (*Hail to the Russian Revolution*), written in 1917 with Pierre Jean Jouve and others, the novel *Clérambault: histoire d'une conscience libre pendant la guerre* (*Clerambault: The Story of an Independent Spirit During the War*), 1920, and additional works.

Among novels published early in the second period of Great War writing in France, which generally have the feel of recent experience, are three by Roland Dorgelès. He had volunteered for combat, convinced the cause was just. Like *Le Feu*, *Les Croix de bois* (*Wooden Crosses*), 1919, was an enormous success, receiving the Prix Fémina, nearly winning the Goncourt. Ignoring the anti-war thought of 1914–18 and refuting by anticipation the widespread indifference and nihilism of the 1920s and appeasement of the 1930s, the work connects pre-1914 patriotism to that of 1939–40. True, war is viewed as deplorable, but it is a necessary response to foreign invasion and thus justified. The structure is episodic, with a first-person narrator who represents the author, but it is not simply a memoir or diary, arranged as pseudo-fiction. The language is not coarse, although colloquialisms appear and spelling indicates uneducated speech. A handful of characters of different backgrounds typify French combatants. Sulphart, a factory worker, is wounded after three years in the trenches and sent home. Pensioned off, he cannot readjust to civilian life: he has no job, and he discovers that Parisians are indifferent to soldiers' sufferings on the Front. Demachy, a former law student who likes books and plays, does not even make it back, bleeding to death instead on the battlefield, where he has been left behind. These losses are absolute, implies Dorgelès, each life being of value; but the nation for which they have died transcends the individual.

Le Cabaret de la belle femme (*The Cabaret Up the Line*), also 1919, which includes three chapters excised by the censors from *Les Croix de bois*, consists of vignettes featuring ordinary soldiers in typical circumstances. It includes some coarse language and popular syntax. Denouncing explicitly a rose-colored view of war and throwing ironic light on the enthusiasm of August 1914, it foresees bitterly the postwar. "On est parti presque joyeux, croyant à l'Aventure. Et l'on est revenu, déçu . . . sans avoir rien vu que des ruines" (We left almost joyous, believing it was an adventure. And we came back, disappointed, without seeing anything but ruins). Before a corpse, the narrator reflects: "N'est-ce pas atroce de penser . . . que la guerre terminée, des milliers de sacrifices pareils tomberont dans l'oubli" (Isn't it atrocious to think . . . that, once war is over, thousands of similar sacrifices will fall into oblivion).[29] Yet its treatment of soldiers' experiences includes humor as well as poetic tenderness.

Le Réveil des morts (Awakening of the Dead), 1923, a novel concerning the postwar rebuilding of a ruined village near Soissons, provides a vivid picture of war's effects in rural France. As if four years of German presence did not suffice, reconstruction brings new scourges – profiteers who grow rich on development schemes and swindle the gullible; incompetent government agencies that provide few services; violation of laws meant to protect the vulnerable; meanness and dishonesty at all levels. In a dream sequence, dead soldiers arise from their graves to challenge the exploiters. The war has not ended injustice, nor prevented future war. "On nous avait promis que ce serait la dernière guerre. Mensonges!" (We had been promised it would be the last war. Lies!).[30] Wartime espionage by women and infidelities with Germans are among other themes. Frequent elsewhere also, they reflect unease over women's behavior during and after the war.

Infidelity is central to Raymond Radiguet's autobiographically inspired psychological novel Le Diable au corps, 1923 (The Devil in the Flesh). Radiguet, an enfant terrible, was too young for service but not too young to enjoy what he termed "quatre ans de grandes vacances" (four years of summer holiday). Revelations about his affair with a woman whose husband was at war reinforced the controversy provoked by the work's casual, even callous attitude. Its tone rings true, however, starting with the tableau, reminiscent of scenes from the Franco-Prussian War, in which enthusiastic civilians send off equally enthusiastic soldiers: "Nous emportions des campanules et les lancions aux soldats. Des dames en blouse versaient du vin rouge dans les bidons et en répandaient des litres sur le quai jonché de fleurs" (We carried bluebells and threw them to the soldiers. Women in smocks poured red wine into cans and spilled liters of it onto the platform strewn with flowers).[31]

Infidelity likewise appears in Joseph Kessel's L'Equipage, 1923 (Pilot and Observer), an early example of French aviation literature. Based on his experiences after he joined the army, aged eighteen, and flew numerous combat missions, the novel includes action scenes and treats themes of friendship and solidarity among pilots. As in numerous other war novels, these frontline scenes are complemented by episodes at the rear, in a rhythm of narrative contrasts. Women are depicted as unable to comprehend the fraternity of battle and its terrible strains, or remain loyal; their affairs with civilians or soldiers on leave reveal and increase their incomprehension.

Henry de Montherlant's war writing is unique. In 1917, having finally passed the physical examination, he succeeded in joining the army, saw active service, and was wounded. Under his pen the conflict becomes an edifying experience of individual development, an end, not a means, almost a sporting event. (*Les Olympiques*, 1924 [*Olympics*], reinforced the analogy between war and sport.) Seeing war in sporting terms was unusual in France: there were few "playing fields" at French lycées. Yet it would be wrong to view him as insensitive: *La Relève du matin*, 1920 (*Morning Changeover*), includes thoughtful observations on the circumstances of 1914, their connection to the past, and the war; he was secretary of the campaign to build an ossuary at Doyaumont; and his *Chant funèbre pour les morts de Verdun* (*Funeral Song for the Verdun Dead*) acknowledges war's tragedy. But in *Le Songe*, 1922 (*The Dream*), of which two-thirds takes place at the Front, the war (a "game") is incidental, the cult of the self central.

Its terms are those of the inherited heroic tradition transferred to a changed setting; danger is a tonic, a spur, and battle a way to win points in struggles within the self. The ethics are thus personal, indeed aristocratic, even aesthetic (beauty of gesture), rather than collective – patriotic, internationalist, or religious. The hero, Alban de Bricoule, excused from service for health reasons, nevertheless volunteers for frontline action through solidarity with a friend and chiefly to test himself in what he calls the holy virile order of battle. (Later readers sense here intimations of Montherlant's homosexuality, never confronted publicly.) The justice of the struggle – Péguy's, Dorgelès's concern – interests him not at all; he rejects the argument that war is justified by the German invasion. Montherlant's glorification of military values – "Il faut faire une paix qui ait la grandeur d'âme d'une guerre" (We must create a peace which has the spiritual grandeur of war) – made him unpopular and later fostered perception of him as a fascist.[32] (He was indeed a right-winger and supported collaboration with the Germans in 1940–44.) This image mattered little to him; his sense of superiority meant that he pleased the public only on his own terms.

Another author who saw the war through a uniquely personal lens is Jean Giraudoux. As an infantry sergeant, he was wounded at the Marne and later served in the Dardanelles before being posted elsewhere. In 1917, already turning his back on war's realities, he had published *Lectures pour une ombre*

(*Campaigns and Intervals*), an idiosyncratic war memoir, characterized by poetic descriptions. It was followed by *Adorable Clio* (1920), whose title is revealing: violent history is transformed, made "adorable," by Giraudoux's vision and witty style, which brushes events with fingertips and clothes them in gauzy fantasy. "Le style de Giraudoux est une évasion" (Giraudoux's style is an escape), noted one critic.[33] *Siegfried et le Limousin* (1922) (*My Friend from Limousin*), a poetic novel in which battlefield amnesia leads to a Frenchman's becoming, temporarily, German, illustrates incompatibilities in temperament between the two peoples; whatever the desire for reconciliation, they are essentially and eternally different.[34]

Criticized for its aestheticism and apparent moral indifference, *Thomas l'imposteur*, 1923 (*Thomas the Impostor*), by Jean Cocteau, offers an artificial, theatrical treatment of the war, termed by some "un désir pervers d'insulter à la mémoire des combattants de 14–18" (a perverse desire to insult the memory of the soldiers of 1914–18).[35] Cocteau's right-wing politics, effete manners, and aesthete's life encouraged such judgments; moreover, he categorized the work as "poésie du roman" (poetry of the novel). For the orphaned hero, Thomas, extraordinary historical circumstances offer an extraordinary opportunity: to live as another in a great game of make-believe. That the setting of this comedy is the Front (Cocteau himself served as a medical orderly in Champagne and Flanders) does not diminish, but rather heightens, its theatricality, as does the confrontation of two archetypical women, personifying goodness and wickedness.

Mistaken for the nephew of a famous general, the underage Thomas soon finds himself in uniform on the Flanders front ("the theatre of war"), where, a pretend soldier, he discovers fraternity in battle, rarified love (for the beautiful Princesse de Bormes, who organizes an ambulance service, and for her daughter), and beauty of spectacle. Cocteau's sea is comparable to Apollinaire's battlefields: "La nuit, cette eau devenait phosphorescente . . . Un projectile y tombant, sa chute allumait au fond un boulevard de magasins splendides" (At night, this water became phosphorescent . . . If a projectile fell into it, its fall lit up at the bottom a boulevard of splendid shops). This child's-fantasy war has, however, a dark side, suggested by a visiting actress, described as a vampire, who gloats on death and suffering. Good and evil and their struggle are real; so are pain and mutilation (a German soldier without hands, a Frenchman whose leg will be amputated without anaesthetic). Thomas witnesses others' deaths before being hit by a German sniper and dying himself. "La nuit froide était constellée de fusées blanches et d'astres . . . Un dernier rideau se lève. L'enfant et la féerie se confondent" (The cold night was starry with white rockets and stars. . . . A final curtain goes up. The child and the enchanting spectacle are one and the same).[36]

Playacting has turned into reality; history cannot be escaped, only transmuted by art.

Proust's *Le Temps retrouvé* (1927) was in manuscript form by 1922, the year of his death. War is not portrayed directly except for a few brief allusions: he had no battle experience (being too old and too ill to serve), and the work is primarily an adventure in aesthetic consciousness, set against a brilliantly analyzed background of high society. However, in street scenes, salons, and the famous male brothel he conveys the atmosphere and treats the effects of war, in aesthetic, social, and political terms – including their consequences for those of modest station – thus complementing writings focused on combat.

Pretenses kept up by some notwithstanding, nothing at the rear is untouched: attitudes, habits, conversation, concert programs, guest lists, fashions, sexual conduct. Even interior decorating is affected: Mme Verdurin has turned against "modern style," judging it *munichois* (Munich-like). Society becomes more fluid: clever climbers succeed in breaching the doors of salons formerly closed to them; certain *Dreyfusards*, formerly *personae non gratae*, earn admission by displays of patriotism. Major characters reveal traits unnoticed or undeveloped before: Charlus can barely conceal his philo-Germanism; Bloch reveals his poltroonery; Saint-Loup shows his patriotism by volunteering for the Front; Brichot writes erudite chauvinistic articles. Proust excels at analyzing speech and journalistic language, identifying the new *poncifs* (clichés) that have replaced the old. His discussions of strategy, European politics, and history (showing, for example, how Great War battles can be seen in Napoleonic terms) are incisive, conveying both commonplaces and his correction of them.

Among his most striking passages are those depicting Paris under wartime conditions. Reduction in night lighting transforms the city; soldiers in uniforms of many nations wander through its streets; snow, left for lack of workers, creates a painterly scene; German airships and French planes against the sonorous background of air-raid sirens provide a Wagnerian experience with an apocalyptic touch; simultaneous activity in the sky and below constitutes a tableau like El Greco's *The Burial of the Count of Orgaz*. Proust's evocations are not, however, retrogressive, but rather constitute a modern, multi-profiled blend of sound and light impressions.

An important war essay of the 1920s is *Mars ou la guerre jugée* (*Mars, or the Truth About War*), 1921, by Alain (Emile Chartier), a lycée philosophy professor who volunteered at age forty-six and spent three years in the artillery, often under fire. Alain belonged to the tradition of *moralistes* – commentators on manners and morals – not that of systematic philosophers; his readership, developed through his daily newspaper columns, was enormous.

The essay, frequently republished, enlarged in 1938 with *Suite à Mars* (*Sequel to Mars*), incorporates portions of a wartime work but takes a broader perspective, encompassing the aftermath of the conflict, or "la guerre continuée par la pompe des cérémonies et l'iniquité des traités en 1919 et 1920" (war continued by the pomp of ceremonies and the iniquity of 1919 and 1920 treaties).[37] Alain's Cartesian approach is to peel away misleading surface appearances and received ideas (about such topics as patriotism, the church in war, corpses) in order to "penser les choses comme elles sont" (think things as they are).[38] Warfare, to him, was a scourge not only repeated but, alas, desired by human beings; yet he argued against its inevitability, insisting that, a human creation, it could be denied by human will.

Two artistic movements indirectly connected to the catastrophe must not go unmentioned. Dada, with roots in Central Europe, migrated to Paris in 1919; and whilst its verbal products – a magazine, experimental poetry – have not proven durable, the phenomenon was important as an insolent, iconoclastic reaction to the war. Surrealism, founded by André Breton, who had frequented the Dada circle, Louis Aragon, and Philippe Soupault, burst forth with tremendous vigor in the 1920s in similar response. The project was to overturn inherited structures and revolutionize the world on a postwar tabula rasa. Apparently nihilistic in its refusal of established values, Surrealism gave rise to manifestos, experimental poetry, strange fiction (such as Breton's *Nadja*, 1928), films, and graphic art (although Cendrars claimed that the Surrealists, "des fils à papa" [Daddy's boys], had produced nothing new[39]). Almost all the Surrealists embraced Communism before the 1920s ended: political utopianism and socialist realism, which Aragon adopted, appeared more practical means of advancing their enterprise.

As the 1920s drew to a close, war was no longer the topic of the day. Increased prosperity after 1926 helped push it into the background; survivors had, in general, already told their stories; the public was surfeited with accounts of the trenches. Julien Benda, in *La Trahison des clercs*, 1927 (*The Intellectuals' Betrayal*), excoriated writers for betraying, through ideological bias or personal passion, the universalist values of reason on which, he argued, literature should be based. The popularity of the brief psychological novel suggests a turning away from history; Gide's masterpiece *Les Faux-Monnayeurs*, 1926 (*The Counterfeiters*), displays little historical sensitivity; Paul Morand's exoticism and Giraudoux's escapism were widely appreciated. Yet political controversies sometimes spilled over into literature and partisanship was rampant. A highly visible, often militant Catholic literature (Claudel's reactionary prose and verse, Jacques Maritain's anti-modern tracts, François Mauriac's fiction) reflected fears of internationalism and moral relativism; conservative critics attacked what they did not like

(Gide, Surrealism) as "foreign" – that is, violating French (nationalist, Catholic) canons.

By the 1930s, the literary landscape was complicated further by historical developments, and *littérature engagée* (committed literature) was the watchword on both left and right. As though removal in time from 1914–18 as well as very recent events offered particular justification or opportunity for their reexamination, a half-dozen major authors devoted novels to the prewar and war. Nearly all had war experience; most were pacifists or anti-nationalists. The burden of history, everywhere present in these works, is powerful: the authors or other voices suffer not only from the war itself but from its legacy, personal and general.

In *Le Grand Troupeau*, 1931 (*To the Slaughterhouse*), Jean Giono denounced the total warfare waged by behemoth powers of modern industrialized Europe. He was, however, concerned less with victimization of the proletariat than that of the peasantry and a jeopardized bucolic way of life – to him, the authentic mode of human existence. The *troupeau* (herd), an echo of countless other French war writings using animal metaphors, is that of men sent off and decimated in battle; it is also the flocks of sheep whose welfare, indeed very life, is compromised by the absence of young shepherds, all at the Front. The war (which Giono saw first-hand as an infantryman for over two years, being gassed in Flanders), is the ultimate anti-pastoral, or dystopia, in one critic's term, carrying farther than any other phenomenon the destructiveness of industrialized nationalism.[40] Giono's revulsion against war was so entrenched that he refused to cooperate after having been called up in 1939 and was imprisoned for two months. (During the purges near the end of World War II he was again imprisoned, for supposed collaboration.)

It could be argued that Céline's *Voyage au bout de la nuit*, 1932 (*Journey to the End of the Night*), derives principally from the Great War, although less than a fifth concerns the conflict itself. Like his creator, Bardamu, the anti-heroic protagonist, is shaped forever by the Front; war is responsible for his cynicism. Céline indicts every figure, every cause, every bit of rhetoric responsible for the war ("Poor Alsace! Poor Belgium"), including its most fundamental grounding, the French republic and its foundations in the Enlightenment. The fatherland is a fiction; patriotism is dupery; the conflict is, literally, madness. (Though Bardamu and scattered other anti-war protesters are confined to an asylum, they alone, the author implies, are sane.) Unlike Barbusse, Céline embraces no internationalist vision that would replace nationalism and end armed conflict; all values, all causes have lost their justification, and Bardamu believes in little henceforth except saving his skin.

Céline underwrites this deconstruction of nationalist idols by a disorderly plot-line and his aggressive style, which, more radically than Barbusse's, incorporates vulgar speech, bad grammar, colloquialisms, sometimes even a hallucinatory quality. This denial of aesthetic and philosophic ideals deeply rooted in French literature and thought – clarity, beauty, control, order, rationality – constitutes a rejection of the entire French humanistic and republican tradition and points to a shattered world. The multiple reprintings and translations and enormous sales of the novel indicate how many readers responded to Céline's disabused vision, although he was later despised because he sought a Franco-German alliance in 1938 and frequented collaborators during World War II (for which, and for his anti-Semitism, he was afterwards condemned *in absentia*).

Whilst less known in English-speaking countries than Céline, his influential contemporary Drieu La Rochelle deserves mention, starting with *Interrogation* (1917), poems based on his experiences at Charleroi, Champagne, the Dardenelles, and Verdun, including two sympathetic to the Germans. His brilliant, bitter satire of the Great War in *La Comédie de Charleroi*, 1934 (*The Comedy of Charleroi and Other Stories*) sold well, although that year he announced his conversion to "social fascism"; like Montherlant, Drieu despised the Third Republic. In these loosely connected autobiographical stories, different narrative voices and shifts in tone offer multiple perspectives. Drieu's sympathy for war, which, like a virile game, allows for cultivation of the will and pursuit of glory, is nonetheless offset by the hero's inability later to find meaning in his experiences. "Je ne croyais plus à la possibilité de réussir la représentation de la journée . . . Ni pour les Allemands ni pour les Français. On se bat pour exprimer quelque chose, pour représenter quelque chose . . . Mais cette représentation était ratée" (I no longer believed it possible for the representation of the day to succeed . . . Neither for the Germans nor the French. One fights to express something, to represent something . . . But this representation was a failure).[41] Such disillusion was surely operative in his embrace of fascism.

Martin du Gard's *L'Eté 1914* (1936) (*Summer 1914*) and *Epilogue* (1940) – the last parts of *Les Thibault* – provide, more than a generation after the fact, a bitter vision of inevitable war. (The author, aged thirty-three in 1914, saw events first-hand as a transport division sergeant.) Through multiple plots, characters, and settings (Paris, Geneva, Berlin, Brussels), *L'Eté 1914* conveys, in a broad sweep, the complexities of European chancelleries, the inertia of human masses, the frightening momentum of war. While personal lives continue, they are at the mercy of politics; the whole of Europe will shortly be carried away in a whirlwind. Though the author was not himself a Socialist, he depicts Socialism with sympathy and perspicacity through his young hero, Jacques Thibault. The orthodox position is to welcome war, which will lead to the collapse of capitalism and Socialist revolution. Jacques cannot accept this policy of expediency. His personal solution is to distribute by plane leaflets calling on soldiers on both sides to lay down their arms. That his gesture is futile – he crashes before the pamphlets can be dropped – and that, his broken leg crudely splinted with a board labeled "FRAGIL," he is shot by a French soldier, underline the novelist's pessimism. The Swedish Academy's award to Martin du Gard of the 1937 Nobel Prize for Literature, albeit thoroughly deserved, was doubtless politically inspired, reflecting fears of a new war.

L'Eté 1914 can usefully be compared to Aragon's novels dealing with the prewar. Whilst Martin du Gard, originally trained as a paleographer, aims at objectivity, Aragon's *Les Cloches de Bâle*, 1934 (*The Bells of Basel*) illustrates a Marxist thesis: that the "internal logic" of industrial capitalism, its fissures dramatized by the Agadir crisis and signaled at the 1912 Socialist congress in Basel, led inevitably to the convulsions of 1914. (Aragon acknowledged his propagandistic intentions.) Two sequels – *Les Beaux Quartiers*, 1936 (*Residential Quarter*) and *Les Voyageurs de l'impériale*, 1942 (*The Century Was Young*) – pursue the analysis of prewar society and the approach of war, depicted directly only at the very end.

Martin du Gard's *Epilogue* (composed 1938–39) warrants its title because Jacques is dead; it applies also to the postwar as epilogue to the world destroyed by 1914–18. The volume centers on Antoine Thibault, Jacques's brother, who is undergoing treatment in 1918 after being gassed. His is the dilemma of the reflective man, someone like Alain: unable to embrace either militant nationalism or pacifism, he believes the war must be pursued to its conclusion, after which new dilemmas will arise. Pessimism and optimism alternate as he contemplates the future. Realizing he will die shortly, the treatment being unsuccessful, he records in his diary his decline (surely suggesting that of Europe), yet writes hopefully of the League of Nations. His death on 18 November coincides with a new era; but readers' awareness of the war's legacy, the League's failure, and the new conflagration kindled in 1939 casts a dark, ironic shadow over Antoine's vision. In Martin du Gard's vision, history, violent, destructive, uncontrollable, has the last word.

Jules Romains's *Prélude à Verdun* and *Verdun* (1938), from *Les Hommes de bonne volonté* (*Men of Good Will*), are among the last Great War novels of the 1930s. Romains did not see battle himself, serving instead in the auxiliary army in a Paris office. Among earlier volumes, *Le 6 octobre* and *Le Drapeau noir* (*The Black Flag*) concern respectively the prophetic Balkan crisis of 1908 and events in summer 1914; the final volumes treat post-1919 disappointments and the rise of fascism. The whole series, intended to bear a pacifistic message, is permeated by historical irony afforded by the chronological vantage point. Hopes reflected in the series title were obviously compromised; the statement that "Ce navire . . . [Europe] voyage avec le drapeau noir" (This ship sails with the black flag) suggests the approach of war in the late 1930s as well as summer 1914.[42]

The scope of *Verdun* reflects Romains's embrace of Unanimism, a pre-1914 literary movement concerned with communal living and crowd identity. His enterprise is not merely to rehearse what had become commonplaces about the battle, but rather to examine it from as many viewpoints as possible, including the worm's-eye view, in order to grasp it wholly in its phenomenal distinctiveness. Using multiple plots, scenes, and characters, he suggests its vastness, complexity, disorder, and various effects. The expository technique is not unlike the simultaneism of Apollinaire and Cendrars, although less fragmented than Jean-Paul Sartre's in *Le Sursis*, 1945 (*The Reprieve*), where scenes and characters change in mid-sentence, historical coherence, being, however, maintained.

Romains's conclusion, like Drieu La Rochelle's, is that comprehension of a modern battlefield and its forces passes human grasp. "Il n'y avait nulle part en Artois ni en Champagne une butte assez haute pour que le champ de bataille pût être embrassé du regard par le chef . . . A plus forte raison n'y avait-il nulle part une tête pour penser cette guerre" (There was nowhere in Artois or Champagne a rise high enough for the commander to see the entire battlefield . . . A fortiori there was nowhere a mind to think this war). The battle cannot even be directed as a whole: "Pas une volonté non plus qui fût d'assez grandes dimensions pour peser vraiment de son propre poids sur l'ensemble de la guerre, ni qui sût se faire assez ferme et perçante pour parvenir telle quelle jusqu'à l'homme de la tranchée" (Nor was there any will great enough to weigh with its own weight on the whole of the war, nor that could become sufficiently steady and sharp to reach men in the trenches).[43] Warfare has escaped from its agents; a totalizing eschatological end – the vindication of war through ending war, demanding total sacrifice of men and matériel – is irrational.

The historian's strategy of retrospective teleology, which links events and conditions so that outcomes appear inevitable, should be used only cautiously, given the limitations of perspective, role of historical contingency, and complexity of any historical field. It was noted that erosion of literary form, rationale, and order was discernible before 1914; character had been subverted and plot challenged. It is tempting, however, to connect further disintegration of form to the Great War and see its delayed, if oblique, effects as late as the mid-century New Novel and Theatre of the Absurd, where fictional conventions are assailed and rationality is denied. Claude Simon's

La Route des Flandres, 1960 (*The Flanders Road*), a novel of the second war centered on the May 1940 debacle and imprisonment in Germany, is illustrative. Plot is both recurrent and indeterminate; point of view multiplies and wavers; punctuation is erratic, syntax strange; history seems recurrent without progress; rationality of human action has imploded into a black hole. This dissolution of fictional meaning and the historical narrative it implies appears as the cultural culmination of the mutilated, exploding bodies and senseless repetitions of the Great War. History, far from having been justified, has become monstrous, autonomous; humanity seems dead.

Yet *human* ingenuity and effort began it all: "La guerre, en se perfectionnant, anéantit sans laisser trace de ce qui vivait . . . Il a fallu l'homme, ses calculs et son travail, pour *tuer* ainsi un pays" (War, in being perfected, annihilates what was living without a trace . . . It required man, his calculations and his labour, to *kill* thus a countryside).[44] In his novel *Les Noyers de l'Altenburg* (1943) (*The Walnut Trees of Altenburg*), concerned with both world wars, André Malraux suggests how humanity can go beyond the deterministic historical cycle of self-destructiveness. The French hero, held prisoner in Chartres cathedral after the fall of France, relives retrospectively the retreat of 1940 and his father's experiences as a German combatant in the Great War. Tentatively, he identifies two means of redemption, fraternity and art, which alike posit the commonality of mankind. His father had witnessed a gas attack against the Russians, when German soldiers, horrified as the gas spread, risked their lives to save their enemies. A generation later, the son experienced fraternity in a Flanders tank battle. Art, illustrated by the cathedral sculptures, similarly transcends the contingencies of events. The idea of essential France, essential Germany, yields to shared humanity, and Valéry's "mortal civilizations" are subsumed into a transcendent and eternal idea of man.

NOTES

1. Victor Hugo, *Les Misérables*, ed. Maurice Allem (Paris: Gallimard, 1951), 1260.
2. Roger Martin du Gard, *Journal*, vol. I (Paris: Gallimard, 1992), 352.
3. Martin Gilbert, *The First World War: A Complete History* (New York: Holt, 1994), 32.
4. Quoted in Jamie H. Cockfield, *White Crow: The Life and Times of the Grand Duke Nicholas Mikhailovich Romanov* (Westport and London: Praeger, 2002), 134.
5. Léon Werth, *Clavel soldat* (Paris: Albin Michel [1917]), 31–32.
6. Marcel Proust, *Le Temps retrouvé*, in *A la recherche du temps perdu*, vol. III (Paris: Gallimard, 1954), 785.
7. Georges Duhamel, *Civilisation, 1914–1917* (Paris: Mercure de France, 1918); Paul Valéry, *Œuvres*, vol. I (Paris: Gallimard, 1957), 927, 988.

8. Eugen Weber, *The Nationalist Revival in France, 1905–1914* (Berkeley and Los Angeles: University of California Press, 1959).

9. Robert Aron, *The Vichy Regime 1940–44*, trans. Humphrey Hare (London: Putnam, 1958), 10.

10. Hans A. Schmitt, *Charles Péguy: The Decline of an Idealist* (Baton Rouge: Louisiana State University Press, 1967), 142.

11. Charles Péguy, *Œuvres poétiques* (Paris: Gallimard, 1957), 1026.

12. Paul Valéry, *La Jeune Parque: étude critique par Octave Nadal* (Paris: Club du Meilleur Livre, 1957), 372.

13. Albert Thibaudet, *Réflexions sur la littérature* (Paris: Gallimard, 1938), 146–47.

14. *Poilu*, the equivalent of "Tommy," literally "hairy," became a term of pride and endearment. Attested in 1910, meaning "soldier," from *poilu* "brave," 1899, it reflects the equivalence between hair and virility (*Le Petit Robert* dictionary). Military policy requiring a mustache, and general filth and lack of hot water, must have reinforced the usage. See Roland Dorgelès, *Le Cabaret de la belle femme* (Paris: Albin Michel, 1919), 46, 52.

15. René Benjamin, *Gaspard* (Paris: Arthème Fayard, 1915), 118–19.

16. Henri Barbusse, *Le Feu: journal d'une escouade* (Paris: Flammarion, 1916), 280.

17. *Ibid.*, 7.

18. *Ibid.*, 35.

19. Maurice Rieuneau, *Guerre et révolution dans le roman français* (Paris: Klincksieck, 1974) gives 1919 as date of publication for *Clavel soldat*. In fact, its first publication was in 1917. See note 5.

20. Werth, *Clavel soldat*, 20, 146, 165.

21. Duhamel, *Civilisation*, 113.

22. André Maurois, *Les Silences du Colonel Bramble* (1918; rpt. Paris: Grasset, 1921), 229.

23. Guillaume Apollinaire, *Œuvres poétiques* (Paris: Gallimard, 1965), 243, 253, 271, 277.

24. Jean Rousselot, *Blaise Cendrars* (Paris: Editions Universitaires, 1955), 42.

25. Blaise Cendrars, *Complete Poems*, trans. Ron Padgett (Berkeley: University of California Press, 1992), 346.

26. Blaise Cendrars, *Selected Writings*, ed. Walter Albert (Westport, Conn.: Greenwood Press, 1978), 184.

27. Rousselot, *Blaise Cendrars*, 44.

28. Paul Claudel, *Œuvre poétique* (Paris: Gallimard, 1957), 526, 529.

29. Dorgelès, *Le Cabaret de la belle femme*, 33, 74.

30. Roland Dorgelès, *Le Réveil des morts* (Paris: Albin Michel, 1923), 300.

31. Raymond Radiguet, *Le Diable au corps* (1923; rpt. Paris: Livre de Poche, 1964), 8.

32. Georges Bordonove, *Henri de Montherlant* (Paris: Editions Universitaires, 1958), 103.

33. R.-M. Albérès, *Histoire du roman moderne* (Paris: Albin Michel, 1962), 156.

34. Giraudoux's play *La Guerre de Troie n'aura pas lieu* (*Tiger at the Gates*), illustrating the inevitability of war, appeared in 1935.

35. Quoted by Jean-Pierre Chauveau, "Tradition et modernité dans les romans de Cocteau," in *Jean Cocteau aujourd'hui: Actes du Colloque de Montpellier* (Paris: Klincksieck, 1992), 86.

36. Jean Cocteau, *Thomas l'imposteur* (Paris: Gallimard, 1923), 114–15, 171.

37. François Foulatier, preface to Alain, *Mars ou la guerre jugée* (1921; rpt. Paris: Gallimard, 1995), 14. The earlier work is *De quelques-unes des causes réelles de la guerre . . .* (On Some Real Causes of War . . .) (composed 1916).

38. Alain, *Mars ou la guerre jugée*, 221.

39. Rousselot, *Blaise Cendrars*, 69; Monique Chefdor, *Blaise Cendrars* (Boston: Twayne, 1980), 53.

40. Walter Redfern, "Jean Giono," in *French Novelists 1930–1960*, ed. Catharine Savage Brosman (Detroit: Gale, 1988), 194.

41. Pierre Drieu La Rochelle, *La Comédie de Charleroi* (Paris: Nouvelle Revue Française, 1934), 69.

42. Jules Romains, *Le Drapeau noir* (Paris: Flammarion, 1937), 201.

43. Jules Romains, *Prélude à Verdun* (Paris: Flammarion, 1938), 29, 31.

44. René Benjamin, *Le Major Pipe et son père* (Paris: Fayard, 1918), 77–78.

8

STANLEY CORNGOLD

The Great War and modern German memory

In an important sense all German literature after 1914 is literature written in the aftermath of the Great War, since it can be held to reflect the horror, despair, and doubtful glory of this event or else to have repressed it. This chapter has much to choose from among "war writings" and has selected those that are explicit in referring to the frontline experience of soldiers, along with other types of writing that arise in an acknowledged, immediate relation to the Great War, including the works of ideological writers, like Thomas Mann, who consider themselves, in Mann's phrase, "soldiers of ideas."

The general reaction to the outbreak of war with Serbia, Russia, France, and England in the great cities of Germany and Austria was a display of enthusiasm in public places by massed crowds so huge as to have the power to draw all observers into their camp. Franz Kafka, for one, was swept along into the street crowds in Prague, in 1914 the capital of the Bohemian Lands of the Austro-Hungarian Empire; but what he afterwards marveled at was the crowd factor, the degree of cohesion, and less the substance of its giant yawp. All throughout Central Europe the weather that summer had been brilliant – unmatchably brilliant in recent memory; and so it is thinkable that if the weather had been foul, and the opportunity for crowds to exert pressure on their rulers less available, the foulness of the war might have been averted: historians like Reiner Stach and Modris Eksteins hold this view.[1]

The moment of war enthusiasm is at the heart of several essays by Robert Musil. In his great, unfinished novel *The Man without Qualities* (*Der Mann ohne Eigenschaften*), 1930–52, Musil went on to record the irony, drift, and malaise of prewar Austria-Hungary. But in September 1914, a month after the German invasion of Belgium, Musil published "Europeanism, War, Germanism" (*Europäertum, Krieg, Deutschtum*) in a leading intellectual journal *Die neue Rundschau*, along with enthusiastic essays by other prominent German writers. The mood of Musil's piece is ecstatic. What comes as a surprise to the reader today is the provocation to this mighty feeling that Musil stresses – the "fantastic outbreak of hatred for us and envy for no fault of our own" – which has had the effect of diminishing the value of everything deeply German – our "world-view and inner equilibrium, our conception of all things human."[2] The mood has been one of a national anxiety, in which every moment of existence, every future project seems shadowed by the threat of death produced by the hostility of others.

But now, with Germany at war, a new set of virtues is alive in the nation – virtues almost unknown to the "art and imagination" of German litera-ture in the preceding fifty years, namely, "loyalty, courage, subordination, performance of duty, simplicity." That these qualities went unmentioned in modernist literature was not entirely "our" fault, writes Musil; after all, "we did not know what a beautiful and fraternal thing war is." But in another sense the culture of modernity was not fundamentally different from this new culture of war, Musil continues, for it was always in opposition, its goal was always "to bend and expose traditional, established, and depend-able psychological attitudes en route to puncturing them." Now that this old aggression informing artistic criticism has surfaced, we realize that our culture has always been inspired by the "same martial and conquering spirit that we feel today in its primordial form in us and around us, astonishing and transporting us with happiness."[3]

Germany has responded to "the conspiracy resolved upon our extermina-tion" with an extraordinary manifestation of cohesion and ardor. These will be the main lines of the dominant "higher" German reading of the war in 1914. Musil concludes:

> a new feeling was born . . . A stunning sense of belonging tore our hearts from our hands . . . Now we feel gathered into a ball, fused together by an inexpressible humility, in which the individual suddenly counts for nothing besides his elementary task of defending the tribe. This feeling must always have been present: it has now awakened . . . a bliss; and over and above its earnestness, a huge security and joy.[4]

Throughout this chapter we will be studying the fate of this moment in German memory in the years following the German defeat. We know the war ended horribly for Germany, especially according to the worst "histori-ans," the right-wing agitators of the Weimar Republic – including especially Ludendorff, the former Chief of Staff of the German High Command – who promulgated the legend of "the stab in the back" delivered to the frontline troops by Socialists, pacifists, and Jewish profiteers. The war ended horribly for Germany, according to more responsible historians as well, such as the revisionist Niall Ferguson, writing around 2000, for whom the "stab" is no

13 Slogans at the start: German recruits setting off for the Front, August 1914

legend at all, though it is in truth a "stab in the Front" delivered by the inde-
fensible defeatism in 1918 of this very Ludendorff and the German High
Command.'

The effort to preserve in its purity the semi-divine moment of national
cohesion, an ecstasy of collective bonding, informs Musil's postwar essay
"The Nation as Ideal and Reality" (*Die Nation als Ideal und als Wirklichkeit*), 1921. He never tires of recalling it; it continues to exhibit a profound meaning. It cannot be dismissed as illusory, as the epiphenomenon of
"mass suggestion." If an order shatters, it shatters really, from its own "involuntary neglected tensions": "That explosive soaring upwards with which
men freed themselves and, on the heights, found one another, found their
kind, was their farewell to bourgeois life, an expression of the will to disorder, to an abandonment of the old order, a leap into adventure – whatever
moral attributes had been attached to it." In the essay of 1914 Musil had been
thrilled by virtues quite consistent with bourgeois life: "loyalty, courage, subordination, performance of duty, simplicity." War on behalf of the nation
was a primordial force; but now it is a movement *a contrario*: the flight
from peace at all costs. It is only in a superficial sense that the German war
enthusiasm was triggered by the hatred flowing in from Germany's enemies;
that piece of propaganda has now been abandoned. The enthusiasm rose up
out of a primordial impulse toward (creative) self-destruction. This reading
of the "moment" makes sense as a step toward the vision of disintegration
informing Musil's *The Man without Qualities*.

The most impressive ideological tractate to have come out of the Great War on either side is the elaborate, labyrinthine defense of Germany by Thomas Mann, subsequently a Nobel-Prize-winning novelist and main representative of German culture. His massive work, *Reflections of a Nonpolitical Man (Betrachtungen eines Unpolitischen)*, was begun in 1915 in, as Mann confesses, a state of considerable agitation. It is a defense and justification of the German cause even through 1917 – two years after the Germans had introduced gas and submarine warfare; but Mann's argument occurs at a great distance from the battlefield: it is concerned with "ideal" issues even as it is driven by personal fury and a need for vindication.

In the background were the bitter propaganda wars being fought between the belligerents. A major provocation was the gruesome events following the German army's occupation in August 1914 of the Belgian city of Louvain, the "Oxford of Belgium." Shots rang out; the German divisions retaliated by going on a rampage that ended with houses looted, 209 civilians dead, and the entire contents of the great library of 230,000 books in flames.[7] The pacifist French writer Romain Rolland, among others, published a series of attacks on the incomprehensibly brutal behavior of the Germans, seeing in these events writ small the text of the entire Prussian imperialist adventure. Rolland's argument did not fail to include an indictment of a "monstrous" article written by Thomas Mann for *Die neue Rundschau*, full of exalted belligerence.[8] In response to such "slanders" in the foreign press, the mayor of Berlin, Georg Riecke, together with the German playwrights Ludwig Fulda and Herman Sudermann, drafted an advertisement, a "Call to the World of Culture," signed by ninety-three scientists and intellectuals, defending German behavior as justified self-defense: the army in Louvain had to answer the provocations of "snipers." And, in the wider sense, German soldiers were charged with the mission of defending German culture against the Anglo-French West, which openly affected to be at war only with Germany's armies but was in truth at war with Germany's soul.[9]

Throughout this critical period, Thomas Mann's older brother Heinrich, also a novelist, sided with Rolland's pacifism and herewith made common cause, in Thomas's eyes, with the party of the Anglo-French. These are the self-blinded "civilization-literati," writers who espouse the "modern ideas" endemic to Anglo-French "civilization" – democratic ideals of political participation based on popular literacy. What values can Thomas Mann have held up as opposite to these and worth defending with a war? They are the German values of depth, irony, pessimism – the values of genuine "culture" (*not* civilization). The Germans are not a political people, he declares; they are an exception to the extension into modernity of Roman, "universalist" values; they are a people not at home "debating and writing, [which is] a republican affair."[10] An important reference – but one that would lead to speculations that would take us off the page – is the philosopher Nietzsche, whom Mann presents as an exemplary upholder of German values: Schopenhauer, Wagner, and Nietzsche form a "triple constellation," illustrious embodiments of the cultural ideals guiding Mann and implicitly lighting the way of this war for German culture.

The great sociologist Max Weber did not need to be provoked by fraternal strife (with his brother Alfred, an important cultural theorist), in order to write, in 1916, like Thomas Mann, an idealistic defense of the German war. In "Germany among the European World Powers" (*Deutschland unter den Europäischen Weltmächten*), Weber analyzes with force and clarity the particular issues of the day, rejecting the extremism of the nationalist party, the proper fate of Belgium (it is *not* to be annexed), the need for a politics driven neither by hate nor vanity but by objective concerns. But he also sees these policy matters in light of the truth about Germany that has conspicuously dawned: Germany is a "national power" (*Machtstaat*), one nation of 70 million whose historical mission cannot be laid aside. Here is "the ultimate, decisive reason for this war": the higher fact that Germany's destiny is that of a great nation called upon to preserve its – and indeed the world's – culture.[11] "It will not be the Swiss, the Danes, the Dutch, and the Norwegians from whom posterity will demand an accounting when it comes to the form of culture on the earth. It is not they whom posterity will blame when on the western half of our planet there is nothing more than Anglo-Saxon conventionality and Russian bureaucracy."[12] The war is not fundamentally an affair of self-defense or even of material aggrandizement: it is an affair of honor, of historical responsibility. That is the point whenever the question of its meaning is raised.

> The mighty weight of the destiny that we must endure leads the nation upwards, past abysses and the danger of decline onto the steep path of fame and honor, on which there is no going back, into the clear, hard air of the rule of world history, into whose fierce but powerful visage it had to, and was allowed to, gaze, so as to become the eternal memory of later generations.[13]

This is the recurrent German vision of the war, persistently "binocular." It registers through the one lens the clash of armies in the service of geo-political and economic interests. Through the other, it witnesses a sublime drama: the unfolding destiny of the mission of German culture; and it tries *to see them together, as one thing.* This belief in the higher value of German culture was continually fostered by the memory of the

14 Old and new warfare: German cavalry prepared for gas attack

miraculous mood of national cohesiveness that accompanied the outbreak
of the war.

This double optic, which tries to hold real-material interests together with
"spiritual" interests in a single frame, can assume extravagant, even monstrous forms. Among Germany's preeminent poets in 1914 was the now
much disremembered Stefan George.[14] George's powerful disciples asked
for a poem on the war, and he wrote "The War" ("Der Krieg"). Its argument attempts to fuse war practices and visionary ends to a mad extreme.
This war, Georg declares – this vile and predictable war – is not the real war.
The real war consists in the struggle to wrest a noble exemplar of masculine
man from the botched and bungled Germany of 1914. What is at stake is
the redeeming type of authentic poet-hero – "whoever shelters the guardian
image in his realm." The real "struggle was already decided on the stars."[15]
And yet it is still important that the Germans win *this* sordid war. Because
if Germany is lost, then the scene and occasion of the real struggle will be
lost along with it. And secondly – and here one's hair stands on end – a
great crime will be allowed to go unavenged, the crime of miscegenation.
This is the danger that the great poet George saw in the French and British
importation of black colonial troops into the war of the Fronts. His fear of

the loss of racial purity among the Germans might be the most disturbing version of Germany's "higher" legacy of thought about the war.

The most influential vehicles of the German cultural response to the war were not poems but plays and novels. Georg Kaiser's powerful Expressionist drama *The Burghers of Calais* (*Die Bürger von Calais*) was published in 1914 but performed to enthusiastic audiences in 1917: it offers a pregnant example of an Expressionist war drama. It is written in a dramatic poetry having Expressionist cadences, and it is a war drama in the sense that it is about a war – the English assault under Edward III on Calais in 1347. This way it manages to codify strong and conflicting attitudes toward the Great War.

The drama centers on the demands of the English king if the port city of Calais is to escape destruction: the city must present to the king six burghers in "beggars' gowns with a rope around their neck." They will be killed – and the city spared.

The extraordinary plot element is that seven not six burghers volunteer as martyrs; and the drama advances by means of the effort to discover a way to separate one from the group who, to his despair, will be denied a role in the city's redemption. But the device produced – a draw on colored balls *all of which* are winners – produces consternation among the seven. The inventor of this device, the burgher Eustache de Saint-Pierre, has been unable to deny to anyone the healing solemnity of the decision to die.

He needs to invent another method, and now it is that the last of the seven to report to the market place at the "first stroke of the clock" will be excluded. All arrive beforetimes except this very Eustache. The six martyrs, and the crowd, mutter betrayal, until, in a heart-stopping scene, the blind father of Eustache appears, carrying the body of his dead son. Eustache has anticipated his fate and in the night killed himself. This is a terrible irony, since at the break of day an English herald announces that the English king has that very night witnessed the birth of a son and in an overflow of lovingkindness determined to spare the city, requiring no sacrifice.[16] What does this drama have to say to the Great War?

Whereas almost all critics of this work have seen in Eustache's suicide a salubrious triumph of the individual will over the group and so a kind of liberation from the "thinking" that flows from conscription and obedience, a more perceptive minority, I think, has seen in it, instead, a crazed readiness for sacrifice that answers exactly to the war enthusiasm of the German cause: it is in reality an enthusiasm for "self"-destruction at the hands of an enemy sworn to kill. The play does not take sides: it compresses in immensely powerful clusters attitudes spawned by the war. But this one attitude may readily be read as dominant: a celebration of the heroism of a mentality of sacrifice for a grand cause apart from any practical consideration. Its audience would have been prepared for a world view that includes the possible loss of the war and all material advantage and yet amounts to a "higher" sort of victory, based on a devotion to death. In the play the cause of death and the cause of the nation (for which the death might be supposed to be useful) fuse in intricate and perplexing ways.

If at this point we spring to a brief account of the cultural phenomenon of Dada, it is with a precise purpose in mind – to stress its cosmopolitan, anti-nationalist, purgative quality. According to legend, Dada begins with a party at the Café Voltaire in Zurich in 1916: Hugo Ball and Emmy Jennings inserted a paper knife into a French–German dictionary (Dada was internationalist in conception right from the start) and landed at the entry "dada," which means, in German, "rocking horse" ("dada" also means "yes" in Rumanian, a definition that can be cheerfully cited for its life-affirming character). In a famous remark about Dada, the situationist philosopher, Guy Debord, wrote that it was beset by "a fatal one-sidedness. For dadaism *sought to abolish art without realizing it* . . ."[17] The "abolition of art," which Dada aimed at, is for the purposes of this chapter an art fueled on "transcendence" covertly in the national interest. The best-known Dada manifesto declares:

> Under the pretext of internalized experience [*Verinnerlichung*], Expressionists in literature and painting have joined ranks in a generation that today already longingly attends its literary-historical and art-historical glorification while stumping for honor-laden bourgeois recognition. Under the pretext of propagating the soul, in their struggle against Naturalism, they have taken the road back to abstract-pathetic gestures, which presuppose a life of comfort empty of incident or emotion . . . For the first time Dadaism no longer adopts an aesthetic stance to life, in that it tears to pieces the elements of all the slogans of ethics, culture, inwardness.

With its assault on "ethics, culture, and inwardness," it could almost have been scripted to refute the mystified elation of *The Burghers of Calais*.[18] We shall encounter, however, a fitful recrudescence of this elation in the work of Ernst Jünger.

To a general readership in the decade following the war, the single work in German most likely to represent the experience of Great War literature was Jünger's *The Storm of Steel* (*In Stahlgewittern*), 1920.[19] The "storm of steel" stands literally for the storm of shells of endless variety raining down on the frontline soldier. Ernst Jünger, who died in 1998 at the age of 102 (!), was himself a frontline infantry officer, distinguished for his daring and his stamina. While in the hospital, recovering from his last wounds – Jünger was wounded seven times, each time in two or more parts of his body – he received the highest military honor then bestowed, the order "Pour le mérite." After its first publication in 1920, *The Storm of Steel* appeared throughout the decades following in much revised editions. The revisions are a many-tracked affair – a matter of commentaries withdrawn when they are exalted but also of embellishments added to aestheticize an overly brutal report of trench warfare. Here is an example of Jünger's provocatively icy objectivity:

> A man of the 76th, close to me, shot off cartridge after cartridge, looking perfectly wild and without a thought of cover, till he collapsed in streams of blood. A shot had smashed his forehead with a report like a breaking board. He doubled up in his corner of the trench, and there he remained in a crouching attitude, his head leaning against the side. His blood poured on to the ground as though poured out of a bucket. The snorting death-rattles sounded at longer intervals and at last ceased. I seized his rifle and went on firing.[20]

The passage says nothing more, consistent with the vow that Jünger makes at the outset: "I made up my mind to omit all comments from this book."[21] A scene like this, which survived all further revisions, is the sort of bare reportage essentially defining *The Storm of Steel*. In the editions of the 1930s, Jünger was intent on removing passages of ultra-nationalist sentiment, such as the concluding paragraph of the first edition:

> We – [the youth of this land who are capable of enthusiasm for an ideal] stand in the memory of the dead who are holy to us . . . Though force without and barbarity within conglomerate in somber clouds, yet so long as the blade of a sword will strike a spark in the light may it be said: Germany lives and Germany shall never go under![22]

If this passage is removed, it may also be because thoughts of the "barbarity within" could invite a visit from the Nazis. But in general all such "heavy," ideological commentary disappears from the editions of the 1930s, which were then republished with a few additional changes in the collected works of 1978 and individually thereafter.

Jünger intends to convey the most immediate sense of the hallucinatory inferno of frontline combat. His text is shocking – shocking to read and shocking to grasp. The story "line," such as it is, is broken – like the broken trench line of the war of position; one is thrust into it, locked into it, as into the war. The "world" of the narrative, as it fitfully emerges, is being shelled to bits. There is scarcely a moment that does not "resonate" with, "report," the explosions of enemy, and sometimes, no less murderous, "friendly" fire. These reports are immediate: the hero-narrator's perception is limited to what one soldier can see in the middle of a field of death. This very narrowing of perspective might be adjudged defensive, as arising from the need to recoil from "open spaces," where one is exposed to the storm – or to the memory – of steel bombs. There is furthermore a sort of defiance in its irrational fixation on the instant, which is the prerequisite for the experience of danger, of adventure. At such moments numbness gives way to aggressive fury, hatred of the enemy, and the thirst to murder.

> The turmoil of our feelings was called forth by rage, alcohol, and the thirst for blood as we stepped out, heavily and yet irresistibly, for the enemy's lines. And therewith beat the pulse of heroism – the godlike and the bestial inextricably mingled . . . In my right hand I gripped my revolver, in my left a bamboo riding-cane. I was boiling with a fury now utterly inconceivable to me. The overpowering desire to kill winged my feet. Rage squeezed bitter tears from my eyes.[23]

And yet for all his avowed concern to reproduce the sensations themselves, Jünger does not suppress a taste for aesthetic effects. A late-interpolated commentary lends an art-character to the battlefield: "The ground in front, wreathed in swathes of smoke, was brightly lit up with light-rockets. These moments, in which all the troops stood in the highest tension, had a magical quality; they recalled those breathless seconds before a major performance, when the music breaks off and the strongest lights are turned on."[24]

Other sorts of aesthetic effects are ingrained in Jünger's vision. When moments of frenzied attack or hasty retreat have subsided, the narrator moves not into or alongside a circumambient civilized world but into the pastoral world of landscapes and weather. This association is forecast in the title of The "Storm" of Steel. The ebb and flow of combat is drawn into the cycle of the seasons:

> The neglected fields were scented with wildflowers. Here and there single trees stood by the wayside . . . They had an air of enchantment, standing alone in the solitude, covered with blossom white or pink or red. It seemed that the war had thrown a heroic and melancholy light over the landscape, and without disturbing its loveliness added a ray to its brightness and a strength to its spell. It is easier to go into the battle in the midst of such beauties of nature . . .[25]

There are a number of such moments, in which Jünger can be seen as aiming to revive the archaic association of art and war.

In its various ways each version strives to give the feel of actual war notes (the novel-memoir shows Jünger stopping to gather his breath, take stock, and write in his notebooks). Because these notes were written under the stress of combat, they must not seem as if they have been constructed to prove a thesis. As a result, the conceptual commentaries that do survive the editing process cry out to be taken seriously.

Here is one deliberately composed for the final version. Following the massive final German attack on the Western Front in 1918, amid scenes of bodies torn and dismembered by shells of all sorts, and with the scent of a German defeat in his lungs, Jünger writes this justification of battle:

> This giant gathering into a ball of powers in the hour of destiny, in which a distant future was being wrestled for, and the discharge which followed it so surprisingly, so dismayingly, had led me for the first time into the depth of suprapersonal regions. That distinguished it from everything that I had experienced till now; it was an initiation, which not only opened the glowing chambers of terror but also led through them.[26]

The impression must survive that for all its horrors, the Great War was ennobling, a scene of honor and a scene of self-discovery.

Such a commentary is, of course, important; and yet the more decisive fact about this memoir-novel is the scarcity of its reflective interludes. This work is above all not about argument: the piecemeal character of Jünger's ideas and cultural references corresponds directly with the subject matter – a world of shrapnel. When they come, they come more like moments of action or of pure sensation – fragmentary, precious, crucial.

Jünger's pictures from the battlefield haunt the conclusion of Thomas Mann's great educative novel *The Magic Mountain* (*Der Zauberberg*), 1924. Although this work is chiefly remarkable for its power to represent characters through their ideas – through their "positions" and "counter-positions" – the last chapter contains some of the most powerful writing in the whole of trench war literature.

> Dusk, rain, and mud, fire reddening a murky sky . . . the damp air rent by piercing, singsong whines and raging, onrushing, hellhound howls that end their arc in a splintering, spraying, fiery crash filled with groans and screams . . .
>
> They rush forward as best they can, with brash cries and nightmarishly heavy feet, clods of earth clinging leadenly to crude boots. They hurl themselves down before projectiles howling toward them, only to leap up and rush on . . . – they have not been hit. Then they are hit, they fall, flailing their arms, shot in the head, the heart, the gut. They lie with their faces in the mire and do not stir . . .
>
> He ["our hero," Hans Castorp] runs with feet weighed down by mud, his bayoneted rifle clutched in his hand and hanging at his side. Look, he is stepping on the hand of a fallen comrade – stepping on it with his hobnailed boots, pressing it deep into the soggy, branch-strewn earth . . . He stumbles. No, he has thrown himself on his stomach at the approach of a howling hound of hell, a large explosive shell, a hideous sugarloaf from the abyss. He lies there,

face in the cool muck, legs spread, feet twisted until the heels press the earth. Laden with horror . . . [it] buries itself in the ground and explodes . . . bursts inside the earth with ghastly superstrength and casts up a house-high fountain of soil, fire, iron, lead, and dismembered humanity.[27]

It is hard to imagine that Mann, who was not physically fit to serve on the Front, could have written these passages without the example of Jünger. As early as 1914 Mann had written that his "prewar" novel would have to end with the war – and just end with it; *The Magic Mountain* would not be about the war; and indeed his narrator, in invoking this "festival of death," shies clear of fully imagining it: the narrator averts his gaze, refusing to "go there" any longer.[28] But not to have ventured to go there at all would have struck this proud writer as the evasion of a challenge.

These pages raise a number of questions about their inner motivation. For one thing, the logic within the novel cannot be that Hans Castorp's sojourn at the mountain sanatorium has to end with the Great War in the sense that everything that he has learned points to the necessity of his going off to war. This logic simply isn't there and would have to be repudiated by every reader in 1924 for whom the monstrous slaughter on the battlefields and Germany's subsequent humiliation was a traumatic memory. We noted before that Mann had decided in whatever case to end the novel with the war; so the "logic of events" must be an affair of rhetorical persuasion, of the suggestion that in some subliminal way it *must* be war that caps the education of our hero and brings him down from the mountain top. The narrative must evoke the coming of the war to the Magic Mountain as something plausible, as an event that makes sense in light of the events that precede it. And here is how this narrative feat is accomplished. In a passage introducing the war pages, we read:

> Then came the rumble of thunder – but modesty and reserve keep us from turning that thundering rumble into a blustering narrative. No bombast, no rodomontade. Here, with appropriately lowered voice, we shall say that the thunderbolt itself (with which we are all familiar) was the deafening detonation of great destructive masses of accumulated stupor and petulance. It was, to speak in subdued, respectful tones, a historic thunderbolt that shook the foundations of the earth; but for us it is the thunderbolt that bursts open the magic mountain and rudely sets its entranced sleeper outside the gates.[29]

The key point is the accumulated "stupor and petulance" that provokes, as it must, a "detonation." The latter word literally means *war*. But the first terms – stupor and petulance – have already been established as precisely the moods that had set in during the last of the seven years of Hans Castorp's stay on the Magic Mountain. And such a stagnation of the spirit surely calls for rectification and change, even violent change; Castorp must go down from those sour heights, even if it requires something like an "explosive" decision on his part to do so. On the Magic Mountain an emotional detonation – leading to a detonation of the will – is reasonable and expectable. And this is in fact exactly what occurs, for "since the moment of his awakening, Hans Castorp had been caught up in the turmoil and confusion of a wild departure, the result of the bursting thunderbolt in the valley."[30]

On the other hand, it would be dubious to propose in 1924 – as indeed many German thinkers did during and immediately after the war (recall Musil in 1921) – that the explosive outbreak of the Great War had been profoundly meaningful, had value as a cathartic purification of a destructive European malaise. Indeed, Mann had himself been such a thinker, writing to Samuel Fischer in August 1914, "This world-at-peace, which has now collapsed with such a shattering uproar – weren't we all basically fed up with it? Hadn't it turned rotten from sheer comfort?"[31]

If we react chiefly to the implicit parallelism (thunderbolt/thunderbolt) between events on the Magic Mountain and events in the flatlands, then Mann makes the war feel inevitable – inevitable as an event, an outcome, in the real course of history.[32] But if we conclude, in light of Hans Castorp's intellectual, moral, and sensuous development on the Magic Mountain, that his descent into the flatlands *as a battlefield* is merely arbitrary – attachable to or detachable from the plot-line – then we will be inclined to view the actual war as superfluous, too, within the course of history. Mann's position is typically equivocal – it encourages both readings – a state of affairs not surprising for the artist who wrote, in the *Reflections*, "Writing as such has always seemed to me the product and expression of problematicalness, of the Here and yet There, the Yes and No, the two souls in one breast, the bad richness of inner conflicts, antitheses, and contradictions."[33]

But this uncertainty raises a basic question about the novel. What alternative might the flatlands have offered in the best of cases to the triviality, licentiousness, and merely speculative character of life on the Magic Mountain? When pressed, the novel offers nothing more compelling than a continual vacating of all positions, ending, finally, with a vacating of the "position" of the Magic Mountain – this is nihilism – and hence again makes the hypothesis more plausible that this *self-destructive* war is the logical and inevitable conclusion of an episode of European nihilism.

Hans Castorp's education has unfolded as in every sense a vacation – a continual vacating of previously entertained positions. Consider the prescriptions of his mentor Naphta, which waver between mystic detachment and the application of terror for the sake of social coherence. This position is implausible for Mann, his hero, and his accomplice, the willing reader.

Castorp's other mentor, Settembrini, appeals to a life of social "action," aiming at "progress," at the betterment of the "people" – an ideal supposedly fueled by a passion for social equality but masking, to Mann's mind, a lust for pedagogical authority and a will to absolutize "the political." This cannot inspire conviction, in light of all the hostility to such a stance that survives in Mann onward from *Reflections* days. Meanwhile, the crucial ideal of artistic creativity is absent from both this "Here and yet There," being barely represented or even intimated on or below the Magic Mountain, except, perhaps, through the arcane suggestion that life on the "mountain" itself is like inhabiting a fiction or that Hans Castorp's indulgence in the pastime of "playing king" over his private domain of thoughts (*Regieren*) is a sort of imaginative fiction-writing. Only Castorp's cousin Joachim's "soldier's honor" projects a real alternative to the life of the Magic Mountain. But Joachim, who escapes to the flatlands once, is delivered back, and dies; and with this, in a sense, for all the world, there dies the very notion of "soldier's honor." For the Great War into which Castorp subsequently descends does not offer even the glimmer of a possibility of honor: Mann's account is brief but visualizes, chiefly, the "howling hounds of hell," whistling shells bringing down atrocious, impersonal death. Again, we are left with the suggestion that nothing other than Europe's self-destruction is available as an option for life in the first decades of the twentieth century.

Finally, however, the novel does at one point teach Castorp, however evanescently, that "man shall grant death no dominion over his thoughts."[34] There remains the fair side of the liberal and life-loving Settembrini, whom Castorp respects the most. Of Hans Castorp's three chief guides, Settembrini is the most influential and the most tenderly remembered; he has repeatedly urged him to flee the sanatorium for the flatlands of civil society in his own country, and Hans, as we see, does. Settembrini, though failing, lives long enough to register that German civil society is now at war.

> I would have wished to see you go in some other way, but it doesn't matter. The gods have decreed it so . . . I hoped to send you off to your work, and now you will be fighting alongside your fellows. My God, you are the one to go, and not our lieutenant [Joachim]. The tricks life plays. Fight bravely out there where blood joins men together.[35]

The figure of Settembrini is important in another way: it contains various coded references to the *Reflections* of 1915–17 – *The Magic Mountain* was begun before the *Reflections* – and in effect reverses its argument. For in taking the route he does, Castorp is also following, to a degree, the advice of a kinder, gentler incarnation of Thomas Mann's older brother Heinrich, whom Settembrini outwardly resembles. Heinrich – the "literary" man, captive of the superficial values of the "civilized" West and hostile to German "culture" – is the implied and much-assaulted addressee of the *Reflections*. And since Heinrich Mann would not have encouraged such a one as Hans Castorp to join the war, the figure of Settembrini, we can conclude, is a fantastic constellation, a masked projection of a benevolent older brother (along with his maddening qualities). Unlike the real Heinrich in 1915–17, Settembrini supports Thomas's position, holding it honorable to fight for Germany. The consideration Mann shows this Latinate figure also prepares the way for Mann's celebrated turn, in the years immediately following the composition of *The Magic Mountain*, to what he was to call "friendship" with the values of Europe, "civilization," and the League of Nations. This turn "southward" and "westward" away from Germany is accomplished for Mann with the help of an example: Nietzsche's own, now awe-inspiring break from Wagner – the same Nietzsche who once figured in the *Reflections*, along with Schopenhauer and Wagner, as a reason to go to war against "civilized" France and England.

Mann's depiction of war at the Front is very likely influenced by the groundbreaking *The Storm of Steel*; but this influence is a matter of content and image and not of the storyteller's art. It is, to use a Kantian distinction, an "imitation" (*Nachahmung*) but not an "emulation" (*Nachfolge*), since there is no fundamental kinship of manner between these writers. Meanwhile, Arnold Zweig's splendid, wide-ranging, and very detailed novel *The Case of Sergeant Grischa* (*Der Streit um den Sergeanten Grischa*) (1927) can be viewed as a work mediating between the two. It is closer to the Front – the Eastern Front – and fighting than the bulk of *The Magic Mountain*, but it deliberately turns in another direction, away from Jünger. Except for brief reminiscences, it does not picture trench warfare, and it has nothing of Jünger's phantasmagoric, modernist rupturing manner. On the other hand, *The Case of Sergeant Grischa* shares a great deal of the narrative art of *The Magic Mountain*: the basis of this style might be termed the "tellability" (*Erzählbarkeit*) of the world. It is plainly insistent on discovering a meaning in the war, even if that meaning should be dispiriting. It is nevertheless an intelligible meaning and a provocation to political revolution.

Zweig's vision of the effect upon the German General Staff of a single persecuted enemy prisoner achieved immense popularity as, first, a play, and thereafter as this much longer novel – efficiently translated into English by Eric Sutton, so efficiently that the English critic J. B. Priestley came to call it the greatest novel to have come out of the war in any language.

The Case of Sergeant Grischa is written from an old-fashioned omniscient perspective. This is owed to the storyteller's principal being-at-home in the world, because it is a world with a sane and healthy (if simple-minded) protagonist, with good men and women in it, old-fashioned characters whose consciousness the author enjoys espousing; and if things turn out badly, it is not by mere chance or contingency; at crucial moments you see the author shrinking back from this "solution" to tricky issues of plot. The work is an encyclopedia of intelligible, humane responses to injustice.

There ought to be a great deal of interest today in this immensely readable, immensely instructive work, to which all college students in the former East Germany were exposed (Arnold Zweig, in his horror of capitalism and fascism, became a sort of literary headman for this pseudo-Communist totalitarian state). One easily admires the tireless, epic range of a work written in the realist tradition of Balzac, Fontane, and Thomas Mann, with its breadth of scene and variety of type and its attempt to present its characters in their very own diction, from the naïve Russian sergeant Grischa Paprotkin to his partisan comrades, such as the "lynx"-like Babka, and from the cultivated Berlin Jewish legal officer Posnanski and his assistant, the Berlin Jewish novelist Bertin, to the elderly Junker general His Excellency von Lychow, the hero of the piece, and his dashing adjutant Paul Winfried. There are East European Jews and young Russian socialist intellectuals and a couple of much-praised army nurses, all of whom are realized with an extreme visual clarity and whose relations are constructed through a continually varied syntax that is hypnotically rich throughout.

In this novel, everything turns on the fate of Grischa, who has escaped from a prisoner of war camp and wandered eastward in an effort to get home. A partisan, his lover Babka, suggests he assume the identity of another soldier, one Bjuscheff, who she believes is a deserter who has died along the way. Babka does not know that in the meantime Bjuscheff, who was spotted meandering through enemy lines, has been sentenced to death as a Russian spy; and when Grischa is apprehended, maintaining that he is Bjuscheff, he is sentenced to death. In desperation he succeeds in establishing to the satisfaction of the legal staff of the division into whose jurisdiction he has wandered that he is not Bjuscheff: this novel could well have been called *I Am Not Bjuscheff*. The case is presented to the old Junker general von Lychow for his approval; and because he has actually been introduced to the ubiquitous Grischa, whose simple handsome strength and life-force remind him of the Russian peasant who taught him to ride as a boy, he is glad to revoke the sentence.

The action turns critical when the plea is rejected by no one less than the Supreme Commander in the East, a certain von Schieffenzahn, who is a respectful parody of Ludendorff, Hindenburg's Chief of Staff. The reply of the Eastern Command Ost reads:

> Even if the identity of the condemned man Bjuscheff with a certain Paprotkin, a prisoner of war . . . has been shown to be to some extent probable, higher considerations make it undesirable that such identity should be successfully established, inasmuch as the Commander-in-Chief . . . is convinced that the legal aspect of the case is of very slight importance compared with the military and political interests involved . . . The execution of the sentence, which was legally imposed and is hereby confirmed, is to be officially reported here.[36]

Below, marked in pencil, are the words: "Seen: Sch." This is von Schieffenzahn himself.

Von Lychow, dreading a head-on collision with von Schieffenzahn and feeling his age (he is over seventy), wavers for a second, but not longer.

> The will of another had dared to impugn his judgment of right and wrong, and within his own domain. Either Germany stood for justice as her rulers saw it, and the conscience of the man responsible, and his sense of law, were the only absolute guarantees of the correctness of his decisions – or else every sort of interference was possible. Anarchy, however disguised, would break forth and rear her hideous, ruthless head . . .[37]

His self-respect, his sense of honor, demand his intervention; von Lychow resolves to take this war to Headquarters, where he confronts the bulldog von Schieffenzahn. Before too long, in this excruciatingly dramatic scene that recalls the fact that this novel first came into the world as a play, von Schieffenzahn is provoked to say: "I prefer . . . to take the plain blunt view of the situation: the State creates justice, the individual is a louse."

This is intolerable for von Lychow – and, indeed, for the narrator.

> No, Sir, it is justice that preserves the State . . . and that alone gives a meaning to life. It is because justice is the foundation of all States that nations have the right to tear themselves to pieces in their defense . . . I know that justice and faith in God have been the pillars of Prussia, and I will not look on while her rulers try to bring her down.[38]

But this argument can have very little relevance for von Schieffenzahn, the Supreme Commander on the Eastern Front.

Throughout the novel, Zweig's energetic, elastic narrator's consciousness penetrates every object, ranging from the lynx in the wood and the horse that the smart young adjutant Brettschneider rides, to the upper echelons of mortal awareness, that of the Supreme Commander, who is bent on creating a vast German empire in the east, in Poland–Russia. Zweig strives to represent difficult minds, difficult personalities. He does not relent until he has taken us into Grischa's consciousness at the very instant of his death before a firing squad. He does not make it easy for himself. Whereas Mann could invoke a certain *pudeur* of the imagination not to venture there, into the scenes of frontline horror, Zweig, with a positive sense of the value of the world, of everything in the world, shrinks back from no task of naming what is the case – including the death agony. (It takes the English translation to bowdlerize Zweig's mentions of genitals and scatological things.)

The novel is plot-driven but shot through with criss-cross skeins of political and erotic desires: the hope for a new Germany in the dream of a new leadership, a symbiosis of the old, reliable Prussian sense of honor and the swiftness of thought of the Berlin Jewish intelligentsia. If, as Mann insisted, *The Magic Mountain* is a prewar novel, then *Grischa* is a thoroughly postwar novel, refracting its imaginative account of the war through the lens of political hope for a Germany that will rise up out of this horror. The striking feature of the action is the collusion of the Jewish and old Prussian "elements" in defense of justice – the justice owed to Sergeant Grischa. Von Lychow says: "These Jewish lawyers . . . I could swear they love law for its own sake as we love our lands and field" – a display of consideration for what matters to the Other, whose concern is put on a par with one's own.[39] This collusion is reinforced by the depiction of a happy, if illicit, love between Bertin the Jewish novelist, who is married, and Sophie, the blue-blooded sister of a family of insensitive Junkers.

In fact there are illicit relations throughout, but they are presented without a grain of worry or remorse by the narrator, for they are chiefly markers of his celebration of the joy of life, of sex and procreation. This reticence appears to function as the marker of a certain disjunction of sensibility in the narration, which is everywhere bent on the positive, even though it cannot blind itself entirely to the horrors of war. Yet when an account is given of the cruelty of the German occupying force, it is told as a distanced story within the story by a woman, Babka, who appears to be well recovered from it: her father and brothers were murdered by German soldiers when they were denounced by a jealous neighbor for hiding a gun they needed for shooting game, but Babka murdered this neighbor in turn, as well as a young German officer, whose splendid clothes she now wears; and now she is richly in love with Grischa, whose child she carries, and cheerful and resourceful throughout.

Throughout this work we have the impression of a world through the telling of it; the act of narration is foregrounded, though without the intensity of refined scrutiny as in *The Magic Mountain*. So the work is modern in the sense of its drive to tell all the world, but it is not modern in the sense that it does without novel devices of narration: unspeakable diction, *à la* Joyce; or elaborately circular referential structures of narration, *à la* Proust; or montage, *à la* the later Thomas Mann. It is serene and forward-moving and replete with the famous plot device of realism: rational coincidence.

And a final political direction. If the first cut is synchronic, showing the German world in its local variety, with all its parts, like pieces in a mosaic, fused together behind Eastern lines under the force of war, it does not fail to emphasize the provenance and the future of these various pieces: the proletariat, the managers of machines, will go forward; the Junker class will die out (though its spirit will continue to rule in new political combinations). Zweig is not overly insistent about the point of a political upheaval from below. It is made in an almost throwaway manner in a final scene in which no high-ranking officer is present. The humble corporal who has guarded Grischa is struggling to catch the train heading west and home; he has been shattered by his duties and is heading for a convalescent leave, but he comes to the station a minute too late. The train has already started to leave the station; and then, to the consternation of the passengers, the two tough engine drivers – the engineer and the fireman – make a quick decision to slow down the train so that little Hermann Sacht can get aboard. It is an unexpected flare-up of solidarity, and in this sense could fit into the cast of characters of Erich Maria Remarque's *All Quiet on the Western Front* (1927–28); but the thrust is different. This train is not heading toward the Front and death; it is leaving the Front for the city, for new life. The solidarity of these lower-class figures is not a feeble stay against an atrocious death – of being blown to pieces by machined steel bombs; their solidarity is a harbinger of another application of machinery, machinery as industrial capital and as engines of class loyalty, and now, as in the case of the engine drivers, in the hands of those who operate these machines. The point is made explicit by one of the officers riding in the officers' carriage: "I fancy an engine-driver today is more indispensable than Schieffenzahn." Another officer, who has protested the behavior of the engine drivers, mutters: "The pack is beginning to be aware of itself, the skilled workmen – all those fellows who have to do with machines." "They don't know it yet," thought a senior army-surgeon, who was allowed to make the fourth in this officers' carriage: "and when they do know it . . ."[40] The novel ends immediately thereafter with this grand filmic symbolic fusion of a political hope and the very machinery of this hope, the instruments guaranteeing the imagined ascendancy of a technically proficient working class. The original moment of communal hope that aimed, in this novel, at a war for *Lebensraum* in the east, now conserves itself in reversing direction as "the interminable train that rolled westward into the brightening noontide."[41]

There is no such salvific postwar moment in Erich Maria Remarque's world-famous *All Quiet on the Western Front*, 1927–28, in which the fortunes of the moment of divine enthusiasm sink to an unheard-of low, for here there is *no* generation left to carry forward what Weber called in 1916 "the cultural forms of the world." This brief, episodic novel – next to Mann's and Zweig's a modest literary effort – rapidly became an object of adoration and contestation throughout Germany, and after its translation, throughout Europe and America.

Its pacifist pathos moved a core of non-politicized readers but also became a political football for the extremes of the proto-Nazi and Communist press. For the Nazis, the book, which lacks propagandistic idealism, dishonored the German war dead and disgracefully erased in advance the possibility of future German military vengeance. For the Communists, the book was inert, unmobilizable, since its perspective was limited to that of the unenlightened petit bourgeois incapable of thinking through the social contradictions that had led to the war and would continue to lead to war. The remarks that follow aim to extract the book from the crossed searchlights of political interests and explain its allure – a peculiar mix of pseudo-naïvety, low-key decency of feeling, lyrical allusion to high German literature, and some complications at their shared borders.

Unlike the writings we have looked at, there is nothing in this book about the "superstructure": no representation of officers, of a cultivated bour-geoisie, of industrialists or ideologues, of persons who continue to read or write. The narrator – or first narrator – the "I" named Paul Bäumer, the graduate of a gymnasium – used to read and write. Now, returned home on furlough, he gazes at the rows of books in his room at home.

> I know them all, and I remember putting them in order. With my eyes I implore them: speak to me – take me up – take me up again, you old life – you carefree, wonderful life – take me up again – . . . My impatience grows.
>
> Suddenly a terrible feeling of isolation wells up inside me. I can't get back, I'm locked out; however much I might, however much I try, nothing moves . . .
>
> I get up wearily and look out of the window. Then I take one of the books and flick through it to try and read. I put it aside and take up another one.
>
> I stand silent in front of them, as if I were on trial.
>
> Dispirited.
>
> Words, words, words – they can't reach me.
>
> Slowly I put the books back in their places on the shelves.
>
> It's over.
>
> I leave the room quietly.[42]

The unwilled detachment from the books of the past mounts into a frenzy of repudiation after he has stayed at a soldier's hospital. He has grasped with horror the fact that there are hundreds of thousands of such places, where agonized bodies lie – in Germany, in France, in Russia. "How pointless all human thoughts, words and deeds must be, if things like this are possible! Everything must have been fraudulent and pointless if thousands of years of civilization weren't even able to prevent this river of blood, couldn't stop these torture chambers existing in their hundreds of thousands."[43]

Because the language of books is withdrawing from the hero, *this* book must strive to speak unobtrusively, and yet the story must be told. So Remarque's main device is to evoke reticence through the indifferent slang of simple soldiers. Paul's conversation with the others is a bit rough or obscene (although this jargon is chiefly presented as spoken to him, not by him). The comrades who survive the slaughter of his schoolmates are semi-illiterate. High literacy – literary quality – is reserved for Paul Bäumer's moments of memory or reflection that float, detached, from the life he actually lives, which consists chiefly of the brute horrors of trench warfare and a struggle, occasionally picaresque, to satisfy drives of hunger, sex, and survival.

This detachment of memory from lived experience – "experience" is saying too much for this exposure to the numbing shocks of storms of steel – is made doubly strong by the claim that Bäumer repeats: he cannot identify his memories as his own. Memories of favored spots – the quiet row of poplar trees in his home town, the inner court of the cathedral at home, full of rosebushes – arise in the midst of the filthy chaos of trench warfare and almost literally float above the battlefield; but most telling is the fact that he cannot connect his present consciousness of life to them; they are his memories and yet they are no longer his.

> Up go the Verey lights [*Leuchtschirme*] – and I see a picture [*Bild*] of a summer evening, and I'm in the cloistered courtyard of the cathedral looking at the tall rose trees that grow in the middle of the little garden there, where the deans of the chapter are buried. All around are stone carvings [*Steinbilder*] for the different stations of the cross. There is nobody there;- this flower-filled square is caught up in a profound silence, the sun shines warm on the thick grey stones, I place my hand on one and feel the warmth . . . Between the slender sunlit columns of the cloisters themselves is that cool darkness that only churches have, and I am standing there and thinking that by the time I am twenty I shall have learnt the secret of the confusion that women cause in men's minds.[44]

This memory has a Rilkean flair: the drama in the shadows of old churches, relics of past devotion, and the vague solicitation of the mysteries of women. But it is framed quite differently from, let us say, the poems in Rilke's *Book of Images*: it is framed by the killing machines of trench warfare.[45] "The picture is astonishingly close, it touches me before it dissolves under the flash of the next Verey light [*Leuchtkugel*, literally, 'flash bomb']."[46]

The conjunction of the framing flare (*Leuchtschirm*) and the involuntary memory image (*Bild*) amounts to a suggestive date stamp for the contemporary reader. Today, in this age of mechanical reproduction, an image (*Bild*) flashing up upon a *Schirm* ("protective cover," also "screen") must suggest the screen (*Bildschirm*) of a television set or a computer. Suddenly, for one moment, the ostensibly harmless, unproblematically everyday character of such medial images appears complicit in the murderous technical conjunctions of experience on the war front. In this passage in Remarque, technology supplies an unwonted light; an image is illuminated *by it* with the colors and moods of strangeness and unavailability – an illumination that we take for granted in our visual culture today and which supplies, in many cases, a surrogate for individual memory. In this moment the novel literally enacts the penetration into the modern mind – into modernism and modernity – of the Great War.

Such unwilled effects of this novel – and there are many odd conjunctions of image and rhetoric – may be more provocative today than its deliberately staged effects, like those produced by doctrinal statements or by all-too-explicit explanations. Here I am referring, in the first instance, to such evocations of a "lost generation" as the one announced on page one of the novel: "This book is intended neither as an accusation nor as a confession, but simply as an attempt to give an account of a generation that was destroyed by the war – even those of it who survived the shelling." [47]

With this, the novel begins drawing the circle that closes on the last page in a passage containing the sentence that gives the novel its name. Here, the novelist, reaching for authority, suddenly transforms the first-person perspective to that of a third:

> He fell in October 1918, on a day that was so still and quiet along the entire front line that the army dispatches restricted themselves to the single sentence: that there was nothing new to report on the Western Front.
>
> He had sunk forwards and was lying on the ground as if asleep. When they turned him over, you could see that he could not have suffered long – his face wore an expression that was so composed that it looked as if he were almost happy that it had turned out that way. [48]

In a way this conclusion displays with finality the novel's faults: its too obvious irony, sentimentality, and will to aestheticize brute reality. Bäumer is dead on the Front, his features may be quietly composed but they are nonetheless due to decompose. Unlike most of Jünger's *The Storm of Steel*, these, and other vignettes, are overexplicit.

The reverberations of the Great War continue to sound today. There is no summing up of its effects any more definitive than a summing up of us who are its survivors; in deep ways we have been made by this war and will never stop being made so. The literature about the war tells us of the horrific degradation of human ideals and aspirations and a horrific degradation of the human body by its collision with the machinery of death. It tells us too of the desperate effort of writers to find something instructive let alone humanly ennobling in scenes of filth and carnage. I conclude by mentioning one effect that has generally gone unnoted. It is not the worst, but it is not for the good either: it is a mentality of calculation, of bookkeeping, of profit-taking, for – as we remember – in its last years the war devolved from thrust and parry and thereafter from the stalemate of the trenches to a war of naked attrition: the victor would be the country that would crush the "competition" by wasting all its stores of men and material. Karl Kraus – in an obnoxious modality of his personality, writing as a Jewish anti-Semite – conjured in *The Last Days of Mankind* "the god of commerce [who] reigns in the war, a god with a human face":

> The Jewish plutocrat, the man who sits at the cash register of world history *collects* victories and daily records the *turnover* in blood. The tenor of his couplings and headlines which shriek with greed for profit is such that he claims the number of dead and wounded and prisoners as assets; sometime he confuses mine and thine with mines and tines (*mein und dein und Stein und Bein*).[49]

But it was not just the vilely conjured "Jewish" plutocrat who did such calculations; this world-view ran up and down Austrian and German society. In 1918 Kaiser William II refused Ludendorff's desperate resignation but added: "I see that we must draw up a balance sheet, we are on the brink of solvency. The war must be ended."[50] It was this sort of rhetoric, this sort of mentality, that prompted the great Austrian novelist Hermann Broch to compose *Huguenau*, the third volume of his trilogy *The Sleepwalkers* (*Die Schlafwandler*), 1931. This novel describes the career of the eponymous hero, an Alsatian profiteer, who makes his way, swindling and killing, to the safe heights of the respectable, wealthy businessman, prompting Broch to write, in his "Historical Excursus" on the "Disintegration of Values": "Modernity's two great rational means of understanding (*Verständigungsmittel*) are the language of science in mathematics and the language of money in bookkeeping."[51] The triumph of these two "languages," under the specific conditions of their perversion in wartime, would mark the final failure of the German dream of "turning and exposing" the brute facts of the war into a justification of a German culture of idealism. In 1933 Walter Benjamin attributed the "poverty" of the wartime experience to the decay of the ecstasy of national bonding.[52] This poverty could be more concretely described as the collapse of an experience of calculation that aimed to impoverish an enemy through his maximum slaughter at minimum expense.[53]

NOTES

1. Reiner Stach, *Franz Kafka – Jahre der Entscheidungen* (Frankfurt A. M.: Fischer, 2002). Modris Eksteins, *Rites of Spring: The Great War and the Birth of the Modern Age* (Boston: Houghton Mifflin, 1989).

2. Robert Musil, "Europäertum, Krieg, Deutschtum," *Die neue Rundschau*, 25 (September 1914): 1303. Unless otherwise indicated, all translations from the German are my own (SC).

3. *Ibid.*

4. *Ibid.*, 1304–05.

5. Niall Ferguson, *The Pity of War: Explaining World War I* (New York: Basic Books, 1999), 314.

6. Musil, "Die Nation als Ideal und als Wirklichkeit" (1921), *Essays und Reden*, in *Robert Musil, Gesammelte Werke, in neun Bänden*, ed. Adolf Frisé, vol. VIII (Reinbeck bei Hamburg: Rowohlt, 1978), 1071.

7. Robert E. Norton, *Secret Germany: Stefan George and His Circle* (Ithaca: Cornell University Press, 2002), 521–22.

8. Romain Rolland, "Pro Aris," *Au-dessus de la mêlée* (Paris: Librairie Paul Ollendorf, 1915), 13.

9. Uwe Reinecke, "Deutsche Kriegskultur," *Ossietsky*, 25 (2002), http://www.sopos.org/aufsaetze/3e15a492b3b8a/1.phtml.

10. Thomas Mann, *Betrachtungen eines Unpolitischen* (Frankfurt A. M.: Fischer Taschenbuch, 2001), 487.

11. Max Weber, "Deutschland unter den Weltmächten," in *Gesammelte politische Schriften* (Tübingen: Mohr, 1971), 175.

12. *Ibid.*, 176.

13. *Ibid.*, 177.

14. George has returned to the center of critical attention for readers interested in modern German poetry and its intellectual background. He is seen as an autocrat cultivating uncritical discipleship and as fostering a mood of irrational servility that prepared the ground for Hitler's seizing power in 1933. See Norton, *Secret Germany*.

15. Stefan George, "Der Krieg," *Das neue Reich*, in *Stefan George, Werke: Ausgabe in zwei Bänden* (München, Düsseldorf: Küpper, 1958), 410–15.

16. Georg Kaiser, *Die Bürger von Calais, Georg Kaiser, Werke*, ed. Walther Huder, vol. I (Frankfurt A.M., Berlin, Vienna: Propyläen, 1971), 579.

17. ". . . and surrealism sought to *realize art without abolishing it.*" Guy Debord, *The Society of the Spectacle* (New York: Zone, 1995), 136.

18. "Dadistisches Manifest," in *Expressionismus und Dadaismus, Die deutsche Literatur in Text und Darstellung*, vol. XIV, (Stuttgart: Reclam, 1974), 293 and 295.

19. Ernst Jünger, *In Stahlgewittern. Ein Kriegstagebuch* (Hanover: Selbstverlag, 1920). This first edition is hard to come by. The English translation *The Storm of Steel* appeared in 1929 (London: Chatto & Windus) and was reprinted in 1996 as a paperback by Howard Fertig publishers, New York: it is based on the German edition circulating in 1924, *In Stahlgewittern. Aus dem Tagebuch*

eines Stoßtruppführers. The German text underwent many changes from 1920 on until becoming the "standard edition" settled on by the author and his publishers: Ernst Jünger, *In Stahlgewittern* (Stuttgart: Klett-Cotta, 1961, 1981). In Germany alone, in the decade following the Great War, various writers were read in numbers that exceeded Ernst Jünger's – Walter Bloem, Werner Beumelberg, Walter Flex, Franz Schauwecker, Hans Magnus Wehner – but they are all but forgotten today. See Wolfgang G. Natter, *Literature at War 1914–1940: Representing the "Time of Greatness" in Germany* (New Haven: Yale University Press, 1999), 69.

20. *The Storm of Steel*, 1996, 273–74.
21. *Ibid.*, 22.
22. *Ibid.*, 318–19. This passage is found in the German text of 1924, 283.
23. *The Storm of Steel*, 1996, 255. This translates *In Stahlgewittern* (1924), 227; in the edition of 1961, the version is much subdued (see 260–61).
24. Ernst Jünger, *In Stahlgewittern* (1978), 87. This passage is not found in the German edition of 1924 and hence not in the English translation.
25. *The Storm of Steel*, 1996, 144.
26. *In Stahlgewittern* (1961), 288; but not in the edition of 1924 and hence not in the English translation.
27. *The Magic Mountain: A Novel*, trans. John E. Woods (New York: Knopf, 1995), 704–05.
28. The fact that *The Magic Mountain* had to end with the outbreak of the war "was definitively settled right from the outset." The quote is from Mann's letter of 21 August 1914, to his publisher Samuel Fischer. Cited in Hanno Helbling, "Vorwort," *Betrachtungen eines Unpolitischen*, 11.
29. *The Magic Mountain*, 699.
30. *Ibid.*, 702.
31. Cited in Helbling, "Vorwort," 8.
32. John E. Woods translates the first occurrence of the word "Donnerschlag" as "thunderbolt" and the second, its repetition, as "thunderclap," thus depriving the reader of the opportunity to perceive the parallel made by Mann between events on the Magic Mountain and events in the real flatlands, Europe in 1914.
33. Mann, *Betrachtungen eines Unpolitischen*, 42.
34. *The Magic Mountain*, 487.
35. *Ibid.*, 702.
36. Arnold Zweig, *The Case of Sergeant Grischa*, trans. Eric Sutton (New York: Viking, 1929), 207.
37. *Ibid.*, 211.
38. *Ibid.*, 285.
39. *Ibid.*, 99.
40. *Ibid.*, 448.
41. *Ibid.*, 449.
42. Erich Maria Remarque, *All Quiet on the Western Front*, trans. Brian Murdoch (London: Jonathan Cape, 1994), 124.
43. *Ibid.*, 186.
44. *Ibid.*, 85–86.
45. After a brief patriotic flare-up, during which he wrote war poems as well as the Fourth of his *Duino Elegies*, Rilke was conscripted in 1915 into the Austrian

army and spent some six months on duty in Vienna. He returned to Munich in a mood of paralyzing despair. One can consult his *Wartime Letters, 1914–1921* (Norton: New York, 1964). The failure of his poetic energies persisted until 1921.

46. Remarque, *All Quiet on the Western Front*, 86.

47. *Ibid.*, 3.

48. *Ibid.*, 207.

49. Cited in J. M. Winter, *Sites of Memory, Sites of Mourning: The Great War in European Cultural History* (1995; rpt. Cambridge: Cambridge University Press, 1998), 187.

50. J. H. Johnson, *1918: The Unexpected Victory* (London: Arms & Armour, 1997), 109. Cited in Ferguson, *The Pity of War*, 313.

51. Hermann Broch, *Die Schlafwandler, Eine Romantrilogie* (Frankfurt A. M.: Suhrkamp Taschenbuch, 1994), 537–38.

52. Walter Benjamin, "Experience and Poverty," trans. Rodney Livingstone, in *Walter Benjamin: Selected Writings, 1927–1934*, ed. Marcus Bullock, Howard Eiland, and Michael Jennings (Cambridge, Mass.: Harvard University Press, 1999), 731–36.

53. The economic basis of modern war persists through its various mutations. According to S. Thamilchelvam – the political leader of the Sri Lankan Tigers, a violent revolutionary organization – the goal of its favored device – suicide bombing – is "to ensure maximum damage done with minimum loss of life." Amy Waldman, "Masters of Suicide Bombing: Tamil Guerrillas of Sri Lanka," *New York Times*, 14 January 2003: A8.

9

JOHN T. MATTHEWS

American writing of the Great War

America's distinctive relation to the Great War originated in its remoteness from the event itself. Both because thousands of miles of ocean lay between the US and the battle in Europe, and because American troops did not participate in major action until the last year of hostilities, the First World War remained a virtual phenomenon to many US residents. The reports of German–Austrian aggression and Belgian–French imperilment did not lack for urgency (there were even German purposes to thwart closer to home, in Mexico and the Caribbean), but they did lack for immediacy. The American side of the Great War necessarily relied on institutions of representation – journalism, print propaganda, fiction, sermons – to make the war real in the place where it was not occurring. In important respects, American writing of the war *was* the war.

In the years before President Wilson abandoned the nation's policy of neutrality and gained a declaration of war from Congress in April of 1917, the American public speculated about European statecraft, debated developments that might draw the US into the hostilities, and imagined the horrific new technologies of modern warfare like poison gas, massive artillery shelling, trench combat, and airplanes used as weapons. The US had already suffered the loss of civilian life in the infamous sinking of the *Lusitania* by a German U-boat in 1915, and that incident, joined with other maritime casualties and escalating reports of German brutalities in the assault on Belgium, produced a climate in which US military intervention on behalf of the Allies (France, England, and Russia) was entertained openly. But as the fighting was still "over there" (in the words of a popular song of the era), the prospect of American engagement more immediately became an opportunity to address pre-existing problems on the home front.

America in 1914 was a country divided by serious struggles of its own. In 1902, Theodore Roosevelt had declared that America's two most urgent difficulties were the conflict between labor and capital, and the problem of the Negro in the South. Through the closing decades of the nineteenth century, large corporations had leapt forward to dominate the commercial and political spheres of the nation, while the situation of workers worsened. In 1915 a congressional commission concluded that the "extent and depth of industrial unrest can hardly be exaggerated."[1] As Americans watched hostilities in Europe from afar during the opening years of the war, conflicts between workers and employers at home heated up: more than 3,000 strikes per year occurred between 1914 and 1920, many of them put down violently by military and police force.[2] In the 1912 presidential elections, progressive candidates split 70 percent of the vote; Woodrow Wilson won as a reform-minded Democrat; third-party Progressive candidate Theodore Roosevelt also beat the Republican Taft; and Eugene Debs attracted nearly a million votes for the Socialist party.[3]

Labor made important gains during Wilson's first term, but in principle his wing of the Democratic party, the Republican oligarchy, and the owning classes in general envisioned America's involvement in the war as a more effective means of addressing the "problem" of labor unrest. Workers might be disciplined through the demands of the war effort, could be Americanized in opposition to European enemies (and hence be cleansed of Old World Socialist leanings), and would have to accept the militarized authority of capitalist ownership. The elite classes, correspondingly, might demonstrate their selfless love of nation by volunteering their sons for duty, as well as by practicing forms of domestic sacrifice and public service that would rehabilitate them in the eyes of their "inferiors." More importantly, as American manufacturing and business supplied the needs of the European war machine, wages would rise. Many workers, on the other hand, saw through such purposes, and staunchly opposed both the European slaughter and American intervention; they understood the war as a contrivance to break the internationalist workers' movement. States at war could justify suppression of subversive labor activities, militarize and send millions of workers to kill each other, rekindle national and ethnic animosities, and strengthen the positions of those holding power.

Theodore Roosevelt's alarm about America's sharpening racial troubles at the turn of the century reflects a crisis brought on by a period of the harshest treatment of blacks in the country's history. By the 1890s, "Jim Crow" laws in the South had relegated African-Americans to official second-class status; they lost access to public facilities and services, were deprived of the right to vote and own property, and were subjected to nightmarish violence. Between 1889 and 1909, an average of eighty-five blacks a year were lynched.[4] Wilson, the first Southerner elected President since the Civil War, prompted the segregation of federal employees for the first time, and avoided speaking

15 African-American troops marching in France

out against Southern vigilantism. Wilson saw the war as an opportunity to display white racial vigor. The "need" for solidarity also allowed the government to sanction the forcible suppression of racial protest and activism. Paradoxically, some African-Americans seized the chance to join the military and insist on combat assignments and officer training, causing confusion to policy makers. Moreover, the requirements of expanded industrial production drew millions of oppressed Southern blacks from farms to Northern cities; the so-called Great Migration permanently altered the face of American demography. Despite the gains held out to African-Americans, however, many rejected the prospect of dying in combat for a nation that continued to practice a killing racism.

Another source of domestic controversy in America before the Great War was a resurgent women's rights movement. In the first decades of the new century, British and American feminists intensified efforts to gain the right for women to vote, to acquire greater legal rights within marriage and through divorce, to provide education about sexual and reproductive matters, and to demand better opportunities in the workplace. Ironically, the conditions of states at war tended to promote such changes; many more women found factory and office jobs, while others volunteered directly for military service.

Though many of the gains were temporary, the war did advance the cause of women's rights; the twentieth amendment granted (non-African-American) women the right to vote in 1920.

As for other subordinated groups, however, many socially progressive American women understood that their advances were being bought with bloodshed. "Social feminists" opposed the war internationally on the grounds that it fed on the disadvantaged. Although never a majority movement, feminist pacifism did voice forceful disapproval of the war, at least up until American troops began to engage in combat. Feminist skepticism of masculinist motives in the war could find support in the history of American foreign exploit. Advocates for American imperial expansion in the late nineteenth century thought that men would benefit from new opportunities for physical combat and conquest. "Teddy" Roosevelt's charge up San Juan Hill with his Rough Riders during the Cuban campaign in the Spanish–American War became the icon for the recovery of men's "barbarian virtues." If many males anticipated the erosion of privilege – in the workplace, courts of law, voting booth, and bedroom – the battlefield might offer fresh occasions to act like men.

As the foregoing account makes clear, most historians remain as skeptical toward the idealism of American war-makers as a disillusioned public became in the 1920s. Since the country's elite figured to benefit so disproportionately from the nation's involvement in the Great War, it is difficult to avoid an historical judgment like Walter Karp's: "The struggle to drag America into the European war was to be a virtual civil war between the powerful, the privileged, and the rich – for 25 years the targets of Populist and progressive reformers – and the overwhelming mass of the American people."[5] The authoritarian policies of the Wilson administration that accompanied the declaration of war and continued after the Armistice in November of 1918 also support this conclusion. Wilson and his congressional supporters took advantage of wartime powers and public anxieties to put down racial and labor unrest with unusual force; sent troops to break strikes; silenced dissent through harsh sedition and espionage laws; and equated anti-capitalism with anti-patriotism. For liberals, the upheavals created in the state at war promised opportunities for progressive reform, but for the advantaged classes, the prospect of war provided a cause for resisting the agitations of modernity.

Imagining the war at home

Although the US populace was largely opposed to intervention until shortly before war was declared, east coast elites supported it earlier and with a keener vision of the good it might accomplish. Much of the earliest imaginative literature about America's relation to the Great War in Europe speculates on how *anticipated* involvement might be good for the nation in its own right. Hopes that a foreign war might sidestep class warfare at home, for example, may be seen in Arthur Train's popular wartime novel *The Earthquake* (1918). Set in New York in the summer of 1917, just after the US has declared war on Germany and is establishing military conscription, but before American troops have left for Europe, *The Earthquake* presents the coming war as a domestic upheaval that will trigger urgent soul-searching, and awaken America to its moral and social decline. Train's fictional narrator, a Manhattan bond-broker, welcomes the opportunity to recover the "eternal verities" upon which the nation was founded – the Christian principles of "honor, humanity, self-sacrifice," the republican ideals of truth and justice. The sacrifices required to prepare for war make John Adams Stanton realize that materialism has become the "impediment" to American freedom.[6] The war to be fought before the war comprises a domestic effort to root out selfishness, social indifference, and neglect of the spirit.

Stanton wishes to see economic disparity as a moral problem, to be fixed by the voluntary reformation of wealthy individuals. If the affluent lead by offering their sons to combat, and by making conspicuous sacrifices in expenditure and consumption, then "this war is going to make the rich respectable again"; "[t]he most obvious reform that the war has occasioned . . . is the annihilation of class distinction and the reverence for wealth"; "the great God Mammon has fallen flat" and "[w]ealth has ceased . . . to have any social significance." Such a "readjustment of values" might have been accomplished by "socialism," the narrator observes, but that would have required "a bitter struggle between the classes," something Train's wartime America congratulates itself on having eluded.[7]

Train looks to restorative effects in other anxious areas of American life, too. If preparation for war can discipline the rich to scale back luxury, become more manly through self-sufficiency (Fire your servants!), and search out more spiritually worthwhile occupations, military participation also benefits the less advantaged. Stanton's son reports that the "sweatshop" workers drafted into his company have been transformed from a "pasty-faced, narrow-chested, and clammy-handed bunch" into clear-complexioned speakers of intelligible English.[8] As it Americanizes ethnic immigrants, so the army inculcates democratic principles into foreigners infected with Socialism; the very fact of universal conscription exemplifies the egalitarian nature of American society. In Train's fantasy, white people will see Negroes with new appreciation because of their war service, blacks will head cheerfully to fight for a country as much theirs as any white person's, sectional difference will evaporate before the sense of a national "we," barbaric mass culture will die stillborn in its moral turpitude, alcohol will be outlawed, women will gain the right to vote, the nation will return to a reverence for producers of goods, fathers will respectfully yield the right to govern to their battle-proven sons, and the great nation will recover its sense of exhilaration at "living on the frontier of the unknown."[9] And all without firing a shot.

Another popular pro-war novelist, Mary Raymond Shipman Andrews, likewise fantasizes the social re-harmonization to be performed by war. Appearing just after hostilities began in Europe, *The Three Things* (1915) is an impatient call for US action. A well-born American decides he cannot wait for his country to do right by invaded Belgium, so he enlists and joins a British unit in France. In the course of his battlefield experiences, three of his principal beliefs come to be challenged: pride in class, atheism, and racial superiority. Phil discovers that the working-class English soldier to whom he grows closest, and who ultimately gives his life saving his American comrade, is actually his cousin. Phil comes to appreciate what it means for America to have given his grandfather, an English valet, the opportunity to make a fortune, become a gentleman, and see his daughter – Phil's mother – marry into American aristocracy. Andrews's novel dreams a reconciliation of the working-class English "Lefty" and the well-off American Phil in its effort to salvage gentility as a merited attainment in a capitalist democracy. Having learned that "class is rot," Phil next goes on to discover the power of prayer (when he is saved in a pile of dying soldiers) and the error of his prejudice against "vulgarian" Huns (when a wounded German does him a kind turn in a field hospital).[10]

As in *The Earthquake*, other benefits to character flow from the abandonment of American isolationism and neutrality. Phil returns home determined to distribute his family fortune philanthropically and spend the rest of his life as a social worker. The war was an especially opportune event through which to hallucinate class reconciliation and capitalist reform since the very opposite result was already observable: the exploitation of European hostilities and American preparation by the nation's owning class. One might argue that the cultural work of pro-war fiction like Train's and Andrews's was to imagine a war that would make the world safe for capitalism.

Andrews's subsequent novel, *Joy in the Morning* (1919), extends this vision of a reinvigorated America by laying to rest matters of historical conscience that might trouble the new century's emergent nation-giant. In literature appearing once America had entered into hostilities, or even after they were over, keepers of the battle faith like Andrews insisted on the good accomplished by the mere contemplation of war. The book assembles ten stories of wartime heroism into a narrative quilt. The fragmentary nature of the book's form models the difficulties of forging a unified war mentality. The stories range across mid-West towns, the Canadian wilderness, Quebec City, England, and a French battlefield. They imagine belief in a common duty to fight arising from disparate and reluctant segments of the North American population. In "Her Country Too," an African-American laundress in a Northern city volunteers her life savings to buy a war bond at the encouragement of her employer. At a critical moment in her foray into the alien terrain of the bank, Aunt Basha is assisted by a stranger, a beautiful white woman who later arranges a social call. The young woman, Aunt Basha, and her employer all discover that they share ties to the same Southern family. Aunt Basha's patriotism earns Andrews's ultimate compliment – she's "the most magnificent old black woman who ever carried a snow-white soul" – and the fairy tales take off from there.[11] In several stories we learn of valor transplanted by French-Indian Canadian natives to the European battlefield; in others Andrews shows a taste for supernatural ratification of North American sacrifice: a soldier son whose ghost keeps a promise to his mother to tell her of his death; a Canadian who awakens from a battlefield wound clutching a silver stirrup and the certainty that Joan of Arc appeared to him; even the story of a dead English hero who returns miraculously to inspire a crowd gathered in Trafalgar Square. *Joy in the Morning* is a frank exercise in wish-fulfillment. It transforms anxieties about African-American resentment over historical mistreatment, for example, into the belief that a German victory will return Negroes to slavery. It lays to rest a continental past of colonizing violence by touting "hybrid" strength. It mediates a spoiling class conflict with tales of class mobility, selfish competition with those of limitless personal sacrifice.

Socialists like Upton Sinclair were not buying the "Hail Britannia" sentiment, yet the most prominent war novel to come out of the political left, his *Jimmie Higgins* (1918), actually arrives at a pro-war point of view too. Sinclair's novel is valuable for its illumination of the American Socialists' dilemma. On the one hand, they understood the war as an event managed by the "War-lords and Money-lords" of Europe.[12] Wartime patriotism exaggerated national and ethnic antagonisms and weakened labor internationalism, while wartime production boosted wages and invited the suppression of labor activism. On the other, Sinclair depicts how American Socialists could choose only among compromised positions: if proletarian pacifism, what of German capitalist domination? If ethnic and family loyalties (with Germans and Irish siding against the Allies), what of "Hun" atrocities against humanity? If pro-democracy militancy, what of Allied violations of civil liberties? If immediate national revolutionism, what of unchecked global imperialism? *Jimmie Higgins* shows the eponymous protagonist, a loyal working-class Socialist, pinballing from position to position in the days before America decides to enter the war. Sinclair's criticism of international capitalism never wavers, but the question of what to do as an American Socialist remains unclear.

Sinclair unambiguously embraces "the vision of a world made over in justice and kindness, the co-operative commonwealth of labour, in which every man should get what he produced, and no man could exploit his fellows." And as "the soul of the movement was its internationalism," the idea of American workers producing the munitions European workers would use to exterminate one another obviously had to be opposed. Rather than seeing the war as an opportunity to tone up capitalist democracy, as Train does, Sinclair presents it as an intensification of the "class-war [that] had been going on for ages." The very language of combat governs working-class plans to gain control of the economy and government: "All such things these men talked about quite casually, as soldiers would talk about the events of the last campaign."[13] Sinclair also exposes the domestic agenda of American militarization by ending his novel with a hideous episode in which Jimmie, having finally rationalized service to his country as a non-combatant mechanic, is assigned to a Russian outpost with the US army, only to be accused of disseminating Bolshevik literature and to suffer torture by his own officers. Sinclair explicitly compares Jimmie's treatment to the repression of dissidents in the US (stricter sedition and espionage laws took effect as Sinclair was writing the novel); the final image of a deranged and mutilated Jimmie Higgins suggests the disfigurement of principle suffered by Socialists regarding the war.

Edith Wharton enlarges the realm of the war's redemptive effects by imagining how America must seize the opportunity to defeat the enemy that is modernity itself. Wharton understands the war as a turning point in history, and constructs narratives in *The Marne* (1918) and *A Son at the Front* (1923, but completed in 1919) that emphasize conserving the achievement of Western civilization. For her, embattled France is less a place in Europe than an ideal for America:

> An Idea: that was what France, ever since she had existed, had always been in the story of civilization; a luminous point about which striving visions and purposes could rally. In that sense she had been . . . [a] spiritual home . . . to thinkers, artists, to all creators, she had always been a second country. If France went, western civilization went with her; and then all they had believed in and been guided by would perish.[14]

16 Image of America's war for "Civilization"

In *Fighting France* (1915), a volume of journalism recording her visits to the French Front during the period of her relief activities in Paris, she concludes that France will ultimately be saved from the barbaric German aggressors because of its distinctive national characteristics: Intelligence, Expression, and Courage. Wharton's first fictional war hero, the American Troy Belknap in *The Marne*, cannot understand the reluctance of his countrymen to spring to France's defense: "*To save France* – that was the clear duty of the world, as he saw it."[15]

For Wharton, the course of modernity itself is bound up with the outcome of the Great War. "To save France" means to defend western society from the invasion of materialism, vulgarity, class upheaval, national and personal self-interest – all of what Wharton considered the ugliness of modern life. Wharton's war fiction centers on how to conserve the best of the past while defeating the barbarities of the modern age. The Great War represents both the threat of modernity, as well as the opportunity to rehabilitate conservative virtues. (A consonant celebration of the premodern virtues of French peasant life endangered by German industrial barbarity may be seen in Dorothy Canfield's *Home Fires in France* [1918].) In *A Son at the Front*, an American painter living in Paris comes to accept his son's voluntary service with the French army and transmutes his grief over his son's death into a memorial work of art.

In a world increasingly coarsened by financial speculation and profiteering, open economic and social competition, lower regard for traditional social institutions like marriage, weakened class distinctions, and decline in the authority of educated taste – subjects Wharton takes up in her most important novels of domestic manners like *The House of Mirth*, *The Custom of the Country*, and *The Age of Innocence* – in such a debased world, the act of personal sacrifice itself becomes the practice of virtue. Paradoxically, what justifies the horrific loss of human life on the battlefield is the magnitude of the sacrifice: for the painter Campton in *A Son at the Front*, "[t]he point was to remember that the efficacy of the sacrifice was always in proportion to the worth of the victims; and there at least his faith was sure."[16] Only willingness to die for a civilization can prove its spiritual value: "There had never been anything worth while in the world that had not had to be died for, and it was as clear as day that a world which no one would die for could never be a world worth being alive in," Troy concludes in *The Marne*.[17] Unlike the Germans, who lust for territory, wealth, and physical gratification, defenders of the Idea of France act on behalf of beauty, selflessness, and spiritual fulfillment.

In her fiction, as well as, even more oddly, in her journalism describing the front line itself, Wharton omits almost all mention of the actual wounding of people. In contrast to battle scenes in later testimonial fiction by ex-combatants, Wharton's seem to have no casualties. They hardly have any soldiers. The trenches she visits are something like Alice's tunnels, and the noteworthy damage is to buildings: "we have passed through streets and streets of such murdered houses, through town after town spread out in its last writhings." Wharton seeks to conquer doubt, moderate conflict, redeem loss; at work is a narrative of spiritual economies. "War is the greatest of paradoxes," she proposes, "the most senseless and disheartening of human retrogressions, and yet the stimulant of qualities of soul which, in every race, can seemingly find no other means of renewal."[18]

Willa Cather's novel *One of Ours* (1922) also concentrates on the period of latency in the American Great War, although the book ends amid the emergence of postwar disillusionment. Cather focuses on a young Nebraskan named Claude Wheeler, who, already chafing under a provincial upbringing, passionless marriage, and purposeless future, warms to the idea of doing something authentic by going to war. Claude flees his middle-class Victorian roots with "a sense of relief at being rid of all [he] had ever been before and facing something absolutely new." Once aboard the transport ship he congratulates himself that the "feeling of purpose, of fateful purpose, was strong in his breast."[19]

Against an American society that disappoints in its preoccupations with commerce and materialism, traits that have made America emotionally "shallow," France and England represent an enduring idea worth dying for. Perhaps the war has come to Americans "for the sins of the fathers"; "[n]o battlefield or shattered country he had seen was as ugly as this world would be if men like his brother Bayliss [a banker] controlled it altogether."[20] Instead, Latin Europe has attained more spiritual heights of civilization. From this standpoint, American involvement in the Great War constitutes another chapter in a national narrative of sacrifice and redemption: the renewal of American greatness through the salvation of European civilization.

Ultimately, though, Cather's war novel refuses to allow such simplicities to stand. Claude may die thinking that "[i]deals were not archaic things, beautiful and impotent; they were the real sources of power among men." But Cather has shown how Claude's idealistic embrace of glorious death sublimates cultural claustrophobia, an outdated masculinism, and a dreary material future. The swift conclusion of the novel deflates the mood of triumph marking the loss of Claude's life in battle. Mrs. Wheeler grows embittered by "the flood of meanness and greed" released in the years after the war (and seen by her in retrospect as responsible for it). To console herself, Mrs. Wheeler "knows what to read into those short flashes of enthusiasm" that appear in the letters – that is, Claude's faith in an idea. But acknowledged as an act of willful reading *into*, Mrs. Wheeler's interpretation underscores how the war's justification requires the suppression of "disillusion."[21]

Like Claude, Alan Seeger, America's only noteworthy poet of the Great War, sustained the dream of the war's good through his dying moment on the battlefield. In 1912 the Harvard-educated Seeger left the US for Paris and began writing poetry. When war broke out, he volunteered for duty with the French infantry, losing his life at the village of Belloy-en-Santerre in 1916, at age twenty-eight. During his two years of service, Seeger composed a set of soldier's sonnets, a number of longer lyrics, and two public poems, one exhorting America to join the war, the other commemorating fellow-citizens already killed in battle.

Seeger's two major poems about the war generally conform to the pattern of enthusiasm we have seen so far. In "Ode in Memory of the American Volunteers Fallen for France," Seeger concentrates on the benefits to be won for individual and nation through fighting. Seeger pictures the US at mid-decade as effete and selfish. Joining the war would put the "sneerers" in their places, give American youth the "privilege of dying well," increase national "manhood," replicate the regenerative violence of the "beckoning frontiers," and generally "vindicate" "us." In "Message to America," he likewise sees the war as an opportunity to revive the "barbarian virtues" Teddy Roosevelt championed: "You are virile, combative, stubborn, hard, / But your honor ends with your own back-yard." Seeger explicitly identifies Roosevelt as just the "prophet" to inspire American males to recover "your honor, your man-hood, and your pride, / And the virtues your fathers dignified."[22] National and personal manliness coincide in Seeger's call to arms – but paradoxically, since the individual must sanction the sacrifice of his own individual survival for the good of the "nation," the "race."

Seeger's appeal to white racial pride to challenge the American public in "Message to America" sounds the imperialist note in American involvement in the Great War. Early in the poem Seeger tries to embarrass Americans for their indifference to assaults said to be committed on US citizens by Mexican revolutionists during recent uprisings there, and he ends by suggesting that Americans should be ashamed of their inaction in allowing "greasers" to have taken "innocent lives / And robbed their holdings and raped their wives."[23] Apparently, America should aspire to the ferocious pride of "little" people like the poorly armed and fiesty Mexicans – who somehow deserve both punishment and emulation. The European conflict allowed the Wilson administration to expand the Monroe Doctrine and lay the groundwork for American intervention in Latin America throughout the century.

As even the few lines quoted above may suggest, the only thing heroic about Seeger's couplets is their determination to find rhymes. The strains in the verse finally owe more to the incoherence of Seeger's appreciation of war than to his being a poetic novice. Seeger's war poems attempt to rationalize standard doubts about combat – the terror of instant death, the worry that governments are deceiving the common soldier. But they do so ultimately in order to sustain a fantasy about the resuscitation of an elite class, rather than the dream of national or personal honor. What "A Message to America" codes as national race virility, other poems insinuate to be the defense of class privilege. In "Bellinglise," for example, Seeger describes a manor in the countryside where he would be content to be laid to rest: "Deep in the sloping forest that surrounds / The head of a green valley that I know, / Spread the far gardens and ancestral grounds / Of Bellinglise, the beautiful chateau." Seeger inserts himself into an "ancestral" order here, "antique" and "untroubled," of a sort that might correspond to Seeger's own prominent New England lineage.[24] The perspective governing his celebrations of soldiering shows Seeger preoccupied, perhaps not fully consciously, with the defense of a class refined enough to appreciate the best of civilization, and rejuvenated in its possession of it.

Reporting home from the war

The will to justify America's entry into the war faded as US combatants began describing the battlefield first-hand. It was not only that ideals of any sort paled against the awfulness of mutilation and death for so many human beings, though such horror was a bitter reproach to all those who thought the war might advance Western civilization. It was also that the very values and institutions in defense of which common Americans were told they were fighting – liberty, patriotism, sacrifice, democratic government, Christianity – seemed to have little to do with the political and military decisions being made over soldiers' heads. Instead, such notions seemed increasingly to look like instruments of ideological manipulation. A generation of writers returned from the war to report that their elders had been mistaken, that the direct experience of war had shaken their confidence in Western faith in progress, reason, technology, and democratic capitalism, and that they would be seeking new artistic ways to express that negative sensibility.

Among the first to contradict the domestic version of the war was John Dos Passos in his novel *One Man's Initiation* (1917). Before America joined the fighting, Dos Passos had volunteered for ambulance duty in Italy. The book he wrote upon his return challenged American beliefs about "the war to end all wars." "How stupid we were before the war," remarks the protagonist, Martin Howe. He and his comrades now profess cynicism about the real purposes of the war, rejecting not only official talk about liberty and democracy as mere hypocrisy, but also the personal gratification sought through military exploit: "I used to think . . . that it was my family I must escape from to be free; I mean all the conventional ties, the worship of success and the respectabilities that is drummed into you when you're young."[25] The novel devotes practically no time to such a state of delusion, the glee over turning a new page on a dull life disappearing as the troop ship heads to sea. It is as if Dos Passos inverts the proportions of Cather's novel to start at the point she leaves off; a long season of homebound tedium like Claude's counts for nothing against the mind-bending atrocities of the battlefield.

Unlike Wharton's accounts of war casualties as strangely unrelated to human bodies, Dos Passos's pages are strewn with ghastly corpses, grotesque wounds. As one soldier speaks to him of his inevitable death, Howe has trouble reconciling the living energy and warmth of the person beside him to "those huddled, pulpy masses of blue uniform half-buried in the mud of ditches." The impersonality of modern combat produces ghoulish jokes about soldiers catching hand grenades that blow them up, of faces so disfigured that lost noses are covered by black patches and missing jaws replaced with "tiny little black metal rods." Such insult to the individual body suggests how all ideological abstractions get "washed out, all the hatreds, all the lies, in blood and sweat."[26] Under the proof that battle is all a matter of bodies – controlling the fear and seeking the safety of your own; feeding it, marching it, cleaning it, keeping it awake; making it kill someone else's – Dos Passos's veterans discredit all the standard justifications for war.[27] They see through "this new particular vintage of lies that has been so industriously pumped out of the press and the pulpit," and zero in on the true interests served by the war. A Frenchman observes that the present tumult is "merely a gigantic battle fought over the plunder of the world by the pirates who have grown fat to the point of madness on the work of their own people, on the work of the millions in Africa, in India, in America, who have come directly or indirectly under the yoke of the insane greed of the white races."[28] *One Man's Initiation* suggests that the world convulsion ought to induce a workers' revolution, the only hope for defeating the root causes of warfare: capitalism, imperialism, militarism.

In *Three Soldiers* (1921) Dos Passos considers the more complex question of whether the war has produced a new form of public mentality. He organizes the novel around the extended metaphor of the war machine, likening the production of a military force to the manufacture of an implement; sections are entitled "Making the Mould," "The Metal Cools," "Machines," etc. Dos Passos worries that the broad-based militarization of the American public, both as civilians and soldiers, has created an overly disciplined, conformist, and desensitized populace – "the people" transformed into "the masses." One of the three soldiers (the title of the novel itself suggests the menace of generic identity) proves to be consciously resistant to homogenization, but early on he registers its appeal as he watches his first propaganda movie with his fellow-recruits:

> They were all so alike, they seemed at moments to be but one organism. This was what he had sought when he had enlisted, he said to himself. It was in this that he would take refuge from the horror of the world that had fallen upon him. He was sick of revolt, of thought, of carrying his individuality like a banner above the turmoil. This was much better, to let everything go, to stamp out his maddening desire for music, to humble himself into the mud of common slavery.[29]

Mass mentality also endangers the chances for a genuinely collective democratic revolution. A public used to following orders and accepting decisions made on behalf of national good conflicted with Dos Passos' vision of democratic Socialism. A despairing revolutionary US soldier points out that the belligerent states will never be brought to class warfare because the mass of soldiers "have no way of learning the truth. And in the tyranny of the army a man becomes a brute, a piece of machinery."[30]

Unsurprisingly, Dos Passos's American army in Europe looks much like home front society. One of the three soldiers awakens from a dream in which his mother's kitchen in Indiana has been the setting for an imaginary act of battlefield violence – against one of his own comrades. Here is confirmation from the psychic lives of combatants that America had actually gone to war against itself.[31] Another of the three, Henry Fuselli, sees the war as an opportunity to rise through the ranks and overcome his working-class origins. He calculates his behavior according to the odds of advancement, and welcomes assignment to the front since it means "he was getting along in the world."[32] Rather than cure social ills, the war seems to Dos Passos merely to allow their replication in new institutional settings; the army provides fresh opportunities for racism, ethnic vilification, sexual immorality, careerism, and exploitation of a wage-earning class.

As conditions increasingly militate against popular revolution, Dos Passos suggests that an alternative form of protest lies in art. Throughout his military experiences, John Andrews attempts to keep alive his devotion to composing music. Toward the end of the novel he realizes that the exercise of his individual imagination constitutes the strongest resistance he can muster to modern regimentation: "Then he thought of his table in his room in Paris, with its piled sheets of ruled paper, and he felt he wanted nothing in the world except to work. It would not matter what happened to him if he could only have time to weave into designs the tangled skein of music that seethed through him."[33] Through indulgence, bodily pleasure, imaginative creativity, and the making of beauty, the inhuman crudeness, violence, and impersonality of modern warfare might be exorcised.

Perhaps the most inspired of all such acts of artistic non-conformity was *The Enormous Room* (1922), E. E. Cummings's fictionalization of his wartime detention in France on charges of sedition. Having volunteered, like Dos Passos, for service in the ambulance corps, Cummings ran afoul of French censors who took exception to American letters home reporting poor conditions and low morale among French troops. Cummings turned his months of incarceration into a merciless satire on every aspect of military bureaucracy, and a withering mockery of the fear and deception required to keep a populace obediently militarized.

Cummings made his career as a poet, with a bent toward formal experimentation. He devotes this work of prose to a defense of the word from corruption by those who use language to misrepresent reality and dominate others. In *The Enormous Room* he suggests how war talk offends both moral and aesthetic sensibilities. He understands that discourse always involves politics, and that especially devious political behavior resorts to especially audacious misuses of language. Cummings suspected the Allies' official-speak during the Great War to be evidence of a new modern menace to truth. Because American involvement in the war required a massive change in public opinion, which ran overwhelmingly against intervention, the "sciences" of propaganda and mass advertising played unprecedented roles in creating a war mentality. Likewise, since President Wilson had not been a career politician and showed little aptitude for cultivating congressional support for his policies, he learned to rely on his rhetorical skills and appeal directly to the American public. Cummings begins *The Enormous Room* with a swipe at Wilson's misleading style:

> To borrow a characteristic cadence from Our Great President: the lively satisfaction which we might be suspected of having derived from the accomplishment of a task so important in the saving of civilization from the clutches of Prussian tyranny was in some degree inhibited, unhappily, by a complete absence of cordial relations between the man whom fate had placed over us and ourselves. Or, to use the vulgar American idiom, B. and I and Mr. A. didn't get on well.[34]

It is important to Cummings throughout his book to use the "vulgar" "idiom" to convey the true thoughts and feelings of common persons. The language of abstraction mystifies the manipulation of subjects by the leaders of nation, government, church, and the military.

The solitary imagination may challenge these forces of corporate discipline and expression by mocking them, and celebrating instead pleasure, beauty, nonsense, and individual distinctness. Cummings pays obsessive attention to the concrete particulars of the space he and the other offenders occupy – the sensations of eating watery broth, sleeping on damp floor pallets, emptying latrine pots. The narrator's refusal to accept the official version of reality, including his alleged guilt, depends on his unwillingness to call things what they are not; eventually, he believes he has "managed to shove my shovel-shaped imagination under the refuse of their intellects."[35] As Cummings revels in the Dickensian variety and squalor of the tiny space allotted to the dissident imagination ("enormous" is used ironically, as well as to underscore the enormity of the government's behavior), he declares that the purpose of art is to attack normative thinking and speaking, to criticize power and authority:

> there is and can be no such thing as authentic art until the *bons trucs* [good tricks] (whereby we are taught to see and imitate on canvas and in stone and by words this so-called world) are entirely and thoroughly and perfectly annihilated by that vast and painful process of Unthinking which may result in a minute bit of purely personal Feeling. Which minute bit is Art.[36]

Cummings associates conventional realistic narrative with western confidence in historical progress and imperial expansion. Once these cultural narratives have been discredited by Europe's plunge into savagery, artists may prefer counter-realistic forms to articulate new mentalities.

Cummings makes the irony of his serving the Allies by serving a term under domestic detention into the basis of a keen insight: that the war functions as the means to discipline deprived, unruly, or eccentric groups at home. The camp at La Ferté Mace repositions the relevant space of combat to the home front; as soon as the narrator becomes an accused "criminal," he is treated like a foreign enemy. The brutalization of domestic populations – from civilians overrun by combat troops, to the Negroes, Jews, Communists, unattached women, and other "misfits" rounded up for detention – turns the war on behalf of democracy into a cruel joke. Treason is preferable: "By treason I refer to any little annoying habits of independent thought or action when *en temps de guerre* [in time of war] are put in a hole and covered over."[37] Cummings reaches the most severe conclusion to be drawn from the event of the Great War when he decides that it invalidates the very "meaning of civilization."

In the mood of desperate flight from Allied self-righteousness and hypocrisy, Cummings hardly welcomes his return to America at the end of *The Enormous Room*. The first sight of Manhattan inspires him with disgust: "My God, what an ugly island."[38] Americans who served in Europe often found that the country they returned to was not the one they had left. Not only had the disillusioning realities of military life and war politics disturbed their confidence in what America was and what it meant to be an American, but the home scene appeared both uncannily the same and also utterly transformed in their absence. Many of the early century's greatest writers – including Hemingway, Fitzgerald, and Faulkner – discovered key sources of inspiration at the outset of their careers in the social and personal conflicts engendered by the upheavals of the Great War.

Ernest Hemingway volunteered for ambulance service in Italy as an eighteen-year-old, suffered a serious wound to his leg, and returned to his home near Chicago to convalesce. A few years later he moved back to Europe and began to write, short sketches and poems at first, and then a startling pair of books in 1924 and 1926. Both *In Our Time* and *The Sun Also Rises* paint the mood of postwar exhaustion. Hemingway not only understood this disillusioned indifference, he also invented a distinctive new way of (not) talking about it. His star characters – Nick Adams and Jake Barnes, both wounded veterans, and Brett Ashley, a war-emancipated new woman – through their dry irony, lost ambitions, and willingness to reduce all of life to a good drink and a pleasant meal, practically invent the ideal of cool. What makes Hemingway's fiction so much more than portraits of hard-boiled cynicism, however, is the mental and even historical turbulence seething under the mask of disenchantment.

In Our Time attempts an experimental narrative form in which brief prose vignettes alternate with more conventional short stories. Each strand possesses internal connections; the vignettes, which appear in italics, present verbal snapshots of the Greek revolt against Turkey in the early 1920s, a Spanish bullfight, and Nick Adams's memories of fighting during the war in Italian villages. These episodes are not identified, however, and it is as if Hemingway deliberately deprives them of context in order to make them feel like undigested, displaced fragments of violence and the fear of death. Hemingway's innovative structure creates the sensation of a psychological palimpsest, in which the barely suppressed trauma of the war deforms the conscious mind of the survivor.

The majority of *In Our Time* deals with young veterans who seek to reenter the lives they have left behind. The most prominent of these, Nick Adams, comes back to his native Michigan, only to discover that he can recover neither his past nor present, to say nothing of a future. In the volume's early Adams stories, Nick recalls childhood memories associated with the places he returns to. Tellingly, what he remembers involves violence and territorial conflict, as if his intervening war memories are sifting through Nick's personal past to reinterpret it. In "Indian Camp," Nick remembers his father, a doctor, helping to deliver an Indian woman's baby in the Michigan wilderness, then discovering that her husband has inexplicably committed suicide – or at least shows up in his bed with a slit throat. Coupled with a subsequent story that in retrospect implicates his father in a scheme to pay Indians to steal logs from a timber company, Nick approaches the recognition that his own and, by extension, his nation's history rest on unacknowledged acts of violence and treachery. Nick's buried memories resurface in the altered domestic landscape he must negotiate.

Notice how the traces of combat stain Nick's return to the unspoiled countryside in the most famous of all the Adams stories, "Big Two-Hearted River." In the first paragraph of Part 1, Nick is heading once again to his favorite fishing spot when he hops off a train at a town that has since burned down. The description might easily double for that of a war-ruined French village:

> There was no town, nothing but the rails and the burned-over country. The thirteen saloons that had lined the one street of Seney had not left a trace. The foundations of the Mansion House hotel stuck up above the ground. The stone was chipped and split by the fire. It was all that was left of the town of Seney. Even the surface had been burned off the ground.[39]

In view of the malaise afflicting Adams on this expedition, such a vision of the Michigan terrain suggests that the devastation of Europe haunts Nick's relation to home. What he seems bent on achieving in the woods is a ritual purification of his contamination by the war, an exorcism that involves both replicating and defusing the mentality of combat. Everything Nick does on the trip might as well be the work of a soldier. He pitches camp expertly, takes pleasure in arranging his supplies, and finds solace in unthinking labor: "Already there was something mysterious and homelike." But the good feeling of ground beneath him, and the sense that "[n]othing could touch him," come at a high price – the cost of suppressing memory itself. "His mind was starting to work. He knew he could choke it because he was tired enough."[40] So the story ends.

As retreat to the wilderness hardly provides an answer, neither do the conventions of prewar domestic life. Gone is any confidence that mid-American small town life will do. Nick breaks off his engagement uncertainly because "It isn't fun any more," though he no more understands what this means than does his fiancée. The gesture typifies many others as characters coma-walk through former lives or restlessly exhaust novelties, only to conclude that "[n]one of it makes any difference."[41]

Among the greatest works to come out of the American writing of the Great War is Hemingway's first full-fledged novel, *The Sun Also Rises* (1926). A work of eerie surface simplicity yet profound insight into how the human condition was changing in the modern world, *The Sun Also Rises* evokes the sense of homelessness felt by many who had experienced their most meaningful, soul-searching moments abroad, and who returned to places and routines that no longer seemed much like home at all. Hemingway extrapolates from his earlier sketches of domestic lostness to create the most memorable of all portraits of postwar futility. Jake Barnes, an expatriate American journalist living in Paris after the war (and the indifferent narrator of the novel), describes a life so diminished that it can be understood as virtually posthumous. Jake has suffered a combat injury that leaves him sexually disabled, and the wound becomes the ironic badge of honor for a war that has already become a boring joke. Incapable of producing a future, Jake lives out his days in a seemingly endless repetition of romances that go nowhere, friendships that break and mend and break, aimless rounds of drinks, excursions, and spectator amusements.

If Hemingway's postwar mood appears defeated, it does not entirely lack consolation. The lasting achievement of Hemingway's writing of the Great War proves to be the literary style he forged to manage its pain. Hemingway's is the consummate art of the unsaid. The pressures contributing to such an aesthetic arise from several sources. There is the emptiness of any effort to generalize about the meaning of an event experienced in as many different ways as there were participants, and largely found lacking in broader meaning by those who registered their reactions. Jake warns early in the novel that there will be no such talk from him: "We would probably have gone on and discussed the war and agreed that it was in reality a calamity for civilization, and perhaps would have been better avoided. I was bored enough."[42] Rather than any such "bilge," Hemingway practices a counter-exercise in language. He reduces assertion to its most fundamental elements, rolling out one simple clause after the next. He distills description to the essence of primary colors, basic shapes, minimal indications of action and state of mind:

> After a while we came out of the mountains, and there were trees along both sides of the road, and a stream and ripe fields of grain, and the road went on, very white and straight ahead, and then lifted to a little rise . . . Then we crossed a wide plain, and there was a big river off on the right shining in the sun from between the line of trees, and away off you could see the plateau of Pamplona rising out of the plain, and the walls of the city, and the great brown cathedral, and the broken skyline of the other churches.[43]

One could find equivalents for this way of depicting the countryside in the abstractionist tendencies of Van Gogh and Cézanne, painters Hemingway had learned to appreciate in Paris at the urging of Gertrude Stein. A passage like this also follows in a tradition of description in war writing that opposes the ugliness of combat to the beauty of nature and organic communities. Here is Dos Passos in *Three Soldiers*:

> They were going into the suburbs of a town. Rows and clusters of little brick and stucco houses were appearing along the roads. It began to rain from a sky full of lights of amber and lilac color. The slate roofs and the pinkish-grey streets of the town shone cheerfully in the rain. The little patches of garden were all vivid emerald-green. Then they were looking at rows and rows of red chimney pots over wet slate roofs that reflected the bright sky. In the distance rose the purple-grey of a church and the irregular forms of old buildings.[44]

Although natural beauty relieves the war-weary eye in both, Dos Passos trusts his prose to search out richness of detail, to re-enliven sensory apprehension. In contrast, Hemingway's version has a random, distracted quality that constitutes a new way of writing nature. Not only does the style originate in the avoidance of deeper reflection by idly attending to the formal beauties of the visible world, but the novelty of such laconic geometrical prose itself offers to compensate for the loss of other reference.

Some readers finish *The Sun Also Rises* without noticing that Jake has disclosed his catastrophic war injury. Jake's method of narration is purposely indirect; in the following sentences, notice how he diverts attention from his wound: "Undressing, I looked at myself in the mirror of the big armoire beside the bed. That was a typically French way to furnish a room. Practical, too, I suppose. Of all the ways to be wounded. I suppose it was funny."[45] Hemingway's style coils around the silence of death, seeking to hold – as he describes his favorite matador's technique – a pure firm line, while working deep in the territory of mortal danger. The danger comes from the suspicion that nothing "makes any difference," that the war has exposed an abyss strewn with fallen ideals and populated by human animals fated to nothing but killing, fucking, dying. Hemingway's writing finds no relief from such darkness, but his minimalist sentences – with their economy of gesture, deadpan irony, and inhuman simplicity – bid to distract the reader from more tragic conclusions.

In 1926, the year *The Sun Also Rises* appeared, William Faulkner made his debut as a novelist with his own book about an injured war veteran. Like Hemingway, Faulkner had also wanted to be part of his era's defining event, but because he was obsessed with the idea of becoming an aviator, his path to action proved more circuitous. Rejected by the army air corps for being too short, Faulkner found he could enlist in the Royal Air Force of Canada. Though he never managed to get beyond training missions in Toronto before the war ended, he returned to his hometown of Oxford, Mississippi, full of stories about the combat missions he had flown in Europe. World War I for Faulkner was the stuff of fiction, as the Civil War had been for the taletellers in his family and would become for his own monumental reimagination of the South's past in his later novels. The Great War represented the drastic, even violent onset of modernity, a change felt all the more acutely in the most distinctive and conservative region of the country. Faulkner's great subject as a mature writer was the tortured history of the slave-owning plantation South, with its continuing legacies of racism and agricultural poverty, as well as its ideals of agrarian self-sufficiency and enduring community. The drama of modernization inspired Faulkner to chronicle a troubled Southern past at the point of its final eclipse, and to probe with all the resources of his genius the new ways of life in the offing. The First World War provided the inaugural occasion for what became a lifelong imaginative project.

Soldier's Pay recounts the return of a wounded veteran to his Southern hometown. Like Nick Adams and Jake Barnes, Donald Mahon's body has suffered symbolic damage, in his case progressive blindness and amnesia. Mahon's condition marks a pivot point from the South's traditional ways to a modern future. A war widow who accompanies Mahon on his return home observes how odd it must be to "feel provincial: finding that a certain conventional state of behavior has become inexplicably obsolete over night." Blind to this induction of "eternal country boys" into "the comparative metropolitan atmosphere . . . diametrically opposed to it," Mahon embodies the inability of a certain order to adjust.[46] The new world's unrecognizability involves familiar novelties of the postwar scene: the unprecedented sexual frankness and behavior of the young, the liberties taken by local blacks after comparing life outside the deep South, the acceptance of national identity and destiny as more important than regional past.

In Faulkner's next novel, *Flags in the Dust* (published as *Sartoris* in 1929), the Great War appears as a replay of the Civil War. The twins John and Bayard Sartoris go off to Europe from Jefferson, Mississippi, as pilots intent on winning valor. One of Faulkner's most distinguished imaginary families, modeled on his own, the Sartorises boast a heroic Confederate colonel as patriarch and a tradition of reckless vainglory. One legendary ancestor dies during the Civil War when on a whim he decides to raid a Yankee camp single-handedly and steal a tin of anchovies in an audacious act of derring-do. Against this background, the twins strive to take the family lust for gallantry to a literally higher level – as jousting knights of the air. John dies when he is shot down over France; Bayard returns to a life devoid of meaning. Eventually Bayard manages to kill himself test-flying an airplane, and the whole deadly arrogant ethos of the family comes into focus: "perhaps Sartoris is the name of the game itself – a game outmoded and played with pawns shaped too late and to an old dead pattern, and of which the Player Himself is a little wearied. For there is death in the sound of it, and a glamorous fatality."[47]

By having removed himself from the South during the Great War, Faulkner gains a critical perspective on his region's great war, on the folly of committing bloodshed in the name of spurious ideals. In *Absalom, Absalom!* (1936) Faulkner portrays the antebellum Southern planter Thomas Sutpen as the incarnation of delusional pride, and the consequences of his design as cruel violence to others and his own destruction. Quentin Compson remarks, after unburdening the story of his South to his Harvard roommate, that had he been there he "could not have seen it this plain." In light of Faulkner's spending the war in Toronto, it may be significant that Quentin's young confessor is a Canadian named Shreve.

Hemingway's fixation on the Great War draws from him yet another novel about a wounded serviceman, *A Farewell to Arms* (1929), though one that differs in having its action transpire during Frederic Henry's actual tour of duty in the war zone. This work revisits even more explicitly Hemingway's own wartime experience in depicting the ambulance driver Frederic Henry's serious leg injury during a battle in northern Italy. Even before his injury, Henry displays Hemingway's trademark irony toward patriotism, the defense of democracy, and battlefield valor. He seems perfectly indifferent to the national interests driving the hostilities, and offers only mild resistance to the complaints of the working-class Italian recruits who understand the war as nothing but a scam to make money for those controlling governments. When he personally witnesses the murderous chaos of a battlefield retreat, and is nearly executed in a random show of discipline by officers of the very Italian forces he is serving, Henry ends up deserting altogether and making "a separate peace" with the war.

More surprisingly perhaps, given the vacancy of emotion in his earlier war fiction, *A Farewell to Arms* counterposes a passionate, if doomed, romance to the impersonality and meaninglessness of the war. Henry admits that he has fallen "in love" with an English nurse after they indulge in a simple battlefront dalliance. The two seek desperately to find in each other balms for incurable wounds – for Catherine Barkley, grief over a fiancé killed in the war; for Henry, the bleak conviction that life "kills the very good and the very gentle and the very brave impartially. If you are none of these you can be sure it will kill you too but there will be no special hurry."[48] It would seem at first that despite, and then because, of their prototypical war damage, these characters are allowed by Hemingway to rediscover their humanity through romantic love. But the novel actually proves less nostalgic than predictive of a modern new method for filling up emotional and philosophical voids: consumption.

Henry does not fall in love with Catherine so much as with the anesthesia of consumption: "I was not made to think. I was made to eat. My God, yes. Eat and drink and sleep with Catherine."[49] From the moment he is wounded, Henry behaves like "our privileged patient," as one taxed nurse puts it, ordering medical personnel around as if they were his personal wait staff. Henry embodies an emergent American consumer culture looking to sate itself on new diversions like the movies (Henry describes combat as like nothing so much as a film), leisured expatriate colonies, luxury goods. The lovers shop and splurge, though they're hardly rich, and care as much about decor as desire, about menu as making love. In an awful way, war's reduction of all that matters to the fate of the body creates a postwar equivalent in the strictly carnal preoccupations of its survivors. *A Farewell to Arms* is not a love story; it is merely a pleasure story. As such it measures the after-effects of war trauma in modern America's numb desertion of immaterial obligations.

With comic excess, F. Scott Fitzgerald envisions how a vast culture of consumption will be built on the cynical hedonism of postwar disillusionment. In *Tender is the Night* (1934), the Armistice redirects wartime energies toward the mass production of novelty goods: Rosemary Hoyt, a teenage movie star, goes shopping with her new friend, Nicole Diver, the heiress of a Chicago financier: there are so many "new things that Rosemary had never seen, from the first burst of luxury manufacturing after the War, and probably in the hands of the first of purchasers."[50] Fitzgerald shows how new industries like Hollywood's will create unheard-of fantasies, how new levels of money-madness will commandeer techniques of adjustment like psychoanalysis, and how America's new economic and cultural might will create an empire more supple and powerful than the political ones that fell in the Great War. Finally, in tracing the outline of postwar modernity, *Tender is the Night* also typifies the ubiquity of key domestic problems left unresolved at war's end, ones that will organize central literary and social projects of the interwar years. In its hyper-sensitivity to reconfigurations of ethnicity and class in the 1920s, for example, the novel reminds us that the upheavals of the war years condition the emergence of both the New Negro Renaissance and the proletarian movement. And in its dissection of patriarchal marriage, *Tender is the Night* evokes the widespread reimagining of gender and sexuality associated with the war era.[51]

NOTES

1. Walter Karp, *The Politics of War: The Story of Two Wars Which Altered Forever the Political Life of the American Republic (1890–1920)* (New York: Harper & Row, 1979), 217.
2. Robert H. Zieger, *America's Great War: World War I and the American Experience* (Lanham: Rowman & Littlefield, 2000), 117.
3. Karp, *The Politics of War*, 143.
4. Zieger, *America's Great War*, 128.
5. Karp, *The Politics of War*, 192.
6. Arthur Train, *The Earthquake* (New York: Scribners, 1918), 115, 230, 234, 43.
7. *Ibid.*, 112, 284, 286.
8. *Ibid.*, 187.
9. *Ibid.*, 297.
10. Mary Raymond Shipman Andrews, *The Three Things* (New York: Curtis, 1915), 19.
11. Mary Raymond Shipman Andrews, *Joy in the Morning* (New York: Scribners, 1919), 80.
12. Upton Sinclair, *Jimmie Higgins* (New York: Boni & Liveright, 1918), 6.
13. *Ibid.*, 67, 15, 140.
14. Edith Wharton, *A Son at the Front* (1923; rpt. Carbondale: University of Southern Illinois Press, 1995), 193.
15. Edith Wharton, *Fighting France* (1915; New York: Scribners, 1917), 38.
16. Wharton, *A Son at the Front*, 105.
17. Edith Wharton, *The Marne* (New York: Appleton, 1918), 44.
18. Wharton, *Fighting France*, 93, 53.
19. Willa Cather, *One of Ours* (New York: Knopf, 1922), 278, 311.
20. *Ibid.*, 406, 409, 419.
21. *Ibid.*, 420, 458, 459.
22. Alan Seeger, *Project Gutenberg Etext of Poems by Alan Seeger* www.firstworldwar.com/poetsandprose/textsseeger.htm.
23. *Ibid.*
24. *Ibid.*
25. John Dos Passos, *First Encounter* (New York: Philosophical Library, 1945), 144, 143. First published as *One Man's Initiation* (New York: George H. Doran Company, 1917).
26. *Ibid.*, 85, 24, 132.
27. *One Man's Initiation* represents a principal genre of postwar fiction that describes in uncompromising detail the horrors of combat and suggests how battlefield cynicism destroys faith in abstractions; other important examples are Thomas Boyd's *Through the Wheat* (1923), Hervey Allen's *Toward the Flame* (1926), James Stevens's *Mattock* (1927), and William March's *Company K* (1933).
28. Dos Passos, *First Encounter*, 30, 147.
29. John Dos Passos, *Three Soldiers* (New York: George H. Doran Company, 1921), 26.
30. *Ibid.*, 92.
31. David M. Kennedy, *Over Here: The First World War and American Society* (New York: Oxford University Press, 1980), 41.

32. Dos Passos, *Three Soldiers*, 68.

33. *Ibid.*, 380.

34. E. E. Cummings, *The Enormous Room* (1922; rpt. New York: Penguin, 1999), 3.

35. *Ibid.*, 227.

36. *Ibid.*, 233.

37. *Ibid.*, 88.

38. *Ibid.*, 252.

39. Ernest Hemingway, *In Our Time* (New York: Scribners, 1925), 133.

40. *Ibid.*, 139, 142.

41. *Ibid.*, 34, 99.

42. Ernest Hemingway, *The Sun Also Rises* (New York: Scribners, 1926), 17.

43. *Ibid.*, 93–94.

44. Dos Passos, *Three Soldiers*, 128.

45. Hemingway, *The Sun Also Rises*, 30.

46. William Faulkner, *Soldier's Pay* (New York: Boni & Liveright, 1926), 198.

47. William Faulkner, *Flags in the Dust* (New York: Random, 1973), 433. (Originally published as *Sartoris* [New York: Harcourt, Brace, 1929].)

48. Ernest Hemingway, *A Farewell to Arms* (New York: Scribners, 1929), 249.

49. *Ibid.*, 233.

50. F. Scott Fitzgerald, *Tender is the Night* (New York: Scribners, 1934), 18.

51. Jessie Redmon Fauset's early novel of the Harlem Renaissance, *There is Confusion* (1924), depicts a scene of racial and familial reconciliation on the battlefield, only to chronicle the decay of race relations in postwar Philadelphia. The emergence of new sexual orders may be glimpsed in the homoeroticism and cross-gendering of war stories like Faulkner's "Turn About" (1932), in Claude's indefinite sexual orientation in Cather's *One of Ours*, and in the lesbianism of Gertrude Stein's *Autobiography of Alice B. Toklas* (1933) and Djuna Barnes's *Nightwood* (1937).

III

POSTWAR ENGAGEMENTS

IO

SHARON OUDITT

Myths, memories, and monuments: reimagining the Great War

When considering the legacy of the Great War, one is inevitably drawn to consider why that war is so frequently reimagined by modern writers. What is to be gained, after nearly a century, from resurrecting the stories embedded in the work of Owen, Sassoon, and Graves? Why does this war haunt the English cultural imagination? And why, specifically, is it the story of the infantry officer on the Western Front that is told and retold by writers as diverse as Stuart Cloete, Susan Hill, and Jennifer Johnston, by Joan Littlewood's Theatre Workshop and the writers of *Blackadder Goes Forth*, and, in the 1990s, by Sebastian Faulks, Pat Barker, and Kate Atkinson?[1]

There are, of course, exceptions to and variations on the theme of subaltern disillusion, some of which are included in the work of writers named above. And there are alternative perspectives – those of women, of the colonial regiments, of the working classes, and of the other fronts on which the war was fought. Even in the 1920s and 1930s, when the rash of memoirs emerged that seemed to solidify the subaltern's story, its universality was questioned. Douglas Jerrold, for instance, objected to what he called the "anti-war" stance as unrepresentative of the young men who experienced the war positively, in terms of adventures and action hitherto unknown.[2] The narrative of bitter disillusionment, according to him, was not the only story.

But perhaps instead of questioning the representative nature of these stories we ought to be considering why those repeated images persist. Late twentieth-century reimaginings of the war are very thoroughly researched (or, in the case of Cloete's, based on personal experience), and return us to familiar terrain: northern France, trenches, gas, rats, lice, moldering corpses, incompetent generals, chlorinated tea, and the all-devouring mud. There are, of course, compelling reasons why these images recur. They were, after all, accurate reflections, both literal and metaphorical, of actual physical and mental conditions. The image of the individual struggling against the effects of a mechanized, dehumanized force is a powerful one. He is doing his best

245

for the men under his care, conscious of a seismic change in world values. This emphasis follows the emotional trajectory of many twentieth-century texts. If the First World War was not the war to end all wars, it was, perhaps, the war that began international, imperial, mechanized conflict. It has become a cultural touchstone, in relation to which we position and measure other military engagements, and through the example of which we feel again the pitching of the individual consciousness into the unknown. It acts as a locus around which the many epistemological, ontological, and heuristic questions torturing (or liberating) the modernist and postmodernist mind can revolve, focusing issues of what is speakable and unspeakable, or what is knowable and unknowable.

These are vehicles for remembrance. They are written in new contexts: the global proliferation of nuclear missiles, the troubles in Northern Ireland, the *fin-de-siècle* preoccupation with memory and identity. To varying degrees, they juxtapose familiar images of the war with newly revealed dimensions of the event. The awful elements of human suffering are recalled to modern consciousness lest anyone should forget the horrors that were endured, and these are recalled in terms that reflect their powerful influence on twentieth-century modes of articulation: irony, alienation, and dissociation. It is part of the duty of remembrance to retell these stories – and often in their own terms, which tend to demand the return of those hauntingly familiar tropes and images. Late twentieth-century remembrance, though, is also about telling or (re)imagining the unspoken stories – those concerning class identity, sexuality, masculinity. Furthermore, it is about the shortcomings of memory, the lack of knowledge, the imperfect nature of interpretation and the need to build monuments, literal or literary, as an objective correlative for loss. The epistemological chasm between past and present that the experience of war apparently revealed is repositioned in late twentieth-century narratives, between "then" and "now." The difficulties of how to know, how to be and how to interpret are worked into narrative form as a tension between the familiar and the unfamiliar, the knowable and the out-of-reach. This tension, as we shall see, is achieved through varying degrees of historical and literary self-consciousness.

The old myths

In order to explore the extent to which the myths of the First World War have been absorbed, reworked, or left behind in modern rewritings, it seems necessary to acknowledge that they form something that looks like shared cultural ground: a common set of events or images that have come to represent the narrative landscape or structure of feeling of the war. Samuel

Hynes, in an attempt to summarize the story of the war, paints it like this:

> a generation of innocent young men, their heads full of high abstractions like Honour, Glory and England, went off to war to make the world safe for democracy. They were slaughtered in stupid battles planned by stupid generals. Those who survived were shocked, disillusioned and embittered by their war experiences, and saw that their real enemies were not the Germans, but the old men at home who had lied to them. They rejected the values of the society that had sent them to war, and in doing so separated their own generation from the past and from their cultural inheritance.[3]

That this point of view privileges the disillusioned perspective of the subaltern is something that Hynes would acknowledge. Whether or not it is representative, the experience of the officer on the Western Front has come to typify the story of the war, and it is a story that has an imaginary coherence composed of numerous narrative tropes and images. Before exploring the more self-conscious departures from that story, it seems appropriate to offer an account of the ways in which its more significant motifs have been replayed in later narratives.

Typically, narratives of the war begin in England, August 1914, with the country so preoccupied with the Irish Troubles and the increasing activity of the suffragettes that events in the Balkans seem to attract little interest. So Ken Follett's bestseller, *The Man from St. Petersburg* (1982),[4] begins, although the apparent civilian calm is undercut by rumors of secret diplomacy and plans for an anarchist assassination. News of the war seems similarly distant in *How Many Miles to Babylon* (1974), Jennifer Johnston's novella. Its build-up is more progressive and gradual in novels dealing with the Russian Front, such as Stephanie Plowman's *My Kingdom for a Grave* (1970), and Solzhenitsyn's panoramic *August 1914* (1971).[5]

For those narratives whose starting point is further into the war, the "virginity" of the soldier is often emphasized (Cloete and William Boyd[6] make much of this – both in military and sexual terms) and a conventional set of activities makes its appearance. Thus Cloete's Jim Hilton commands his company bravely, but with the help of his more experienced sergeant. He takes part in routine wire-mending patrols, experiences movement up and down the line for no apparent reason, deals sensitively with his men, censors their letters, and even captures an enemy trench. The General Staff sends men out on suicidal missions (see the chapter called "Plain Bloody Murder" – Cloete has little time for subtlety), blind to the real conditions of trench warfare. In Susan Hill's *Strange Meeting* (1971) the military strategy is based on archaic cavalry maneuvers; no general appears on the front lines to ascertain

whether or not the "surprise element" is attainable. There are frequent dis-
quisitions on rats, on lice, and on latrines ("By God, having a crap in war
was a frightening affair"[7]). The pastoral, familiarized as antithetical to war's
horrors by Edmund Blunden and Edward Thomas, is hauntingly present in
the orchard apple loft, in which Hill's Hilliard and Barton are billeted during their rest period. Roses, wildflowers, birdsong ("All the bloody larks in
the world were singing"[8]) attract Cloete's Jim Hilton and Faulks's Stephen
Wraysford.

The turning point in the conventional narrative of the war, and often in
their reimaginings, comes with the battle of the Somme. Cloete describes the
men staggering across no man's land, after a week-long barrage that was
"certain" to break down the enemy wire but didn't, only to be decimated by
machine guns. Faulks's Stephen Wraysford experiences the whole thing, from
the walking pace "attack," to the men crawling out of shell-holes amongst
a ghostly wailing sound from the wounded, once night has fallen. Kate
Atkinson's Frank Cook gets stuck in one of those shell-holes, from which
he sees a beatific vision of his pal, Arthur, who has been killed. Susan Hill's
David Barton remains one of the "missing." Those who survive feel both
lucky and guilty. Jim Hilton, shot through the shoulder, is shipped home
with his "blighty" to convalesce, only to confront further horrors when the
shell shock sets in. Briefly, as in all these stories, savagery and civilization
become inseparable, but in his case, he is "restored," rather as nineteenth-
century heroes are "saved," by a pretty young VAD nurse, whom he returns
to marry – with perfect narrative closure – on Armistice Day.

The fortuitous combination of war and romance in this novel guaranteed
a popular audience. Yet the material on which these writers build is usually
derived from detailed research. Susan Hill is quite open about this, explaining
not only what she read, but also her method.[9] As her title, *Strange Meeting*,
suggests, she was heavily influenced by Wilfred Owen. Her book also reflects
attitudes voiced by Siegfried Sassoon and Robert Graves. As for these writers,
there is from the beginning a gap in understanding between those at the Front
and those at home: John's family – his mother and sister – take only a formal
interest in what he is doing, and can respond to him only in clichés. For his
part, John cannot speak to them, despite a formerly close relationship with
his sister. The newspapers mystify what is going on in France, yet construe
the battles in terms of victory. Sebastian Faulks's Stephen Wraysford, in his
fearless approach to raids, is known as "mad," echoing Sassoon's persona
as "Mad Jack"; his friend Michael Weir, while home on leave, imagines a
tank coming in to squash the apathetic, uninterested civilians on the home
front (Pat Barker's Billy Prior entertains a similar fantasy, one derived from
an image by Sassoon); Wraysford "dies" – in that is he is so badly wounded

as to be mistaken for one of the dead: he comes back to life, thus imitating Graves's experience of having his death reported.

Is it a failing, then, that these texts reveal the traces of their sources? It is not clear, for example, whether Geoff Dyer is complimenting Susan Hill when he comments on the "judiciousness" of her research.[10] Ben Shephard, on the other hand, writing in the *Times Literary Supplement*, is openly critical of Pat Barker's reliance in *The Regeneration Trilogy* on secondary sources. He derides her use of "mainly feminist" historians, whose work enables her to "recycle modern academic clichés" rather than undertaking "real research" among the more obscure, primary historical sources that might have made of her a Tolstoy, rather than merely a modern novelist "in search of a story-line."[11]

Barker acknowledges her sources with the integrity of one who wishes to make available to her readership the extent to which she has imagined the material, and to which it draws on scholarly research. Those familiar with Graves and Sassoon on the one hand, and with the cultural historians Elaine Showalter and Eric Leed on the other, will easily spot these resonances.[12] To some extent, then, the same old stories are being rehearsed. But Barker, in combining fact and fiction, is contributing to the postmodern genre of "faction." Furthermore, the emphasis in *The Regeneration Trilogy* has shifted: toward Rivers and toward Billy Prior, one of the entirely imagined characters in the trilogy. The issues on which she concentrates – masculinity, class, nightmares, civilization – all draw on conventional images to establish a level of familiarity, but also articulate what was originally "unspeakable." In doing this Barker contextualizes historical issues in present-day discourse. Blake Morrison registers some dissatisfaction with the predictability of her concern with the "very nineteen-nineties" issues of gender and emasculation,[13] but the specificities in the novels – the relationship between Rivers, Sassoon, and Owen; the prosecution of homosexuals, pacifists, and trades unionists on the home front; the death of Owen in November 1918 – draw out a combination of the well known and the barely documented. In the second volume, for example, the treatment of prisoners is dealt with in some detail: the lack of privacy (the eye in the door), the humiliation and, in the case of pacifists and strikers, the violence to which they were subject become a logical extension of the horrors of the Front. Thus Billy, rejecting the contamination of civilian rights by military values, describes the Front as the only "clean" place to be and Barker, in pursuing this analysis, undermines one of the war's more prevalent tropes: the chasm between war zone and home front.

Other writers moved further away from the familiar narratives of mud and trenches. For some the war on other fronts, or through means of combat other than artillery, provided usable material. Some wrote purely to appeal to a popular market: fantasy tales buying into the power and the pity to provide a lurid backdrop to conventional narrative. Two novels that deal with aviation, for example, *The Blue Max* (Jack D. Hunter, 1965) and *In the Company of Eagles* (Ernst K. Gann, 1966),[14] provide compelling action sequences that imagine the war not as bleak stasis but reinvest it with the chivalric glamor for individual acts of heroism that the trench narratives had subdued. Thomas Keneally's *Gossip from the Forest* (1975), on the other hand, analyzes the characters responsible for signing the Armistice, imagining their motives and envisaging the imminent horrors for a humiliated Germany.[15]

Whether bestsellers, prize-winners, novellas, or narratives of the whole of the twentieth century, these are all vehicles for remembrance and reflection. Some choose to dwell entirely on the war's futility and the need to heed Owen's warning of its enormous cost. Others, as we may go on to see in greater detail, deviate from the established myths and open up alternative contexts as a means of speaking the unspeakable and encouraging a late twentieth-century audience to observe the continuities as well as the chasms between then and now.

Sexuality, masculinity, class: burdens of manhood

In most early renderings of the war, sex and sexuality were alluded to rather than described. D. H. Lawrence, along with the increasing influence of Freud, began to change all that in the immediate aftermath of the war, but *Women in Love* (1920) is only obliquely a war novel, and younger writers such as Orwell, Waugh, Heller, and Mailer, turned their attention to other scenes of conflict. It was only in the "liberated" 1960s that writers about the Great War began to conjoin those natural accomplices, sex and death, in ways that might create a modern war hero whose sexual life was self-consciously a part of his masculine identity.

Heterosexual activity, from the masculine perspective, is often seen as a means of confirming the manhood of a young protagonist. Stephen Wraysford, and the would-be assassin, Feliks, in Follett's novel, both attract women who are the "property" of their social superiors. Cloete's Jim Hilton, in *How Young They Died* (1969), is similarly initiated, but through the offices of a call girl. This novel has been described by Hugh Cecil as a "vigorous tale of shellfire and fornication . . . a fantasy about the kind of sexual opportunities he missed when a capable young officer."[16] Here, war and sex (a paler coupling than sex and death) complement each other in a way that condones rape as a means of succouring the war-ravaged psyche of the temporarily brutalized male ("He had to do it. He was like a bent spring" [17]). Read in the context of the "sexual revolution" of the 1960s, forty years after the other war fictions and fifty years after the experience itself, this can be seen deliberately to lack the subtlety and innocence of, for example, *All Quiet on the Western Front*. Read in the context of the second wave of feminist writing (late 1960s and 1970s) it might be seen as an attack on feminism. Even Jim's mother muses on the fact that frilly underwear grants women more power than the vote ever could. Erotic need (male erotic need) is presented as a sub-Lawrentian life force – "the seed of life that had to be planted" – which allows Jim to categorize his women according to his needs. The only one disapproved of is the professional military nurse, whose "milk-less breasts flat with efficiency" mark her out as unaccommodating: a "big bitch."[18] Cloete's "argument" rather opportunistically echoes Freud: that sexual drives underpin all of human activity, and are particularly stimulated by the threat of death. The kind of hero that emerges is a rather stereotyped action hero, whose needs are met by a conspicuously obliging array of female "types."

In *Gossip from the Forest* sex and death are brought together in an unusually imaginative way. Here we are barely introduced to the couple concerned. At some distance from the fighting lines, and during the closing stages of the war, the sex act is seen not as the self-defining drive of an action hero, but as an ordinary human activity that takes on a regenerative symbolic power. A man and a woman break into the train carriage in which the terms of the Armistice have been discussed, and make love on the table around which the negotiations had been taking place:

> Even if they had not already had their minds on it, they would have found coitus the obvious recourse. Simply because it was insufferable to think that in such a little space, round a table no bigger than a family dinner table, with notepaper and pencils, it was possible for eight men to weave a scab over that pit of corpses four years deep.[19]

These two are seen as "the wiser visitors to 2417D" who, in a small, unheroic, transgressive act mock the futility and the arrogance of the Armistice negotiators, who seem impervious to the scale of the disaster they have overseen.[20]

Gossip from the Forest, then, abstracts sexuality from the interiority of the individual, presenting instead a tableau where, symbolically, eros confronts thanatos. The more common response in late twentieth-century accounts – and one that Blake Morrison finds predictable – is to probe the construction of masculinity in the subaltern. Homoeroticism is, of course, central to Fussell's study of trench experience, and is implicit in a great deal of the writings and poetry of the war. It is implicit also in Susan Hill's *Strange Meeting*, and Jennifer Johnston's *How Many Miles to Babylon*, and, to a lesser degree, in Faulks's *Birdsong* (1993) and Atkinson's *Behind the Scenes at the Museum* (1995). In *Strange Meeting* the relationship is (as in *Journey's End*), between two officers. The novel provides a sensitive exploration of the capacity for same-sex love between two men of the same class who experience the war according to the tropes which have now become familiar. It does not ask or answer questions that have not been posed before. The exploration of masculinity becomes more variegated when issues of national allegiance, class identity, and personal friendship are brought into conflict with a construction of masculinity predicated on English public school discipline. Alec and Jerry in *How Many Miles to Babylon* are both Irish and thus already considered potentially seditious. Their cross-class friendship – Alec is a gentleman, later an officer; Jerry a local lad – has always been difficult to maintain and, in the context of a British army regiment, becomes inadmissible. The inhuman military solution – to sentence Jerry to death by a firing squad under Alec's command – represents a clear indictment of public school, militarist masculinity.

Part of Alec's problem is that he has never been to (public) school and so has never learned the "burdens of manhood": "leadership and service." Lacking this training (which would have been available to Sassoon, Graves, Hilliard, and Barton, if not to Wraysford and Billy Prior), Alec remains relentlessly, if quietly, opposed to the military machinery. He admits to fear, but not of the conventional misfortunes of war: "I was afraid that one day I might wake up and find that I had come to accept the grotesque obscenity of the way we lived." He values those things that image freedom: horses galloping across open fields, swans flying freely, poetry. He is aware that his family and his superior officer "all wanted me to become a man," but is resistant to what this might entail.[21]

Alec stands outside the codes of public school masculinity and actively resists them. Those officers under the care of Rivers in the *Regeneration* trilogy, on the other hand, have to be persuaded to undo the muting tendencies of traditional masculine behavior in order to accept that their response to the war – breakdown, grief, tenderness for other men – is normal. Like them, though, Rivers has been "trained to identify emotional repression as the essence of manliness." In treating mutism, memory loss, verbal and somatic displacements, he is brought up against the reality that he, too, exhibits a neurotic symptom in the form of a stammer, and that his role as "male mother" to these suffering men argues for a renegotiation of masculinity.[22] But it is the form of masculinity on which his own identity is somewhat perilously constructed.

If Alec rejects the "responsibilities" of his class, Rivers begins to examine and renegotiate them. Both characters can be seen as being motivated at some level by love of someone of their own sex, and both find that the combined conventions of class and masculinity provide no clear defense against the "crumbling world."[23] Perhaps now we are beginning to hear the unspeakable being spoken. But if this sound is tentative, exploratory, involving a stammer and a story told from a military jail, Barker's narrative elsewhere provides graphic descriptions of what was not merely unspeakable but open to prosecution in the England of 1914–18: homosexual acts. The plot of The Eye in the Door, of course, revolves around the alleged threat to national security posed by 47,000 homosexual men in high office. Sassoon's homosexuality is frequently alluded to, but the issues centering on class, masculinity, and sexuality are focused most clearly in the relationship between Prior, who is a working-class officer, and Captain Charles Manning. Prior's class origins determine the narrative for his sexual relationship with Manning, which is dominated by role-playing – Prior assuming a "rough" working-class persona – and by scenes of working-class life. The maid's bedroom, not the drawing room, seems the appropriate place to Manning for enacting scenes that are "unspeakable" in his world, and Prior is content to play along with that. Within a private world, then, there is free and open exchange. But outside that world prosecution and public disgrace are the least that might be expected.

Old and new orders

Part of the myth of the First World War suggests that the war revealed a new way of seeing: that it broke down class barriers, separated generations, cut off the transmission of cultural inheritance, and permitted men and women to see each other plainly for the first time. If the old order was based on land, class, and capital, dominated by a chivalric code and inflected by Victorian values, the new order looked forward to mechanization, new forms of political organization, the redistribution of power, and new forms of weaponry. Inevitably in writing dating from the 1960s and more recently, those notions are complicated by the preoccupations of the age. In Gann's In the Company of Eagles we see an interesting conjunction when the ideals of a chivalric code meet the instruments of modern warfare in a moment of national reconciliation. The narrative follows a revenge plot in which a French pilot seeks to bring down his rival German flying "ace." The final dogfight represents, as it were, the conflict of the best in both national characters. Each has at least one opportunity to kill the other. But neither does. Ultimately, they fly alongside one another, look each other in the eye and salute. This echoes the common mockery of the generals who, by contrast, appear gross and murderous. It also alludes to a deconstructive ideology in which each fighter sees the other in himself, recognizes the "horror" that is the savagery of war, and pulls away from it, to restore civilized and human emotions. And so we are left with an image of mutual respect, a chivalric admiration for the ability, control, and power that each has displayed, and a refusal to allow the barbarism of this war to overcome a code at once ancient and modern – of shared humanity and respect for national differences.

Keneally's *Gossip From the Forest*, on the other hand, depicts the old order unwilling to give way to the new. Indeed, the former is pitched against the latter. The novel constructs the meeting between opposing nations as oppositional and bullying.

In this novel the power, inflexibility, and determination of the Allies is set against the inexperience of the Germans, who are just ordinary men drafted in to do an extraordinary job. As news reaches them of the Kaiser's abdication and of Communist revolutions all over the country, it is not even clear to them for whom, and in whose name, they are negotiating the Armistice. The terms laid down by the Allies are, of course, crushing. They choose not to believe the statistics relating to the poverty and malnutrition presently suffered by ordinary German civilians. There is no wisdom, no insight, no political imagination in evidence among the victors. The German representative Erzberger's only hope is that, once peace negotiations start, then "German plenipotentiaries will be negotiating not with an insane old soldier and obsessive British sailors, but with men of wider ideas."[24] *Gossip*, then, instead of dwelling on the pity of war, shows it as the gateway to the evils of the twentieth century: Erzberger's faith in the disinterestedness of international diplomats is seen to be misplaced. We see the seedbed of the famine, influenza, depression, and other depredations that were shortly to provide the context for Hitler's popularity, and for all the actual and potential wars that followed. Keneally's epigraph – "In the season in which this book was written, the French government persisted in exploding nuclear devices above the ocean where my children swim" – says much about the staying power of the values of "old Europe."

In the *Regeneration* trilogy, Rivers is seen as a member of the "old order" confronting the challenges of the new. But he is conscious of his own complicity with the inflexible forms of militarism, which inevitably form part of his "cure." When Sassoon departs from Craiglockhart for the Front with an admittedly ironic "Thank you, sir," Rivers is reminded of Yealland and his brutal, coercive treatment of Callan. He knows that the public has complacently renounced reason and settled for being told what to think, and that the bargain on which the stability of all patriarchal societies is struck (if the young and strong will obey the old and weak, they too will peacefully inherit, one day) is being broken. "A society that devours its own young," Rivers acknowledges, "deserves no automatic or unquestioning allegiance." He too has come to question his role in keeping the war going, in upholding something that is called civilization but which seems more like barbarism. His frequent memories of his Eddystone experiences force us to contrast a culture committing suicide with one in demise because of, among other things, the absence of war. "We weren't the measure of all things," Rivers is forced to admit when reexamining his capacity to make judgments as an anthropologist.[25] Implicitly he is also wondering whether he is any more justified in adhering to conventional military judgments in his role as an army doctor.

Nightmares, memories, and monuments

Although the works of Sigmund Freud were not readily available in translation until after the war, professionals like Rivers would have had some access to them. Freudian ideas are alluded to in *How Young They Died*, in *Birdsong*, and, with more effect, in *The Blue Max* and the *Regeneration* trilogy as a means of representing a world fragmented and disjointed in which narrative progression is frequently disrupted by stories that compete with it for attention. Psychoanalysis provided a language with which to describe personality disorders, fugue states, dissociation, and the forms of repression that are commonly seen in nightmares. Nightmares, recollections under hypnosis, or hallucinations are seen in themselves to offer a narrative of an idea or sequence of events unavailable to the conscious mind. They are also used as metaphors for chaos.

Keneally initially uses chaos as a metaphor for a nightmare, representing Erzberger's attempt to set off for France in terms of "impossible time-tables, nebulous instructions, undisclosed fellow-travellers and destinations." Erzberger's actual nightmare images a repulsively "clammy and fungoid" forest. Here he finds himself under fire, and the mood of threat and ambush, the suggestion of rebirth, ironically prefigures the conclusion in which he is indeed killed, his body left overnight in a forest. There is another image in that dream, though, which is not contained by the temporal sequence of the novel's narrative. Erzberger fruitlessly attempts to defend himself by holding up an umbrella. From its tattered shards appear wounded soldiers, climbing out of bullet holes as they might once have struggled out of shell holes in no man's land: reborn in the unconscious (and in the narrative) if not in the grim reality of war's sequence. Even the formidable Marshall Foch finds himself dreaming about soldiers, silenced, with medal ribbons sewn onto their foreheads, walking naked in the forest. "They were sombre children returned to a playroom after a long winter. Behind the trees, somewhere, cunningly amongst leaves, were the utterly adequate toys of childhood." This is a striking image in a novel that is principally concerned with the rituals of diplomacy. These ghostly creatures, tagged and voiceless, seek in death their lost childhoods. The conjunction of images, the "affect" of loss, waste, "doomed youth," haunts the novel, even if the inflexible Foch declines responsibility for them, taking comfort rather in the idea that he is "the most powerful man in the world" and preparing to impose his will on any one who might dare to disagree with him.[26]

Nightmares, though, not only wound and frighten, they also permit healing: the retelling of a distressing story brings into the narrative present something that may have been buried in the past. John Hilliard finds himself at home, recovering from wounds, experiencing the inability to connect with those around him, and reliving, through vivid nightmares, the horrors of the Front. "He did not retch at the real things, only the memory of them, here in his old room above the rose garden."[27] On one level this anticipates the element of the plot that deconstructs the opposition between Hilliard's chilly reserve and Barton's garrulous self-disclosure by having Hilliard break down Barton's temporary silence using the techniques of listening and encouragement that he has learned from Barton himself. Thus Hilliard persuades his friend that it is not true that he does not feel, and he persuades him of this by encouraging him to narrate, to remember, to recreate his response to witnessing the sudden death of eleven of his fellow-men. On another level perhaps the suggestion is that it is the part of the mind that narrates that experiences the horror, as it recreates (or anticipates) the experience. Thus narration itself becomes therapy and plays its part in reconciling the past with the present and in pacifying the feelings of guilt, pain, and dissociation that arise when the unspeakable is confronted.

Billy's memories, of his frontline experience, of his father's treatment of him, of the fact that he used to "go into the shine on the glass" in order to escape from intolerable violence as a child, help him to make sense of his past. This would be, in Rivers's terms, the "epicritic" function taking over from the "protopathic" one. It is part of Rivers's role as analyst, rationalist, and listener, to help his patients confront those repressed experiences and feelings in order to accommodate them to the patient's conscious experience. Occasionally these narratives – memories, dreams, hallucinations – may not seem sufficient to fill the psychological gap created by their absence. At other times, they may come unbidden (like Sassoon's haunting by Orme, or Billy's alter ego). Both disrupt the present and simultaneously, if painfully, make some sense of the past. Bidden or otherwise, they fracture chronology, unsettle the present by introducing buried fears, horrors, violence, or memories of other kinds. Rivers the rationalist attempts to aid his patients in managing this, by encouraging them to talk. The cost of this is his own necessary silence which paradoxically drives him toward breakdown.

Is there an analogy to be drawn between Billy's or Sassoon's nightmares or memories and the effect of these books in our own culture? Do these reimagined stories represent the return of our culture's repressed horrors? Like nightmares they bring with them, in narrative form, the powerful affect of the original events, obscured, reworked, but nevertheless redolent of waste, loss, horror, pity. Manning's story about Scudder (who finally drowns in mud); Billy's "unmediated" diary, which tells us of his and Owen's last days – these narratives within the narrative continue to retell First World War horror stories, to disinter that which we might prefer to forget. And what of the analytical framework within which we judge them? Rivers's task as an army doctor is to encourage his patients to remember and thus resolve their traumas, in order that they might return to the Front and to almost certain death. His broader interests in anthropology, however, alert us to the western tendency to make reductive judgments about "civilization," according to hierarchical conventions. "We weren't the measure of all things," he says of his own imperial investigative team; "Shotvarfet" ("it's not worth it") says the dying Hallett.[28] Between them these two statements speak (one with the reflective cadence of the rational mind, the other through the fractured physiognomy of the war victim) of the absence of any clear or lasting value system that might make sense of the experience both have endured.

Faulks's *Birdsong* catches, perhaps more self-consciously, a commemorative mood similar to that of *The Ghost Road*. In its before/during/after structure, the novel places the war as a central reference point for the twentieth century. It opens in Amiens, 1910, the Somme with its canals, flat-bottomed boats, water-gardens, and drowsy fishermen part of the provincial landscape. English teas at Thiepval, a fishing trip to the Ancre, and a train journey heading along the Marne to the Meuse and then down to Verdun set up an Edenic topography, but one in which no reader can fail to register the sites of the future killing fields. It is only a matter of time before Stephen Wraysford finds himself back in them wearing the uniform of a British army officer.

From the outset, then, the novel is about the way in which we conceptualize the past, and how narratives are constructed to anticipate, contain, or resurrect a well-known field of traumatic events. At the end of his ordeal, Stephen experiences "deliverance" from that part of his life, and this representation, as if to acknowledge the structuring influence of the subaltern poets, recasts images from Owen's "Strange Meeting." Trapped in one of the "profound dark tunnels" that form so much of the novel's symbolism,

Stephen and Jack Firebrace become aware of the "gallery of ghosts," of "all the needless dead" of the war reproaching and mocking them, as they fight for life. Jack dies, but not before they succeed in setting off some explosives and half-blowing an escape hole. The explosion causes the death of one of Stephen's would-be rescuers, a German who, with his brother, was trying to reach the trapped men. Stephen emerges from his "coffin," ready to fight the hated enemy. Instead he finds himself opening his arms ("lifting distress-ful hands as if to bless") and embracing the German-Jewish doctor, whose brother he has just killed. The enemy he has killed would have been his friend, and those who are living, at the end of the war, weep together over the "bitter strangeness of their human lives" but have no other resources with which to interpret that strangeness.[29]

This deliverance or rebirth is echoed some sixty years later when Stephen's granddaughter, Elizabeth, tries to uncover his story. She finds her grandfa-ther's diaries and with some detective work, manages to decipher the code in which they were written. Thus the "secrets" of the war are made apparent to her. And like many of her generation (and those since), she feels the need to make reparation by feeling the losses for herself. It is instructive to read this alongside Geoff Dyer's account of *The Missing of the Somme* (1994). Both the fictional Elizabeth and the writer/journalist Dyer visit the monument for the missing of the Somme at Thiepval. "Nobody told me," Elizabeth finds herself saying, overwhelmed by the huge numbers of the dead and missing from those fields alone.[30] "Thiepval is not simply a site of commemoration but of prophecy, of birth as well as of death," says Dyer: "a memorial to the future, to what the century had in store for those who were left, whom age would weary."[31] Elizabeth is pregnant. Her way of "completing the circle" is to name her child "John," after the dead son of Jack Firebrace. Her grand-father had promised the dying Jack that he, at least, would go on having children. In the event he doesn't, but Elizabeth's decision to keep his promise for him allows her to pick up the displaced, obscured threads of his story and to repay something of the debt she feels she owes.

In Kate Atkinson's *Behind the Scenes at the Museum* (1995), the First World War, although a powerful presence, is not the focal point. It sees the death of the main character's great-uncle – and of, seemingly, a whole gener-ation of men, epitomized by a photograph of a football team, of which there is only one member still living at the war's end. Like *Birdsong*, it is a narrative of the twentieth century, driven by a lost memory. The resulting picture is made up from incomplete recollections, photographs without contexts, and partial testimonies, and is therefore fragmentary.

Elizabeth's "lost memory" in *Birdsong*, that of her grandfather, is more or less restored to her by the end of the narrative. But what it means, or how she is to interpret it, is not necessarily any clearer. Geoff Dyer, visiting monuments, finds himself struggling to arrive at some kind of interpretation of the words inscribed in the visitors' book by a Dutch woman in 1986: "It is because of the lonelyness [*sic*]." Eventually he lets them stand for themselves, "their mystery and power undisturbed, these words that explain everything and nothing."[32] The meaninglessness of the First World War is, of course, one of its major tropes and most searing agonies. In that it makes no sense from the perspective of the alienated individual, no "meaning" can be extracted from it. Countless narratives thus circulate around it sometimes only to reinforce – and reproduce – the emptiness at the center, sometimes to fill the void with meaning as an act of reparation and interpretation. "Lest We Forget" becomes sympathetically ironical while the term "the Great War" gives way to the more anodyne "The First World War" for, as these texts remind us, this was not the war to end all wars, but the beginning of endless wars.

Can these writers do anything with this conflict other than reproduce its established myths? For the most part, it seems that Owen, Sassoon, Graves, and others have told us how to remember it, and it seems disrespectful to betray them. Perhaps we do not want those myths to be shattered. They are part of our cultural landscape and we need them to be reinforced rather than dispersed: the "Great War," futility, murderous absurdity, the old lie, satire, savagery, and sadness, and, at its heart, the brave, innocent white male. If this picture becomes too complicated we lose a founding image of western twentieth-century irony. But the picture *is*, nevertheless, incomplete, fragmented. Women's story of the war, for example, is barely represented here. That of the colonial regiments is absent. So too are the many fronts other than the Western Front, which is where all the imagery, all the poetry seems to be located – and where actual monuments and acres of cemeteries stand in remembrance of those millions of individuals who, in their national, regional, and religious diversity, can only partially be assimilated into the myth.

NOTES

1. Stuart Cloete, *How Young They Died* (1969; rpt. London: Fontana Books, 1971); Susan Hill, *Strange Meeting* (1971; rpt. Harmondsworth: Penguin, 1974); Jennifer Johnston, *How Many Miles to Babylon* (1974; rpt. London: Coronet Books, 1975); Pat Barker *Regeneration* (London: Viking, 1991); *The Eye in the Door* (London: Viking, 1993); *The Ghost Road* (London: Viking, 1995); all three volumes published together in *The Regeneration Trilogy* (London: Viking, 1996); Sebastian Faulks, *Birdsong* (1993; rpt. London: Vintage, 1994); Kate Atkinson, *Behind the Scenes at the Museum* (1995; rpt. London: Black Swan, 1996).

2. See Bernard Bergonzi, *Heroes' Twilight: A Study of the Literature of the Great War* (London: Macmillan, 1965), 195–97; Samuel Hynes, *A War Imagined: The First World War and English Culture* (London: Bodley Head, 1990), 451–54.

3. Hynes, *A War Imagined*, x.

4. Ken Follett, *The Man from St. Petersburg* (London: Hamish Hamilton, 1992).

5. Stephanie Plowman, *My Kingdom for a Grave* (London: Bodley Head, 1970); Alexander Solzhenitsyn, *August 1914* trans. Michael Glenny (London: Bodley Head, 1972).

6. William Boyd, *The New Confessions* (London: Hamish Hamilton, 1987).

7. Cloete, *How Young They Died*, 132.

8. *Ibid.*, 309.

9. There is an explanation, aimed at students of her work, of Hill's approach to researching the novel on her web page, at www.susan-hill.com.

10. Geoff Dyer, *The Missing of the Somme* (London: Hamish Hamilton, 1994).

11. Ben Shephard, "Digging Up the Past," *Times Literary Supplement*, 22 March 1996: 12–13.

12. Eric Leed, *No Man's Land: Combat and Identity in World War One* (Cambridge: Cambridge University Press, 1981); Elaine Showalter, *The Female Malady: Women, Madness, and English Culture, 1830–1980* (London: Virago, 1985).

13. Blake Morrison, "War Stories," *The New Yorker*, 22 January 1996: 82.

14. Jack D. Hunter, *The Blue Max* (1965; rpt. London: Corgi Books, 1966); Ernst K. Gann, *In the Company of Eagles* (London: Hodder & Stoughton, 1966).

15. Thomas Keneally, *Gossip from the Forest* (1975; rpt. London: Coronet Books, 1984).

16. Hugh Cecil, *The Flower of Battle: British Fiction Writers of the First World War* (London: Secker & Warburg, 1995), 6.

17. Cloete, *How Young They Died*, 214.

18. *Ibid.*, 337, 174.

19. Keneally, *Gossip from the Forest*, 167–68.

20. *Ibid.*, 168.

21. Johnston, *How Many Miles*, 110, 78, 113.

22. Barker, *Regeneration*, 44, 97.

23. Johnston, *How Many Miles*, 23.

24. Keneally, *Gossip from the Forest*, 210.

25. Barker, *Regeneration*, 134, 133, 218, 212.

26. Keneally, *Gossip from the Forest*, 31, 25, 11, 14.

27. Hill, *Strange Meeting*, 14.

28. Barker, *Ghost Road*, 212, 58.

29. Faulks, *Birdsong*, 368, 390.

30. *Ibid.*, 211.

31. Dyer, *Missing of the Somme*, 128.

32. *Ibid.*, 130.

11

JAMES CAMPBELL

Interpreting the war

In his acceptance address for the 1980 Theodore Adorno Award, the widely influential essay "Modernity – An Incomplete Project," Jürgen Habermas marks the twentieth century as the historical moment during and after which widespread faith in the progressive improvement of human culture through the means of secular enlightenment becomes increasingly untenable. In his context, he is stating an obvious fact and thus provides no details.[1] Yet it is useful occasionally to belabor the obvious: what specific events of the twentieth century have made the project of modernism, understood as a trajectory of historical improvement, so vexed? Certainly, the Holocaust is one inevitable meaning of this twentieth-century interruption. The specter of the tools of enlightened technology turning the factory from a site of production to a site of sheer destruction haunts any subsequent evocation of the inevitability, or even probability, of human progress. No other single event of the twentieth century may have the interruptive power of Auschwitz. Yet in many ways the unprecedented mass slaughter of the First World War inaugurates the twentieth century as a disruption of enlightenment. The products and techniques of industrial culture turn on their users: what had been tools for the efficient production of goods become weapons in the efficient production of death. Mass armies of draftees are marched to their mechanized destruction with all the organization that industrial capitalism has learned from the factory and the abattoir. The machine has produced the machine gun, and the human individual, supposed heir to Tennyson's "one far-off divine event, / to which the whole creation moves," becomes merely one of the more vulnerable parts of that machine.

The fact that a majority of citizens of industrialized Europe prior to 1914 could legitimately be seen as serving a machine more than as being served by the machine should give us pause, but not cancel the significance of the differences between industrialized war and industrialized peace. At least when viewed from an appropriate distance, the working conditions of the nineteenth century laborer could be seen as an inevitable price to be paid on the difficult road to full enlightenment. In fact, with a few adjustments, such a position was tenable for either the liberal Kantian or the radical Marxist. Moreover, the reforming tendencies of the western European governments, whether expressed in terms of legislation (Britain) or revolution (France), could be arranged in such a way that a trajectory toward increased individual freedom for all citizens looked inevitable. Some might be progressing faster than others, and certain hurdles proved momentarily difficult, but the shape of the future was nonetheless clearly visible and ultimately attainable. The Great War made violence no longer an anomaly to be solved, but a glimpse into a truer, if more chilling, reality. With the trajectory of history looking less and less like a gentle upward slope, the individual as cog in the great wheel became the rule rather than the exception.

Such is one interpretation of the meaning of the Great War, though by no means the only one. This chapter provides an overview of interpretations of the literature of the war developed over the last forty years. My main focus, therefore, lies in the criticism of war literature, however that latter term may be defined. In fact, the question of what constitutes the literature *of* the Great War is one of the central concerns at stake in such an investigation, and we will discover a number of contrasting answers to it. I divide the subject into three sections that are roughly chronological: first, the early work (1964–75) that assigns itself the task of defining the canon of Great War literature and defending its aesthetic and ethical status; second, a post-1975 emphasis on gender and sexuality that focuses both on widening the definition of war literature and on rereading the canonical figures in ways informed by Foucauldian insights on sexuality; third, a strain that seeks to break the relative isolation of the first two movements and put Great War literature in direct relation to more mainstream forms of literary modernism existing on both chronological sides of 1914–18. Because I am limiting my account to texts written in English, the primary texts addressed in these interpretations lean heavily toward British sources. However, comparative studies have become more prevalent since the early 1980s, and the reader will find a few of them mentioned below.

Excluded for the most part, however, are interpretations of the war itself as historical event rather than as viewed through the literary texts it produced. The distinction is not so easy to maintain as it may initially appear. History "itself" is known through texts, whether those texts be literary or cultural, and the Great War is now sufficiently recessed in time to be inaccessible to most living memories (those memories themselves constituting texts of a sort). It is thus now impossible to remember the war without in some way remembering through its literary texts, especially, for Anglophone audiences at least, the lyric poetry of two or three junior officers in the British army who fought on the Western Front. The Great War was the first to send a large number of educated, non-professional soldiers into combat, several of whom considered themselves poets well before they became soldiers. Thus, rather than depend on a Tennyson or a Kipling to represent their feelings and attitudes, the First World War produced literary artists who articulated experiences ostensibly their own: these figures become the basis of the war literature canon delineated below. But, largely as a result of the shock of hearing these voices as it were straight from the trenches, directly from the experience itself, the Great War's literary representations are inextricable from its status as raw happening. In order to make some distinctions, however, I attempt to include in my account books that take up the war as a cultural event with clear and significant links to non-military culture while excluding those whose focus seems more strictly military or political in the small sense of those words.

The years between the Armistice and 1964 are, of course, not accounted for in the scheme I have outlined above. This is partially due to the state of literary research in the first half of the twentieth century: contemporary literature was not widely considered a legitimate subject for academic concern at the end of the war. When contemporary writing did make its way into scholarly acceptability, it did so largely under the rubric of formalism, either of the US New Criticism or the British practical criticism of I. A. Richards. Both these approaches thrive on isolation from historical context, which is not the type of environment in which literature overtly tied to a specific moment in cultural history can expect to receive a sympathetic reading. The primary immediate critical afterlife of Great War literature was provided by British poets: C. Day Lewis edited the first complete edition of Wilfred Owen's poems, accompanying it with a generous introduction, while the poets killed in the war (primarily Owen, Isaac Rosenberg, and Edward Thomas) form an important part of an indigenous tradition constructed in preference to high modernism by the Movement poets Donald Davie and Philip Larkin. In this version of British poetry, the death of these heirs of Thomas Hardy opened the door for the foreign opportunists Pound and Eliot. Another dominant non-English modernist, Yeats, was famously unkind to Great War poetry, excluding it systematically from his 1936 *Oxford Book of Modern Verse*. This difficult relationship between modernism and war literature lies behind much of the material covered in the third section below.

Establishing the canon

By 1964, due no doubt in part to the Cold War, its accompanying specter of an impending Third World War, and the distant rumblings from southeast

Asia, the literature of the first total war gradually became more relevant to the academy. The scholarly publications of the first decade of Great War criticism (1964–75) had as their main purpose the establishment and defense of a canon of literary texts. For the most part, the texts in question represented combatant experience of the war on the Western Front. The foundation of the canon was quickly defined as the lyric poetry of the British junior officer class, with such figures as Wilfred Owen, Siegfried Sassoon, and Charles Sorley seen as representative. Autobiography was generally treated as a secondary genre, again with junior officer memoirs, especially Robert Graves's *Good-bye to All That*, predominating. Fiction was relegated to a tertiary role: when discussed at all, Ford Madox Ford's series of novels *Parade's End*, R. H. Mottram's *The Spanish Farm Trilogy*, and Richard Aldington's *Death of a Hero* became the touchstones.

Interestingly, a certain pattern soon becomes evident in this hierarchy of genres, especially when the lyric poetry is treated, as it tends to be in this early stage of the criticism, as strictly autobiographical. The eyewitness poetry is privileged because of its speed: it is the genre that comes closest to allowing a kind of real-time representation of trench experience. The poetry that gains critical attention, with one notable exception, is that written during the war and that by extension is the voice of the war itself, both geographically and temporally. When one considers as well the number of poets killed in the war (Rupert Brooke, Julian Grenfell, Wilfred Owen, Isaac Rosenberg, Charles Sorley, Edward Thomas), the logic becomes clear: only lyric poetry captures the moment, not recollected in tranquility, but experienced, as it were, just as the poem is being written. Thus lyric war poetry becomes synonymous with poetry written during the hostilities. The single exception is David Jones's long narrative *In Parenthesis*, which is significantly treated by some sources as a memoir, by others as a novel, and in the field of poetry as an exception. Following 1918, the poetry fades and the memoirs take over. After a ten-year hiatus, the late 1920s and 1930s see the war memoir become an established genre, with Edmund Blunden, Graves, C. E. Montague, and Sassoon its exemplars. These texts are by definition survivors' accounts and the products of a decade's more or less peaceful reflection. A wave of Great War fiction was published at approximately the same time as the memoirs though fiction further suffers under the criterion of immediacy. These books were as removed chronologically from the war as were the memoirs, but they also bore the burden of fictional characters and events imposing themselves between the reader and the supposedly real experience with which the reader was seeking a connection.

For it is access to the war itself that is the primary value of the literature for this first wave of criticism. The war poetry of Owen and Sassoon is privileged on the basis of its factual nature, its refusal to hide behind poetic cliché and continue to mask the realities of combat from a naïve audience. Great war literature is a soldier's literature in this formulation, but rather than the militarisms of a Kipling, these uniformed poets provide us with the unvarnished and unpopular truth of military action that has heretofore been hidden from civilian experience. Thus poetry becomes a more direct conduit to raw experience than either fiction or nonfiction prose. Although only tacitly, such a stance refutes formalist assumptions about poetry, and Great War criticism can thus be seen as part of the story of literary criticism's gradual detachment from New Critical principles.

The inaugural text for this first wave is John H. Johnston's *English Poetry of the First World War* (1964). This book establishes the soldier poets as synonymous with the Great War canon, but more famously it critiques all Great War poetry, with the exception of Jones's *In Parenthesis*, as failing to move beyond lyric reaction and into narrative form. Johnston seems to require a Homer of the trenches, and Owen and Sassoon do not meet the need. Johnston's significance to later war critics lies in his setting up their insistence that the lack of epic form in combatant poetry is precisely the point. While foregrounding the poetry's intimate connection to actual events, he denigrates the poetry for failing to rise above the immediate conditions of its making. He thus sets up subsequent critical reactions that will stress the immediacy of the poetry, its mud and bloodstains, as its most prominent feature. He is a significant, if chiefly contrasting, influence on three further texts appearing before 1975.

Bernard Bergonzi's *Heroes' Twilight* was first published in 1965, seeing minor revisions in 1980 and 1996. His scope is broader than Johnston's as he takes on poetry, fiction, and nonfiction prose, but the pride of place unquestionably goes to poetry. Noncombatant responses are limited to a brief chapter covering established writers (Kipling, Shaw, Pound, Lawrence): war literature is combatant literature and more or less isolated from previous and subsequent literary movements (Georgianism, Imagism, Vorticism, modernism). Bergonzi introduces the book through a contrast between roughly pro- and anti-war attitudes as expressed through Shakespeare's characters Hotspur and Falstaff. Hotspur is killed in *Henry IV* while Falstaff survives, setting up Bergonzi's narrative of the death of heroic and epic ideals in the face of the reality of the trenches.

Bergonzi's narrative of the war as the sudden elimination of military glory and epic martial tone thus places the book, published as the first official US troops were sent to South Vietnam, as implicitly anti-war: Jon Silkin's *Out of Battle* (1972) is much more overt in its political orientation and much more overtly critical of Johnston's implied politics. Silkin narrows his focus to include only poets, all but the first two of whom (Hardy and Kipling) are combatants. He situates his tour of the combatant poets by way of a history of nineteenth-century poetry's relation to radical and internationalist politics. Notwithstanding this polemic, even his readings of Kipling are well balanced and resolutely fair-minded, while his chapter on Isaac Rosenberg remains among the most significant pieces of criticism ever published on this under-represented figure. Likewise, his reading of compassion as Owen's primary poetic and political virtue has been immensely influential on most subsequent readings of Owen's verse.

Only slightly more narrowly focused than Silkin, Arthur Lane's *An Adequate Response: The War Poetry of Wilfred Owen and Siegfried Sassoon* (1972) advertises itself as a book about Owen and Sassoon, but a good half of the volume is dedicated to representing the title figures' immediate contexts of Georgian poetry and the combatant verse of the early war. Lane stresses Owen and Sassoon as realists, poets able to address the unique realities of twentieth-century warfare in a way that other more Georgian war poets could not. Theirs is a poetry of direct witness and truth-telling, and Lane's ideological stance is humanist: Owen's and Sassoon's central belief "was a faith in the endurance of man's humanity."[2] Though his book is generally not as insightful as Silkin's, *An Adequate Response* is perhaps the paradigmatic book of this initial category of Great War criticism. It argues that the validity and the values of the war poets lie in their relation of direct experience, that their combatant lyrics provide the least mediated path between the realities of the trench and the innocence of the civilian reader. It establishes an aesthetic of truth and justifies war literature insofar as that literature adheres to this aesthetic/ethical criterion.

Several books published after 1975 continue along the same lines as the ones just described, among them John Lehman's *English Poets of the First World War* (1982) and Fred D. Crawford's *British Poets of the Great War* (1988). Both texts maintain a trajectory firmly established by Bergonzi, Silkin, and Lane, stressing a combatant poetry of first-hand experience and consolidating the lyric poem as the dominant literary form of the war and the junior officer poets, especially Owen and Sassoon, as its dominant practitioners. Generally speaking, this is still the prevailing interpretation of the war and its literature for a non-specialist audience whose primary mode of access remains the literary text rather than the historical one. The canonical war poets are heard as the voices of protest against military and governmental incompetence culminating in pointless slaughter. Their voices are sincere, realistic, and truthful. They operate as a conduit to the genuine meaning of the war, dispelling the patriotic cant of civilian ignorance. They protest the war from the inside, and they provide a politically relevant warning to those who continue to support national belligerence without regard to its probable real-world consequences.

Paul Fussell's *The Great War and Modern Memory* (1975) both reinforces this view and moves far beyond it. Quite simply, it is difficult to underestimate Fussell's influence. The book's ambition and popularity move interpretation of the war from a relatively minor literary and historical specialization to a much more widespread cultural concern. His claims for the meaning of the war are profound and far-reaching; indeed, some have found them hyperbolic. Yet, whether in spite of or because of the enormity of his assertions, Fussell has set the agenda for most of the criticism that has followed him. In the terms of this chapter, *The Great War and Modern Memory* marks a fork in the road for Great War criticism. After 1975, criticism largely becomes divided between questions of gender and sexuality and questions of the war's relationship to modernist culture. Both of these directions are present in Fussell in a way they had not been in previous scholarship. His dramatic contentions for the central importance of the war for all subsequent western culture has been nothing if not controversial: more than twenty-five years later, these controversies, though altered over time, continue to dominate current investigations into the war and its lingering significance.

The basic premise of Fussell's book is that the war had a much more profound impact on modern culture than has heretofore been presumed. It is probably not an exaggeration to state that Fussell claims that modern culture is a direct product of the war; in other words, those aspects of culture that make it uniquely modern were, if not given birth in, then at least raised to a higher pitch by, the Great War. The broader stakes of Fussell's project are evident in the organization of the book. It is clear from the beginning that Fussell is making a break from his predecessors: he provides close readings of the canonical combatant writers, including significant sections dedicated to Sassoon, Robert Graves, David Jones, and Owen, but rather than proceed on a chapter by chapter basis through a guided tour of the established groupings, Fussell embeds his close readings within an organization founded on thematic structures. Sassoon, for instance, is addressed at length within the context of the war's imposition of a psychological binarism on its participants, while Owen is taken up within a chapter dedicated to the homoeroticism of the war. The literature thus becomes less an end in itself than a means through which to interpret the war as a kind of literary text. The war is to be read as an artifact, full of symbolic resonance and prophetic power. It fulfills the dark forebodings of the literary nineteenth century and provides the vocabulary through which the postwar world will articulate itself. Fussell is the first to read the war in this manner, or at least to do so in anything like a systematic way. Rather than playing a role in the American importation of structuralism or cultural studies, however, Fussell justifies his hermeneutics by stressing the literary (rather than textual) nature of the war. "Oh What a Literary War" is the title of his fifth chapter, and in the Preface he offers as a possible subtitle to the book as a whole "An Inquiry into the Curious Literariness of Real Life."[3] If the First World War is a phenomenon to be read, then, it is to be read as a specifically literary work, paying special attention to form, symbols, and above all, irony.

Irony is the controlling motif of *The Great War and Modern Memory*. Above all, the Great War in its grim reality was infinitely worse than any prewar imagination, even that of Thomas Hardy (though he comes closest), could possibly predict. For Fussell, the expectation of ever worsening conditions and the inability to conceive of the totality of proceedings so complex that no one mind can possibly encompass them are indications of the modern condition, and they are products of the war. The war met a population raised on the ideologies of Victorian and Edwardian progress and smug self-confidence and introduced it to a world of chaos and paranoia. To use a literary example upon which Fussell relies in several instances, Thomas Pynchon, with his conspiracy theories and dark complexities, is an heir to the tradition of the war, which is to say, the true tradition of the modern.

The emphasis on irony as a specifically literary mode points out what doubtless seems now to be a weakness in the book. To those more used to the widespread use of cultural history and cultural studies in late twentieth-century criticism Fussell, despite his unprecedented use of non-literary material in his construction of the war, nonetheless comes off as too literary, in the high culture, aesthetic sense. In a chapter comparing the setting of the war to literary traditions of the pastoral, Fussell remarks parenthetically "Sometimes it is really hard to shake off the conviction that this war has been written by someone."[4] Readers coming to Fussell after having been exposed to Walter Benjamin, Hayden White, Michel Foucault, or any number of other thinkers on the subject of history and its epistemological difficulties may be likely to question to what extent Fussell is discovering literary tropes that actually inhere within his subjects. These readers would be inclined to see Fussell constructing these literary tropes because they represent the primary manner in which his mind makes meaning. The fact that it may well be the writers he is reading who construct the war as a literary artifact at least partially addresses this question but raises another: since the texts from which Fussell draws his meanings are almost completely the products of educated junior officers, do their readings of the war as an ironic confrontation between the ideals of the classical pastoral and the realties of battlefield conditions have the same resonance for the far less educated enlisted men who form the vast majority of the army? David Jones, a spectacular auto-didact who fought as a private soldier, is the exception that proves the rule here, and Fussell ultimately decides that Jones's epic *In Parenthesis* misses the point of the war's modernity. The contemporary reader may decide that Fussell wants to read the war as a poem without admitting that he is con-structing it as a poem, and that the difference is critical. The reader may also decide that Fussell overstates his case and that not all specifically modern aspects of post-Great War culture have their genesis in the Great War itself. Nonetheless, *The Great War and Modern Memory* remains the single most significant interpretation of the war and an unavoidable point of reference for all subsequent work.

The general tendency of Fussell's book is to solidify previous interpreta-tions of the war and provide them with far more copious justification and rationale. Fussell's subject, for instance, remains the combatant representa-tion of the war. Though the war seeps into the cultural subconscious of the modern mind at large, "the war" here means the frontline soldier's expe-rience of the trenches. This war is an exclusively military endeavor; even within the military, the warfare that counts, that provides the insights that will haunt the modern memory, emerges from the frontline soldiers. Civilian culture exists, as in the angry protest poems of Owen and Sassoon, merely as a foil, its complacency setting off the sufferings of the soldiers that it dare not comprehend. British home front culture, therefore, is seen as uniformly blinkered and belligerent while the unique cultural elements that will come to dominate postwar civilian life are ironically developed exclusively in the trenches.

Perhaps the single most influential aspect of Fussell's expansion of the cul-tural terms of Great War literature was his inclusion of sexuality as one of the modern themes on which the war had such a great impact. His eighth chapter, "Soldier Boys," delineates what he calls the "homoeroticism" of the war, its appreciation for "a sublimated (i.e., 'chaste') form of tempo-rary homosexuality."[5] Fussell traces the genealogy of homoeroticism back to underground poetry of the *fin de siècle* and a more overt, though dis-guised, expression in A. E. Housman's *A Shropshire Lad*. The war, however, provides a moment in which at least masculine homoeroticism is tolerated if not positively celebrated. As mentioned above, Fussell reads Owen's poetry within this context, but he demonstrates that most of the junior officer poets on whom the Great War canon is based expressed an unembarrassed erotic attachment to "their" men. The effects of this observation have been far-reaching and form the basis of the following section.

Queer invasions: gender and sexuality

For literary and cultural studies generally, an appreciation of approaches to scholarship based on sexuality has largely been a product of feminism, something made clear in the work of such foundational figures as Eve Kosofsky Sedgwick and Judith Butler. In Great War criticism, the feminist phase is skipped: gender becomes an active concern only after Fussell's introduction of homoeroticism into the discourse. After Fussell, the traditional canon of war literature becomes subject to a reappraisal on the basis of sexuality, while the canon itself is revised and expanded by a feminist archaeological project of the rediscovery of civilian texts about the war. The introduction of gender and sexuality into the subject has meant that neither the war writers themselves nor the genres of which they had been seen as the exclusive practitioners can any longer be seen in the same manner as they were prior to 1975.

In addition to *The Great War and Modern Memory*, the text that enabled the feminist expansion of the canon was an instance of that ordinarily most mechanical of scholarly apparatus, the bibliography. In 1978, Catherine Reilly published *English Poetry of the First World War* with a minimum of interpretative introduction. Nonetheless, she made several issues readily apparent: first, the war had occasioned a phenomenal quantity of verse (most of it aesthetically quite dreadful); second, the preponderant majority of this verse was the product of civilian pens; and third, a significant portion of those civilian pens had been wielded by women. Reilly followed up the bibliography in 1981 with an anthology of women's Great War poetry, *Scars upon My Heart*. The mere existence of the collection stands as a testimony to the inadequacy of the assumptions of Great War criticism up to this time. The first decade of critics, including if not especially Fussell, had assumed that war experience was identical with combat experience, with the result that, however much influence the war might be said to have on subsequent culture, from 1914 to 1918 the war seemed to have absolutely no significant effect on those not doing the shooting. Reilly's texts demonstrate the meagerness of such claims. They do so, interestingly enough, non-confrontationally: Reilly merely counts the poetic products of the war and presents (quite well, it might be added) some of the most thematically and aesthetically significant of these products. It is left to others to spell out the cultural implications, but these explanations were not long in coming.

In 1988, Sandra Gilbert and Susan Gubar began publishing their massive follow-up to 1979's *The Madwoman in the Attic*. Eventually comprising three sizable volumes, they choose the name *No Man's Land* for the title of the entire project. Although they address the sum of twentieth-century

English-language literary writing by women, their choice of title reveals a fundamental connection with the First World War. The portion of *No Man's Land* most immediately relevant to our purposes here, however, is the seventh chapter of the second volume, *Sexchanges*, entitled "Soldier's Heart." Gilbert and Gubar construct the war as a critical moment in women's history, one that opened up innumerable new opportunities of social and economic progress. As a matter of historical fact, the war mobilized women as well as men on a grand scale and thus incorporated women's labor into the cause of the state. And the granting of women's suffrage, the galvanizing feminist cause before war, was largely perceived as a reward for a job well done in support of the war effort. Such progress came at the price of massive masculine resentments, which equated women's opportunity with the cost (exacted vampire-like) of men's blood, and Gilbert and Gubar trace this response through numerous male writers, both combatants and non-combatants. They also read many women's texts of the war and develop an idea of a feminine bad conscience, a generational feeling of guilt over the apparent opportunism the war came to represent for women's culture. In their reading, such internalizations ultimately become part of a postwar anti-feminist backlash that accompanies modernist cultural dominance. This argument has proved controversial: Jane Marcus rejects Gilbert and Gubar's thesis in her article "The Asylums of Antaeus," claiming that the war did inestimable harm to a burgeoning women's culture and that the cause of feminism is better served by looking at women's self-representations, especially those stemming from the prewar suffrage movement. Nonetheless, as they had in the 1970s with nineteenth-century literature, Gilbert and Gubar were among the first feminist scholars to revisit the canon and reread texts from an unapologetically feminist standpoint.

In 1988, Nosheen Khan brought forth the first book-length study of women's Great War poetry. A product both of Reilly's and her own painstaking archival research, Khan offers an exhaustive tour through a variety of poetic responses to the war by women poets. This variety is her point: Khan sees a reading of women's poetry as part of a larger project of revising our view of war literature from the narrow focus inherent in the emphasis that the canonical soldier poets have received. True war poetry, which is to say any verse that responds to the war's cultural effects on the writer, cannot be prejudged according to the acceptability of its content to a later audience: "There is no standard response to war; the romantic and the realistic both are representative responses, and so far as the First World War is concerned neither one can be rejected or disclaimed."[6] Khan elsewhere makes clear that she finds the realistic, anti-war poetry more humane than its jingoist counterpart, but her general tendency is to present the poetry in its bulk and contradiction in order to establish that women in wartime do not speak with one voice. Her argument, in other words, is that women's Great War poetry has no single argument.

While Khan for the most part showers the reader in excerpts from lost primary texts without much in the way of interpretation, Claire Tylee's *The Great War and Women's Consciousness*, appearing two years later, is much more systematic in stating its reasons for revision. As is obvious from the title, Tylee has in mind a revision of Fussell. Although his insistent if tacit exclusion of women's voices – from not only the Great War but also the modern memory in which it survives so formatively – constitutes one field of contention, others are perhaps even more important. Her objections are methodological as well. Fussell's work rests on ahistoric, idealist assumptions: "not merely did Fussell treat time, memory, and the past as if entirely separate from the political and economic developments of any concrete society. He treated memory and culture as if they belonged to a sphere beyond the existence of individuals or the control of institutions."[7] Tylee's criticism arises from a characteristically British combination of feminism and Marxian cultural studies, and her emphasis on the ideological control of women and the war's effect on their consciousness is consistently informed by this foundation. She also stresses the connections between the suffrage movement and the war, as well as the significant minority of women who wrote in favor of pacifism and negotiated peace. Though Tylee's analysis includes both world wars and extends up to 1964, the Great War remains her focal point and thus the definitive moment in the ideological formation of women's consciousness in the modern world.

Lynne Hanley's *Writing War* (1991) is even more directly condemnatory of Fussell's assumptions. Hanley's book is not, strictly speaking, about World War I specifically; rather, it intersperses critical essays with creative nonfiction pieces, all of them focused on women's relationship to war in the twentieth century. The first critical essay, "The War Zone," takes up *The Great War and Modern Memory* as a paradigmatic exercise in the justification of masculinist ideas of modern war. Hanley critiques Fussell's exclusion of civilian voices generally and women's specifically from his canon of war literature and contends that, though Fussell goes a long way in questioning war as a noble and ennobling activity, his "stunningly narrow"[8] focus nonetheless remains heavily and unopposedly biased in favor of white, well-educated British officers. Moreover, Fussell's insistence on limiting the writing of war to soldiers fosters an interpretation wherein men are not so much the agents of war as they are the victims. This is the image of the passive soldier, and Hanley reads it as a kind of anodyne for masculine guilt. It tends, however, to obscure other victims of modern war, especially women, and deny their right to speak of their experience and to put it in circulation alongside the soldiers' stories. In all, Hanley sees Fussell's version of war experience as confining the war to a delimited zone, outside of which it has little impact. For Hanley, this is a misleading and dangerous idea. Admittedly, Hanley is using Fussell as a stand-in for ideas he did not invent, but the reader unfamiliar with feminist critiques of first-wave Great War criticism might well want to begin with this succinct yet probing essay.

Sharon Ouditt's *Fighting Forces, Writing Women* (1994) is less concerned with masculinist exclusions of first-wave criticism than with questioning the feminist revision of which it forms a part. Specifically, Ouditt questions Gilbert and Gubar's reading of the war as a liberating experience for women. Ouditt sees this insistence on feminine empowerment as constructing a too monolithic effect of the war on women's culture. Ouditt stresses the competing ideologies that metaphorically fought over women's identities during the war and make any simplistic rendering of women's reaction to the war problematic. As a case in point, Ouditt rereads *Testament of Youth*, Vera Brittain's extremely popular account of her coming of age as a VAD nurse, in traditional terms of her bereavements and increased work opportunities, but addresses also the manner in which the VAD organization was both a symptom and a further enforcement of patriarchal class structures which Brittain herself does not or cannot avoid. Interestingly, by this time in Great War criticism, a woman's canon of war writing is beginning to form, and the VAD memoir is certainly an established subgenre within it. Though Ouditt's concern is as much with nonliterary as with literary works, most significant writers (in addition to Brittain) include Enid Bagnold, May Sinclair, Helen Zenna Smith (Evadne Price), and Olive Schreiner. She also provides a major reappraisal of Virginia Woolf's relation to the war (the final chapter is on Woolf).

Two texts in 1995 serve to consolidate further the feminist revision. Joan Montgomery Byles's *War, Women, and Poetry* covers both world wars. It reads women's war verse in the context of the suffrage movement; her second chapter consists mainly of extended commentary on Reilly's *Scars upon My Heart* anthology, which is juxtaposed with readings of canonical male trench poets. Byles evinces a similar skepticism to Gilbert and Gubar as does Ouditt. A Twayne's series book by Dorothy Goldman entitled *Women Writers and the Great War* provides a balanced overview of recent issues in Great War criticism. Goldman tends to stress a continuity between men's and women's war writing.

The post-1975 development of sexuality (as opposed to gender) as a branch of Great War criticism is a road a bit less traveled but nonetheless important for that. Fussell's emphasis on the war's homoeroticism was followed in 1981 by Eric Leed's *No Man's Land*, a wide-ranging study of the psychology of the war. Among several insights Leed perceived that combatant shell shock was symptomatically identical to prewar hysteria; in other words, war caused men to suffer from disorders previously thought to be exclusively female. Elaine Showalter made more of this point in *The Female Malady* (1985). The physical conditions of trench warfare inflicted upon men confinement and passivity, two standard features of feminine culture under the separate spheres ideology of the nineteenth century. Motivated by a vision of active heroism, soldiers were introduced to a world in which visible motion was literally death; junior officers soon discovered they were more likely to be concerned with feeding their men and inspecting the state of their boots than with leading a glorious charge. The war, advertised as the supreme masculine adventure, turned out to be an exercise in feminizing domestication.

Two books of the 1980s complicated previous readings of canonical trench poets. Siegfried Sassoon's diaries were published in 1983 and revealed that Sassoon during the war was a comfortable, if chaste, homosexual; Dominic Hibberd's *Owen the Poet* (1986) convincingly demonstrated Owen's sexual identity along similar lines. Both texts are products of an increasingly tolerant attitude within literary criticism generally, not only of gay and lesbian writers, but of the centrality of sexuality itself as both a subject and a mode of inquiry. Martin Taylor's anthology *Lads* (1989), inspired by Fussell, collected poetic examples of combat homoeroticism. Less celebratory was Adrian Caesar's *Taking It Like a Man* (1993), which seeks to demonstrate that the canonical war poets have too much invested in the sexuality of masculine sacrifice to be truly as anti-war as earlier criticism had painted them. Caesar's remains one of the few book about male trench poetry to provide a truly revisionist take on the canon.

Joanna Bourke's *Dismembering the Male* (1996) provides an in-depth analysis of the war's effects on constructions of British masculinity or, as she puts it, men's bodies during the war. Contrary to Fussell, Bourke seeks connections between military and civilian masculine culture, emphasizing especially working-class experience. She radically questions the absolute separateness of the war years from surrounding culture, a position that becomes a crux for many of the books we will see in the following section. Bourke also stresses the limits of male bonding during the war, drawing a harder line between the homoerotic and the homosexual than Fussell had set up. She contends that masculine camaraderie during the war did not reconstruct masculine intimacy.

Enter the modern

Part of Fussell's impact was his insistence on connecting the war to wider cultural movements, especially his definition of "the modern." Where previous war criticism had tended to place Great War literature only in the context of the literature of other wars, Fussell made the war an integral if not inaugural part of the modern world. This correlation to "the modern" forms the other branch of post-Fussell criticism, and perhaps the most forceful proponent of a view in basic congruence with Fussell is Modris Eksteins in *The Rites of Spring* (1989). Eksteins departs from Fussell's exclusively literary definition of "the modern" and embraces a more historically and culturally broad version. For Eksteins, the war reversed the balance between the cultural forces of modernism and of traditional humanist culture that had obtained in 1914. On the eve of the war modernism, symbolized by the Stravinsky ballet referenced in Eksteins's title, was an avant-garde movement of a minority, stressing energy, violence, interiority, and a break with the bourgeois past. By 1918, such was the widespread condition of Europe. Eksteins identifies modernism most closely with Germany and thus presents a postwar Europe in which, though Germany lay defeated, its cultural mode became dominant.

Similar in scope, Samuel Hynes's *A War Imagined* (1990) stresses what he terms "the Myth of the War," which is a narrative that emphasizes the war's creation of a gap in history between modern (that is to say, postwar) culture and all that preceded it. Hynes uses the term "myth" not to accuse the narrative of dishonest representation, but to call attention to its status as a construction: the Myth of the War as a process of disenchantment with previous history and the disburdening of the illusions of nineteenth-century culture is an evolving story, and one that arises mostly from the war books published a decade after the Armistice. It has, however, since been accepted as the truth of the war (it is difficult not to see this distinction between cultural myth and critical commonplace as a tacit corrective to Fussell). The connection to postwar modernism is very strong for Hynes; as he puts it: "By the end of the Twenties, the War Myth and the Waste Land Myth were simply two versions of the same reality."[9]

A comparable skepticism runs through Daniel Pick's *War Machine*, a farreaching and sophisticated analysis of the history of thought about European war since Clausewitz. Pick looks with great suspicion at all claims of absolute cultural break and turns an especially doubtful eye on such declarations about the Great War. His argument with Fussell is not tacit. Jay Winter's dispute in *Sites of Memory, Sites of Mourning* (1995) runs along similar lines and is at least as much with Eksteins as with Fussell. Winter looks closely at styles of remembrance, from official cenotaphs to very unofficial séance sessions. Herein he finds evidence for the continuity of earlier languages and traditions, as opposed to the utter rejection of such forms that the modernist school tends to emphasize. Winter's focus remains primarily an anti-elitist attempt to locate the continuity of memory among the non-avant-garde majority populations of Germany, France, and Britain. Winter, of course, does not discount the war as an aspect of the history of modernism, but he does see, as with Hynes and Pick, a more continuous process than the jarring rupture portrayed by Fussell.

Recent books on this topic have tended to read the works of canonical modernism within the context of the war, thus engaging the question of the war's impact outside the narrow field of "war literature" while avoiding the question of interpretation of the war itself as a definitive break from the culture of realism. Allyson Booth in *Postcards from the Trenches* (1996) takes up an impressive array of different canonical modernist texts, including architecture as well as literature, finding hidden traces of the war in poems, novels, and buildings not obviously connected to it. Trudi Tate in *Modernism, History and the First World War* (1998) concentrates on modernist fiction by H.D., Ford Madox Ford, William Faulkner, and Virginia Woolf, among others. She constructs modernism as a type of war writing along similar lines to those of Booth, but Tate's emphasis lies on material technology and its impact on literary and cultural representation. Her chapter on the tank as an artifact of more cultural than military importance is exemplary. Angela Smith's *The Second Battlefield* (2000) looks at women's war writing in prose as a link between nineteenth-century realism and experimental modernist literature. For Smith, the newness of the war forced writers to employ new forms of writing – even private modes such as the diary attest to the strain of the war by breaking the old conventions. Finally, Vincent Sherry's *The Great War and the Language of Modernism* (2003) traces the origins of modernism in three canonical practitioners: Pound, Eliot, and Woolf. Each of these figures was an outsider to British tradition from before the war, Pound and Eliot on account of nationality, Woolf for reasons of gender. Sherry finds their influential versions of modernism in their reaction to the war as a crisis in English Liberal discourse. As the war worsened, the rhetoric of the ruling Liberal party became increasingly strained and self-parodic, until the language of Liberal rationalism seemed a form without substance. Modernism thus becomes, in Sherry's view, a reaction to the intellectual bankruptcy of English Liberalism. As the war emptied out the meaning behind Liberalism's words, the modernists took the now vacant form and appropriated it for new ends in a new world.

The last forty years in First World War scholarship thus encapsulate several of the trends of literary scholarship more generally. We have witnessed the formation of a canon and the expansion and/or abandonment of that canon due to its blind spots in gender and sexuality. We have seen war literature initially defined as a realm entirely apart from other forms of literary expression only to be recuperated in a revision of modernism. And we have experienced the gradual movement from placing Great War literature in a narrow version of literary history to a much broader cultural account of history. As we enter a fifth decade of interpretation of the war and its literature, we confront one aspect of its place in cultural history: nearly everyone who personally experienced the events of 1914–18 is now dead, yet we live in a world that is still very much a product of those years. These ghosts will not speak for themselves: the process of interpretation continues.

NOTES

1. "Enlightenment thinkers of the cast of mind of Condorcet still had the extravagant expectation that the arts and sciences would promote not only the control of natural forces but also the understanding of the world and of the self, moral progress, the justice of institutions and even the happiness of human beings. The twentieth century has shattered this optimism." Jürgen Habermas, "Modernity – An Incomplete Project," in *The Norton Anthology of Theory and Criticism*, ed. Vincent B. Leitch (New York: Norton, 2001), 1754.
2. Arthur E. Lane, *An Adequate Response: The War Poetry of Wilfred Owen and Siegfried Sassoon* (Detroit: Wayne State University Pres, 1972), 174.
3. Paul Fussell, *The Great War and Modern Memory* (Oxford: Oxford University Press, 1975), ix.
4. *Ibid.*, 241.
5. *Ibid.*, 272.
6. Nosheen Khan, *Women's Poetry of the First World War* (Lexington: University Press of Kentucky, 1988), 9.
7. Claire M. Tylee, *The Great War and Women's Consciousness: Images of Militarism and Womanhood in Women's Writings, 1914–64* (Iowa City: University of Iowa Press, 1990), 6.
8. Lynne Hanley, *Writing War: Fiction, Gender, and Memory* (Amherst: University of Massachusetts Press, 1991), 26.
9. Samuel Hynes, *A War Imagined: The First World War and English Culture* (London: Bodley Head, 1990), 459.

MAJOR WORKS OF CRITICAL REFERENCE

Bergonzi, Bernard. *Heroes' Twilight: A Study of the Literature of the Great War.* London: Constable, 1965.
Booth, Allyson. *Postcards from the Trenches: Negotiating the Space between Modernism and the First World War.* New York: Oxford University Press, 1996.

Bourke, Joanna. *Dismembering the Male: Men's Bodies, Britain, the Great War*. Chicago: University of Chicago Press, 1996.

Byles, Joan Montgomery. *War, Women, and Poetry, 1914–1945: British and German Writers and Activists*. Newark: University of Delaware Press, 1995.

Caesar, Adrian. *Taking It Like a Man: Suffering, Sexuality and the War Poets: Brooke, Sassoon, Owen, Graves*. Manchester: Manchester University Press, 1993.

Crawford, Fred D. *British Poets of the Great War*. Selinsgrove, Penn.: Susquehanna University Press, 1988.

Eksteins, Modris. *The Rites of Spring: The Great War and the Birth of the Modern Age*. Boston: Houghton Mifflin, 1989.

Fussell, Paul. *The Great War and Modern Memory*. Oxford: Oxford University Press, 1975.

Gilbert, Sandra M. and Susan Gubar. *Sexchanges*. Volume II of *No Man's Land: The Place of the Woman Writer in the Twentieth Century*. New Haven: Yale University Press, 1989.

Goldman, Dorothy, with Jane Gledhill and Judith Hattaway. *Women Writers and the Great War*. Twayne's Literature and Society Series 7. New York: Twayne–Simon and Schuster, 1995.

Hanley, Lynne. *Writing War: Fiction, Gender, and Memory*. Amherst: University of Massachusetts Press, 1991.

Hibberd, Dominic. *Owen the Poet*. Athens: University of Georgia Press, 1986.

Hynes, Samuel. *A War Imagined: The First World War and English Culture*. London: Bodley Head, 1990.

Johnston, John H. *English Poetry of the First World War: A Study in the Evolution of Lyric and Narrative Form*. Princeton: Princeton University Press, 1964.

Khan, Nosheen. *Women's Poetry of the First World War*. Lexington: University Press of Kentucky, 1988.

Lane, Arthur E. *An Adequate Response: The War Poetry of Wilfred Owen and Siegfried Sassoon*. Detroit: Wayne State University Press, 1972.

Leed, Eric. *No Man's Land: Combat and Identity in World War I*. Cambridge: Cambridge University Press, 1981.

Lehmann, John. *The English Poets of the First World War*. New York: Thames and Hudson, 1982.

Marcus, Jane. "The Asylums of Antaeus. Women, War and Madness: Is There a Feminist Fetishism?" *The Difference Within: Feminism and Critical Theory*. Eds. Elizabeth Meese and Alice Parker. Amsterdam: John Benjamins, 1989. 49–83.

Ouditt, Sharon. *Fighting Forces, Writing Women: Identity and Ideology in the First World War*. London: Routledge, 1994.

Pick, Daniel. *War Machine: The Rationalisation of Slaughter in the Modern Age*. New Haven: Yale University Press, 1993.

Reilly, Catherine W. *English Poetry of the First World War: A Bibliography*. London: George Prior, 1978.

Reilly, Catherine W., ed. *Scars upon My Heart: Women's Poetry and Verse of the First World War*. London: Virago, 1981.

Sassoon, Siegfried. *Diaries 1915–1918*. Ed. Rupert Hart-Davis. London: Faber and Faber, 1983.

Sherry, Vincent. *The Great War and the Language of Modernism*. New York: Oxford University Press, 2003.

Showalter, Elaine. *The Female Malady: Women, Madness, and English Culture, 1830–1980*. New York: Pantheon, 1985.

Silkin, Jon. *Out of Battle: The Poetry of the Great War*. London: Oxford University Press, 1972.

Smith, Angela K. *The Second Battlefield: Women, Modernism and the First World War*. Manchester: Manchester University Press, 2000.

Tate, Trudi. *Modernism, History and the First World War*. Manchester: Manchester University Press, 1998.

Taylor, Martin, ed. *Lads: Love Poetry of the Trenches*. London: Constable, 1989.

Tylee, Claire M. *The Great War and Women's Consciousness: Images of Militarism and Womanhood in Women's Writings, 1914–1964*. Iowa City: University of Iowa Press, 1990.

Winter, Jay. *Sites of Memory, Sites of Mourning: The Great War in European Cultural History*. Cambridge: Cambridge University Press, 1995.

12

LAURA MARCUS

The Great War in twentieth-century cinema

"Of all the arts," Modris Eksteins writes, "the one that may best express the conflicts in the twentieth-century soul is film."[1] The years of World War I were those in which film was becoming increasingly accepted as a legitimate source of entertainment, as a serious art form, as a crucial medium for education, and as the most effective propaganda instrument. In one sense, the relationship between World War I and cinema is a matter of historical and temporal concurrence or coincidence; in another, modern war and film have a complex and profound interconnection, as twin technologies of modernity. World War I was, Paul Virilio has argued, not only "bloody conflict" but a pyrotechnic *"lighting war,"* a "continuous performance, all day and all night."[2]

The question of what defined "war films" during the years of the First World War is a complex one. In her study of US cinema and World War I, Leslie Midkiff DeBauche notes that film producers, distributors, exhibitors, and reviewers took up varying positions on the question of the role of popular culture in periods of national crisis, and were often divided between the view that films should provide escape from contemporary realities, with comedy tending to be favored as the proper film genre in wartime, and the conviction that it was the role of film to reflect historical immediacies. Yet even when the themes of the feature films themselves were unrelated to the war, the contexts of cinema exhibition were often highly war-related, as in the case of the "Four Minute Men" in the US, who would speak on patriotic themes during intermissions and reel changes.[3]

The trajectory of American "war films" has been outlined by film historians, including Michael Isenberg and Andrew Kelly, as a series of stages that could be summarized as neutrality, preparedness, intervention, war as adventure, rejection of war.[4] Thomas H. Ince's *Civilization* (1915) upheld the ideal of religious pacifism, but its anti-German stance and its vilifications of a Kaiser figure anticipated some of the most lurid of the US "preparedness" and militancy films, which included such titles as *The Kaiser – Beast of Berlin*, *To Hell with the Kaiser*, *The Hun Within*, and *Escaping the Hun*. On its 1916 release in Britain, Ince's film was given the title *Civilization: What Every True Briton is Fighting For*, and its original pacifist message was considerably altered through the addition of material from another Ince film, *The Purple Cross*. J. Stuart Blackton's pro-war and anti-German *The Battle Cry of Peace* (1916) was, in Blackton's words, "a call to arms" during the period in which President Wilson was "arguing for neutrality and peace";[5] the end of 1916 saw the release of the last significant US peace film of the war period, Herbert Brenon's *War Brides*, which deployed allegory to suggest that the German people were opposed to conflict. At the start of the war, documentary film footage was deemed dangerous for security purposes by the British War Office, and cinema cameramen, like press photographers, were excluded from the Front. Documentaries using home-front material were, however, central to cinema programming in the first two years of the war. Michael Hammond discusses the Roll of Honour films, locally produced films of photographs of men who had been killed, wounded, or taken prisoner, or who were still serving at the Front. Such films were screened with an accompaniment of patriotic songs and music as part of cinema programs, at least until 1917. Hammond suggests that their function was largely to write the local into the narrative of the nation; their appeal depended both on the possibility of recognition of individuals and on the incorporation of the individual soldier into an overarching heroic narrative. As the war went on, however, with no sign of cessation, and with unprecedented casualty figures, such "rolls" began to lose their inspirational quality for audiences.[6]

By early 1916, official attitudes in Britain to film had changed, and its significance for propaganda and education was increasingly recognized. During the three years in which official films were produced, some 240 were released, together with 152 issues of the official newsreel. It has been estimated that *Battle of the Somme* (1916) was seen by some 80 percent of the British adult population: Nicholas Reeves argues that it was one of a trilogy of official films whose impact can only be explained "by the fact that they gave the domestic audience its first images of the terrible physical devastation of war – the ruined buildings, the battle-scarred landscape and, much more important, a sense of the human cost of war."[7] While a significant part of *Battle of the Somme* is given over to shots of the dead and wounded, commentators at the time almost invariably focused on the "over the top" sequence, in which two British soldiers fall instead of advancing. Of this scene (and appearing to condense the two men into one), Rider Haggard wrote in his diary:

The most impressive [of the pictures] to my mind is that of a regiment scrambling out of a trench to charge and of the one man who slides back shot dead. There is something appalling about the instantaneous change from fierce activity to supine death. Indeed the whole horrible business is appalling. War has always been dreadful, but never, I suppose, more dreadful than today.[8]

Rebecca West's war novella, *The Return of the Soldier*, linked dreams and war films in a clear reference to the "over the top" sequence in *Battle of the Somme*:

Disregarding the national interest and everything except the keen prehensile gesture of our hearts towards him, I wanted to snatch my cousin Christopher from the wars and seal him in this green pleasantness his wife and I now looked upon. Of late I had had bad dreams about him. By night I saw Chris running across the brown rottenness of no man's land, starting back here because he trod upon a hand, not even looking there because of the awfulness of an unburied head, and not till my dream was packed full of horror did I see him pitch forward on his knees as he reached safety – if it was that. For on the war films I have seen men slip down as softly from the trench parapet, and none but the grimmer philosophers would say that they had reached safety by their fall.[9]

It is now believed that the "over the top" scene was the only "faked" scene in the film, but for the audience at the time its authenticity seems to have been unquestionable. Samuel Hynes argues that its appeal to journalists and historians of the scene was that it was "the one melodramatic moment in the film,"[10] though it is striking that, in the quotations above, Rider Haggard and Rebecca West called attention to the muted nature of the death or deaths they saw represented: "I have seen men slip down as softly from the trench parapet," in West's words. Rider Haggard's account of "the instantaneous change from fierce activity to supine death" suggests that the impact of the scene was that it appeared simultaneously both to represent and to occlude the moment of death and the process of dying. A further dimension of the response may have been to a perceived reversal of direction from movement to stasis, and to the slipping or sliding back from the inexorable advance both of troops and of celluloid.

The success of *Battle of the Somme* was followed up with *The King Visits His Armies in the Great Advance* (a forty-minute film of the visit of George V to the Somme battlefields, released October 1916), *Battle of the Ancre* (released January 1917), which included, for the first time, footage of the movement of tanks, and *The German Retreat and the Battle of Arras* (released June 1917). By this stage of the war, however, feature-length factual war films were clearly waning in popularity, and official film production began to be concentrated on newsreels and short factual films. Official and propaganda films became increasingly sanitized in the last eighteen months of the war, as popular support for it became less secure, with growing privations at home and increasing pessimism about the lack of progress at the Front.[11]

A new perception of the power of the film medium for propaganda purposes, and varying official, commercial, and artistic perceptions of the most appropriate and most compelling genre for war film – fiction or nonfiction, epic or romance – emerged in a striking way at this time, with the making of D. W. Griffith's *Hearts of the World*. In 1917, Griffith received an invitation from the British government to make a war film in Europe, at the instigation of Lord Beaverbrook, the new chairman of the War Office Cinematograph Committee, and a tour of the war zone in France was arranged for him. The project's original purpose was, Russell Merritt writes, "to convince America to join the war on England's side, and then when the United States entered of its own accord, to help set the emotional tone for America's pursuit of that war."[12]

Griffith's Civil War film *The Birth of a Nation* (1915) had received an overwhelming response, although it also generated a good deal of controversy over its racial politics and its representation of the Civil War from the Southern point of view. *Hearts of the World* was, William Everson suggests, virtually a remake of *The Birth of a Nation* transposed to World War I: "the same family structure, the same separations and reunions, the same editing pattern. A brigade of French volunteers substituted for the Ku Klux Klan, and their leader again arrived in time to save Lilian Gish from rape at the hands of George Siegmann."[13] *Hearts of the World* focused on the situation of women and children in a French village behind the lines, and on the romance between the children of American neighbors living on the Rue de la Paix in a French village. It was the longest-running film produced during the period of US involvement, and was enormously successful in the States, though less so in Britain. Its sentimental patriotism has come in for criticism, but it should be remembered that Griffith was selected to make the film on the basis of his abilities to represent the spectacle of battle, evidenced in *The Birth of a Nation*, whose battle sequences, Everson argues, "have never been equalled in terms of realism or excitement."[14]

Griffith's comments on war and film in this period indicate both the perception that the medium of film had the power to prevent war, and a view that World War I was not essentially a "cinematic" war. His assertion that "if moving pictures properly done of the horrors of war had been inoculated [*sic*] in all the nations of Europe, there would be no bodies of men lying on European battlefields" reveals a view of film as an international language, the force of whose representations had the potential to prevent nation states from waging war.[15] The phrase "properly done," however, raises unresolved questions; it is not clear if Griffith was alluding to the force of documentary realism, to the affective power of cinematic imagery, or to film as modern epic, of the kind that Griffith had himself created in *The Birth of a Nation* and *Intolerance*.

In 1918, Griffith asserted that the war was "in some way disappointing" as a drama. Modern conflict was:

> neither romantic nor picturesque . . . Everyone is hidden away in ditches. As you look out across no man's land there is literally nothing that meets the eye but an aching desolation of nothingness – or torn trees, ruined barbed wire fence and shell holes . . . There is nothing but filth and dirt and the most soul sickening smells. The soldiers are standing sometimes almost up to their hips in ice cold mud . . . It is too colossal to be dramatic. No one can describe it. You might as well try to describe the ocean or the milky way. A very great writer could describe Waterloo. But who could describe the advance of Haig? No one saw it. No one saw a thousandth part of it.[16]

These comments have particular significance for the ways in which subsequent directors would represent the war, and their depictions of what "meets the eye" across no man's land. Griffith continued to represent a panoramic and movement-filled view of war, despite the stasis on the Western Front. Directors in the 1920s and 1930s would often work with the fact that "everyone [was] hidden away in ditches" to restage the war less, or not only, as large-scale combat waged across a terrain, but through encounters, often to the point of death, in shell-holes or trenches. Hence the increasing use, for example, of scenes between two soldiers, wounded or dying, on opposing sides, to which I will return in discussing films of the 1920s and 1930s, such as King Vidor's *The Big Parade* (1925) and Lewis Milestone's *All Quiet on the Western Front* (1930).

Before leaving the context of films made during the war years, however, we should turn to a figure who, by this period, had come to emblematize cinema itself, and to the very significant role of comedy in representing the soldier's life on the front line. Charlie Chaplin's *Shoulder Arms* went into production on 29 May 1918, and was exhibited in America and Canada at the end of October; it thus coincided with the end of the war in ways that undoubtedly contributed to its box-office success. The film was, however, made against the background of contention over the issue of Chaplin and enlistment. Attitudes toward Chaplin during the years of the war in both Britain and the US had been mixed. Chaplin's decision in August 1914 not to return to his country of birth and join the army had created significant bad feeling in Britain, and his labeling in the press as "Chaplin the Slacker." He was spared from call-up in part because he contributed so substantially to war funds, while his reputation was saved by the overwhelming success and appeal of his films to British troops at the Front, so that his role could be framed as that of morale booster to the soldiers.

Chaplin's iconic status by this stage of the war has particular significance for the issue of the role of cinema in World War I. Kevin Brownlow and others have pointed to the use of Chaplin's image on the Front; Brownlow records that cut-out figures of Charlie were popular with the troops, who would stand them on the parapet during the attack, while, in prison camps, "every hut had its Chaplin impersonator."[17] Such scenes were deployed in *Oh, What a Lovely War* to make popular culture central to war experience (thus providing an alternative "voice," as I later discuss, to the dominant one of the war poets), and the film includes the soldiers' song "The moon shines bright on Charlie Chaplin":

> The moon shines bright on Charlie Chaplin
> His boots are cracking,
> For want of blacking,
> And his little baggy trousers
> They want mending
> Before we send him
> To the Dardanelles.

Makeshift cinemas were a regular feature of life at the Front from August 1915, and by mid-1916 there were twenty cinemas within the British sector. American pictures were most in demand, above all Chaplin's films. Brownlow quotes an American observer who saw motion pictures run in an old dugout that held fifty men:

> Those ragged, dirty fellows, caked with mud and covered with vermin, did not want to look at the pictures that well-intentioned folks thought they would be interested in, but were eagerly enthusiastic over scenes of city streets of Paris, London, New York. You see, they had got in a state of mind where none of them believed they would ever see a city street again, and a city street with well dressed crowds walking about. Love plots didn't seem to interest them much, but a comedy – I mean regular slapstick stuff – started them shouting with glee.[18]

Cinema as dream, as fantasy, and as comedy is incorporated in multiple and complex ways into *Shoulder Arms*. Like the soldiers "enthusiastic over scenes of city streets," Private Charlie, standing in a trench, daydreams (in a split screen sequence) of a modern city with traffic and skyscrapers and then of a bartender mixing a cocktail, as if the soldier's dream were that of the promise and the energies of modern, metropolitan America. The trench in which he stands is signposted "Rotten Row" and "Broadway." The film also accommodates the soldier's dream of nurture, as in the scene in which a beautiful young Frenchwoman (Edna Purviance) enters the room in a bombed-out house in which Private Charlie has fallen asleep, and tends the sleeping man, whom she believes to be wounded. The overt "dream" of the film is, however, the dream of heroic action. In the first scenes of the film we see Private Charlie (an American soldier) as the most awkward of "the awkward squad," his wayward feet rendering him incapable of marching in a straight line. He goes to his tent and falls asleep, and the intertitle comes up "Over there."

The scene moves to a trench on the front line, and to a series of gags on the familiar experiences of the soldier in the trenches. Constant bombardment by shells subjects the body to a series of mechanical tics (Charlie's tin hat lifts from his head every time a shell drops), but the comedy also lies in his implacable responses to the shocks of war. Private Charlie's dugout becomes so flooded that the soldiers have to sleep up to their necks in water, Charlie using a gramophone horn as a snorkel. Increasingly, we see the object world and the war world conforming to his wishes. Going "over the top," he captures a German trench: "I surrounded them," he says casually, as the enormous German soldiers (and their tiny officer) are herded into captivity. Back in his trench, he opens a bottle and lights a cigarette by holding these objects aloft and waiting for a passing shell to do the work for him. Nonchalantly firing from the trench while smoking the cigarette, he scores direct hits every time, notching them up on a board. Camouflaged as a tree within the enemy's line, he saves an Allied soldier from the German firing squad; disguised as a German officer, he captures the Kaiser, and is cheered by the Allies. "Peace on earth – good will to all mankind" is the intertitle, suggesting that Charlie's actions have ended the war. The film ends with Private Charlie's awakening from his dream, and his finding himself again in the tent in which he had fallen asleep before going "Over there" in his dream-world. Dreams in *Shoulder Arms* are wish-fulfillments, as they were for Freud. It was, however, the dreams of World War I soldiers which required Freud to revise his theory of dreams, to posit a model of "repetition-compulsion," as shell-shocked soldiers had recurrent dreams of their worst waking nightmares, and to theorize the death-drive in *Beyond the Pleasure Principle*.

Chaplin's comedy rests in large part on the machine–body equation and the shocks of modernity, something that cinema (with its powers to animate the object world and to turn human bodies into objects) has at its core. But cinema can also be understood as a ghost-world, as it was for its very first viewers: "Last night I was in the kingdom of shadows," Maxim Gorki wrote, of his viewings of the Lumière brothers' films in 1896.[19] This perception of the spectrality of cinematic, and photographic, images reemerged with striking force for many viewers of the war films, in a context in which the soldiers pictured on the screen were very likely to be corpses by the time the films were viewed, granted a ghostly posthumous existence on the screen: "Oh, living pictures of the dead," as Henry Newbolt wrote in his 1916 poem "The War Films."[20]

In 1916, the French film director Abel Gance wrote in his diary: "How I wish that all the dead of the war would rise up one night and return to their country into their houses, to discover if their sacrifices were for anything. War would stop on its own, strangled by the immensity of the horror."[21] Gance began writing the scenario for his war film *J'accuse* in the summer of 1917, under the influence of Henri Barbusse's war novel *Le Feu* (1916), and in competition with D. W. Griffith, whose *Intolerance* he had seen, and whom he knew to be working on *Hearts of the World*. The title of Gance's film, Richard Abel has argued, with its echo of Emile Zola's attack on the court martial that condemned Dreyfus, "announced a provocative film treatment of the war, completely different from the propagandistic and pacifist films seen in such abundance. And it did so with the assistance of the French Army."[22]

At the close of the film, the shell-shocked hero, Jean, summons a troop of phantom soldiers, who rise up to confront the horrified villagers; the people beg their forgiveness and affirm their sacrifice, and the dead move off and finally disappear. Jean too dies, accusing, as Abel puts it, "even the sun for its complicity in the war's destruction."[23] Yet the ending, echoed in so many subsequent films, from *All Quiet on the Western Front* to *Oh, What a Lovely War*, is an ambiguous one, open to a range of readings. Marcel Oms, for example, wrote of the close of *J'accuse* that "it is less the war that is denounced than the pleasure, cupidity, and immorality of the living as opposed to the nobility of the dead soldiers who have known true valor."[24]

Few films about the war were made between 1918 and 1925. Of the British context, Andrew Kelly writes: "Generally the subject was disliked, though this was as much to do with recession in the industry as realisation that the public wished to avoid the subject."[25] Exceptions here were Maurice Elvey's *Comradeship* (1919), which portrayed a lasting destruction of social barriers in the camaraderie engendered by the war. This theme was pursued in Adrian Brunel's 1927 film *Blighty* which, in Brunel's words, "fulfilled the requirements of a 'war' picture, though we never showed the war, but rather the reactions to it on the home front. And, it was, quietly, an anti-war picture rather than a pro-war picture."[26] The "quietly" here is significant, suggesting the need of films and their makers to tread a careful line between pro- and anti-war stances, and, by the late 1920s, to help preserve the delicate balance of Anglo-German relations, a line and a balance which Herbert Wilcox's 1928 film *Dawn* (recounting the highly charged story of Nurse Edith Cavell, shot at dawn for helping the Allied soldiers to escape) was seen to transgress.

Rex Ingram's *The Four Horsemen of the Apocalypse* (1921) was a significant popular success and a key film of this period in that, in Ivan Butler's words, "it exactly caught the mood of the moment, bridging the gap between exhausted satiety and nostalgia, and also affording a last enjoyable indulgence in Hun-phobia."[27] The 1920s and early 1930s also saw the production of popular war reconstructions by Harry Bruce Woolfe's company British Instructional Films, from *The Battle of Jutland* (1921) to *The Battles of the Coronel and Falkland Islands* (1927), films matched in France by Leon Poirier's *Verdun, visions d'histoire* (1928) and in Germany by *The Emden* (1927), the compilation film *Der Weltkrieg (The World War)* (1927) and Heinz Paul's battle reconstructions in *Douaumont* (1931) and *Tannenberg* (1932). Following on from the somewhat romanticized view of war in the BIF films came a number of British fiction films which represented the war as adventure and as romance, including Elvey's *Mademoiselle from Armentières* (1926) and *Roses of Picardy* (1926), a dramatization of R. H. Mottram's *Spanish Farm* trilogy, in which a British officer and a Flemish farmer's daughter fall in love.

Writing of his 1925 film *The Big Parade*, the American director King Vidor stated:

> I wanted it to be the story of a young American who was neither over-patriotic nor a pacifist, but who went to war and reacted normally to all the things that happened to him. It would be the story of the average man in whose hands does not lie the power to *create* the situations in which he finds himself but who nevertheless feels them emotionally. I said that the soldier doesn't make war. The average American is not overly in favour of it, nor abnormally belligerent against it. He simply goes along for the ride and tries to make the most of each situation as it happens.[28]

The film critic Paul Rotha, in his 1931 study *The Film Till Now*, wrote of *The Big Parade* that: "Its power lay in the opening sequences, where an immense feeling that hundreds of thousands of people were being howled into war, none of them knowing its meaning, the women regarding it as a thing of romance, the young men as a chance of gallant heroism, was dramatically spread across to the spectator."[29] In these opening sequences, war, or its declaration, both interrupts the images of industrial process and progress – the machinery of modern America – and is inseparable from them, as the most powerful of modern technologies and the one that would line the pockets of the army contractors. When we first encounter the idle young mill-owner's son Jim (John Gilbert), the film's central protagonist, he is reassuring his mother that he will not enlist. The film sympathetically portrays, at its beginning and its end, the attachment between mother and son, and the fact that, for mothers (as Olive Schreiner explored in her 1911 *Women and Labour*), war is all the more terrible for its destruction of the bodies that they bring into the world. Jim's decision not to join up is, however, reversed by the expectations of his fiancée, the exhortations of his friends, and, most forcefully, by the insistent rhythms of a marching military band. Once we see Jim's feet tapping in time to the martial music, we know that they will soon be marching to war.

The rhythms of war are central to the "silent music" of the film. In his autobiography, Vidor described his use of a metronome to film the march through the Bois Belleau:

> I instructed the men that each step must be taken on a drum beat, each turn of the head, lift of a rifle, pull of a trigger, in short, every physical move must occur on the beat of the drum . . . One British veteran wanted to know if he were performing in "some bloody ballet." I did not say so at the time, but that is exactly how it was – a bloody ballet, a ballet of death.[30]

An earlier scene deployed a different but no less powerful rhythm, that of counterpoint, as the troops depart from their billets in a French village for the Front line. "Each part," Vidor writes, "the specific movement of trucks, motor-cycles, horse-drawn artillery, and men – could be given an individual tempo of its own . . . these were distinctive rhythms which could be blended into a total symphonic effect."[31] There is a further dynamic to the sequence, in the shots of Jim and the French village girl, Mélisande (Renée Adorée), with whom he has fallen in love, searching for each other to say goodbye, their figures seen in glimpses between the lumbering vehicles of the war machine. When Mélisande eventually finds Jim, and as his army truck pulls away, she clings to him and to it, as if to hold it back from its inexorable drive forward, which will transmute into the death march to the Front.

This is the tension of the film: the orchestrated marching and the epic sweep of the battle scenes in counterpoint with the intensity of the film's desire to locate meaning and value in the intimacies of love and of comradeship. Like many later war films, *The Big Parade* gives over much of its narrative time to army life remote from combat; in this case the soldiers' existence in the French village, the friendships that develop across the class divide, and a rural life which is both physically uncomfortable and liberating. The concern of the film is indeed with war from the ordinary soldier's point of view, and the intertitling deploys soldiers' popular songs to punctuate and articulate the silent film narrative. The class leveling aspect of the war is at the heart of *The Big Parade*, linking it back to numerous American war films of 1917 and 1918, and forming a connection, in Michael Isenberg's words, "between democratisation and the American fighting man," which is one of the more enduring themes in film history.[32]

After the lengthy, pastoral sojourn, the sudden plunge into war at the frontline is shocking. Here Vidor presents scenes of a type that would become central to subsequent war films: the three friends trapped in a shell hole; Jim alone with a wounded German soldier; his coming round after being shot, in a cathedral turned makeshift hospital. It is camaraderie that spurs Jim on to a reckless heroism, after his friend Slim is fatally wounded, and it is this loss that leads him to express the only anti-German feeling in the film – "They got him, God damn their souls. You got my buddy," reads the intertitle – and the only direct anti-war sentiment – "What the hell do we get out of this war anyway?"

Of the scene in which Jim is alone with the wounded German soldier, Vidor wrote:

> Up until this picture, that type of scene never happened. There's not going to be any animosity directed towards some young German fellow just because he happened to be born in Germany and then was drafted. He might be a school teacher, an accountant, or even a screen actor. You can't put animosity down to two individuals facing each other. That's what the picture says.[33]

The scene in *The Big Parade* stages the face-to-face encounter; Jim is on the point of cutting the young German's throat when he realizes that the man is badly wounded, withdraws his knife, and gives him a cigarette. His response is one of pity and disgust, as he twice pushes away the dying man's face as it falls towards him. This scene uses the human face, so central to cinematic representation, to depict war death (in the context of the forced meeting between two soldiers on warring sides) as a terrible and distorted intimacy. The "face-to-face" is a recognition of a shared humanity, but the proximity of the face of the dying other threatens to destroy the subject, and survival demands that it be rejected.

The destruction of faces in a very literal sense has also been represented in some of the most significant of World War I films. In trench warfare the worst wounds tend to be sustained to head and face. The effects of such disfigurement were explored in Piquard's *Pour la paix du monde*, a documentary film representing the hidden existence of "les gueules cassées," the faceless ones, or "broken mugs." The cinema theorist Béla Bálazs, for whom film was an essentially physiognomic medium, revealing, in his phrase, "the face of things," described *Pour la paix du monde* in these terms:

The director who compiled the film strips in the archives of the armed forces was Colonel Piquard, chairman of the organization of the "Faceless Ones," the men who lived like lepers in an isolated, secret community of their own, because the sight of them would have been unbearable for their fellow-men. The film begins by showing these faceless ones in close-up, their mutilations covered by masks. Then they take off their silken masks and with it they tear the mask off the face of war.

Those whom the war has robbed of their faces show the true face of war to those who know nothing about it. And this physiognomy of film is of an emotional power, a force of pathos no artistic feature film about the war had ever attained. For here war is presented by the horrified, torture by the tortured, deadly peril by the endangered – and it is they who see these things in their true colours.[34]

"The face of war" is also central to François Dupeyron's recent film *The Officer's Ward* (2001), the story of a World War I lieutenant who is horribly disfigured at the start of the war while on reconnaissance. With half his face blown away by a German shell, he spends four years in a ward reserved for officers with serious head wounds on the top floor of the Val-de-Grâce military hospital in Paris, helped to recovery by a nurse for whom he becomes a surrogate son. For the patients in this ward, the Armistice means leaving the enclave of the hospital to face the world, and learning to deal with the responses that their damaged faces – "the face of war" – produce in others. The film contains strong echoes of the earlier, more brutal *Johnny Got His Gun* (Dalton Trumbo, 1971), in which a soldier is all but destroyed by an exploding shell, helped back to life and the possibility of communication by a devoted nurse, and then consigned again to darkness and to silence when it becomes apparent that he wishes to use his experiences to disseminate an anti-war message.

The foreword to Erich Maria Remarque's 1928 novel *All Quiet on the Western Front*, placed at the start of the 1930 film of the same title, reads: "This book is to be neither an accusation nor a confession, and least of all an adventure, for death is not an adventure to those who stand face to face with it. It will try simply to tell of a generation of men who, even though they may have escaped shells, were destroyed by the war."[35]

Lewis Milestone's *All Quiet on the Western Front* (an American film of the German novel) was the most influential of a group of World War I films produced in 1930, which included Howard Hughes's *Hell's Angels*, Howard Hawks's *The Dawn Patrol* (both of which were, like William Wellman's 1927 *Wings*, aviation dramas), James Whale's *Journey's End* (from R. C. Sherriff's play), and G. W. Pabst's *Westfront 1918*. Samuel Hynes writes of these films that:

Each shared something of the essential Myth: each told a war story that was individual, violent, and mortal – a story not of battles won, but of lives lost. It was an international story – not because American actors played German soldiers and Germans played Frenchmen, but because there was only one story, in which young men went to war, fought there and died. Audiences of any nationality could see that story and respond to it.[36]

Yet there were differences between the ways in which British, German, and French films in the 1930s represented the war. Andrew Kelly suggests that Britain turned against the war to a lesser extent than other countries, the realism of its representations of conflict muted by conservatism and class interests. "British cinema," he argues, "was more Rupert Brooke than Siegfried Sassoon: the war was bloody slaughter, but the deaths that resulted were not necessarily wasted."[37]

All Quiet on the Western Front and *Westfront 1918* (based on Ernst Johanssen's book *Vier von der Infanterie*, which was dedicated "In Memory of the Slain") were the most anti-war of the 1930 films (while *Hell's Angels* and *The Dawn Patrol* represented the brutality of war, they also lay stress on heroism and adventure) and the nearest, in Hynes's words, "to the dark realism of the great war memoirs."[38] While *Journey's End* and Anthony Asquith's 1931 *Tell England* (which represented the events at Gallipoli) focused on the experiences of the officer class, *All Quiet* and *Westfront* told the stories of ordinary infantrymen in the trenches of the Western Front. They also depicted the ways in which the soldier experiences alienation from home and family.

Remarque's novel was, Kelly argues, the most widely read of all the hundreds of novels published about the war, and "the one most influential in laying the foundations for a new view of the war as brutal, pointless waste."[39] The film opens with scenes of mobilization in a small German town; the patriotic schoolteacher, Kantorek (Arnold Lucy) seeks to persuade his pupils to join up. Persuaded by dreams of glory, the whole class, led by Paul Baumer (Lew Ayres), enlists. At training camp, they endure the humiliations inflicted by a sadistic drill sergeant, Himmelstoss; in the trenches, they are bombarded in an attack which leaves half of them injured or dead. In a further attack, Paul is trapped in a shell-hole with a French soldier, Duvall (Raymond Griffith), whom he stabs. He is forced to stay with the dying man for two days; Duvall dies and Paul makes a promise to help his family after the war: "Oh, God! Why did they do this to us? We only wanted to live – you and I – why should they send us out to fight each other? If we threw away these rifles and these uniforms you could be my brother . . . You have to forgive me, comrade."

Paul is later injured and sent home on leave; he finds his parents struggling to survive in wartime Germany, and Kantorek, the schoolteacher, again persuading his class to enlist. Paul is greeted by Kantorek as a returning hero, and expected to endorse his patriotic rhetoric, but instead Paul delivers an angry speech: "It's dirty and painful to die for your country. When it comes to dying for your country, it's better not to die at all." Paul bitterly returns to the Front, to find almost all the soldiers in his company have been killed; his friend Kat, one of the few remaining, is injured while out searching for food. As Paul carries his wounded friend on his back, he speaks to him of the future, not realizing that Kat has in fact died, the trope of talking to the now-dead a repetition of the scene with the Frenchman Duval in the shell-hole. Paul himself dies in the last weeks of the war; reaching out from his trench toward a butterfly, he is killed by a sniper's bullet. The film ends (echoing the close of *J'accuse*, as *Oh! What a Lovely War* will in turn echo it), with a shot of the ghostly figures of dead soldiers marching over ranks of crosses and graves.

"There is no silence at the Front and the spell of the Front is so strong that we are never far away from it. Even in the depots way behind the lines, or in the rest areas, the buzz and the muted thundering of the shellfire is always in our ears. We are never so far away that we can't hear it any more," Remarque wrote in his novel.[40] *All Quiet* and *Westfront 1918*, along with the French *The Wooden Crosses* (1931) and Asquith's *Tell England* (1931), were among the first war films to deploy fully the new technologies of sound cinema, in particular to reproduce the noise of battle and, in the case of *The Wooden Crosses*, to recreate the cries of the wounded. *All Quiet* and *Westfront* were the first sound films for both their directors: the Russian-born Milestone, and the Austrian-born Pabst, whose silent films of the 1920s included *The Joyless Street* (1925), which portrayed the desperation, desolation, and corruption of life in postwar Vienna.

Such representations are also at the heart of Pabst's *Westfront 1918*. After sequences showing a group of soldiers billeted in a French house, scenes at the Front, and a long sequence at a front theatre, in which Pabst demonstrated the possibilities of the new sound medium, we see the central protagonist, Karl, returning home from the Front on leave. His mother does not go to greet him, because she has been queuing for many hours outside the butcher's shop and cannot risk losing her place in the line. Karl, meanwhile, enters his apartment to find his wife in bed with another man, the butcher's son, who has bought her affections with food; human relationships have become entirely subordinated to hunger and survival. Karl returns to the Front without becoming reconciled with his wife. He volunteers for a dangerous mission, and is fatally wounded. At the close of the film, we see him in an army hospital inside a church; the wounded bodies of the men are juxtaposed with broken statues. Before he dies, Karl hallucinates an image of his wife, who accuses him of having left without a reconciliation. "It isn't my fault," she says, in a repetition of the words she uttered after Karl had discovered her with the butcher's son. "We are all guilty," Karl responds; his last words, indeed. A wounded Frenchman, not realizing Karl has died, takes his hand, and speaks to him: "Moi, camarade. . . . pas enemi, pas enemi . . ."

Michael Geisler has argued that *Westfront 1918*, along with other German World War I films and novels of the late 1920s and early 1930s, represented a renewed debate about the war which "amounted to a displaced attempt at coming to terms with the problems of 1929–30," while the pervasive rhetoric of war "points to an awareness among Weimar intellectuals of living in an uncertain peace beneath which the real conflicts behind World War I remained unresolved."[41] Any World War I film made outside the immediate context of the war must, indeed, have dual referents: firstly, the war itself, and, secondly, the period in which the film is made, whose cultural and political contexts will shape the ways in which the war is represented. As Martin O'Shaughnessy writes of Jean Renoir's First World War film *La Grande Illusion* (1937):

> It had to be seen as an "authentic" expression of the mentality of the combatants of World War I. Yet it also had to be an adequate response to its own period, particularly the threat of Fascism. Without putting anachronistic sentiments into the minds of the characters, it had to negotiate a path between the antimilitarist pacifism that the war had generated among so many and the anti-Fascism and left-wing nationalism that were such prominent features of the Popular Front.[42]

Although one of the contexts for *La Grande Illusion* was the cluster of anti-war films of the 1930s, it maintains a distance from the representation of actual warfare, deploying none of the familiar iconography – trenches, shells, barbed wire – that had accreted around World War I. Most of the action of the film takes place in two prisoner-of-war camps, Hallbach and Wintersborn. At the opening of the film Maréchal (Jean Gabin), who represents the "ordinary" Frenchman, and the career officer, the aristocratic De Boieldieu, have their plane shot down. In the POW camp to which they are taken, they join a group of Frenchmen (including the wealthy Jew Rosenthal), who are engaged both in digging an escape tunnel and in preparing for a camp revue, one of the numerous theatrical performances in World War I cinema, and indeed war films more generally. The preparations for the revue are interrupted by news of Verdun and the fall of the key fort of Douaumont to the Germans; during the performance itself, the prisoners hear that it has been recaptured, and, in defiance of their guards, they sing "La Marseillaise." We then learn that Douaumont has again been taken by the Germans; Verdun was the battle which had come to represent the waste and horror of World War I for the French, as the Battle of the Somme did for the British. The ebb and flow around Verdun also suggests, O'Shaughnessy argues, "the succession of wars between France and Germany, begun in 1870, continuing in 1914 and threatening to go into a new phase as the film was being made."[43]

Maréchal, Rosenthal, and Boieldieu are subsequently sent to Wintersborn, a bleak fortress, whose commandant is Rauffenstein (Erich von Stroheim), first encountered at the film's opening. His bond is with Boieldieu, an alliance of class that cuts across nationality. Both men represent an old, and declining, aristocratic order, and their relationship is contrasted with the alliance between Maréchal and Rosenthal, the commoner and the Jew. Boieldieu enables the two men to escape by creating a disturbance and is shot, with great reluctance, by Rauffenstein. Maréchal and Rosenthal, on the run, are given shelter by a young German widow, Elsa, whose husband and brothers were all killed at Verdun. At the close of the film Maréchal and Rosenthal are depicted in long-shot, walking in a vast expanse of snow; a German soldier's attempt to shoot them is halted when it is realized that the two Frenchmen are over the German border and into Switzerland, though the unmarked landscape points up the arbitrary nature of all such borders and boundaries.

"I made *La Grande Illusion* because I am a pacifist," Renoir wrote in 1938.[44] The film's title is never fully explained, but it would seem that, on the brink of World War II, the greatest illusion maintained by the film's characters was that World War I would be the last such war. The Second World War had a major impact on the ways in which the events of 1914–18 were perceived; for the Allied countries, the morality and justice of the causes for which World War I was fought suffered by comparison with those of World War II. For German society, Rainer Rother suggests: "The First World War cannot compete in scale with the horrors of Nazi period . . . It is part of the especially German view of the First World War that it is seen as belonging utterly to the past. As a consequence of this very few post-1945 films ever let that 'distant' war play a part."[45]

In the British context, the fiftieth anniversary of the war in the 1960s was the occasion for a renewed preoccupation with the Great War, marked by a major BBC series, which attracted very substantial audiences. Stanley Kubrick's *Paths of Glory* (1958) was the first of a cycle of films, including David Lean's *Lawrence of Arabia* (1962), Joseph Losey's *King and Country* (1964), and Richard Attenborough's *Oh! What a Lovely War*, to represent the soldiers' enemies as their own corrupt leaders and to depict the workings of hierarchy and power within the army. *Paths of Glory* was based on an event that took place in the French army, but the film is to a large extent a Hollywood courtroom drama. The anti-war tone is set at the start with a voice-over (to a scene of soldiers training for combat) giving an account of the start of the war: "Successful attacks were measured in hundreds of yards and paid for by lives in hundreds and thousands." The French generals live in luxury while the men shiver in the trenches; the battle plans of the leaders are ill considered and they are utterly indifferent to the loss of life. When one impossible attack ends in chaos, three men are arbitrarily selected to serve as examples to the rest, and sentenced to death by firing squad. The film's focus on their captain's (Kirk Douglas) determined but hopeless attempts to defend them in the kangaroo court, and on the anguish of the condemned men's last hours before their execution, puts on trial the cynicism and corruption of the Allied army's upper echelons.

This representation of the war, with its central focus on class as the most significant divide, was pursued in Losey's *King and Country*, in which a "deserter," Private Hamp (Tom Courtenay), in the British army is condemned to death when, after three years at the Front, he decides he can take no more. He is defended by Captain Hargreaves (Dirk Bogarde); initially unsympathetic to the soldier, Hargreaves comes to see that he is suffering from shell shock. This defence is inadmissible in the court-martial ("There is no such thing as shell shock," the French general in *Paths of Glory* declares, when face-to-face with a soldier who has clearly been driven out of his mind) and Hamp's death-sentence is a foregone conclusion. When the firing-squad botches the execution, Hargreaves himself has to fire the shot that puts an end to Hamp's life.

In *Oh! What a Lovely War* the ordinary soldier becomes the dupe of the powerful, "howled into war" (to borrow Paul Rotha's phrase) by cynicism masked as patriotism. The film, closely based on the stage play by the radical Theatre Workshop, uses music-hall sketches and seaside entertainments both to represent the war as a form of tragic burlesque and to give voice to the popular imaginary, rejecting the poetic patriotism of a Rupert Brooke in favor of the subversions of the soldiers' songs, which speak both of the immediacy of their experiences and of their ultimate incommunicability. At the center of the film is the truce, the exchange of gifts, and the football match between the opposing armies on Christmas Day 1914 in No Man's Land, around which so much historical and mythical meaning has accreted. The final scenes of the film show the ghost of a soldier following the "red tape" that stands for the negotiations by the crowned heads of Europe and state leaders in the weeks before the Armistice was finally declared, as soldiers on both sides continued, now wholly needlessly, to be killed.

Here we might recall the soldier-poet Wilfred Owen, killed in the final days of the war, one of the protagonists of Pat Barker's war trilogy (*Regeneration, The Eye in the Door, The Ghost Road*), on which the film *Regeneration* (1997) is based. *Regeneration* is staged through an interplay of competing or interlocking discourses: psychiatry/psychoanalysis, symptoms/dreams, words/silence. The central argument is with W. H. R. Rivers (the psychiatrist at Craiglockhart, the hospital to which both Siegfried Sassoon and Wilfred Owen were sent during the course of the war) or, at least, with his conflicted attitudes toward war. Owen's poem *Anthem for Doomed Youth* ("Anthem" was the title adopted by Owen at Sassoon's suggestion), written at Craiglockhart in September–October 1917, is to a substantial extent the "voice" of the film. We see Sassoon working with Owen on his poetry, his revisions a marker of the profound revisions Owen himself undertook on his attitudes toward war. Owen's poem *Dulce et Decorum Est* (which owed much to Sassoon) was a repudiation of an early poem he had written originally entitled "The Ballad of Peace and War," in which "the old lie" of the Latin quotation is offered as a *truth*: "Oh it is meet and it is sweet / To live in peace with others. / But sweeter still and far more meet / To die in war for brothers.[46]

The film of *Regeneration* closes with Rivers reading Owen's "The Parable of the Old Man and the Young," the poem ending Sassoon's letter to Rivers, in which he recalls telling Owen that returning to the Front would benefit his poetry, and writes of his feelings of guilt over Owen's death, which occurred only a few days before the Armistice. In Owen's poem, Abram binds Isaac with "belts and straps, / And builded parapets and trenches there." The Angel appears to Abram and tells him to offer the ram in place of Isaac: "But the old man would not so, but slew his son, / And half the seed of Europe, one by one."

Regeneration is a striking indication of the ways in which understandings of World War I have become mediated and represented through the languages of psychoanalysis (in particular the psychoanalytically informed concept of "shell shock" as trauma) and of poetry, in particular that of Wilfred Owen. The film also contains echoes of Benjamin Britten's *War Requiem*, which interspersed settings for Owen's poetry with the Latin Mass *Missa pro Defunctis* and was first performed on 30 May 1962 to celebrate the consecration of Basil Spence's new Coventry Cathedral, built to replace the medieval cathedral all but destroyed by bombing in the Second World War. Like the anti-war films of the same period, the pacifist message of Britten's *War Requiem* was fully in tune with the marches of the Campaign for Nuclear Disarmament and the increasing protest against the Vietnam War.

In 1988, Derek Jarman made a film version of the *War Requiem*, his cinematic images accompanying Britten's music and Owen's poetry. He wrote in his commentary on the making of this low-budget film: "I've built a loose story around Wilfred Owen, a Nurse, and the Unknown Soldier, which incorporates found (or documentary) footage, and flashbacks filmed with my Super-8 camera . . . It's possible to create a loose narrative until the poem 'The Parable of the Old Man and the Young,' which could illustrate Owen's death in the last week of the Great War, sacrificed for the sake of the Nation's pride." The figure of the Nurse was, Jarman wrote, his version of Britten's addition of "a female presence in the soprano role,"[47] and we could point here to the ways in which filmmakers have divided between those, like Peter Weir in *Gallipoli* (1981), who continued to represent the war in exclusively masculine terms, and those, like Dupeyron in *The Officer's Ward*, for whom women's experiences of the war are as significant as men's. In *War Requiem*, Jarman also included a sequence "built around snowballs, and the legendary Christmas Day when the English and German soldiers exchanged greetings and played football in no man's land."[48] As in *Oh! What a Lovely War*, this event, in which the camaraderie between the opposing forces gives the lie to the dynamic of warfare, comes to emblematize the pity and the waste of war.

The figure of the Unknown Soldier is also, though in far more ironic ways, at the heart of Bertrand Tavernier's *Life, and Nothing But* (1988). The central protagonist of the film is an officer who, after four years of fighting, has committed himself to locating and identifying the "missing" of the war; at the same time, he is deputed to find an unclaimed body that can serve as the official "unknown soldier" for France. Tavernier's complex film in part sets out to show that all soldiers could at some level be said to be "unknown"; in the course of the film, it becomes clear that the same missing soldier is being searched for by two women, one his wife, the second his mistress, neither of them aware of each other's relationship to the missing man.

Set in 1919, *Life, and Nothing But* suggests the rapidity with which the demand for memorialization came into being after the war's end. At the same time the film shows that official remembrance also functioned as a way of forgetting, and of representing the most violent and extreme of historical events in ways that could be more readily and less painfully accommodated.

NOTES

1. Modris Eksteins, "The Cultural Impact of the Great War," *Film and the First World War*, eds. Karel Dibbets and Bert Hogenkamp (Amsterdam: Amsterdam University Press, 1995), 208.

2. Paul Virilio, *War and Cinema: The Logistics of Perception*, trans. Patrick Camiller (London: Verso, 1989), 70.

3. Leslie Midkiff DeBauche, *Reel Patriotism: The Movies and World War I* (Madison, University of Wisconsin Press, 1997), 38.

4. See Michael Isenberg, *War on Film* (East Brunswick, N.J.: Associated University Presses, 1981) and Andrew Kelly, *Cinema and the Great War* (London: Routledge, 1997).

5. In a lecture given at the University of Southern California, 20 February 1929. Quoted Lewis Jacobs, *The Rise of the American Film* (New York: Teachers College Press, 1968), 251.

6. See Michael Hammond, *The Big Show: Cinema Exhibition and Reception in Britain in the Great War*, diss., Nottingham Trent University, 2001, 27–33.

7. Nicholas Reeves, "Official British Film Propaganda," in *The First World War and Popular Cinema: 1914 to the Present*, ed. Michael Paris (Edinburgh: Edinburgh University Press, 1999), 43.

8. D. S. Higgins, ed., *The Private Diaries of Sir H. Rider Haggard* (London: Cassell, 1980), 84. Quoted in Samuel Hynes, *A War Imagined: The First World War and English Culture* (London: Bodley Head, 1990), 125.

9. Rebecca West, *The Return of the Soldier* (London: Virago, 2003), 13–14.

10. Hynes, *A War Imagined*, 125.

11. See Reeves, "Official Film Propaganda," 41–42.

12. R. Merritt, "D. W. Griffith Directs the Great War: The Making of *Hearts of the World*," *Quarterly Review of Film Studies*, 6 (1981): 45–65.

13. William K. Everson, *American Silent Film* (New York: Da Capo Press, 1998), 98.

14. *Ibid.*, 81.

15. Kelly, *Cinema and the Great War*, 25.

16. Harry Carr, "Griffith, Maker of Battle Scenes, Sees Real War," *Photoplay*, March 1918, 23.

17. Kevin Brownlow, *The War, the West and the Wilderness* (New York: Alfred Knopf, 1979), 41.

18. *Ibid.*, 45.

19. Maxim Gorki, "The Kingdom of Shadows," in *Movies*, ed. Gilbert Adair (London: Penguin, 1999), 10.

20. Newbolt's poem is included in *Up the Line to Death: The War Poets 1914–18*, ed. Brian Gardner (London: Methuen, 1964), 75.

21. Abel Gance, *Prisme* (Paris: Gallimard, 1930), 108–9, as quoted in Jay Winter, *Sites of Memory, Sites of Mourning* (Cambridge: Cambridge University Press, 1995), 137.

22. Richard Abel, *French Cinema: The First Wave 1915–1929* (Princeton: Princeton University Press, 1984), 296.

23. *Ibid.*, 297.

24. *Ibid.*, 302.

25. Kelly, *Cinema and the Great War*, 31.

26. Adrian Brunel, *Nice Work: Thirty Years in British Films* (London: Forbes Robertson, 1949), 127.

27. Ivan Butler, *The War Film* (London: Tantivy Press, 1974), 30.

28. King Vidor, *A Tree is a Tree* (London: Longmans, 1954), 73.

29. Paul Rotha, *The Film Till Now* (London: Jonathan Cape, 1931), 124.
30. Vidor, *A Tree is a Tree*, 77.
31. *Ibid.*, 77.
32. Isenberg, *War on Film*, 90.
33. N. Dowd and D. Shephard, *King Vidor: A Directors' Guild of America Oral History Project* (Metuchen, N.J. and London: Directors' Guild of America and The Scarecrow Press, 1988), 57–58. Quoted in Kelly, *Cinema and the Great War*, 39.
34. Béla Bálazs, *Theory of the Film*, trans. Edith Bone (London: Dobson, 1952), 169.
35. Erich Maria Remarque, *All Quiet on the Western Front*, trans. Brian Murdoch (London: Vintage, 1996).
36. Hynes, *A War Imagined*, 447.
37. Andrew Kelly, *Filming All Quiet on the Western Front* (London: I. B. Tauris, 1998), 24.
38. Hynes, *A War Imagined*, 447.
39. Kelly, *Filming All Quiet on the Western Front*, 39.
40. Remarque, *All Quiet on the Western Front*, 87.
41. Michael Geisler, "The Battleground of Modernity: *Westfront 1918*," in *The Films of G. W. Pabst*, ed. Eric Rentschler (New Brunswick, N.J.: Rutgers University Press, 1990), 99, 102.
42. Martin O'Shaughnessy, *Jean Renoir* (Manchester: Manchester University Press, 2000), 124.
43. *Ibid.*, 127.
44. A. Sesonske, *Jean Renoir: The French Films, 1924–1939* (Cambridge, Mass.: Harvard University Press, 1980), 287.
45. Rainer Rother, "The Experience of the First World War and the German Film," *The First World War and Popular Cinema*, ed. Paris, 217–18.
46. See Jon Stallworthy, *Anthem for Doomed Youth: Twelve Soldier Poets of the First World War* (London: Constable, 2002), 15.
47. Derek Jarman, *War Requiem: The Film* (London: Faber, 1989), xii, 1
48. *Ibid.*, 24.

FILMOGRAPHY

All Quiet on the Western Front. Dir. Lewis Milestone. Universal, 1930.
The Battle Cry of Peace. Dir. J. Stuart Blackton. Vitagraph, 1915.
The Battle of the Somme. Dir. Geoffrey Malins, J. B. McDowell. 1916.
The Battle of Arras; The Battle of Ancre; The Battle of St. Quentin. Dir. Geoffrey Malins, J. B. McDowell, 1917.
The Battle of Jutland. Dir. H. Bruce Woolfe. British Instructional Films, 1921.
The Big Parade. Dir. King Vidor. MGM, 1925.
Blighty. Dir. Adrian Brunel. Gainsborough, 1927.
The Blue Max. Dir. John Guillermin. Fox, 1966.
Civilization. Dir. Thomas Ince. Ince, 1916.
Dawn. Dir. Herbert Wilcox. BD, 1928.
The Emden (Kreuzer Emden). Dir. Louis Lalph. Emelka Company, Germany, 1927.
A Farewell to Arms. Dir. Frank Borzage. Fox, 1957.
The Four Horsemen of the Apocalypse. Dir. Rex Ingram. MGM, 1921.

Four Sons. Dir. John Ford. Fox, 1928.

Gallipoli. Dir. Peter Weir. Paramount, 1981.

La Grande Illusion. Dir. Jean Renoir. Réalisations d'Art Cinématographique, 1937.

Hearts of the World. Dir. D. W. Griffith. Art, 1918.

The Hun Within. Dir. Chester Withey. Paramount, 1918.

J'accuse. Dir. Abel Gance. Pathé, 1918.

Johnny Got His Gun. Dir. Dalton Trumbo. Cinemation, 1971.

Journey's End. Dir. James Whale. Tiffany, 1930.

The Kaiser, or the Beast of Berlin. Dir. Rupert Julian. Jewel, 1918.

King and Country. Dir. Joseph Losey. BHE, 1964.

Lawrence of Arabia. Dir. David Lean. Columbia, 1962.

Life, and Nothing But (La Vie et rien d'autre). Dir. Bertrand Tavernier. Hachette Premiere/AB Films/Little Bear/Films AZ, 1989.

Mademoiselle from Armentières. Dir. Maurice Elvey. Gaumont, 1926.

Nurse Edith Cavell. Dir. Herbert Wilcox. RKO, 1939.

Oh! What a Lovely War. Dir. Richard Attenborough. Paramount, 1969.

The Officer's Ward (La Chambre des officiers). Dir. Francois Dupeyron. ARP/France Z Films, 2001.

Paths of Glory. Dir. Stanley Kubrick. United Artists, 1957.

Regeneration. Dir. Gillies MacKinnon. Rafford Films/Norstar/BBC Films, 1997.

Roses of Picardy. Dir. Maurice Elvey. Gaumont, 1927.

Sergeant York. Dir. Howard Hawks. Warner Bros., 1941.

Shoulder Arms. Dir. Charles Chaplin. First National Pictures, Inc., 1918.

Tell England. Dir. Anthony Asquith. British Instructional Films, 1931.

Verdun, visions d'histoire. Dir. Léon Poirier. 1927.

Westfront 1918. Dir. G. W. Pabst. Emelka, 1930.

What Price Glory?. Dir. Raoul Walsh. Fox, 1926.

Wings. Dir. William A. Wellman. Paramount, 1927.

Wooden Crosses (Les Croix de bois). Dir. Raymond Bernard. Pathé-Natan, 1932.

Military history

Audoin-Rouzeau, Stéphane. *Men at War, 1914–1918: National Sentiment and Trench Journalism in France during the First World War.* Trans. Helen McPhail. Providence, R.I.: Berg, 1992.

Barnett, Correlli. *The Swordbearers: Studies in Supreme Command in the First World War.* London: Eyre & Spottiswoode, 1963.

Bond, Brian. *The First World War and British Military History.* Oxford: Clarendon Press, 1991.

Castle, Harold. *Fire over England: The German Air Raids of World War I.* London: Secker & Warburg, 1982.

Fewster, Kevin, Vecihi Basarin, and Hatice Hurmuz Basarin. *Gallipoli: The Turkish Story.* London: Allen & Unwin, 2003.

Gudmundson, Bruce I. *Stormtroop Tactics: Innovation in the German Army, 1914–1918.* New York: Praeger, 1989.

Hickey, Michael. *Gallipoli.* London: John Murray, 1995.

Keegan, John. *The Face of Battle.* Harmondsworth: Penguin, 1978.

  The First World War. New York: Vintage, 2000.

Leed, Eric. *No Man's Land: Combat and Identity in World War I.* Cambridge: Cambridge University Press, 1981.

Leese, Peter. *Shell Shock: Traumatic Neurosis and the British Soldiers of the First World War.* New York: Palgrave, 2002.

Liddle, Peter. *The Soldier's War, 1914–18.* London: Blandford, 1988.

Liddle, Peter, and Hugh Cecil, eds., *Facing Armageddon: The First World War Experienced.* London: Leo Cooper, 1996.

McEntee, Girard Lindsley. *Military History of the World War: A Complete Account of the Campaigns on All Fronts.* New York: Scribner's, 1937.

McKenzie, Compton. *Gallipoli Memories.* London: Cassell, 1929.

Mosier, John. *The Myth of the Great War: A New Military History of World War I.* New York: HarperCollins, 2001.

Philpott, William James. *Anglo-French Relations and Strategy on the Western Front, 1914–1918.* New York: St. Martin's, 1996.

Samuels, Martin. *Doctrine and Dogma: German and British Infantry Tactics in the First World War.* New York: Greenwood, 1992.

Sheffield, G. D. *Leadership in the Trenches: Officer–Man Relations, Morale and Discipline in the British Army in the Era of the First World War.* Basingstoke: Macmillan, 2000.

Shephard, Ben. *A War of Nerves: Soldiers and Psychiatrists, 1914–1994.* London: Pimlico, 2002.

Snyder, Jack L. *The Ideology of the Offensive: Military Decision Making and the Disasters of 1914.* Ithaca: Cornell University Press, 1984.

Travers, Timothy. *The Killing Ground: The British Army, the Western Front, and the Emergence of Modern Warfare, 1900–1918.* London: Allen & Unwin, 1987.

Tuchman, Barbara. *The Guns of August.* New York: Macmillan, 1962.

Verhey, Jeffrey. *The Spirit of 1914: Militarism, Myth, and Mobilization in Germany.* Cambridge: Cambridge University Press, 2000.

Ward, Rutherford. *The Russian Army in World War I.* London: Gordon Cremonesi, 1975.

Zuber, Terence. *Inventing the Schlieffen Plan: German War Planning, 1871–1914.* Oxford: Oxford University Press, 2002.

Political history

Berghahn, Volker Rolf. *Germany and the Approach of War in 1914.* 2nd edn. New York: St. Martin's, 1993.

Bosworth, R. J. B. *Italy and the Approach of the First World War.* New York: St. Martin's, 1983.

Carsten, F. L. *War against War: British and German Radical Movements in the First World War.* Berkeley: University of California Press, 1982.

Ferguson, Niall. *The Pity of War: Explaining World War I.* New York: Basic Books, 1999.

Geiss, Immanuel, ed. *July 1914, the Outbreak of the First World War: Selected Documents.* Trans. Geiss and Henry Meyric Hughes. London: Batsford, 1967.

Gregory, Adrian, and Senia Paseta, eds. *Ireland and the Great War.* Manchester: Manchester University Press, 2002.

Hayne, M. B. *The French Foreign Office and the Origins of the First World War.* Oxford: Clarendon Press, 1993.

Henig, Ruth. *The Origins of the First World War.* 3rd edn. London: Routledge, 2002.

Hoover, Alice. *God, Germany, and Britain in the Great War: A Study in Clerical Nationalism.* New York: Praeger, 1989.

Jahn, Hubertus. *Patriotic Culture in Russia during World War I.* Ithaca: Cornell University Press, 1995.

Jeffery, Keith. *Ireland and the Great War.* Cambridge: Cambridge University Press, 2000.

Kennan, George Frost. *The Fateful Alliance: France, Russia, and the Coming of the First World War.* New York: Pantheon, 1984.

Langhorne, Richard. *The Collapse of the Concert of Europe: International Politics, 1890–1914.* London: Macmillan, 1981.

Laqueur, Walter, and George L. Mosse, eds. *1914: The Coming of the First World War*. New York: Harper & Row, 1966.

Lincoln, W. Bruce. *Passage through Armageddon: The Russians in War and Revolution, 1914–1918*. New York: Simon and Schuster, 1986.

MacMillan, Margaret. *Peacemakers: The Paris Conference of 1919 and its Attempt to End War*. London: J. Murray, 2001.

Paris 1919: Six Months that Changed the World. New York: Random House, 2002.

Martel, Gordon. *The Origins of the First World War*. 2nd edn. London: Longmans, 1996.

Messinger, Gary S. *British Propaganda and the State in the First World War*. Manchester: Manchester University Press, 1992.

Mombauer, Annika. *The Origins of the First World War: Controversies and Consensus*. London: Longman, 2002.

Morel, E. D. *Truth and the War*. 3rd edn. London: National Labour Press, 1918.

The Secret History of a Great Betrayal. 6th edn. London: "Foreign Affairs," 1925.

Mosse, George L. *The Jews and the German War Experience, 1914–1918*. New York: Leo Baeck Institute, 1977.

O'Donnell, Charles James. *Ireland in the Great War: The Irish Insurrection of 1916 Set in its Context of the World War*. Belfast: Athold Books, 1992.

Padfield, Peter. *The Great Naval Race: The Anglo-German Naval Rivalry, 1900–1914*. London: Hart-Davis, MacGibbon, 1974.

Peterson, Horace Cornelius. *Opponents of War, 1917–1918*. Madison: University of Wisconsin Press, 1957.

Propaganda for War: The Campaign against American Neutrality, 1914–1917. Port Washington, N. Y.: Kennikat, 1968.

Sharp, Alan. *The Versailles Settlement: Peacemaking in Paris, 1919*. New York: St. Martin's, 1991.

Simpson, William. *The Second Reich: Germany, 1871–1918*. Cambridge: Cambridge University Press, 1995.

Smith, Leonard V., Stéphane Audoin-Rouzeau, and Annette Becker. *France and the Great War, 1914–1918*. French sections trans. Helen McPhail. Cambridge: Cambridge University Press, 2003.

Steiner, Zara S. *Britain and the Origins of the First World War*. London: Macmillan, 1977.

Stevenson, David. *French War Aims against Germany, 1914–1919*. Oxford: Clarendon Press, 1982.

Thompson, John M. *Russia, Bolshevism, and the Versailles Peace*. Princeton: Princeton University Press, 1967.

Vaughn, Stephen. *Holding Fast the Inner Lines: Democracy, Nationalism, and the Committee on Public Information*. Chapel Hill: University of North Carolina Press, 1980.

Williamson, Samuel R. *Austria-Hungary and the Origins of the First World War*. New York: St. Martin's, 1991.

July 1914: Soldiers, Statesmen, and the Coming of the Great War. Boston: Bedford, 2003.

The Politics of Grand Strategy: Britain and France Prepare for War, 1904–14. Cambridge, Mass.: Harvard University Press, 1969.

Cultural and social history

Becker, Anne. *War and Faith: The Religious Imagination in France, 1914–1930.* Trans. Helen McPhail. New York: Berg, 1998.

Becker, Jean Jacques. *The Great War and the French People.* Trans. Arnold Pome. New York: St. Martin's, 1986.

Bourke, Joanna. *Dismembering the Male: Men's Bodies, Britain, and the Great War.* Chicago: University of Chicago Press, 1996.

Culleton, Claire A. *Working Class Culture, Women, and Britain, 1914–1921.* New York: St. Martin's, 1999.

Daniel, Ute. *The War from Within: German Working-Class Women in the First World War.* New York: Berg, 1997.

Darrow, Margaret H. *French Women and the First World War: War Stories of the Home Front.* New York: Berg, 2000.

DeBauche, Leslie Midkiff. *Reel Patriotism: The Movies and World War I.* Madison: University of Wisconsin Press, 1997.

Dibbets, Karl, and Bert Hogenkamp, eds. *Film and the First World War.* Amsterdam: Amsterdam University Press, 1995.

Dombrowski, Nicole Ann, ed. *Women and War in the Twentieth Century: Enlisted With or Without Consent.* New York: Garland, 1999.

Eksteins, Modris. *Rites of Spring: The Great War and the Birth of the Modern Age.* Boston: Houghton Mifflin, 1989.

Grayzel, Susan R. *Women and the First World War.* London: Longman, 2002.
  Women's Identities at War: Gender, Motherhood, and Politics in Britain and France during the First World War. Chapel Hill: University of North Carolina Press, 1999.

Greenwood, Maurine Weiner. *Women, War, and Work: The Impact of World War I on Women Workers in the United States.* Ithaca: Cornell University Press, 1990.

Higonnet, Margaret, *et al.*, eds. *Behind the Lines: Gender and the Two World Wars.* New Haven: Yale University Press, 1987.

Horne, John. *Labour at War: France and Britain, 1914–1918.* Oxford: Clarendon Press, 1991.

Isenberg, Michael. *War on Film.* East Brunswick, N.J.: Associated University Presses, 1981.

Keene, Jennifer. *Doughboys, the Great War, and the Remaking of America.* Baltimore: Johns Hopkins University Press, 2001.

Kelly, Andrew. *Cinema and the Great War.* London: Routledge, 1997.

Kennedy, David M. *Over Here: The First World War and American Society.* New York: Oxford University Press, 1980.

LeBon, Gustave. *Psychology of the Great War: The First World War & its Origins.* New Brunswick, N.J.: Transactions Publishers, 1999.

Lebovics, Herman. *True France: The Wars Over Culture and Identity, 1900–1945.* Ithaca: Cornell University Press, 1992.

Lerner, Paul Frederick. *Hysterical Men: War, Psychiatry, and the Politics of Trauma in Germany, 1890–1930.* Ithaca: Cornell University Press, 2003.

Long, Rose-Carol Washton, ed. *German Expressionism: Documents from the End of the Wilhelmine Empire to the Rise of National Socialism.* Berkeley: University of California Press, 1993.

Markov, Vladimir. *Russian Futurism: A History.* Berkeley: University of California Press, 1968.

Marlow, Joyce, ed. *The Virago Book of Women and the Great War, 1914–1918.* London: Virago, 1998.

Marwick, Arthur. *The Deluge: British Society and the First World War.* Boston: Little, Brown, 1966.

Women at War, 1914–1918. London: Fontana (with the Imperial War Museum), 1977.

Melman, Billie, ed. *Borderlines: Genders and Identities in War and Peace, 1870–1930.* London: Routledge, 1998.

Paris, Michael, ed. *The First World War and Popular Cinema: 1914 to the Present.* Edinburgh: Edinburgh University Press, 1999.

Reeve, Nicholas. *Official British Film Propaganda during the First World War.* London: C. Helm (with the Imperial War Museum), 1986.

Schivelbusch, Wolfgang. *The Culture of Defeat: On National Trauma, Mourning, and Recovery.* Trans. Jefferson Chase. New York: Metropolitan Books, 2003.

Smith, Page. *America Enters the World: A People's History of the Progressive Era and World War I.* New York: McGraw-Hill, 1985.

Tisdall, Caroline, and Angelo Bozzolla. *Futurism.* New York: Oxford University Press, 1978.

Ward, Larry Wayne. *The Motion Picture Goes to War: The U. S. Government Film Effort During World War I.* Ann Arbor, Mich.: UMI Research Press, 1985.

Watkins, Glenn. *Proof through the Night: Music and the Great War.* Berkeley: University of California Press, 2003.

Whalen, Robert Weldon. *Bitter Wounds: German Victims of the Great War, 1914–1939.* Ithaca: Cornell University Press, 1984.

Wilson, Trevor. *The Myriad Faces of War: Britain and the Great War, 1914–1918.* Cambridge: Polity Press, 1986.

Winter, Jay. *Sites of Memory, Sites of Mourning: The Great War in European Cultural History.* Cambridge: Cambridge University Press, 1995.

Winter, Jay, and Jean-Louis Robert, eds. *Capital Cities at War: Paris, London, Berlin, 1914–1919.* Cambridge: Cambridge University Press, 1997.

Literary history

Ayers, David. *English Literature of the 1920s.* Edinburgh: Edinburgh University Press, 1999.

Bergonzi, Bernard. *Heroes' Twilight: A Study of the Literature of the Great War.* 2nd edn. Basingstoke: Macmillan, 1980.

Booth, Allyson. *Postcards from the Trenches: Negotiating the Spaces between Modernism and the First World War.* New York: Oxford University Press, 1996.

Brearton, Fran. *The Great War in Irish Poetry: From W. B. Yeats to Michael Longley.* Oxford: Oxford University Press, 2000.

Bridgwater, Patrick. *The German Poets of the First World War.* New York: St. Martin's, 1985.

Brosman, Catharine Savage. *Images of War in France: Fiction, Art, Ideology.* Baton Rouge: Louisiana State University Press, 1999.

Buitenhuis, Peter. *The Great War of Words: British, American, and Canadian Propaganda and Fiction, 1914–1933.* Vancouver: University of British Columbia Press, 1987.

Byles, Joan Montgomery. *War, Women, and Poetry, 1914–1945: British and German Writers and Activists.* Newark: University of Delaware Press, 1995.

Caesar, Adrian. *Taking It Like a Man: Suffering, Sexuality and the War Poets.* Manchester: Manchester University Press, 1993.

Cardinal, Agnes, Dorothy Goldman, and Judith Hattaway, eds. *Women's Writing on the First World War.* Oxford: Oxford University Press, 1999.

Cecil, Hugh. *The Flower of Battle: British Fiction Writers of the First World War.* London: Secker & Warburg, 1995.

Cobley, Evelyn. *Representing War: Form and Ideology in First World War Narratives.* Toronto: University of Toronto Press, 1993.

Cohen, Debra Rae. *Remapping the Home Front: Locating Citizenship in British Women's Great War Fiction.* Boston: Northeastern University Press, 2002.

Cole, Sarah. *Modernism, Male Friendship, and the First World War.* Cambridge: Cambridge University Press, 2003.

Cooperman, Stanley. *World War I and The American Novel.* Baltimore: Johns Hopkins University Press, 1967.

Crawford, Fred D. *British Poets of the Great War.* Selinsgrove, Penn.: Susquehanna University Press, 1988.

Cruickshank, John. *Variations on Catastrophe.* Oxford: Clarendon Press, 1982.

Field, Frank. *Three French Writers and the Great War.* Cambridge: Cambridge University Press, 1975.

Fussell, Paul. *The Great War and Modern Memory.* Oxford: Oxford University Press, 1975.

Gale, Maggie B. *West End Women: Women and the London Stage 1918–1962.* London: Routledge, 1996.

Gilbert, Sandra M., and Susan Gubar. *Sexchanges.* Volume II of *No Man's Land: The Place of the Woman Writer in the Twentieth Century.* New Haven: Yale University Press, 1989.

Goldman, Dorothy, with Jane Gledhill and Judith Hattaway. *Women Writers and the Great War.* New York: Twayne–Simon and Schuster, 1995.

Hager, Philip, and Desmond Taylor. *The Novel of World War I.* New York: Garland, 1981.

Hanley, Lynne. *Writing War: Fiction, Gender, and Memory.* Amherst: University of Massachusetts Press, 1991.

Hanna, Martha. *The Mobilization of Intellect: French Scholars and Writers During the Great War.* Cambridge, Mass.: Harvard University Press, 1996.

Hueppauf, Bernd, ed. *War, Violence, and the Modern Condition.* Berlin, New York: de Gruyter, 1997.

Hynes, Samuel. *A War Imagined: The First World War and English Culture.* London: Bodley Head, 1990.

Johnston, John H. *English Poetry of the First World War: A Study in the Evolution of Lyric and Narrative Form.* Princeton: Princeton University Press, 1964.

Khan, Nosheen. *Women's Poetry of the First World War.* Lexington: University of Kentucky Press, 1988.

Kingsbury, Celia Malone. *The Peculiar Sanity of War: Hysteria in the Literature of World War I*. Lubbock: Texas Tech University Press, 2002.

Klein, Holger Michael, ed. *The First World War in Fiction: A Collection of Critical Essays*. New York: Barnes & Noble, 1977.

Lehmann, John. *The English Poets of the First World War*. New York: Thames and Hudson, 1982.

Linder, Ann. *Princes of the Trenches: Narrating the German Experience of the First World War*. Columbia, S.C.: Camden House, 1996.

Marsland, Elisabeth A. *The Nation's Cause: French, English and German Poetry of the First World War*. London: Routledge, 1991.

Mosse, George. *Fallen Soldiers: Reshaping the Memory of the World Wars*. New York: Oxford University Press, 1990.

Natter, Wolfgang G. *Literature at War 1914–1940: Representing the "Time of Greatness" in Germany*. New Haven: Yale University Press, 1999.

Norris, Margot. *Writing War in the Twentieth Century*. Charlottesville: University of Virginia Press, 2000.

North, Michael. *Reading 1922: A Return to the Scene of the Modern*. New York: Oxford University Press, 1999.

Norton, Robert. *Secret Germany: Stefan George and His Circle*. Ithaca: Cornell University Press, 2002.

Onions, John. *English Fiction and Drama of the Great War, 1918–39*. Basingstoke: Macmillan, 1990.

Orel, Harold. *Popular Fiction in England, 1914–1918*. Hemel Hempstead: Harvester Wheatsheaf, 1992.

Ouditt, Sharon. *Fighting Forces, Writing Women: Identity and Ideology in the First World War*. London: Routledge, 1994.

Parfitt, George. *Fiction of the First World War*. London: Faber & Faber, 1988.

Perloff, Marjorie. *The Futurist Moment: Avant-Garde, Avant-Guerre, and the Language of Rupture*. Chicago: University of Chicago Press, 1986, 2003.

Pick, Daniel. *War Machine: The Rationalisation of Slaughter in the Modern Age*. New Haven: Yale University Press, 1993.

Quinn, Patrick J. *The Coming of America: The Great War and American Popular Literature*. Amsterdam and Atlanta: Rodopi, 2001.

Quinn, Patrick J., and Steven Trout. *The Literature of the Great War Reconsidered*. New York: St. Martin's, 2001.

Raitt, Suzanne, and Trudi Tate, eds. *Women's Fiction and the Great War*. Oxford: Oxford University Press, 1997.

Ramazani, Jahan. *Poetry of Mourning: The Modern Elegy from Hardy to Heaney*. Chicago: University of Chicago Press, 1994.

Reilly, Catherine W. *English Poetry of the First World War: A Bibliography*. London: George Prior, 1978.

Sherry, Vincent. *The Great War and the Language of Modernism*. New York: Oxford University Press, 2003.

Showalter, Elaine. *The Female Malady: Women, Madness, and English Culture, 1830–1980*. London: Virago, 1985.

Silkin, Jon. *Out of Battle: The Poetry of the Great War*. London: Oxford University Press, 1972.

Smith, Angela K. *The Second Battlefield: Women, Modernism and the First World War.* Manchester: Manchester University Press, 2000.

Tate, Trudi. *Modernism, History and the First World War.* Manchester: Manchester University Press, 1998.

Tylee, Claire. *The Great War and Women's Consciousness: Images of Militarism and Womanhood in Women's Writings, 1914–1964.* Iowa City: University of Iowa Press, 1990.

Tylee, Claire, ed. *Women, The First World War, and the Dramatic Imagination: International Essays (1914–1999).* London: Edwin Mellen Press, 2000.

Van Wyk Smith, Malvern. *Drummer Hodge: The Poetry of the Anglo-Boer War.* Oxford: Clarendon Press, 1978.

Weber, Eugen. *The Nationalist Revival in France, 1905–1914.* Berkeley & Los Angeles: University of California Press, 1959, 1968.

Wetzel, Heinz, ed. *The First World War in German Narrative Prose: Essays in Honour of George Wallis Field.* Toronto: University of Toronto Press, 1980.

INDEX

CAMBRIDGE COMPANIONS TO LITERATURE

CAMBRIDGE COMPANIONS TO CULTURE

Management Accounting

Management Accounting

CATHERINE GOWTHORPE

SOUTH-WESTERN
CENGAGE Learning™

Australia • Brazil • Japan • Korea • Mexico • Singapore • Spain • United Kingdom • United States

SOUTH-WESTERN
CENGAGE Learning™

Management Accounting
Catherine Gowthorpe

Publishing Director: Linden Harris

Publisher: Stephen Wellings

Production Editor: Lucy Mills

Head of Manufacturing: Jane Glendening

Production Controller: Eyvett Davis

Marketing Manager: Anne-Marie Scoones

Typesetter: Newgen, India

Cover design: Adam Renvoize

Text design: Design Deluxe, Bath, UK

For product information and technology assistance,
contact emea.info@cengage.com.
For permission to use material from this text or product,
and for permission queries,
email clsuk.permissions@cengage.com.

The Author has asserted the right under the Copyright, Designs and Patents Act 1988 to be identified as Author of this Work.

British Library Cataloguing-in-Publication Data
A catalogue record for this book is available from the British Library.

ISBN: 978-1-84480-204-3

Cengage Learning EMEA
Cheriton House, North Way, Andover, Hampshire, SP10 5BE, United Kingdom

Cengage Learning products are represented in Canada by Nelson Education Ltd.

For your lifelong learning solutions, visit
www.cengage.co.uk

Purchase your next print book, e-book or e-chapter at
www.ichapters.co.uk

Printed by Seng Lee, Singapore
2 3 4 5 6 7 8 9 10 – 11 10 09

Brief contents

Contents

Preface

Who is this book aimed at?

This book is aimed primarily at students who are studying management accounting for the first time, although it may also be useful as a refresher course for those who last studied the subject some years ago. The book is likely to be useful to:

- Undergraduate students in their first and/or second year of study for a degree in accounting.
- Undergraduate students on degree courses in business studies, international business, business and accounting or similar subject combinations.
- MBA students.
- Post-graduate Masters students in accounting and related disciplines.
- Professional managers who would like to improve or bring up to date their knowledge of management accounting.

What makes this book different from the others?

There are many excellent textbooks on management accounting, and, indeed, some of them will be referred to from time to time in this book. So why add to the number? First, many of the best texts on the subject are very large volumes, mostly because they cover the subject matter in great depth and detail. The detailed approach is excellent for advanced study but can be daunting for new students. Besides, some students simply do not need to know the subject in great detail. Those studying for masters level qualifications in business administration (MBA) need to know quite a lot about management accounting, but in their subsequent professional lives they will require an informed overview rather than detailed knowledge. Students who are embarking on an undergraduate degree in accounting will, by the time they graduate, know a great deal about management accounting and many other useful things besides, but at the first year stage, they and their tutors may find it helpful to start with a text that aims to *introduce* management accounting. The more advanced and more detailed textbooks can be added at second or third year level, building upon the knowledge gained from this book.

The second reason for adding to the ranks of textbooks on management accounting is that the approach taken in this book is distinctive in certain respects. This book aims to provide a solid grounding in both practical management accounting techniques and in related, relevant, theory including a brief introduction to some of the historical context of the subject. One of the early chapters of the book is specifically devoted to examining relevant theoretical frameworks, but in addition, the explanation of practical techniques in other chapters is often blended with theoretical perspectives. A combination of practice and theory helps to provide a context for the study of the material, and this is particularly important for those who have had little experience of management accounting in particular, or of business in general. The inclusion of theoretical perspectives also (in the author's opinion, at least) makes the study much more interesting. Further relevance is added by the use of real world examples in most of the chapters, and references to recent research work. Students are encouraged to follow up these references and to become accustomed to reading academic journal papers. This approach will allow them to explore certain topics in depth where they wish to do so, and to have access to current developments and thinking.

Features of this book

Chapter structure

All of the chapters in this book, with the exception of the final, summary, chapter, start with the overall chapter aim and a list of learning outcomes. The first ten chapters conclude with a chapter summary, which is followed by a list of references, a summary of the additional material included on the book's website, and end of chapter exercises.

The end of chapter exercises are, in most cases, numerous. Students are often worried, and may become demotivated, if the end of chapter exercises are too difficult. Therefore, the exercises are designed to test the full range of learning points in the chapter, from simple to complex. Even more exercises are included on the book's website (see below).

The website

The website can be found at: www.cengage.co.uk/gowthorpema. The lecturer section is password protected and the password is available free to lecturers who confirm their adoption of the book. Lecturers should complete the registration form on the website to apply for their password or contact their local Cengage Learning sales representative.

For students and lecturers (open access) Question bank: this contains supplementary questions for every chapter. In many cases a multiple choice quiz is provided. Glossary: An electronic copy of the book's glossary, with explanations of all the key terms.

For lecturers (password protected) Lecturers' Guide: this provides answers to the end of chapter questions for which answers are not provided in the book.

Additional questions and answers.

Case studies and solutions.

Overhead transparencies and PowerPoint presentations to accompany each chapter.

Electronic copies of all the figures in easily downloadable form.

Supplementary resources: Examview®

This testbank and test generator provides a huge amount of different types of questions, allowing lecturers to create online, paper and local area network (LAN) tests. This CD-based product is only available from your Cengage Learning sales representative.

Virtual Learning Environment

All of the web material is available in a format that is compatible with virtual learning environments such as Blackboard and WebCT. This version of the product is only available from your Cengage Learning sales representative.

A note about international context and currencies

Similar management accounting techniques are found in many different countries. There is no need, therefore, for a management accounting textbook to be restricted to a single national context. Although this book is written in the UK by a British author, most of its content can be applied equally elsewhere in the world. In order to emphasise this point, the principal currency used for examples in the book is the euro (€), but other currencies are used within specific examples.

Acknowledgements

I would like to thank all those who reviewed the original proposal for the book, and the individual chapters. Special thanks are due to Professor Deryl Northcott who reviewed the first draft of the completed book in its entirety. Her comments were invariably constructive and helpful and subsequent drafts were much improved by following her guidance. Any errors are, of course, my own.

Thanks to Alice Gallagher and Charlotte Loveridge, the Development Editors, for their invaluable guidance and exemplary patience. Many thanks also to Patrick Bond, the publisher, who has given me much useful advice and encouragement in publishing over a period of several years.

The publisher wishes to thank the following academics who reviewed the draft chapters and provided invaluable feedback which helped shape the book:

Seppo Ikaheimo, Helsinki School of Economics
Deryl Northcott, AUT Business School
Simon Pallett, Newcastle University Business School
Vesa Partanen, Turku School of Economics
Graeme Reid, Hull University Business School
Liz Warren, University of Greenwich Business School

Walk through tour

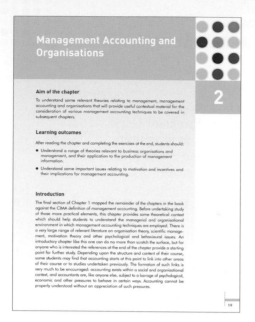

Aim of Chapter and Learning Outcomes These appear at the start of each chapter to help you monitor your understanding and progress through each chapter.

Chapter Summary Each chapter ends with a comprehensive summary that provides a thorough re-cap of the issues in each chapter, helping you to assess your understanding and revise key content.

Example Real-world examples with broad international and sector spread demonstrate the principles set out in the book and link theory to practice.

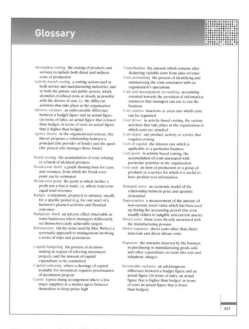

Marginal Definitions and Glossary Key terms are highlighted in colour throughout and explained in the margin. They are also compiled in full in the Glossary at the end of the book, enabling you to find explanations of key terms quickly.

Exercises Appearing at the end of each chapter, these help reinforce and test your knowledge and understanding, and provide a basis for group discussions and activities. The answers are available to lecturers on the companion website.

Self-assessment Exercises and Self-test Questions Answers to these questions are provided at the back of the book, to help test yourself and assess your understanding.

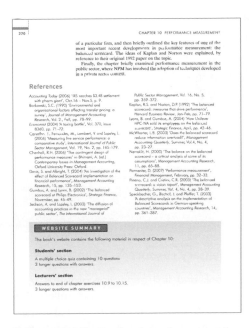

Website Summary This directs the reader to the relevant material on the companion website and lists the extra resources available for each chapter.

References Comprehensive references at the end of each chapter allow you to explore the subject further, and act as a starting point for projects and assignments.

A COMPANION WEBSITE ACCOMPANIES

Visit the supporting website at www.cengage.co.uk/gowthorpema to find further teaching and learning material, including:

Students

- MCQs to test your learning
- Additional questions and answers
- Links to useful companies, news and other relevant sites
- Glossary explaining key terms.

Lecturers

- Additional questions and answers
- Case studies and solutions
- Overhead transparencies and PowerPoint presentations to accompany each chapter.

Supplementary resources: Examview®

This testbank and test generator provides a huge amount of different types of questions, allowing lecturers to create online, paper and local area network (LAN) tests. This CD-based product is only available from your Cengage Learning sales representative.

Virtual Learning Environment

All of the web material is available in a format that is compatible with virtual learning environments such as Blackboard and WebCT. This version of the product is only available from your Cengage Learning sales representative.

Introduction to Management and Cost Accounting

Aim of the chapter

To explain the nature, purpose and historical development of management and cost accounting, and the principal uses of management and cost accounting information in the business environment.

Learning outcomes

After reading the chapter and completing the exercises at the end, students should:

- Understand in principle the nature and purpose of management and cost accounting.
- Appreciate some of the important developments in the history of management accounting.
- Know about some of the principal features of management and cost accounting.
- Appreciate the usefulness of management and cost accounting in helping management to make decisions, and to plan, control and monitor business activity.

Introduction

This chapter sets the scene for the book. It first establishes some important features and characteristics of management accounting. It examines definitions of the key terms 'management accounting' and 'cost accounting' and explains a model of the principal steps involved in management, and a description of the management information that, in general terms, is required at each step. Finally, the scope of the rest of the book is described by mapping most of the subsequent chapters against the key definition of management accounting.

What is management and cost accounting?

There are two distinct strands to accounting by organisations: **management accounting** and financial accounting. For the benefit of newcomers to accounting, it is helpful at the outset to distinguish between the two strands. Management accounting processes are concerned with the provision of information for use internally, within the organisation, for functions such as decision-making by managers, and the control of business activities. Management accounting reports can be as abundant as necessary. For example, a small business that employs few staff and is engaged in the provision of a single service is unlikely to need a great deal of information for decision-making and control purposes. Management accounting systems in such cases are likely to be rudimentary and informal. By contrast a complex multinational business engaged in a range of activities must take a much more formal and organised approach to information gathering and processing.

Virtually all organisations, regardless of size, have external **stakeholders** who are interested in how well the business is performing. In the case of small businesses the stakeholders are often limited to the tax authorities, and perhaps, the providers of finance in the form of loans and overdrafts. Larger businesses may have numerous shareholders and lenders who take no active part in the running of the business and so do not have access to the management accounting information used for functions such as decision-making and control. The external stakeholders do not need very frequent or abundant information, but they do have an interest in receiving periodic reports at least annually. The provision of such periodic reports is the purpose of financial accounting.

Public sector and not-for-profit organisations also have a potentially wide range of external stakeholders, for example, the public, government, regulators and contributors of funds. Such organisations are often required to publish external financial reports.

Although management and financial accounting are distinct from each other in terms of consumer, style and content, they often use the same sources of data, and the same accounting system may be used to produce much of the information. Figure 1.1 below expresses the relationship between management and financial accounting information and reporting, showing the boundary between the organisation and the external world. The consumers, or users, of the different reports are shown at the bottom of the diagram. While there is a range of users who are interested in financial reports, management reporting information is used solely by management and is rarely distributed outside to anyone in the external environment.

Characteristics of management accounting information

The typical characteristics of management accounting information are identified in the table on the following page by means of contrasting such information with the periodic financial reports that are oriented towards external users.

FIGURE 1.1

The relationship between management and financial reporting

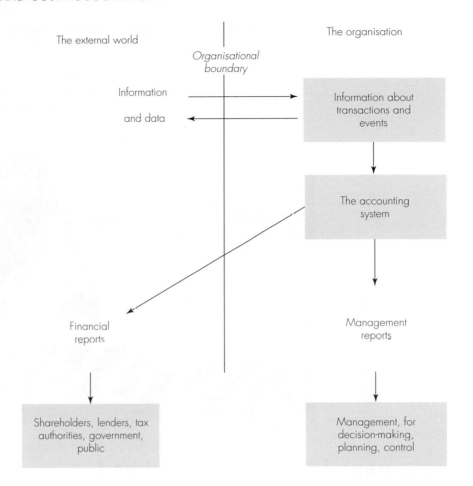

Characteristics of management reports

Characteristic	Financial reports	Management reports
Frequency	Usually produced annually	As frequently as necessary for management purposes
Timeliness	Usually there is a significant time lag between the period covered by the report and the date of publication	Can be produced with minimal delay, provided that appropriate systems are in place
Orientation to future or past	Summarise transactions and events that have already taken place; they are not oriented towards the future	Can be oriented towards future or past, depending upon managers' information requirements
Level of detail	The information is not detailed: transactions are summarised under a few headings	Can be as detailed or as aggregated as necessary
Non-financial performance information	More likely to be included in the reports of larger, not smaller, organisations, but often limited in scope and content	Non-financial performance information and/or indicators are often very important elements

As the figure suggests, management information is much more flexible in nature. Financial reports tend to be highly standardised, because of regulatory requirements, but the nature of management reports is variable because managers can specify the information that they need and the frequency with which it is produced. These useful and flexible features of management accounting information are summarised and discussed further below.

Some useful features of cost and management accounting information

Lack of regulation

Cost and management accounting
accounting oriented towards the provision of information resources that managers can use to run the business

Cost and management accounting, being internal to the organisation, is unregulated, and can therefore be geared towards the specific needs of the organisation and its managers. The cost and management accounting system can be tailored specifically to organisational own needs; information can be produced in whatever form, and in whatever quantity, is appropriate for the organisation and its managers.

Orientation towards past and future

Management accounting information draws upon past events for information but is also oriented towards the future. It considers such questions as, for example:

- How much profit is the business likely to make next year?
- How much additional business might we pick up if we lower our prices by 5%?
- Should we close down a part of the business that is making losses?

- We need a new machine in the factory. Should we buy it or lease it?
- How much does this department cost to run?
- Which divisions in the organisation are, relatively speaking, more cost-effective?

Timely production

The overriding objective of the production of cost and management information is that it should be useful. Management can set up systems that produce useful information quickly. For example, in most businesses it will be useful to have monthly sales figures reported as quickly as possible. Such figures do not necessarily have to be completely accurate. Also, they do not necessarily have to be accompanied by detail of other income and **expenses** (because this would probably slow up the production of information). There is no reason why simple sales figures could not be available a day or two after each month end. Managers would thus be in a position to respond very quickly to changing circumstances, as illustrated in the following example.

Expenses
the amounts incurred by the business in purchasing or manufacturing goods sold, and other expenditure on items like rent and telephone charges

EXAMPLE 1.1

Duckworths sells household alarm systems in do-it-yourself installation kits. Until recently there have been two types: the Standard and the De-Luxe systems. This year, from 1 January, the business has introduced the Super-De-Luxe, which has much more sophisticated circuitry and an extra alarm box for external installation. The gross margins on the three types are 38%, 40% and 46% respectively, and Duckworths' directors are keen to promote sales of the higher-specification and more profitable products.

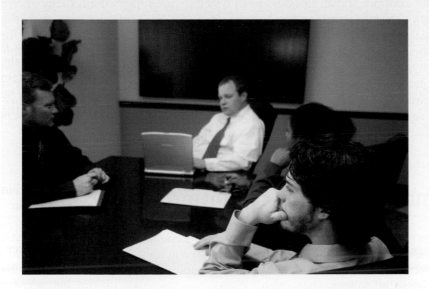

Each month the sales director holds a meeting with the sales force on about the fifth or sixth day of the month. On 5 April he discusses the sales figures (in units) for January, February and March, which are as follows:

	Standard	De-Luxe	Super-De-Luxe	Total
January	2038	1604	213	3855
February	2175	1598	344	4117
March	2240	1634	28	3902

At the meeting he asks his staff why they think that sales of the Super-De-Luxe, after a promising start in January and February, have nosedived in March. A couple of the sales reps tell him that Duckworths' principal competitor has brought out a de-luxe system that is not only cheaper than Duckworths' but which also has some extra features. The Duckworths' product is more expensive and is of poorer quality.

The sales director now has quite a lot of information to take with him to the next main board meeting: concrete evidence in the form of the sales figures of problems with the Super-De-Luxe sales, and some reasons for the drop in sales. The information he has available does not solve the problem, but the rapid provision of figures has at least allowed him to identify that a problem exists. It is then up to the board of directors to discuss the problem and possible solutions to it.

Frequent reporting

Financial reporting
the regular reporting of financial information to interested parties external to the organisation

In the example above, sales of alarm systems were reported internally once a month. This is clearly a much more frequent basis of reporting than the annual **financial reporting** undertaken by businesses. It is common for businesses to organise their internal management reporting on a monthly basis, producing often quite detailed reports. However, it is possible to produce internal cost and management information as frequently as it is required. In larger businesses some important elements of internal information may be reported as frequently as once a day. For example, large retailers are likely to produce sales figures daily.

A definition of management accounting

A fairly lengthy definition of management accounting is provided by CIMA (the Chartered Institute of Management Accountants), 2005. The definition is given in full in the box below, as it is useful in setting the scene for the chapters that follow.

Courtesy of CIMA

Management accounting is the application of the principles of accounting and financial management to create, protect, preserve and increase value for stakeholders of for-profit and not-for-profit enterprises in the public and private sectors.

Management accounting is an integral part of management. It requires the identification, generation, presentation, interpretation and use of relevant information to:

- Inform strategic decisions and formulate business strategy.
- Plan long, medium and short-run operations.
- Determine capital structure and fund that structure.
- Design reward strategies for executives and shareholders.
- Inform operational decisions.
- Control operations and ensure the efficient use of resources.
- Measure and report financial and non-financial performance to management and other stakeholders.
- Safeguard tangible and intangible assets.
- Implement corporate governance procedures, risk management and internal controls.

Cost accounting
the process of identifying and summarising the costs associated with an organisation's operations

What about **cost accounting**? CIMA (2005) defines cost accounting as the 'Gathering of cost information and its attachment to cost objects, the establishment of budgets, standard costs and actual costs of operations, processes, activities or products; and the analysis of variances, profitability or the social use of funds'.

In practice, there is a considerable overlap in the terms 'management accounting' and 'cost accounting', and indeed they are often used together as in this chapter's title. This book will not attempt to demarcate the terms rigorously. 'Management accounting' will be used as a general term to cover the production and uses of information within the business. 'Cost accounting' will be referred to in areas that specifically consider the identification and accumulation of costs.

Management accounting: the historical context

The beginnings of management accounting can be traced back a very long way indeed. As soon as business activity is conducted at anything other than the individual or perhaps family, level, organisation-type structures come into being, followed rapidly by some form of accounting. Mathews and Perera (1996) note that Mesopotamian civilizations were keeping accounting records of property ownership and business transactions from as early as 4500BC. There is plentiful evidence, too, of accounting systems in ancient Greece, Rome and China. As commercial activity became more complex, larger organisational forms developed. It is probably fair to say that the precursors of the modern corporation did not properly emerge until the Industrial Revolution, but even before this time, management accounting techniques were in use.

The Industrial Revolution involved changes in the nature of manufacturing, labour management, the use of technology and the development of new approaches to the organisation of business enterprises. Jones (1995) explains the transformation from cottage-type activity (small scale, family-based, reliant principally on human and animal power) to the factory (usually large-scale and oriented towards the exploitation of technology). The move to larger scale operations demanded new forms of commercial organisation in order to gain access to the necessary finance to fund the increased level of activity: notably the **joint-stock corporation**, precursor of the modern limited liability company. From the point of view of parties external to the organisation, including shareholders who did not take an active part in management, the joint-stock corporation gave rise to a need for increased accountability in the form of periodic financial statements. This was paralleled by an increased need for accountability within larger and more complex organisations, which resulted in significant developments in cost and management accounting techniques.

Johnson (1981) states that: 'The first modern business organisations to require internal accounting information for decision-making and control were the mechanised, multi-process, cotton textile factories that appeared in England and the United States around 1800' (p. 511). He goes on to describe the use of cost accounts in such businesses to record the conversion costs of raw material into finished yarn and cloth. This (as we will see in subsequent chapters) was a technically complex record-keeping activity. What was the purpose of such accounting? Kaplan (1984) describes some of the managerial activities that were enabled by cost accounting, for example:

- Monitoring of the efficiency of a textile mill's conversion of **raw materials** into **finished goods**.
- Using operating statistics for evaluation and controlling performance of sub-units in railroad organisations.
- Using detailed data organised by sales department and geographic areas, to monitor sales performance.

In summary, with the development of larger organisations undertaking more complex activities than were possible under pre-Industrial Revolution conditions, a need arose for cost and management accounting techniques that would assist managers to plan, control and to make decisions.

More recent developments

The 1980s saw the emergence of a great deal of criticism of prevailing management accounting practices. It was argued that management accounting

---

Joint-stock corporation
the precursor to the modern limited liability company

Raw materials
materials which are bought in by a business and then put through a manufacturing process

Finished goods
inventory items which have been through a complete manufacturing process and which are now ready for sale

had failed to develop throughout most of the twentieth century and that its ingrained practices were increasingly irrelevant to modern business. The most influential critics were Johnson and Kaplan, whose book *Relevance Lost: The Rise and Fall of Management Accounting* (1987) observed that the continued use of outmoded and irrelevant management accounting practices had contributed significantly to the relative decline in US business success. The changing nature of business activity in the USA and other developed economies meant that management accounting techniques geared to large-scale manufacturing industry were of less and less practical use. The business environment was changing because of the move away from manufacturing and towards the provision of services, because of increased levels of auto-mation and computer usage, and because of the increased importance of advanced human skills in many businesses. Johnson and Kaplan's (1987) critique was highly influential and in the following decade there were many innovations in management accounting practice, some of which will be discussed in the course of this book.

The management accounting process

The process of management, and related management information needs, can be summarised in a neat, linear form, as set out in Figure 1.2.

The objectives of the organisation

Much of the content of the forthcoming chapters is concerned with techniques and mechanisms that allow managers to make decisions and then plans, to control activities and to monitor outcomes. It is important, though, to bear in mind that these activities operate within an overarching organisational objective, and that managerial efforts should always be geared to achieving that objective. The principal objective of a private sector business might seem obvious: to make a profit. Naturally, all businesses within an essentially capitalist system need to make a profit in order to survive: profitability is therefore important. However, business objectives and priorities go far beyond the simple desire to make money. Profitability and positive cash flow are by-products that tend to arise when a business's key objectives are met. Typical objectives might be expressed as follows:

- 'We want to be the market leader in plumbers' fittings'.
- 'This company aims to be the best travel agent in the business'.
- 'We aim to operate according to the highest ethical standards at all times'.

Public sector and not-for-profit organisations also tend to gauge their success against overarching objectives or principles. For example, the UK's National Health Service holds to the following fundamental principles: 'The provision of quality care that meets the needs of everyone, is free at the point of need, and is based on the patient's clinical need, not their ability to pay'.

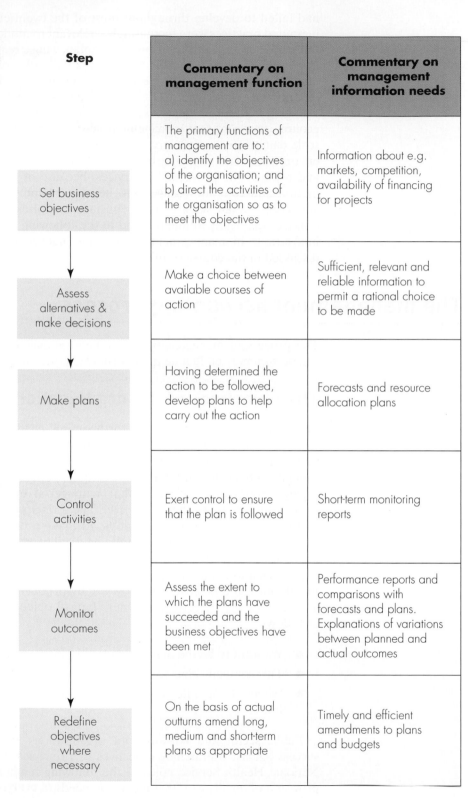

FIGURE 1.2

The process of management

Step	Commentary on management function	Commentary on management information needs
Set business objectives	The primary functions of management are to: a) identify the objectives of the organisation; and b) direct the activities of the organisation so as to meet the objectives	Information about e.g. markets, competition, availability of financing for projects
Assess alternatives & make decisions	Make a choice between available courses of action	Sufficient, relevant and reliable information to permit a rational choice to be made
Make plans	Having determined the action to be followed, develop plans to help carry out the action	Forecasts and resource allocation plans
Control activities	Exert control to ensure that the plan is followed	Short-term monitoring reports
Monitor outcomes	Assess the extent to which the plans have succeeded and the business objectives have been met	Performance reports and comparisons with forecasts and plans. Explanations of variations between planned and actual outcomes
Redefine objectives where necessary	On the basis of actual outturns amend long, medium and short-term plans as appropriate	Timely and efficient amendments to plans and budgets

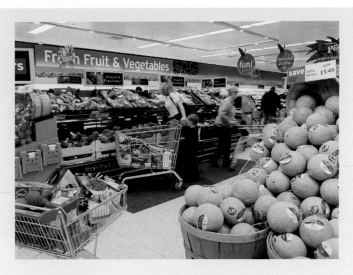

*Courtesy of
J. Sainsbury plc*

Some real-life examples of what businesses say about their objectives:

J. Sainsbury plc: 'At Sainsbury's we will deliver an ever improving quality shopping experience for our customers with great product at fair prices. We aim to exceed customer expectations for healthy, safe, fresh and tasty food making their lives easier everyday'.

*Courtesy of
GlaxosmithKline
plc*

GlaxoSmithKline plc: 'We have a challenging and inspiring mission: to improve the quality of human life by enabling people to do more, feel better and live longer'.

Courtesy of Balfour Beatty plc

Balfour Beatty plc: 'We are committed to customer satisfaction, first-class service, safety and a responsible approach to the environment'.

The effect of uncertainty

The diagram in Figure 1.2 comprises the textbook version of how decision-making, planning and control should take place. Needless to say, the process in real life is somewhat messier and less precise. Managers spend much time and effort in an attempt to anticipate future events and trends, but of course information on such matters is highly speculative. Even understanding current events and trends can present significant challenges. Managers work in rapidly changing environments beset by difficulties and uncertainties. It may be necessary to alter plans at short notice in response to unanticipated events (e.g. shortage of raw materials, war, civil unrest, new competitors, new product inventions and so on). The information systems that serve managers should be efficient and responsive to rapidly changing needs but in the real world this is not always the case. Management accounting systems can often, in practice, be quite inflexible and managers may have to make decisions at short notice with sub-optimal levels of information at their disposal. Luck and a favourable combination of circumstances may subsequently validate the decisions (or maybe not).

Although the textbook model of management is rarely, if ever, completely reflective of reality, the model does approximate in some degree to the process that intelligent managers follow. As for information, although it can rarely be complete and is always subject to uncertainties, some information is usually better than no information. The existence of information may help to give managers the confidence they need to engage in strategic planning and decision-making, and will help them, at least to some degree, to follow through and monitor their decisions. It will be helpful, though, to bear in mind that the management and costing information explained in some detail in the rest of the chapters will not necessarily be complete, or sufficient or timely enough, for managers' needs.

Organisation of the rest of the book

The chapters that follow will deal with many, although not all, of the elements of the CIMA definitions of management and cost accounting. The elements of the CIMA definitions can be mapped against the chapters as follows:

Chapter	Elements of the CIMA definitions
3 Product and services costing	Cost accounting: gathering of cost information and its attachment to cost objects . . . actual costs of operations, processes, activities or products . . .
4 ABC (Activity-based costing)	Cost accounting: gathering of cost information and its attachment to cost objects . . . actual costs of operations, processes, activities or products . . .
5 Pricing	Management accounting: inform operational decisions
6 Marginal costing and decision-making	Cost accounting: gathering of cost information and its attachment to objects. Management accounting: plan medium and short-run operations; inform operational decisions; ensure the efficient use of resources
7 Capital investment decisions	Management accounting: plan long and medium-run operations; ensure the efficient use of resources
8 Budgets	Cost accounting: the establishment of budgets. Management accounting: plan long medium and short-term operations; control operations and ensure the efficient use of resources
9 Accounting for control	Cost accounting: the establishment of standard costs, and actual costs of operations, processes, activities or products; and the analysis of variances. Management accounting: control operations and ensure the efficient use of resources
10 Performance measurement	Management accounting: measure and report financial and non-financial performance to management and other stakeholders

Before looking at these specific areas of management accounting, however, the next chapter examines the broader issue of managerial behaviour with particular reference to accounting. It introduces some important ideas and theories about how human behaviour affects managerial decision-making and control.

Although the table above deals with most aspects of the CIMA definition of management accounting, a few elements of it are beyond the scope of this introductory level book. For example, the book does not cover the design of reward strategies for executives and shareholders (but note that theories relating to motivation and incentives are briefly covered in Chapter 2). The determination of capital structure and the funding of that structure is usually regarded as occupying the domain of finance. The implementation of corporate governance procedures, risk management and internal controls are also regarded as beyond the scope of this book. However, the chapter mapping table above demonstrates that the rest of this book will cover most aspects of the definitions of management and cost accounting. The CIMA definition of management accounting encompasses a wide range of types of organisation (public and private sector, for-profit and not-for-profit). The principal orientation of this book is towards private sector, profit-making businesses, but it should be appreciated that many of the techniques and practices discussed can be found across all sectors. Some of the examples in the chapters that follow reflect the wide applicability of management accounting techniques in different sectors.

The final section of the book comprises a conclusion which:

- Summarises the important aspects of management accounting covered in the book.
- Briefly examines current issues of interest.
- Provides a gateway for further study of management accounting.

Chapter summary

This chapter has introduced some important ideas about, and definitions of, management accounting, and has sketched in some background about its historical development. Students should at this point have gained some idea of the nature of the subject and the extent of coverage that is supplied in this introductory text. The framework suggested for study is based upon a professional accounting body's definition of management accounting, and so has a distinctly practical orientation. However, in addition, it should be recognised that there is a rich and varied theoretical underpinning to the subject, some aspects of which will be introduced at various points in the book. Chapter 2 proceeds to examine some relevant elements of management, organisational and motivational theory.

WEBSITE SUMMARY

The book's website contains the following material in respect of Chapter 1:

Students' section

Two questions with answers.

Lecturers' section

Answers to end of chapter exercises 1.4 to 1.6
Two questions with answers.

References

CIMA (Chartered Institute of Management Accountants) (2005) *Official Terminology*, 2005 edition, Elsevier/CIMA Publishing: Oxford.

Johnson, H.T. (1981) 'Toward a new understanding of nineteenth-century cost accounting', *The Accounting Review*, Vol. LVI, No. 3, July, pp. 510–518.

Johnson, H.T. and Kaplan, R.S. (1987) *Relevance Lost: The Rise and Fall of Management Accounting*, Harvard: Boston.

Jones, T.C. (1995) *Accounting and the enterprise: a social analysis*, Routledge: London.

Kaplan, R.S. (1984) 'The evolution of management accounting', *The Accounting Review*, Vol. LIX, No. 3, July, pp. 390–418.

Mathews, M.R. and Perera, M.H.B. (1996) *Accounting theory and development*, Thomas Nelson Australia: Melbourne.

SELF-ASSESSMENT EXERCISES

Note that because this chapter is a relatively short introduction to management accounting, there is only a limited number of end-of-chapter exercises. The intention is that the exercises should be answered in fairly general terms, drawing upon both common sense and imagination. Students have to try to think their way into the situations described in order to specify the kind of management information that would be useful. The objective behind the questions is to get students accustomed to thinking about typical decisions that have to be made in business.

If this book is being studied as part of a taught course, any of the questions that follow could be used as a basis for class discussion.

1.1 Cueline Limited manufactures furniture at factory premises held on a lease. The lease is due to end next year, but it could probably be renegotiated. The company's directors are also considering the possibility of buying freehold premises. What items of management information would be useful to the directors in reaching a decision?

1.2 Putt plc owns several shops selling golfing and other sporting equipment. It operates principally in the area around London. The company's directors will be meeting next month to discuss a proposal for a major change in business strategy. The sales director has observed that gross margins on golf-related items are much higher than those on other stock lines, and he is proposing that the company should in future sell only golfing equipment. What items of information, financial and non-financial, are likely to be useful to the directors in assessing the pros and cons of the proposed change in strategy?

1.3 Bulstrode, Barker and Bennett is a successful firm of solicitors operating in a small town. Bulstrode died some years ago, Barker has retired, but Dexter Bennett still works in the business as senior partner. There are three junior partners, and Dexter has called a meeting of the partners to discuss the decisions they should make on the following proposals:

a) The conveyancing department is very busy. Would it make economic sense for the firm to employ another solicitor in that department?

b) The firm currently specialises in conveyancing and litigation work. The town's principal specialist in divorce work has just retired, and Bennett thinks there is an opportunity to pick up some extra business. He knows a highly experienced divorce specialist who is currently working for a large firm in London. She could be persuaded to move if she were offered a position as a junior partner.

What information are the partners likely to need (both financial and non-financial) in order to reach the right decisions on these proposals?

EXERCISES

1.4 Cyclostyle Limited makes metal parts for bicycles. The metal press machine, which has been used in the business for several years, is now reaching the end of its useful life. The directors are looking at two replacement options. One is a German machine at a cost of £54 000. The other is a British machine at a cost of £38 500.

What items of information, financial and non-financial, are likely to be useful to the directors in deciding between the two machines?

1.5 Preedy Price Limited is a small fashion company run by two sisters, Anne Preedy and Amelia Price. They have been very successful in marketing a range of very exclusive and expensive knitwear through small specialist retail outlets. The company has been approached by a large retailer, Shield & Flagg plc, which would like to market a cut-price version of some of the sisters' exclusive designs. Shield & Flagg's buyer assures the sisters that this would be a very good opportunity for them to make high volume sales and to make a lot of money. She estimates that volumes of up to 35 000 garments per year are quite feasible. The maximum number of garments the sisters have produced and sold in one year to date is 5600.

Production could be handled by some of Shield & Flagg's regular knitwear production factories, or the sisters could set up their own large-scale production facilities. In order to make the launch of the new lines successful, however, inventories of around 20 000 items would have to be available in advance of the items going on sale in Shield & Flagg's 35 stores around the country.

What factors (both financial and non-financial) should the sisters take into consideration in deciding whether or not to take up this new opportunity?

1.6 Denver runs a restaurant business, operating from rented premises in the centre of a large town. His business has been relatively successful; he has succeeded in making a small profit each year, but he feels that he could do better if he expanded the business.

Denver is a sole trader and the only person with whom he can really discuss business strategy, in complete confidence, is his accountant, Dylan. He has arranged a meeting with Dylan to discuss possible future directions for the business. He starts the meeting by explaining some of the ideas he's had to improve the business:

'The fundamental point is that I need to expand the number of covers. I can't do this in my current premises at Hanover Road, and I would need to move. There's a freehold building for sale on Cross Street with a restaurant on the ground floor. If I bought that I could have half as many covers again as I have now. I could sell my house and then move into the upper part of the building. That would help to keep the mortgage down to a reasonable level.

I've also been wondering about making some fairly major changes to the menu. My net profit margin, as you know from the annual accounts you've just prepared for me, is only about 6%. I would like to cut out the less profitable menu items. I think I know which ones are less profitable but I can't be sure. As you know, I'm open six evenings a week at the moment. I'm wondering about starting weekend lunches as well, but I don't know whether I could make enough money to justify keeping the place open.'

Advise Denver on the type of information – financial and non-financial – he needs in order to make decisions on the three points above (the advice can be given in fairly general terms).

Management Accounting and Organisations

2

Aim of the chapter

To understand some relevant theories relating to management, management accounting and organisations that will provide useful contextual material for the consideration of various management accounting techniques to be covered in subsequent chapters.

Learning outcomes

After reading the chapter and completing the exercises at the end, students should:

- Understand a range of theories relevant to business organisations and management, and their application to the production of management information.

- Understand some important issues relating to motivation and incentives and their implications for management accounting.

Introduction

The final section of Chapter 1 mapped the remainder of the chapters in the book against the CIMA definition of management accounting. Before undertaking study of those more practical elements, this chapter provides some theoretical context which should help students to understand the managerial and organisational environment in which management accounting techniques are employed. There is a very large range of relevant literature on organisation theory, scientific management, motivation theory and other psychological and behavioural issues. An introductory chapter like this one can do no more than scratch the surface, but for anyone who is interested the references at the end of the chapter provide a starting point for further study. Depending upon the structure and content of their course, some students may find that accounting starts at this point to link into other areas of their course or to studies undertaken previously. The formation of such links is very much to be encouraged: accounting exists within a social and organisational context, and accountants are, like anyone else, subject to a barrage of psychological, economic and other pressures to behave in certain ways. Accounting cannot be properly understood without an appreciation of such pressures.

The theories discussed in this chapter fall into two principal categories: first, theories of organisations and management; and second, theories of motivation and incentives. Both of these categories of theory have implications for the practice of management accounting. The first set of theories is concerned with how organisations work, and are structured. A strict hierarchical structure, for example, is likely to require strict accountability through the different levels of hierarchy, using formal methods of information collection and reporting. Management and cost accounting techniques are used in such environments to collate, calculate, summarise and report.

Theories of motivation and incentives seek to describe, predict and explain human behaviour within organisations. Management accounting, because it is carried out by human beings, may be affected by management bias, and economic self-interest. For example, management accounting often involves the setting of targets or budgets, but these could be biased towards being easily achievable where managers wish to give themselves an easy life.

Students may find it helpful to use this chapter principally as a point of reference, to be returned to after study of subsequent chapters. However, it is likely to be helpful to read it before engaging on the more technical work that begins with the next chapter.

Theories of organisations and management

Puxty (1986) comments that 'management as a skill was not developed to any great extent in the nineteenth century'. However, from the early years of the twentieth century the activity of management was subject to much greater scrutiny than previously, and theories were developed to explain and to prescribe the process of management.

Scientific management

Scientific management
a theory of management propounded by Frederick Taylor, sometimes nowadays referred to as 'Taylorism'

Early in the twentieth century the notion of the organisation as something akin to a machine developed. The theory of 'scientific management' was propounded by Frederick Taylor (and is now sometimes referred to as 'Taylorism'); the basic tenet of this theory, as the name implies, was that management could be refined to a precise science. Managers' responsibility was to identify the precise nature of each element of a task and to ensure that workers were selected and trained to carry out these tasks, and that work and responsibility should be shared between management and workers according to their skills. Managerial skills involved thinking, prescribing and ordering whereas the workforce was simply paid in order to carry out the tasks prescribed by management. In order to ensure the co-operation of the workforce, incentives would be provided in the form of rewards for higher productivity. Taylor had the opportunity as a senior engineer in a steel company to test his theories in the workplace. His early successes, both as a manager and a consultant to other businesses, in making radical improvements in productivity ensured that his theories attracted the attention of a wider audience, and scientific management proved to be an immensely influential idea that was applied in many different industries. Despite its widespread influence, it was unpopular in many quarters. Puxty (1986) explains why: 'Taylor's system was disliked, although he never seems to have understood why. The workforce was opposed because the implications seemed to be widespread unemployment (since more efficient methods meant fewer people being employed). Both workers and management opposed the system because of its dehumanizing effect on the individual' (p. 22).

Administration and bureaucracy

Henri Fayol, a French engineer and business manager, was an important management theorist of the early and mid-twentieth century (although his book on management principles was published in 1916, it did not appear in English until over thirty years later and so was of limited influence at first in the English-speaking world). He identified five elements of management roles and actions: planning, organising, commanding, co-ordinating and controlling. Some of these roles should look familiar – it might be helpful at this point to refer back to Figure 1.2 in the previous chapter which sets out the steps involved in the process of management, and their related management information needs. Fayol named 14 principles of management, as follows:

1 Division of work – individuals are to specialise in a limited number of tasks, so as to increase productivity.
2 Authority – the right to issue commands, balanced by an obligation to take responsibility.
3 Discipline – employees must obey the commands of management, but equally, managers must provide good leadership.
4 Unity of command – there should be a hierarchical system of command constructed in such a way that no-one in it is responsible to more than one manager.
5 Unity of direction – people in an organisation should work to a common set of objectives.
6 Subordination of individual interest – individual interests should be subordinated to general interests.
7 Remuneration – should be fair.
8 Centralisation – to the degree appropriate to the nature of the business.
9 Line of authority – the line of authority running through the hierarchy from top to bottom should not be too long. Communication should work up and down the hierarchy, but in the interests of efficiency, lateral communication (between people on the same level in the organisation) should also take place, provided that the communication process is properly supervised.
10 Order – both materials and labour should be managed in an orderly way.
11 Equity – people should be treated both justly and kindly.

12 Stability of tenure of personnel – people need to be secure in their job tenure in order to give of their best.

13 Initiative – creating conditions in which employees can give of their best and show initiative is in the best interests of the organisation.

14 Esprit de corps – managers should ensure that employees work well together as a co-ordinated team.

Properly applied these principles should create a sound system of business administration. Fayol's approach involves the establishment of rigid hierarchies and is consistent with the view of the organisation as a machine operated along scientific principles. However, his approach is not devoid of humanity, and several of the principles demonstrate an awareness of the importance of creating conditions in which people can give of their best. Fayol's theories about management are firmly rooted in his own practice and experience.

Several of Fayol's principles have implications for management and cost accounting. For example, the line of authority suggests the need for accountability by departments within an organisation to more senior managers. Such accountability could be achieved by the submission of formal reports on matters such as costs incurred and outputs achieved. The principle of order applied to materials and labour also suggests accountability and the need for formalised internal reporting.

Another key thinker on management issues of the early twentieth century was Max Weber, a sociologist of wide-ranging interests. His publications include works on sociology, religion, politics, capitalism and economics, but also on **bureaucracy** which is the element of particular interest in the context of organisations and management. While Taylor and Fayol were principally involved in the prescription of managerial methods, Weber's theories serve rather to explain the workings of bureaucracy. As Puxty (1986) points out, the term 'bureaucracy' these days generally has a pejorative meaning, but Weber did not use the term in this sense. In his writing, 'bureaucracy' describes a systematic approach to management involving a series of rules and procedures. The management of businesses was only one of a range of possible bureaucratic contexts – Weber was also concerned with government and ecclesiastical authorities.

Bureaucracy
(in the sense used by Max Weber) a systematic approach to management involving a series of rules and procedures

The human element

Although Taylor's scientific management theories identified the individual (whether manager or worker) as the key element in increasing productivity, the application of his theories was regarded as inhumane, and tending to lead to confrontation and conflict. Fayol's principles and Weber's theories relating to bureaucracy do not ignore the human element, but both are concerned with hierarchy and rationality. The theories of Taylor, Fayol and Weber are generally identified with the concept of the organisation as a machine. In due course, however, this concept was challenged. According to Scott (2004): 'In reaction to these technocratic versions, social scientists entered the workplace during the 1930s and 1940s, talked to and observed participants, and began to challenge the conception of organisation as dominated by rational, instrumental behaviour' (p. 2). An important protagonist in the development of the human relations approach was an Australian researcher, Elton Mayo.

In the 1920s and 1930s he conducted with colleagues an extensive research programme at the Hawthorne Works, part of an American energy company. An early set of experiments were conducted at the request of management as part of an attempt to combat poor productivity and worker dissatisfaction. One set of experiments tested whether or not changing the level of illumination provided in rooms where workers assembled telephones would aid productivity. The workers were divided into two groups, a control group whose level of illumination would remain unchanged, and an experimental group which was subject to altered levels of illumination. The study yielded the unexpected result that productivity increased in both groups. The level of illumination was proven to be irrelevant. The conclusion drawn from the experiments was that participants' behaviour had changed purely because of their involvement in the experiment. According to Haslam (2004), an organisational psychologist [Note: this section of the chapter draws extensively upon Haslam's account, and explanation, of Mayo's work]: 'the "Hawthorne effect" has become a widely recognized phenomenon in psychological research – referring to the capacity for peoples' behaviour to change as a result of their participation in research, rather than as a result of the nature of the research' (p. 9).

> **Hawthorne effect** describes the phenomenon, commonly noted in psychological research, where people's behaviour changes when they are under observation as part of a research project

Subsequent research by Mayo and colleagues at Hawthorne examined the effects of changing other working conditions, for example, introducing regular rest periods. As with the illumination experiment, productivity increased and working relationships improved, but these effects were proven to be unrelated to the changes in conditions themselves. The factor that made the difference was what Haslam (2004) refers to as 'the changing *state of relations* between management and the workers'. The experiments had the unlooked for effect of helping to build effective teams and helped to create feelings of involvement and commitment amongst workers.

The Hawthorne experiments did much to establish a new approach to thinking about the nature of organisations and the people who work in them. The work of Mayo and others suggested that the view of the organisation as a machine and the people who work in them as machine components was overly simplistic. People and, therefore, their organisations, are much more complicated.

Managers could be helped to be more effective by being aware of the Hawthorne effect when building teams and setting up lines of authority and reporting. Implications for management accounting include, for example, the advisability of taking people's need for involvement into account when setting targets. Effective reporting may need to involve non-financial information in order to capture the human element of activities. This would be especially important in those organisations (the majority in many countries) that rely for their success on intellectual capital and the successful interaction of people.

Summary: two ways of thinking about the organisation

By the middle of the twentieth century, then, two distinct ways emerged of thinking about the organisation. Selznick (1948) characterised these as follows: 'On the one hand, any concrete organisational system is an *economy*;

at the same time, it is an *adaptive social structure'* (Selznick's emphasis) (pp. 25–26). Viewed as an economy, the function of the organisation is to use the scarce resources available to it in as effective and efficient a manner as possible. To this end, rational systems, such as cost and management techniques, can be devised which allow managers to control the activities of the organisation. This is the view advocated by Taylorism and scientific management theory of the organisation as machine. The alternative view of the organisation, however, recognises additional layers of complexity because of the social and psychological factors that are inevitably involved whenever people work together. The formal systems of an organisation cast individuals in designated roles; however, as Selznick points out, individuals do not operate in this way:

'From the standpoint of organizations as a formal system, persons are viewed functionally, in respect to their *roles*, as participants in assigned segments of the cooperative system. But in fact individuals have a propensity to resist depersonalization, to spill over the boundaries of their segmentary roles, to participate as *wholes'* (p. 26).

Perrow (1973), in a classic (and very readable) paper, identifies a similar polarity between views of the organisation which he describes as the '**mechanical school**' and the '**human relations school**' of theory. The first paragraph of his paper is as follows:

'From the beginning, the forces of light and forces of darkness have polarized the field of organizational analysis, and the struggle has been protracted and inconclusive. The forces of darkness have been represented by the mechanical school of organizational theory – those who treat the organization as a machine. This school characterises organizations in terms of such things as:

- centralised authority
- clear lines of authority
- specialization and expertise
- marked division of labour
- rules and regulations
- clear separation of staff and line.

The forces of light, which by mid-twentieth century came to be characterized as the human relations school, emphasizes people rather than machines, accommodations rather than machine-like precision, and draws its inspiration from biological systems rather than engineering systems. It has emphasized such things as:

- delegation of authority
- employee autonomy
- trust and openness
- concerns with the "whole person"
- interpersonal dynamics.'

Mechanical school
in organisation theory, those who treat the organisation as a machine. This contrasts with the 'human relations school' of theory

Human relations school
in organisation theory, those who emphasise the role of people in organisations, contrasted with the 'mechanical school' of theorists who treat the organisation as a machine

Perrow proceeds to examine these characterisations thoroughly, in the light of subsequent developments in organisational research which challenged both approaches. Organisations, he concludes, are extremely complex and variable. In some types of organisation the work is routine and predictable and thus they lend themselves to highly structured and bureaucratic management styles, but some organisations will respond better to different approaches.

Naturally, cost and management accounting has been associated with the 'economic' or 'mechanical' school of organisation theory. It lends itself to organisational situations in which activities are predictable, repetitive and structured. Where the organisational environment changes rapidly, where products and services are variable and fast changing, it is more difficult to define a distinct role for cost and management accounting. The lack of a distinct role was referred to in Chapter 1, where some of the criticisms of management accounting that emerged in the 1980s were noted. Although there have been many interesting recent developments in the area, the relevance of much management accounting is still open to query.

Recent trends in organisation and management theories

The changing nature of economic activity in the developed world

Although Perrow's views of the organisation retain much of their validity, there have, clearly, been enormous changes in organisations in the period of over 30 years that has elapsed since the publication of the paper cited above. Highly developed economies such as those of the USA and Western Europe have witnessed a huge change in the nature of their industrial economies with a move away from manufacturing and towards service industries. The table below illustrates the point.

Value added in agriculture and industry as a percentage of total value added

	1974	1984	1994	2004
France	25.8	23.0	18.4	15.8
Germany	36.8	32.4	25.9	25.0
Japan	33.2	30.9	25.0	22.7*
Spain	32.7	28.0	22.1	18.5
UK	32.9	33.0	25.6	25.3
US	27.9	27.1	22.2	17.4

*This figure for Japan is for 2003.
Source of information: OECD Factbook 2005, available online at www.oecd.org. In the countries selected for comparison, agriculture is a relatively insignificant factor, and the decline in the percentage of total value added is largely attributable to a decline in industrial activity.

The trend for many years has been for developed countries to lose their manufacturing capacity, which has been gradually transferred to developing countries where wage costs are much lower. The bulk of GDP in developed countries is now derived from the provision of services. The changing nature of economic activity has an effect on the nature of management and cost accounting practice. Cost accounting practice was developed in large-scale enterprises, principally concerned with the manufacture of goods from raw materials utilising labour and machinery for the conversion process. Such processes are increasingly irrelevant to the economic activity of many of the world's major economies (although they continue to be highly relevant in some national environments). The type of information required for planning, control and decision-making purposes may vary widely across service industries, and it is perhaps less easy now than it was to consider management accounting as a set of unvarying techniques that can be applied in a wide range of institutional contexts.

Changing organisational boundaries

Organisational boundary theory is concerned with the establishment of limits between the organisation and the environment in which it operates. Scott (2004) points out that 'in recent decades the boundaries of organisations have become more open and flexible' (p. 10). He gives the examples of staff working under diverse contractual arrangements (temporary, seconded or on contract), teams and project groups incorporating members from independent firms, organisations entering into partnerships and alliances with others. He also describes the trend towards externalisation where, for example, services that were formerly carried out by the organisation are now contracted out to other organisations. Services such as cleaning, data handling, customer enquiries, information technology management, accounting and property management which would at one time have been service divisions within an organisation are nowadays frequently transferred beyond organisational boundaries. Such externalisation has important implications for management; rather than directly managing a diverse range of services, they are now more likely to be responsible for the processes involved in handling, tendering, monitoring and controlling a varied set of contractual arrangements. In consequence there are important implications for management and cost accounting: for example, a proposal to contract out services that were formerly performed in-house will require detailed management information about the alternatives (e.g. contract-out to Contractor A, or Contractor B, or retain the service in-house).

Scott (2004) also identifies a change in 'power processes'. The hierarchical organisational structures described by Weber and prescribed by Fayol are becoming obsolete in many commercial organisations because of the blurring of organisational boundaries described above. He says: 'As the operational boundaries of firms and agencies extend outwards to include temporary workers and contractors, managers are obliged to learn to manage horizontally (without authority) as well as vertically' (p. 12). Burns and Vaivio (2001) summarise some of the recent changes that have implications for management accounting: '. . . business environments exhibit a variety of structures and processes – including flat and horizontal organisational forms, multidimensional matrix structures, networks of "virtual" organisations and self-directed work teams' (p. 389). Management and control in such circumstances become more problematic; it is more a case of juggling competing interests than of exerting control over people and processes. Similarly, accounting for control is likely to present difficult challenges, for example because of the problems involved in gathering relevant information for decision-making.

Motivation and incentives

So far, this chapter has examined the organisation and its management as a whole. This section of the chapter turns to an examination of managerial motivations and incentives as they affect the individual. Theories of motivation and incentives are relevant in the context of management accounting as they help to predict and explain managerial behaviour in the essential functions of planning, controlling and decision-making.

Agency theory

Agency Theory
in the organisational context, this theory proposes a relationship between a principal (the provider of funds) and the agent (the person who manages those funds)

Utility
in an economic context, a measurement of consumption of goods and services. Agency theory assumes that all individuals want to maximise their utility, that is, their ability to consume

Agency theory proposes a relationship between a principal, and an agent acting on behalf of the principal. The principal in the corporate context is the investor in shares, who takes no part in the management of the business, while the agent is the manager who runs the business on behalf of the investor. Agency theory assumes that both the principal and agent seek to 'maximise their utility'. **Utility** in the economic context is a measurement of consumption of goods and services. It is assumed that all individuals want to maximise their ability to consume. In non-economic terms it means that they want to earn as much as possible for their work (this may be in money or in goods and services or other types of advantage like occupying the best office), and that this is their sole motivation. If agency theory correctly reflects normal human preferences, it means that the agent (manager) will act in the best interests of the principal (investor) only where it suits his or her own purposes to do so. Agency theory assumes that costs (known as 'agency costs') are an inevitable part of the agency relationship. In the particular context of the investor/manager relationship, the production of periodic financial statements, and their verification by auditors, represents an agency cost. Other agency costs may include the provision of incentives to persuade managers to act in a way that promotes the interests of the principal.

Agency theory predicts that managers will act in their own best interests at all times and that they are motivated purely by economic considerations. In the context of management accounting, economic self-interest could have, for example, the following adverse consequences:

- Managers might set themselves easy targets in budgets so that they can obtain performance related rewards.
- Managers might make exaggerated predictions of a proposed project's success in order to secure the funds to carry it out, and thus enhance their reputation.
- Divisional managers could exaggerate the results of their division in order to gain profit-related pay, or enhance their promotion prospects.

Agency theory can be criticised on the grounds that it embodies an incomplete reflection of human motivation. It may be argued that people are not motivated purely or even mostly by economic incentives. Other factors that could affect attitudes to work and relationships include personal morality, adherence to professional ethical codes and motivation through other factors such as achieving job satisfaction. The incomplete nature of the economic approach has been reflected in the work of many researchers.

McGregor's theories

Douglas McGregor developed two models of human behaviour which encapsulated alternative sets of beliefs about the nature of workers, which he identified as **Theory X and Theory Y**. The principal features of these theories are as follows:

Theory X: The average human being inherently dislikes work and will seek to avoid it if possible. People must therefore be controlled and threatened in order to make them work. Most people prefer to be told what to do and dislike taking responsibility.

Theory Y: Control and punishment are not the only way to make people work. Ideally, people want to use their imagination and creativity, and they are willing, in appropriate conditions, to accept responsibility. People like work and are willing to do it. Self-direction and self-actualisation through work are achievable.

The first set of beliefs assumes that people are naturally idle, and that they require crude incentives to make them engage in activity. Theory Y, on the other hand, reflects a more complicated, and optimistic, view of human nature. Theory X can be identified with the scientific management and economics-based theories described earlier: people must be made to do things, and effective incentives embody threats or tangible rewards, or both. Theory Y suggests an altogether more subtle approach to human relations and management. The implications of these theories for management accounting include the following:

- Control systems have to be carefully designed in order to elicit positive responses from the workforce;

- If theory Y is applied to managers themselves, their motivations may be more subtle than the purely economic one inherent in agency theory. A system of managerial incentives should reflect this complexity;

- Purely financial systems of 'keeping score' within the organisation may be too crude. Non-financial performance indicators are likely to be of importance too.

Herzberg's theories

One of Frederick Herzberg's (1968) fundamental insights into the issue of motivation was that 'the factors involved in producing job satisfaction (and motivation) are separate and distinct from the factors that lead to job dissatisfaction' (p. 56). He divided human needs into two different sets: one set derived from basic animal needs such as the need to avoid pain and hunger (e.g. by earning a salary sufficient to prevent such adverse outcomes).

Theory X and Theory Y

two models of human behaviour proposed by McGregor. Theory X proposes that people actively dislike working and therefore must be controlled and directed in order to make them work. Theory Y proposes that people are self-motivated, will accept responsibility, and do not need to be threatened or punished to make them work

He called this set of needs 'hygiene factors': those factors that led to the avoidance of dissatisfaction. The second set of needs were related to the ability to achieve, and to experience psychological growth: these growth and motivator factors include recognition, responsibility and advancement. Herzberg demonstrated through empirical research work that the growth and motivator factors were responsible for job satisfaction. The existence of other factors such as good working conditions, good relationships with supervisors and reward in the form of salary could prevent dissatisfaction, but could not (or would not necessarily) promote satisfaction. Practical applications of the theory reported by Herzberg involved the 'loading' of existing jobs with increased opportunities for responsibility and personal achievement, for example, by removing some controls, and granting additional authority to the individual.

The adoption of job enrichment programmes which emphasise individual autonomy and responsibility has some obvious implications for managerial control. Herzberg's theory suggests that control systems should be more diffuse and subtle rather than simply authoritarian, in order to be effective. Hierarchical control systems might need to be deconstructed and the lines of reporting and responsibility might therefore be less rigid.

Incentives and motivation: summary

A striking feature of many theories (and not just those related to organisations, or incentives, or motivating factors) is that they are expressed as polarities, inviting a judgement as to whether one or the other is 'correct' or in some way preferable. Theoretical models reduce a complex reality to a set of relatively simple propositions and there is a danger of over-simplification. Students may be thinking by now: 'yes, but money is important' (and especially to students who tend to be impoverished and working, if they work at all for money, in minimum wage employment). As Puxty (1986) says: 'There is a danger in discussing theories like this that some very basic things get missed. Your employer can enrich your job all he likes: but if the factory over the road is paying twice the wages, you will likely leave and go there' (pp. 174–5).

Work is more important for some people than others. It is not necessarily the primary means of self-actualisation in life; people may find the true expression of themselves in, say, birdwatching or charitable activities undertaken in their spare time. Work may be part of a compromise – a means to support the rich and meaningful aspects of their existence.

Another problem is that models describing opposites tend to feel too uncompromising and extreme. It's unlikely that many people really conform to the rational economic utility maximiser that is integral to agency theory. A lot of us find that we're quite keen to maximise monetary reward some of the time, but that other less tangible factors are also important. We don't necessarily have consistent attitudes at all times in our working lives. Lewis (1989), musing on his decision to stop being a bond trader earning ludicrous sums of money, observes:

'For me . . . the belief in the making of dollars crumbled; the proposition that the more money you earn the better the life you are leading was refuted by too much hard evidence to the contrary . . . . The funny thing is that I was largely unaware of how heavily influenced I was by the money belief until it had vanished'.

And that's another thing: our own true motivations may be hidden to us not to be revealed until much later when we take the opportunity for reflection.

However, theoretical models are often useful as a means of clarifying thinking and reducing complex realities to a manageable set of propositions. The brief summary of a few motivational theories provided in this chapter hardly begins to address a complex and well-researched topic. Those wishing to read further could try the chapters on motivation in Haslam (2004) and Puxty (1986).

Chapter summary

This chapter has discussed some theories about the organisation and management that should provide useful background for the study of management accounting that follows in the next few chapters of the book. In order to help to make the links, various examples and suggestions about the implications for management accounting have been made in respect of the theories discussed.

The theories identified above are well-known classics, which are referred to by many textbooks. For this reason they may well be encountered in other parts of students' programmes of study, although they may be dealt with from a slightly different perspective. Those who wish to read more about any of them will find that there is plenty of material available.

Management and cost accounting involves a good deal of work with figures, as we are about to find out, but it's useful and may well make the subject more interesting, to bear in mind the human, social and psychological perspectives that have been covered briefly here.

References

Burns, J. and Vaivio, J. (2001) 'Management accounting change', *Management Accounting Research*, 12, pp. 389–402.

Haslam, S.A. (2004) *Psychology in organisations: the social identity approach*, (2nd edition), Sage: London.

Herzberg, F. (1968) 'One more time: how do you motivate employees?', *Harvard Business Review*, January–February, pp. 53–62.

Lewis, M. (1989) *Liar's poker*, Coronet Books: London.

Perrow, C. (1973) 'The short and glorious history of organisational theory', *Organisational Dynamics*, Summer, Vol. 2, Issue 1, pp 2–15.

Puxty, A.G. (1986) *Organisation and management: an accountant's perspective*, Pitman: London.

Scott, W.R. (2004) 'Reflections on a half-century of organisational sociology', *Annual Review of Sociology*, 30, pp. 1–21.

Selznick, P. (1948) 'Foundations of the theory of organisation', *American Sociological Review*, Vol. 13, No. 1, February, pp. 25–35.

SELF-ASSESSMENT EXERCISES

The exercises following most of the chapters in this book are divided into those for which answers are provided at the end of the book, and those whose answers are available to lecturers via the book's website. However, the exercises below often do not have a definitively correct answer. Many of them might best be attempted via discussion in a group. Some guidance is provided at the end of the book, but it is not intended to be comprehensive.

2.1 Taking an organisation that you know about as an example (preferably an organisation where you have undertaken paid employment) discuss the extent to which you think Fayol's principles of management apply in modern organisations.

2.2 The quotation from Perrow's (1973) paper given in the chapter characterises organisations in two distinct ways: what Perrow refers to as the 'mechanical' and 'human relations' school of thinking. Identify which of the two approaches seems more valid to you, and discuss the reasons for your choice.

2.3 BigCorp runs a chain of fast food establishments. The company's finance director has suggested to other board members that it might be cost-effective to close down the in-house cleaning department which organises the employment of cleaning staff for the restaurant outlets. Both the cleaning department administrative staff and the cleaners themselves are employed on permanent contracts. Instead, the work could be contracted out to one of the large national firms of cleaning contractors.

Identify the costs that might be relevant in comparing the two options, and in reaching a decision on whether or not to contract out the cleaning. Identify and briefly discuss any non-financial factors that should be taken into account.

2.4 Which of the McGregor theories about human behaviour most closely accords with your own view of human behaviour? Explain the reasons for your choice.

2.5 What are the implications for management and cost accounting if it is assumed that agency theory accurately describes managerial motivation?

Product and Services Costing

3

Aim of the chapter

To achieve an understanding of how costs are gathered and attached to cost objects, and knowledge of the terminology and classifications used in costing.

Learning outcomes

After reading the chapter and completing the exercises at the end, students should:

- Recognise and understand a range of basic costing terminology.
- Be able to classify costs into direct and indirect costs.
- Understand the build-up of materials, labour and production overhead into full production cost.
- Be able to apportion costs between cost centres.
- Be able to calculate and apply suitable overhead absorption rates.
- Understand some important issues in relation to the costing of services.

Introduction

This chapter introduces some aspects of cost and management accounting practice, and thus provides a significant contrast to Chapter 2 which discussed exclusively theoretical issues. As this chapter develops, however, students will find that the discussion of practice is expressly linked to some of the theoretical issues identified in the previous chapter.

Chapter 1 introduced the CIMA definition of cost accounting, the first part of which is the 'Gathering of cost information and its attachment to cost objects . . .'. This chapter and Chapter 4 examine these processes. This chapter deals with the more traditional approach to costing, whereas Chapter 4 will examine a more recent innovation in costing practice: Activity-Based Costing (ABC).

The first section of this chapter defines the term 'cost object' and examines the reasons why managers might find it useful to be able to identify costs. The chapter then proceeds to examine a range of relevant techniques for the costing of products, including costs of materials, labour and overheads. The final section of the chapter examines the particular problems and issues associated with the costing of services, as opposed to products, and the application of costing techniques in a public sector context.

Costing in business

Cost object
any product, activity or
service that requires
costing

Costing involves the gathering of cost information and its attachment to cost objects. A cost object is any item or activity which requires costing; any product or service provided by a business could be a cost object. Costing can be useful to management in many aspects of its roles of planning, assessing alternatives, controlling activities and monitoring outcomes:

Planning – in forecasting future commercial transactions it is necessary to have some idea of the cost of products and services in order to be able to estimate reliably future outflows of resources.

Assessing alternatives and decision-making – for example, according to Baxter (2005) costing 'acts as a handy guide to many decisions. Thus, it can be compared with a product's sale price; if cost of a unit is less than price, the product may be worth making' (p. 89).

Monitoring outcomes – information about expected and actual costs of a product or service is required in order to effectively monitor outcomes.

In addition, product costing has traditionally been used to provide essential inputs into financial accounting and reporting. For example, the valuation of inventories in a manufacturing business typically requires detailed information about product costs, especially where work-in-progress constitutes part of the value of inventories.

The next major section of the chapter examines the techniques involved in costing products.

Product costing

In a manufacturing environment there are three basic components of cost:

- materials cost
- labour cost
- production overheads.

Direct costs
those costs directly
associated with the
manufacturing process

Direct expenses
direct costs other
than direct materials
and direct labour costs

Indirect costs
those costs which are not
directly identifiable with
a unit of production

Direct inputs into the manufacturing process usually include both materials and labour costs. Production overheads are indirect inputs. They are costs involved in running a production facility but which are not themselves identifiable with individual items produced; they may include both indirect labour and indirect materials costs.

Costs are often classified as direct (direct materials, direct labour and any other direct expenses and indirect (overheads)). If in doubt about whether a cost is direct or indirect, ask the question: 'Can this cost be traced directly to the product?'

The following example will help to illustrate the point.

EXAMPLE 3.1

© geogphotos / Alamy

GHP Limited, a company based in New Zealand, manufactures greetings cards. The production process involves the following stages:

1 a design is produced
2 the design is printed onto card in a run of 1000 cards per production run
3 the card is cut and folded
4 other processes such as embossing, gilding and over-printing are then undertaken, depending upon the design of the card
5 the cards are matched with envelopes of a suitable size
6 each card and envelope is individually packaged in a cellophane wrapper.

What are the direct costs involved in this process?

Direct costs

Direct materials

Materials costs include: the cost of card, ink, possibly metal-leaf, envelopes and cellophane and, perhaps, a label.

Direct labour

Labour is required to: set up and operate the printing machine (this is a computerised process, but it involves some input of time), operate the machine which cuts and folds the card, package the card together with the envelope (at GHP Limited this is a completely manual process).

▶

Direct expense

GHP Limited buys in designs from freelance designers. The company pays the designer NZ$100 for the design under an agreement which allows it to produce 1000 cards of each design. The production of each card therefore includes a direct expense of 10¢ per card.

Indirect production costs (overheads)

Indirect production costs include all of those costs of running the production facility which cannot be directly identified with units of production. These would include such items as:

Factory rental

Production supervisor's wages

Factory cleaning costs

Maintenance and repair of factory and machinery

Other indirect costs (overheads)

As well as indirect costs incurred in running the production facility, GHP incurs many other costs. For example:

Administration salaries

Rental of the office

Depreciation of the office computer

Salespersons' salaries

All of the costs taken together add up to the total cost of running the business, summarised as follows:

Direct materials
+
Direct labour   } DIRECT COSTS
+
Direct expenses
=

PRIME COST
+

Production overheads
=
PRODUCTION COST } INDIRECT COSTS
+
Other overheads
=

TOTAL COST

Note that the terms 'indirect costs' and 'overheads' mean the same thing. Either term can be used. '**Prime cost**' is a term sometimes used in practice: it simply refers to the total of direct costs (direct materials, direct labour and direct expenses).

SELF-TEST QUESTION 3.1

Beeching Plumstead has a factory which produces babies' pushchairs. The following is a list of some of the costs which the company incurs:

Canvas material	
Metal spokes for wheels	
Spare parts for sewing machine repairs	
Advertising expenditure	
Machine oil	
Electricity bill for factory	
Wages of assembly line workers	
Wages of factory canteen staff	
Wages of assembly line supervisor	
Secretary's salary	
Delivery vehicle depreciation	

Classify each item of expense as one of the following:

Direct labour

Direct materials

Direct expenses

Indirect production overheads

Other indirect overheads

The next example fits some figures into the structure:

EXAMPLE 3.2

Julienne Benoit SARL is a company which produces socks from a small rented factory space. In the month ending 31 August 2008 it incurs the following costs:

	€
Depreciation of knitting machines	420
Knitting machine repair	68
Machine operators' wages	6330
Wool	4850
Sticky labels for socks	93

Plastic ties for sock pairing	133
Factory rental	1230
Electricity costs – factory	216
Electricity costs – office	38
Part-time secretary's wages	540
Office stationery and supplies	21
Factory cleaner's wages	123
Telephone – office	83
Delivery costs	436
Other office costs	214
Other factory costs	130

Required: rearrange the information given above into a cost statement for August 2008.

Julienne Benoit SARL: cost statement for the month ending 31 August 2008

	€	€
Direct materials		
Wool	4 850	
Sticky labels for socks	93	
Plastic ties for sock pairing	133	
		5 076
Direct labour – Machine operators' wages		6 330
Prime cost		11 406
Production overheads		
Depreciation of knitting machines	420	
Knitting machine repair	68	
Factory rental	1 230	
Electricity costs – factory	216	
Factory cleaner's wages	123	
Other factory costs	130	
		2 187
Production cost		13 593
Other overheads		
Electricity costs – office	38	
Part-time secretary's wages	540	
Office stationery and supplies	21	
Telephone – office	83	
Delivery costs	436	
Other office costs	214	
		1 332
Total costs		14 925

Prime cost
the total of all direct costs associated with manufacture

Product costs
those costs relating to the production of goods or services for sale by a business

Period costs
costs incurred during the accounting period

Cost classification: product and period costs

Another way of looking at costs is to classify them as product or period costs.

Product costs are those related to production of goods or services for sale by the business. Using the terminology we have already established, product costs include direct and indirect production costs.

Period costs are those costs which are incurred in the period of account, for example, salaries of sales and marketing personnel.

Note that the principle of accruals or matching operates in management accounting, just as in financial accounting. For example cost of sales used in management accounting must be adjusted for opening and closing inventories. In a manufacturing business, this means bringing forward opening inventories and carrying forward closing inventories, both valued at production cost. Next we will consider product costs in more detail.

Approaches to costing

Absorption costing
the costing of products and services to include both direct and indirect costs of production

Job costing
an accumulation of costs relating to one identifiable job or task

Product costing
the accumulation of costs relating to the production of a large number of identical units

Batch costing
the accumulation of costs relating to a batch of identical products

Cost unit
an item of production or a group of products or a service for which it is useful to have product cost information

In order to keep track of costs, to be able to plan and control business activity and to be able to value work in progress and finished goods inventories, costs should be allocated to products. Work in progress and finished goods inventories are carried forward to the next accounting period at production cost (i.e. including materials, direct labour and production overheads costs). This accumulation of costs is known as **absorption costing**.

Where the cost information relates to a single piece of work chargeable to one client or customer the accumulation of costs may help in establishing the price at which the goods or services are to be invoiced. In costing terminology this is known as **job costing**.

Often in manufacturing industries goods of a generic type are produced to replenish general inventories of finished goods. Costing information is gathered for each type of product manufactured. In costing terminology this is known as **product costing**.

Sometimes in manufacturing industries it is appropriate to produce goods in batches or production runs of convenient sizes. Costs are allocated to each batch or run. In costing terminology this is known as **batch costing**.

All product and service costing involves the allocation of costs to cost units. A **cost unit** is an item of production or a group of products or a service for which it is useful to have product cost information. Three examples of cost units follow, each illustrating a different type of costing method.

EXAMPLE 3.3

Clement is a sole trader who owns a small factory. He and his team of skilled workers produce high quality furniture to order. He has been given an order for 12 dining chairs by a luxury hotel chain. Clement keeps a job card record for each order on which he records prime cost details.

▶

This order (Code ref: 3223) has had the following materials and labour booked to it:

Direct materials	Booked
Mahogany	18 pieces
Seat padding	12 pieces
Leather cloth	6 metres

Direct labour	Booked
Grade 1	115 hours
Grade 2	86 hours

Mahogany is purchased at €36 per piece, each piece of seat padding costs €3.50 and the leather cloth is €42.00 per metre.

Clement employs two grades of labour: grade 1 for which direct labour cost is €8.50 and grade 2, for which direct labour cost is €9.25.

The job cost record for Job number 3223 would be as follows:

Job number 3223 12 dining chairs	Cost	€	€ total
Direct materials			
Mahogany	18 @ €36	648.00	
Seat padding	12 @ €3.50	42.00	
Leather cloth	6 metres @ €42.00 per m.	252.00	
			942.00
Direct labour			
Grade 1	115 hours @ €8.50	977.50	
Grade 2	86 hours @ €9.25	795.50	
			1773.00
TOTAL			2715.00

This example illustrates job costing.

EXAMPLE 3.4

Peirce Waterworth plc manufactures a range of components for the motor industry. The company keeps a constant inventory of its 100 or so most popular lines so that it can respond immediately to orders. For example, once inventories of component XL046, an air filter, fall to 50 units, production is scheduled to replenish the inventories of the component. The input of materials is logged, and the number of hours and minutes that people spend operating the machines. These are charged to production of the XL046 and the inventory value is built up by successive inputs of materials, labour and overheads.

This example illustrates product costing.

EXAMPLE 3.5

In the example of the greeting cards company used earlier (see example 3.1), a production run of 1000 cards was assumed. This is likely to be quite a reasonable size for a cost unit. Treating each individual card as a cost unit would involve a pointlessly detailed set of calculations. Given that the 1000 cards are identical and are all produced in one run, the cost unit in this case will be the run of 1000 cards. Having established the costs for the cost unit, the cost of an individual card is easily calculated by dividing total costs by 1000.

This example illustrates batch costing.

The next three sub-sections of the chapter will examine the allocation of the three broad areas of cost – materials, labour and production overheads – to cost units. This is illustrated in the context of a manufacturing environment.

Materials costs

Inventory
items bought by a business to sell on to somebody else, or to process or transform in some way to make saleable goods

Raw materials are bought in and an **inventory** maintained as necessary in order to ensure that shortages, which would slow up production, do not occur. Direct materials are issued to production in appropriate quantities and the cost is allocated to the appropriate cost unit.

How do we establish the cost of raw materials transferred into production?

The answer to this question is not, perhaps, as straightforward as it seems, especially where there is a fairly large volume of identical items moving in and out of inventory, and where prices are changing. Businesses usually employ one or other of the two following valuation conventions in dealing with this matter.

First In, First Out (FIFO)

This convention assumes that the items which have been in inventory the longest are the first to move out into production. (Note that this is a theoretical assumption for valuation purposes only – it may not be born out by the actual physical movements in inventory.)

Weighted average cost (AVCO)

Under this convention the value of each individual item of inventory is a weighted average of the value of all items in inventory.

EXAMPLE 3.6

Parben et Cie runs a business manufacturing pencils. These are placed in presentation boxes which hold 48 pencils. The boxes are purchased from the same supplier in batches of between 100 and 200. The inventory record for February 2008 shows the following details of deliveries with, it can be assumed, relatively few employees. In more complex businesses, labour time booking is often a quite elaborate procedure involving careful observation and record-keeping. A production operative may work on a range of different cost units during a day, and a method must be found for ensuring that the work is accurately booked. If errors are made product costs will be misstated and incorrect decisions may result.

In the previous chapter it was noted that cost accounting was associated with the 'economic' or 'mechanical' school of organisation theory. Certain aspects of cost accounting, as they relate to labour, are allied to scientific management thinking. Taylorism involved close observation and timing of routine tasks in manufacturing processes, the type of observation that later became known as 'time and motion' study. If costing is to be undertaken successfully in complex manufacturing processes that involve the use of direct labour, some level of time and motion study is likely to be involved. However, managers need to be aware of the risks and potentially demotivating effects that can result from treating people as if they were machines.

The following are some of the practical issues and complexities which may arise in respect of the identification and allocation of direct labour.

Employee performs a combination of direct and indirect labour tasks

An employee may spend part of his or her time on a production line engaged in specific aspects of production which can be allocated to cost units. However, in addition he or she may have more general tasks, such as cleaning machinery, sweeping up, engaging in routine maintenance and so on. Therefore, it may be necessary to allocate time between direct and indirect labour tasks.

Variation in methods of payment

There are several ways of paying employees. Usually there is a basic rate element, but in addition there may be special payments for working overtime or unsocial hours. Sometimes, for example in garment production, direct labour employees are paid piece rates for work (a fixed amount, say, for each shirt sewn); in addition they may be paid a bonus for achieving a particularly high level of output.

Idle or non-productive time

If a machine breaks down or there is some other kind of hitch in the production process employees may not be able to be employed in productive activity. This is sometimes known as idle time. Employees are entitled to be paid for the time, but how should it be treated?

It is often the case that the management accountant takes into account all of the complexities of labour costs, averages them, and produces an hourly rate for each grade of labour, which can then be applied to all direct labour time spent in production.

EXAMPLE 3.7

This example demonstrates the allocation of direct material and labour costs to a particular job.

Barker and Clyde produce machine parts for the airline industry. They have an order from an aircraft manufacturer for 150 units of component BYA570. This work is assigned job code V477848.

This involves the following transfers from raw materials inventories:

650 kg of material V, valued at AVCO which is currently €3.60 per kilo

125 kg of material G, valued at AVCO which is currently €5.50 per kilo

Three grades of direct labour are involved:

Grade 7, which is to be recorded at the rate of €5.50 per hour

Grade 13, recorded at the rate of €7.60 per hour

Grade 14, recorded at the rate of €7.80 per hour.

The cost accountant collects information about direct labour time spent from the factory and summarises it onto computer input forms, which identify the job codes, labour grade and hours spent.

When the job is completed the computer record shows the following summary for prime cost:

Job number: V477848	Date: 12.11.07		
Component number: BYA 570	Supervisor: ASHTON		
Quantity: 150 units			
		€	€
Direct material			
Material V (650kg × €3.60)		2340.00	
Material G (125kg × €5.50)		687.50	
			3027.50
Direct labour			
Grade 7 – 26.5 hours booked @ €5.50 per hour		145.75	
Grade 13 – 12 hours @ €7.60 per hour		91.20	
Grade 14 – 3.75 hours @ €7.80 per hour		29.25	
			266.20
Prime cost			3293.70

This information allows us to calculate prime cost per component:

$$\frac{€3293.70}{150} = €21.96$$

SELF-TEST QUESTION 3.3

Harvey & Cork produces photograph frames in batches of 500. The following materials and labour are booked to batch number 30453A:

100 kg of metal @ €4.50 per kilo

Paint – 2 litres of blue @ €6.80 per litre

Glass – 500 pieces at 30¢ each

22 hours of direct labour at A grade (charged at €4.80 per hour)

19 hours of direct labour at B grade (charged at €6.00 per hour)

Prepare a batch costing record to show the prime cost of batch number 30453A. What is the cost per picture frame?

Production overheads

Allocation of production overheads is one of the most difficult costing problems for the management accountant. Production overheads are part of the overall production cost, and it is usually necessary to allocate them in order to produce useful information for management and for inventory valuation. However, as we have seen, they are not directly identifiable with cost units. Where production goes through several stages, the first step in dealing with production overheads is usually to allocate them to cost centres.

Allocation to cost centres

Cost centres
functions or areas into which costs can be organised

Often, production is organised methodically into **cost centres** to which costs can be allocated. Cost centres are functions or areas into which costs can be organised.

EXAMPLE 3.8

Choremaster produces industrial cleaning machines. There are three distinct stages in the production process:

Metal machining

Brush fitting

Paint and finishing

The metal machining shop has its own full-time production supervisor. The other production supervisor employed by the company splits her time in a 60:40 ratio between the brush fitting shop and the painting and finishing shop. The cost of employing each supervisor, including benefits and employer's health insurance contribution is €17 360 per annum. (NB Production supervisors' salaries are part of the company's indirect production overheads.)

What is the allocation of supervisors' salaries to each of the three production areas?

Metal machining	17 360
Brush fitting (60% × €17 360)	10 416
Paint and finishing (40% × €17 360)	6 944

Apportionment to cost centres

In the above example the indirect cost of supervisors' salary could be allocated because precise information was available about the use of the supervisors' time. Where indirect costs cannot be allocated, they must be apportioned. Cost apportionment often involves some fairly arbitrary decisions about the split of costs between cost centres.

We will expand the Choremaster example to illustrate what is involved in cost apportionment.

EXAMPLE 3.9

Choremaster incurs the following indirect production overheads in the year ending 31 December 2007:

	€
Factory rent	33 970
Production supervisors' salaries	34 720
Canteen costs	13 440
Cleaning and other indirect labour	8 885
Factory rates	12 480
Insurance	8 760
Electricity – factory	10 770
Building maintenance	2 490
Machine maintenance and repair	3 423
Depreciation of machinery	12 220
Depreciation of canteen fixtures and fittings	1 792
Total	142 950

The indirect production overheads have to be apportioned between the three production areas: metal machining, brush fitting and painting and finishing. Usually, different methods of apportionment are used depending upon the nature of the cost. Some common approaches to apportionment are listed below:

Type of cost	Typical method of apportionment
Factory rent, rates, insurance, building maintenance, electricity, indirect labour and cleaning	Floor area
Depreciation of machinery	Machinery value
Canteen costs	Number of employees
Machinery maintenance and repair	Number of call-outs
Production supervisor's salaries	Number of employees

It is important to note that these methods of apportionment do not constitute precise rules. Much depends upon the nature of the expense, and the amount of detail that can be collected about how it is incurred. In the case of Choremaster, for example, we know that the production supervisors' salaries can be allocated neatly across the three departments. In other companies, it might not be possible to make such an allocation, and a basis of apportionment (such as number of employees, as suggested in the table above) would be more appropriate.

We need some further information in order to be able to apportion Choremaster's costs. This is given in the table below:

		Cost centre		
	Total	Metal machining	Brush fitting	Paint and finishing
Floor area (sq metres)	10 000	6 000	2 000	2 000
Number of employees	28	17	6	5
Machinery value	122 200	103 000	8 400	10 800
Maintenance and repair call-outs	7	6	0	1

We can now apportion costs to each cost centre, as follows:

Factory rent is apportioned to each cost centre on the basis of floor area. For example, the part of cost to be apportioned to the metal machining cost centre is:

$$\frac{6\ 000}{10\ 000} \times €33\ 970 = €20\ 382$$

Brush fitting:

$$\frac{2\ 000}{10\ 000} \times €33\ 970 = €6\ 794$$

Paint and finishing:

$$\frac{2\ 000}{10\ 000} \times €33\ 970 = €6\ 794$$

(Note that €20 382 + 6 794 + 6 794 = €33 970, i.e. all of the cost is apportioned.)

We can use the same approach to apportioning all the other costs:

	Basis	Total €	Cost centre		
			Metal machining €	Brush fitting €	Paint and finishing €
Factory rent	Floor area	33 970	20 382	6 794	6 794
Production supervisors' salaries	Actual	34 720	17 360	10 416	6 944
Canteen costs	Employees	13 440	8 160	2 880	2 400
Cleaning and other indirect labour	Floor area	8 885	5 331	1 777	1 777
Factory rates	Floor area	12 480	7 488	2 496	2 496
Insurance	Floor area	8 760	5 256	1 752	1 752
Electricity – factory	Floor area	10 770	6 462	2 154	2 154
Building maintenance	Floor area	2 490	1 494	498	498
Machine maintenance and repair	Call outs	3 423	2 934	–	489
Depreciation of machinery	Machinery value	12 220	10 300	840	1 080
Depreciation – canteen	Employees	1 792	1 088	384	320
Totals		142 950	86 255	29 991	26 704

SELF-TEST QUESTION 3.4

Swift Metals Limited produces machine parts. Its factory space is divided into three areas: preparation, tooling and finishing. These three functional areas are used as cost centres. Swift's management accountant has asked you to prepare a schedule showing the apportionment of the company's production overheads between the three cost centres for the year ending 31 December 2008.

The production overhead totals are as follows:

	£
Factory costs (rental, insurance, cleaning etc.)	700 000
Canteen costs	18 496
Machinery depreciation	17 650
Machinery maintenance and repair	2 961
Supervisory salaries	23 358
	762 465

Factory costs are to be apportioned on the basis of floor area.

Canteen costs and supervisory salaries are to be apportioned on the basis of number of employees.

Machinery depreciation is to be apportioned on the basis of the net book value of machinery used in each cost centre.

Machinery maintenance and repair is to be apportioned on the basis of the number of call-outs.

Relevant data is included in the following table:

	Total	Preparation	Tooling	Finishing
		Cost centre		
Floor area (sq metres)	20 000	7 000	9 000	4 000
Number of employees	34	16	12	6
Machinery value	176 500	26 000	112 000	38 500
Maintenance and repair call-outs	9	2	6	1

Prepare the overhead apportionment schedule for the management accountant.

Overhead absorption

In the previous sub-section of this chapter we examined the allocation and apportionment of costs to cost centres. This allows us to say, for example, that overheads of €29 991 were allocated to Choremaster's brush fitting cost centre, but we are no closer to identifying the total production overhead cost of an individual cost unit.

Overhead absorption
a method of allocating an appropriate portion of production overheads to cost units

We need to find some way of transferring overhead costs to cost units. Traditionally, the way this has been done in manufacturing industries is via overhead absorption, a method of allocating an appropriate portion of production overheads to cost units. A logical way of doing this might be on the basis of the number of units of production. Suppose that Choremaster produces 5400 cleaning machines in the period during which it incurred total production overheads of €142 950. The total production overhead attributable to each cleaning machine could then be calculated as:

$$\frac{€142\ 950}{5\ 400} = €26.47 \text{ (rounded)}$$

Overhead absorption rate
a rate used to estimate the amount of production overhead incurred in manufacturing

€26.47 becomes the overhead absorption rate applied to each machine in respect of production overhead. It would be added to the materials and direct labour costs for each cleaning machine to arrive at a total production cost per machine. Note that this is a 'blanket' overhead rate; it is appropriate where a business produces only one product. Where there is more than one product the overhead absorption procedures become more complicated.

In this example, the information could only be calculated accurately once the accounting period was over and total costs could be summed and allocated to cost centres. Management accounting information, as we have seen, needs to be produced very quickly in order to be useful and a retrospective exercise in overhead absorption is not likely to be very helpful. For this reason, overhead absorption is done in practice on the basis of figures budgeted in advance; a budgeted overhead absorption rate is calculated and then applied to production. (Note that we will examine budgeting in more detail in Chapter 8.)

The next example will demonstrate some of the techniques involved in calculating overhead absorption rates and will examine three possible approaches to overhead absorption: number of units of production, machine hours, and labour hours.

EXAMPLE 3.10

Stahl-produkt GmBH produces large metal storage containers in one size only. The production process involves three stages:

Cutting department: large metal sheets are cut into standard sizes, and are shaped and drilled.

Assembly department: the standard pieces are attached together by screwing and welding.

Painting and finishing: the containers are smoothed down and spray painted.

Each department is treated as a cost centre.

The management accountant is working out appropriate overhead absorption rates for the next financial year (the year to 31 December 2006). She estimates that total production overheads will be €136 000, allocated as follows between the cost centres:

Cutting	€56 000
Assembly	€48 000
Painting and finishing	€32 000

Total production in units for 2009 is estimated at 16 000 containers. The management accountant has also worked out budgeted materials and labour costs per container, as follows:

Prime cost of container	€
Direct materials (metal, fixings, paint)	15.50
Direct labour:	
Cutting – 10 minutes (@ €6 per hour)	1.00
Assembly – 1 hour 30 minutes (@ €6 per hour)	9.00
Painting and finishing – 20 minutes (@ €4.50 per hour)	1.50
Total prime cost	27.00

Note that the cutting department processes are mostly mechanised; there is a relatively low input of labour. Assembly processes, by contrast, are mostly manual. The extent to which processes are labour intensive influences the choice of overhead absorption method.

The management accountant now needs to work out an overhead absorption rate to be applied to each of the three cost centres. She will use three different rates, one for each department, and each worked out on a different basis.

Cutting department: overhead rate per machine hour

Where manufacturing processes depend more upon machines than upon labour input, it is usually most appropriate to work out an overhead absorption rate based upon machine hours available. The number of machine hours is estimated by reference to factory working hours and number of machines. For example, in this case, suppose that the accountant estimates that a total of 16 000 hours of machine time will be available over the next year. The cutting department overhead for the year is estimated at €56 000. The estimated overhead absorption rate for the cutting department for 2009 will therefore be:

$$\frac{€56\ 000}{16\ 000} = €3.50 \text{ per machine hour}$$

For every machine hour used in production €3.50 will be charged in production overheads.

How many machine hours will be used to produce one container? Assuming that all of the available machine hours (16 000) are required to produce 16 000 containers, each cost unit uses up 1 machine hour. €3.50 will, therefore, be included in the production cost of a container.

Assembly department: overhead rate per labour hour

In this department the manufacturing processes are labour intensive. The accountant estimates that 24 000 direct labour hours will be used in this department in 2009. The assembly cost centre overhead for the year is estimated at €48 000. The estimated overhead absorption rate for the assembly department for 2009 will therefore be:

$$\frac{€48\ 000}{24\ 000} = €2.00 \text{ per labour hour}$$

How many assembly labour hours will be used to produce one container? Each container requires 1 hour 30 minutes in labour time. 16 000 containers would therefore require 24 000 hours (which just happens to be the number of direct labour hours available in this department). The overhead to be absorbed in respect of assembly for each cost unit will be 1.5 × €2.00 – i.e. €3.00.

Painting and finishing: rate per unit of production

The painting and finishing cost centre overhead for 2009 is estimated at €32 000. This will be spread over an estimated 16 000 units of production (cost units). The estimated overhead absorption rate for the assembly department for 2009 will therefore be:

$$\frac{€32\ 000}{16\ 000} = €2.00 \text{ per unit}$$

Finally, we will work out an estimated total production cost per unit, as follows:

Production cost of container	€	€
Direct materials (metal, fixings, paint)		15.50
Labour:		
Cutting – 10 minutes (@ €6 per hour)	1.00	
Assembly – 1 hour 30 minutes (@ €6 per hour)	9.00	
Painting and finishing – 20 minutes (@ €4.50 per hour)	1.50	
		11.50
Production overhead:		
Cutting	3.50	
Assembly	3.00	
Painting and finishing	2.00	
		8.50
Total production cost		35.50

Overhead absorption rates: some other approaches

The example of Stahl-produkt demonstrated the use of three different approaches to calculating overhead absorption rates: rate per unit, rate per machine hour and rate per labour hour. There are other possibilities as below.

Percentage of direct labour

The overhead absorption rate would be calculated as follows:

$$\frac{\text{Production overheads}}{\text{Direct labour cost}} \times 100$$

Example 3.11 explains how the overhead absorption rate is calculated and applied on this basis.

EXAMPLE 3.11

The fabrications cost centre of Millom Holz uses two grades of direct labour. Grade A is paid at €6.70 per hour and Grade B is paid at €5.90 per hour. The production estimates for the 2008 accounting year require 30 000 hours of Grade A and 28 000 hours of Grade B labour. The management accountant has already carried out an allocation and apportionment exercise which resulted in estimated production overheads of €208 000 for the fabrications cost centre in 2008. What is the overhead absorption rate to be used for fabrications?

Direct labour =
Grade A: 30 000 hours × €6.70 = 201 000
Grade B: 28 000 hours × €5.90 = 165 200
                                                  366 200

Overhead absorption rate for fabrications:

$$\frac{\text{Total budget production overheads}}{\text{Direct labour cost}} \times 100$$

$$= \frac{208\ 000}{366\ 200} \times 100 = 56.8\% \text{ (to one decimal place)}$$

So, 56.8% of the direct labour charge for any batch, job or cost unit will be added to represent production overheads.

Taking the example a little further. Millom Holz manufactures components for the shipbuilding industry on a job costing basis. The job cost card for an order of 120 units of component 177Z2A is as follows:

▶

Component number: 177Z2A
Quantity: 120 units

	€	€
Direct materials		370.00
Direct labour		
Grade A: 25 hours @ €6.70	167.50	
Grade B: 39 hours @ €5.90	230.10	
		397.60
Prime cost		767.60
Production overheads		
56.8% × direct labour cost = 56.8% × 397.60		225.84
Total cost		993.44

Percentage of direct materials cost

This approach to overhead absorption works in the same way as the percentage of direct labour cost. An overhead absorption rate is worked out in advance by using **budget** figures. Production overheads for an individual job, batch or product are then calculated by reference to the input of materials cost.

Both this method and the percentage of direct labour cost method can be particularly useful where a range of different products is made.

It must be recognised, however, that there are no fixed rules about which method to use. The ultimate test to be applied to all management accounting information is whether or not it is useful in managing the firm. Management should use the methods and techniques which they find most efficient and effective in achieving the overall objectives of the business.

Budget
a statement, prepared in advance, usually for a specific period (e.g. for one year) of a business's planned activities and financial outcomes

Traditional costing: is it still relevant?

The long section of the chapter above sets out the fundamentals of a traditional costing system of type that has been in common use in manufacturing environments throughout the twentieth century. However, recent years have seen major changes in manufacturing methods. For example, Brown et al. (2006) describe some of the problems of traditional batch manufacturing systems where large numbers of identical items are produced. 'Traditional batch manufacturing focuses on one main theme or production philosophy – run as large a batch as is economically feasible in order to avoid changing over equipment' (p. 3). However, this approach leads to high inventory storage costs, and perhaps more importantly, is inflexible in providing a sufficient level of customer choice and service:

'. . . The rapid product changes and varieties created by global competition allows the customer to insist on an increased number of product features. If a company is holding a large inventory of finished goods, then it is limited in its capacity to react to a shift in customer demand' (p. 4).

In response to these problems manufacturing businesses have tended to adopt more flexible manufacturing procedures, involving a more focused and less cost-driven approach to measurement, and/or outsourcing. Outsourcing devolves many of the responsibilities of production to outside suppliers, and dispenses with at least some of the complexities involved in costing what can be a very complex multi-stage production procedure. For example, outsourcing has been particularly popular in the automotive industry.

A move towards more flexible and responsive manufacturing techniques has tended to emphasise the weaknesses of traditional costing: it tends to be rigid and inflexible, and to reinforce an organisational system with fixed hierarchies and barriers between departments.

Nevertheless, surveys of management accounting practice continue to provide evidence that quite traditional approaches to costing are alive and well. For example, Hughes and Paulson Gjerde (2003) report a survey of US manufacturing companies which finds that traditional costing is used by 35% of respondents, and traditional costing in combination with activity based costing (which will be covered in Chapter 4) is used by a further 30%. So, despite recent innovations in management accounting techniques, traditional costing does appear to be still widely used.

Costing of services

Contribution
the amount which remains after deducting variable costs from sales revenue

As noted in Chapter 2, the **contribution** of manufacturing industries to overall GDP has been falling steadily in developed countries and the provision of services is now far more important in many economies. Costing of services is important for many of the reasons given at the beginning of the chapter, and the same principle of identifying costs with cost objects is valid both for services and products. However, depending upon the circumstances and nature of the business, the process of identification may be more difficult. The element of direct materials input is absent, but there may be elements of labour input that are more or less direct in nature. The problem of allocating overheads is common to both services and product costing.

Take the example of an advertising agency that works for various clients on a range of campaigns using different media. An employee may work on a single project over a long period of time in which case all of the costs associated with that employee are attributable to the project. However, some employees will be involved with the project only for brief periods, and others are likely to be employed in administrative functions that are not directly associated with any particular project. The cost object in such a case is the advertising campaign and it is a matter for debate, depending upon circumstances, whether any useful purpose is served by allocating overhead costs to it. In all cases, the benefits of a particular management accounting technique should not be outweighed by the costs associated with it.

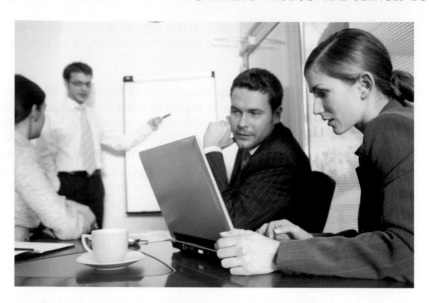

By contrast, some services involve a large number of identical items or processes, and in such cases it may well be worth allocating overheads to them. For example, retail banking involves the processing of very large numbers of identical transactions in the form of direct debits, automated teller transactions and so on.

Some service businesses employ job costing in order to control costs and to assist with billing of services. For example, professional firms of accountants, auditors, solicitors, surveyors and so on, need to keep detailed records of costs associated with particular clients. This is a form of job costing as illustrated by the example below.

EXAMPLE 3.12

Gulam, a conveyancing solicitor, spends time on work for various different clients in the course of a day. Each piece of work for a client represents a cost unit. For example, Gulam's client, Maisie, is moving house and is also selling a commercial property. Each of these two matters represents a cost unit. Each of the matters Gulam deals with has its own unique code; for example, Maisie's house move is coded 0376 and her commercial property sale is coded 0375. During the day, Gulam keeps a time record of each unit of 5 minutes that he spends on each matter. On a particular day, extracts from his time records look like this:

Name: Gulam		Date: 15 October 2007	
Time	Time units	Client and code	Details
2.05 – 2.15	2	Maisie 0376	Phone call to discuss possible completion dates
2.15 – 2.30	3	Bryan 0412	Dictate letter re Land Registry search
2.30 – 2.40	2	Maisie 0375	Dictate letter to commercial agents

The above form serves as a computer input document. At the end of the day, all the solicitors in Gulam's firm submit their time sheets, and the details are input to the computer system. In respect of the day recorded above, 2 time units of 5 minutes each will be logged to each of Maisie's file codes. The time is costed by the computer at Gulam's charge-out rate – so, if his charge-out rate is €60 per hour, each file will receive a charge of €10 (i.e. 10 minutes at €1 per minute) in respect of the solicitor's time spent on 15 October 2007. Other types of cost will be logged against the codes, for example, the cost of Land Registry searches and similar fees, which in this context constitute direct costs.

Once the conveyancing is successfully concluded Gulam will be able to generate an invoice to send to Maisie from the information that is logged on the computer.

Earlier in the chapter the tendency to outsource elements of production was noted. This tendency is also noticeable in some areas in the provision of services where it has similar beneficial effects in the simplification of costing and control for the outsourcer. The box below explains a real-life example of outsourcing of services.

Homeshoring: a new phenomenon

In recent years it has become common in many large businesses to locate call centres in developing countries in order to save costs. Some countries, notably India, have a resource of well-educated English speakers who can be employed at far lower labour rates than in more developed economies such as the UK and the USA. However, this development has not been completely successful and now some companies in the USA are exploring a new approach to handling calls. A recent article (Frase-Blunt, 2007) explains that companies such as JetBlue Airways are starting to employ home-based call agents in the USA. The agents work in their own homes, thus eliminating the costs involved in provision of offices and computers. The article quotes an estimate that using home-based agents can cut property and IT costs by as much as 80% compared to locating call centres off-shore.

From a costing perspective, outsourcing the service makes costing much more straightforward. Agents are paid an hourly rate for their work which is the basic cost of the service to the organisation. Other costs of training, and employee benefits, are involved, but because many elements of service provision are devolved to the employees, far fewer overheads are involved. The outsourcing organisation has an on-going responsibility for ensuring quality standards are maintained, and that the wage rate offered remains sufficiently attractive to attract staff. However, the homeshoring experience of organisations reported in the article suggests that this is not a problem; there is a large pool of potential employees.

SELF-ASSESSMENT EXERCISES

3.1 Paige Peverell produces plastic casings for telephones. The following is a list of some of the costs which the company incurs:

Plastic moulding machine depreciation
Sales office fixtures and fittings depreciation
Plastic materials
Advertising expenditure
Depreciation of factory building
Electricity bill for factory
Wages of assembly line workers
Wages of factory canteen staff
Wages of assembly line supervisor
Secretary's salary
Delivery vehicle depreciation
Factory consumables
Royalty payable per item produced to telephone designer
Mobile phone bill – sales director

Classify each item of expense as one of the following:

Direct labour
Direct materials
Direct expenses
Indirect production overheads
Other indirect overheads

3.2 ArtKit Supplies manufactures metal paint tins for the artist's supplies industry. The company operates from a small rented factory unit. In the year ending 31 August 2008 it incurs the following costs:

	€
Sundry factory costs	2 117
Hinge fittings for boxes	960
Secretarial and administration salaries	12 460
Delivery costs	1 920
Machine operators' wages	18 250
Machinery repair	176
Factory cleaning	980
Lacquer paint for boxes	1 600
Rental of factory	6 409

cont.

Continued	
	€
Finishing operative's wages	10 270
Sundry office costs	904
Salesman's salary	18 740
Metal	18 006
Electricity – factory	1 760
Office supplies	2 411
Depreciation – machinery	1 080
Office telephone	1 630

Required: rearrange the information given into a cost statement for the year ending 31 August 2008.

3.3 Porter Farrington Limited is a New Zealand based company that imports components for input into its production process. In May 2008 the following deliveries into inventory and transfers to production take place in respect of component PR430:

Date	Activity	Units
1 May	Balance of inventory @ NZ$3.00 per unit	30
2 May	Delivery of inventory @ NZ$3.30 per unit	50
18 May	Transfer to production	(40)
31 May	Balance of inventory	40

What is the value of closing inventory, assuming that Porter Farrington Limited adopts the FIFO convention?

a) NZ$23

b) NZ$126

c) NZ$120

d) NZ$132.

3.4 Jersey Brookfield & Co is a manufacturer of soap powders and detergents. Each of the products moves through two stages: bulk production and then packaging.

In the year ending 31 December 2007 Jersey Brookfield incurred production overheads which it plans to allocate and apportion as follows between the two departments:

	€	Basis of apportionment
Factory building depreciation	5 670	Floor area
Factory rates	11 970	Floor area
Factory insurance	7 980	Floor area
Canteen costs	18 876	Number of employees
Supervisory salaries	29 480	Number of employees
Other indirect labour	18 275	Machinery net book value
Machinery depreciation	21 500	Machinery net book value
Cleaning	17 850	Floor area
Electricity	30 290	Actual
Building maintenance	5 040	Floor area
Total	166 931	

The following information is relevant for the apportionment of overheads:

	Total	Bulk production	Packaging
Floor area	10 500 sq. m.	6 000 sq. m.	4 500 sq. m.
Employees	22	10	12
Machinery NBV	215 000	146 000	69 000
Electricity	30 290	18 790	11 500

Required: produce a schedule apportioning the overheads between the two departments (cost centres).

3.5 Barley Brindle produces a single product, Product B. One unit of Product B has a prime cost of €10.20, which included 1 hour of direct labour @ €6.20, and each unit uses 0.5 hours of machine time.

Estimated production of B in 2008 is 60 000 units.

Total production overheads are estimated at €218 000.

Required: calculate the overhead recovery rates (to the nearest cent) for 2008, based on:

i)   direct labour hours

ii) machine hours

iii) units of production.

3.6 WGB GmBH produces two types of metal shelving in their factory – one for domestic use, and one, which is produced to a higher quality standard, for commercial use (in factories and hotel kitchens, for example).

Each shelf unit passes through two processes – first, metal machining and second, painting and finishing (P&F). Commercial shelving is made of stronger material, has extra bracing bars and is given an additional coat of paint in the painting shop.

Cost structures for the two products are as follows:

Domestic shelves	Dept	€
Materials	Machining	18.00
	P&F	3.30
		21.30
Direct labour	Machining 0.75 hours × €6	4.50
	P&F 1 hour @ €6	6.00
		10.50
Prime cost		31.80

Commercial shelves	Dept	€
Materials	Machining	27.00
	P&F	4.60
		31.60
Direct labour	Machining 1 hour @ €6	6.00
	P&F 1.5 hours @ €6	9.00
		15.00
Prime cost		46.60

Production overheads are estimated at the following apportioned amounts for next year:

Machining   €172 490
Painting and finishing   €116 270

The company plans to produce 6000 units of each product next year.
Required: calculate overhead absorption rates based upon:

i) Percentage of direct materials cost

ii) Percentage of direct labour cost.

Discuss which basis of overhead absorption might be preferable for each cost centre.

3.7 (NB no answer is provided for this question.) This chapter cites work by Hughes and Paulson Gjerde, 2003. There are other studies of the incidence of management accounting practices.

Required: research the use of costing techniques in manufacturing industry using academic journal sources, and write a brief paper summarising the findings. The paper should be fully referenced using the Harvard system of referencing (if this is unfamiliar, a web search will produce many comprehensive explanations of the system) or another system recommended by your lecturer.

3.8 Identify the cost object that is likely to be used in an architect's practice which employs 15 architects and 15 support staff. List the principal costs that are likely to be incurred by the practice and explain how the costs might be identified with the cost object for management accounting purposes.

3.9 David has recently been elected as a local councillor for an area in England served by two primary schools (note: English primary school education lasts for seven years). The council has threatened to close the smaller of the two schools (School A) on the grounds that it provides poor value for money compared with the larger school (School B). The biggest single item of cost is teaching staff salaries. David has asked for, and received, a summary of the salary cost for both schools for the 2007/8 financial year (see Appendix). There is substantial local opposition to the threatened closure. David has asked you, as a preliminary step in his investigation of the issue, to:

a) tell him whether or not, on this evidence, School A does appear to provide poor value for money;

b) suggest possible reasons for any discrepancy in salary costs between the schools.

Appendix: data on Schools A & B for 2007/8

	School A	School B
School roll	75	132
Average numbers of teaching staff	4.3	6.2
Teaching staff salary cost	£166 200	£210 000

EXERCISES

3.10 Xiang Products produces motherboards for PCs from a range of bought in components. The following is a list of some of the costs which the company incurs:

Depreciation of factory work benches	
Bank interest charges	
Administration salaries	
Sundry factory expenses	
Factory insurance	
Supervisor's salary	
Assembly operatives' wages	
Managing director's salary	
Production office computer depreciation	
Purchase of silicone chips	
Factory rental	
Depreciation of sales representatives' cars	
Purchase of circuit boards	
Factory cleaning	

Classify each item of expense as one of the following:

Direct labour

Direct materials

Direct expenses

Indirect production overheads

Other indirect overheads

3.11 Brisbane Pinker Limited manufactures a range of containers for cosmetics in metal and plastic. In the year ending 31 December 2007 the company incurs the following costs:

	Au$
Selling department sundry expenses	1 899
Metal	21 444
Depreciation of factory building	1 500
Factory cleaning	6 440
Metal moulding machine: operators' wages	12 222
Factory power	8 370

Finishing operative's wages	10 240
Sales department salaries	39 434
Security guard to factory	4 290
Dyes and paint	2 490
Sundry factory expenses	4 284
Depreciation of office building	1 100
Telephone charges	4 338
Factory canteen costs	12 234
Plastics	63 570
Distribution costs	18 777
Factory insurance	6 960
Plastics machine: operators' wages	15 249
Machinery depreciation	3 950
Administrative salaries	21 496
Stationery and other office admin. supplies	2 937
Other administrative expenses	6 422
Depreciation of office fixtures and fittings	1 929

Required: rearrange the information given into a cost statement for the year ending 31 December 2007.

3.12 Wensleydale Woollen Waistcoats Limited (WWW Ltd) buys in wool to manufacture into waistcoats on its weaving machines. The inventory card for wool code 78X4A shows the following movements in June 2008:

Date	Activity	Kg
1 June	Balance of inventory @ £2 per kilo	38
2 June	Issue to production	(8)
6 June	Delivery into inventory @ £2.10 per kilo	50
20 June	Issue to production	40

There were no other transactions in the month.

What is the value of the issue to production on 20 June if WWW Ltd uses the AVCO inventory valuation convention?

a) £82.50

b) £84.00

c) £80.00

d) £81.00.

3.13 Ravenna & Michele produces components to order for specialist motor manufacturers. An order for 100 components, code 1187AB6, was received from one of the business's principal customers. A job code, X4721, was assigned and over the following month various items of direct material and labour were booked to the job:

Material J	21.4 kg
Material Q	3.7 kg
Grade IV labour	16 hours
Grade VIII labour	8 hours

Material J was booked out of stores on 21 September 2008. The store card for material J contains the following details for September 2008:

Date	Activity	Kg
1 September	Balance of inventory @ €14.30 per kg	28.7
8 September	Delivery of inventory @ €14.20 per kg	30.0
18 September	Transfer to production job code X4692	(20.6)
21 September	Transfer to production job code X4721	(21.4)

Ravenna & Michele apply the FIFO method of inventory valuation.
Material Q costs €2.75 per kg.

Grade IV direct labour cost	= €4.78 per hour
Grade VIII direct labour cost	= €8.21 per hour

Required: produce a job cost record for Job number X4721, calculating:

i) total prime cost

ii) prime cost per component.

3.14   Curtis Bedford is managing director of the family business, Bedford Bowler. The company manufactures children's wooden trainsets. Recently Curtis has been on a course about costing and he is keen to apply his new knowledge to the business. Thinking through the production process, he can identify three principal cost centres: machining, assembly and painting, and packaging.

Curtis's accountant supplies the following summary of production overheads incurred by the business to the most recent year end, 31 December 2007. Curtis adds a note of what he thinks is the most appropriate method of apportionment between cost centres.

	€	Basis of apportionment
Factory rental	21 105	Floor area
Packaging machine leasing charges	5 500	Actual (see note)
Cleaners' wages	17 991	1/3 to each cost centre
Factory rates	6 930	Floor area
Electricity – factory	8 280	Actual
Supervision	21 456	Number of employees
Machinery maintenance and repair	4 472	Call outs
Machinery depreciation	12 250	Net book value
Total	97 984	

Note: the packaging machine leasing charges relate only to machinery used in the packaging cost centre. There is no other machinery in the packaging department.

The following information is relevant for the apportionment of overheads:

	Total	Machining	Assembly	Packaging
Floor area	6 300 sq. m.	2 500 sq. m.	1 700 sq. m.	2 100 sq. m.
Employees	18	5	9	4
Machinery NBV	61 250	35 000	26 250	–
Electricity	8 280	3 905	1 892	2 483
Call outs	8	5	3	–

Required: produce a schedule apportioning the overheads between the two departments (cost centres).

3.15   A manufacturing business, Oakshield Carver, organises its production into four cost centres. In the coming financial year the company plans to produce 115 000 items of product. Further details of its plans are included in the following table:

Cost centre	Production overhead €	Machine hours	Direct labour hours
Machining	297 000	80 000	3 000
Assembly	136 000	20 000	6 000
Finishing	121 500	15 000	9 000
Packaging	76 000	5 000	2 000
Totals	630 500	120 000	20 000

Calculate the overhead absorption rate for each department on the following basis:

i)   machining – machine hours

ii) assembly – units of production

iii) finishing – direct labour hours

iv) packaging – units of production.

3.16   Facts as in 3.15
       The prime cost and timing details for one unit of production are:

	€
Materials	14.20
Direct labour	18.00
Prime cost	32.20

Each unit uses 2 hours of machine time in the machining department.
Each unit uses 1.5 direct labour hours in the finishing department.
Required: calculate the total production cost for one unit of the company's product, using the overhead absorption rates calculated in exercise 3.15.

3.17   Bushey Travel is an on-line travel agent. Clients can book on-line or by phoning the company's headquarters which are located in a business park. Bushey Travel operates as an agency only (i.e. it does not provide holidays itself). It obtains commission on the cost of the holiday from the supplier of the holiday.

   Required: identify the principal categories of cost involved in Bushey Travel's operations.

3.18   Northcott & Llewellyn (2002) cite costing statistics for primary hip replacement operations across a range of Health Trusts in the UK. The cost of the procedure in 1999/2000 varied from £480 to £9337, with an average cost of £3899.

   Required: suggest at least five reasons to account for the very large differences in the cost of the procedure between health care providers. (Hint: obtain and read the paper!)

Activity-Based Costing

4

Aim of the chapter

To understand activity-based costing (ABC) systems, to be able to compare and contrast activity-based costing with traditional costing methods, and to be able to discuss issues relating to its adoption in practice.

Learning outcomes

After reading the chapter and completing the exercises at the end, students should:

- Understand the nature of ABC and be able to apply its principles to straightforward costing examples.
- Be able to contrast ABC with traditional costing methods.
- Know about the research evidence on the use of ABC in practice.
- Understand the nature of the benefits, constraints and problems involved in the application of ABC in practice.

Introduction

The previous chapter introduced and explained traditional costing techniques. It noted that while such techniques are still in widespread use, traditional costing is subject to criticism for its inflexibility and failure to keep up with a changing business environment. Traditional absorption costing techniques, where overheads are 'absorbed' into products using a basis of, for example, machine or labour hours, were developed at a time when direct labour, materials and machine time constituted the most significant inputs into manufacturing processes. However, as processes in both manufacturing and many service business environments have become increasingly mechanised, the prime importance of direct labour inputs has diminished significantly. In those cases where direct labour remains as a major product constituent the function is often exported to a country where low-cost labour is available. Machine-based processes have themselves often become more streamlined and efficient, using less energy and other types of resource. At the same time the relative importance of indirect overheads in many businesses' cost structures has tended to grow. The effect is that increasing amounts of overhead have been allocated to shrinking numbers of machine hours or direct labour hours. This results in questionable allocations of costs. For example, if the overhead absorption rate is €200 per direct labour hour, then every additional fraction of a minute spent on the production of a cost unit will result in a significant additional burden of overhead cost.

During the 1980s business managers and academics expended considerable effort in exploring alternative approaches to costing that offered more meaningful allocations of cost to products and services. A very important alternative to traditional costing emerged in the form of **activity-based costing** (usually referred to as ABC), the adoption of which has been widespread. This chapter explains the principles of ABC, using examples to demonstrate its application in a practical context. It also looks at the incidence of ABC adoption, and some of the problems and constraints involved in its adoption.

Activity-based costing
a costing system used in both service and manufacturing industries, and in both the private and public sectors, which identifies overhead costs as closely as possible with the drivers of cost, i.e. the different activities that take place in the organisation

Principles of ABC

The fundamental principle of ABC is that overhead costs should be identified with cost objects as accurately as possible. Costs are caused or 'driven' by the various activities that take place in the business environment. Such activities in a manufacturing environment might include, for example:

- Materials ordering
- Materials storage
- Setting up production runs
- Testing the quality of production
- Organising production.

Although ABC was originally developed in the context of manufacturing industry its use is by no means limited to that environment. Activities in a service environment might include:

- Appointments system (in, say, a medical or legal practice).
- Cheque processing (in a bank).

Cost driver
in activity-based costing, the various activities that take place in the organisation to which costs are attached

Cost pools
in activity-based costing, the accumulation of costs associated with particular activities in the organisation

Each activity can be identified with one or more **cost drivers**. (A cost driver is defined by CIMA as a 'Factor influencing the level of cost. Often used in the context of ABC to denote the factor which links activity resource consumption to product outputs'.) So, for example, in the case of materials ordering, the cost driver might be the number of orders placed. The first part of the ABC process would require allocation of overheads to the identified activities in the form of so-called **cost pools**. In the second part, overheads in the cost pool attributable to the materials ordering process would be divided by the number of orders placed to give a value for the cost of placing an order. Total product costs could be determined by aggregating the costs of all activities relating to the product, together with any direct elements of cost.

© *SHOUT / Alamy*

It is claimed by the proponents of ABC, that this approach to costing produces better results than traditional costing. For example, Damitio et al. (2000) say that:

'ABC can provide businesses with better answers to questions such as . . .

- Which products and services should be carried in our product line?
- What does it cost to produce them?
- How profitable are they?
- What are my product costs by plant?
- Where can we reduce costs?
- Which customers should we pursue?
- Where should we invest resources to maximise shareholder value?
- How does our performance compare to that of our competitors?
- How can we improve our performance to obtain a competitive advantage?' (p. 4)

Activity-based management (ABM)

Activity-based management (ABM) is a development closely related to ABC. This approach to management involves managing the firm's usage of indirect overheads. Because, as noted earlier, indirect overheads have become relatively much more important in most organisations, it is very important that they should be managed effectively in order to ensure the success of the business operation. Using ABM managers should be equipped to make better quality business decisions.

ABC: implementation

This section of the chapter is divided into two sub-sections. The first sub-section includes a detailed example to demonstrate how overheads are identified with cost drivers, contrasting the ABC approach with overhead allocation under a traditional system. The second sub-section focuses upon a real-life example of applying ABC in a service industry context.

Applying ABC in a manufacturing business

The following example demonstrates the application of ABC in a simplified manufacturing context. The first part of the example costs products using overhead absorption based on direct labour hours. The second part uses the same data, but applies ABC principles.

EXAMPLE 4.1

Sallis Weller produces two products: product X and product Y. Until now, it has adopted traditional absorption costing techniques, transferring overheads to production via an overhead absorption rate based on direct labour hours. The company's managing director has recently read an article about ABC, a revolutionary costing technique. He asks the finance director to organise a comparison by applying ABC alongside normal absorption costing for a month.

A – Using absorption costing

During November 2007 the company produces 2000 units each of product X and product Y, and incurs the following indirect production overhead costs:

	€
Factory cleaning	2 000
Power	16 000
Factory rental	23 000
Factory insurance	5 000
Supervisory salaries	12 000
Canteen charges	3 000
Machinery depreciation	21 000
Machinery maintenance	5 000
Production consumables	6 000
Other indirect labour costs	12 000
Other factory costs	8 000
	113 000

Total direct labour hours for the month are 5000, resulting in an overhead absorption rate of:

$$\frac{€113\ 000}{5\ 000} = €22.60$$

Relevant details for the two products are as follows:

	Product X	Product Y
Hours of direct labour (per unit)	1	1.5
	€	€
Direct materials (per unit)	17.50	12.00
Direct labour (per unit)	7.00	10.50
Prime cost	24.50	22.50
Overhead		
1 direct labour hour x €22.60	22.60	
1.5 direct labour hours x €22.60		33.90
Production cost per unit	47.10	56.40

B – Using Activity Based Costing

ABC involves the identification of key activities and their drivers. The finance director carefully examines the activity bases of the factory operations and establishes five basic activities which take place:

- Machining
- Finishing
- Materials ordering
- Materials issue to production
- Scheduling, control and quality testing of production.

The fundamental cost driver for each activity, together with quantities, is established as follows:

Activity	Cost driver	Total	Product X	Product Y	€
Machining	Machine hours	3 000	2 000	1 000	45 000
Finishing	Direct labour hours	5 000	2 000	3 000	25 000
Materials ordering	Number of orders placed	25	16	9	4 000
Materials issue to production	Number of materials issues made	75	47	28	12 000
Scheduling etc.	Number of production runs	36	22	14	27 000
					113 000

This table shows that the production of X involves more activity in several respects than that of Y. Materials ordering appears more complicated (more orders have to be placed) and the number of production runs is far greater.

The final column of the table shows the results of the finance director's re-classification of the total of €113 000 indirect production overheads for the month into appropriate cost pools. The individual items for rental, insurance, supervision, etc. have been apportioned into cost pools relating to the five activities.

▶

The use of ABC in practice

ABC has consistently attracted much interest from academic researchers, with the result that there is a great deal of research evidence about the incidence and use of ABC in practice, in many different countries. Findings generally have been that ABC adoption is much more likely to occur in larger firms, and that firms are reluctant in many cases to adopt it. In a leading paper in the area, Innes et al. (2000) report the results of a survey of the 1000 largest UK companies, comparing their results with those obtained five years earlier. Their results in respect of current levels of adoption are summarised in the table below:

Firms	1999		1994	
	n	%	n	%
Currently using ABC	31	17.5	74	21.0
Currently considering ABC adoption	36	20.3	104	29.6
Rejected ABC after assessment	27	15.3	47	13.3
Had not considered ABC to date	83	46.9	127	36.1

Source: Innes et al. (2000) – adapted from table 2, p. 352.

Of the 31 ABC users in the 1999 survey, 12 were manufacturing companies, 8 were non-manufacturing and the remaining 11 were financial companies. The researchers observed that around one quarter of the users regarded their ABC adoption as 'pilot testing'. A majority of those firms using ABC were running it in parallel with an existing costing system.

Using ABC in the public sector

Recent research by Jackson and Lapsley (2003) suggests that ABC has been adopted in many public sector organisations. The researchers surveyed public sector accountants in Scotland about whether or not a range of management accounting practices had been adopted in their employer organisation. Of the local authority accountants who responded to the survey, 54% reported that ABC had been adopted in their organisations. The comparable figures for healthcare organisations and government agencies were 55% and 17% respectively.

The process of adoption in a public sector context is illustrated in a case study by Arnaboldi and Lapsley (2005). They studied the adoption of ABC in one of the UK's Regional Blood Transfusion Services, part of the National Health Service. The adoption of ABC was voluntary rather than arising through regulatory requirements. The Blood Transfusion Service is a 'mixed' organisation, in that it is both public sector and market-oriented because it sells some of its products and services to organisations outside the National Health Service. The adoption of ABC allowed the organisation to determine, for the first time, which products and clients were unprofitable, and to take remedial action.

In summary, it appears that a significant number of large organisations, both in the public and private sector, do use ABC, but that there are many more that do not, either because they have considered its adoption and rejected it, or because they had never even considered it. So, there appear to be significant factors preventing ABC adoption. The next section of the chapter includes, as well as a discussion of the potential benefits of ABC systems, a consideration of the problems that may arise in adopting ABC.

Benefits, constraints and problems in applying ABC

Benefits

It is argued that the application of ABC results in significant improvement in the quality of information obtained from the costing system, and consequently, in better control and planning of activities. The Innes et al. (2000) survey found that those adopting ABC rated highly the system's ability to reduce costs overall, to improve product/service pricing, to achieve better analysis of profitability and budgeting, and to improve measurement of the business's performance. However, success ratings by the people who are deeply involved in implementing new systems may be biased, whether consciously or not. Some researchers have focused on more objective measures of success. For example, Cagwin and Bouwman (2002) examined the relationship between the adoption of ABC systems and financial performance. They found that where ABC systems are used with other innovative management techniques there is a net improvement in financial performance. Generally, 'ABC contributes positive benefits, but not in all firm-specific circumstances' (p. 27).

In another study, Kennedy and Affleck-Graves (2001) found that in a sample of UK businesses, those firms adopting ABC techniques outperformed non-adopters in terms of profitability. In summary, there are, apparently, substantial benefits to be derived from successful adoption of ABC systems.

Constraints and problems

ABC, as even the relatively straightforward example earlier in the chapter showed, is a system of considerable complexity. The constraints and problems that have been identified in using ABC include the following:

Expense: A great deal of information has to be collected and administered, and the system is costly to implement. Costs might include the buying in or development of software, payments for consultancy time, reorganisation and perhaps redundancy costs. Such costs may not be perceived as outweighing the benefits to be derived from a more sophisticated costing system. For example, Damitio et al. (2000), explaining the adoption of ABC/ABM systems by the Dow Chemical company in the USA, point out that 'In driving ABC/ABM to lower and lower levels of detail, the cost/benefit issue becomes a factor . . . . The time required to understand and manage individual activities needs to be determined by the macro view of the cost and benefits to be gained with the use of ABC/ABM' (p. 5).

Resistance by staff: Staff may be suspicious of the implementation of ABC systems if they are concerned that new approaches to costing are likely to change the priorities of a business. They may fear redundancy or at least change because of the likely disruption to their working lives. If senior managers force through the types of changes required to introduce ABC they risk alienating the workforce, and staff resistance could result in more or less deliberate attempts to sabotage the new system. For example, in the Soin et al. (2002) study referred to earlier in the chapter, the researchers noted that:

> 'The productivity management consultants were already in the Clearing Department when the ABC project started and it was rumoured that they were looking to cut 40–50 per cent of the workforce. Many members of the Clearing Department were suspicious of *any* new systems seeing ABC as just one more means of justifying reductions in the work force' (p. 262).

Identification and selection of cost drivers: Typically, in the large and complex organisations that tend to adopt ABC, a large number of separate activities and cost drivers can be identified. Using a very high number of cost drivers might well produce more accurate cost allocation, but would be expensive and complicated to administer and understand. Homburg (2001) points out that 'an ABC-system of low complexity, i.e. a system with a small number of cost drivers, is not only less costly but also easier for management to understand . . . . Furthermore, it is often desirable to focus management attention on only a few main cost drivers' (p. 198). However, if the number of cost drivers in a system is kept to manageably low levels, the process of selection of appropriate drivers is very important. If the selection is made badly, the results of the ABC system may be erroneous and misleading.

Continuing focus on quantifiable costs only

ABC involves the identification of a broader range of cost pools and cost drivers, but in essence, it can be argued that it does not differ very radically from traditional costing systems. Major (2007) points out that ABC/ABM 'has been criticised for being only a marginal refinement of traditional costing techniques' (p. 170). In establishing costs for decision-making purposes ABC fails to encompass the qualitative, non-financial factors that are almost always significant in taking decisions.

Chapter summary

This chapter has introduced the topic of activity-based costing which was developed in the 1980s in an attempt to address the shortcomings of traditional costing systems. The application of ABC is complicated, as demonstrated even in the very straightforward example used in the chapter. However, survey evidence has shown that it has been adopted by a significant minority of large businesses operating in both manufacturing and service environments, and in the public sector. Its adoption is often controversial in practice, meeting resistance from staff, and there are many examples in the accounting research literature of ABC failures. Despite the failures, ABC continues to attract considerable interest in practice because of the superior quality of information it is capable of providing in a well-designed system.

References

Arnaboldi, M. and Lapsley, I. (2005) 'Activity based costing in healthcare: a UK case study', *Research in Healthcare Financial Management*, Vol. 10, No.1, pp. 61–75.

Cagwin, D. and Bouwman, M.J. (2002) 'The association between activity-based costing and improvement in financial performance', *Management Accounting Research*, 13, pp. 1–39.

Damitio, J.W., Hayes, G.W. and Kintzele, P.L. (2000) 'Integrating ABC and ABM at Dow Chemical', *Management Accounting Quarterly*, Winter, pp. 1–5.

Homburg, C. (2001) 'A note on optimal cost driver selection in ABC', *Management Accounting Research*, 12, pp. 197–205.

Innes, J., Mitchell, F. and Sinclair, D. (2000) 'Activity-based costing in the U.K.'s largest companies: a comparison of 1994 and 1999 survey results', *Management Accounting Research*, 11, pp. 349–362.

Jackson, A. and Lapsley, I. (2003) 'The diffusion of accounting practices in the new "managerial" public sector', *The International Journal of Public Sector Management*, Vol. 16, No. 5, pp. 359–372.

Kennedy, T. and Affleck-Graves, J. (2001) 'The impact of activity-based costing techniques on firm performance', *Journal of Management Accounting Research*, Vol. 13, pp. 19–45.

Major, M. (2007) 'Activity based costing and management: a critical review', in Hopper, T., Northcott, D. and Scapens, R. (eds) *Issues in Management Accounting*, 3rd edition, FT Prentice Hall; Harlow.

Soin, K., Seal, W. and Cullen, J. (2002) 'ABC and organizational change: an institutional perspective', *Management Accounting Research*, 13, pp. 249–271.

WEBSITE SUMMARY

The book's website contains the following material in respect of Chapter 4:

Students' section

2 longer questions with answers.

Lecturers' section

Answers to end of chapter exercises 4.4 to 4.6.
2 longer questions with answers.

SELF-ASSESSMENT EXERCISES

4.1 Activity based costing (ABC) is a costing system that was developed in the 1980s as a result of an increasing awareness in businesses of the deficiencies of traditional approaches to production overhead absorption.

Required:

i) Describe the principal deficiencies in the traditional product costing system which ABC seeks to correct.

ii) Describe the key features of ABC.

iii) Identify and comment upon a significant advantage *and* a significant disadvantage associated with the typical implementation of an ABC system.

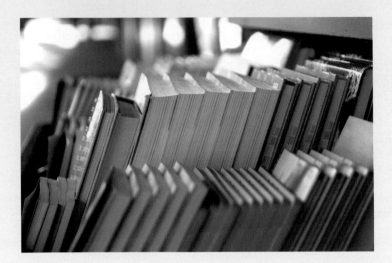

4.2 Arbend is an internet-based bookseller which uses an ABC system. The chief management accountant and his team have produced the following information about expected annual overhead cost pools, activities and cost drivers:

Activity	Cost driver	Total for year	Total overhead pool per cost driver €000
Receipt of books, unpacking and shelving	Number of book orders received from publishers	250 000 orders	1 000
Storage	Number of books	12 million books, each spending on average 1 month in storage	6 800
Customer order processing, packaging	Number of orders received from customers	4 million orders	2 400
Inventory picking	Number of items on picking list	12 million items	800
Total			11 000

Each book order to a publisher comprises on average 48 books.

Required: using the above information, calculate the overhead cost associated with an order of 4 books from a customer.

4.3 Hallett Penumbra Systems produces a range of building products at several factories. The company's directors have decided to pilot an activity based costing system at one of its factories.

The factory produces products C and D. After a substantial amount of preliminary work, the finance controller at the factory produces the following list of cost drivers, with overhead cost pool allocations to each driver, and an estimate of the relevant quantities involved for the 2009 financial year:

Activity	Cost driver	Total	Product C	Product D	Total cost per cost driver €
Planned units of production			6 000	5 000	
Machining	Machine hours	6 000	2 500	3 500	148 200
Finishing	Labour hours	12 000	7 200	4 800	136 440
Materials ordering	Number of orders	186	124	62	12 183
Materials issues	Number of issues	120	70	50	11 592
Machine set up	Number of hours used in set up	70	26	44	19 915
Total					328 330

A unit of product C uses one machine hour, whereas a unit of product D uses 1.4 machine hours. One unit of C has a prime cost of €28.50, and a unit of D has a prime cost of €32.70. Required:

a) calculate the overhead absorption rate based on the company's traditional system of using machine hours as a basis for overhead absorption

b) calculate the overhead per unit of product C and product D using the data provided for the new ABC system

c) calculate the production cost of one unit of product C and one unit of product D under the old and new costing systems

d) explain the principal reasons for the difference in the product costs produced by the old and the new costing systems.

EXERCISES

4.4 Research evidence shows that the use of ABC in service industries appears to be more widespread than in manufacturing industries. Identify and discuss the possible reasons for ABC's relative popularity in service industries.

4.5 Combe Cullen Systems manufactures two products in its Oldfield division. Traditionally the company has used an overhead absorption system based on machine hours. However, following a management consultancy exercise in which outside consultants reviewed the management information systems, the directors have decided to pilot an activity-based costing (ABC) system at the Oldfield factory. For the coming year, 2009, Oldfield's production overheads are estimated as follows:

	€
Factory rent and rates	42 200
Heat and light to factory	23 950
Factory insurance	7 100
Supervisory salaries	38 540
Other indirect labour	18 030
Canteen charges	6 100
Machinery depreciation	18 000
Machinery maintenance	5 520
Production consumables (e.g. machine oil)	2 050
Other factory costs	7 480
Total	168 970

Following a detailed review of the production processes, the finance director and the divisional accountant identify a set of key cost drivers, together with cost allocations to each, and estimates of the relevant quantities involved for products A and B in the 2009 financial year:

Activity	Cost driver	Total	Product A	Product B	Total cost per cost driver €
Planned units of production			6 000	5 000	
Machining	Machine hours	11 000	6 000	5 000	63 030
Assembly	Labour hours	9 000	3 000	6 000	43 020
Packing	Labour hours	4 000	2 000	2 000	31 000
Materials ordering	Number of orders	111	86	25	9 990
Materials issues	Number of issues	150	103	47	12 000
Machine set up	Number of hours used in set up	33	25	8	5 940
Quality inspection	Number of inspections	35	10	25	3 990
Total					168 970

Each planned unit of production of both product A and product B uses one machine hour. One unit of A has a prime cost of €12.50, while one unit of B has a prime cost of €16.00.
Required:

a) calculate the overhead absorption rate based on the company's traditional system of using machine hours as a basis for overhead absorption

b) calculate the overhead per unit of product A and product B using the data provided for the new ABC system

c) calculate the production cost of one unit of product A and one unit of product B under both the old and the new costing systems

d) comment on the difference between the production costs for each product under the old and the new costing systems.

Work to two decimal places (i.e. the nearest cent).

© Jack Sullivan / Alamy

4.6 Queen's Move plc is a listed business that specialises in household removals and storage services. The business runs its own fleet of removal vehicles and also has freehold premises used for storage in many major towns and cities. The directors are undertaking an exercise to identify the principal cost drivers in both aspects of the business with a view to implementing ABC on a two-year trial basis.

Required: identify the principal cost pools and activities and related cost drivers in both the removals and storage sides of the business.

Pricing

5

Aim of the chapter

To understand the principal factors involved in the price-setting decision by reference to a broad range of industry examples.

Learning outcomes

After reading the chapter and completing the related exercises students should:

- Understand the interaction between supply and demand and the interdependence of price and quantity.
- Understand the various additional factors which play a part in pricing decisions.
- Understand the interface between pricing and costing, with especial reference to cost-plus pricing.
- Be able to apply knowledge of pricing issues across a range of industries and commercial activities.

Introduction

The two previous chapters examined methods of cost accumulation which are employed to determine, with a reasonable degree of accuracy, the total cost of a product or service. In both chapters references were made in passing to the potential usefulness of cost information for determining prices. This chapter will examine the pricing decision in much more detail. The issue of pricing is sufficiently important to merit a chapter to itself: after all, if prices are set too low a business will experience sub-optimal levels of profitability, and in the medium to long-term may even fail. Conversely, where a business sets its prices too high, its revenue is likely to fall as its competitors gain market share at its expense. The chapter starts by examining some relevant economic theory.

The relationship between price and quantity

In fundamental economic terms, supply and demand are critical elements in the determination of prices. In a pure market environment, scarcity of supply of a commodity pushes up prices. Conversely, plentiful supply results in lower prices. There is, therefore, a theoretical interaction between quantity and price, which can be illustrated graphically as follows.

FIGURE 5.1

Demand

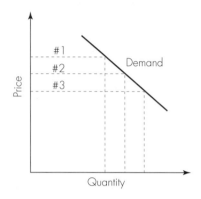

Three sets of lines have been drawn on the graph. Set #1 describes the supply of a lower quantity of goods; the relative scarcity is reflected in a higher price. Sets #2 and #3 describe position of progressively higher supply which results in a relatively lower price. If a large number of price/quantity relationships are plotted the price/quantity relationship emerges. This is usually referred to as the **demand curve**.

Demand curve
an economic model of the relationship between price and quantity demanded

The relationship described in the graph is an economist's representation of reality; it is an economic model of the relationship between price and quantity. How well does this neat graphical representation relate to reality? In practice, much depends upon the nature of the commodity traded, the degree of competition in the market, and the context in which it is supplied. It is possible to observe, in general terms, examples of such a relationship in the real world. For example, in the UK the price of strawberries in the summer months (when strawberries grown in the UK are available in large quantities) tends to be lower than in the winter months when the supply is smaller (because the only available strawberries are imported). However, it is usually quite difficult to observe the classic relationship between price and quantity in operation.

Elasticity and inelasticity

Demand is described by economists as elastic where:

- Customers are relatively indifferent about the product (because, for example, there are many identical or close substitutes in the market).
- The demand is highly sensitive to changes in price.

Products for which demand is elastic would include, for example, most household commodities (washing up liquid, soap, tea and so on).

By contrast, demand is inelastic where:

- Customers place a high value on the product.
- Demand is relatively insensitive to price (i.e. it takes a substantial increase in price to have any effect on demand).

Luxury goods and services tend to demonstrate inelastic demand. For example, if a customer shopping for a new suit has the resources and inclination to buy one from Armani, he is not likely to be satisfied by a cheap substitute from a chain store. The price of the Armani suit would have to increase by a substantial margin in order to deter such a customer.

© *Lourens Smak / Alamy*

Problems in applying the economic model to the real world

The model represented by the graph above takes account of only two variables – price and quantity. However, in the real world other complexities frequently come into play. For example, the effects of:

> *Advertising* – if advertising is effective it can affect both demand and the price that people are willing to pay for a commodity or service.

Novelty – a new product on the market can often command higher prices initially simply because of its novelty value.

Fashion – an item that is widely perceived as more fashionable may be able to command a premium price.

Reputation – a good brand name may command a premium price.

Sometimes, in practice, several of these factors interact.

In addition to the complex combinations of factors which affect price, there are other problems which arise in real-world attempts to apply the simple economic model:

Lack of information:　in most cases, it is very difficult to obtain accurate information as to the effect on prices of a change in demand, because these are theoretical effects. The model may be useful in helping to broadly predict the direction of price movements, but it is difficult to know with any degree of precision how much a change in price, for example, will affect demand.

Product range:　as noted, it is very difficult to obtain accurate information about the interaction of price/quantity/demand. This becomes even more difficult where large numbers of products are concerned. Most businesses produce a range of products or services, some of which may differ only slightly from each other. Management, in most cases, will simply lack the huge resources which would be required to accurately estimate demand over a range of conditions.

State of competition in the market:　the number and nature of competitors in the market will affect prices. These effects are examined in more detail below.

Competition in the market

Perfect competition
a hypothetical economic condition where no player in a market has the power to change prices

The more suppliers in the market, the more competitive the environment. In such conditions, a state approaching 'perfect competition' is likely to exist. **Perfect competition** describes the hypothetical economic condition where no player in the market, whether provider or purchaser, has the power to change prices. Where there are many suppliers, no individual supplier can set prices at a significantly higher level. Prices and supplies will easily reach an equilibrium state in which dramatic movements are unlikely to take place.

There may be special competitive conditions, however, in the markets for some products:

Monopoly
a market condition where only one supplier supplies the market with a particular good or service

Monopoly:　a **monopoly** exists where only one supplier supplies the market with a particular good or service. The monopolist can take advantage of this unique position in raising prices to a high level. Regulation by the state often seeks to ensure that a monopoly position cannot arise. For example, proposed mergers between businesses are often carefully examined by regulatory authorities who have the authority to block any merger which would lead to a single, monopoly, supplier in a market.

Oligopoly
a market condition where there are few suppliers (about three to five) of a particular good or service. Typically, the market shares between the suppliers are fairly evenly spread

Oligopoly: an oligopoly exists where there are few suppliers (between, say, three and five) in the market for the supply of a particular good or service, and where market shares are fairly evenly spread out. An example of oligopoly exists in the provision of accounting services. Although there is a proliferation of accounting firms in the UK and worldwide, most of them are very small practices. There are only four major international firms which can genuinely compete for the business of accountancy advisory services to multinational corporations. Where oligopoly exists, there is a danger of reduced competition in the market, and stagnation of prices. Regulators often take a keen interest in oligopolistic market conditions, and will carefully assess the competitive implications of proposed mergers between members of an oligopoly. Nevertheless, oligopolies are found in many industries.

Cartel
a price-fixing arrangement where a few major suppliers in a market agree between themselves to keep prices high

Cartel: a cartel is a price-fixing arrangement where a few major suppliers in a market agree between themselves to keep prices high. This is widely regarded as anti-competitive and in most market economies regulations exist to outlaw cartels. Currently, in the UK the law allows for very substantial fines to be levied on companies involved in price-fixing arrangements. The Office of Fair Trading (OFT) is the government department in the UK responsible for consumer and competition issues. One of its functions is to enforce legislation with a view to eliminating anti-competitive behaviour and unfair trading. (The work of the OFT is described in detail on its website: www.oft. gov.uk.) A recent example of a cartel case is described in the box below.

Replica shirt pricing

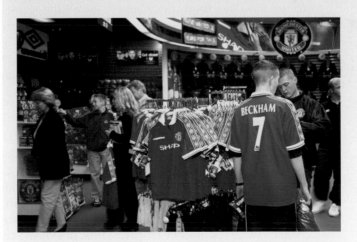

© Ingolf Pompe/Alamy

In 2000 and 2001 a cartel of several companies (including JJB Sports, Manchester United plc and the Football Association Limited) agreed between them to rig the prices of England, Manchester United and other teams' replica football shirts. An OFT investigation resulted in the imposition of penalties amounting to a total of £16 million on the companies concerned. The penalties did nothing to compensate individual consumers but recently (early 2007) a change in the law allowed Which?, the consumer

◀ organisation, to make a claim against JJB Sports for compensation to individual consumers. Consumers who overpaid for a replica shirt in 2000 and 2001 were invited to stake their claim via the Which? website (www.which.co.uk).

More information on the case can be found on the OFT and Which? websites, and in Tait (2007) and Elliott (2007).

Price taker
a supplier in a market with little or no influence over the level of prices charged for a product or service

Price setter
an influential supplier in a market with the power to influence the level of prices for a product or service

Price setters and price takers

The position of an individual business in the market may determine whether or not it has any control over prices. In an intensely competitive market with many suppliers of goods or services, there may be little scope for an individual supplier to separate from the pack. Sometimes markets are dominated by a few large suppliers, trailed by a large number of smaller providers. In such cases, a small provider of goods or services is unlikely to be able to influence prices; this type of provider is known as a **price taker**; they have to take the prices determined by the more powerful players in the market. By contrast, a **price setter** does not have to accept the prices set by other people.

How do producers decide on prices?

As we have just seen, price takers have little scope for making decisions on prices. What about price setters? Theoretically, producers and suppliers of goods and services should have regard to demand and to market conditions. Some producers do examine the market, although many continue to rely upon cost-based pricing. This section of the chapter examines both market-based and cost-based pricing.

Market-based pricing

If market information is available or can be obtained at relatively low cost, businesses should use it. Sometimes pricing is based upon perceptions, and experience, of market demand which have little, if anything, to do with costs.

In some circumstances competition is important and pricing by competitors may be clearly visible. For example, supermarket businesses frequently compete with each other on price. It is, obviously, easy to determine what the competition is charging for a basket of products because prices are visibly displayed. There are relatively few supermarket businesses, and it is not clear that people will always go to the cheapest – other factors such as the range of goods on sale and the general brand identity matter, too. Nevertheless, the level of pricing in such markets is often an important factor in securing sales.

In some markets, the availability of prices via the internet to retail consumers has meant that pricing has become more transparent and the providers of certain types of goods and services have had to become more aware of market conditions and competition. The box in the following page provides an example.

Cross channel ferry pricing

© Troika / Alamy

The rapid growth of budget airlines such as Ryanair and easyJet which provide cheap short-haul fares to many European destinations has presented a major challenge to the providers of cross-channel ferry services. A newspaper article (Butler, 2006) points out that 2006 ferry fares have fallen to half the price that would have been payable five years previously in 2001, and that many more bargain fares are available from the ferry operators' websites than previously.

The provision of comparison websites for budget flights and ferry fares has exposed travel costs to unprecedented scrutiny by consumers. Service operators, because of the easy availability of market information, have been obliged to respond much more rapidly to changes in competitors' prices.

Cost-based pricing

Cost-based pricing, as the term implies, is the fixing of the price for a product or service based upon the cost of providing it. However, cost-based pricing cannot usually be undertaken without any reference at all to the market, especially in the longer-term. If a cost-based price results in a product with a very much higher price than similar or identical products in the market, there is likely to be a problem. If the higher costs result from inherent inefficiencies or defects in the manufacturing process the business is likely to fail.

Sometimes international inequalities, very often in the price of labour, result in businesses either being priced out of a particular market, or having to change their source of supply. As noted in an earlier chapter, one of the reasons for the relative decline of manufacturing industry in the UK has been the availability of cheaper labour elsewhere. Firms have often moved their entire manufacturing operation into other countries where labour costs are lower.

Cost-plus pricing

As the name implies, this approach to pricing first establishes the cost and then adds on a 'plus' factor – the required level of profit.

EXAMPLE 5.1

Binnie Fairweather makes a range of commercial ovens for sale to hotels and restaurants. The company uses a cost-plus approach to pricing. Direct costs of producing an oven are:

	€
Direct materials	49.60
Direct labour	61.30
Other direct costs	21.50
	132.40

The company absorbs production overheads on the basis of machine hours used. Fixed production overheads for the current year are estimated at €695 000 and total machine hours are 25 000 for the year. Each oven uses 1.5 machine hours.

Binnie Fairweather requires a profit of 25% on total cost.

The fixed production overhead absorption rate is: $\dfrac{€695\ 000}{25\ 000}$

$$= €27.80$$

Selling price is calculated as follows:

	€
Direct costs	132.40
Production overheads	
€27.80 × 1.5 machine hours	41.70
Total costs	174.10
Profit mark up: €174.10 × 25%	43.53
Selling price	217.63

Binnie Fairweather may be more or less flexible in relation to this calculated selling price. If the company looks around the other suppliers in the market it may see that selling prices for similar ovens are no more, generally, than €200. The company then has a choice: if it is in a price setting position it may decide to go ahead and market the product at approximately €218 or even higher, based upon factors such as:

● Good brand name

● Better quality (perceived or actual)

● A carefully targeted marketing campaign.

In fact, the selling price which is arrived at through application of cost-plus pricing may be simply a starting-off point in a long process of determining an appropriate price.

There are several disadvantages of cost-plus pricing:

● Absorption costing may not give a particularly accurate estimate of the overhead costs related to a product. As we have seen in

Chapters 3 and 4, allocation and apportionment of costs can be quite arbitrary and may, therefore, lead to incorrect decisions.

- The absorption rate is set in advance; it may prove to be quite seriously inaccurate, in which case pricing decisions based on full cost plus calculations may prove, in retrospect, to be less than optimal.

- The emphasis on costs may result in firms failing to consider market conditions properly. Where the market is highly competitive, even a small price differential could result in a large fluctuation in sales. Fluctuations in volume of sales and production could result in significant misallocation of fixed costs, thus adding to the absorption costing problem already identified.

- In industries where cost-plus pricing is widely accepted as a basis for establishing contractual arrangements, inefficiency may actually be rewarded. Under cost plus pricing arrangements, the higher the cost, the higher the profit margin.

In order to address the problem of the unreliability of absorption costing for this type of decision-making, the company could add a higher mark-up to the variable elements of cost only, such as direct materials and labour. This approach is known as variable cost-based pricing. (Chapter 6 will examine the issue of variable costs in much more detail.)

EXAMPLE 5.2

The directors of Binnie Fairweather have concluded that cost-plus pricing on the basis of total cost is simply too unreliable. They have therefore decided to use variable cost as a base, with a mark-up of 55% of the variable cost total.

This approach produces the following selling price:

	€
Variable costs	132.40
Add: profit mark up: €132.40 × 55%	72.82
Selling price	205.22

Whether or not this selling price is more realistic, given current market conditions for the company, would be a matter for the directors to decide. Again, this price might just be a starting point for the decision-making process.

Examples 5.1 and 5.2 illustrate cost-plus pricing in a manufacturing environment. This method is also commonly found in retail and service businesses. For example, a retailer may apply a standard mark-up to products in a particular category. In the case of service businesses a standard hourly charge is often applied to time spent on a particular customer's business. This is likely to be based upon an allocation of total costs of the business over the number of productive service hours available, plus a mark-up. Provided the resulting standard hourly charge is reasonably competitive, the cost-plus approach is likely to work well.

The management accountant clearly has a key role to play in pricing decisions, and especially where pricing is based upon cost. The determination of cost, as demonstrated in the previous two chapters, is far from straight-forward in most business activities but it takes on an additional importance where it is used in making pricing decisions.

Special cases

Tendering

Some types of commercial contracts for goods and services are arranged by tender. This is a process which involves several businesses competing for a contract; usually it involves the submission of sealed bids by a certain date and time. The customer opens the tenders on the same occasion, compares prices and conditions, and decides which tender to accept.

The sealed bid system is intended to allow for fair competition, and to give the customer the best opportunity of obtaining a fair price. In this situation, from the supplier's point of view, information about prices in the market is likely to be non-existent or limited (unless the suppliers have banded together in an illegal cartel to artificially adjust prices). Tendering is, therefore, likely to be done on the basis of a cost-plus approach, using information derived from the business's costing system, together with some guesswork about the prices likely to be offered by the competition.

The customer is not obliged to choose the lowest tender price. Sometimes, a supplier will submit a price that is obviously under-estimated, perhaps because they wish to obtain the business at very low cost (this may be worth doing, for example, if labour is underemployed at a slack period). Alternatively, they may simply have under-estimated what is involved in the contract.

Highly restricted supply of unique products

Some products do not fit particularly easily into either the market-based or cost-based approaches to pricing.

EXAMPLE 5.3

Pricing original works of art

An original work of art is, by definition, unique. In a sense, each work of art creates its own demand because, until it is created, nobody can know with certainty that they want it or need it. However, once a certain class of works of art is established, a market of a sort may be created, and the market price is tied into intangible factors such as reputation and more obvious and quantifiable factors such as scarcity of supply. For example, the works of Vermeer, the seventeenth century Dutch artist are so scarce (there are only 36 definitively attributed paintings) that prices become almost irrelevant; there is, effectively, no supply, although the demand would, presumably, be very high were one of his paintings to reach the market. Demand, in economists' terms, is highly inelastic.

The relationship between supply of works of art and prices does follow the classic economic model to some extent. When an artist with a reputation dies, the prices of his or her works will tend to increase because the supply has now definitively ceased.

Art pricing rarely has anything to do with cost, however great or small the reputation of the artist. A painting, for example, is a piece of stretched canvas, board or paper with pigments in some kind of medium applied to it; variable raw materials costs are unlikely in most cases to be very high. The labour required to produce it is rarely costed by the artist; if it were, the hourly rate would, in most cases, be laughably small. Cost-plus pricing in this case is hardly an option – information is lacking and the intrinsic cost of the product is rarely an issue in a decision to purchase in any case.

Target pricing and costing

This approach to pricing turns cost-plus pricing on its head. A target price is established by reference to the market, not cost. This may not be straight-forward, especially where the product is highly differentiated, and will involve research into prices of similar products, consumer preferences and relative level of price elasticity. Once a target price has been established, the firm will then deduct the desired profit margin on selling price. The residual amount then represents the maximum amount of cost which the firm can incur in producing the product or service – the target cost. If this amount appears to be too small to accommodate all the associated costs, then the firm makes strenuous efforts to reduce those costs so that the target can be met. This may involve:

- Engaging in general cost reduction programmes to reduce overheads to a minimum.
- Re-engineering a product.
- Investing to create additional production efficiencies.
- Making compromises on quality of materials.
- Planning for additional volumes of production so as to reduce unit costs (by means of, for example, taking advantage of discounts for large-scale purchases).

Discounting

Many businesses will give discounts on selling price to reward customer loyalty or to ensure early payment for goods or services supplied on credit. Usually, such discounting reduces the supplier's profit margin by a small amount, but the reduction is balanced by a commensurate benefit.

However, sometimes a business may make a rational decision to sell goods or services at less than the cost of producing them. On the face of it this strategy appears foolish; it would clearly lead to the rapid downfall of the business if done too often over too wide a product range. However, it can make sense where:

- There is a large quantity of stock with a short shelf-life to clear.
- The goods or services are being treated as a loss leader.

Some stock is, by its nature, perishable: food and soft drinks, for example. In other cases, the life of stock is limited by fashion considerations. It usually makes sense for retailers to sell fashion items at the end of a season for whatever they can raise, so that room can be made for the new season's stock.

A loss leader product or service is used to attract customer attention to a range of goods or to a particular supplier. Although it does not make long-term sense to provide goods or services at less than cost, a loss leader may help a business to break into a particular market. This occasionally happens on a large scale, as demonstrated by the following fictional example:

Loss leader
a product or service which is used to attract customer attention to a range of goods or to a particular supplier

EXAMPLE 5.4

Mills Greaves plc is a supermarket group based in one of England's regions. It has turned in a high level of profits relative to other supermarket businesses, and is currently rich in cash. The company's directors are ambitious for the future of the group, and have planned in detail an expansion programme which will in due course mean that its supermarkets are found in all parts of England and Wales. The directors have targeted a series of smaller towns which do not currently have a supermarket. They will open relatively large premises and will provide a huge range of goods at extremely low prices. The company can afford to bear the losses because of its previous profitability, and because it is mostly still owned by members of the Mills and Greaves families (most of the directors are family members and shareholders) it is not under pressure to pay a dividend. The strategy is fundamentally to drive out the competition by undercutting prices. Once competitors have been forced into closure, Mills Greaves will be able to raise prices in the new areas and return to previous levels of profitability.

The ethics of this type of business decision may cause some concern, especially because of the proposed scale of the operation. However, any new entrant to a market is likely to try a modified version of this approach, especially if price is the principal distinguishing feature in consumer choice.

Auction

Where prices are established at auction the seller abandons part of his or her control over price setting. For some types of commodity (e.g. art, antiques, certain categories of real estate) selling at auction is the accepted method of contracting; it would not normally apply for new goods. Usually the seller can stipulate a reserve price. For example, a seller sends an antique vase to auction, setting a reserve on it of €1500. This means that if the bidding does not reach that price, the item will not be sold by the auctioneer.

© Trip / Alamy

More issues in pricing decisions

Product life-cycle

Revenue
the amount of goods
and/or services sold in
an accounting period by
a business, expressed in
terms of monetary
amounts

The discussion and examples earlier in the chapter about cost-plus pricing took into account only direct and indirect costs of the current period. This approach is perfectly valid in some types of business. Sometimes, however, it is necessary to take a longer view of costs in order to determine an appropriate price. If a firm is to stay in business, the total **revenue** streams from a given product must normally exceed the total costs arising. This means that, where there has been a substantial up-front investment in developing a product or services, the cost of the investment must be taken into account when deciding on a selling price. Management accounting uses life-cycle costing and pricing in order to ensure that all costs are taken into account, and that the level of pricing is capable of covering these costs. The example below illustrates the process.

EXAMPLE 5.5

Glock Systems is a computer games developer. The company's management accountant is preparing for a meeting with the sales director in order to discuss the pricing of Glock's forth-coming game, codenamed XX23. The game has been in development for the last six months, and the following costs have been accumulated to date:

	€
Cost of games developers' time	503 000
Out-sourced product and advertising design	177 000
Advertising agency billings	195 000
Allocation of general business overhead	138 000
	1 013 000

▶

(and be able) to charge more. Usually, a percentage recovery figure will be calculated to indicate the extent to which the fees indicated by the charge-out rate have been recovered. If recovery falls much short of 100% the partners may need to rethink their rates.

Competition Traditionally, solicitors' fees have been shrouded in mystery. However, with the advent of advertising by solicitors (it used to be prohibited in the UK) and a greater willingness on the part of the public to challenge solicitors' bills, competition has become more of a factor. Word of mouth is an important factor for professional practices in gaining new business; if word gets round that Haringey, Fisker and Blott's bills are much higher than average, they could lose business. So, to some extent, price affects demand, and market conditions should be taken into account.

Chapter summary

The chapter began with a brief discussion of the classical economist's model of demand. The real world application of the classical model is complicated by many different factors, including special competitive conditions such as monopoly, oligopoly and cartel. The disadvantage experienced by consumers and customers in such conditions are often addressed by regulation. In a UK context, the OFT seeks to ensure compliance with relevant legislation.

In practice, there are various approaches to the important decisions involved in price-setting. Market-based approaches are likely to be used in competitive conditions, but cost-based pricing, despite its several disadvantages, is also widely used in practice. There are many special cases of approaches to pricing decisions, including tendering, unique product pricing, target pricing, discounting and auction. Policies such as price-skimming and price discounting may be adopted depending upon the stage a product has reached in its life-cycle.

The management accountant is involved in many aspects of pricing. Prices must be set so that, in the long run, a product or service's revenue exceed its costs. The role of the management accountant is to determine costs and to provide the information necessary for making pricing decisions.

Pricing is a difficult area of management decision-making. Despite the attractions of the simple demand model, it appears in practice that pricing in many industries is more of an art than a science.

References

Butler, S. (2006) 'Cross-channel ferry operators knew they'd be sunk if they didn't cut their prices, but is it still cheaper to fly?', *The Sunday Telegraph*, 5 February, p. 4.

Elliott, V. (2007) 'Payback time for fans who lost their shirt', *The Times*, 9 February, p. 12.

Tait, N. (2007) 'Sports companies face penalty threat as Which? puts the boot in', *Financial Times*, 9 February, p. 3.

WEBSITE SUMMARY

The book's website contains the following material in respect of Chapter 5:

Students' section

A multiple choice quiz containing 5 questions
2 longer questions with answers.

Lecturers' section

Answers to end of chapter exercises 5.7 to 5.10.
2 longer questions with answers.

SELF-ASSESSMENT EXERCISES

5.1 Which statement is correct? The demand curve plots the relationship between:

   a) Selling price and cost

   b) Quantity and cost

   c) Quantity and selling price

   d) Selling price and discounts.

5.2 Which statement is correct? Demand is described as elastic where it:

   a) Is highly sensitive to changes in price

   b) Seldom increases or decreases

   c) Cannot be met

   d) Increases only where there is a substantial change in price.

5.3 Which statement is correct? An oligopoly exists in cases where:

   a) One supplier controls the market

   b) About three to five suppliers control the market

   c) There are many suppliers of about equal size in the market

   d) New suppliers enter the market frequently.

5.4 Auger Ambit is a manufacturing company which sets prices based on total costs plus a mark-up.
   For the year ending 31 December 2009 the company is forecasting total fixed costs of
   €788 000. Direct materials costs will be €18.00 per unit and direct labour costs will be
   €27.56 per unit. The company expects to produce 20 000 units, and normally looks for a
   profit mark up of 25%.
   Suggest a suitable cost-based selling price per unit of product for 2009.

5.5 Belvedere, Bharat & Burgess are in partnership together as accountants. They have recently enlarged their practice and have taken on extra staff. The partners meet to discuss charge-out rates, which currently stand at €110 per hour for each of the three partners, €85 per hour for senior staff and tax specialists and €50 per hour for all other grades of qualified accountant. The partnership operates on the assumption that 75% of hours worked will be chargeable to clients as fees, and that a 43 week year is worked, at 8 hours per working day. Costs are expected to amount to €1 275 000 in the coming year, 2008.

    i)   If the partners' assumptions are correct, how much in fees could the partnership expect to bill in 2008?

    ii)   If hours are worked exactly as planned, the average recovery rate on billing is actually 94%, and total actual costs are 1% above budget in 2007 how much profit or loss would the partnership make?

5.6 Discuss the key factors which would arise in determining selling prices for:

A garden centre

A small grocery store which is open for 24 hours.

EXERCISES

5.7 Ainsley Witt manufactures old-fashioned dolls houses. The manufacturing process is labour intensive, and involves a cost of €54 per house. Materials costs are €22 per house, and in addition, the company pays a royalty per house manufactured of €1 to the designer.

The company's usual level of overhead costs is €125 000 per year. In an average year about 2400 dolls houses will be produced. Ainsley Witt's sales manager has suggested that the company should carry out an exercise to compare the current selling price of €150 for a dolls house with a cost plus calculation, based upon a target mark-up on cost of 23%.

Calculate the difference between the current selling price and a selling price based upon the cost plus calculation.

5.8 Burke and Harpur are solicitors who have recently set up in partnership together and are working hard to establish themselves in a town which already has several solicitors. Both have a charge out rate per hour of €65. They are preparing a bill for Mrs Henrietta Higgs, for whom they have recently drafted a will.

The bill contains the following items:

Fees for time: 43 hours @ €65	2795
Taxation specialist's charges for advice	650
Other sundry charges	240
Total	3685

The partners disagree about how much to charge. Burke thinks that €3685 is a ridiculously high amount to charge for drafting a will, and that if word gets out that the firm charges that much for the service, it will badly damage their chances of increasing business. He says they should charge €1500 and be prepared to take the loss.

Harpur worked the majority of the 43 hours noted on the bill. He defends the high charge on the grounds that it is only so high because Mrs Higgs wasted such a lot of time changing her mind about who should inherit her considerable wealth. Also, because she is so rich, she should be able to afford the charges. He adds that he personally doesn't care if Mrs Higgs doesn't use their services again because she was so difficult to deal with.

Discuss the points of view of the two partners on this pricing problem. Which partner do you think is correct?

5.9 Discuss the key factors which would arise in determining selling prices for:

A plumber (sole trader)

A biscuit manufacturer.

5.10 Earlier in the chapter the case successfully brought by the Office of Fair Trading against various sports related businesses was explained. The companies found guilty were required to pay a substantial fine for running an illegal cartel to supply over-priced replica football shirts. However, it might be argued that the regulation against cartels interferes with the operation of a free market and the economists' demand/supply model.

Discuss the pros and cons of this argument.

Marginal Costing and Decision-Making

6

Aim of the chapter

To understand some of the important elements in decision-making with particular reference to marginal costing.

Learning outcomes

After reading the chapter and completing the related exercises, students should:

- Understand the principal factors involved in decision-making, including the importance of relevant costs and of risk and uncertainty.
- Understand the nature and classification of costs as variable, fixed or semi-variable.
- Be able to use cost-volume-profit analysis to establish a break-even point and to assist in business decision-making.
- Understand the issues involved in making decisions in special circumstances.
- Understand the limitations of marginal costing for decision-making.

Introduction

The previous chapter examined the important decisions involved in setting product prices. This chapter expands the topic of decision-making with particular reference to decisions about such questions as, for example, whether or not it is worthwhile to produce a particular product, the amount that must be sold in order to break even or to make a profit and whether or not to accept contracts at special prices. This type of decision is often referred to as 'short-term', by contrast with decisions that affect future periods such as the purchase of major items of equipment (decisions like the latter are generally referred to as 'long-term'; they are covered in Chapter 7 of this book). However, all such decisions are important and may have consequences that stretch far into the future. For example, the decision to cease manufacture of a particular product is not really short-term; a dropped product cannot necessarily be easily reinstated.

The type of decision-making covered in this chapter relies upon a close examination of costs, in order to determine which costs are relevant to the decision. The first section of the chapter examines the idea of relevant costs and revenues, along with some other important factors such as risk and uncertainty, and varying attitudes to risk. The second section covers the issue of cost variability which is often important when determining relevant costs. The topic of **marginal costing** is introduced, together with cost-volume-profit analysis and break-even analysis which can be helpful to accountants and decision-makers. The chapter then examines certain special cases of decision-making, and then concludes with a review of the limitations of analysis based on marginal costing.

Marginal costing
an approach to costing which excludes fixed costs

Issues in decision-making

This first section of the chapter establishes some important principles in costing for decision-making.

Relevant costs and revenues

Relevant costs and revenues are those that change as a result of a decision. Past costs cannot be relevant for decisions made now, because they have already been incurred; in the context of the type of decision-making covered in this chapter, such costs are described as **sunk costs**. Future revenues may be, but are not always, relevant to a decision. For example, suppose that a decision is required as to the preferable production method (out of two possibilities) for 1000 units of product B which will sell for €100 each. There are two possible decisions in this case if production is to go ahead, but revenue will be the same under either decision and so is not relevant.

The example below examines some aspects of relevant costs and revenues for decision-making.

Sunk cost
a cost which is irrelevant to a decision, because it has already been incurred

EXAMPLE 6.1

Georgetown Systems is in business as a computer dealer. A recent inventory count showed that some of the business's inventory was becoming outdated. For example, there are five ATB2000 computers, purchased over two years ago at a cost of €1000 each. One of Georgetown's technical managers has been researching various possibilities for disposing of the computers. She has come up with three options:

1 Give the computers to a local school for disadvantaged children. The school is under funded and is always pleased to receive gifts of money or equipment. Georgetown Systems' directors are well known supporters of local and national charities and the company's annual report always contains at least a page providing details of charitable activities during the year.

2 A discount trader has offered €200 each for the machines.

3 For an outlay of €400 each, the machines' processors could be upgraded. If this were done each machine could be sold for €700.

When considering this type of decision, it is easy to be distracted by the original outlay of €1000. For anyone who has absorbed and fully understood the techniques of financial accounting, it seems somehow wrong to ignore such a significant amount. However, it must be understood that the amount is not being ignored in the financial accounts; a total outlay of €5000 for the computers was no doubt properly recorded when the original transaction took place, and unless a provision for loss of value has been made subsequently, the €5000 remains as an amount in inventory in the balance sheet. But, for the purposes of the decision that now has to be made the historic cost of the machines is irrelevant; it represents an event that happened in the past and which remains the same whichever decision is made.

The relevant costs and revenues are shown in the table below:

	Option 1	Option 2	Option 3
Relevant revenues	0	5 × €200 = €1000	5 × €700 = €3500
Relevant costs	0	0	5 × €400 = €2000
Net revenue	0	€1000	€1500

Note that all relevant revenues and costs represent future outflows and inflows of resources. Which is the correct decision? On the face of it, the decision requires no thought at all: option 3 produces the best net revenue figure of the three. It is certainly preferable to the other commercial option, option 2. However, it is worth pausing to consider option 1 in the light of Georgetown's apparent objectives. It seems that the business does not exist solely to make profits, but that it also has charitable objectives in mind, as evidenced by the nature and prominence of its reporting on charitable activities. The question in this case is whether the commercial objective outweighs the charitable objective. It is up to the business's managers to weigh up the factors involved. If they do decide to give the computers away, the management accounting procedures involved in determining relevant costs equip them with the knowledge of the value of the gift, which is the net potential revenue achievable under option 3.

Opportunity cost

Opportunity cost
in decision-making, the potential benefit that is given up when a particular course of action is taken in preference to an alternative

Opportunity cost, according to CIMA's Official Terminology is: 'the value of the benefit sacrificed when one course of action is chosen in preference to an alternative. The opportunity cost is represented by the foregone potential benefit from the best rejected course of action'. In the example above, if Georgetown decides to give the computers away, the opportunity cost of this action is the €1500 that could be realised if the computers were modified and sold.

In summary, the following principles are applicable when determining relevant costs and revenues:

- Past (sunk) costs are not relevant
- Fixed costs are not relevant

- Future costs and revenues are relevant where they vary under different decision scenarios
- Costing for decision-making is not the same as financial accounting for costs
- Opportunity cost may be relevant to the decision
- Non-financial factors may play an important part in decision-making, especially where the business has objectives other than the making of profits.

Risk and uncertainty

Any business decision, beyond the very trivial, is likely to involve elements of both risk and uncertainty. Definitions of these two terms are taken from Bullock and Trombley (2000) as follows:

Risk: 'In economics, risk means something slightly different from its everyday meaning: it refers to a situation where there are different possible outcomes, each of which has a known probability of occurring . . .' (p. 760).

Uncertainty: 'In economics, a decision or course of action is subject to uncertainty if the probabilities of the different possible outcomes are not known. Decision-making under pure uncertainty is difficult to analyse and, in this way, is to be distinguished from risk . . .' (p. 893).

In most business and accounting contexts it is not possible to know the probabilities of the different possible outcomes, and so, from the economist's perspective, businesses tend to face uncertainty rather than risk. Despite this, risk is generally perceived as an important factor in the business environment, and it is more likely that managers and accountants will refer to the risk inherent in a situation than to its uncertainty. Because accountants like to quantify factors for decision-making they may well make a guess, even a fairly informed guess, as to the range of possible outcomes and their probabilities, but it is important to bear in mind that the accountant is only guessing (or estimating, to use a slightly more respectable term). This may seem a trivial point, but once a range of outcomes has been quantified, even if the underlying uncertainties are great, the fact of quantification lends a certain aura of respectability to the figures that may be quite unjustified.

Attitudes to risk and uncertainty differ between individuals, and indeed, may vary within an individual, depending upon context. The board of directors of a company may decide upon a corporate stance in respect of risk and uncertainty which will help to condition their approach to decision-making; this stance is often referred to as 'risk appetite'. It is important to appreciate, though, that risk-taking and decision-making are affected by individual psychology. It is beyond the scope of this book to examine this area in detail, but it is worth noting that there is a substantial body of research in economic psychology that demonstrates that people do not always, or even often, make decisions in a rational manner. The principal academic figures in this area are probably Amos Tversky and Daniel Kahneman; the latter was awarded the Nobel prize for economics in 2002. The Nobel citation (Nobel, 2002) makes the point as follows: 'In a series of studies, Kahneman – in collaboration with the late Amos Tversky – has shown that people are incapable of fully analyzing complex decisions when the future consequences are uncertain. Under such circumstances, they rely instead on . . . rules of thumb'.

Students who would like to explore this field further could try reading some of the relevant academic work, for example: Tversky and Kahnemann, 1986; Fox and Tversky, 1998; Thaler et al., 1997. These papers are not especially easy to read, but they are rewarding and informative.

Cost variability

In the discussion of relevant costs for decision-making earlier in the chapter it was noted that future costs and revenues are relevant for decision-making where they vary depending upon the decision scenario. With reference to costs, it is important to be able to distinguish between those costs that vary depending on such factors as level of output, and those that do not. Chapter 3 on product and services costing introduced the notion of direct and indirect costs; it could be observed there that direct costs tend to increase proportionately with the level of output whereas indirect overhead costs are likely to remain unchanged. Full absorption costing (as explained in Chapter 3) is therefore not useful for decision-making purposes.

This section of this chapter refines these initial observations by introducing variable, semi-variable and fixed costs.

Variable costs

Variable cost
a cost which varies in proportion to the level of business activity

A fully **variable cost** is one that varies in line with the level of business activity. For example, direct materials costs tend to be fully variable. The relationship between level of activity and variable cost is shown in the graph below.

FIGURE 6.1

Graph of variable cost behaviour

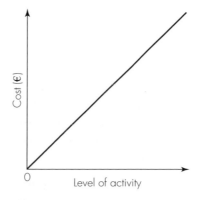

Variable costs increase as the level of activity increases; the relationship between costs and activities is linear. As activity increases (e.g. the number of units of production) variable costs increase. The line on the graph begins at 0 because at this point zero activity = zero variable cost. Example 6.2 demonstrates how a variable cost graph is created.

EXAMPLE 6.2

Sparks Kitchenware produces various types of kitchen equipment. A basic metal spatula requires 300 grams of metal at a cost of €1.00. The cost of metal to make two spatulas is exactly twice as much: 600 grams at a total cost of €2.00.

To make 10 spatulas, 3kg (300 grams × 10) of metal is required at a total cost of €10.00. For each additional spatula, the cost increases by €1 (i.e. the same amount every time). This is an example of a fully variable cost.

Earlier we noted that direct materials costs tend to be fully variable. When might they not be fully variable? Well, in practice, it is usually possible to obtain lower prices per unit of material as volumes increase. In the case of Sparks Kitchenware, suppose that a quantity discount of 5% is available for purchases of metal in quantities over 100kg. This means that a higher volume of production will be relatively a little cheaper than a low volume. However, it is often quite realistic to make an assumption that direct costs are fully variable with the level of output.

We can plot the variable cost data onto a graph similar to that in Figure 6.1. The variable materials cost of the spatulas produced by Sparks Kitchenware is shown at three different levels of activity in the following table.

Number of units produced	Variable cost total (€1 × number of units produced)
0	0
10	€10
20	€20

FIGURE 6.2

Sparks Kitchenware: Variable materials cost graph

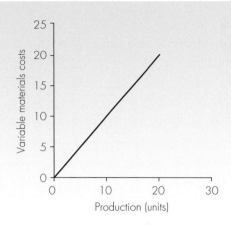

Fixed costs

A fixed cost is one that does not vary with the level of business activity. The relationship between level of activity and fixed cost is shown in the graph below.

FIGURE 6.3

Fixed cost behaviour

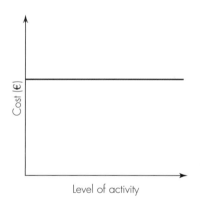

EXAMPLE 6.3

Sparks Kitchenware rents a factory unit. It pays rent of €28 000 each year for the unit, and insurance of €4360 each year. These are both examples of costs that do not vary with the level of output of the factory. Whether 1 or 1 000 000 metal spatulas are produced, the cost of factory rent and insurance remains the same. We can plot the fixed cost of the factory rental (€28 000) onto a graph. See Figure 6.4.

Of course, even fixed costs vary eventually. Suppose that the maximum number of spatulas Sparks Kitchenware can produce in its factory is 1 million per annum. If the business is successful and expands beyond this level of production it will need to obtain bigger production facilities – so factory rent and insurance would go up. It is only possible to describe costs as fixed within certain levels of activity.

FIGURE 6.4

Sparks
Kitchenware:
Fixed
cost (factory
rental) graph

Stepped costs

Where a business reaches the level of activity where a fixed cost must increase, the increase is sudden (see Figure 6.5).

FIGURE 6.5

Stepped cost
behaviour

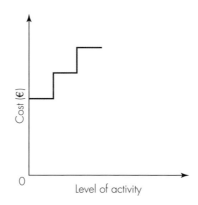

EXAMPLE 6.4

Sparks Kitchenware employs production supervisors at an annual salary cost of €12 500 each. The company's health and safety policy requires a certain level of supervision in the factory, and so the directors have decided that a supervisor must be employed for every 10 machine operators. So, if the number of machine operators is 50, 5 supervisors will be employed at a total cost of (5 × €12 500) €62 500. If the number of machine operators rises to 51, the company's policy requires that 6 supervisors will be employed. The total cost rises to (6 × €12 500) €75 000. We can plot this stepped cost onto a graph. See Figure 6.6.

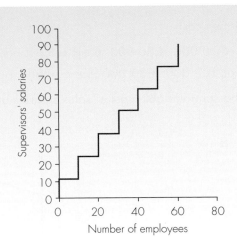

FIGURE 6.6

Sparks Kitchenware: Supervisors' salaries cost graph

Semi-variable costs

Semi-variable cost
a cost which varies to some extent with the level of business activity; it has both fixed and variable elements

A **semi-variable cost** is one that varies to some extent with the level of business activity; it has both fixed and variable elements. For example, telephone bills have both fixed and variable elements. There is a line rental charge that is fixed; it remains the same regardless of the number of calls made. In addition to the fixed line rental, however, there is a variable element that depends upon the number of phone calls made. The graph of a semi-variable cost (in Figure 6.7 below) shows that, even at a zero level of activity, some cost is incurred. That is why the cost line starts part way up the vertical axis.

FIGURE 6.7

Semi-variable cost behaviour

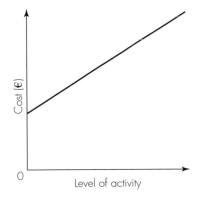

EXAMPLE 6.5

Sparks Kitchenware employs two sales staff. Each is paid a basic salary of €15 000 per year. In addition, each member of staff is paid a commission of 10% of sales value for every sale they make. Sales of €10 000, therefore, incur commission charges of €10 000 × 10% = €1000. Sales of €100 000 incur commission charges of €100 000 × 10% = €10 000.

▶

Total sales salaries costs:

- Sales level of 10 000: €30 000 (basic salary) + €1000 (commission) = €31 000.
- Sales level of 100 000: €30 000 (basic salary) + €10 000 (commission) = €40 000.

We can plot the semi-variable cost of sales salaries onto a graph. See Figure 6.8.

FIGURE 6.8

Sparks
Kitchenware:
Semi-variable cost
(sales salaries)
graph

Typical cost behaviour in different business sectors

In some types of business there are few, if any, variable costs. Even in businesses where a substantial proportion of cost is apparently variable with levels of activity, the reality may be that the costs are fixed in nature. We will look at some examples to illustrate these points.

A manufacturer

Usually, the direct materials used in manufacturing production tend to be variable; a progressively larger amount of material is used as the level of activity increases. By the same token, we would expect direct labour to be a variable cost. However, in practice, an employer's obligations to employees under employment regulations are often such that the labour cannot necessarily be regarded as variable. In many of the examples up to this point in the book, we have assumed that the supply of direct labour, like water from a tap, can be turned on or off at the convenience of management. This assumption, in many circumstances, is unrealistic. While a long-term downturn in an industry is likely to result in reductions in employees, short-term reductions in activity do not result in workers being laid off.

Therefore, in determining whether or not labour is a variable cost, the circumstances must be examined carefully. For example, sometimes, especially in garment manufacture, workers are paid piece rates – i.e. a sum for each completed item. Where this forms the whole of a worker's pay, the cost is truly variable. In some cases, however, there will be a basic, fixed level of wages plus a piece rate. This arrangement constitutes a semi-variable cost.

A commercial airline

Very few of the costs involved in running a commercial airline are variable. There are some very significant fixed costs, though:

Depreciation
a measurement of the amount of non-current assets value which has been used up during the accounting period (the term usually relates to tangible non-current assets)

- **depreciation** of aircraft
- employment of pilots and cabin crew
- aircraft maintenance and safety charges
- airport charges
- interest costs (on borrowing money to finance the purchase or lease of the planes).

A commercial aircraft service running scheduled flights must run the advertised flights even if there are very few passengers (in fact, because the planes have to be in certain places at scheduled times, a plane is likely to make the flight even if there are no passengers at all). Any variable costs are likely to be very minor indeed compared to the high level of fixed costs incurred. Variable costs would include, for example, the cost of any drinks supplied free during flights (the fewer passengers the fewer the drinks served, by and large).

Restaurant

Running a restaurant usually involves incurring a high level of fixed costs. For example:

- premises rental
- cost of employing staff
- depreciation of equipment.

What about food costs? To some extent these are variable, but because of the perishable nature of many food items there may be a fixed element of cost involved. If food is not sold to customers it will have to be thrown away sooner or later.

Labour costs may be variable to some extent, depending upon the basis of employment. If the restaurant proprietor expects a quiet evening he may be able to reduce the level of waiting and kitchen staff to some extent, but he will have to schedule at least some staff. Even if no customers at all turn up, he will still have to pay the staff for their time, and this basic minimum of staff time would represent a fixed cost.

Holiday tour operator

A holiday tour operator incurs fixed costs such as rental of offices, employment of staff to take bookings and deal with ticket administration, and so on. However, some of the costs are likely to be variable with the level of bookings taken from the public. A total of 37 couples booking a resort holiday will require 74 flight tickets and 37 rooms. There could, however, be some fixed elements to these costs; for example, where the contract with a hotel owner stipulates that, say, a minimum of 30 rooms will be paid for each week by the tour operator, regardless of whether or not they are used. In a case like this, the tour operator is being obliged to share with the hotel owner the risk of unused rooms.

Clearly, categorising costs neatly into 'fixed' and 'variable' categories is not always as simple in practice as it may at first appear. In many businesses genuinely variable costs are rare.

Marginal costing for decision-making

Marginal cost
the cost of one
additional unit

A **marginal cost** in economics is the cost of one additional unit. If a factory produces 1000 units of a product, the marginal cost of the product is the cost that would be incurred in producing the 1001st unit. If fixed costs remain the same at a production level of both 1000 and 1001 units, the marginal cost of the

1001st unit comprises variable costs only. Marginal costing is an accounting term that describes an approach to costing that excludes fixed costs. It provides a superior basis for decision-making, as the next example demonstrates.

EXAMPLE 6.6

Modena Mayhew plans the following budget income and expenditure for May 2008:

	€
Sales: 1000 units × €10 each	10 000
Costs	
Direct materials and labour	(4 000)
Production overheads, absorbed at €3 per unit	(3 000)
	3 000
Selling and administrative costs	(1 500)
Net profit	1 500

The business is not working to full capacity and it would be possible to produce more units of product. Modena Mayhew's sales director is approached by a contractor who wishes to order 100 units, to be produced and delivered in May for a special price of €8.50 per unit. In deciding whether or not to accept the order, the sales director needs information on the cost of a unit of product. What does it cost to produce one unit?

It might be tempting to take the total costs in the statement above (€4000 + €3000 + €1500 = €8500), divide by 1000 and come up with the figure of €8.50 per unit. However, this approach would be incorrect, unless all the costs were variable (and that is highly unlikely to be the case). Those costs that are fixed remain fixed unless the level of activity changes radically.

Really, the sales director needs to know the marginal cost of manufacturing one additional unit. Assuming that the production, selling and administrative costs are all fixed, and that all the direct costs are variables, this means that the business incurs €4000 of variable cost to produce 1000 units of product. The marginal cost of the 1001st unit of product is therefore €4 per unit.

If the sales director incorrectly calculated that the additional cost of the 100 unit order would be €850 (€8.50 × 100) he would conclude that it would not make sense to accept the order because the sales revenue from it would be no greater than cost. However, if he uses marginal cost, he may conclude that the order should be accepted.

Contribution

Contribution refers to the amount that remains after variable costs have been deducted from sales. Referring back to the information in Example 6.6, the additional contribution per unit of product that would be made on the special order for 100 units would be: €8.50 − 4.00 = €4.50 (sales price per unit less variable cost per unit = contribution per unit).

If contribution is a positive figure it contributes towards meeting the fixed costs of the business. Once sufficient contribution is made to cover all of the fixed costs, any remaining amount contributes to net profits.

Contribution can be calculated per unit, and can also be shown as a total (number of units sold × contribution per unit).

Break-even

Break-even point
the point at which neither a profit nor a loss is made, i.e. where total costs equal total revenues

The **break-even point** is the point at which no profit or loss is made in a set of business transactions. For example:

	€
Sales: 10 000 × €3	30 000
Less: variable costs: 10 000 units × €1	(10 000)
Contribution	20 000
Fixed costs	(20 000)
Net profit	Nil

SELF-TEST QUESTION 6.1

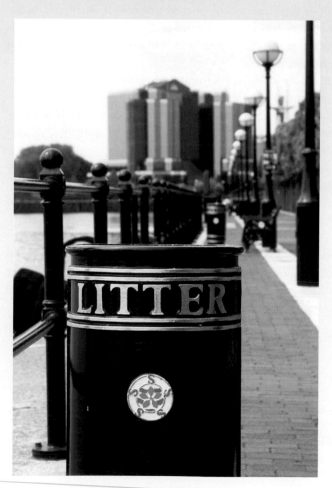

© Philip Corbluth / Alamy

Brinn Bartholomew sells municipal litter bins for €250 each. The bins cost €97 in direct materials (all variable cost) and €36 in direct labour (all variable cost). In June 2008 the company plans to sell 1400 bins. Its budgeted fixed costs for the month are €120 400.

- What is the company's budgeted contribution for June 2008?
- What is the company's budgeted net profit for June 2008?

Cost-volume-profit analysis

It is important to understand the relationships between the level of business activity and the different types of cost and profitability. The analysis of the interaction of these factors is known as cost-volume-profit analysis (CVP analysis). We will examine CVP relationships further, first by charting cost, volume and profit in graphical form, and then by using formulae to express the relationships between the factors. First, we will look at the construction of **break-even charts**.

Break-even chart
a graph showing lines for costs and revenues, from which the break-even point can be estimated

Break-even charts

Step 1

Earlier in the chapter we constructed graphs for each different type of cost. Developing that approach further, we can show both fixed and variable costs on the same graph (see Figure 6.9). An alternative presentation is shown in Figure 6.10.

Fixed costs, as we have seen, are those that remain at the same level regardless of the volume of activity. Variable costs increase steadily as the volume of activity increases. Showing the two together on a graph gives the result illustrated. The upper sloping line represents total costs. Where there is zero activity (i.e. no production or sales) the only costs incurred are fixed costs (which is why the total cost line starts part way up the vertical axis). As activity increases, so do total costs.

FIGURE 6.9

Graph of total costs, split into fixed and variable

Showing profit on a graph

Up till now we have not focused specifically on the graphical representation of profit. Suppose that Mulberry Piggott can make and potentially sell up to 7000 raincoats per year without any change to fixed costs. We can plot the following points on a graph:

Production level	Fixed costs €	Total costs €	Total revenue €
0	60 000	60 000	0
7 000	60 000	130 000 (€60 000 + [7 000 × €10])	210 000 (7 000 × €30)

This gives the result shown in Figure 6.12. The areas of profit and loss are marked on the graph. Beyond break-even point, as production increases, the area between the revenue and total costs lines is occupied by profit. The first dotted line shows sales in units and in revenue to produce profits of €30 000 (as calculated above).

FIGURE 6.12

Mulberry Pigot: Cost-volume-profit graph

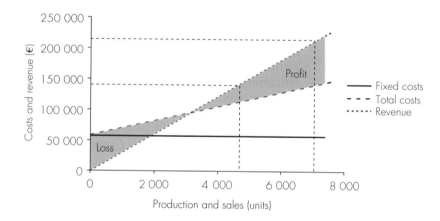

The second dotted line shows the maximum activity level that is possible at expenditure on fixed costs of €60 000. Profits at this level (the difference between the total revenue and total costs lines) would be much higher than at a level of 4500 sales; we can prove this by doing the calculation of profit at the maximum activity level of 7000 units:

	€
Sales (7 000 × €3)	210 000
Variable costs (7 000 × €10)	(70 000)
Contribution	140 000
Fixed costs	(60 000)
Profit	80 000

Margin of safety
the excess of planned or actual sales above the breakeven point.

Margin of safety

Margin of safety is the excess of planned or actual sales above the break-even point. In example 6.7 we calculated the Mulberry Piggott break-even point in units as 3000 raincoats. If we suppose that the sales of 4500 units targeted by the directors (as in example 6.8) are a realistic target, the margin of safety, expressed both in units and in sales value, is as follows:

	Units of sales	Sales
		€
Actual sales estimate	4 500	135 000
Break-even point	3 000	90 000
Margin of safety	1 500	45 000

The margin of safety can also be expressed as a percentage of the sales estimate:

$$\frac{1\ 500}{4\ 500} \times 100 = 33.3\%$$

Special decisions

Accepting contracts

In this section we look more closely at business decisions involving acceptance or non-acceptance of contracts on special terms. Marginal costing analysis can be useful in reaching the appropriate decision.

If an order or contract at a special price would produce a positive contribution to fixed costs, then the business should accept the order. However, there may be other factors to take into consideration. A business needs to have regard to factors such as maintaining its brand image and its position in the marketplace as, for example, a producer of high quality goods or as a firm with a serious commitment to minimising its environmental impact. A special price contract could damage a business's image and its relationships with other organisations.

EXAMPLE 6.9

of €6000 has been charged in depreciation. An offer has been received of €12 000 from a local firm. Wetwang's directors would like to be sure that they receive the best price for the machinery. They could advertise the machinery in a trade magazine for €500.

If the directors decide to advertise the machinery what is the minimum price they should accept for it?

6.3 Billericay Ashworth makes tennis racquets. In an average month it produces about 3000 racquets. The following are some of the costs the company incurs:

- Cost of raw materials. Each racquet uses €13.00 of raw materials.
- Factory insurance. The cost for a month is €800.
- Telephone charges. The company has several telephone lines. Its line rental charges per month are €1000. If no calls are made, the call charge is €0. On average 500 calls cost a total of €250 and 1000 calls, on average, cost €500. In most months about 1500 calls are made in the company.

You are required to:

i) Classify each of the above costs as one of the following:

- variable
- fixed
- stepped
- semi-variable.

ii) Using either graph paper or a spreadsheet program graphing facility, plot each of these costs onto a separate graph. Activity levels should be on the horizontal (x) axis and costs on the vertical (y) axis.

6.4 Classify each of the following costs as:

- variable
- fixed
- stepped
- semi-variable.

i) Sales staff members' mobile phone charges. There is a basic rental cost irrespective of the number of phone calls made, plus a charge for each phone call made, based on the number of minutes the call lasts.

ii) Factory machine oil.

iii) Metered water charges. The bill comprises a charge per unit for the number of units consumed.

6.5 For each of the following types of business, list at least two fixed and two variable costs that might typically be incurred:

- self-employed taxi driver
- solicitor

- shirt manufacturer
- beauty salon.

Try not to repeat the same examples of costs for the different businesses.

6.6 Porton Fitzgerald manufactures wardrobes. The selling price of a wardrobe is €210. Each wardrobe costs €52 in direct materials (all variable) and €34 in direct labour (all variable). In April 2008 the company expects to sell 450 wardrobes, and it has budgeted for fixed overheads of €43 200.

What is the company's budgeted contribution for April 2008?

What is the company's budgeted net profit for April 2008?

6.7 Fullbright Bognor, a manufacturing business, has the following cost structure:

Selling price per unit: €85

Variable costs per unit: €41

The company's directors expect to incur fixed costs of €62 000 in the year ending 31 December 2008. The maximum level of production which the company can reach is 3000 units per year.

You are required to:

i) Draw a break-even chart recording: fixed costs; total costs; total revenue.

ii) From the chart estimate the break-even point in units and in sales value for Fullbright Bognor for the year ending 31 December 2008.

iii) Use the break-even formula to find the break-even point in units and in sales value for Fullbright Bognor for the year ending 31 December 2008.

6.8 Foster Beniform makes mannequins for shop window displays. The company's directors are meeting to discuss sales budgets for 2008. The business has struggled to make a profit in recent years, but the finance director has made strenuous efforts in the last year or so to reduce the level of fixed costs and the directors hope to be able to make a profit in 2008. The production facilities can produce a maximum of 2000 mannequins per year.

The selling price of a mannequin is €55, with variable costs of production of €25 per unit. In order to be able to make plans for 2008 the directors would like to know the break-even point in units if (a) fixed costs in 2008 are €40 000; (b) fixed costs in 2008 are €50 000.

You are required to:

i) draw two break-even charts, one for each estimate of fixed costs, recording:

- fixed costs
- total costs
- total revenue.

ii) From the charts estimate the break-even point in units and in sales value for Foster Beniform for 2008 at each projected level of fixed costs.

iii) Use the break-even formula to calculate the break-even point in units and sales value at each estimated level of fixed costs for Foster Beniform for 2008.

6.9   Gropius Maplewood manufactures a single product that it sells for €150 per unit. Variable costs of each unit are €62, but are expected to rise at the beginning of 2008 to $63; because of severe competition the company will not be able to pass on this increase in costs to its customers. Fixed costs for 2008 are expected to be €90 000.

Break-even point for 2008 is estimated (to the nearest whole unit) at:

a)   1023 units

b)   1429 units

c)   1452 units

d)   1034 units.

6.10   Gimball Grace manufactures a single model of electric fan heater. Each heater sells for €21. Variable costs of manufacture are €7.50. Fixed costs of the business are estimated at €54 000 for the 2009 financial year. The net profit of the business in 2008 was €36 500, and the directors hope to increase that by 10% in 2009. How many fan heaters will they have to sell to reach their target net profit (to the nearest whole unit)?

a)   6974

b)   4000

c)   6704

d)   7374.

6.11   Garbage Solutions makes wheelie bins. In the 2009 financial year each bin will sell to local authorities for €25, with variable labour costs of €3.20 per bin and variable raw materials costs of €4.20. Fixed costs are budgeted at €178 900. The company's directors have budgeted net profit of €83 150 in 2009.

What is the company's margin of safety in units (to the nearest whole unit)?

a)   10 165

b)   9448

c)   5441

d)   4724.

6.12   Hubert et Hix Cie makes rucksacks. It has developed and patented a highly effective waterproof material and a revolutionary design. These make the company's products very much sought after, and the rucksacks sell at a premium price of €68.50 to camping shops and hiking organisations. Annual sales are 20 000 rucksacks. Variable costs of manufacture are €29.00. The company's current level of fixed costs is €382 420.

Most of the company's sales are within France and the UK, but there has been growing interest in Scandinavia and last financial year export sales to Norway and Sweden accounted for 10% of total sales.

The company has just received an enquiry from a Moroccan hiking organisation. The director of the organisation, Raoul, tried out one of the company's rucksacks on a recent hiking trip in the Atlas mountains, and is convinced that it's the best rucksack he's ever used. He would like to start supplying the rucksack in Morocco. However, he knows that there will be very few buyers in Morocco at the premium prices charged by retailers in Western Europe for the company's products. Raoul suggests that a reasonable price would be €50.00 and that the specification could perhaps be lowered, as the weather conditions are rather better in Morocco than in many parts of Europe. He estimates that annual sales in Morocco would be around 1000 units. Hubert et Hix's production director modifies the design slightly, and estimates that the variable costs of the new design would be €26.30. You are required to advise the directors on whether or not they should accept the order, taking into consideration both financial and non-financial factors.

6.13 Inez & Pilar Fashions is a fashion manufacturing and wholesale business operating from rented premises. The business is well established and has operated successfully for several years. However, Inez and Pilar, the company's directors, realise that they have reached maximum production capacity in their present building. They have an opportunity to expand into neighbouring premises. This would involve some minor reorganisation of production but could be achieved quite easily. Inez and Pilar have worked out that given extra production capacity their sales could increase, at an optimistic estimate, from the existing level of €310 000 per year to as much as €345 000. However, if there is a downturn in the economy the increase might be only €20 000.

Inez and Pilar estimate that variable production costs constitute 30% of sales value. If they take over the neighbouring premises there will be additional fixed costs of €15 000 per year.

You are required to advise Inez and Pilar on whether or not they should expand their production facilities, using calculations to support your arguments.

6.14 Juniper Jefferson manufactures two models of baby buggy: the De Luxe and the Super De Luxe. There is currently a shortage of the special grade of aluminium required for the buggy frame. This is unlikely to be a long-term problem, but it will affect production over the next three months. The cost and selling price information for each model is as follows:

	De Luxe	Super De Luxe
	€	€
Selling price	150	165
Variable cost of raw materials	38.25	42.50
Aluminium (at €8.50 per kg)		
Other raw materials	12.50	15.00
Variable cost of labour	13.65	15.60

The company has 350kg of aluminium in stock and expects to be able to buy no more than a further 1000kg per month for the next three months.

You are required to:

i) Calculate the contribution per unit of limiting factor for both models of buggy.

ii) Advise the directors on the production plan they should follow, assuming that:

   a) demand for the De Luxe will be 800 units over the next three months, with demand for the Super De Luxe at 300 units over the same period; or

   b) demand for the De Luxe will be 600 units over the next three months, with demand for the Super De Luxe at 400 units over the same period.

EXERCISES

6.15   The directors of Darlene Fabrik are considering whether or not to start up a new production process. The process would use a machine that is no longer required for the purpose for which it was originally bought. It cost €45 000 four years ago, and accumulated depreciation at the decision date was €13 000. Similar machines of the same age can be sold for €38 000. The same model of machine would now cost €50 000 if purchased new.

What is the amount of the opportunity cost for input into the decision process?

6.16   [Suitable for class discussion]

Tversky and Kahneman (1986) conducted an experiment on decision-making. Respondents were given a series of problems expressed (or 'framed') in different ways. Consider the following paired problems:

1 Assume that you are €300 richer than you are today. You have to choose between

   i) a sure gain of €100

   ii) a 50% chance of gaining €200 and a 50% chance of gaining nothing.

2 Assume that you are €500 richer than you are today. You have to choose between

   i) a sure loss of €100

   ii) a 50% chance of losing nothing and a 50% chance of losing €200.

First, decide your own answers to these questions. Second, compare your answers with the results obtained by the researchers. They found that in respect of the first problem, 72% of their 126 respondents chose the sure gain of €100, and the remaining 28% chose the second option. In respect of the second problem they found that 36% of 128 respondents chose the sure loss of €100, and the remaining 64% chose the second option.

Discuss the implications of the research findings, referring where appropriate to your own responses.

6.17   A tour operator, Colby Overland, is organising a coach trip to Russia as one of its new season's forthcoming attractions. Two of the major costs incurred are described as follows:

i) Coach costs. Each coach holds up to 40 passengers. The total cost of hiring a coach for the fortnight long trip is €14 000. The company will book only as many coaches as it needs. When the 41st holiday reservation is made, another coach is booked (and a further coach is booked upon receipt of the 81st holiday reservation, and so on). Because of constraints imposed by the limited availability of hotel rooms in Omsk, no more than four coachloads of passengers would be taken on the trip.

ii) Hotel costs. Each time a holiday reservation is made the company faxes the hotel in Omsk to make the extra booking. If no more rooms are available, the hotel refuses the booking and the tour is regarded as full. The hotel cost per passenger is €280.

Required:

i) Using either graph paper or a spreadsheet program graphing facility plot each of these costs onto a separate graph. The number of holiday reservations should be shown on the horizontal (x) axis and cost on the vertical (y) axis.

ii) Classify each of the costs as one of the following:

- variable
- fixed
- stepped
- semi-variable.

6.18 For each of the following types of business, list at least two fixed and two variable costs that might typically be incurred:

- milk delivery business
- coffee bar
- stationery manufacturer
- cross channel ferry operator.

Try not to repeat the same examples of costs for the different businesses.

6.19 Vernon is a xylophone manufacturer. The direct materials cost of a xylophone is €300; the direct labour process is intensive and costs €450 per xylophone. Both direct materials and direct labour are fully variable. Each xylophone sells for €1500. In August 2008 the company expects to sell 120 xylophones, and it has budgeted for fixed overheads of €54 000.

What is the company's budgeted contribution for August 2008?

What is the company's budgeted net profit for August 2008?

6.20 Finch Fletcher manufactures trumpets. Each trumpet sells for €350, and has variable costs of manufacture of €120. The company can produce no more than 1200 in a year. In the year ending 31 March 2008 the company's directors expect to incur fixed costs of €172 000.

You are required to:

i) Draw a break-even chart recording:

- fixed costs
- total costs
- total revenue.

ii) From the chart estimate the break-even point in units and in sales value for Finch Fletcher for the year ending 31 March 2008.

iii) Use the break-even formula to calculate the break-even point in units and in sales value for Finch Fletcher for the year ending 31 March 2008.

6.21 Fallon Frodsham manufactures and installs small prefabricated building structures that are sold to people who want to establish a home office using part of their gardens. Each prefabricated building sells at €13 000, including installation costs. The variable costs of manufacture are €7300 per building. The company's directors have set a sales target of 150 buildings for the 2008 accounting year.

i) Using a break-even chart, estimate the maximum level of fixed costs the company can incur in 2008 without making a loss, on the assumption that the sales target is met.

ii) Apply the break-even formula to calculate the maximum level of fixed costs.

Tutorial note: This question may require some thought. Known factors are total revenues (sales revenue per unit × number of units sold), and total variable costs (variable costs per unit × number of units sold). The point on the horizontal (x) axis at which break-even point is reached is also known (150 units). The line must be drawn from that point upwards to the point where it intersects with the total revenue line.

6.22 Gulf Gadgets manufactures chess sets. Each chess set sells for €185. Variable costs of manufacture are €78. The company's directors are currently setting the budget for 2009. Fixed costs are expected to be €65 000. The selling price of a chess set will rise to €187 and the variable costs of manufacture are expected to increase by 10%.
Break-even point for 2009 is estimated (to the nearest whole unit) at:

a) 607
b) 655
c) 642
d) 596.

6.23 Gecko Grimsby sells specialist aquaria. In the 2008 financial year each aquarium sold for €1320. The variable costs of manufacture were €321 per aquarium and the total fixed costs incurred were €85 750.
If the selling price, variable costs and fixed costs are all expected to increase by 10% in the 2009 financial year, how many aquaria (to the nearest whole unit) will the company have to sell to make net profits of €50 000?

a) 131
b) 144
c) 136
d) 124.

6.24 Gospodin Grimshaw manufactures hiking boots for sale which it sells principally in Russia and other parts of eastern Europe. Each pair of boots sells for €15. Variable costs are €5.50 per pair. Fixed costs are budgeted at €87 900 for the 2008 financial year. The company expects to sell 15 000 pairs of boots in 2008. What is its margin of safety in €s (to the nearest €)?

a) €54 597
b) €86 205

    c) €138 795

    d) €62 520.

6.25   Ince Pargeter manufactures padded carrying cases for laptop computers. The market is currently buoyant, and the company's factory is working to capacity. The company has been offered the opportunity to compete for a contract for 10 000 cases per year at a selling price of €15 per case. This is below the company's usual selling price of €17.25. Variable costs of manufacture would be the same as for existing cases, i.e. €5.63. However, in order to be able to take on the contract the company would need to expand its production facilities. For technical reasons it would be impossible to expand production to increase capacity to produce exactly 10 000 additional units. The expansion of facilities would increase capacity to the point where 20 000 additional units could be manufactured. Ince Pargeter's sales director thinks it is possible that he may be able to obtain additional orders that will use up the spare capacity. If production facilities were expanded, fixed costs would rise from €283 000 to an estimated €390 000.

    You are required to advise the company on whether or not it should expand its production facilities.

6.26   Jackson Demetrios manufactures three different types of office desk. Type A has extra drawers, type B has a printer shelf and type C has a moveable footrest.

    In the company's present factory, production facilities are limited and there is a restriction on the number of machine hours available. The directors have considered moving to larger premises, but they are unwilling to make the move just at the moment because of fears of a downturn in the office furniture market.

    Cost and selling price information for each type of desk is as follows:

	Type A €	Type B €	Type C €
Selling price per unit	175	160	165
Variable materials costs			
Wood	37	35	35
Plastics	16	15	18
Screws and fixings	2	2	2
Variable labour costs	18	16	16
Machine hours required per unit	2.5 hours	2.0 hours	2.1 hours
Sales demand for 2008	1400	1600	1550

Machine hours available are 4000 hours during 2009. You are required to:

i) Advise the directors on the most profitable production plan available to them without further expansion of the premises.

ii) Calculate the overall contribution to fixed costs (to the nearest €) if your recommended production plan is followed.

Capital Investment Decisions

Aim of the chapter

To understand some of the techniques used in longer-term decision-making on capital investment.

Learning outcomes

After reading the chapter and completing the exercises at the end, students should:

- Understand the need for control over capital investment decision-making.
- Understand and be able to apply two simple methods of capital investment appraisal: payback and accounting rate of return.
- Understand the time value of money.
- Understand and be able to apply more complex methods of capital investment appraisal: net present value and internal rate of return.
- Understand some of the limitations of capital investment appraisal techniques in theory and practice.

Introduction

The two previous chapters have examined various aspects of decision-making relating to pricing and short-term decisions about production, undertaking contracts and so on. This chapter continues the decision-making theme by examining the methods and techniques used by businesses to decide on longer-term investment decisions. Managers are frequently called upon to make important decisions, often involving large sums, about expenditure on capital items. Capital expenditure involves investment in items such as tangible non-current assets, investment in other businesses, and the acquisition of holdings in the form of financial instruments that will be held for the longer term. Capital expenditure decisions involve the appraisal of profits and cash flows that will be generated into the future, usually over a relatively long time period.

This chapter examines a range of techniques used in practice to appraise capital investment projects. The early part of the chapter explains the use of two relatively straightforward techniques: accounting rate of return (ARR) and

Net present value
the aggregate of a set of cash inflows and outflows forecast to take place at future dates, discounted to present values

payback. The chapter then proceeds to consider the issue of the valuation of cash flows that may extend well into the future. The time value of money and the techniques used for estimating it are explained in the context of two more advanced appraisal techniques: **net present value** (NPV) and internal rate of return (IRR). The chapter's concluding sections examine the extent to which these capital investment appraisal techniques are used by firms, and the limitations and problems which may arise in practice and theory.

Capital investment in context

Capital budgeting
the process of decision-making in respect of selecting investment projects, and the amount of capital expenditure to be committed

All organisations, whether business, public sector, or not-for-profit, are likely at some time or other to be involved in decisions about the deployment of resources in longer-term investments. The operations of some businesses are capital intensive in that they require substantial investment in premises and machinery in order to facilitate production of goods. As noted in earlier chapters the proportion of such activities in highly developed economies has tended to fall during the late twentieth century. Nevertheless, even in service industries it is common to find that some level of capital investment is required. Because of the relatively long-term impact of such investments it is important that they should be made in conformity with the strategic objectives of the business. It is part of the role of senior management to ensure that sufficient resources are made available in order to achieve their objectives. They must decide on the amount of capital expenditure that is appropriate and feasible. The process referred to as **capital budgeting** is, according to CIMA's Official Terminology, 'concerned with decision-making in respect of the choice of specific investment projects and the total amount of capital expenditure to commit'. The box below gives an example of a real business's capital budget and its deployment.

Tesco's capital budget

As reported in the *Financial Times*, Tesco, which is the world's fifth-largest retailer, is currently increasing its investment outside the UK. '. . . Tesco will be investing more than half its capital outside the UK in two years . . . although the time when it achieves more sales abroad than at home is some time off.' The following excerpt from the article gives some idea of the scale of investment:

> 'In the next 18 months, Tesco will launch its convenience chain in California. Sir Terry [Leahy] has dispatched Tim Mason, head of marketing and a board member, to the US along with a dozen Tesco staff. The supermarket group is spending €250m a year on the project – just under 10 per cent of its entire capital budget this year.'

Extrapolating from this information, Tesco's entire capital budget must be in the region of €2,500 million. (Source of information: Rigby, 2006.)

Capital rationing

Capital rationing
where a shortage of
capital available for
investment requires
prioritisation of
investment projects

Because resources are limited, there may be significant levels of competition for funds within organisations. For example, divisions within the organisation may have to compete with each other in order to win funding for capital projects. If funds are employed for a particular capital project they cannot, clearly, be used for anything else: each potential use of funds involves an opportunity cost. In conditions of **capital rationing** it is important that management has clear criteria, linked to overall strategic objectives, in order to make the best possible investment decisions. Capital rationing is defined by CIMA as follows:

'Restriction on an entity's ability to invest capital funds, caused by an internal budget ceiling being imposed on such expenditure by management (soft capital rationing), or by external limitations being applied to the company, as when additional borrowed funds cannot be obtained (hard capital rationing).'

In order to ensure that scarce capital resources are deployed as effectively and as efficiently as possible, senior managers should establish their decision-making criteria in advance. Some, although not necessarily all, of these criteria are likely to be expressed in quantitative terms. For example, a firm's board may say to its middle managers that it will consider any potential investment project that is projected to exceed certain cash flow or profitability criteria. The criteria may be set in terms of some of the investment appraisal techniques set out in this chapter: for example '. . . we will consider any project that is budgeted to generate an internal rate of return (IRR) in excess of 8.5% . . .'.

The next section of the chapter examines some simple techniques that can be used to appraise potential capital investments.

Simple appraisal techniques

Two techniques will be explained in this section of the chapter: accounting rate of return (ARR) and payback. A single example will be used to explain both these and the more complex techniques later in the chapter. The example contains, necessarily, quite a lot of detail and this is explained first.

EXAMPLE 7.1

Proctor Hedges manufactures a wide range of gardening equipment. It has recently developed a new design of compost bin. A market research project costing €20 000 was undertaken in which the prototype was demonstrated to a large number of gardeners at show gardens around the country. Results of the market research have been very promising. In addition, the company's marketing director has used his contacts to have the new design prominently featured in a prime-time television gardening programme. The programme is due to appear in three months' time, and the company expects to receive a large number of orders very soon afterwards. The directors have decided that they must gear up production to be ready for the anticipated demand for the new product. The principal capital expenditure involved would be the purchase of an advanced do introduce further elements of imprecision and estimation into the appraisal calculations.

Assembling information for the appraisal

First, it will be helpful to establish an estimated production and sales schedule for each of the two machines. It is assumed that revenue and expenses approximate to cash flows.

Year	Demand	Machine A production and sales	Machine B production and sales
1	60 000	40 000	60 000
2	48 000	40 000	48 000
3	42 000	40 000	42 000
4	25 000	25 000	25 000
5	25 000	25 000	25 000

Because Machine A has a maximum production capacity of 40 000 units per year, it cannot meet demand. It will produce up to capacity for the first three years (120 000 units as opposed to demand of 150 000). It is assumed that dissatisfied customers will not wait for a compost bin (people are not likely to put their name down on a waiting list for this type of product) and will simply buy another type.

Once we have established sales and production figures, we can estimate profits before depreciation for each of the five years, as follows:

Year	Machine A	Machine B
1	40 000 × €4.00 = €160 000	60 000 × €4.10 = €246 000
2	40 000 × €4.00 = €160 000	48 000 × €4.10 = €196 800
3	40 000 × €4.00 = €160 000	42 000 × €4.10 = €172 200
4	25 000 × €4.00 = €100 000	25 000 × €4.10 = €102 500
5	25 000 × €4.00 = €100 000	25 000 × €4.10 = €102 500
Total profit	€680 000	€820 000

Accounting rate of return

The accounting rate of return (ARR) method uses projections of accounting profit to calculate the expected rate of return on capital invested into an asset or project. It is calculated as follows:

$$\frac{\text{Average expected return (accounting profit)}}{\text{Average capital employed}} \times 100 = ARR\%$$

Calculating average expected return (accounting profit)

Accounting profit takes depreciation into account. Therefore, we must deduct depreciation from each of the annual profit figures calculated earlier, before calculating the average profit over five years:

	Machine A	Machine B
Year	€000	€000
1	160 − 80 = 80	246 − 100 = 146
2	160 − 80 = 80	196.8 − 100 = 96.8
3	160 − 80 = 80	172.2 − 100 = 72.2
4	100 − 80 = 20	102.5 − 100 = 2.5
5	100 − 80 = 20	102.5 − 100 = 2.5
Total profit	280	320

The average profit per year generated by Machine A is:

$$\frac{280\ 000}{5} = €56\ 000$$

The average profit per year generated by Machine B is:

$$\frac{320\ 000}{5} = €64\ 000$$

Calculating average capital employed

The capital employed figure to be taken into account is the capital employed by the project or investment (not the capital employed by the whole business).

In this particular example, because the straight-line method of depreciation is adopted, the capital investment is assumed to be depleted by the same amount each year (€80 000 for Machine A and €100 000 for Machine B). Therefore, we take initial capital employed (at Time 0) and capital employed by the end of the final year of operation (Time 5) and average the two figures, as follows:

	Machine A	Machine B
Time	€000	€000
0	450	600
5	50	100
Average	$\frac{450 + 50}{2} = €250$	$\frac{600 + 100}{2} = €350$

We now have both elements necessary for the calculation (average accounting profit and average capital employed) of ARR. For Machine A:

$$ARR = \frac{56\ 000}{250\ 000} \times 100 = 22.4\%$$

For Machine B:

$$ARR = \frac{64\ 000}{350\ 000} \times 100 = 18.3\%$$

The ARR calculation shows Machine A as the better of the two options. Although Machine B is estimated to produce more profit, the average investment is considerably higher. If the directors were to use only this one method of investment appraisal they might very well opt for Machine A. Note, however, that the comparison of ARR ignores the fact that Machine B actually produces a higher absolute profit (€64 000) than that produced by Machine A (€56 000). This is a notable weakness of the ARR technique.

Students may well have spotted the similarity between the calculation of ARR and that of return on capital employed (ROCE). ROCE is calculated for a business as a whole. If Proctor Hedges' ROCE is substantially in excess of the ARR of 22.4% the directors may wish to think again about the whole project. If a project is undertaken that produces an ARR that is lower than ROCE, the ROCE percentage will be reduced overall.

The Proctor Hedges' example requires comparison between two investments. However, sometimes only one possible investment is appraised (because the choice is simply between making the investment and not making the investment). In such cases it is common to find ARR being judged against a yardstick or target return percentage. If the proposed investment's ARR is less than the target then the investment may well be rejected.

Payback

Payback is a simple and unsophisticated investment appraisal technique that involves estimating the length of time it will take for cash inflows to cover the initial investment outflow. This can be a useful technique where one of the management's principal criteria is the ability of a project to 'pay for itself' quickly, so that proceeds can be reinvested in other projects.

Note that payback appraises investments in terms of cash inflows and outflows. Because depreciation is neither an inflow nor an outflow (remember: depreciation is an accounting adjustment) it is not taken into account.

Payback is relatively simple to calculate:

Time	Machine A €000	Machine B €000
Initial outflow		
0	− 450	− 600
Inflows		
1	+160	+246
2	+160	+196.8
3	+160	+172.2
4	+100	+102.5
5	+100	+102.5
5*	+50	+100

*Note that at the end of year 5 the machine will be sold, or transferred into alternative production at net book value. An inflow of the amount of the net book value is therefore included.

Payback is calculated by taking cumulative cash flows into account, and identifying the point at which the net cumulative cash flow reaches zero.

For Machine A:

Time	Cash flow €000	Cumulative cash flow €000
0	−450	−450
1	+160	−290
2	+160	−130
3	+160	+30
4	+100	+130
5	+100 + 50	+280

Cumulative cash flow reaches the zero position sometime during the third year. We can estimate a figure for payback expressed in years and months as follows:

Payback = 2 years + (130/160 × 12 months) = 2 years and 10 months (to nearest whole month)

For Machine B:

Time	Cash flow €000	Cumulative cash flow €000
0	−600	−600
1	+246	−354
2	+196.8	−157.2
3	+172.2	+15
4	+102.5	+117.5
5	+102.5 + 100	+320

Cumulative cash flow reaches the zero position sometime during the third year (as for Machine A). Estimating a figure for payback expressed in years and months:

Payback = 2 years + (157.2/172.2 × 12 months) = 2 years and 11 months (to nearest whole month)

Comparing the payback measures, we can see that Machine A pays back only slightly more quickly than Machine B. Payback, then, is unlikely to play a major part in this particular investment decision.

Payback is a popular method of appraisal in practice, but it has a major limitation in that it concentrates attention on only one important aspect – the ability of an investment to pay back quickly. As we can see from the Proctor Hedges example, cash flows beyond the point of payback are completely ignored. Surely these later cash flows should be taken into account in investment appraisal?

Net present value, which we examine next, does take into account all of the cash flows associated with an investment.

More complex appraisal techniques

In order to understand the more complex appraisal techniques, it is first important to gain an appreciation of the factor of time in longer-term investments.

The time value of money

The principle of the time value of money rests on the observation that, because of interest, €1 now is not the same as €1 in a month's time or a year's time, or ten years' time. The effect of interest is illustrated below.

Compounding

A saver puts €100 in the bank on 1 January 2007. The bank's interest rate is 10% throughout the whole of the year which follows. Consequently, when the interest is paid on 31 December 2007 the saver now has €110 in the account. If €110 is kept in the account for the whole of the next year following – 2008 – and the interest rate remains stable at 10%, by 31 December 2008 the saver has accumulated:

€110 (at 31 December 2007) + Interest for 2008 (10% × €110) = €121

Each year, provided the saver keeps both the original investment and the accumulated interest in the bank, the interest compounds. The amount of interest earned each year gradually increases. The five-year effect, assuming a constant interest rate of 10%, as follows:

Year	Balance at start of year	Interest for year	Balance at end of year
1	100.00	10.00	110.00
2	110.00	11.00	121.00
3	121.00	12.10	133.10
4	133.10	13.31	146.41
5	146.41	14.64	161.05

So, €1 at Time 0 (the beginning of year 1) is the equivalent of €1.61 at the end of year 5.

The compounding effect can be expressed via a formula derived as follows. Using 10% as an example:

€1 + (€1 × 10%) = €1.10

So, the initial sum invested × (1 + the rate of interest) = amount at the end of year 1. That is:

$1 \times (1 + i)$

where i = the interest rate (expressed as a decimal, e.g. 0.10 rather than 10%).

What about a formula for year 2? For the total at the end of year 2 we take the amount at the end of year 1 × (1 + the rate of interest) = amount at the end of year two. That is:

$1 \times (1 + i) \times (1 + i)$

Or:

$1 \times (1 + i)^2$

Test this out by reference to the example of €100 invested at a rate of 10% per year for two years:

€100 × (1 + 0.10)^2 = €100 × (1.21) = €1.21

The formula for year 3 adds another compounding factor:

$$1 \times (1 + i) \times (1 + i) \times (1 + i)$$

Or:

$$1 \times (1 + i)^3$$

And so on. The formula for the compounding factor is expressed as follows:

$$(1 + i)^n$$

where i = the rate of interest and n = the number of years. For each combination of interest rate and number of years, we can work out a compounding factor. For example, what is the compounding factor for €1 invested at a constant rate of 4% over three years? Answer:

$$(1 + 0.04)^3 = (1.04) \times (1.04) \times (1.04) = 1.125$$

So €1 invested at a constant rate of 4% over three years will result in a balance at the end of year 3 of €1.125.

SELF-TEST QUESTION 7.1

1 Write down the formula for €1 invested at a constant rate of 8% for four years and work out the compounding factor.

2 Write down the formula for €1 invested at a constant rate of 7% for five years and work out the compounding factor.

3 Write down the formula for €1 invested at a constant rate of 6% for six years and work out the compounding factor.

Discounting

In the discussion of compounding above we noted that, at a constant rate of 10%, €1 invested now (at Time 0) is the equivalent of €1.61 by the end of year 5. Conversely, we could say that €1.61 at the end of year 5 is the equivalent of €1 now. In order to have €1.61 at the end of year 5 we would need to invest €1 now. How can this be expressed in a formula?

Discounting formulae are the reciprocals of compounding formulae. So, we noted earlier that, at a constant rate of 10% the initial sum invested $\times$ (1 + the rate of interest) = amount at the end of year 1. That is:

$$1 \times (1 + i)$$

We can turn this round to discount back from the end of year 1:

$$\text{Amount at the end of year } 1 \times \frac{1}{(1+i)} = \text{amount of the initial sum invested}$$

Similarly, taking the reciprocal of the year 2 compounding formula:

$$\text{Amount at the end of year } 2 \times \frac{1}{(1+i)^2} = \text{amount of the initial sum invested}$$

We continue to discount the cash flows using discount factors that decrease as the cash flow events recede into the future. Setting the figures out neatly in a table:

Time	Cash flow €	Discount factor (from table)	Discounted cash flow €
0	(450 000)	1	(450 000)
1	160 000	0.909	145 440
2	160 000	0.826	132 160
3	160 000	0.751	120 160
4	100 000	0.683	68 300
5	150 000	0.621	93 150
Total			109 210

The total of €109 210 is known as the net present value (NPV); it is the total of the cash inflows and outflows associated with the investment (hence 'net'), all discounted and expressed in terms of €s at Time 0 (hence 'present value').

Present value
the discounted value at the present time (i.e. now) of a cash flow expected to arise in the future

Machine B

Time	Cash flow €	Discount factor (from table)	Discounted cash flow €
0	(600 000)	1	(600 000)
1	246 000	0.909	223 614
2	196 800	0.826	162 557
3	172 200	0.751	129 322
4	102 500	0.683	70 008
5	202 500	0.621	125 752
Total			111 253

The net present value of the investment in Machine B is estimated at €111 253.

The basic decision rule that is employed in respect of NPV is:

If NPV > 0 accept the project or investment

Or, where there is more than one alternative project or investment:

Accept the project or investment with the larger (largest) NPV

In this case, Machine B produces a slightly larger NPV, and so looks preferable to the investment in Machine A. (Note that both ARR and payback indicate that Machine A is the better investment!)

Ratio of cash inflows to initial investment

In deciding between investment projects it can be helpful to look at the relationship between the discounted cash flows generated by a project against the initial outflow of cash.

Machine A

Total positive discounted cash flows generated = NPV + initial investment:

= €109 210 + €450 000 = €559 210

(If this step seems complicated, just add up all the positive present values of cash flows from years 1 to 5 inclusive – it will give the same answer.) The ratio of the positive cash flows to the initial investment is:

$$\frac{€559\ 210}{450\ 000} = 1.24$$

Machine B

Total positive discounted cash flows generated = NPV + initial investment:

= €111 253 + €600 000 = €711 253

The ratio of the positive cash flows to the initial investment is:

$$\frac{€711\ 253}{600\ 000} = 1.19$$

Machine A gives the higher ratio. This means that it produces more positive cash inflow relative to the initial investment. Although the NPV of Machine B is, overall, slightly higher, the calculation of this ratio points towards Machine A as a better investment.

Internal rate of return

The final investment appraisal technique that we will examine is the internal rate of return (IRR). This technique is closely related to the NPV technique that we have just examined. The IRR of an investment or project is the expected yield (expressed as a percentage). IRR is the discount rate, which, applied to expected cash flows, produces an NPV of zero.

This is easier to understand if presented graphically. Using the example of Machine A, we can see that at a discount rate of 10%, a positive NPV of €109 210 results. What happens if we calculate NPV using, say, 12%, 14%, 16%, 18% and 20%? The following NPVs have been calculated at each of these rates:

Interest rate	NPV €
10%	109 210
12%	82 790
14%	58 410
16%	35 960
18%	14 990
20%	(4 540)

FIGURE 7.2

Net present value of
Machine B cash
flows at various
discount rates

Expressed diagrammatically:

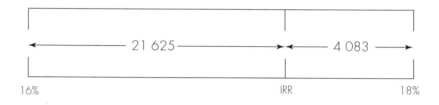

The distance between 16% and IRR is:

$$\frac{21\ 625}{25\ 708} \times 2\% = 1.68\%$$

The distance between IRR and 20% is:

$$\frac{4\ 083}{25\ 708} \times 2\% = 0.32\%$$

IRR is 16% + 1.68% = 17.68%
(or alternatively: IRR is 18% − 0.32% = 17.68%: it amounts to the same).

Using a computer: Machine B

For the Machine B data, the IRR calculated by the computer is 17.68%.

Significance of IRR for decision-making

Where IRR is greater than the business's cost of capital the project is acceptable. If, as in the example, a choice has to be made between two possible projects, the one with the higher IRR is preferable.

In the Proctor Hedges example, the Machine A project produces an IRR of 19.53%, whereas the Machine B project produces an IRR of 17.68%. Both are well in excess of the 10% used by the company and so both projects would be acceptable. However, Machine A produces the better IRR rate, and so is preferable.

Choosing between projects

The application of the four methods of investment appraisal to the example of Proctor Hedges produces the following results:

Method	Machine A result	Machine B result	Choice
ARR	22.4%	18.3%	Machine A
Payback	2 years 10 months	2 years 11 months	Machine A
NPV	€109 210	€111 253	Machine B
IRR	19.54%	17.68%	Machine A

Three out of the four sets of results point towards the choice of Machine A (but note that there is little to choose between them in terms of payback). NPV is the exception but in this case the results for the two machines are very similar.

It would seem that Machine A may be the better choice. However, as with all business decisions, the solution indicated by the figures may not be preferred once other factors are taken into consideration. A key point for consideration by the directors is that Machine A does not have sufficient capacity to meet demand in the first three years or so of the project. This means that a significant part of customer demand will be unfulfilled. Possible consequences include loss of customer goodwill, bad publicity and a knock-on effect on sales of the company's other products.

On the other hand, if demand for the compost bins proves to have been over-estimated, Machine A will emerge, with the benefit of hindsight, as a very much better choice. None of the investment appraisal techniques we have examined in the chapter take account of the relative riskiness of the alternatives. This is a weakness that needs to be recognised by decision-makers.

Which of the four techniques provides the most reliable results? The strengths and weaknesses of each of them are examined in the following section.

Strengths and weaknesses of the common investment appraisal techniques

There are some weaknesses common to all of four of the techniques examined. As noted above, the relative risk attached to future cash flows is not taken into account. Also, all of the appraisal techniques are based upon future estimates. As the estimates of cash flow recede into the future they become progressively less reliable. It is possible to accept, for example, that experienced managers are able to make a reliable prediction of the coming year's sales figures, but can they really predict sales figures five years from now with any degree of reliability? The imprecision that inevitably surrounds future figures means that they are open to manipulation by unscrupulous managers.

A further problem about attaching apparently precise values to future predictions is that managers may give the figures more credence than they really merit. The figures can only ever provide a guide to decision-making.

The principal strength of all of the techniques described is that they are better than nothing. Managers sometimes make decisions based on 'gut feeling' or 'instinct' or 'experience'. These may not be reliable qualities upon which to base decisions; at least by making some effort to formally appraise projects, managers may be able to avoid making really big mistakes.

In addition to these general points, each of the techniques has its own strengths and weaknesses.

Accounting rate of return (ARR)

Strengths

- Calculation of ARR is very straightforward.
- ARR is a widely used measurement (in the form of ROCE); it is easy to compare the ARR of a particular project with the overall ROCE for a business.
- It is a measurement that non-financial managers can readily understand.

Weaknesses

- ARR treats all future cash flows as equal in weight; it takes no account of the time value of money.
- ARR is calculated on the basis of accounting profits rather than cash flow. It includes the effect of depreciation, an accounting adjustment the nature and timing of which is determined by management.
- As noted on pp. 149/150, ARR fails to take into account the relative size of competing projects.

Payback

Strengths

- Calculation of payback is very straightforward.
- It can be useful where rapid recovery of funding is a priority.
- It is a measurement that non-financial managers can readily understand.

Weaknesses

- Payback treats all future cash flows as equal in weight; it takes no account of the time value of money.
- Where rapid recovery of funding is not a major priority, payback provides little useful information.
- All cash flows beyond the payback point are simply ignored.

STRENGTHS AND WEAKNESSES OF THE COMMON INVESTMENT APPRAISAL TECHNIQUES

Net present value (NPV)

Strengths

- NPV builds the time value of money into calculations.
- Unlike payback, NPV takes all of the future projected cash flows into account.
- NPV is very useful for ranking different projects as it deals in absolute values rather than percentages (which, as in the case of ARR, can give unreliable results).

Weaknesses

- It can be difficult to explain NPV to non-financial managers.
- There are significant practical difficulties in determining an appropriate discount rate.

Internal rate of return (IRR)

Strengths

- IRR builds the time value of money into calculations.

Weaknesses

- It can be difficult to explain IRR to non-financial managers.
- Because IRR is expressed in percentage terms it ignores absolute values: 15% return on an investment of €100 000 is fine (€15 000), but not as good in absolute terms as a 12% return on €1 000 000 (€120 000).
- There are significant practical difficulties in determining an appropriate target discount rate.
- It is not always possible to calculate IRR.

The last point perhaps needs explanation. In the Proctor Hedges example, the pattern of cash flow was an initial major outlay of cash, followed by several years of inflows. Where the pattern of cash flows is more irregular (for example, a net inflow in years one and two followed by a net outflow in year three, followed by another inflow in year four) IRR cannot be used.

The best technique?

Of the four techniques examined in the chapter, NPV appears to have the fewest significant weaknesses and the most obvious strengths. The widespread availability of computers, and the fact that many business managers are now highly computer literate, means that the calculations of NPV and IRR no longer present any difficulties.

The social context of decision-making

Reading a book like this, which, amongst other things, explains in detail certain quantitative techniques for decision-making, might lead the reader to the conclusion that decision-making is straightforward provided that the techniques are employed correctly. This conclusion would ignore, however, the context in which decisions are made and techniques and technologies are employed. In practice, it is rarely, if ever, a simple matter of putting figures into a spreadsheet, doing the calculation and following a decision-rule. It is important to understand the powerful influence of the social context in which decisions are made.

The theory of technological determinism assumes that technological developments impact on society, and that society, being a passive recipient of technology, will change in predictable ways as a result of such developments. So, if a set of sound techniques for decision-making are developed, the theory of technological determinism would predict that managerial behaviour will alter, and that better decisions will naturally result. However, there is abundant evidence to suggest that this is not, in practice, how technologies (using the word to encompass techniques) actually operate. While it is undoubtedly the case that technology impacts on society, the consequences of the impact are not necessarily predictable.

An alternative theoretical approach is embodied in the idea of 'social shaping' of technology. This theory is based on the idea that technological development and society are inextricably entwined with each other. Because society is complex the adoption of technology is also, naturally, complex and technologies may not conform to predictions about their use.

> 'Successful practising engineers have always known that their work is as much economic, organizational, even political, as it is "technical". They know that a design that works technically will still fail if it is too expensive, if it is unattractive to employers or customers, if its "fit" to the structure of an organization is poor, or if it falls foul of powerful political forces. The most enterprising among engineers even know that these are not simply constraints to be met. Costs can be manipulated, both in projections and in reality; employers can be swayed; markets can be created and shaped; organizations can be restructured . . . and so on' (Mackenzie and Wajcman, 1999, p. xv).

In the context of decision-making using the appraisal techniques explained in this chapter, social shaping theory suggests that they may be misunderstood, misinterpreted, or used to further the agenda of a group of individuals within an organisation. Thomas (1999) relates the (true) story of the adoption of a complex and expensive machining system in an organisation. The machining system cut down on labour input, and involved much new computer technology. Thomas's story focuses upon the process that produced the decision to make this particular investment, and to reject alternatives. A group of research and development (R&D) managers championed this particular solution and engaged in a process of persuading top management to make the investment. This involved representing the facts in a particular way.

Thomas commented: 'I was puzzled by the difference between R&D's confident portrayal of [the system] to upper management and its private tentativeness, uncertainty and possible understatement of the system's true costs' (p. 200). In order to justify the acquisition, managers had to present figures that would present the proposed investment in a good light. One of the engineers involved commented:

'I had to come up with a payback . . . and the best I could come up with was four years. Around here, the corporate rule, the ground rule, is if the thing can't be paid back in two years, preferably one year, your request has a chance of a snowball in hell of flying. Well, now that either makes you damned smart or a good liar' (p. 207).

Essentially, if the figures did not prove the case that the managers wanted to make, then the figures had to be changed so that they did support the investment.

Social shaping theory does not negate the potential usefulness of decision-making techniques, but it does suggest that in practice the application of such techniques is unlikely to be completely rational, and that it will be shaped and influenced by complex and sometimes unpredictable factors. In particular, managers who are responsible for making decisions based on data and calculations supplied by other people should be appropriately critical of the process that produces the figures.

Investment appraisal in practice

Several research studies have investigated the extent to which the capital investment appraisal techniques explained in this chapter are used in practice. Over time, researchers have found that more firms are using the more

Management accountants
specialists in the provision of financial information for use within the business

complex discounted cash flow techniques, a tendency which is attributed to the more widespread use of computers by managers. A survey by Drury and Tayles (1997) of UK **management accountants** in manufacturing organisations revealed the following usage of investment appraisal techniques.

Extent of use of investment appraisal techniques (percentage of 303 respondents)

	Never/rarely %	Sometimes %	Often/always %
Accounting rate of return	39	20	41
Payback method	23	14	63
Net present value	41	16	43
Internal rate of return	32	11	57

Source: adapted from Drury and Tayles (1997).

The researchers did find some differences in the responses between larger and smaller organisations. As might be expected, larger organisations are more likely to use formal capital budgeting techniques. It is clear from the research that many organisations use multiple appraisal techniques, despite the weaknesses of the simpler techniques that were identified earlier in the chapter. The use of payback and ARR instead of, or alongside, discounted cash flow techniques tends to suggest that managers do not always undertake investment appraisal on a completely rational basis.

Finally, it is worth noting that the research results suggested that capital investment appraisal involving discounted cash flow (DCF) techniques is often done incorrectly. The effects of inflation were often not taken into account properly, and managers often appeared to be using excessively high discount rates because they were over-estimating the risk associated with projects. If too high a discount rate is used, potentially profitable projects may be incorrectly rejected. The authors conclude that managers should be better educated in the proper use of DCF techniques.

Chapter summary

The focus of this chapter has been decision-making in the longer term. Capital budgeting and capital rationing were explained in order to set the scene for the explanation of appraisal techniques which occupied most of the chapter. Businesses need to have clear criteria upon which to base capital investment decisions, especially where capital is rationed.

Two relatively straightforward techniques are often used: accounting rate of return and payback. After explaining some of the factors involved in establishing relevant information for the appraisal, the chapter turned to an explanation of these simple techniques. There are many significant drawbacks to both of these techniques: for example, they rely upon accounting measurement of profits, they ignore cash flow beyond the end of the payback period, they do not take into account the time value of money, and are economically non-rational. Discounted cash flow techniques, which have become more widely used in recent years, are more sophisticated approaches which do take time value into account. After a brief consideration of the importance of selecting a suitable discount rate, net present value and internal rate of return were explained.

As with other areas of accounting, it is important to appreciate the limitations of the information presented. The strengths and weaknesses of the common appraisal techniques were listed and explained. The risk of fundamental misapplications of the techniques was discussed in the context of the theories of social shaping and technological determinism. Finally, the chapter briefly examined the incidence of the use of the four appraisal techniques in practice, as evidenced by research.

Management accountants and managers should of course be alert to the possible misuse and misrepresentation of information used in investment appraisal. Provided that managers thoroughly understand the information, the techniques explained in this chapter can be used to improve the quality of decision-making.

References

Coombs, H.M, and Jenkins, D.E. (2002) *Public sector financial management*, Thomson Learning: London.

Drury, C. and Tayles, M. (1997) 'The misapplication of capital investment appraisal techniques', *Management Decision*, 35/2, pp. 86–93.

Horngren, C.T., Bhimani, A., Datar, S.M. and Foster, G. (2005) *Management and cost accounting*, FT Prentice Hall: Harlow.

Mackenzie, D. and Wajcman, J. (1999) *The social shaping of technology* (2nd edition) Open University Press: Maidenhead.

Rigby, E. (2006) 'Operations overseas are where every little helps to improve returns for Tesco, *Financial Times*, 2 May, p. 21.

Thomas, R.J. (1999) 'What machines can't do: politics and technology in the industrial enterprise', in Mackenzie, D. and Wajcman, J. (eds) *The social shaping of technology*, (2nd edition) Open University Press: Maidenhead.

WEBSITE SUMMARY

The book's website contains the following material in respect of Chapter 7:

Students' section

A multiple choice quiz containing 10 questions
4 longer questions with answers.

Lecturers' section

Answers to end of chapter exercises 7.10 to 7.19.
5 longer questions with answers.

SELF-ASSESSMENT EXERCISES

7.1 A business is considering whether or not to invest in a new building. The managers have incurred expenditure of €15 000 on an initial land survey. For capital investment appraisal purposes this expenditure is:

a) a fixed cost

b) a relevant cost

c) a sunk cost

d) an estimated cost.

7.2 Mellor & Ribchester, a health drinks company, is considering whether or not to invest in a project to develop and sell a new range of fruit teas. Initial expenditure on a range of development expenses will be €150 000 at Time 0 to get the project up and running. Sales of the products will start in year 2, and it is anticipated that annual net cash inflows will be as follows:

	€
Year 2	68 000
Year 3	71 000
Year 4	54 000
Year 5	28 000
Year 6	10 000

Demand for the product is expected to decline after year 6 to the point where it will not be worth continuing production. The €150 000 of initial expenditure is treated as a non-current asset, to be depreciated on a straight-line basis over six years, with an assumption of nil residual value at the end of six years.

i) Calculate ARR for the project.

ii) Calculate the payback period for the project.

7.3 The compounding factor for an investment over four years at 3% per year is (to 3 decimal places):

a) 0.888

b) 1.093

c) 0.915

d) 1.126.

7.4 At the end of year 4, €312 invested now at an annual rate of 6% interest over four years will be worth (to the nearest €):

a) €394

b) €387

c) €372

d) €418.

7.5 The discounting factor for an investment over three years at 10% is (to 3 decimal places):

a) 0.700

b) 0.751

c) 0.100

d) 1.093.

7.6 Assuming a constant discount rate of 12%, the present value of €1300 receivable at the end of year 5 is (to the nearest €):

a) €563

b) €520

c) €2293

d) €737.

7.7 Naylor Coulthard is considering investing in a major advertising promotion of one of its skincare products. The advertising campaign would cost €250 000, all of which is assumed to be spent at Time 0. The effectiveness of the advertising would be short-lived; it would produce incremental cash inflows only in years 1 and 2. The year 1 net cash inflow is estimated at €196 000. The net cash inflow for year 2 is estimated at €168 000. After the end of year 2 another major advertising campaign would probably be needed to produce further incremental revenues.

   The company's cost of capital is 9%. What is the NPV of the advertising promotion project? Does the NPV suggest that the project should be accepted or rejected?

7.8 A company estimates the following net cash inflows and outflows for a capital investment project that is currently under consideration:

Time	€000
0	(680 000)
1	180 000
2	200 000
3	240 000
4	350 000

   The company's cost of capital is 12%.

   i) Calculate the NPV of the project.

   ii) Calculate the IRR of the project.

7.9 Outhwaite Benson Limited runs a chain of hairdressing salons. The company's directors, Linda Outhwaite and David Benson, are considering a proposal to add sunbed facilities to their salons. They have surveyed staff and customers and have found that 55% of their existing customers would consider using the facilities. On the basis of this finding they have constructed a set of costings and revenue projections. The sunbeds would cost £180 000 in total to buy and install; they would have an estimated useful life of five years after which they could be sold for £15 000 in total. Linda and David estimate that the net cash inflow arising each year from the sale of time on the sunbeds would be £46 000.

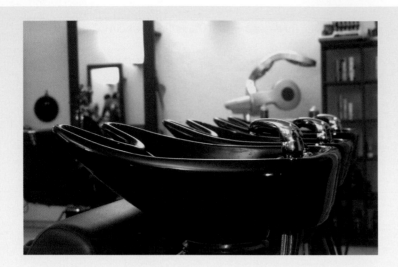

The £180 000 will be lent to the company by the two directors; it is the proceeds of the sale of their second home in Italy. If the money is not put into the sunbed project it would be invested in the opening of a new salon. The average yield from a salon is 14% per year, and the directors decide to use this as the cost of capital in appraising the proposed sunbed investment.

i) Calculate the NPV of the sunbed investment project.

ii) Calculate the IRR of the sunbed investment project.

iii) Advise the directors on whether or not they should make the investment, considering any other relevant factors that might have a bearing on the decision.

EXERCISES

7.10   Montfort Spelling operates a chain of health clubs. Each year the company opens a club in a new location. For 2008, the company is examining two possible locations: Broughton Town and Carey City. The directors have collected information about costs and local demographics, and have come up with the following summary of the initial investment required, and cash flows for the subsequent five years. The company's normal policy is to completely refurbish its clubs every five years; it remodels and redecorates the clubs and sells off all the old equipment.

   Initial outlay includes the cost of taking out a five-year lease on premises, buying in all the equipment and paying architects and builders to remodel the premises. The net cash inflows from years one to five include estimated takings in annual subscriptions and joining fees, less the costs of employing staff, and various other fixed costs of running the club.

   The table below summarises the costs for the two locations:

	Broughton Town €000	Carey City €000
Time 0: initial investment	(630)	(540)
Time 1: net cash inflows	250	242
Time 2: net cash inflows	275	250
Time 3: net cash inflows	280	260
Time 4: net cash inflows	295	270
Time 5: net cash inflows	310	280
Time 5: inflow from sales of equipment	35	30

The initial capital expenditure less the anticipated residual values is to be depreciated on a straight-line basis, in accordance with the company's policy, over five years.

i) Calculate ARR for each project.

ii) Calculate the payback period for each project.

iii) Advise the directors as to which location should be preferred.

7.11   The compounding factor for an investment over six years at 8% per year is (to 3 decimal places):

a) 1.587

b) 0.627

c) 1.595

d) 0.630.

7.12   At the end of year 6, NZ$1900 invested now at an annual rate of 17% interest over six years will be worth (to the nearest NZ$):

a) NZ$3838

b) NZ$741

c) NZ$4874

d) NZ$2223.

7.13 The discounting factor for an investment over five years at 19% is:

a) 0.419

b) 0.190

c) 0.950

d) 0.810.

7.14 Assuming a constant discount rate of 14%, the present value of €85 000 receivable at the end of year 4 is (to the nearest €):

a) €50 320

b) €47 600

c) €49 045

d) €73 100.

7.15 Nuria Collezione is a fashion clothing company. Nuria, the chief executive, regularly attends major fashion events in order to spot trends in the market. She has recently returned from a show that featured fake fur waistcoats and she thinks these could be next season's big fashion story. Unfortunately, fake fur tends to clog up the production machinery used in the company's factory, and it will be necessary to make an additional investment of €28 000 in new cutting and sewing machinery. Nuria thinks it is quite likely that sales of 6000 waistcoats are achievable in the first year, and possibly up to 2000 in the second year. Her knowledge of fashion trends tells her that after that point the waistcoats will probably be unsaleable except at very heavy discounts. The first 5000 waistcoats will almost certainly sell at full price, and should produce a net cash flow of €4 each. The final 3000 of production may have to be sold at a discount and it is safest to assume that net cash flow will be only €3 per waistcoat. The machinery will be saleable at the end of the second year for around €10 000.

i) Assuming that the company's cost of capital is 13%, what is the NPV of the project?

ii) If Nuria's initial projections were wrong, and only 5000 of the waistcoats could be sold, all in the first year and producing net cash flow of €4 each, what would be the NPV of the project? Assume in this case that the machinery is saleable at the end of the first year for €13 000.

7.16 A company estimates the following net cash inflows and outflows for a capital investment project that is currently under consideration:

Time	€000
0	(1 650 000)
1	480 000
2	450 000
3	390 000
4	360 000
5	450 000

The company's cost of capital is 8%.

i) Calculate the NPV of the project.
ii) Calculate the IRR of the project.

7.17 Oppenheim Zimmer sells sofas, armchairs and other furniture items from its premises in a retail park. Customers often ask for home delivery to be arranged, and the company has contracted out the service to a series of small delivery firms. The delivery services are of inconsistent quality; customers often ring Oppenheim's to complain that the delivery was late, or that the goods were damaged in transit. Oppenheim's directors have decided that the delivery problem must be properly addressed because the company is losing sales and acquiring a reputation for unreliability. The company's finance director has examined three options:

- Option 1. Buy three new delivery vehicles and employ full-time drivers. The initial outlay for the vehicles would be €76 000, and the annual incremental costs of employment, fuel and other motor expenses would be €82 000. At the end of their five-year useful life the vehicles could be sold for €9000 in total.
- Option 2. Contract the service out to a single, high quality provider who would take on full responsibility for van purchase, maintenance and other costs, including the employment of drivers. Quotations for the service have been obtained; a good quality service can be purchased under a five-year contract for €105 000 per year.
- Option 3. Lease the three vehicles required for the service at a cost of €10 000 per year per vehicle for a term of five years. Fuel and other running costs, and the costs of employing three drivers, would be incurred direct under this option at a total cost of €77 000 per year.

The finance director estimates that an improved service would boost sales. Incremental sales of €113 000 per year would be made under all three options. Oppenheim's cost of capital is 12%.

i) Calculate the NPV for each option.
ii) Advise the directors on the most appropriate course of action, taking into account any other relevant factors.

7.18 Identify two factors that are likely to influence the discount rate selected by managers to appraise capital investment proposals.

7.19 You have recently started a new job as a management accountant in a medium-sized unlisted business. The board of directors makes all significant capital investment decisions using the payback method and written reports from department heads. Write a memo explaining the advantages offered by DCF techniques.

Appendix: discount factors

The table gives the present value of a single payment received a number of years in the future discounted at x% per year. For example, with a discount rate of 7% a single payment of €1 in six years' time has a present value of €0.6663 or 66.63¢.

Years	1%	2%	3%	4%	5%	6%	7%	8%	9%	10%
1	0.9901	0.9804	0.9709	0.9615	0.9524	0.9434	0.9346	0.9259	0.9174	0.9091
2	0.9803	0.9612	0.9426	0.9426	0.9070	0.8900	0.8734	0.8573	0.8417	0.8264
3	0.9706	0.9423	0.9151	0.8890	0.8638	0.8396	0.8163	0.7938	0.7722	0.7513
4	0.9610	0.9238	0.8885	0.8548	0.8227	0.7921	0.7629	0.7350	0.7084	0.6830
5	0.9515	0.9057	0.8626	0.8219	0.7835	0.7473	0.7130	0.6806	0.6499	0.6209
6	0.9420	0.8880	0.8375	0.7903	0.7462	0.7050	0.6663	0.6302	0.5963	0.5645
7	0.9327	0.8706	0.8131	0.7599	0.7107	0.6651	0.6227	0.5835	0.5470	0.5132
8	0.9235	0.8535	0.7894	0.7307	0.6768	0.6274	0.5820	0.5403	0.5019	0.4665
9	0.9143	0.8368	0.7664	0.7026	0.6446	0.5919	0.5439	0.5002	0.4604	0.4241
10	0.9053	0.8203	0.7441	0.6756	0.6139	0.5584	0.5083	0.4632	0.4224	0.3855
11	0.8963	0.8043	0.7224	0.6496	0.5847	0.5268	0.4751	0.4289	0.3875	0.3505
12	0.8874	0.7885	0.7014	0.6246	0.5568	0.4970	0.4440	0.3971	0.3555	0.3186
13	0.8787	0.7730	0.6810	0.6006	0.5303	0.4688	0.4150	0.3677	0.3262	0.2897
14	0.8700	0.7579	0.6611	0.5775	0.5051	0.4423	0.3878	0.3405	0.2992	0.2633
15	0.8613	0.7430	0.6419	0.5553	0.4810	0.4173	0.3624	0.3152	0.2745	0.2394
16	0.8528	0.7284	0.6232	0.5339	0.4581	0.3936	0.3387	0.2919	0.2519	0.2176
17	0.8444	0.7142	0.6050	0.5134	0.4363	0.3714	0.3166	0.2703	0.2311	0.1978
18	0.8360	0.7002	0.5874	0.4936	0.4155	0.3503	0.2959	0.2502	0.2120	0.1799
19	0.8277	0.6864	0.5703	0.4746	0.3957	0.3305	0.2765	0.2317	0.1945	0.1635
20	0.8195	0.6730	0.5537	0.4564	0.3769	0.3118	0.2584	0.2145	0.1784	0.1486
21	0.8114	0.6598	0.5375	0.4388	0.3589	0.2942	0.2415	0.1987	0.1637	0.1351
22	0.8034	0.6468	0.5219	0.4220	0.3418	0.2775	0.2257	0.1839	0.1502	0.1228
23	0.7954	0.6342	0.5067	0.4057	0.3256	0.2618	0.2109	0.1703	0.1378	0.1117
24	0.7876	0.6217	0.4919	0.3901	0.3101	0.2470	0.1971	0.1577	0.1264	0.1015
25	0.7798	0.6095	0.4776	0.3751	0.2953	0.2330	0.1842	0.1460	0.1160	0.0923
26	0.7720	0.5976	0.4637	0.3607	0.2812	0.2198	0.1722	0.1352	0.1064	0.0839
27	0.7644	0.5859	0.4502	0.3468	0.2678	0.2074	0.1609	0.1252	0.0976	0.0763
28	0.7568	0.5744	0.4371	0.3335	0.2551	0.1956	0.1504	0.1159	0.0895	0.0693
29	0.7493	0.5631	0.4243	0.3207	0.2429	0.1846	0.1406	0.1073	0.0822	0.0630
30	0.7419	0.5521	0.4120	0.3083	0.2314	0.1741	0.1314	0.0994	0.0754	0.0573
35	0.7059	0.5000	0.3554	0.2534	0.1813	0.1301	0.0937	0.0676	0.0490	0.0356
40	0.6717	0.4529	0.3066	0.2083	0.1420	0.0972	0.0668	0.0460	0.0318	0.0221
45	0.6391	0.4102	0.2644	0.1712	0.1113	0.0727	0.0476	0.0313	0.0207	0.0137
50	0.6080	0.3715	0.2281	0.1407	0.0872	0.0543	0.0339	0.0213	0.0134	0.0085

11%	12%	13%	14%	15%	16%	17%	18%	19%	20%	Years
0.9009	0.8929	0.8850	0.8772	0.8696	0.8621	0.8547	0.8475	0.8403	0.8333	1
0.8116	0.7972	0.7831	0.7695	0.7561	0.7432	0.7305	0.7182	0.7062	0.6944	2
0.7312	0.7118	0.6931	0.6750	0.6575	0.6407	0.6244	0.6086	0.5934	0.5787	3
0.6587	0.6355	0.6133	0.5921	0.5718	0.5523	0.5337	0.5158	0.4987	0.4823	4
0.5935	0.5674	0.5428	0.5194	0.4972	0.4761	0.4561	0.4371	0.4190	0.4019	5
0.5346	0.5066	0.4803	0.4556	0.4323	0.4104	0.3898	0.3704	0.3521	0.3349	6
0.4817	0.4523	0.4251	0.3996	0.3759	0.3538	0.3332	0.3139	0.2959	0.2791	7
0.4339	0.4039	0.3762	0.3506	0.3269	0.3050	0.2848	0.2660	0.2487	0.2326	8
0.3909	0.3606	0.3329	0.3075	0.2843	0.2630	0.2434	0.2255	0.2090	0.1938	9
0.3522	0.3220	0.2946	0.2697	0.2472	0.2267	0.2080	0.1911	0.1756	0.1615	10
0.3173	0.2875	0.2607	0.2366	0.2149	0.1954	0.1778	0.1619	0.1476	0.1346	11
0.2858	0.2567	0.2307	0.2076	0.1869	0.1685	0.1520	0.1372	0.1240	0.1122	12
0.2575	0.2292	0.2042	0.1821	0.1625	0.1452	0.1299	0.1163	0.1042	0.0935	13
0.2320	0.2046	0.1807	0.1597	0.1413	0.1252	0.1110	0.0985	0.0876	0.0779	14
0.2090	0.1827	0.1599	0.1401	0.1229	0.1079	0.0949	0.0835	0.0736	0.0649	15
0.1883	0.1631	0.1415	0.1229	0.1069	0.0930	0.0811	0.0708	0.0618	0.0541	16
0.1696	0.1456	0.1252	0.1078	0.0929	0.0802	0.0693	0.0600	0.0520	0.0451	17
0.1528	0.1300	0.1108	0.0946	0.0808	0.0691	0.0592	0.0508	0.0437	0.0376	18
0.1377	0.1161	0.0981	0.0829	0.0703	0.0596	0.0506	0.0431	0.0367	0.0313	19
0.1240	0.1037	0.0868	0.0728	0.0611	0.0514	0.0433	0.0365	0.0308	0.0261	20
0.1117	0.0926	0.0768	0.0638	0.0531	0.0443	0.0370	0.0309	0.0259	0.0217	21
0.1007	0.0826	0.0680	0.0560	0.0462	0.0382	0.0316	0.0262	0.0218	0.0181	22
0.0907	0.0738	0.0601	0.0491	0.0402	0.0329	0.0270	0.0222	0.0183	0.0151	23
0.0817	0.0659	0.0532	0.0431	0.0349	0.0284	0.0231	0.0188	0.0154	0.0126	24
0.0736	0.0588	0.0471	0.0378	0.0304	0.0245	0.0197	0.0160	0.0129	0.0105	25
0.0663	0.0525	0.0417	0.0331	0.0264	0.0211	0.0169	0.0135	0.0109	0.0087	26
0.0597	0.0469	0.0369	0.0291	0.0230	0.0182	0.0144	0.0115	0.0091	0.0073	27
0.0538	0.0419	0.0326	0.0255	0.0200	0.0157	0.0123	0.0097	0.0077	0.0061	28
0.0485	0.0374	0.0289	0.0224	0.0174	0.0135	0.0105	0.0082	0.0064	0.0051	29
0.0437	0.0334	0.0256	0.0196	0.0151	0.0116	0.0090	0.0070	0.0054	0.0042	30
0.0259	0.0189	0.0139	0.0102	0.0075	0.0055	0.0041	0.0030	0.0023	0.0017	35
0.0154	0.0107	0.0075	0.0053	0.0037	0.0026	0.0019	0.0013	0.0010	0.0007	40
0.0091	0.0061	0.0041	0.0027	0.0019	0.0013	0.0009	0.0006	0.0004	0.0003	45
0.0054	0.0035	0.0022	0.0014	0.0009	0.0006	0.0004	0.0003	0.0002	0.0001	50

Source: Drury, C. (2001) *Management Accounting for Business Decisions*, Second Edition, London: Thomson Learning.

Budgets

8

Aim of the chapter

To understand the reasons for, and the processes involved in, setting a budget for a business organisation, and to be able to prepare and evaluate budget statements.

Learning outcomes

After reading the chapter and completing the exercises at the end, students should:

- Understand the role of budgeting in planning and controlling business organisations.
- Know about the stages involved in setting a budget.
- Be able to prepare straightforward budget statements.
- Understand the issues involved in evaluating actual outcomes against budget plans.
- Be able to discuss some of the behavioural and other issues involved in budgeting.

Introduction

In Chapter 1 the principal features of cost and management accounting were introduced by reference to the CIMA definitions of these terms. It was noted that cost accounting encompasses the establishment of budgets, and management accounting the planning of long, medium and short-term operations, the control of those operations and the efficient use of resources.

A budget is a plan, expressed in financial and/or more general quantitative terms, which extends forward for a period into the future. Budgets are widely used in organisations of all types and sizes. This chapter concentrates principally on the use of budgets in profit-making organisations, but it should be recognised that budgets are used in all kinds of organisations, including health trusts, schools, charities and government departments.

Budgeting, for most organisations, is an important dimension of the processes of planning, controlling and evaluating outcomes. The three chapters preceding this one have been principally concerned with decision-making and the processes involved in assessing alternative courses of action. To recap some of the information in Chapter 1, the relevant processes are as follows:

- Once the key decisions are made, it is usually necessary to formulate plans to help carry out the action: these involve management information such as forecasts and resource allocation plans.

- Having set the plans in motion, managers then need to control activities in order to ensure that the plan is followed: this involves management information such as short term monitoring reports.

- Managers then need to assess the extent to which the plans have succeeded and the business objectives have been met. This involves performance reports, comparisons with forecasts and plans and explanations of variations between planned and actual outcomes.

- It may be necessary to redefine objectives on the basis of actual outturns. Long, medium and short-term plans may require amendment.

This chapter proceeds as follows: first the relationship between strategic, longer-range, planning and short-term budgets is explored, using an example as an illustration of the type of thinking and processes involved in turning strategic plans into feasible short-term budgets. The different possible approaches to budgeting are then discussed, followed by an example that illustrates the stages that are likely to be involved in setting a budget in a manufacturing business. The chapter then proceeds to examine, using a detailed numerical example, the work involved in setting a budget. This is followed by a consideration of some of the issues involved in monitoring outcomes. Finally, the chapter examines the benefits and drawbacks of budgeting with particular reference to behavioural issues, drawing, where appropriate, from relevant research evidence.

The relationship between strategy and budget setting

In order to be able to meet the key objectives of their business, managers need to determine the appropriate long-term strategies to adopt. Some organisations formulate a strategic plan that reaches forward into the future over a period of, say, three to five years. Using the strategic plan as a framework, managers will then set budgets, most probably on an annual basis. The rest of this section of the chapter uses an example to illustrate what might be involved in such a process.

Budgeting is not, as the example above implies, a simple process. However, if the business sets its strategic objectives sensibly, the budget, to some extent, emerges naturally from higher level management decisions.

EXAMPLE 8.1

© Helene Rogers / Alamy

Calder Calloway Cards, a greeting cards manufacturer, was established eight or nine years ago by two brothers who continue to hold the majority of the shares in the company. The company has grown steadily over the period since its formation, but its management information systems have remained rudimentary, mostly because of resistance from one of the founders who has been managing director (MD) throughout the company's life.

Following pressure from junior managers and the company's two non-executive directors the MD has finally become convinced, during the 2008 financial year, that a more formal planning and management control process is required. He and his fellow directors have met several times with a view to deciding upon a set of strategic objectives for the business. They have also decided to recruit a management accountant to help in the formal process of budget setting and evaluation.

The directors determine the following key strategic objectives:

- To grow the company to the point where it is a credible competitor with the largest producers in the greetings card market.
- To produce cards of high quality with a distinctive company design identity.

Out of these two key objectives a long-term plan develops. The directors decide that the plan should cover the next five years. It is a written document that identifies the strategy for achieving the key objectives. An extract from it includes the following principal actions (together with more detailed actions for achieving the key action):

- Increase sales by at least 30% per annum
  - Recruit new members of the sales team

- ○ Encourage and motivate by use of commission and reward schemes
- ○ Identify new outlets.
- Reduce unit costs and increase gross profitability to 45% within five years
  - ○ Improve and expand production facilities by investment in 'state of the art' printing machinery
  - ○ Implement a system of capital expenditure control and evaluation
  - ○ Improve production logistics.
- Improve, and keep improving, the quality of the product
  - ○ Recruit quality supervisor
  - ○ Improve supervision
  - ○ Implement a Total Quality Management system to motivate all staff.
- Create a distinctive design identity for the company's products
  - ○ Recruit a design team under the strong leadership of a design director who will be a full member of the board of directors
  - ○ Identify and recruit staff at an appropriate level and remuneration
  - ○ Identify key elements of design policy in conjunction with design director.

Some of the points are likely to be acted upon within the next 12 months; others will produce action over the longer term.

The directors, working together with the new management accountant, will produce a budget for the next 12 months. This will identify financial and other quantitative measurements that represent the changes proposed. The immediate financial implications of the plan will be recognised in the budget. For example:

- Personnel budget: it seems likely that recruitment of the design team will take place within the next 12 months. Costs of recruitment and of the new salaries will be included in the budget. Consequential savings (for example, in respect of the payments made to freelance card designers) will also be estimated and their effect taken into account. The personnel budget will be expressed both in terms of numbers of staff and financial costs.

- Capital expenditure budget: a detailed budget taking account of the effects of likely short-term decisions will be required. For example, if the production director decides that a printing machine should be scrapped and should be replaced during the year with a new machine costing around €20 000, the decision has an impact on production speed and quality, volume of production, cash (€20 000 has to be found) and depreciation.

- Sales budget: if the company aims to increase sales by at least 30% the budget should reflect this aim. The planned increase involves extra costs (for example, in recruiting additional staff, in creating and implementing a commission scheme and in planning a campaign to expand into new sales outlets).

All of these implications (and more) must be reflected in the budget for the following financial year.

Principal types of budget

Budgets are often prepared for a budget period of one year, coinciding with the business's annual reporting period. However, the budget period can extend over a shorter or even, occasionally, a longer period. The annual budget is usually further split into shorter periods of quarters, months, four-week periods, or even single weeks.

Rolling budget
a budget which is updated on a regular basis as each period of time (usually one month) elapses

Some organisations use a system of rolling budgets. The budget is initially prepared for a period, probably of one year. With each month that elapses, another month is added on to the end of the budget so that at any given point in time, there is a full 12 month budget ahead. For example, a company sets a budget for the 12 months between 1 September 2009 and 31 August 2010. At the end of September 2009 another month (September 2010) is added. And so on.

In the public sector the achievement of objectives via resource allocation is an essential part of organisations' activities. The budget preparation process in most public sector organisations is likely to be more or less a year-round activity.

Approaches to budgeting

It is common to find organisations using an incremental approach to budgeting. Incremental budgeting involves the establishment of a new budget using a previous budget as a base upon which to work. So, for example, in setting a new budget a business might simply increase all expenditure headings by 5% in line with the general rate of inflation in the economy. This approach is simple and cuts down on the amount of time spent on the budgeting process. However, it may have disadvantages, too:

Incremental budgeting
budget setting by taking a previous period's budget total and adding a standard percentage increase

- Where a uniform level of increment is made across many budget headings, as in the example given, it may be less applicable to some than to others. While a 5% general increase might be quite appropriate in some areas, other types of expenditure may be subject to greater or less than average inflation. Some departments or activities might be disadvantaged by such a broad and general approach.

- An incremental approach continued over more than one budget period can result in some parts of the budget being seriously out of kilter with real world conditions.

- This approach involves very little scrutiny of the budget, and may result in inefficiencies being perpetuated over several years.

Zero-based budgeting (ZBB)
a budget process that ignores any previous budgets and requires that budgetary allocations must be justified in full by managers

By contrast, zero-based budgeting (ZBB) ignores any previous budgets and requires that budgetary allocations must be justified by managers. So, for example, if a manager has had a budget allocation for business travel and entertaining expenses in the past, an incremental approach would simply reallocate the expense, with possibly an additional increment to take account of inflation. A ZBB approach, on the other hand, would require the manager to justify an allocation. ZBB has the significant benefit of requiring

managers to think carefully about expenditure, but of course there are some
drawbacks too:

- The process of justifying expenditure is likely to take up the resource
  of managerial time, and there is an opportunity cost attached to that
  time. It could be argued that managers could more usefully employ
  their time elsewhere.
- ZBB can produce adverse reactions from managers who view the
  process as a threat to their authority or status.

There is no reason, of course, why some combination of the two approaches
could not be used – perhaps a thorough budget overhaul every two or three
years from a ZBB perspective, with a less challenging and time-consuming
approach being adopted in the interim.

ZBB was first adopted by the US firm, Texas Instruments, and was widely
used in the public sector during the 1970s, mostly because it was championed
by President Jimmy Carter. However, it has not been much used outside the
USA and, generally, its importance has diminished since the 1970s (Jones and
Pendlebury, 2000).

The budget process

The starting point for budgets in most commercial organisations is the sales
budget, because sales volume is usually the principal factor that determines
the scale of the business's activities. In a manufacturing organisation the
production, direct materials, direct labour and production overheads budget
are directly dependent upon projected sales volumes and inventory levels.
Budgets are likely to be required for the less direct areas too: research and
development, administration expenses, capital expenditure and marketing
and advertising. Figure 8.1 sets out some of the principal budgets that are
likely to be required in a manufacturing business.

The diagram presents the sales budget in the centre at the top, signifying
its importance to all other budgets. The sales budget links in directly to the
production budget which, in turn, drives budgets for raw materials, direct
labour and production overheads. The link with other costs is a little more
tenuous, as denoted by the broken lines. However, all of these costs are related to some extent to the general volume of activity generated by the business.
All functional areas may have capital expenditure requirements: a capital
budget is shown separately below. Finally, all of the budget information
(sales, production, expenses and capital expenditure) is brought together in
the form of three principal budget statements: budget cash flow statement,
income statement and balance sheet.

**Responsibility
accounting**
accounting within the
business which identifies
the person or department
responsible for particular
outcomes

Who sets the budget?

The principle underlying much of the budgeting that takes place in commercial organisations is that of responsibility accounting. Managers are held to
be answerable for the performance against budget of the areas and functions
for which they are responsible. Broadly, two approaches to budget setting can

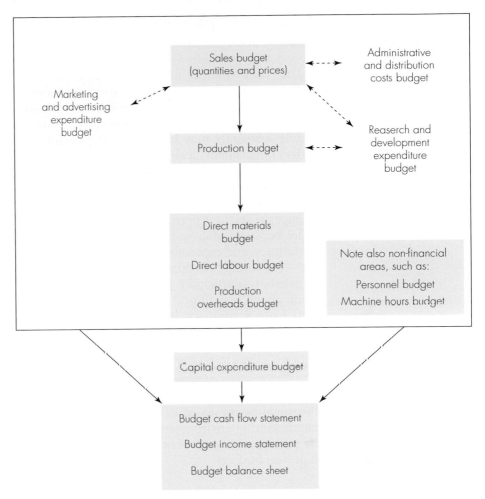

FIGURE 8.1

Principal budget areas within a manufacturing business

be taken: the budget can be imposed from above, or a more participative approach can be taken in which managers are involved in the budget setting process at a detailed level. There are advantages and drawbacks to both approaches.

Imposition of budgets

The process of imposing budgets from above is likely to be less time-consuming than a more participative approach. Senior managers are able to impose their view of the best way to achieve the organisation's objectives without the distraction of detailed consultation with lower levels of management. Some managers may prefer this approach because it saves their own time, and also gives them a validated target to work for. If bonus levels are directly linked with managerial performance against budget it is probably preferable to have the budget imposed from above in order to avoid managers setting themselves targets that are too easy to achieve. However, the drawback is that an imposed budget can create resentment if it is felt to be unachievable or if it fails to take into consideration the real world complexities that face middle management.

Participative approach

If middle managers and staff are invited to participate in the budget setting process they are more likely to feel that they have 'ownership' of the budget, and to work towards meeting it. They may be aware of constraints and limitations that are too minor to affect the views of senior management but which may well be sufficiently significant to impact on the budget at a departmental or divisional level. However, there are some potential drawbacks: middle managers may be motivated principally by a desire to keep their budget targets manageable, especially if their bonus payments are dependent upon meeting targets. A further problem is that participative processes take time, and the budget process may absorb too much managerial attention at the expense of other activities. This is especially likely to be the case where managerial status is perceived as depending upon the resources controlled.

To be successful, a participative budgeting process must be genuine. Sometimes, and especially in large bureaucratic organisations, the process is one of pseudo-participation. Staff are apparently encouraged by senior managers to participate in decisions about the budget, but the process is a sham: all the real, important, decisions will be taken at a senior level, and the participatory approach is a façade only. Pseudo-participation fools no-one and serves only to antagonise staff.

Stages involved in setting a budget

The principal stages that are typically involved in setting the budget will be illustrated by means of an example. This example is set in a fairly complex manufacturing environment that is organised into departments. It illustrates the participative style of budgeting where departments are asked to propose their own budgets.

EXAMPLE 8.2

Arbus Corporation manufactures and sells cosmetics and skincare products. It operates in a highly competitive market in which there is a culture of constant scientific development. The company's basic strategic objective is to improve market share by the development of improved products, innovating more quickly and effectively than the competition. Each year the research and development department finds new ways of improving products (for example, by changing the feel and consistency of a skin make-up).

Stage 1: Discussing the sales budget

For this company, in a very competitive environment, the most important constraint on its activities is the level of sales. Therefore, the budget process starts here.

In June 2009 work starts on setting the budget for the accounting year that runs from 1 March 2010 to 28 February 2010. The directors meet to talk about the sales budget. Their discussion is influenced by the fact that a new improved face cream has recently been introduced by a competitor. Arbus Corporation has responded to this by changing the advertising and packaging of their equivalent product, emphasising the scientific soundness of the formula. The directors feel that the advertising is likely to prove fairly effective, and they are optimistic about the sales projections for the coming year. They agree that the budget volume of sales (i.e. number of items sold in the various categories of product) should increase by an average of 5%, and that prices can be increased by 3%. They are aware, however, that their competitors are working on anti-ageing products for both men and women; in order to keep up with the market Arbus Corporation is going to have to increase its R&D activities.

Stage 2: The production budget

The next stage is that the detailed analysis of the sales budget is used to project production requirements. If sales volumes are expected to increase by 5% it is reasonable to suppose that a corresponding increase in production will be required. However, other factors can influence the production budget; for example, if a special product promotion is planned, linked to an advertising campaign, it will probably be necessary to plan for additional production. The optimum levels of inventory must be determined, and this decision may well impact on production targets.

Stage 3: Communication of budget guidelines

At this point it is probably appropriate to broaden the scope of the budget process. The directors have made the strategic decisions relating to objectives and they have decided upon the broad general approach to be taken in the following year's budget (e.g. an increase of 5% in sales volume, some price increases, etc.). Budgeting guidelines will then be communicated to the various departments around the company.

Stage 4: Submission of departmental budgets

Individual departments or divisions can now be asked to submit their budgets for approval. These should be prepared in accordance with the corporate objectives, and so it is important that senior management communicate these effectively. The R&D department, for example, is clearly being directed to expand its activities; the head of R&D will probably revise personnel requirements and may start work on presenting a proposal for an expansion of laboratory facilities. The marketing department may respond to the call for a 5% increase in sales volume by planning additional marketing campaigns.

Stage 5: Approval of budgets

A well-organised budget process will have a range of submission deadlines for parts of the budget. Once the departmental budgets have been submitted they can be coordinated and considered together to judge the extent to which they are reasonable and achievable given the inevitable operational constraints that apply to all businesses. For example, suppose that the head of R&D submits an ambitious budget based upon a planned expansion of numbers of personnel by 30%. He also requests capital expenditure of €1.5 million. These proposals may be quite reasonable in the context of management expectations (or not: the head of R&D might be trying to build up his personal prestige and organisational status). Senior managers will accept, reject or modify such proposals and then return them to the originator. In some processes, budget proposals may be discussed and modified several times before the final budget is agreed.

Stage 6: Agreement of budget

Once the budget has been extensively negotiated and discussed, the final agreed version can be drawn up, together with the projected income statement, balance sheet and cash flow statement (sometimes referred to as the master budget). The budget is then disseminated across the business and then people can get on with the business of implementing it. If the process has been genuinely participative and a feeling of 'ownership' has been achieved, the budget may prove to be a very useful co-ordinating and motivating tool.

The process described above mainly describes the planning aspect of budgeting. Control is principally achieved by close monitoring of actual outcomes against budget. Monitoring is discussed later in the chapter.

Setting the budget: a practical example

This section of the chapter examines the mechanics of budget setting using a simple illustrative example based on a company that manufactures one product only. The budget period is reduced from the more usual 12 months to 6 months. Even though the setting is deliberately simplified the example produces many interlinked numbers. It works from the initial sales budget through to the production of master budget statements.

EXAMPLE 8.3

Macey Nelson manufactures a single product: vacuum cleaners. The company is in the process of preparing a budget for the six months ending 30 June 2010. The balance sheet at 31 December 2009 is as follows:

	€	€
ASSETS		
Non-current assets		
Machinery at cost	96 000	
Less: accumulated depreciation	(38 400)	
		57 600
Office fixtures and fittings and computer	15 000	
Less: accumulated depreciation	(3 000)	
		12 000
Current assets		
Inventories: finished goods (200 units)	15 000	
Inventories: raw materials	3 750	
Receivables (December 2009 sales, all on credit)	40 000	
Cash at bank	8 000	
		66 750
		136 350
EQUITY AND LIABILITIES		
Equity		
Share capital	20 000	
Reserves	93 350	
		113 350
Current liabilities		
Payables for raw materials (1 month's purchases)	10 000	
Payables for production overheads (1 month's purchases)	9 000	
Payables for administrative expenses (1 month's purchases)	4 000	
		23 000
		136 350

At the end of every month the figure for debtors equals the total sales for the month just ended (e.g. debtors at the end of December are December's sales). At the end of every month creditors equals the total purchases for the month just ended (e.g. creditors at the end of December are December purchases).

Macey Nelson's selling price and cost structure for one vacuum cleaner is as follows:

	€
Selling price	100
Raw materials	25
Direct labour	20
Prime cost	45

The business uses full absorption costing based upon the number of units planned for production.

The company's sales director produces a forecast for sales (in units) for the first six months of 2010 on the basis of discussions he has held with fellow directors and with his sales team.

The production director then works out projected production in numbers of units. Projections for sales and production in units, together with opening and closing inventories of finished goods for each month are as follows:

Month	Opening inventories in units	Number of units: sales	Number of units: production	Closing inventories in units
January	200	250	300	250
February	250	280	280	250
March	250	280	330	300
April	300	300	350	350
May	350	300	350	400
June	400	300	350	450
Total		1710	1960	

Production in July is estimated at 350 units.

Production is planned in such a way as to build up stocks of finished goods towards the autumn; this is to ensure that the company has sufficient stock to respond to a potential increase in demand following a major advertising campaign that is planned for the latter half of the year. At the beginning of each month the production director plans to have half of the raw materials in stock which will be required for the coming month's production schedule. In order to simplify the budgeting exercise it is assumed that there is no work-in-progress at each month-end.

Production overheads forecast for the first six months of 2010 are:

	€
Factory rental	16 000
Supervisory salaries	12 450
Other direct labour	6 250
Cleaning	3 900
Insurance	2 600
Power	5 800
Depreciation of machinery	4 800
Maintenance	1 000
Canteen costs	2 500
Business rates	2 800
Other factory expenses	700
Total	58 800

Production overheads accumulate evenly over the six-month period.

Monthly administrative costs total €4000, plus €250 of depreciation of office fixtures and fittings and computer. Each month's expenses are paid in the following month (remember that this does not include depreciation, which is a non-cash adjustment).

No capital expenditure is planned for the six months ending 30 June 2010 and there will be no disposals of non-current assets.

The requirement is to prepare the following budgets for the first six months of 2010:

a) Raw materials purchases budget.

b) Budget overhead absorption rate.

c) Budget income statement for each of the six months ending 30 June 2010 and a summary income statement for the six-month period.

d) Budget balance sheet at 30 June 2010.

e) Budget cash flow statement for each of the six months ending 30 June 2010.

a) Raw materials purchases budget

Each unit of product uses €25 of raw material, and we need to ensure that raw material sufficient for half of each month's production is available in inventories at the beginning of the month. We can work out the opening and closing inventories for each month, the utilisation of raw materials in production and hence (by means of a balancing figure) the amount of raw materials purchases each month:

First, opening inventories:

		€
January	Given in balance sheet at 31.12.09	3750
February	50% × 280 (Feb. production) × €25	3500
March	50% × 330 (Mar. production) × €25	4125
April	50% × 350 (Apr. production) × €25	4375
May	50% × 350 (May production) × €25	4375
June	50% × 350 (June production) × €25	4375

Each month's opening inventories are the closing inventories of the previous month. A figure for closing inventories in June is still required. We know that July production is estimated at 350 so the opening inventories for July will need to be 50% × 350 × €25 = €4375 (remember that opening inventories for July are the same as closing inventories for June).

Utilisation of raw materials in production:

		€
January	300 units × €25	7500
February	280 units × €25	7000
March	330 units × €25	8250
April	350 units × €25	8750
May	350 units × €25	8750
June	350 units × €25	8750

Bringing all this information together we can calculate the expected level of raw material purchases.

Opening inventories + Purchases of raw materials − Raw materials used in production = Closing inventories

This formula contains four pieces of information; we now know three of them so we can calculate the fourth. Purchases of raw materials is the balancing figure, which we can calculate for each month as follows:

Closing inventories + Raw materials used in production − Opening inventories

▶

	Opening inventories of raw materials €	Purchase of raw material (balancing figure) €	Raw materials used in production €	Closing inventories of raw materials €
January	3750	7250	(7500)	3500
February	3500	7625	(7000)	4125
March	4125	8500	(8250)	4375
April	4375	8750	(8750)	4375
May	4375	8750	(8750)	4375
June	4375	8750	(8750)	4375

b) Budget overhead absorption rate

Total production overheads for six months: €58 800.
   Total number of units to be produced: 1960.
   Therefore the budget overhead absorption rate per unit is:

$$\frac{€58\ 800}{1\ 960} = €30 \text{ per unit}$$

We now know the total budgeted production cost per unit:

	€
Prime cost	45
Production overhead absorbed	30
Total production cost per unit	75

We need this information in order to calculate the budget income statement for each of the six months in the budget period.

c) Income statement

Macey Nelson: Budget income statement for each month January–June 2010

	Jan €	Feb €	Mar €	Apr €	May €	June €
Sales	250 × €100 =	280 × €100 =	280 × €100 =	300 × €100 =	300 × €100 =	300 × €100 =
	25 000	28 000	28 000	30 000	30 000	30 000
Cost of sales (= production cost)	250 × €75 = (18 750)	280 × €75 = (21 000)	280 × €75 = (21 000)	300 × €75 = (22 500)	300 × €75 = (22 500)	300 × €75 = (22 500)
Gross profit	6 250	7 000	7 000	7 500	7 500	7 500
Admin expenses (including depreciation)	(4 250)	(4 250)	(4 250)	(4 250)	(4 250)	(4 250)
Net profit	2 000	2 750	2 750	3 250	3 250	3 250

Macey Nelson: Summary budget income statement for the six months ending 30 June 2010

		€
Sales	1710 units @ €100 each	171 000
Cost of sales	1710 units @ €75 each	(128 250)
Gross profit	1710 units @ €25 each	42 750
Admin expenses	6 months × €4250	(25 500)
Net profit		17 250

d) Budget balance sheet at 30 June 2010

Workings are as follows:

1 Non-current assets

	At 31 December 2009 €	Depreciation – 6 months to 30 June 2010 €	At 30 June 2010 €
Machinery			
Cost	96 000		96 000
Accumulated depreciation	(38 400)	(4 800)	(43 200)
Net book value	57 600		52 800

8.5 Reinhart has his own wholesale business selling goods to retailers. His sales are made entirely on credit. In respect of the sales in any given month he expects 75% to be paid for in the next following month, and 25% in the month after that. (So, for example, sales made on credit in March would be paid for in April as 75% and May as 25%.) Budget data relating to four months of Reinhart's sales are as follows:

	€
November 2009	25 000
December 2009	26 800
January 2010	21 000
February 2010	21 300

Reinhart is preparing his cash flow forecast for the month of February 2010. How much should he include as sales receipts?

a) €21 000

b) €21 250

c) €22 450

d) €21 225.

8.6 Skippy is about to set up in business as a tour operator, after several years of working in the travel industry. He is starting out on a small scale, working from a room in a friend's office. The friend has agreed to let him have the room rent-free for six months in order to get him started.

In his first quarter of operations, January–March 2009, Skippy plans two tours, both coach trips to Austria. He advertises the trips in November and December 2008, paying the cost of €3000 out of his own money. He also pays €2000 for a computer. He intends that both of these amounts should constitute his initial capital contribution to the new business. The computer will be depreciated over its estimated useful life of five years on the straight-line basis.

The revenue and cost structure of each trip is as follows:

	€
The trip will cost €530 per person. The coach carries a maximum of 60 people and Skippy expects an 80% load factor – that is, 48 people. So 48 × €530 = sales revenue per trip	25 440
Hotel costs = €42.50 per person for 7 nights half board accommodation: 7 × €42.50 × 48	14 280
Coach travel costs	2 600
Insurance bond	1 500

Notes

- The first trip is planned for 17 February, and the second for 15 March. The sales revenue from the trips will be received in advance – receipts from trip one will be received in January, and from trip two in February.

- The hotel requires a non-returnable deposit of 50% in advance, with the remainder paid at the end of the stay. Advance payments will be made in January for trip one and in February for trip two.

- The coach costs must also be paid in advance: trip one will be paid for in January and trip two in February. The insurance bond for both trips will be paid in January.
- Other costs are: phone – the bill for an estimated €360 will be paid in March; and sundry office costs – €200 paid in cash each month.
  Prepare for Skippy:

  i) A budget cash flow statement for the three months of January, February and March 2009.
  ii) A budget income statement for the three months ending 31 March 2009.
  iii) A budget balance sheet at 31 March 2009.

8.7 Referring to the information given in exercise 8.6, at the beginning of April 2009 Skippy reviews the past three months. Bookings on the first coach trip to Austria were not as good as planned: he sold only 42 places on the coach. However, the second trip was very popular with sales of 50 places. The hotel charged Skippy based upon the actual, not the budgeted number of people. Coach and insurance costs remained the same.

Actual office costs were higher than budgeted: in January Skippy paid €230, in February €350 and in March €270. The phone bill of €455 was paid in March. Prepare an income statement for the three months ending 31 March 2009 showing columns for actual results, budgeted results and the variation between the two. Also prepare an actual balance sheet at 31 March 2009 showing an extra column for the budgeted figures. Overall, has Skippy's business performed better or worse than budget?

8.8 Lamar Bristol plc is a large trading organisation with retail premises in most major towns and cities in the UK. The key budget factor is sales; the company's main board sets the sales budget by agreeing an annual fixed percentage increment which is applied to all stores. The increment varies from year to year and is dependent upon the directors' assessment of current economic conditions and competitors' published sales figures. Generally it varies between 2% and 4%.

Discuss the likely effectiveness and efficiency of this method of setting a sales budget, identifying strengths and weaknesses of the approach.

EXERCISES

8.9 It is widely recognised that budget setting can be mishandled in organisations and may result in some undesirable effects that work against an organisation's best interests. Write a short report that describes potential problems that may arise if budgeting is not handled properly.

8.10 Hildebrandt St. Martins manufactures a single product. Its budget sales (in units) for December 2008 are 9350. Opening inventory of finished goods for the month is budgeted at 12 360 units and closing inventory is budgeted at 13 475 units.

Each unit of finished goods inventory uses 2kg of a raw material that is forecast to cost €3 per kilo. Opening inventory of raw material at the beginning of December 2008 is forecast at 18 000 kilos, but closing inventory for the month should fall to 16 000 kilos.

What is the budget amount in €s of purchases of this raw material for December 2008?

a) €56 790

b) €68 790

c) €49 410

d) €55 410.

8.11   Colney Brighouse Limited makes office furniture. The company's directors are preparing sales and production forecasts for January, February and March 2009. Sales forecasts in units for its two principal products, tables and office chairs, are as follows for the relevant months:

	Tables	Chairs
January 2009	13 000	28 000
February 2009	15 000	31 000
March 2009	16 000	35 000
April 2009	18 000	36 000

Opening inventory at 1 January 2009 is forecast at 7500 (tables) and 19 000 (chairs). The directors have decided to aim for closing inventory at the end of each month amounting to exactly 50% of the following month's sales requirements. Prepare the production budget for tables and chairs for January–March 2009 (inclusive).

8.12   Corby Thirlwell manufactures ornamental birdbaths made out of reconstituted stone. The company works on a rolling budget system, and its senior management is currently examining forecasts for the month of June 2009. June is a big month for sales in the birdbath business, and the directors are optimistically forecasting sales of 3250 units. They intend to launch a sales incentive scheme to encourage the sales staff to sell more birdbaths; from the beginning of 2009 each birdbath sold will result in a payment of €1.50 to the salesperson. The selling price of each birdbath is €65. The production cost structure of one birdbath is as follows:

Per unit	€
Direct materials	18.00
Direct labour	12.57
Production overhead recovery	13.86
Production cost	44.43

Administrative overheads for June 2009 are forecast at €12 479, and selling and distribution overheads (excluding the cost of commission) are forecast at €10 220.

i) Identify two advantages of the system of rolling budgeting.

ii) Prepare a budget income statement for the month of June 2009.

8.13   Discuss the advantages and drawbacks of a participative approach to budgeting.

8.14 Roxanne's budgeted year-end accounts at 31 December 2008 include a figure for receivables of €23 600. This represents:

	€
20% of November sales of €28 000	5 600
60% of December sales of €30 000	18 000
	23 600

This calculation is based upon the normal pattern of receipts for the business: 40% of sales on credit are paid for within the same month, and 40% are paid for in the following month, with the remaining 20% paid for in the month after that.

If January 2009 sales are budgeted at €28 000, how much will be included for sales receipts in the cash flow forecast in January 2009?

a) €28 800

b) €23 600

c) €24 000

d) €19 520.

8.15 Silas is starting out in business on his own, running a shop selling scuba diving gear. He has gained a lot of free publicity for his new venture by writing articles in specialist trade and enthusiasts' magazines, and he is well known as a leading expert on scuba diving. He is therefore fairly confident that he will be able to start selling in reasonable quantities straight away.

Silas is renting shop premises, and his principal start-up cost has been the cost of equipping the shop with stock. He has also invested in an electronic till, a computer for keeping track of stock and dealing with correspondence, and some general shop fixtures and fittings. His expenditure just prior to start up is:

	€
Inventory	42 000
Computer	2 500
Till	1 000
Fixtures and fittings	3 500
Total	49 000

Silas also transfers €6000 from his own bank account into a new business bank account. He has sold his house to finance the new venture and is currently living in the flat above the shop.

In his first year in trading Silas plans the following sales and purchases of inventory:

	Sales €	Purchases €
April	1 500	2 250
May	4 500	3 750
June	8 250	6 750
July	9 000	7 500
August	12 000	7 500
September	12 000	7 500
October	12 000	6 750
November	10 500	6 750
December	12 000	6 375
January	7 500	6 375
February	9 000	5 625
March	10 500	6 000
	108 750	73 125

It is expected that most sales will be for cash, but 25% are planned to be made on credit to scuba diving organisations. Credit sales are expected to be settled in full in the month after invoicing.

Purchases of inventory will be on credit, with payment made in full in the month following purchase. Closing inventory at the end of March is budgeted at €42 045.

Silas has budgeted for the following expenses:

Expense item	€	Payment details
Rent	6000	Payable in quarterly instalments in April, July, October and January
Insurance	1200	Payable in April
Phone	600	Quarterly bills of €150 to be paid in June, September, December and March
Water rates	750	Payable in May
Business rates	1500	Payable in April
Wages	1800	€150 to be paid each month
Subscriptions	300	€150 in May and €150 in November
Sundry admin and other expenses	2400	€200 to be paid each month

Silas plans to draw €1000 from the business in cash each month.

The computer will be subject to depreciation on a straight-line basis over four years. Fixtures and fittings and the electronic till have an estimated useful life of 10 years and will be depreciated on a straight-line basis. No residual values are expected at the end of the assets' useful lives.

Prepare the following statements for Silas:

i) Budget cash flow statement showing the cash movement in each of the first 12 months of business.

ii) Budget income statement for the 12 months ending 31 March.

iii) Budget balance sheet at 31 March.

8.16 Working with the information from 8.15, put the cash flow information into a spreadsheet. Use the spreadsheet to perform 'what if' calculations to answer Silas's questions as follows:

i) 'What would happen to my estimated cash at bank balance at the end of March if my receivables took two months, instead of one month, to be settled? Would the bank account go overdrawn at any point in the year?'

ii) 'I think I may have underestimated my sundry admin expenses. What would happen to the cash at bank balance at the end of March if my expenses each month were €400 rather than €200?'

iii) 'What would happen to the end of March cash at bank balance if both of these things happened – i.e. receivables take two months to pay me, not one, and admin expenses increase to €400 each month? Would I have an overdraft at any point, and if so, what would be the maximum budget overdraft figure?'

Accounting for Control

9

Aim of the chapter

To establish a context for the understanding of control in organisations, and to examine in detail one specific approach to accounting control in the form of standard costing, flexible budgeting and variance analysis.

Learning outcomes

After reading the chapter and completing the exercises at the end, students should:

- Know about a classification of control mechanisms within organisations.
- Know about some of the problems of control in firms.
- Understand the use of a standard costing system in a manufacturing environment.
- Be able to compare actual results against flexed budgets.
- Understand and be able to analyse some of the possible reasons for variances that emerge from the comparison of actual with standard costs.
- Understand the pros and cons of standard costing systems.

Introduction

The previous chapter on budgeting referred to the use of budgeting in controlling as well as planning and monitoring business activity. This chapter continues the theme of control by examining a relevant theory of control mechanisms, and then briefly examines an important critique of the nature of accounting controls. The early part of the chapter thus provides a context for the detailed consideration of a mechanism of accounting control that is widely adopted in organisations: standard costing. Most of the rest of the chapter is devoted to an examination of the mechanisms of standard costing, flexible budgeting and variance analysis. Naturally, there are advantages and drawbacks to this particular approach to control, and these are briefly discussed towards the end of the chapter.

Organisational control mechanisms

Ouchi (1979) poses the question: 'What are the mechanisms through which an organisation can be managed so that it moves towards its objectives?' Based on work study in a large organisation, Ouchi identified three mechanisms:

Market mechanism	Decision-making based on prices; where market information is available, there is little need for any more formal control mechanism
Bureaucratic mechanism	Characterised by close personal surveillance and direction of subordinates by superiors
Clan mechanism	Control through informal social structures, based upon shared values

Ouchi gives the example of materials purchasing to illustrate the market control mechanism. The best outcome for the organisation is achieved through a competitive bidding process, and relatively little managerial input is required to ensure that the best result is obtained. However, other business activities cannot easily be controlled in the same way. Once the materials are purchased, their use, storage and movement within the organisation need to be controlled but there is no market mechanism available to help. Depending upon context, it is possible that some kind of social control is possible, where, for example, employees subscribe to the same set of organisational values which encourages them to get the job done on time and done well. However, it is also very likely that some form of bureaucratic control mechanism is required as well. As Ouchi puts it: 'if the price requirements of a market cannot be met, and if the social conditions of the Clan are impossible to achieve, then the Bureaucratic mechanism becomes the preferred method of control'. In practice, in any given profit-making organisation, there are likely to be some elements of all three mechanisms in place.

Earlier, in Chapter 2, the growth of scientific management in the twentieth century was described, and the tendency to think of the organisation as a machine, in which people are subject to rules that are supposed to make them behave like machine components. A set of bureaucratic control mechanisms for regulating human activity forms part of this characterisation of the organisation. However, the development of the human relations school was also noted. The tendency in this view of the organisation is to emphasise the human element. In practice, though, it is likely that most organisations display aspects of both scientific and humanistic approaches to management.

Top-down, bottom-up

In recent years, more formal, bureaucratic approaches to managerial control have been criticised frequently for their inefficiency and ineffectiveness. It is argued that 'top-down' managerial control leads to some unfortunate outcomes, in the form of manipulation of processes and results. Johnson, an important management accounting theorist, argued in 1992 that top-down control was a key factor in America's inability to compete globally. He contrasted it with 'bottom-up' empowerment. The following table is reproduced from his book on the subject:

Bottom-up	Top-down
Information technology empowers the customer and gives the customer CHOICE	Companies learn and change in 'big steps' that draw on knowledge from the outside
The customer's power of choice makes it necessary for companies to quickly CHANGE	Information is owned by top management who PLAN AND DECIDE
To change quickly, everyone in a company must continually LEARN	Top management passes down INSTRUCTIONS to subordinates and workers who MANAGE RESULTS by manipulating processes
Constant learning and adaptation to change require the workforce to have OWNERSHIP of information from processes. That ownership of information generates the worker EMPLOYMENT	

Source: Johnson (1992) p. 156.

The top-down approach described in the table is consistent with much organisational management. Despite some movement in recent years towards flatter management structures, many businesses continue to be organised in hierarchies with lines of command and information moving in a vertical direction. Agency theory (as described in Chapter 2) supports the idea that people will tend to manipulate processes in order to achieve certain results, so that information cannot be relied upon to be accurate. People hold objectives that are likely to be divergent from those of the organisation and will tend to be preoccupied by issues such as their own promotion prospects and remuneration. Johnson's argument is, essentially, that American organisations are hampered by the 'top-down' control that predominates, and that their competitiveness could be transformed by the transfer of empowerment to the workforce who would be enabled to respond rapidly to the exercise of customer choice. Johnson's thinking has been very influential, but it is worth noting that the scale of change required has been too much of a challenge to most organisations who continue to employ 'top-down' control mechanisms. Bureaucratic control exercised through hierarchical management systems continues to be a major factor in the way organisations are run in practice in many countries.

Bureaucratic control and management accounting

Traditional management accounting, in the form of budgetary and costing systems and so on, is an intrinsic element of the type of control systems that are based on the view of the organisation as a machine and employees as cogs within it. However, as illustrated by Ouchi's (1979) analysis, control mechanisms are likely to overlap in practice. Therefore, even where control mechanisms are predominantly bureaucratic in nature, other elements will come into play. For example, the budgeting chapter that preceded this one illustrated the interdependent elements of formal control and human behaviour.

The remainder of this chapter describes a control system, standard costing, that is primarily bureaucratic in nature. However, it may in practice also be subject to market and/or social (or 'clan') controls.

Standard costing, flexible budgeting and variance analysis

Introduction to the analysis of variances

The previous chapter examined the setting of budgets and the comparison of actual with budgeted results. Often the identification and analysis of the difference between actual and budgeted performance is quite straightforward. For example, suppose that a business budgets to spend €10 500 on business insurance, on the basis that the previous year's charge was €10 000 and the general level of price inflation suggests that 5% would be a likely level of increase. But in fact, the business's insurers, in common with the rest of the insurance industry, raise charges by 10%. The actual bill for insurance totals €11 000, €500 more than was budgeted. Investigation of other insurers shows that it is not possible to obtain cover for less than €11 000.

Adverse variance
an unfavourable difference between a budget figure and an actual figure (in terms of sales, an actual figure that is lower than budget; in terms of costs an actual figure that is higher than budget)

The **adverse variance** of €500 against budget in this case can be easily explained. It is a general price increase, not attributable to any internal factor such as poor purchasing or failure to control expenditure properly. In terms of control mechanisms, as discussed earlier in the chapter, the market control mechanism (looking for the best price) ensures that the best price is obtained for the service required.

In the insurance example above, it is easy to establish the reasons for the variance against budget. But in a relatively complex manufacturing environment, it can be difficult to track down the reasons for variances unless some quite detailed analysis is carried out.

EXAMPLE 9.1

Sugden Harkness, a manufacturing business, sets a budget based upon a sales forecast for July of 5000 units. Each unit of product is budgeted to use 3 metres of raw material (15 000 metres in total) at a cost of €4.20 per metre (15 000 × €4.20 = €63 000). The actual business performance statement for July shows that, although exactly 5000 units were sold, the total cost of the raw material element of cost of sales was €68 000.

What has happened here?

Clearly, raw material costs have increased; there is an adverse variance of €68 000 − €63 000 = €5000. The reasons, however, are not clear, unless further analysis is undertaken. It could be that:

- The price has increased to a level higher than the €4.20 budgeted.
- The production process has been less efficient than expected and has used more than 3 metres of raw material per unit of product.
- Both of these factors are present in some combination.

The management accountant of Sugden Harkness needs to be able to analyse the variance in more detail in order to be able to:

- Find out if there is a problem that needs attention.
- Attribute responsibility for the adverse variance to the appropriate department or person.

The process of responsibility accounting ensures that problems are tracked to their source. Having correctly identified the source, it is then the responsibility of management to ensure that problems are dealt with via appropriate corrective action. As we saw in the previous chapter, one of the possible adverse consequences of a budgeting system arises where responsibility is incorrectly attributed, leading to resentment and demotivation. Sometimes, the reason for the occurrence of a problem seems obvious, but further investigation may be required to look beyond the apparently obvious and to uncover true causes and effects.

Taking the example of Sugden Harkness a little further, suppose that the adverse variance were found to be attributable to extra usage of the raw material. This looks, on the face of it, as though it should be the responsibility of the production manager and his team. It may well result from inefficiencies in the use of raw materials (too much wastage, for example). However, the picture changes if we find out that the regular supplier of the raw material had increased prices, and that, in response to the increase, the purchasing manager had purchased inferior quality material but at the budget price. The poorer quality resulted in more wastage as the material was put through the production process. The adverse variance now appears to be attributable to the purchasing manager rather than the production manager.

Despite problems of this type in attributing responsibility for variances, variance identification and analysis are very common procedures in manufacturing industry. Variances are often identified and quantified by using a standard costing system.

Standard costing

Standard costing is a system of costing which can be used in business environments where a repetitive series of standardised operations are carried

Standard costing
a system of costing
which attributes
consistent costs to
elements of production

out. In such systems each element of production involves a consistent input of resources at prices that can be predicted with a fair degree of accuracy.

Standard costs are the budgeted costs of individual units of production. The standard cost is compared with actual cost in order to calculate an overall variance. This overall variance can then be broken down further in order to identify:

- The effects of variation in volume of the resource inputs.
- The effects of variation in price of the resource inputs.

Standard costing and variance analysis are widely used in industries where mass production is carried out. Managers in such industries are frequently presented with financial reports including information about variances, and it is important even for non-financial managers to understand something about the fundamentals of standard costing systems.

Establishing standard costs

Establishing budget information can be a time-consuming and potentially expensive task. Standard costs may also require a substantial investment of time in research and observation. For example, in order to establish standard costs for the direct materials component of a product, it is necessary to examine two aspects:

- The purchase price of the material inputs.
- The expected rate at which material is used in the product.

The purchase price may be variable depending upon the supplier used, quantities available, movements on commodities markets and so on. The standard cost will probably reflect a price which can be obtained with a reasonable amount of effort on the part of those responsible for materials purchasing. If too low a standard price is set purchasers will not have to make much of an effort to better it. On the other hand, if the standard price set would be obtainable only rarely, then purchasers may become demotivated.

Establishing the rate of usage will require careful observation of the manufacturing process, probably on a number of separate occasions. Again, the rate of materials consumption which is adopted as the standard is likely to reflect a realistic achievable target, set neither too low nor too high.

However, standard cost setters need to be wary of relying upon too many established precedents and practices. There may be a need to challenge lax and wasteful production procedures in setting standards.

Each element of cost of production is broken down and costed. Even for an apparently simple product, there may be many different elements of cost. Take a tin of beans, for example. Materials input per batch includes: beans, tomatoes, salt, sugar, flavourings, tins and labels. Each part of the processing involves labour and machine times which must be timed to the second in order to produce accurate costs and forecasts.

For each product a standard cost card is built up, as shown in the comprehensive demonstration example which follows.

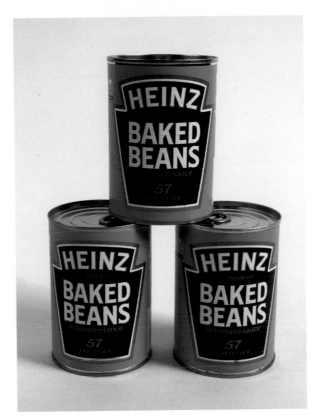

© Barry Bland / Alamy

EXAMPLE 9.2

A comprehensive example will illustrate the application of variance identification in a standard costing system. Although the basic facts in the example are straightforward there are several calculations. The whole example takes up several pages, because each step is explained in full. Students should work through it slowly and ensure that each point is understood before moving on. It will seem difficult, if not impossible, at first, but it does all hang together quite logically.

Zamboni & Zeuss manufactures a specialised metal component which is sold to manufacturers of heavy lifting machinery.

The standard cost card for one component is as follows:

	€
Selling price	150.00 Per unit
Costs:	
Direct materials	35.00 7kg of metal @ €5 per kilo
Direct labour	15.00 3 hours @ €5 per kilo
Prime cost	50.00

▶

The company's budget for January 2009 is as follows:

	€
Sales: 1000 units @ €150	150 000
Costs:	
Direct materials: 1000 units × (7kg × €5)	(35 000)
Direct labour: 1000 units × (3 hours × €5)	(15 000)
Production overhead	(50 000)
	50 000
Selling and administrative overhead	(20 000)
Net profit	30 000

The production overhead, as we have seen in previous chapters, is usually absorbed via an overhead absorption rate. For the purposes of this particular demonstration we will assume that the overheads are simply recorded, and also, that they remain at the same level regardless of changes in the level of production, i.e. they are fixed overhead costs. Later in the chapter we will examine overhead variances in more detail, but for the moment, we will simplify the overheads aspects of the question.

Simple comparison of budget with actual results

After the end of January 2009, the management accountant identifies the variances between the budget and actual results.

Actual results are as follows:

	€
Sales: 1100 units @ €145	159 500
Costs:	
Direct materials: 1100 × (7.5kg × €4.50)	(37 125)
Direct labour: 1100 units × (2.8 hours × €5.50)	(16 940)
Production overhead	(52 000)
	53 435
Selling and administrative overhead	(21 250)
Net profit	32 185

A very brief comparison of the statements shows us that the company has produced higher profits than expected. Good news, surely? Well, yes, but has the business made as much extra profit as might be expected, given that it has sold an extra 100 components? The answer to the question is not immediately obvious; it requires further analysis of the variances.

Flexing the budget

One problem with comparing the two statements shown above is that we are not really comparing like with like. The initial budget was produced on the assumption that 1000 units would be sold. The actual outcome is that 1100 units were sold. In order to make a more useful comparison, we need to adjust the budget to reflect the additional volume of sales. This is known as flexing the budget.

The flexed budget income statement (flexed to reflect the actual level of activity of 1100 units sold) is as follows:

	€
Sales: 1100 units @ €150	165 000
Costs:	
Direct materials: 1100 × (7kg × €5)	(38 500)
Direct labour: 1100 units x (3 hours × €5)	(16 500)
Production overhead	(50 000)
	60 000
Selling and administrative overhead	(20 000)
Net profit	40 000

The flexed budget shows the sales revenue that would have been expected from sales of 1100 units, and all the costs adjusted for the additional volume of sales. Remember that we are working on the assumption that production overheads do not increase in line with the volume of sales. Selling and administrative overheads, also, are not assumed to increase in line with the volume of sales; they are also regarded as fixed overhead costs. (Note: The distinction between variable costs and fixed costs will be examined in more detail later in the chapter.)

We now have three income statements: the original budget, the flexed budget and the statement of actual results. It will help at this point to place them side by side:

	Original budget €	Flexed budget €	Actual €
Sales	150 000	165 000	159 500
Direct materials	(35 000)	(38 500)	(37 125)
Direct labour	(15 000)	(16 500)	(16 940)
Production overhead	(50 000)	(50 000)	(52 000)
	50 000	60 000	53 435
Selling and administrative overhead	(20 000)	(20 000)	(21 250)
Net profit	30 000	40 000	32 185

Calculating variances

The original budget net profit was €30 000. Actual net profit is €32 185. The overall variance is a favourable variance of €2185. We will break this figure down into its constituent variances which will allow us to identify possible problem areas.

Sales profit volume variance

A key element of the difference is the sale of more units than originally anticipated. This variance is the difference between the original budget profit and the flexed budget profit: €40 000 − €30 000 = €10 000. It is clearly in the interests of the company to sell more components, and so this is a favourable variance.

Sales price variance

The actual profit is affected by the fact that, although extra sales have been made, the selling price is actually lower than budgeted.

This variance is calculated as follows:

Actual volume of sales at actual selling price: 1100 × €145	€159 500
Less: actual volume of sales at budget selling price: 1100 × €150	165 000
Sales price variance	5 500

This represents an undesirable outcome for the firm; it would have been better to sell at the higher, budgeted, price, so this is an adverse variance.

At this stage refer back to the three statements presented side by side, and note that we are comparing the flexed budget statement with the actual statement in order to calculate this variance.

Direct materials variances

Comparing the figure for direct materials in the flexed budget statement with the figure in the actual statement:

Flexed budget for direct materials	€38 500
Actual direct materials	37 125
	1 375

The actual amount is less than budget; this is a good outcome and so this is classified as a favourable variance.

We can analyse this variance further by looking at the budget input of resources against actual input. Management accountants are able to calculate two direct materials variances: direct materials price variance and direct materials quantity variance. These relate, respectively, to price effects and volume effects.

Direct materials price variance

We compare:

- The actual quantity of raw materials used at the price actually paid (actual price).
- The actual quantity of raw materials used at the price budgeted (standard price).

Using the same measure of quantity (actual) ensures that we isolate the price effect.

Actual quantity at actual price	
7.5kg was used for each of 1100 components:	
actual quantity used is 7.5kg × 1100 = 8 250kg.	
8250kg × price actually paid (€4.50)	37 125
Actual quantity at standard price	
8250kg × standard price (€5.00)	41 250
Direct materials price variance	4 125

The business has paid less per unit for direct materials than it expected; this is therefore a favourable variance.

Direct materials quantity variance

We compare:

- The actual quantity of materials used at standard price.
- The standard quantity of materials used at standard price.

Actual quantity at standard price	
Actual quantity used (already worked out) – 8250kg	
Standard price per kg – €5	
Actual quantity at standard price = 8250 × €5	41 250
Standard quantity at standard price	
Standard quantity: 7kg × 1100 components = 7700kg	
Standard price per kg – €5	
Standard quantity at standard price = 7700 × €5	38 500
Direct materials quantity variance	2 750

The business has used more materials per component than budgeted; this is therefore an adverse variance.

In summary, the direct materials variances are:

Direct materials price variance	4125 (F)
Direct materials quantity variance	2750 (A)
Direct materials variance	1375 (F)

Note: 'F' stands for 'Favourable'; 'A' stands for 'Adverse'.

▶

Direct labour variances

Comparing the figure for direct labour in the flexed budget statement with the figure in the actual statement:

Flexed budget for direct labour	€16 500
Actual direct labour	16 940
	440

The actual amount is more than budget; this is not a good outcome and so is classified as an adverse variance.

As with direct materials, we can break down this overall variance into two variances, one quantifying the price effect and the other quantifying the volume effect. These are traditionally known as the direct labour rate variance, and the direct labour efficiency variance, respectively.

Direct labour rate variance

We compare:

- The actual hours of direct labour used at the wage rate actually paid (actual rate).
- The actual hours of direct labour used at the wage rate budgeted (standard rate).

Using the same measure of hours (actual) ensures that we isolate the rate effect.

Actual hours at actual rate	
Actual hours was 2.8 hours for each of 1100 components:	
2.8 × 1100 = 3 080 hours	
3080 hours × rate actually paid (€5.50)	16 940
Actual hours at standard rate	
3080 hours × standard rate (€5.00)	15 400
Direct labour rate variance	1 540

The business has paid more per hour for direct labour than it budgeted; this is therefore an adverse variance.

Direct labour efficiency variance

We compare:

- The actual hours of direct labour used at standard rate.
- The standard hours of direct labour used at standard rate.

Actual hours at standard rate	
Actual hours used (already worked out) – 3080 hours	
Standard rate per hour – €5	
Actual hours at standard rate = 3080 × €5	15 400
Standard hours at standard rate	
Standard hours: 3 hours × 1100 = 3300	
Standard rate per hour – €5	
Standard hours at standard rate = 3300 × €5	16 500
Direct labour efficiency variance	1 100

The business has used fewer hours per component than budgeted; this is therefore a favourable variance.

In summary, the direct labour variances are:

Direct labour rate variance	€1540 (A)
Direct labour efficiency variance	1100 (F)
Direct labour variance	€440 (A)

Production overhead variance

Budget figure for production overhead:	50 000
Actual figure for production overhead:	52 000
Production overhead variance	(2 000) (A)

The company appears to have spent more than initially planned; therefore, this is an adverse variance.

Selling and administrative overhead variance

Budget figure for selling and administrative overhead:	20 000
Actual figure for selling and administrative overhead:	21 250
Selling and administrative overhead variance	(1 250) (A)

Having calculated this long list of variances, they can now be presented in the form of a standard cost operating statement, as follows:

Zamboni & Zeuss: standard cost operating statement for January 2009

	Favourable €	(Adverse) €	Total €
Original budgeted net profit			30 000
Sales profit volume variance			10 000
Flexed budget net profit			40 000
Other variances			
Sales price variance		(5 500)	
Direct materials price variance	4 125		
Direct materials quantity variance		(2 750)	
Direct labour rate variance		(1 540)	
Direct labour efficiency variance	1 100		
Production overhead variance		(2 000)	
Selling and administrative overhead variance		(1 250)	
Total	5 225	(13 040)	(7 815)
Actual net profit			32 185

What does this statement tell us? Remember that we started out with the simple observation that there was an overall favourable variance between budgeted profit and actual profit of €2185. The standard cost operating statement above allows us to identify the component parts of that overall variance, and to pinpoint the areas where problems may have arisen. There are several adverse variances:

Sales price variance: although the volume of sales has increased, the beneficial effect on profit is not as great as it might have been because the selling price has fallen. Of course, these two factors may very well be related; it could be that the company has made a deliberate attempt to boost sales by setting a lower selling price. If that was the intention, the objective appears to have been met.

Direct materials quantity variance: it appears that the production process is less efficient in terms of usage of materials than was originally intended. There may be good reasons why this has happened; indeed, the problem may be that the original standard set for quantity was too ambitious. Further investigation of the variance would probably be necessary. This adverse variance, however, is more than offset by a favourable *direct materials price variance*. Perhaps a special purchase of materials has been made, but, of course, if the quality is slightly poorer, it may be more difficult to use the materials efficiently.

Direct labour rate variance: production staff appear to have been paid at a higher rate than allowed for in the standard cost calculations. If this is a permanent change, the standard cost needs changing. If it is a temporary change, the reasons for it should be investigated. It is noticeable, however, that the *direct labour efficiency variance* is positive; perhaps higher paid staff are working more quickly, or perhaps the supervision process is more effective than originally anticipated.

While the standard cost operating statement certainly provides management with more information than a simple statement like 'profits have gone up', it does not, clearly, answer all the questions. However, it serves a useful purpose in directing management's attention to areas which may require investigation and in suggesting the kind of questions which should be asked.

Before moving on try this self-test question which runs through the same variance calculations as the demonstration example above.

SELF-TEST QUESTION 9.1

Bridge and Blige make metal casings for lawn mowers in one standard size. In February 2009 the company's budget for sales and related costs is as follows:

	€
Sales: 800 units × €35	28 000
Costs:	
Direct materials: 800 units × (2kg × €6)	(9 600)
Direct labour: 800 units × (1 hour × €7.50)	(6 000)
Production overheads	(4 000)
	8 400
Selling and administrative overheads	(2 300)
Net profit	6 100

The actual figures for February 2009 are as follows:

	€
Sales: 900 units @ €36	32 400
Costs:	
Direct materials: 900 units × (1.9kg × €5.50)	(9 405)
Direct labour: 900 units × (1.2 hours × €7.00)	(7 560)
Production overheads	(4 400)
	11 035
Selling and administrative overheads	(2 450)
Net profit	8 585

iii) calculate the actual figures for sales, direct materials, direct labour, variable overheads, fixed overheads and profit.

9.11   BLP Limited is a small, but rapidly growing, manufacturing organisation. In the early days following start-up there were few formal controls, because the small number of employees worked as a closely knit team, but it has become obvious recently that management needs to exert more control over operations. Last month a fraud was discovered: the purchasing officer had been working in collusion with one particular supplier, XM Limited. Instead of searching for the best price available, the purchasing officer had directed all orders to XM, in exchange for a commission of 2% of the order value.

Required:

i) Explain BLP's current control environment in terms of the three control mechanisms identified by Ouchi (1979).

ii) Explain how the establishment of standard costs for materials purchases could help to prevent and/or identify a fraud of the type described above.

9.12   The directors of Bellcraft are due to meet to discuss a proposal to implement a standard costing system to control their manufacturing operations. One of the directors has been reading a book about management systems which contains a chapter about the drawbacks of standard costing systems. He has circulated a paper in advance of the meeting suggesting that the proposed system would be excessively expensive and bureaucratic. He says that standard costing systems fail to produce information on a sufficiently timely basis, so that variance investigation is bound to be ineffective. You are the management accountant of Bellcraft, and you are due to attend the directors' meeting as an adviser.

Required: make notes to take into the meeting which address the criticisms of standard costing in the director's paper.

EXERCISES

9.13   Dorchester Slugg manufactures plastic refuse bins. Its monthly budget for August 2009 is as follows:

	€
Sales: 4000 units × €18	72 000
Direct materials: 4000 × (7kg × €1)	(28 000)
Direct labour: 4000 × (0.5 hours × €6.00)	(12 000)
Production overhead	(10 000)
	22 000
Selling and administrative overhead	(4 000)
	18 000

Dorchester Slugg does not absorb production overheads using an overhead absorption rate. It may be assumed that all of its overheads are fixed in nature.

Required: flex the budget for a sales and production level of 4500 units.

9.14   Dillinger Dalonghi produces a line of leather bags. Although they vary slightly in design the cost structure is the same for each bag. The company's budget for January 2009 is as follows:

	€
Sales: 4000 units × €22.00	88 000
Direct materials: 4000 × (1 square metre × €6.50)	(26 000)
Direct labour: 4000 × (0.5 hours × €7.80)	(15 600)
Production overhead	(24 000)
	22 400
Selling and administrative overhead	(6 000)
Net profit	16 400

Dillinger Dalonghi does not absorb production overheads using an overhead absorption rate. It may be assumed that all of its overheads are fixed in nature.

If the company flexes its budget for 3600 units, what will be the revised net profit figure?

a)   €11 760

b)   €17 760

c)   €14 160

d)   €7 600.

The following information is relevant for questions 9.15 to 9.20.

Estella Starr produces garden sheds which are sold direct to the public in kit form. March is one of the company's best months for sales, and in March 2009 the directors have set some ambitious targets. These are summarised in the following budget for the month:

	€
Sales: 900 units × €217.00	195 300
Direct materials: 900 × (16 metres × €4.00)	(57 600)
Direct labour: 900 × (4 hours × €6.30)	(22 680)
Production overhead	(62 300)
	52 720
Other overheads	(10 600)
Net profit	42 120

Estella Starr does not absorb production overheads using an overhead absorption rate. It may be assumed that all of its overheads are fixed in nature.

The company's actual results for the month are as follows:

	€
Sales: 830 × €214.00	177 620
Direct materials: 830 × (15 metres × €4.10)	(51 045)
Direct labour: 830 × (4.1 hours × €6.00)	(20 418)
Production overhead	(61 400)
	44 757
Other overheads	(8 950)
Net profit	35 807

9.15 What is the sales profit volume variance for the month?

a) €6313 (A)

b) €8946 (A)

c) €8946 (F)

d) €6313 (F).

9.16 What is the sales price variance for the month?

a) €2490 (F)

b) €2490 (A)

c) €15 190 (F)

d) €15 190 (A).

9.17 What is the direct materials price variance for the month?

a) €6555 (A)

b) €1245 (A)

c) €6555 (F)

d) €1245 (F).

9.18 What is the direct materials quantity variance for the month?

a) €3320 (F)

b) €3320 (A)

c) €7800 (A)

d) €7800 (F).

9.19 What is the direct labour rate variance for the month (to the nearest €)?

a) €360 (A)

b) €360 (F)

c) €1021 (F)

d) €1021 (A).

9.20   What is the direct labour efficiency variance for the month (to the nearest €)?

a) €523 (A)

b) €523 (F)

c) €340 (F)

d) €340 (A).

9.21   Finkel and Stein is a manufacturing company. For the month of August 2009 it budgeted for 780 units of production, each to use 4 hours of machine time. Production overhead absorption rates were budgeted as follows:

Variable production overhead: €2.80 per machine hour
Fixed production overhead: €7.60 per machine hour

The actual level of production in the month was 760 units.

The original production overhead budget, the flexed budget and the actual expenditure are shown in the following table:

	Original budget €	Flexed budget €	Actual €
Variable production overheads	8 736	8 512	8 476
Fixed production overheads	23 712	23 104	24 160
	32 448	31 616	32 636

Required:

i) Calculate the total variable production overhead variance

ii) Calculate the total fixed production overhead variance.

9.22   Explain the implications of agency theory in the context of 'top-down' systems of control.

9.23   Andrea Ellison is managing director of Francis & Follett, an unlisted company that manufactures wooden bedframes. After a few difficult years in the last decade the company has managed to secure half a dozen contracts with major home furnishings retailers. This has significantly expanded the volume of trade and has allowed the company to repay its long-term loans. The company's accountant and business adviser suggested last year that it is now time to improve the quality of management control systems. Andrea and her brother, Phil, the sales director, are the two active directors in the business. In the past they have been able to keep tight control over the business by close supervision. However, as the business has taken on more staff that kind of control has lessened, although Andrea and Phil try to maintain a 'small company' ethos by holding monthly informal breakfast meetings with staff where members of staff are encouraged to discuss business issues. A few months ago the company appointed a management accountant, Sylvie, who has worked hard to establish a budgetary control system in time for the start of the financial year on 1 January 2009. Sylvie has carefully monitored the production process and has established standard costs and times for all parts of the process. The annual budget is split into 12, and actual performance is monitored each month. It is now the end of March 2009.

The budget for March 2009 is as follows:

	€
Sales: 1600 units × €103	164 800
Costs:	
Direct materials: 1600 units × (12 metres × €2.50 per metre)	(48 000)
Direct materials: 1600 units × 1 bag of metal components × €4.50	(7 200)
Direct labour: 1600 units × 1 packaging box × €3.50	(5 600)
Direct labour: 1600 units × (2.5 hours × €6.00 per hour)	(24 000)
Variable production overheads: 1600 units × (1.5 machine hours per unit × €4)	(9 600)
Fixed production overheads: 1600 units × (1.5 machine hours per unit × €10)	(24 000)
	46 400
Selling and administrative overheads	(16 600)
Net profit	29 800

The pieces for each bedframe are flat-packed in the factory. Each pack contains the necessary metal components for assembling the bedframe. Francis & Follett buys in the components ready packaged in plastic bags. Production overheads are absorbed on the basis of machine hours. Machine hours for March are budgeted at 2400 hours. Actual figures for March are as follows:

	€
Sales: 1650 units × €103	169 950
Costs:	
Direct materials: 1650 units × (12.2 metres × €2.70 per metre)	(54 351)
Direct materials: 1650 units × 1 bag of metal components × €4.50	(7 425)
Direct materials: 1650 units × 1 packaging box × €3.50	(5 775)
Direct labour: 1650 units × (2.4 hours × €6.00 per hour)	(23 760)
Variable production overheads	(10 050)
Fixed production overheads	(23 960)
	44 629
Selling and administrative overheads	(16 420)
Net profit	28 209

This chapter examines some important aspects of internal performance reporting in business, with particular emphasis on reporting issues in businesses that are split into divisions. The earlier part of the chapter is concerned with ways of measuring and reporting performance in quantitative (principally financial) terms. In recent years, though, the importance of reporting using a combination of financial, other quantitative, and non-quantitative measures has been increasingly appreciated, and this type of reporting occupies the latter part of the chapter. It concludes with a brief review of performance measurement issues and practices in the public sector.

Performance reporting and organisational objectives

This first section of the chapter examines an example of performance reporting in a service sector organisation. This illustrates some important features of performance reporting within a fairly large organisation. The larger a business becomes, the greater the complexity of its internal accounting and reporting processes. Very large businesses are likely to employ many full-time staff in a management accounting department with a responsibility to produce reports useful for management.

Activities should be oriented towards achieving organisational objectives, and, similarly, the reporting of activities should demonstrate the extent to which those objectives have been met. Most organisations, whatever their size, find it useful to develop key performance indicators (sometimes referred to as KPIs) which help to measure the extent to which objectives are being achieved.

Illustrative example 10.1 indicates some of the performance indicators, and reports, that might be useful in an estate agency business.

EXAMPLE 10.1

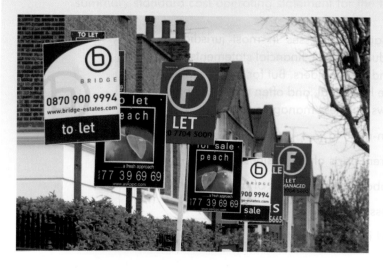

© Justin Leighton / Alamy

Wisharts is a national firm of estate agents, with 180 branches around the country. The market for estate agency services is highly competitive in most locations, with several national and local firms competing for business. At the company's head office a small team of management accountants collates information submitted via the firm's intranet in a standard form. Each time a new instruction is received, or a property is sold, details are logged onto the computer system.

Senior managers at head office require weekly updates on the following key performance indicators:

- Number of new instructions.
- Number of houses/flats sold, in total, and by each agent.
- Value of sales made.
- Average turnover of instructions in days (i.e. the average length of time a house remains on the books of the agency).

Each Saturday at close of business, the branch manager enters the information into standard formats that are submitted to head office via the intranet. Senior managers at head office meet on the following Monday afternoon to discuss the results for the week which are presented on hard-copy report forms, summarised into 14 regions. The management accounting team also updates a set of graphs showing the movement over a rolling 12 month period of indicators such as average house price in each region and number of sales made per region. Where a region appears to be under-performing, managers are able to drill down into the regional data to identify individual office performance. The performance of individual agents is accumulated and a national ranking is produced at the end of each month. The top five agents in the country receive a substantial financial bonus and an allocation of points towards Wisharts annual agents' awards. Where branch or individual performance gives cause for concern, a member of the senior management team calls or visits the branch to determine the reasons and to take remedial action.

At the end of each four-week period, senior managers are presented with monthly management accounts showing total revenue and expenditure for the month, together with the totals for the key regional indicators of new instructions, number of houses/flats sold and average selling price. The Wishart management accounting system is designed to be flexible and responsive so that managers are able to request special purpose reports which they normally receive within 24 hours. Recently, for example, the chief executive requested a special report listing the details of all individual house sales in excess of €300 000 for region 12.

Hardly any of the information reported internally to the senior managers in the example above would be reported in the external annual report to stakeholders. Important indicators such as new instructions received are for internal use only.

Internal performance reports can take any form: they might be a one page monthly summary in a small business, or, for a large business, could run to many pages of detail. The key point, as always with management information, is that they should provide information that is useful to managers in their planning, controlling, monitoring and decision-making functions. Information reported to managers should ideally have the following characteristics:

- It should be produced quickly so that managers can respond rapidly to it.
- It should be easily comprehensible, useful, accurate and reliable.
- The costs of producing it should not outweigh its benefits.

Also, the lines of responsibility within an organisation should be clearly set out and understood by all concerned, and they should be oriented towards achieving the objectives of the business. For example, in the Wishart organisation described in the example above, senior managers are likely to be concerned most with growing their market share in a highly competitive market. Having determined that growth in market share is a key objective, they must communicate the objective clearly to all the business's employees so that every individual understands their role in achieving it. Internal reporting should be oriented towards measuring the organisation's success in pursuing its key objectives.

SELF-TEST QUESTION 10.1

Dreamstay runs a chain of eight luxury hotels, all located in prime city centre sites throughout Great Britain. One of its key business objectives is to maximise the revenue from both sale of rooms and additional value-added services such as in-house hairdressing and beauty salons. Suggest three key performance indicators linked to this objective.

KPIs are important indicators of achievement, or lack of it, in many organisations. They will be considered further later on in the chapter.

Divisional responsibility in large business organisations

In some cases the sheer size and complexity of a business organisation may make it difficult for a single management team to control all of the operations of the business. Where this is the case, part of the control can be devolved to divisional managers, leaving the most senior level of management free to deal with issues of major strategic importance (for example, a decision to launch a takeover bid). Divisions may be established, for example, by reference to the nature of their function or their geographical location, or both. A business that produces four major product groups might organise their activities into four divisions: one for each group. A major multinational car maker such as Nissan or Volkswagen might organise its activities into geographical groups such as North American, Asia-Pacific and Europe. Example 10.2 shows how a manufacturing business might organise its operations into divisions.

EXAMPLE 10.2

Popps is a manufacturer and bottler of soft-drinks operating in France and Spain. The French operations comprise the bottling of naturally sourced mineral water, and, at a separate location, the manufacturing and bottling of fizzy cola drinks. The Spanish operation is based at one location, manufacturing and bottling a similar range of cola drinks to those produced in France.

It would be possible to create two simple geographical divisions – one based in France and one in Spain. However, the two French operations differ somewhat from each other; they operate at different locations and are probably selling in slightly different markets. Therefore, Popps might find it advantageous to split operations into three divisions: Spain, France (cola) and France (water).

Divisions operate with varying degrees of autonomy. Highly decentralised organisations devolve a great deal of control to divisions, whereas, by contrast, in centralised organisations control is retained at the centre. There are advantages and disadvantages to both approaches.

Centralisation and decentralisation

The advantages of decentralisation include the following:

- Managers of decentralised parts of a business are likely to be given a high level of autonomy in decision-making. This is likely to lead to a more flexible and rapid response to problems.

- Managers in decentralised businesses may be highly motivated if they are given sufficient responsibility in the running of their divisions.
- The comparisons made by senior management between the performances of different divisions in a decentralised business can help to generate a healthy level of competition between divisional managers.

However, there are some drawbacks, too. Healthy competition, if left unchecked, can result in a short-termist approach to decision-making. Managers may take decisions that are not in the best overall interests of the organisation for the sake of gaining some short-term advantage for their own division. Also, decentralised organisations can be more expensive to run where, for example, a separate sales department is required for each division. It would probably be cheaper and might be more efficient to run a single centralised sales department.

The advantages of a centralised approach to organisational management are:

- The operations of the business remain under close scrutiny and control by senior managers.
- There are none of the inter-divisional rivalries that can lead to sub-optimal decision-making.
- By centralising functions such as accounting, marketing and selling, cost savings can be made.

However, highly centralised operations are very demanding of senior management time, and may operate relatively inefficiently as a result. The opportunity of motivating staff by assigning divisional responsibilities to them is lost.

SELF-TEST QUESTION 10.2

Identify each of the following statements about centralisation and decentralisation as TRUE or FALSE:

1 Inter-divisional rivalries can lead to sub-optimal decision-making.

2 Decentralisation means that divisional managers are always motivated to make decisions that are in the best interests of the organisation as a whole.

3 By decentralising, senior managers may be able to concentrate more on the overall strategy of the organisation.

4 Decentralisation is likely to result in a more flexible and rapid response to problems in specific parts of the business.

Assessing divisional performance

The nature of divisional performance assessment varies depending upon the degree of autonomy assigned to the division. A key principle is that divisional managers should be assessed only in respect of elements of performance that are under their control. A highly autonomous division will be responsible for virtually all aspects of its operations within a general framework of overall business strategy. Such responsibilities would include, for example, determining the level of investment in assets, the nature and direction of marketing strategies and fixing selling prices. By contrast, divisional control might be limited to minor issues.

Broadly, three levels of autonomy can be recognised under the following descriptions:

Cost or revenue centre: at cost centre level divisional managers are responsible for controlling costs, but not revenue or investment. Decisions on matters such as fixing selling prices, determining sales mix targets and making capital investments would be made by more senior managers at a higher level in the organisation. Revenue centre managers are responsible for revenue and possibly sales-related expenses, but not for the costs of making the product or providing the service, or for capital investment decisions.

Profit centre
a method of divisional organisation where managers are able to determine pricing strategy and control costs, but do not determine investment strategy.

Profit centre: divisional managers have more autonomy than in a cost centre; they decide on selling strategies and fix their own prices. Also they are responsible for managing assets assigned to them by head office in the most cost effective way. They are not, however, responsible for determining capital investments.

Investment centre
a method of divisional organisation where managers are able to control costs, pricing strategy and investment strategy

Investment centre: this describes the highest level of autonomy where divisional managers are responsible for costs, revenue and capital investment decisions.

SELF-TEST QUESTION 10.3

Division Beta is part of the Glenpool organisation. Beta division manufactures kit radios for export. The divisional management team is able to set prices for its products. An allocation of capital expenditure funds is made from head office each year, and the divisional managers are able to spend this as they choose.

Is Beta a profit centre, a cost centre, a revenue centre or an investment centre?

The method of assessment of divisional performance varies, depending upon whether the division is a cost/revenue, profit or investment centre.

FIGURE 10.1

Scope of divisional
control

INVESTMENT CENTRE

Make capital investment decisions

PROFIT CENTRE

Fix selling prices
Decide sales strategy

COST/REVENUE CENTRE

Control   Increasing autonomy
costs/revenues →

Cost/revenue centre

In a cost centre divisional performance should be assessed only in respect of costs, because revenue is beyond the control of managers at a divisional level. Reporting in such divisions would therefore focus principally upon analyses of costs that can be controlled by divisional managers. This would exclude any depreciation charges (because depreciation is controlled at head office level) and probably any sales related costs because the division has no autonomous control over sales strategies. In a revenue centre such as, for example, a regional sales office, performance would be assessed in terms of sales and sales-related costs.

Profit centre

Divisional performance in a profit centre is likely to be assessed by using an income statement which shows the profit or loss made for the period under review. Remember, though, that an income statement used for reporting within an organisation may not bear a very close resemblance to the financial accounting statements that are produced for use by people outside the business organisation.

A divisional performance statement should distinguish clearly between the categories of costs controllable at divisional level and those that are controllable at head office level.

Divisional performance statement for a profit centre

	€000
Sales	X
Less: variable costs	(X)
Contribution	X
Less: Controllable fixed costs	(X)
Controllable profit	X
Less: Non-controllable fixed costs	(X)
Divisional profit before allocation of head office costs	X
Head office cost allocation	(X)
Divisional profit before tax	X

Some of the terminology in this statement should be familiar from earlier chapters. There are, though, some new elements in the form of the distinction between controllable and non-controllable costs, and in the allocation of head office costs. The following example illustrates the nature of some of the important figures.

EXAMPLE 10.3

Delta division is a profit centre of Otranto, a listed company with a diverse range of manufacturing activities. The controllable profit of all the company's divisions is required to be at least 35% of sales. The division's accountant has summarised the following performance figures for the year ended 31 December 2008:

	€000
Variable costs of production	3588
Sales	6782
Depreciation of non-current assets	982
Head office charge for central training, administration and IT costs	1033
Delta's administration costs (all fixed)	433

If we arrange this information into the form of a divisional performance statement we will be able to assess Delta's performance, and to see whether or not it has achieved the required performance criteria for the year.

Delta: divisional performance statement for a profit centre

	€000
Sales	6782
Less: variable costs	(3588)
Contribution	3194
Less: Controllable fixed costs	(433)
Controllable profit	2761
Less: Non-controllable fixed costs	(982)
Divisional profit before allocation of head office costs	1779
Head office cost allocation	(1033)
Divisional profit before tax	746

▶

Note that the depreciation charge for the year has been treated as a non-controllable fixed cost. Delta is a profit centre, not an investment centre, and its managers have no authority over investment decisions. It would therefore be unfair to treat depreciation as a controllable item.

Has Delta met the group criterion for controllable profit? Controllable profit (€2 761 000) as a percentage of sales (€6 782 000) is 40.7%. So we can see that the division has returned a controllable profit well in excess of the target. This result is beneficial to the division, its managers (whose reputation within the business is likely to be enhanced) and to the business as a whole.

This example is very straightforward so as to illustrate the principles involved in preparing a divisional performance statement. In practice, however, the distinction between controllable and uncontrollable costs may be difficult to determine. Taking training costs as an example: suppose that the head office of Otranto is responsible for organising and running training courses. Divisions can choose whether or not to participate in training activities: if divisional staff wish to attend training courses they must ask their manager if the division is prepared to bear the cost. The courses are not charged at full cost; the element of cost that is not covered by fees paid is treated as part of the head office cost allocation. In this case, some element of training cost is controllable at a divisional level, but some of it is not. The amount of head office allocation depends upon the popularity of the training courses, and the willingness of divisional management to fund attendance by staff. If a division's managers decide that their staff will not participate in centrally organised training activities, an element of controllable cost is saved, the overall amount of head office training cost allocation increases and other divisions are penalised (even if only marginally).

Depreciation may be another grey area. In practice, divisional managers may be able to influence head office allocations and decisions on investments. Where this is the case, depreciation expense cannot truly be said to be non-controllable at divisional level.

The allocation of costs may be highly significant to managers, where their own performance appraisal is based upon divisional results. Where, for example, managerial bonuses are paid on the basis of controllable profit, senior managers at head office should carefully scrutinise the divisional performance statements to ensure that costs have been fairly allocated under the different headings in accordance with group policy.

Investment centre

Return on Investment (ROI)
a commonly used method of assessing divisional performance; it expresses divisional net profit as a percentage of the investment in divisional net assets

The managers of an investment centre control both costs and the level and nature of capital investment. Therefore it is possible to assess divisional performance in this case on the basis of **Return on Investment (ROI)**. This is a commonly used form of divisional performance measurement in cases where the divisions operate as investment centres. ROI is calculated as follows:

$$\frac{\text{Divisional net profit}}{\text{Investment in net assets}} \times 100$$

The advantages of using this type of simple measure are that it:

- Relates net profit to the resources used to produce it.
- Is easy for managers to understand.
- Provides a benchmark for comparison across corporate divisions.

However, as with most measurements based on the relationship between accounting numbers, there are problems in ensuring that ROI provides a valid and consistent measure of divisional performance. Each of the components of ROI is examined in turn below.

Determining investment in net assets

Where ROI is used for comparison purposes, it is important to ensure that investment in net assets is calculated on a consistent basis across divisions. Also, the investment in net assets should represent those resources involved in generating divisional profit that are controllable by divisional management. Investment in net assets may not always provide a useful basis for measurement; in service businesses, the principal 'asset' often comprises the members of staff who provide the service and their value is not usually quantified for reporting purposes.

Another problem is that the working of the ROI calculation contains, potentially, an incentive to divisional management to delay investment, as example 10.4 illustrates.

EXAMPLE 10.4

Scala Main conducts most of its business activities via five operational divisions. Division Gamma manufactures a well-established range of laboratory benches and other equipment. Investment strategy is determined at divisional level. The three principal managers of Gamma division are rewarded partly in salary and partly in bonuses that are dependent upon year-on-year improvements in ROI. The three managers have met to discuss a proposal to replace a significant piece of machinery. The proposed investment will cost €1.3 million, to be depreciated on a straight-line basis over ten years, with an assumed residual value of NIL. The existing machinery is ten years old and has reached the end of its originally estimated useful life. In the year ended 31 December 2007, the depreciation charge relating to the existing machine was €80 000, and its net book value at that date was €0. Normally, machinery is replaced when it reaches the end of its useful life. However, one of the managers suggests that the division should defer the investment. He points out that the machine is still working fairly well. Repair costs of €20 000 were incurred in the year ended 31 December 2007, and it is reasonable to suppose that repair costs in 2008 probably would not be any higher. A new machine would not incur repair costs during the first three years of ownership because it would be covered by a repair warranty.

Divisional profits were €1 600 000 for 2007 (before taking into account depreciation and repair costs relating to the machine), and are likely to be at the same level in 2008. Investments

▶

in net assets at 31 December 2007 totalled €12 000 000. If the new machinery is purchased, investment in net assets at 31 December 2008 is forecast to be €13 470 000. If the purchase is deferred, investment in net assets is forecast to be €12 580 000. ROI in the division is calculated as follows:

$$\frac{\text{Divisional net profit}}{\text{Investment in net assets at year end}} \times 100$$

Assess the effects on ROI, and upon the business, of

a) replacing the machine

b) deferring its replacement.

We can compare the effects of the alternative strategies as follows:

	2007 Actual	2008 (replacing machine)	2008 (deferring replacement)
Profits before depreciation and repair of the machine	1 600 000	1 600 000	1 600 000
Depreciation	(80 000)	(130 000)	0
Repairs	(20 000)	0	(20 000)
Divisional profits	1 500 000	1 470 000	1 580 000
Investment in net assets	12 000 000	13 470 000	12 580 000
ROI	12.5%	10.9%	12.6%

Deferring the replacement of the machine is forecast to produce a significantly higher level of divisional profits, and a small increase in ROI over the 2007 figure. If the investment is made, however, the ROI decreases. The divisional managers are likely to be tempted to defer investment so as to earn additional rewards in the form of bonuses. In 2008, the strategy is likely to work reasonably well, provided that the machine continues to function at the required level of reliability. However, in one year's time the managers are likely to be tempted to adopt the same strategy in respect of this machine, and possibly other assets. If this approach is taken consistently, the efficiency of the asset base is likely to decline. All other things being equal, ROI is likely to increase, and managers will be rewarded for failing to keep the non-current asset base up to date.

Determining divisional net profit

Often, divisions within a company sell to each other, and these inter-divisional sales and purchases have an impact on the profits of the divisions involved. A suitable selling price for such transactions has to be agreed between the divisions, and this can have a significant impact on the level of profits in the divisions involved. Anything that impacts on divisional profit affects perceptions of divisional managers' performance, and so it is difficult to overstate the importance of determining fair internal prices.

EXAMPLE 10.5

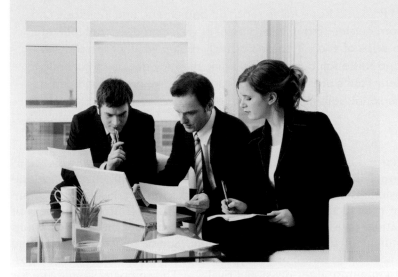

Bartolemi divides its operations into various divisions. Division P produces components that are used in the production process of Division R – these components are sold by P and by other companies for €20.00 per unit, and are readily available at all times. Up till now, R has purchased these components from other companies, but Paul, the divisional manager of P, has suggested that the profit from the sale of these components might as well stay within Bartolemi, so as to boost overall corporate profit, rather than being earned elsewhere. R's manager, Rosie, agrees, but argues that a discount on the market price would be appropriate given that P will have a captive market and will not have to expend any effort on marketing the components to R. She suggests that a price of €18 per unit is more appropriate. Variable costs per unit are €10, and fixed costs would not be affected by the extra production in Division P. The number of units purchased annually by R is 16 000. What will be the effect on the profit of the two divisions if P sells at:

a) €20 per unit

b) €18 per unit?

Because fixed costs would not change, the additional profit made by division P would be the contribution from the sales of 16 000 extra units. Depending on which selling price is used, the additional profit could be either:

16 000 × (20 – 10 variable costs) = €160 000

16 000 × (18 – 10 variable costs) = €128 000

There is a difference of €32 000 between these profit figures. If P sells to R, an additional profit of €160 000 is made for the company, Bartolemi, as a whole, and a profit of at least €128 000 for division P. But the key question to be resolved is which division obtains the benefit of the €32 000 profit figure. Clearly, Paul would prefer to sell at €20 so that the additional €32 000 remains in his division. Equally, Rosie wants to buy at €18, thus saving €2 per unit on the market price, and therefore adding €32 000 to her division's profit. The discussion between the two managers would have added importance for them if their personal bonuses depended upon divisional performance.

The danger for Bartolemi is that Paul and Rosie fail to reach an agreement, and that Rosie continues to source the component from outside. From Rosie's point of view as a divisional manager, if she sources the component at a price of €20, it doesn't actually matter whether the supplier is division P or an outsider. If Paul and Rosie fall out over this issue, she may decide to continue to source from outside, in order to deny Paul's division the opportunity to make profits (and perhaps to deny him the opportunity for personal gain in the form of bonus).

Transfer pricing
the method of pricing sales of goods or services between divisions in an organisation

Goal congruence
ensures that all divisions within an organisation work together to maximise returns for the organisation as a whole

The scenario outlined in example 10.5 illustrates what is usually known as the transfer pricing problem which is often an important practical consideration in divisionalised organisations. Transfer pricing is considered in more detail in the next section. The example also illustrates a further problem of divisionalisation: divisional managers may identify closely with their divisions to the detriment of the company as a whole. Senior management at head office level need to be aware of this type of problem, and should take all possible steps to minimise inter-divisional rivalries. The company should aim for goal congruence, which means that all divisions should be working together to maximise returns for the company as a whole. It should be noted that these problems provide practical illustrations of the application of agency theory to the internal workings of organisations. ROI can be a useful measure, but it needs to be treated with some caution, especially where divisional managers' rewards are based on achieving a specified ROI performance. Agency theory would predict that managers will always act to maximise their own utility, an effect that is exacerbated where remuneration is dependent upon performance.

Divisionalisation can lead to a lack of goal congruence in the organisation, where divisions compete against each other, divisional managers spend too much time and effort on internal politics, and less than optimal decisions are made. Also, there is a danger that divisional managers will focus upon short-term gains and will neglect longer-term strategic considerations. Senior managers in the organisation need to be sensitive to the factors that affect divisional performance, and should be aware of the problems that may arise because of divisionalisation.

Transfer pricing

The example of Bartolemi (example 10.5) illustrates some of the complexity and risk involved in transfer pricing decisions. Transfer pricing is a complex area of management accounting, and some aspects of it are beyond the scope of this book. However, the topic is briefly examined in this section of the chapter so that it is familiar in outline to those who progress to more advanced study. The Bartolemi example demonstrates a classic problem which, if not carefully resolved, would lead to sub-optimal results for the organisation as a whole. An optimal transfer price is one that would:

● allow divisional managers to make a profit without placing the organisation as a whole at a disadvantage;

- provide information that can be used in managerial performance assessment;
- allow the profit of an organisation to be distributed equitably between divisions.

An often problematic aspect of the transfer pricing issue arises in multinational organisations operating in countries that are subject to differing tax regimes. If country A has an effective corporate tax rate of 20%, compared to the 30% charged in country B, then multinational corporation X has a powerful incentive to move profits into its country A division where they will be subject to a lower tax rate. Transfer pricing arrangements in multinationals may therefore attract the attention of taxing authorities, which adds an additional layer of complexity to the original problem of equitable distribution between divisions. This is not a minor problem: the example in the box below indicates how significant transfer pricing can be in businesses.

Glaxo SmithKline Holdings (GSK)

This major multinational pharmaceutical business, based in the UK, has had a long-running dispute with the Internal Revenue Service (IRS) in the United States. The case goes back to 1989, and was finally settled out of court late in 2006 with the multinational agreeing to pay around $3.4 billion (reported in *Accounting Today* (2006)). The amount sought by the IRS was even greater than the amount finally agreed in settlement: the *Economist* (2004) reported that the bill presented to GSK was $5.2 billion. The article explained:

'Even though Glaxo had paid taxes on its profits in Britain, and although there is a "double-taxation" agreement between Britain and America, which means that a company should not have to pay tax on the same profits in both countries, the IRS decided that much of this profit had, in fact, been made in America' (p. 71).

How can organisations determine transfer prices? Possible methods include the following:

1 Variable or total cost. Total cost would include the allocation of fixed overheads. Neither approach would allow any profit to be made by the selling division, although this method has the advantage that it is likely to be fairly straightforward.

2 Cost plus an allowance for profit. The selling division in this case would make a profit but it would be determined on the basis of a fixed formula and might therefore create conditions in which managers were demotivated. If the formula is a fixed percentage on cost, it might even create an incentive to incur unnecessary cost in order to increase profit. This is the potential problem with all cost-plus arrangements that depend upon a percentage of cost.

3　Market price. Where a market price exists, this may well be the optimal solution to the problem because the price is easily established and applied. However, the Bartolemi example demonstrates that using market price would not necessarily remove conflict between divisions. In some cases, where goods are transferred from one division to another in a part-completed state, there may simply not be a market price.

4　Negotiated price. The best solution may be to negotiate between interested parties in order to set a price. However, such negotiation is likely to be time-consuming, and may have to be repeated frequently. Where, for example, raw materials prices change rapidly or are subject to change because of movements in exchange rates, the amount of overall profit to be allocated may alter quickly.

Borkowski (1990) surveyed large businesses in the US on the topic of transfer pricing. Of the 236 survey respondents, 168 used some form of transfer pricing. The table below summarises her findings:

Method	Frequency (number of businesses using this method)	Percent
Market based	55	32.7%
Negotiated	38	22.6%
Full cost	69	41.1%
Variable cost	6	3.6%
	168	100%

Transfer pricing is a significant problem for many businesses and the consequences of poor transfer pricing decisions may include reduced profitability, staff demotivation, time-consuming disputes and even, as in the Glaxo case, legal challenges. Where problems arise from the performance measurement aspect of transfer pricing, one possible means of addressing them lies in changing the nature of performance measurement by shifting the emphasis from purely financial and quantitative measurements, as discussed in the following sections of the chapter.

Non-financial performance measures

Some of the drawbacks of financial performance measures such as ROI can be addressed by assessing performance using a set of non-financial measurement. Example 10.1 early in the chapter demonstrated how a range of performance measures, including both financial and non-financial, can be used to provide valuable management information in the form of Key Performance Indicators. The rest of this chapter examines the use of a combination of measures in performance evaluation.

Some examples of non-financial performance indicators at a divisional level are given in the example that follows.

EXAMPLE 10.6

© DAVID NEWHAM / Alamy

Tony has recently been appointed to head the Light Aircraft division of a major aeronautical manufacturer, Lipp & Smeeton. Lipp & Smeeton's other principal divisions manufacture passenger aircraft and corporate jets, and build engines for the defence industry. The company's stated aims are to grow market share, and to maintain outstanding levels of quality and service to customers. The activities of the Light Aircraft division comprise manufacture of small aircraft for sale to private owners and clubs, and of powered gliders and hang-gliders. Whereas the other divisions have been consistently good performers, Light Aircraft has turned in losses for the last three years under poor quality divisional management, despite buoyant market conditions. Although the basic engine quality of the products has remained high, there have been complaints from customers about the long lead-time for delivery, high prices, and poor quality interior finish. Tony's task is to turn the division around, returning it to profit within 18 months.

What performance measures are likely to be appropriate in assessing both divisional performance and Tony's own performance?

Financial performance measures will be of importance in assessing how quickly the division can be returned to profit. Measures such as ROI, gross profit margin and sales revenue growth will be useful. The measures should correspond, as far as possible, with the aims of the company as a whole. Its first stated aim is to grow market share, and so it is important to ensure that the Light Aircraft division, and Tony, as its head, are assessed on market share measurement.

The division has maintained reasonable quality standards, but has failed on several aspects of customer satisfaction. The second stated aim of Lipp & Smeeton is to maintain 'outstanding levels of quality and service to customers'. Tony needs to ensure that the division first achieves those levels, before he need worry about maintaining them. The measurement of quality and service standards is likely to involve the following:

Customer service

Post-sales questionnaires to elicit customer satisfaction levels in respect of:

Competence of sales staff

Availability of sales staff

▶

Effectiveness of staff in dealing with complaints (if any)

Delivery schedules

Product finish and quality

Product pricing compared to competitors

Quality

Number of defects detected during quality inspection

Number of defects detected post-delivery

Customer satisfaction levels in respect of quality

Number of customer complaints per month/year

The most appropriate non-financial measurements to use naturally vary from one organisation to another. In the aircraft business, the safety and quality characteristics of the product are of surpassing importance, and measures of performance are likely to focus heavily on quality issues. In another context, for example, on-line travel booking, performance measures are likely to focus upon ease of use and accessibility of the service, efficiency and speed of information processing, and the appearance and design of the website. Where customers are being provided with a face-to-face service, for example, travel booking using a high street travel agent, other factors come into play. Customers are likely to value not only efficiency, but also the friendliness and helpfulness of the staff and their competence in making bookings. Performance measures are likely to reflect these factors.

SELF-TEST QUESTION 10.4

HB is the handbag division of a luxury goods manufacturer, BYPH. HB's business objective is to lead the market in the sales of very high quality, exclusive leather handbags. Each season HB changes most of its designs, apart from a small number of classic items.

Discuss whether or not the following performance indicators are likely to be appropriate non-financial measures of success:

1 Market share

2 Number of defective products

3 Volume of sales by product line

4 Customer perceptions of exclusivity

5 Competitiveness of product pricing.

The balanced scorecard

As noted in the previous section of the chapter, the best way of assessing the performance of an organisation or division is likely to be via a combination of financial and non-financial measures. In this section, we examine a popular method of performance measurement and reporting using financial and non-financial measurements that can be tailored to individual organisations.

The 'balanced scorecard' is an idea developed by two US academic researchers, Robert Kaplan and David Norton. The term describes an easily understood set of performance measures that can be used to provide managers with a relevant and thorough summary of complex information about the business. Kaplan and Norton (1992) likened the scorecard to the dials and indicators in an aeroplane cockpit:

> 'For the complex task of navigating and flying an aeroplane, pilots need detailed information about many aspects of the flight. They need information on fuel, air speed, altitude, bearing, destination, and other indicators that summarize the current and predicted environment. Reliance on one instrument can be fatal. Similarly, the complexity of managing an organisation today requires that managers be able to view performance in several areas simultaneously.'

The balanced scorecard uses both financial and non-financial measures to examine the performance of the business. Kaplan and Norton identify four fundamental perspectives that can be applied to any business, in the form of questions:

- How do customers see us? (Customer perspective.)
- What must we excel at? (Internal perspective.)
- Can we continue to improve and create value? (Innovation and learning perspective.)
- How do we look to shareholders? (Financial perspective.)

These four perspectives are represented on the balanced scorecard as set out in Figure 10.2.

In order to use the balanced scorecard managers must be able to identify the key performance measures under each of the four perspectives. It is important that these should be linked in to the overall business strategy, and, as suggested in the figure, to each other. The balanced scorecard emphasises the interdependence of the measurements in its four perspectives. Kaplan and Norton illustrate the chain of cause and effect using the example of a real business: growth in employee morale was correlated to customer satisfaction which was linked to faster settlement of invoices, resulting in improvements in financial perspective indicators such as return on capital employed. In principle, a virtuous circle is established, where improvements in one perspective result in improvements elsewhere. Certain other advantages are claimed for the balanced scorecard:

- It minimises information overload by limiting the number of performance measures used, ensuring that only really important measurements are reported.

FIGURE 10.2

The balanced
scorecard

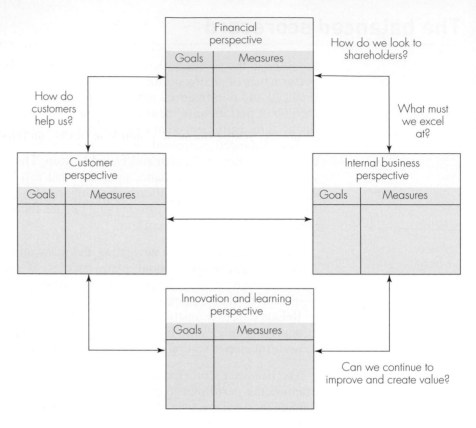

- It brings key aspects of a business's performance together into a single management report.
- It ensures that managers are obliged to consider all of the really important measurements together, so that if good performance in one area has been achieved at the expense of diminishing performance in another area, the trade-off should be obvious.

The four key perspectives of the balanced scorecard

Customer perspective

Customer satisfaction is a critical area for all businesses. Kaplan and Norton observe in their paper that customers' concerns tend to relate to time (for example, time taken to fulfil orders), quality, performance and service, and cost. In putting the balanced scorecard into operation, a business might, for example, identify two key goals: increasing market share and improving the delivery schedule. In this case relevant performance measures are likely to include:

- Number of new customers gained
- Percentage of sales from new customers

- Percentage of total market share
- Average time lapse between order and delivery.

Internal business perspective

In order to achieve the goal of customer satisfaction, a business's managers must be able to identify the key internal processes that contribute to success or failure. Taking the same example as above, increased market share might hinge upon the business's relative success in introducing new products into a competitive market. If this is the case, business goals might include meeting a schedule of planned product innovations. The relevant performance measurement might be performance against this schedule.

Innovation and learning perspective

As Kaplan and Norton point out, the intense nature of global competition means that businesses must continually innovate in order to survive and to create value for customers and shareholders. If a business is to grow, it needs to invest in its infrastructure in order to create the right conditions. This could involve investment in people (in the form of recruitment and training), organisation of the business in order to maximise creativity and motivation amongst staff and investment in systems (such as computer systems) that will help to achieve the business's strategic objectives. A specific business goal could be, for example, to create the conditions necessary for first-class product innovation and development. Relevant performance measures might include:

- Retention rate of employees in key areas
- Number of new appointments in relevant departments
- Satisfaction levels amongst key employees.

(Note that the 'innovation and learning' perspective identified by Kaplan and Norton is referred to in some subsequent writings as the 'learning and growth' perspective.)

Financial perspective

The way in which shareholders see the business from a financial perspective is heavily influenced by the contents of the important financial statements such as the balance sheet, cash flow statement and income statement. Such statements provide a summary of the financial effects of decisions made by managers in pursuing the goals they have identified for the business. The financial statements can be viewed as the acid test of success or failure. It may take time for the effects of innovative strategies to filter through and to be evidenced in the financial statements presented to shareholders. However, the success or failure of the strategies must eventually be judged by financial measurements. As Kaplan and Norton put it:

'A failure to convert improved operational performance, as measured in the scorecard, into improved financial performance should send executives back to their drawing boards to rethink the company's strategy or its implementation plans.'

Relevant performance measures might include some of the measurements explained earlier in the chapter and other widely used accounting ratios such as earnings per share and return on capital employed.

Choosing the right measures

Parmenter (2007) argues that there are only a handful of genuine key performance indicators in any firm. He distinguishes between Key Result Indicators that demonstrate managerial performance in respect of a critical success factor and Key Performance Indicators that focus upon 'those aspects of performance that are the most crucial for the continued success of an organisation'. Managers need to be able to distinguish between the two, so that they concentrate efforts upon the factors that will significantly enhance performance. Parmenter lists the following characteristics of true Key Performance Indicators:

- 'They are non-financial measures.
- They are measured frequently.
- They are acted upon regularly by the chief executive and the top management team.
- All employees understand them and what corrective action they indicate.
- Responsibility for KPIs can be attributed to teams or individuals.
- They have a significant impact on the organisation – e.g. they affect most of the core critical success factors and aspects of a balanced scorecard.
- Positive results on KPIs affect other measures positively' (p. 32).

In essence, managers should take care to identify, measure and act upon a set of indicators that reflect the really important elements of a business's activities, and this process should be pervasive throughout the organisation, led by the most senior of its managers.

The balanced scorecard in practice

The balanced scorecard idea has proved to be very pervasive and influential. Kaplan and Norton published their first paper in 1992, but have followed it with several others and a couple of books. Around the world, many organisations, in both the private and public sector, use the balanced scorecard as an essential management tool. Pineno and Cristini (2003) cite evidence that it is used by approximately 50% of the companies in the US Fortune 1 000 listing, and by about 40% of companies in Europe. A study by Speckbacher et al. (2003) of listed companies in Germany, Switzerland and Austria found that about 25% of their respondent companies were actually using the balanced scorecard, although a further 13% were in the process of actively undertaking a project to introduce it or had taken initial steps towards it. The box below shows two examples of large multinationals that have adopted a balanced scorecard approach to performance measurement.

Philips Electronics

Gumbus and Lyons (2002) describe the process of implementation of the balanced scorecard at Philips Electronics. They comment that 'The tool has helped Philips Electronics focus on factors critical for their business success and align hundreds of indicators that measure their markets, operations and laboratories'. The business identifies four critical success factors on its balanced scorecard: competence, processes, customers and financial.

Unilever (Home and Personal Care – North America)

Lyons and Gumbus (2004) describe the balanced scorecard as enabling managers to measure progress against a company's strategy in a simple, straightforward manner. The article focuses upon an important issue relevant to any management innovation: how it is communicated to people inside the company in a way that will make them want to use it. Within Unilever HPC-NA the project was instigated by senior board level management. Part of the initial process was identifying key measures: from an initial list of 80 measures, 'about a dozen' were identified as being of critical importance. A significant part of the project overall was communicating the project to employees.

Is the balanced scorecard successful?

Since its introduction 15 years ago, the balanced scorecard has attracted a great deal of attention and has been the subject of many academic and professional journal articles. Many large businesses, as discussed above, have adopted it enthusiastically, but the scale of adoption does not necessarily prove success. Business managers are as likely as anyone else to take up the latest fad. So, is the balanced scorecard more than a passing fad? Of course, it is not easy to prove a causal link between the adoption of any new measure and improved (or deteriorated) performance. However, some studies have suggested that adoption of the balanced scorecard has been successful. Davis and Albright (2004) found, in a study of bank branches, that the balanced scorecard could be used to improve performance. McWhorter (2003) used a survey to ask managers about their use of the balanced scorecard. The findings concluded that 174 out of 763 managers used the balanced scorecard and one of the important survey findings was that 'they perceive that more relevant information is available to them in making work-related decisions' (p. 27). It is certainly the case that some commentators are quite convinced that the balanced scorecard is a major step forward in organisational performance measurement: '. . . the balanced scorecard is a powerful strategic tool – not the latest management fad – for strategic planning, goal setting, goal alignment, and measurement' (Gumbus and Lyons, 2002, p. 49).

of a particular firm, and then briefly outlined the key features of one of the most important recent developments in performance measurement: the balanced scorecard. The ideas of Kaplan and Norton were explained, by reference to their original 1992 paper on the topic.

Finally, the chapter briefly examined performance measurement in the public sector, where NPM has involved the adoption of techniques developed in a private sector context.

References

Accounting Today (2006) 'IRS reaches $3.4B settlement with pharm giant', Oct.16 – Nov.5, p. 9.

Borkowski, S.C. (1990) 'Environmental and organizational factors affecting transfer pricing: a survey', *Journal of Management Accounting Research*, Vol. 2., Fall, pp. 78–99.

Economist (2004) 'A taxing battle', Vol. 370, Issue 8360, pp. 71–72.

Carvalho, J., Fernandes, M., Lambert, V. and Lapsley, I. (2006) 'Measuring fire service performance: a comparative study', *International Journal of Public Sector Management*, Vol. 19, No. 2, pp. 165–179.

Chenhall, R.H. (2006) 'The contingent design of performance measures' in Bhimani, A. (ed.) *Contemporary Issues in Management Accounting*, Oxford University Press: Oxford.

Davis, S. and Albright, T. (2004) 'An investigation of the effect of Balanced Scorecard implementation on financial performance', *Management Accounting Research*, 15, pp. 135–153.

Gumbus, A. and Lyons, B. (2002) 'The balanced scorecard at Philips Electronics', *Strategic Finance*, November, pp. 45–49.

Jackson, A. and Lapsley, I. (2003) 'The diffusion of accounting practices in the new "managerial" public sector', *The International Journal of*

Public Sector Management, Vol. 16, No. 5, pp. 359–372.

Kaplan, R.S. and Norton, D.P. (1992) 'The balanced scorecard: measures that drive performance', *Harvard Business Review*, Jan–Feb, pp. 71–79.

Lyons, B. and Gumbus, A. (2004) 'How Unilever HPC-NA sold its employees on the balanced scorecard', *Strategic Finance*, April, pp. 42–46.

McWhorter, L.B. (2003) 'Does the balanced scorecard reduce information overload?', *Management Accounting Quarterly*, Summer, Vol.4, No. 4, pp. 23–27.

Nørreklit, H. (2000) 'The balance on the balanced scorecard – a critical analysis of some of its assumptions', *Management Accounting Research*, 11, pp. 65–88.

Parmenter, D. (2007) 'Performance measurement', *Financial Management*, February, pp. 32–33.

Pineno, C.J. and Cristini, C.R. (2003) 'The balanced scorecard: a vision report', *Management Accounting Quarterly*, Summer, Vol. 4, No. 4, pp. 28–39.

Speckbacher, G., Bischof, J. and Pfeiffer, T. (2003) 'A descriptive analysis on the implementation of Balanced Scorecards in German-speaking countries', *Management Accounting Research*, 14, pp. 361–387.

WEBSITE SUMMARY

The book's website contains the following material in respect of Chapter 10:

Students' section

A multiple choice quiz containing 10 questions
3 longer questions with answers.

Lecturers' section

Answers to end of chapter exercises 10.9 to 10.15.
3 longer questions with answers.

SELF-ASSESSMENT EXERCISES

10.1   Identify three key characteristics of management information.

10.2   Golfstore Retail plc was established five years ago by a small team of golf enthusiasts in Scotland. The company retails a range of quality golfers' clothing and equipment from stores around Scotland. Last year it expanded its stores into the north of England and into Wales. The management team has ambitions to open stores throughout the UK and Ireland, with the ultimate aim of expanding into Western Europe within the next eight years. The board has met to discuss the best way of managing the expansion, and to consider a proposal to establish relatively autonomous divisions based on geographical areas so that eventually, for example, there will be a Golfstore France with its own divisional management team.

Explain to the directors the principal advantages of divisionalisation within the context of their business.

10.3   The managers of division Alpha of Burntwood and Down Holdings determine selling prices for the division, and control almost all costs. Decisions on non-current assets purchases are made at head office level. Is Alpha

a)   a profit centre

b)   a cost centre

c)   a revenue centre

d)   an investment centre?

10.4   Perkora Bains manufactures household fittings. The company uses a system of divisional management, with divisions split by product type. All divisions are treated as profit centres. The accountant in the bathroom division (BD) has gathered the following data for production of the quarterly performance statement which is due for submission to head office:

	€000
Direct materials cost	280
Direct labour cost	311
Sales	1671
Depreciation of non-current assets	112
Fixed costs excluding depreciation	580
Head office cost allocation	337

Of the fixed costs, €37 000 is non-controllable at divisional level. The head office cost allocation relates to research and development and marketing expenditure.

a)   Prepare a divisional performance statement for BD

b)   Identify the amount of profit that should be used as an indicator of divisional performance.

10.5   Identify and explain two reasons why Return on Investment (ROI) may be an unreliable measurement of divisional performance.

© PCL / Alamy

10.6   Tripp and Hopp Limited is a booking agency that specialises in selling London theatre tickets. Until this year the business ran four central London booking offices and a website. But in late 2008, the company decided to transfer all its operations to the website. The company's objective is 'to provide a competitive, efficient and secure service to London's theatregoers'.

Draw up a list of six appropriate non-financial performance indicators that will help Tripp and Hopp's management to assess the extent to which the company is meeting its objectives. For each indicator, suggest a way of measuring it.

10.7   Brookmaye is a manufacturer of diving equipment. Its manufacturing activities are split into several divisions operating as profit centres. During the most recent financial year the company introduced a system of profit-related pay for its divisional managers. The chief financial officer has recently received a memo from the manager of Plastics division which supplies parts to Materials Assembly. Until now, supplies have been valued at cost when transferred from one division to another. However, the manager has pointed out in the memo that this is unfair because it means that his division is denied any profit on the transactions, unlike the Materials Assembly division. He has been reading up on the topic of transfer pricing in his old management accounting textbook, and suggests that the transfer price should be based on actual cost of production plus a fixed percentage of 10% to provide his division with profit.

Required: explain why the divisional manager of Plastics feels that the current transfer pricing arrangements are unfair, and identify any problems that could arise if his suggestion for cost-plus transfer pricing is adopted.

10.8 Your company is considering the introduction of a Balanced Scorecard system. Your head of department has attended a briefing session on the new system and has circulated the following memo:

To: Marketing department staff
From: Head of department
BALANCED SCORECARD
You may have heard by now that our chief executive wants to introduce a so-called 'Balanced Scorecard' system for performance measurement. Frankly, even after attending the briefing I'm still a bit clueless on the subject. I don't think it involves any figures, which would be good news, but we would have to measure things like customer satisfaction. Brian, the accountant, said that lots of companies have tried this system and it's well known. I think he also said it's like flying an aeroplane but perhaps I'd dozed off at that point. Have any of you heard of it? I'd like to hear from anyone who can provide me with a brief, comprehensible account of the Balanced Scorecard.

Reply to the memo, explaining the Balanced Scorecard as concisely as possible.

EXERCISES

10.9 Identify and briefly discuss the principal drawbacks to divisional organisation within large businesses.

10.10 The management team of Florian Space Products are meeting to discuss a proposal to divide the company's operations into three divisions. Each division will deal with one of the business's three principal products. The finance director proposes that the divisions should be given cost centre status. The marketing director, however, argues that if divisionalisation is to be effective, the divisions should operate on a fully decentralised basis as investment centres.

Identify and explain two arguments supporting each of the directors' views.

10.11 Identify one from each list of words given below to fill in the missing words in the following sentence:

A divisional performance statement for (1) _____ centre identifies contribution, (2) _____ profit, divisional profit before allocation of (3) _____ costs and divisional profit before tax.

List 1	List 2	List 3
A profit	Non-controllable	Interest
A cost	Operating	Divisional
An investment	Controllable	Head office

10.12 Spall Spelling operates several manufacturing divisions, with each division treated as a profit centre. Division D's accountant has drawn up the following list of data prior to preparing the monthly performance statement for submission to head office.

	€
Sales	272 600
Fixed costs	72 400
Depreciation	36 000
Variable materials	47 000
Variable labour	63 700

Of the depreciation charge for the month, 25% relates to non-current assets over which the division has complete control. Of the fixed costs, 15% are non-controllable. The accountant has been notified that the head office cost allocation for the month is €43 200.

Prepare a divisional performance statement for Division D.

10.13 Explain the application of agency theory to the transfer pricing problem that arises when goods or services are transferred between divisions.

10.14 Answer TRUE or FALSE to the following statements about the Balanced Scorecard method of performance measurement.

1 The Balanced Scorecard is helpful to managers who are not accountants because it uses only non-financial measurements of performance.

2 The Balanced Scorecard can help managers by cutting down information overload.

3 A problem with the Balanced Scorecard is that it uses the same performance measurements across all companies, and sometimes these are not appropriate.

4 In order to use the Balanced Scorecard effectively, managers must be able to link performance measurement to the overall business strategy.

10.15 As part of its implementation of the Balanced Scorecard method of performance appraisal, the directors of Bretton Tallis have met to discuss the key question: 'Can we continue to improve and create value?' The company, which is engaged in the manufacture and sale of replacement windows and doors, faces tough competition: recent entrants to the market have introduced a range of innovative product improvements, with the result that Bretton Tallis's product range is starting to look old-fashioned. The directors conclude that the company can continue to improve and create value only if it takes urgent steps to improve the quality and design of its product ranges. Two specific goals are identified: to promote the rapid development of new plastics (in order to produce better and more distinctive products), and to create conditions in which innovative design can flourish.

For each of these goals suggest four performance measurements that could assist the company's directors in assessing progress towards the goals.

Themes and Issues in Management Accounting

11

As explained in the preface, the overall aim of this book is to introduce management accounting. It provides both a foundation for further study and a contextual background that will be helpful in business practice. This conclusion is intended to set the scene for future study or practice by:

- Identifying and briefly describing some current issues and themes in management accounting.

- Suggesting further reading that will help students to deepen their knowledge and understanding of the fundamentals of management accounting that have been introduced in this book.

Current themes and issues in management accounting

As in many fields of human activity, management accounting in recent years has been, and continues to be, subject to rapid and pervasive change. The changing nature of organisations is discussed first below, and is followed by a brief section dealing with the contemporary role of the management accountant.

The changing organisation

Earlier in the book, evidence was cited to show that manufacturing in the highly developed economies of the world has fallen into steep decline in recent years. For this reason, some people suggest that much of the content of textbooks like this one is defunct and outdated because manufacturing is no longer of importance. It is undoubtedly the case that less and less of the national product of the developed economies derives directly from manufacturing. However, shops, houses, apartments and public buildings are full of things that have been manufactured somewhere by someone, and much economic activity in the advanced economies continues to take the form of selling and purchasing material objects. A big change in recent years has undoubtedly been the accelerating move of manufacturing from higher cost to lower cost economies, but in a globalised economy a great deal of manufacturing activity remains under the control of powerful multi-national organisations based in the USA or Europe. A management accountant located in Rotterdam, say, may be concerned with accounting for large manufacturing operations in distant locations. An important trend has been the growth of international management accounting which, in part, is concerned with sourcing and using management information from many locations for the familiar purposes of planning, controlling and decision-making. For many major corporations the international control of information flows presents formidable challenges, although the parallel developments that have taken place in data capture and IT have helped to facilitate the rapid production of information.

But not all management accountants work for multinational manufacturing corporations. In some parts of the world manufacturing continues to be a major part of economic wealth but those who work, for example, in Western Europe or the USA are increasingly likely to be engaged in service sector activities. Many of the techniques described in earlier chapters in this book, such as absorption costing, were developed in the context of manufacturing industries, and sometimes their application to a service environment is less obvious. Many service businesses have very few assets, in the traditional sense, and it is more and more the case that the principal business 'asset' is that of the skills, experience and know-how of its staff. The determination of relevant costs, and cost allocation in such businesses is often problematic. There has been much discussion, especially over the last ten years, of the issue of **intellectual capital**, of how, and whether, to account for it, and how it can best be measured and controlled. While the balanced scorecard approach

Intellectual capital the resources available to an organisation in the form of, for example, the technical know-how of employees and established relationships with other organisations explained in Chapter 10 provides some pointers towards a broader range of non-quantitative indicators it does not expressly address the intellectual capital issue, and practice in this area remains a challenge for management accountants.

The development of New Public Management in the public sector, especially in the UK but in other countries too, has been referred to at various points in this book. Management accounting has taken on an increasingly prominent role in public sector organisations because of concerns over accountability for public funds. Research evidence shows the growing prevalence of management accounting techniques, such as activity-based costing in publicly funded organisations. Not everyone agrees that the costs of implementing these quite advanced management accounting techniques in the public sector is outweighed by the benefits derived, but the problem of demonstrating accountability is likely to ensure that management accounting in such organisations continues to grow rather than to diminish.

The contemporary role of the management accountant

In the first chapter of the book, reference was made to the discussion that took place in the 1980s stimulated by Johnson and Kaplan's 1987 book *Relevance Lost*. The recent history of management accounting has comprised a continuing search for relevance and a struggle to define the role of the management accountant and the purpose of management accounting information. Much has been written about the role of the management accountant in strategic decision-making – a field of study loosely defined as **strategic management accounting**. Information input at the strategic level might involve analysis of markets for products, comparative monitoring of existing business strategy against the strategies of competitors, and a range of techniques such as target costing, value-chain management and activity-based management. Detailed consideration of these techniques falls outside the scope of this book but students should find that they are equipped to engage upon further reading about them.

The range of activities associated with strategic management accounting suggests a broader role for the management accountant than that of number-cruncher or scorekeeper. Earlier in the professional evolution of management accountants the calculation and presentation of numbers formed a significant part of their role. Typically, management accountants were corralled into discrete departments, performing a service function to other parts of the organisation. Nowadays, because information technology takes care of a much greater proportion of the routine number processing tasks, it is more likely that the accountant will be working as part of a team running business operations. This change has implications for the professional education and development of management accountants, who, it can be argued, need a broader range of analytical and interpersonal skills than was once the case.

A final issue of importance relates to ethical considerations and this is one of the dimensions of professional activity that remains, essentially, a constant. Thus, business and accounting ethics are always a current issue of importance.

Strategic management accounting
the role played by management accountants and management accounting in strategic decision-making, involving, for example, analysis of markets and the business strategy of competitor organisations

Accounting and business scandals emerge with almost metronomic regularity, despite the attempts of legislators and other regulatory bodies to prevent them. This book has mentioned behavioural issues in management accounting in several different places, and the dangers to optimal business performance suggested by, for example, agency theory. Accountants within organisations are often under pressure to bend the rules or to misrepresent or conceal information. One approach to tackling dysfunctional behaviour is through the promulgation within business and, especially, the accounting profession, of ethical standards. The major professional accounting bodies in the UK and elsewhere have demonstrated increasing awareness in recent years of the place of ethics in accounting professionals' education and practice development. Whether such education and development ultimately results in an improvement in ethical standards is difficult to prove. The frequent occurrence of accounting scandals tends to suggest that ethical awareness and education makes no difference to those who are bent upon criminal activity, but it is at least possible that strong ethical standards in the accounting profession could have an influence on improving the ethical climate in business.

Further reading

This book contains many references to relevant professional and academic literature. By this point, students should find that they are able to read with understanding and appreciation many of the articles about management accounting in the journals of professional accounting bodies. One of the best examples is CIMA's monthly journal *Financial Management*, which frequently publishes articles on the topics covered in this book. For example, recent issues have included readable and interesting articles on Performance Measurement, Transfer Pricing, and Forecasting.

Academic papers tend to be lengthy and sometimes more difficult to read. It takes practice to read them, and to become familiar with the conventions and methodologies typically used in academic research. An academic paper reflects years of accumulated knowledge and study by its author(s), and any individual research project is likely to involve thousands of hours of concentrated work. Therefore it is hardly surprising that a paper emerging from all this detailed study is long and often complex in its arguments and theories. Nevertheless, it is worth persisting with this type of reading because of its unparalleled ability to elucidate and inform. At this point, having understood the fundamentals of management accounting practice and theory conveyed in this book, students should find that they are able to read with understanding academic papers published in a range of journals. A good place to start would be by searching the contents of *Management Accounting Research* or any of the other journals referenced in this book.

Edited collections of contributions by academics and others can be very useful in bridging the gap between textbooks (like this one) and heavyweight academic articles. Typically, contributors, who are all eminent in their field, provide an overview of a particular area or theme, such as, for example, the Balanced Scorecard, or Activity Based Costing. Those wishing to read more can follow up the chapter references to more detailed journal articles. For a detailed review of contemporary issues in management accounting, readers are advised to look at Hopper et al. (2007) or Bhimani (2006) both of which contain excellent chapters on some of the themes introduced in this book.

References

Bhimani, A. (2006) *Contemporary Issues in Management Accounting*, Oxford University Press: Oxford.

Hopper, T., Northcott, D. and Scapens, D. (eds) (2007) *Issues in Management Accounting*, 3rd edition, FT/Prentice Hall: Harlow.

Answers to self-test questions and assessment exercises

Chapter 1

Note: the answers to the Chapter 1 questions are guidelines only. There are many relevant points that could be made in respect of each of the questions, and they may not all be included in the guideline answers given below.

Answers to self-assessment exercises

1.1 Cueline Limited's directors are looking at two options: renewal of the lease and purchase of freehold premises. They need to examine projected financial information for both options in order to ensure that they reach the right decision.

Renewal of the lease

The following items of information would be useful:

- The estimated cost of any lease premium (a lease premium is a capital sum payable at the start of a lease).
- The regular annual rental and any service charges that will have to be paid over the lease term.
- If a large sum has to be paid at the start of the lease, the directors need to examine financing options. Does Cueline Limited have the cash available? Will it need to borrow? If it does have the cash available are there better uses to which it can be put?
- If a loan has to be taken out, how much will the regular charge for interest be?

Purchase of freehold premises

The directors need to identify a range of possible properties for purchase by contacting local commercial property agents. By doing this, they will be able to estimate an approximate capital outlay for the purchase. They need to plan any necessary financing, taking into consideration the following points:

- Will a mortgage loan be available for this type of property?
- What effect will a loan have on the company's gearing?
- How much will the regular charge for interest be?
- What are the implications of the loan and interest repayments for the company's cash flow?

1.2 Putt's directors need to make a thorough assessment of the consequences of a change in strategy. They should obtain information on the following:

- The state of the market for golf-related items and the outlook for sales over the next few years. This may involve commissioning specific market research.

- An estimate of the impact of the change on the future performance of the company. How profitable is the company likely to be in the future? Will future performance be an improvement on past performance? How big a difference will the change in strategy make?

- An assessment of the competition. How successful have competitor businesses been in obtaining market share? Are there any new entrants to the market who are likely to pose a threat to Putt plc?

- The likely effects of the proposed change on the need for selling space. Would the existing shops expand their range of golf-related items if more space were to be made available? Would shops need to move (for example, nearer to golf courses)? Are there any implications for staffing (for example, would some staff need to be made redundant)?

- Disposal of existing non-golf inventory items. Would these items need to be sold quickly, and would they have to be sold at a loss? If so, what is the projected effect on the company's income statement?

1.3 Bulstrode, Barker and Bennett

a) Employing a new solicitor in the conveyancing department

The obvious financial impact of employing another member of staff is the cost of the salary, plus other costs such as employer's national insurance, employer's contributions to the pension scheme (if any) and any other incidental costs of employment such as health benefits. It would appear to make sense to employ another person if the department's income would, in consequence, increase by enough to cover the additional costs, and the partners would require information about the effect on both income and costs.

However, there are other relevant considerations. If the conveyancing department is genuinely short-staffed, either or both of the following effects could occur:

- Existing staff will be overworked and may become disgruntled. If sufficiently dissatisfied they may seek to change employment.

- There might be an adverse effect on quality. If a serious mistake is made in conveyancing, the firm could lay itself open to legal action, or to criticism from regulators. If it acts inefficiently in dealing with client business, the consequence could be a loss of reputation. Prospective clients may take their business elsewhere.

b) This involves a significant strategic decision. The existing partners will seek information on:

- The likely cost of bringing in another partner. The new partner would be entitled to a share of the profits of the business, although this could be made dependent upon performance to some extent. She would also expect the same range of benefits (health benefits, pension scheme and so on) as the existing partners. There would, presumably, also be other knock-on effects on staffing (for example, she would almost certainly need some secretarial assistance).

- The expected benefits in terms of increased fees. How much extra business could a divorce specialist be expected to generate? Would she be able to contribute any capital to the business?

- How many solicitors experienced in divorce law actually operate in the area? Is there really a gap in the market for another one? Are there any cross-selling opportunities (for example, people who are getting a divorce often sell property jointly, and there may be new opportunities for generating extra conveyancing work)?

- It is important that partners (as joint proprietors of a business) are able to agree among themselves. Would the proposed new partner be an easy person to work with?

Chapter 2

Answers to self-assessment exercises

Guidance on Chapter 2 questions
Note: no guidance is provided in respect of the content of answers to questions 2.1, 2.2 and 2.4 as the questions require the expression of personal opinions. However, try to make sure that you answer the questions as fully as possible.

2.3   BigCorp

Costs

The cost of running the current cleaning operations would include wages, salaries and benefits payable. Any other expenses associated with the cleaning operations, that would be saved by contracting out, should be taken into account. This may include, for example, the cost of providing premises for the staff.

The amount payable to a cleaning contractor for providing the same level of service could be established by getting suitable contractors to submit tenders. However, it would be important to ensure that like was compared with like and that the service level was the exact equivalent.

Other costs might be incurred in closing down the cleaning department. If it were possible that some staff could be redeployed elsewhere, they might require retraining which would incur further costs. The costs of making a large number of staff redundant could be significant as they all appear to be employed on permanent contracts.

Non-financial considerations are often important in decision-making. Because BigCorp is in the restaurant business, where cleanliness is particularly important, the directors would have to be convinced that the level of service provided by a contractor would be at least as good as that provided by the in-house service. Poor levels of cleanliness could lead to bad publicity which could affect revenue and profitability. If staff were deployed elsewhere to avoid having to make them redundant it would be important to ensure that they were properly fitted for their new roles. If staff are redeployed simply in order to find them something else to do, dissatisfaction and demotivation could result, with adverse effects on the business.

(Note: this is a suggestion only as to how the question might be tackled: many other valid points could be made. The criteria for identifying relevant costs for decision-making will be dealt with in subsequent chapters.)

2.5 If agency theory accurately describes managerial motivation, the following are some of the implications for management and cost accounting that could arise:

1 Managers would act in the best interests of the principal only where it suits their own purposes to do so. Where the interests of the principal and the manager diverge, managers might, for example, exaggerate figures or report selectively to bias the view given by accounting reports in order to boost their own chances of promotion, or a bonus.

2 Where principals suspect that managers are acting to maximise their own utility, they might want to institute additional reporting and monitoring of reports. This could have the effects of increasing management accounting activity, and of requiring more frequent and complex reports. Additional agency costs would thus be incurred.

Chapter 3

Answers to self-test questions

3.1 Beeching Plumstead

Canvas material	Direct materials
Metal spokes for wheels	Direct materials
Spare parts for sewing machine repairs	Indirect production overheads
Advertising expenditure	Other indirect overheads
Machine oil	Indirect production overheads
Electricity bill for factory	Indirect production overheads
Wages of assembly line workers	Direct labour
Wages of factory canteen staff	Indirect production overheads
Wages of assembly line supervisor	Indirect production overheads
Secretary's salary	Other indirect overheads
Delivery vehicle depreciation	Other indirect overheads

3.2 Gonzalez Perez

a) FIFO

Date	Deliveries into inventory			Transfers to production			Balance	
	Units	€	€	Units	€	€	Units	€
1 Mar							55	165.00
10 Mar	160	3.20	512.00				215	677.00
12 Mar				35	3.00	105.00	180	572.00
25 Mar				20	3.00	60.00	160	512.00
				50	3.20	160.00	110	352.00

Tutorial note: the 110 items remaining in inventory after the transfer to production on 25 March are all assumed to belong to the batch of items delivered on 10 March, and so are valued at €3.20 each (110 × €3.20 = €352.00).

b) AVCO

	Deliveries into inventory			Transfers to production			Balance		
Date	Units	€	€	Units	€	€	Units	AVCO €	€
1 Mar							55	3.00	165.00
10 Mar	160	3.20	512.00				215	3.149	677.00
12 Mar				35	3.149	110.21	180	3.149	566.79
25 Mar				70	3.149	220.42	110	3.149	346.37

3.3 Harvey & Cork

Batch No: 30453A

	€	€
Direct materials		
Metal: 100kg @ €4.50 per kilo	450.00	
Paint: 2 litres @ €6.80 per litre	13.60	
Glass: 500 pieces @ 30¢ per piece	150.00	
		613.60
Direct labour		
Grade A: 22 hours @ €4.80	105.60	
Grade B: 19 hours @ €6.00	114.00	
		219.60
Prime cost		833.20

$$\text{Cost per picture frame} = \frac{€833.20}{500} = €1.67 \text{ (to two decimal places).}$$

3.4 Swift Metals Limited: apportionment of production overheads – year ending 31 December 2008

			Cost centre		
	Basis	Total £	Preparation £	Tooling £	Finishing £
Factory costs	Floor area	700 000	245 000	315 000	140 000
Canteen costs	Employees	18 496	8 704	6 528	3 264
Machinery depreciation	Net book value	17 650	2 600	11 200	3 850
Machinery maintenance and repair	Call-outs	2 961	658	1 974	329
Supervisory salaries	Employees	23 358	10 992	8 244	4 122
Totals		762 465	267 954	342 946	151 565

Tutorial note: note that, by contrast with the Choremaster example, supervisory salaries for Swift Metals are apportioned on the basis of the number of employees supervised. Remember, there are no fixed rules about the way in which costs are apportioned – the basis of apportionment is whatever is most appropriate for the business.

Answers to self-assessment exercises

3.1   Paige Peverell

Expense	Classification
Plastic moulding machine depreciation	Indirect production overheads
Sales office fixtures and fittings depreciation	Other indirect overheads
Plastic materials	Direct materials
Advertising expenditure	Other indirect overheads
Depreciation of factory building	Indirect production overheads
Electricity bill for factory	Indirect production overheads
Wages of assembly line workers	Direct labour
Wages of factory canteen staff	Indirect production overheads
Wages of assembly line supervisor	Indirect production overheads
Secretary's salary	Other indirect overheads
Delivery vehicle depreciation	Other indirect overheads
Factory consumables	Indirect production overheads
Royalty payable per item produced to telephone designer	Direct expenses
Mobile phone bill – sales director	Other indirect overheads

3.2   ArtKit Supplies: cost statement for the year ending 31 August 2008

	€	€
Direct materials		
Metal	18 006	
Lacquer paint	1 600	
Hinge fittings	960	
		20 566
Direct labour		
Machine operators' wages	18 250	
Finishing operative's wages	10 270	
		28 520
Prime cost		49 086
Production overheads		
Rental of factory	6 409	
Machine repair	176	
Depreciation – machinery	1 080	
Electricity – factory	1 760	
Factory cleaning	980	
Sundry factory costs	2 117	
		12 522
Production cost		61 608

cont.

Continued

	€	€
Other overheads		
Secretarial and administration salaries	12 460	
Salesman's salary	18 740	
Office supplies	2 411	
Office telephone	1 630	
Sundry office costs	904	
Delivery costs	1 920	
		38 065
Total costs		99 673

3.3 Because Porter Farrington adopts a FIFO policy for inventory valuation, the 40 items left in inventory at the end of May 2008 are deemed to be those most recently delivered. The most recent delivery before the end of the month was the 50 items delivered on 2 May at a cost of 3.30 per unit. The correct valuation is, therefore:

40 units @ NZ$3.30 = NZ$132.00

The correct answer, therefore, is d).

3.4 Jersey Brookfield & Co: apportionment of production overheads for the year ending 31 December 2007

			Cost Centre	
	Basis	Total €	Bulk production €	Packaging €
Factory building depreciation	Floor area	5 670	3 240	2 430
Factory rates	Floor area	11 970	6 840	5 130
Factory insurance	Floor area	7 980	4 560	3 420
Canteen costs	No. employees	18 876	8 580	10 296
Supervisory salaries	No. employees	29 480	13 400	16 080
Other indirect labour	Machinery NBV	18 275	12 410	5 865
Machinery depreciation	Machinery NBV	21 500	14 600	6 900
Cleaning	Floor area	17 850	10 200	7 650
Electricity	Actual	30 290	18 790	11 500
Building maintenance	Floor area	5 040	2 880	2 160
		166 931	95 500	71 431

3.5 Barley Brindle

i) Overhead absorption rate based on direct labour hours

Each unit uses 1 hour of direct labour; production of 60 000 units is planned, therefore 60 000 direct labour hours will be used.

Overhead absorption rate: $\dfrac{€218\ 000}{60\ 000} = €3.63$

ii) Overhead absorption rate based on machine hours

Each unit uses 0.5 hours of machine time. Anticipated total machine time is, therefore 60 000 × 0.5 = 30 000

Overhead absorption rate: $\dfrac{€218\ 000}{30\ 000} = €7.27$

iii) Overhead absorption rate based on units of production

Overhead absorption rate: $\dfrac{€218\ 000}{60\ 000} = €3.63$

(i.e. the same rate as calculated on the basis of direct labour hours).

3.6   WGB GmBH

Totals for direct materials based on production of 6000 of each product

	€
Metal machining dept	
Domestic shelves: €18.00 × 6 000	108 000
Commercial shelves: €27.00 × 6 000	162 000
	270 000
Painting and finishing dept	
Domestic shelves: €3.30 × 6 000	19 800
Commercial shelves: €4.60 × 6 000	27 600
	47 400

Totals for direct labour based on production of 6000 of each product

	€
Metal machining dept	
Domestic shelves: 0.75 × €6 × 6 000	27 000
Commercial shelves: 1 × €6 × 6 000	36 000
	63 000
Painting and finishing dept	
Domestic shelves: 1 × €6 × 6 000	36 000
Commercial shelves: 1.5 × €6 × 6 000	54 000
	90 000

i) overhead absorption rates based on % of direct materials:

Metal machining dept: $\dfrac{172\ 490}{270\ 000} = 63.9\%$

Painting and finishing dept: $\dfrac{116\ 270}{47\ 400} = 245.3\%$

ii) overhead absorption rates based on % of direct materials:

Metal machining dept: $\dfrac{172\ 490}{63\ 000} = 273.8\%$

Painting and finishing dept: $\dfrac{116\ 270}{90\ 000} = 129.2\%$

Materials are relatively much more significant than labour hours in the machining department. Therefore, it would probably make sense to use an overhead absorption rate based on the % of direct materials consumed.

By contrast, in the painting and finishing department, direct labour is relatively more important than the input of materials. Therefore, it would probably make sense to use an overhead absorption rate based on the % of direct materials consumed.

Because the machining department probably involves use of a relatively high level of machine hours it may be worth considering the calculation of an overhead absorption rate based on machine hours.

3.8   The cost object with which costs are identified in an architects' practice is likely to be a job for a specific client.

The principal costs incurred by the practice are likely to be:

- Architects' and support staff salaries and related benefits such as health insurance, travel allowances, and car parking.
- Premises costs, including rental, power, business rates, water rates, and service charges.
- Sundry supplies such as paper, computer consumables, and magazines.
- Depreciation of capital items such as premises (if owned not rented), computer equipment, desks, tables, and chairs.

Architects' salaries and the salaries of any ancillary staff directly associated with a particular job can be identified with the cost object using a record keeping system that records time spent on a particular job. Salaries of staff that are not specifically identified with particular jobs plus all other expenses would fall into the general category of overheads. These might be allocated on a 'direct labour hour' basis according to the amount of time directly spent by the professional staff on particular jobs.

3.9   David

a) Does School A, on this evidence, provide poor value for money?

The average salary cost per child taught in 2007/8 was £2216 in School A whereas in School B it was £1591. The average salary per member of staff was £38 651 in School A, and £33 871 in School B. Salary costs in School A are certainly relatively higher than in School B. However, on its own, this information says little about relative value for money.

The ratio of staff to children is 17.4 in School A and 21.2 in School B. This suggests that School B is somewhat more efficient. However, it would be necessary to look at other costs and educational outcomes before being able to draw any firm conclusions.

b) Possible reasons for the discrepancy between salary costs in the two schools.

It is likely that each school has a head teacher, and probably a deputy head teacher as well. These are senior posts for which higher salaries are payable. However, the burden of higher salaries is proportionately greater in School A because it has fewer staff.

Nearly half of the average teaching staff number is accounted for by the head teacher and deputy.

It is quite possible that the higher average salary in School A is entirely accounted for by the head teacher/deputy issue. However, differences can arise between schools in this respect where one employs more newly and recently qualified teachers who are at the lower end of the standard salary scales.

Where schools allocate their own budgets (as is the case in England) they can choose, within certain parameters, to spend more on some categories of expenditure than others. It is possible that School A is able to spend more on salaries because of spending less on another category of spending. For example, it may be better supported by charitable contributions than School B and therefore perhaps spends less on computer equipment and books.

Chapter 4

Answers to self-assessment exercises

4.1   i) The traditional product costing system is based upon a rather outdated industrial model of labour intensive production processes allied to the use of large, relatively slow machinery. Overhead absorption rate calculations are typically based upon either machine hours or direct labour hours. However, in modern industry, both of these factors may be relatively insignificant. At the same time, indirect overheads have tended to increase in importance. The use of high technology machinery, for example, may result in high annual depreciation charges and staff may be used in a supervisory rather than a direct labour capacity.

The effect has been that increasing amounts of production overheads have been allocated to a steadily shrinking base of labour or machine hours. This results in very high absorption rates which are highly sensitive to very small changes in labour or machine time spent.

ii) The basic principle of ABC is that cost units should bear the cost of the activities which they cause. A much higher level of investigation into the nature of production activities and related costs is undertaken in the application of ABC. Costs are seen as 'driven' by activities, and so it is clearly important to establish what those activities are. Activities include:

Materials ordering, handling and control

Testing and supervising quality

Preparing machinery for production runs.

A cost driver is established for each activity; for example, in the case of materials ordering it is likely to be the number of orders placed. A production activity that involves high levels of materials ordering will, under the application of ABC, bear a higher proportion of ordering costs than a production activity which involves relatively few materials orders.

iii) In a modern production environment, ABC, properly applied, is likely to result in a much more realistic way of allocating overheads to products. It may help to avoid some of the incorrect decisions which can easily result where traditional product costing is used.

However, a significant disadvantage of ABC is that it is costly and complicated to implement. Firms must be sure that the potential benefits of installing ABC outweigh the substantial costs of implementing it properly.

4.2 Arbend

Overhead cost for a customer order of 4 books

Activity		Cost amount €
Receipt of books	$\dfrac{€1\,000\,000}{250\,000} \times 4/48$	0.33
Storage	$\dfrac{€6\,800\,000}{12\,000\,000}$	0.57
Customer order processing	$\dfrac{€2\,400\,000}{4\,000\,000}$	0.60
Inventory picking	$\dfrac{€800\,000}{12\,000\,000} \times 4$	0.27
Total		1.77

4.3 Hallett Penumbra Systems

a) Overhead absorption rate based on machine hours
Estimate of production overheads for 2009: €328 330
Total machine hours = 6 000

Rate per machine hour $= \dfrac{€328\,330}{6\,000} = €54.72$ per hour

b) Overhead per unit using ABC system

Cost per unit of cost driver

Activity		Cost amount €
Machining	$\dfrac{\text{Overhead}}{\text{Machine hours}} = \dfrac{148\,200}{6\,000}$	€24.70 per machine hour
Finishing	$\dfrac{\text{Overhead}}{\text{Labour hours}} = \dfrac{136\,440}{12\,000}$	€11.37 per labour hour
Materials ordering	$\dfrac{\text{Overhead}}{\text{No. of orders}} = \dfrac{12\,183}{186}$	€65.50 per order
Materials issue	$\dfrac{\text{Overhead}}{\text{No. of issues}} = \dfrac{11\,592}{120}$	€96.60 per issue
Machine set up	$\dfrac{\text{Overhead}}{\text{No of hours}} = \dfrac{19\,915}{70}$	€284.50 per hour

Allocation of overhead between product C and product D

	Product C €		Product D €	
Machining	2 500 × €24.70	61 750	3 500 × €24.70	86 450
Finishing	7 200 × €11.37	81 864	4 800 × €11.37	54 576
Materials ordering	124 × €65.50	8 122	62 × €65.50	4 061
Materials issues	70 × €96.60	6 762	50 × €96.60	4 830
Machine set up	26 × €284.50	7 397	44 × €284.50	12 518
Total		165 895		162 435

c) Production cost of one unit of each product under ABC system
Number of units planned for production:

C uses 1 machine hour per unit, so 2500 units are planned for production.

D uses 1.4 machine hours per unit, so 3500/1.4 = 2500 units are planned for production.

	C	D
Total production overhead	€165 895	€162 435
Number of units planned for production	2 500	2 500
Production overhead per unit	€66.36	€64.97
Prime cost per unit	28.50	32.70
Production cost per unit	94.86	97.67

Production cost of one unit of each product under the old costing system

Prime cost per unit	€28.50	€32.70
Production overhead for 1 machine hour	54.72	
Production overhead for 1.4 machine hours		
1.4 × €54.72		76.61
Production cost per unit	83.22	109.31

d) Product D uses significantly more (1.4 compared to 1) machine hours per unit than product C. So, any system of overhead absorption based on machine hours will result in a disproportionately larger charge to product D than to Product C. It can be argued that, in this case, ABC produces a more equitable result that is more appropriate for decision-making than the old system of overhead absorption.

Chapter 5

Answer to self-assessment exercises

5.1 The demand curve plots the relationship between quantity and selling price. The correct answer, therefore, is c).

5.2 Demand is described as elastic where it is highly sensitive to changes in price. The correct answer, therefore, is a).

5.3 An oligopoly exists in cases where about three to five suppliers control the market. The correct answer, therefore, is b).

5.4 Auger Ambit

Fixed costs per unit: $\dfrac{€788\ 000}{20\ 000} = €39.40$

Cost-plus calculation:

	€
Variable materials cost per unit	18.00
Variable labour costs per unit	27.56
Fixed costs per unit	39.40
Total costs per unit	84.96
Profit mark-up: €84.96 × 25%	21.24
Selling price	106.20

5.5 Belvedere, Bharat and Burgess

i) The partnership could expect to bill fees as follows:

Time available: 43 weeks × 5 days × 8 hours × 75% = 1290 hours per person	€
Accountants: 6 × 1290 × €50	387 000
Senior staff and tax specialists: 5 × 1290 × €85	548 250
Partners: 3 × 1290 × €110	425 700
	1 360 950

ii) If the average recovery rate on billing is 94% this means that the partnership has not been able to recover all of the hours charged by its staff and partners.

	€
Billed: €1 360 950 × 94%	1 279 293
Costs: €1 275 000 × 101%	1 287 750
Loss for 2008	(8 457)

5.6 **A garden centre**

The managers of a garden centre will have regard to local competition in setting selling prices. If there is little competition it may be possible to charge higher prices. In the long run, of course, the business must be able to cover all of its costs. It would be normal practice for the management of such a business to apply a standard mark-up on cost.

Probably, cost-based pricing will be the principal price-setting strategy, but management will also keep an eye on the competition. Even if competitors are charging lower prices, management may feel justified in charging more if, for example, it offers complementary services such as garden design, a coffee shop and a bookshop.

A small grocery store, open for 24 hours

Generally, convenience stores are able to charge relatively high prices, simply because of the additional convenience they offer. Much depends upon the competition, of course. Now that many large supermarkets are offering 24 hour service, a small grocery store may find that it has to bring down prices in order to be able to compete.

There is a cost element to take into account in setting pricing; in a 24 hour business labour must be employed at highly unsocial hours, and there may be a wage premium to pay (although the extent of this depends upon the local employment market, availability of hard-up students to work through the night, and so on). Additional costs have to be met either by increasing selling prices or reducing profit margins.

Chapter 6

Answers to self-test questions

6.1   Brinn Bartholomew: Budget for June 2008

	€
Sales: 1 400 bins × €250 each	350 000
Variable costs	
Direct materials: 1 400 bins × €97	(135 800)
Direct labour: 1 400 bins × €36	(50 400)
Contribution	163 800
Fixed costs	(120 400)
Net profit	43 400

6.2   The following points can be plotted onto the graph:

Level of production	Fixed costs €	Total costs €
0	50 000	50 000
10 000	50 000	100 000

We do not need to plot any other points in order to draw the graph, because variable costs increase at a steady rate in line with the level of production. The data produces the graph shown in Figure 1.

FIGURE 1

Marshall Mexico: Total costs, split into fixed and variable, for 2008

6.3 From Figure 2 we can see that the break-even point is 5000 units. In terms of sales value this is between €60 000 and €80 000 on the vertical axis – probably at approximately €75 000.

We can check this answer by working out a profit statement at a production and sales level of 5000 units:

	€
Sales (5 000 × €15)	75 000
Variable costs (5 000 × €5)	(25 000)
Contribution	50 000
Fixed costs	(50 000)
	0

FIGURE 2

Marshall Mexico: Break-even chart for 2008

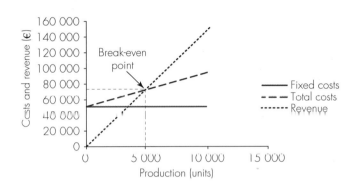

6.4 Calculating Neasden Northwich's break-even point (in units):

Sales revenue per unit = €20.00
Variable costs per unit = €6.00

Contribution per unit is, therefore, €14.00 (sales minus variable costs).

$$\text{Break-even point (in units)} = \frac{\text{Fixed costs}}{\text{Contribution per unit}}$$

$$= \frac{70\ 000}{€14} = 5\ 000 \text{ units}$$

Answers to self-assessment exercises

6.1 Bubwith Girolamo

Relevant revenues = 1 000 units × €27 = €27 000
Relevant costs = direct materials cost (1000 units × 4kg × €4.50) = €18 000.

Relevant revenues less relevant costs produces a positive figure, and so it appears that the special contract should be accepted. Note: the direct labour cost is not relevant to the decision because the direct labour force is currently underutilised but is paid for a full working week. The staff will be paid whether or not the contract is accepted.

A relevant non-financial factor might be the relationship with the regular customer. It might even be worth taking unprofitable work on occasion in order to maintain goodwill.

6.2   Wetwang

The information about original purchase cost and depreciation is irrelevant. If the Wetwang directors decide to try to sell for more than the existing offer, the opportunity cost of that decision is €12 000. Any new offer must at least meet the €12 000 plus the cost of advertising of €500. The minimum acceptable price is €12 500 on the information given.

6.3   Billericay Ashworth

i) Cost classification

The cost of raw materials is a variable cost; the cost of factory insurance is a fixed cost; telephone charges are a semi-variable cost.

ii) Graphs

For the graph of raw materials cost, two points are plotted:

- cost of raw materials at zero production: €0
- cost of raw materials at 3000 production level: 3000 × €13 = €39 000.

FIGURE 3

Billericay Ashworth: Raw materials cost

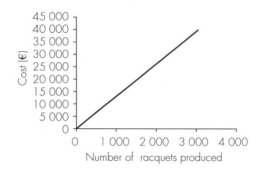

For the graph of factory insurance, two points are plotted:

- cost of factory insurance at zero production level: €800
- cost of factory insurance at 3000 production level: €800.

FIGURE 4

Billericay Ashworth: Factory insurance

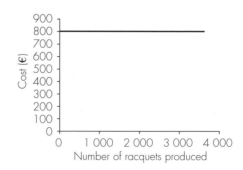

For the graph of telephone charges, three points are plotted:

- Telephone charges where no calls made: €1000 (i.e. basic rental charge).
- Telephone charges where 500 calls are made: €1250 (i.e. basic rental charge of €1000 + €250 in call charges).

● Telephone charges where 1000 calls are made: €1500 (i.e. basic rental charge of €1000 + €500 in call charges).

FIGURE 5

Billericay Ashworth:
Telephone charges

Note that the activity level in this case is the number of calls made: we have no information that links call charges with the level of production or any other measurement of activity.

6.4   Cost classification

i)   Sales staff members' mobile phone charges: semi-variable cost.

ii) Factory machine oil: it depends! This would probably be a relatively minor cost and would, in practice, be treated as part of fixed factory costs. However, the more the machines are used, presumably the more oil they consume, so it could be argued that this cost is variable with production. It would depend upon the particular circumstances.

iii) Metered water charges: this is a variable cost based upon the number of units consumed.

6.5   Examples of fixed and variable costs

Type of business	Examples of fixed and variable costs
Self-employed taxi driver	*Variable costs* Petrol or diesel Replacement parts for cab *Fixed costs* Accountancy and tax advisory services Cab licence
Solicitor	*Variable costs* Stationery costs (e.g. files for holding documents) Overtime payments to staff called out to attend clients in police custody *Fixed costs* Rental of office premises Employment costs of secretarial staff
Shirt manufacturer	*Variable costs* Cost of shirt material Labour costs (if variable such as piece rates) *Fixed costs* Sewing machine depreciation charges Factory heating charges

Beauty salon

Variable costs
Cost of beauty products
Stationery costs (e.g. cost of appointment cards)
Fixed costs
Staff salaries
Business rates

Note how difficult it is, especially in service businesses, to think of significant variable costs.

6.6   Porton Fitzgerald

Porton Fitzgerald: Budget statement for April 2008

	€
Sales: 450 wardrobes × €210 each	94 500
Variable costs	
Direct materials: 450 wardrobes × €52	(23 400)
Direct labour: 450 wardrobes × €34	(15 300)
Contribution	55 800
Fixed costs	(43 200)
Net profit	12 600

6.7   Fullbright Bognor

i) Break-even chart
For the break-even chart for the year ending 31 December 2008 the points plotted are:

Production level	Fixed costs	Total costs	Total revenue
	€	€	€
0	62 000	62 000	0
3 000	62 000	185 000	255 000
		(€62 000 in fixed costs + [3000 × €41])	(3000 × €85)

FIGURE 6

Fullbright Bognor:
Break-even chart

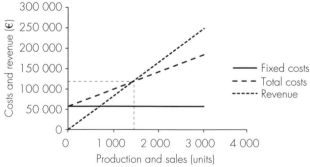

ii) Break-even point estimates
Reading from the chart, the break-even point in units lies somewhere between 1000 and 2000 units, at around 1400 to 1500 units. The sales value appears to be around €120 000. (Note: the larger the scale chosen for the graph, the more accurate the estimate of break-even is likely to be.)

iii) Break-even points for year ending December 2008

	€
Selling price per unit	85.00
Variable costs per unit	41.00
Contribution per unit	44.00

$$\text{Break-even point (in units)} = \frac{\text{Fixed costs}}{\text{Contribution per unit}}$$

$$= \frac{62\ 000}{44.00} = 1\ 409 \text{ units (to nearest whole unit)}$$

The break-even point in sales value = 1 409 units × €85 = €119 765.

6.8   Foster Beniform

a) Where fixed costs are €40 000

i) Break-even chart

For the break-even chart for 2008 (fixed costs at €40 000) the points plotted are:

Production level	Fixed costs	Total costs	Total revenue
	€	€	€
0	40 000	40 000	0
2 000	40 000	90 000	110 000
		(€40 000 + [2000 × €25])	(2000 × €55)

FIGURE 7

Foster Beniform:
Break-even
chart (fixed costs at
€40 000)

ii) Break-even point estimates

Reading from the chart, the break-even point in units appears to be around 1300 units; the break-even point in sales value appears to be around €73 000.

iii) Formula calculations

	€
Selling price per unit	55.00
Variable costs per unit	25.00
Contribution per unit	30.00

$$\text{Break-even point (in units)} = \frac{\text{Fixed costs}}{\text{Contribution per unit}}$$

$$= \frac{40\ 000}{30.00} = 1\ 333 \text{ units (to nearest whole unit)}$$

Break-even point in sales value = 1 333 units × €55 = €73 315.

b) Where fixed costs are €50 000

i) Break-even chart
For the break-even chart for 2008 (fixed costs at €50 000) the points plotted are:

Production level	Fixed costs	Total costs	Total revenue
	€	€	€
0	50 000	50 000	0
2 000	50 000	100 000	110 000
		(€50 000 + [2 000 × €25])	(2 000 × €55)

FIGURE 8

Foster Beniform: Break-even chart (fixed costs at €50 000)

ii) Break-even point estimates
Reading from the chart, the break-even point in units appears to be around 1700 units; the break-even point in sales value appears to be around €90 000.

iii) Formula calculations

	€
Selling price per unit	55.00
Variable costs per unit	25.00
Contribution per unit	30.00

$$\text{Break-even point (in units)} = \frac{\text{Fixed costs}}{\text{Contribution per unit}}$$

$$= \frac{50\ 000}{30.00} = 1\ 667 \text{ units (to nearest whole unit)}$$

Break-even point in sales value = 1 667 units × €55 = €91 685.

6.9   Gropius Maplewood

	€
Selling price per unit	150
Variable costs per unit	(63)
Contribution per unit	87

$$\text{Break-even point (in units)} = \frac{\text{Fixed costs}}{\text{Contribution per unit}}$$

$$= \frac{90\ 000}{87} = 1\ 034 \text{ units}$$

The correct answer, therefore, is d).

6.10   Gimball Grace

Target net profit for 2009: €36 500 × 110% = €40 150.
Contribution per unit = €21.00 (selling price) – €7.50 (variable costs) = €13.50.

$$\text{Target sales in units} = \frac{\text{Fixed costs} + \text{Target profit}}{\text{Contribution per unit}}$$

$$= \frac{54\ 000 + 40\ 150}{13.50} = 6\ 974 \text{ units}$$

The correct answer, therefore, is a).

6.11   Garbage Solutions
       Contribution calculation:

	€
Selling price per unit	25.00
Less: variable labour costs	(3.20)
Variable raw materials costs	(4.20)
Contribution per unit	17.60

$$\text{Break-even point} = \frac{\text{Fixed costs}}{\text{Contribution per unit}}$$

$$= \frac{178\ 900}{17.60} = 10\ 165 \text{ units}$$

$$\text{Target sales in units} = \frac{\text{Fixed costs} + \text{Target profit}}{\text{Contribution per unit}}$$

$$= \frac{178\ 900 + 83\ 150}{17.60} = 14\ 889$$

The margin of safety is the difference between target sales and break-even sales:

14 889 – 10 165 = 4 724

The correct answer, therefore, is d).

6.12   Hubert et Hix Cie

The contribution per unit from the rucksack designed for the Moroccan market would be:

	€
Selling price per unit	50.00
Variable costs per unit	(26.30)
Contribution per unit	23.70

The contribution per unit is a positive figure, therefore the advice to management, based solely upon the accounting figures, would be to accept Raoul's order. This advice would be appropriate provided that spare production capacity was available and provided the level of fixed costs would not increase. What non-financial factors should be taken into consideration?

The sales of this special order are all to Morocco; therefore it is quite likely that French and British buyers would not find out that similar rucksacks were available at a substantially lower price. The fact that the specification is lower also helps; if Western European buyers were to ask why the rucksacks were priced so much lower in Morocco, it would be quite reasonable to point out that the product was of a different quality (although the difference in variable costs is only €2.70 between the two grades of product, suggesting that the quality difference is not very great).

Would the company suffer if it became known that it was offering a product of lesser quality? This is a factor that needs to be borne in mind by producers of high quality goods. However, as noted above, the quality differential is not likely to be very noticeable.

In the circumstances, the company should consider seriously accepting Raoul's order, although the sales director might like to investigate Raoul's assertions regarding the Moroccan market. Is it really true that there would be few buyers in Morocco at the company's normal prices? Or is Raoul just saying this to beat the company down on price?

6.13 Inez & Pilar Fashions

Because fixed costs increase with the increase in production capacity, it is necessary to look at the level of incremental profits that could be made. We can examine these at two levels:

Optimistic incremental sales forecast

	€
Sales (€345 000 – 310 000)	35 000
Incremental variable costs: €35 000 × 30%	(10 500)
Incremental fixed costs	(15 000)
Incremental net profit	9 500

Pessimistic incremental sales forecast

	€
Sales	20 000
Incremental variable costs: €20 000 × 30%	(6 000)
Incremental fixed costs	(15 000)
Incremental net loss	(1 000)

Clearly, if the pessimistic forecast is accurate, a net loss will be incurred by expanding the production facilities. However, at most levels of incremental sales some profit would be made. Unless the directors are very averse to taking risks, and/or they feel that the pessimistic forecast is the most likely outcome, it is probably worth expanding production facilities.

Other factors to take into account would be:

- Could the additional capacity be used to produce new product lines?
- Is the current constraint on production capacity causing problems with customers? (If customers are becoming impatient because of delays in production there may be a loss of goodwill; this could be an argument in favour of expanding the facilities even if there is a small risk of an incremental loss.)

6.14   Juniper Jefferson

i) Contribution per unit of limiting factor

	De Luxe	Super De Luxe
	€	€
Selling price	150	165
Variable cost of raw materials		
Aluminium (at €8.50 per kg)	(38.25)	(42.50)
Other raw materials	(12.50)	(15.00)
Variable cost of labour	(13.65)	(15.60)
Contribution per unit	85.60	91.90
Kilos of material used		
De Luxe (€38.25/8.50)	4.5	
Super De Luxe (€42.50/8.50)		5.0
Contribution per unit of limiting factor	85.60/4.5 = €19.02	91.90/5 = €18.38

ii) Production plan
The directors should follow a production plan that produces the De Luxe model in preference to the Super De Luxe, where possible.
   The availability of the raw material in the next three months is:

	kg
Already in stock	350
3 month's purchases	3000
	3350

If all of this material were to be used in the production of De Luxe buggies, it would be possible to make 3350/4.5 = 744 De Luxe buggies (rounded down to the nearest whole number).

a) If demand for the De Luxe is 800 units, then it makes sense to turn production over completely to the production of the De Luxe (800>744).

b) If demand for the De Luxe is 600 units, then the maximum 600 should be produced. This would mean using 600 x 4.5kg = 2700kg of the scarce raw material, leaving 3350 – 2700 = 650kg for producing Super De Luxe buggies.

So 650kg would produce 650/5 = 130 Super De Luxe buggies at a rate of usage of 5kg per buggy. The production plan would thus be:

De Luxe = 600
Super De Luxe = 130.

Chapter 7

Answers to self-test questions

7.1   **1** Formula for €1 invested at 8% over 4 years:
€1 $\times$ $(1.08)^4$
Compounding factor = $(1.08) \times (1.08) \times (1.08) \times (1.08)$ = 1.360

2 Formula for €1 invested at 7% over 5 years:
€1 $\times$ $(1.07)^5$
Compounding factor = $(1.07) \times (1.07) \times (1.07) \times (1.07) \times (1.07)$ = 1.403

3 Formula for €1 invested at 6% over 6 years:
€1 $\times$ $(1.06)^6$
Compounding factor = $(1.06) \times (1.06) \times (1.06) \times (1.06) \times (1.06) \times (1.06)$ = 1.419

7.2   **1** Present value (PV) at Time 0 of €1 at the end of year 3 at a discount rate of 2%:

$$PV = €1 \times \frac{1}{(1.02)^3}$$

$$\text{Discounting factor} = \frac{1}{(1.02)} \times \frac{1}{(1.02)} \times \frac{1}{(1.02)}$$
$$= 0.942$$

2 Present value (PV) at Time 0 of €1 at the end of year 5 at a discount rate of 4%:

$$PV = €1 \times \frac{1}{(1.04)^5}$$

$$\text{Discounting factor} = \frac{1}{(1.04)} \times \frac{1}{(1.04)} \times \frac{1}{(1.04)} \times \frac{1}{(1.04)} \times \frac{1}{(1.04)}$$
$$= 0.822$$

3 Present value (PV) at Time 0 of €1 at the end of year 2 at a discount rate of 9%.

$$PV = €1 \times \frac{1}{(1.09)^2}$$

$$\text{Discounting factor} = 1 \times \frac{1}{(1.09)} \times \frac{1}{(1.09)}$$
$$= 0.842$$

Answers to self-assessment exercises

7.1   The €15 000 spent on the initial land survey is irrelevant to the business decision because the expenditure has already been made. This is an example of a sunk cost; the correct answer, therefore, is c).

7.2   Mellor & Ribchester

i) ARR calculations

$$\frac{\text{Average expected return (accounting profit)}}{\text{Average capital employed}} \times 100 = \text{ARR\%}$$

€150 000 of non-current asset expenditure, depreciated over 6 years on a straight line basis, results in an annual depreciation charge of €150 000/6 = €25 000. This must be taken into account in calculating accounting profit.

Year	€000
1	0 − 25 = (25)
2	68 − 25 = 43
3	71 − 25 = 46
4	54 − 25 = 29
5	28 − 25 = 3
6	10 − 25 = (15)
Total profit	81

The average profit per year generated is:

$$\frac{€81\ 000}{6} = €13\ 500$$

Time	€000
0	150
6	0
Average	150/2 = 75

$$ARR = \frac{€13\ 500}{75\ 000} \times 100 = 18\%$$

ii) Payback period

Time	Cash flow €000	Cumulative cash flow €000
0	(150)	(150)
1	0	(150)
2	68	(82)
3	71	(11)
4	54	43
5	28	71
6	10	81

Cumulative cash flow reaches the zero position sometime during the fourth year. Payback to the nearest month is:

3 years + (11/54 × 12 months) = 3 years and 2 months (to nearest whole month).

Note: the cash inflows in this example do not start until the second year. This does not change the methods of working out ARR or payback.

7.3   The compounding factor for an investment over 4 years at 3% per year is:
$(1.03)^4 = (1.03) \times (1.03) \times (1.03) \times (1.03) = 1.126$. The correct answer, therefore, is d).

7.4   The compounding factor is: $(1.06)^4 = 1.263$.
$1.263 \times €312 = €394$ (to the nearest €). The correct answer, therefore, is a).

7.5   The discounting factor is:

$$\frac{1}{(1.1)^3} = 0.751$$

The correct answer, therefore, is b).

7.6   The correct discount factor (from tables) is: 0.567.
PV of €1300 receivable at the end of year 5, assuming a constant discount rate of 12% is:

€1300 × 0.567 = €737 (to nearest €).

The correct answer, therefore, is d).

7.7   Naylor Coulthard

Calculation of NPV of the advertising promotion project

Time	Cash flow €	Discount factor (from table)	Discounted cash flow €
0	(250 000)	1	(250 000)
1	196 000	0.917	179 732
2	168 000	0.842	141 456
TOTAL			71 188

The NPV is positive which suggests that the project should be accepted.

7.8   *i) NPV at 12% cost of capital*

Time	Cash flow €	Discount factor (from table)	Discounted cash flow €
0	(680 000)	1	(680 000)
1	180 000	0.893	160 740
2	200 000	0.797	159 400
3	240 000	0.712	170 880
4	350 000	0.636	222 600
			33 620

ii) IRR
12% cost of capital produces a positive NPV. The IRR (the point at which NPV = 0) must therefore be higher than this. Calculating NPV at 16%:

Time	Cash flow €	Discount factor (from table)	Discounted cash flow €
0	(680 000)	1	(680 000)
1	180 000	0.862	155 160
2	200 000	0.743	148 600
3	240 000	0.641	153 840
4	350 000	0.552	193 200
			(29 200)

IRR must, therefore, lie somewhere between 12% and 16%.

Using a discount rate of 12% NPV = €33 620
Using a discount rate of 16% NPV = €−29 200.

The total distance between these two figures is €33 620 + 29 200 = €62 820.
Expressed diagramatically:

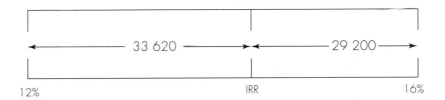

The distance between 12% and IRR is $\dfrac{33\ 620}{62\ 820} \times 4\% = 2.14\%$

IRR is 12% + 2.14% = 14.14%
(NB: the IRR according to computer calculation is 14.07%.)

7.9 Sunbed investment project

i) NPV at 14% cost of capital

Time	Cash flow £	Discount factor (from table)	Discounted cash flow £
0	(180 000)	1	(180 000)
1	46 000	0.877	40 342
2	46 000	0.769	35 374
3	46 000	0.675	31 050
4	46 000	0.592	27 232
5	46 000 + 15 000	0.519	31 659
			(14 343)

ii) IRR

14% cost of capital produces a negative NPV. The IRR (the point at which NPV = 0) must therefore be lower than this. Calculating NPV at 10%:

Time	Cash flow £	Discount factor (from table)	Discounted cash flow £
0	(180 000)	1	(180 000)
1	46 000	0.909	41 814
2	46 000	0.826	37 996
3	46 000	0.751	34 546
4	46 000	0.683	31 418
5	46 000 + 15 000	0.621	37 881
			3 655

IRR must, therefore, lie somewhere between 10% and 14% (but much nearer to 10% than to 14%).

Using a discount rate of 10% NPV = £3 655
Using a discount rate of 14% NPV = £−14 343.

The total distance between these two figures is £3 655 + 14 343 = £17 998

The distance between 10% and IRR is $\dfrac{3\ 655}{17\ 998} \times 4\% = 0.81\%$

IRR is 10% + 0.81% = 10.81%
(NB: the IRR according to computer calculation is 10.77%.)

iii) On the basis of the results of the NPV and IRR calculations it appears that the directors should not make the investment in the sunbeds. The company's cost of capital is 14% and this investment falls well short of that target.

However, the directors may consider other factors in making their decision. For example:

● How important is it to the future of the business that it diversifies its range of services? Will the hairdressing business continue to produce strong returns? If there is some uncertainty, it may make sense to diversify.

● Are competitors offering sunbeds? If they are, the existing hairdressing business could be damaged if Outhwaite Benson does not do the same.

● Is it possible that the provision of the sunbed service will attract new customers who may also use the hairdressing services? If so has this potential for additional sales been taken into account in the projected cash flow figures?

Finally, how reliable are the estimates? If the projected cash flows are put into a spreadsheet the directors can perform a series of 'what if' calculations to test out various levels of projection (optimistic, pessimistic, average).

Chapter 8

Answers to self-assessment exercises

8.1   Subject: Summary of the benefits of effective budgeting
To: The directors of Brewster Fitzpayne
From: Management accountant
A budgeting system assists senior management in its tasks of planning and controlling business activity by ensuring that a detailed plan is laid out and quantified for a specified period (usually one year). The budget should help the company to attain its longer-term objectives, and it is important to ensure that there is a clear relationship between the budget and the longer-term business strategy determined by the directors.

Budgets allow for coordinated efforts on the part of all personnel and departments. Once the key elements of the budget have been determined (usually starting with the sales budget) budget guidelines can be issued to all departments and managerial staff. They will then be required to submit draft budgets for their own areas. Senior management must then ensure that these drafts are amended where necessary to ensure proper coordination of plans. Senior staff have an overview of the business objectives and should be able to ensure that individual budgets mesh together to achieve optimal outcomes.

If properly used, budgets can inspire and motivate staff to greater efforts. It is important that staff lower down the hierarchy feel a sense of 'ownership' of the budget so that they will be more inclined to make the extra effort to achieve targets.

Actual business performance should be monitored carefully against budget. If this is done properly and on a timely basis, senior managers are able to control operations much more effectively than is possible without a budget. Timely and effective control allows for higher quality decision-making.

Finally, it is possible to use budgets as a basis for individual and group performance evaluation. For example, sales staff could be rewarded by means of bonuses or extra commission for exceeding budget targets. This use of budgets must be handled carefully, however. If targets for achievement are set too high then dissatisfaction and demotivation may well result.

8.2   Pirozhki Products.
The forecast for opening inventory at 1 March 2009 is 75% of forecast sales in March:

75% × 12 000 units = 9 000 units

The forecast for closing inventory at 31 March 2009 is 75% of forecast sales in April:

75% × 14 800 units = 11 100 units.

Transfers out of finished goods inventory will be 12 000 units in March (i.e. the quantity sold), so production required is:

	€
Opening inventory	9 000
Production (bal. fig.)	14 100
Transfers out of inventory	(12 000)
Closing inventory	11 100

The correct answer, therefore, is b).

8.3   Luminant Productions

a) *Production budget July–September 2009*

	Opening inventory: units	Production: units	Transfers out of production (for sales): units	Closing inventory: units
July	6000	8100	(8600)	5500
August	5500	7700	(8200)	5000
September	5000	8500	(9000)	4500

b) *Raw materials purchases budget: July–September 2009*

Closing inventory + Raw materials used in production – Opening inventory
  = Raw materials purchases

	Opening inventory of raw material €	Purchases of raw materials (bal. fig.) €	Raw materials used in production €	Closing inventory of raw material €
July	2 800	16 400	€2 × 8 100 = €16 200	3 000
August	3 000	15 500	€2 × 7 700 = €15 400	3 100
September	3 100	17 100	€2 × 8 500 = €17 000	3 200

8.4   Barfield Primrose

Budget overhead recovery rate, based on machine hours:

$$\frac{\text{Budget production overheads}}{\text{Machine hours}} = \frac{312\ 390}{17\ 355} = €18.00 \text{ per machine hour}$$

The total production cost of one ice cream maker is, therefore:

	€
Prime cost	61.00
1.5 machine hours × €18.00 per hour	27.00
Production cost	88.00

Barfield Primrose: Budgeted income statement for three months ending 31 March 2009

	Jan €	Feb €	March €
Sales	620 × €145 = 89 900	610 × €145 = 88 450	640 × €145 = 92 800
Cost of sales (= production cost)	620 × €88 = (54 560)	610 × €88 = (53 680)	640 × €88 = (56 320)
Gross profit	35 340	34 770	36 480
Admin and selling expenses	(18 400)	(19 250)	(18 900)
Net profit	16 940	15 520	17 580

8.5 In February Reinhart's budget sales receipts will be estimated as follows:

	€
In respect of sales made in January: 75% × €21 000	15 750
In respect of sales made in December: 25% × €26 800	6 700
Total	22 450

The correct answer, therefore, is c).

8.6 Skippy's tour operating business

i) Budget cash flow

Skippy: Budget cash flow statement for January–March 2009

	January €	February €	March €	Total €
Receipts				
Trip 1	25 440	–	–	25 440
Trip 2	–	25 440	–	25 440
	25 440	25 440		50 880
Payments				
Hotel: Trip 1	7 140	7 140	–	14 280
Trip 2	–	7 140	7 140	14 280
Coach	2 600	2 600	–	5 200
Insurance bond: 2 × €1 500	3 000		–	3 000
Phone bill	–	–	360	360
Office expenses	200	200	200	600
Total payments	12 940	17 080	7 700	37 720
Opening balance	0	12 500	20 860	
Add: receipts	25 440	25 440	–	
Less: payments	(12 940)	(17 080)	(7 700)	
Closing balance	12 500	20 860	13 160	

ii) Budget income statement

Skippy: Budget income statement for the three months ending 31 March 2009

	€
Sales	50 880
Expenses	
Hotel costs (€14 280 × 2)	28 560
Coach	5 200
Insurance bonds	3 000
Phone	360
Office costs	600
Advertising	3 000
Computer depreciation: €2 000 × 20% = 400 – for 3 months =	100
	40 820
Net profit	10 060

iii) Budget balance sheet

Skippy: Budget balance sheet at
31 March 2009

	€
Computer at cost	2 000
Less: accumulated depreciation	(100)
Net book value	1 900
Cash at bank	13 160
	15 060
Capital introduced	5 000
Profit	10 060
	15 060

Note that capital introduced by Skippy consists of the advertising expenditure paid for before January 2009 (€3000) and the computer (€2000).

8.7 Skippy's tour operating business

Working 1: Actual sales

	€
Trip 1: 42 × €530	22 260
Trip 2: 50 × €530	26 500
	48 760

Working 2: Hotel costs

	€
Trip 1: 42 × 7 nights × €42.50 per person	12 495
Trip 2: 50 × 7 nights × €42.50 per person	14 875
	27 370

Skippy: Actual and budgeted income statement for the three months ending 31 March 2009

	Actual €	Budget €	Variance €
Sales (working 1)	48 760	50 880	(2 120)
Expenses			
Hotel costs (working 2)	27 370	28 560	1 190
Coach	5 200	5 200	–
Insurance bonds	3 000	3 000	–
Phone	455	360	(95)
Office costs (€230 + €350 + €270)	850	600	(250)
Advertising	3 000	3 000	–
Computer depreciation: €2000 × 20% = 400 – for 3 months = €100	100	100	–
	39 975	40 820	845
Net profit	8 785	10 060	(1 275)

* Variance is the term used in costing for differences between actual and budget figures. Adverse variances are shown in brackets in the comparison and favourable variances are shown without brackets. Variances are examined in more detail in Chapter 9.

Skippy: Actual and budgeted balance sheet at 31 March 2009

	Actual €	Budget €
Computer at cost	2 000	2 000
Less: accumulated depreciation	(100)	(100)
Net book value	1 900	1 900
Cash at bank (see working 3)	11 885	13 160
	13 785	15 060
Capital introduced	5 000	5 000
Profit	8 785	10 060
	13 785	15 060

Working 3: Actual cash at bank

	€	€
Receipts (same as sales revenue)		48 760
Payments	39 975	
Less: depreciation (non-cash item)	(100)	
Less: advertising paid for by Skippy	(3 000)	
		(36 875)
		11 885

Overall, Skippy's business has performed slightly worse than budget: actual sales are 95.8% of budget, but there has been a related saving on hotel costs which helps to offset the variance. Office and telephone costs are higher than budgeted. However, overall, the differences are fairly minor and Skippy is likely to be quite pleased with his first three months in business.

8.8 Lamar Bristol plc

This is a relatively efficient approach to budget setting. While some external research into competitors' sales figures and general economic conditions is required, the resource input to the research process is unlikely to be extensive. Because the budget is market led it is based upon economic reality, and is therefore quite likely to provide a realistic target for stores.

However, there are some problems with this approach. It is incremental in that it builds upon the sales budget for the previous year. However, if this budget amount was less than could have been achieved with greater effort, the directors approach to budgeting does not question or challenge it.

It ignores differences between stores. Some stores will struggle more than others to achieve this across the board target because of, for example, local competition which is stronger in some locations than others. A percentage increase that is easily achievable by one store might be impossible for another. A further problem is likely to arise if store managers' remuneration is linked to performance. If a store manager is set a target that is impossible to achieve, resulting in no bonus payment, he or she is likely to feel resentful and demotivated.

Chapter 9

Answers to self-test questions

9.1   Bridge and Blige

i) Flexed budget for 900 units

	€
Sales: 900 units @ €35	31 500
Costs:	
Direct materials: 900 units × (2kg × €6)	(10 800)
Direct labour: 900 units × (1 hour × €7.50)	(6 750)
Production overheads	(4 000)
	9 950
Selling and administrative overheads	(2 300)
Net profit	7 650

ii) Calculation of variances

Summary of budget, flexed budget and actual statements

	Original budget €	Flexed budget €	Actual €
Sales	28 000	31 500	32 400
Direct materials	(9 600)	(10 800)	(9 405)
Direct labour	(6 000)	(6 750)	(7 560)
Production overhead	(4 000)	(4 000)	(4 400)
	8 400	9 950	11 035
Selling and administrative overhead	(2 300)	(2 300)	(2 450)
Net profit	6 100	7 650	8 585

The overall variance is:

Original budget net profit	6100
Actual net profit	8585
	2485 (F)

Sales profit volume variance

This variance is the difference between the original budget profit and the flexed budget profit: €6100 – €7650 = €1550. The flexed budget profit is greater than the original budget profit, so this is a favourable variance.

Sales price variance

Actual volume of sales at actual selling price: 900 × €36	€32 400
Less: actual volume of sales at budget selling price: 900 × €35	31 500
Sales price variance	900 (F)

Direct materials variances

Comparing the figure for direct materials in the flexed budget statement with the figure in the actual statement:

Flexed budget for direct materials	€10 800
Actual direct materials	9 405
	€ 1 395 (F)

Direct materials price variance

We compare:

The actual quantity of materials used at the price actually paid (actual price).

The actual quantity of materials used at the price budgeted (standard price).

Actual quantity at actual price	
1.9kg was used for each of 900 casings: actual quantity	
used is 1.9kg × 900 = 1 710kg.	
1 710kg × price actually paid (€5.50)	9 405
Actual quantity at standard price	
1 710kg × standard price (€6.00)	10 260
Direct materials price variance	855 (F)

Direct materials quantity variance

We compare:

The actual quantity of materials used at standard price.

The standard quantity of materials used at standard price.

Actual quantity at standard price	
Actual quantity used (already worked out) – 1 710kg	
Standard price per kg – €6	
Actual quantity at standard price = 1 710 × €6	10 260
Standard quantity at standard price	
Standard quantity: 2kg × 900 casings = 1 800kg	
Standard price per kg – €6	
Standard quantity at standard price = 1 800 × €6	10 800
Direct materials quantity variance	540 (F)

In summary, the direct materials variances are:

Direct materials price variance	855 (F)
Direct materials quantity variance	540 (F)
Direct materials variance	1395 (F)

Direct labour variances

Comparing the figure for direct labour in the flexed budget statement with the figure in the actual statement:

Flexed budget for direct labour	€6 750
Actual direct labour	7 560
	€ 810 (A)

Direct labour rate variance

We compare:

The actual hours of direct labour used at the wage rate actually paid (actual rate).

The actual hours of direct labour used at the wage rate budgeted (standard rate).

Actual hours at actual rate	
Actual hours was 1.2 hours for each of 900 casings:	
1.2 × 900 = 1080 hours	
1080 hours × rate actually paid (€7.00)	7560
Actual hours at standard rate	
1080 hours × standard rate (€7.50)	8100
Direct labour rate variance	540 (F)

Direct labour efficiency variance

We compare:

The actual hours of direct labour used at standard rate.

The standard hours of direct labour used at standard rate.

Actual hours at standard rate	
Actual hours used (already worked out) – 1080 hours	
Standard rate per hour – €7.50	
Actual hours at standard rate = 1080 × €7.50	8100
Standard hours at standard rate	
Standard hours: 1 hour × 900 = 900	
Standard rate per hour – €7.50	
Standard hours at standard rate = 900 × €7.50	6750
Direct labour efficiency variance	1350 (A)

In summary, the direct labour variances are:

Direct labour rate variance	€ 540 (F)
Direct labour efficiency variance	1350 (A)
Direct labour variance	€ 810 (A)

Production overhead variance

Budget figure for production overhead:	4000
Actual figure for production overhead:	4400
Production overhead variance	(400) (A)

Selling and administrative overhead variance

Budget figure for selling and administrative overhead:	2300
Actual figure for selling and administrative overhead:	2450
Selling and administrative overhead variance	(150) (A)

ii) Bridge and Blige: standard cost operating statement for February 2009

	Favourable €	(Adverse) €	Total €
Original budgeted net profit			6100
Sales profit volume variance			1550
Flexed budget net profit			7650
Other variances			
Sales price variance	900		
Direct materials price variance	855		
Direct materials quantity variance	540		
Direct labour rate variance	540		
Direct labour efficiency variance		(1350)	
Production overhead variance		(400)	
Selling and administrative overhead variance		(150)	
Total	2835	(1900)	935
Actual net profit			8585

9.2   Singh and Waterhouse

i) Flexed budget for 2000 units

	€
Sales: 2 000 × €45	90 000
Costs:	
Direct materials: 2 000 × (16 metres × €1)	(32 000)
Direct labour: 2 000 × (2 hours × €5.00)	(20 000)
Variable production overheads: 2 000 units × (2 machine hours per unit × €1)	(4 000)
Fixed production overheads: 2 000 units × (2 machine hours per unit x €6)	(24 000)
Profit before other overheads	10 000

ii) Variance calculations

First of all, we will set the original budget, flexed budget and actual side by side:

	Original budget €	Flexed budget €	Actual €
Sales	81 000	90 000	90 000
Direct materials	(28 800)	(32 000)	(32 000)
Direct labour	(18 000)	(20 000)	(20 000)
Variable production overhead	(3 600)	(4 000)	(3 800)
Fixed production overhead	(21 600)	(24 000)	(23 400)
	9 000	10 000	10 800

The overall variance is:

Original budget net profit	9 000
Actual net profit	10 800
	1 800 (F)

Sales profit volume variance

This variance is the difference between the original budget profit and the flexed budget profit: €9000 − 10 000 = €1000 (F). The variance is favourable because the flexed budget profit is higher than the original budget profit.

There are no variances for sales price, direct material, direct labour and selling and administrative overheads. Once the budget is flexed, it becomes clear that sales prices, direct material and direct labour costs are exactly as would have been predicted if 2000 units had been budgeted for.

Variable production overhead variance

The overall variance can be calculated in the same way as, say, the total direct materials variance: by comparing the totals in the flexed budget statement with the actual statement:

Flexed budget for variable overhead   €4000
Actual variable overhead   3800

€ 200 (F)

Fixed production overhead variance

The overall variance is calculated in the same way as by comparing the totals in the flexed budget statement with the actual statement:

Flexed budget for fixed overhead   €24 000
Actual fixed overhead   23 400

€ 600 (F)

iii)   Singh and Waterhouse: standard cost operating statement for April 2009

	Favourable €	(Adverse) €	Total €
Original budgeted net profit			9 000
Sales profit volume variance			1 000
Flexed budget net profit			10 000
Other variances			
Sales price variance	–	–	
Direct materials price variance	–	–	
Direct materials quantity variance	–	–	
Direct labour rate variance	–	–	
Direct labour efficiency variance	–	–	
Variable overhead variance	200	–	
Fixed overhead variance	600		
Selling and administrative overhead variance	–	–	
Total	800	–	800
Actual net profit			10 800

Answers to self-assessment exercises

9.1   Stalkompania

March 2009: budget for XP04/H flexed for 1300 units

	zl
Sales: 1 300 units × zl30 per unit	39 000
Direct materials: 1 300 units × (3kg × zl1.20)	4 680
Direct labour: 1 300 units × (2 hours × zl8.50)	22 100
Prime cost	26 780

9.2   Darblé et Cie

November 2009: budget flexed for 2600 units

	€
Sales: 2 600 units × €19.50	50 700
Direct materials: 2 600 × (2 metres × €2.00)	(10 400)
Direct labour: 2 600 × (1 hour × €6.00)	(15 600)
Production overhead	(10 000)
	14 700
Selling and administrative overhead	(3 000)
Net profit	11 700

The correct answer, therefore, is c).

Edwards and Sheerness: general information for the answers to questions 9.3 to 9.8:

Flexed budget for 2650 units

	€
Sales: 2 650 units × €29.00	76 850
Direct materials: 2 650 × (3 kg × €3.00)	(23 850)
Direct labour: 2 650 × (1.5 hours × €4.40)	(17 490)
Production overhead	(17 000)
	18 510
Other overheads	(3 500)
Net profit	15 010

Comparison of original budget, flexed budget and actual:

	Original budget €	Flexed budget €	Actual €
Sales	72 500	76 850	74 200
Direct materials	(22 500)	(23 850)	(24 486)
Direct labour	(16 500)	(17 490)	(18 921)
Production overhead	(17 000)	(17 000)	(16 900)
	16 500	18 510	13 893
Other overheads	(3 500)	(3 500)	(3 600)
Net profit	13 000	15 010	10 293

9.3   Sales profit volume variance

Flexed budget net profit   15 010
Original budget net profit   13 000
                               ─────────
                               2 010 (F)

The correct answer, therefore, is d).

9.4   Sales price variance

Actual volume of sales at actual selling price: 2 650 × €28   74 200
Actual volume of sales at standard selling price: 2 650 × €29   76 850
                                                                ─────────
                                                                2 650 (A)

The correct answer, therefore, is d).

9.5   Direct materials price variance

Actual quantity of materials used at actual price:
    2 650 × 2.8kg = 7 420 × €3.30   24 486
Actual quantity of materials used at standard price: 7 420 × €3.00 22 260
                                                                   ─────────
                                                                   2 226 (A)

The correct answer, therefore, is b).

9.6   Direct materials quantity variance

Actual quantity of materials used at standard price: 7 420 × €3.00   22 260
Standard quantity of materials used at standard price:
    2 650 × 3.0kg = 7 950 × €3.00   23 850
                                                                    ─────────
                                                                    1 590 (F)

The correct answer, therefore, is c).

9.7   Direct labour rate variance

Actual hours at actual wage rate: 2 650 × 1.7hrs = 4 505 × €4.20   18 921
Actual hours at standard wage rate: 4 505 × €4.40   19 822
                                                                   ─────────
                                                                     901 (F)

The correct answer, therefore, is d).

9.8   Direct labour efficiency variance

Actual hours at standard wage rate: 4 505 × €4.40   19 822
Standard hours at standard wage rate:
    2 650 × 1.5hrs = 3 975 × €4.40   17 490
                                                        ─────────
                                                        2 332 (A)

The correct answer, therefore, is b).

9.9 Ordoñez and Fernando

i) Total variable production overhead variance

	€
Actual variable production overhead	26 250
Flexed budget variable production overhead	25 200
	1 050 (A)

ii) Total fixed production overhead expenditure variance

	€
Actual fixed production overhead	48 750
Flexed budget fixed production overhead	50 400
	1 650 (F)

9.10 WNZH

i) The variances which are regarded as significant according to the company's 5% criterion are:

Direct materials price variance (Yuan 1 650 000 (A) – 5.8% of flexed budget)

Variable production overhead variance (Yuan 1 400 000 (F) – 16.2% of flexed budget).

ii) Possible reasons for the variances:

Direct materials price variance

Successful negotiation for lower prices

Obtaining quantity discounts for large orders

Variation in material quality

Volatile market for material, leading to unexpected increases or decrease in price.

Variable production overhead variance

Price changes because of events in the wider economy

Improved management control over costs.

It is also possible in this case (the variance being so large) that some items of expense have simply gone unrecorded.

iii) Actual figures can be derived from the information given by adding the flexible budget amount to the variances, as follows:

	Yuan 000
Sales 123 470 + 1 030	124 500
Direct materials: 28 250 + 1 650 + 106	(30 006)
Direct labour: 29 900 – 200	(29 700)
Variable production overheads: 8 640 – 1 400	(7 240)
Fixed production overheads: 19 780 – 339	(19 441)
Actual profit	38 113

9.11 BLP Limited

i) In the early life of a business, when the number of employees is small and the directors of the business keep close personal control over all activities, social or clan mechanisms are likely to be important. As the business grows, the nature of control is likely to change as senior managers become remote and have less knowledge of the day to day operations of the business. Bureaucratic controls are likely to be found more useful as the business grows larger. Control through price, or markets, is important wherever such prices are available. The function of purchasing should involve some element of market control. In the case of BLP's purchasing officer, this control has obviously been circumvented, and it seems likely that the control environment will be improved by some form of bureaucratic control.

ii) Establishing standard costs for materials purchases will require the involvement of people other than the purchasing department. It is likely that management accounting staff will be involved, and this involvement will, in itself, be a useful preventive control. It means that people other than those directly involved in purchasing are aware of market prices for materials and so it will be more difficult to perpetrate a materials price fraud. Once the standard is established, the investigation of variances should mean that a consistent pattern of purchasing at inflated prices becomes evident to managers outside the purchasing department. A fraud of the type described could be identified by careful examination of the causes of variances. Such frauds are also likely to be prevented if employees in the purchasing department know that their actions will be subject to scrutiny. However, managers need to be prepared to examine even quite small variances; if employees know that only variances larger than a rule-of-thumb figure (e.g. 5% of the budget amount) will be closely scrutinised, then it would be quite possible to organise a fraud that would not be picked up by the control.

9.12   Bellcraft

Expense and bureaucracy

It is undeniably the case that standard costing systems involve some expense. However, the benefits of any good system should outweigh the costs. It will be important to monitor the costs of implementing the system to make sure that they do not get out of hand. Quantifying the benefits of the system is not easy, but better control should ultimately result in benefits such as improved profitability, less wastage and reduced storage costs. The system is bureaucratic in that it involves the production of reports. However, the quantity of information could be reduced by using an exception reporting basis.

Lack of timeliness

This has traditionally been a problem associated with standard costing systems, especially where reporting is normally done on a monthly basis. However, reporting can be done much more frequently than that, especially now that computer capacity has increased so much. We could aim for weekly, or even more frequent, reporting of variances so that timeliness is not a problem. Even if there is a passage of time between events and their reporting, it does not have to mean that variance investigation is useless. The cause of the variance can be identified, and remedial action taken to ensure that its causes are tackled.

Chapter 10

Answers to self-test questions

10.1   ● Average price per room sold as a percentage of rack rate (NB rack rate is the full published price of a hotel room, before deduction of any discounts).

- Occupancy rate (number of rooms actually occupied as a percentage of the total rooms available).
- Average revenue per customer from provision of additional services.

10.2 Statements 1, 3 and 4 are TRUE.
Statement 2 is FALSE.

10.3 The divisional management of Beta appears to have considerable autonomy over its operations, including control over investment strategy. This indicates that Beta is an investment centre.

10.4 In any business, appropriate non-financial measures of success are those that relate to the overall business strategy. There is a contradiction hidden in HB's business objective: it wants to lead the market, which implies a greater market share than its competitors. On the other hand, it also aims to provide exclusive products, that is luxury products that people can own, safe in the knowledge that they belong to an elite. This contradiction epitomises the luxury goods business. Of the five performance indicators listed, all except the fifth are likely to be appropriate. Market share (1) and sales volume (3) relate directly to the strategic objective of leading the market. Defective product items (2) relates to the objective of supplying high quality items. Customer perceptions of exclusivity (4) again links directly to the business strategy. However, competitive pricing (5) is not really an issue. In the luxury goods business, the perception of exclusivity is likely to be assisted by high prices.

Answer to self-assessment exercises

10.1 Three key characteristics of management information:

1 It should be produced quickly so that managers can respond rapidly to it.
2 It should be useful, and easily comprehensible.
3 The cost of producing the information should not outweigh its benefits.

10.2 Golfstore Retail plc
The advantages of divisionalisation for this company include the following:
Divisions based on regions or (eventually) countries in Western Europe will ensure that management can exploit local opportunities that might not come to the attention of head office management. For example, a regional management team should be better aware of the trading conditions in their area, and if, say, a new golf course is planned for a particular town, they could ensure that a new store is opened in the area.
Divisionalisation can result in better motivated managers. This can be enhanced if senior divisional managers are rewarded at least partly on the basis of results achieved. A degree of competition between divisions can be healthy and productive.
In this particular case, the company is beginning to expand. If divisionalisation is instituted now along a geographical split within the UK, a pattern is established which could make the addition of future divisions within Europe relatively straightforward.

10.3 Division Alpha is a profit centre.

10.4   a) Quarterly divisional performance statement for BD

	€000
Sales	1671
Less: variable costs (280 + 311)	(591)
Contribution	1080
Less: Controllable fixed costs (580 − 37)	(543)
Controllable profit	537
Less: Non-controllable fixed costs (37 + 112)	(149)
Divisional profit before allocation of head office costs	388
Head office cost allocation	(337)
Divisional profit before tax	51

b) The division's performance should be judged on the basis of the amount of profit over which it has control. Controllable profit is €537 000.

10.5   1 Transfer pricing can have an impact on divisional performance. Where divisions sell goods to each other, it is necessary to identify an appropriate price for the goods. The level of price affects the allocation of profit between divisions and so may affect profit-related remuneration. Where it is difficult to agree realistic transfer prices divisions have an incentive to source goods from outside the company and in this case the profit goes outside the company. If divisional performance is affected by transfer pricing agreements, there is a knock-on effect on the Return on Investment measurement.

2 The calculation of Return on Investment can also be affected by the valuation of net assets. Higher asset valuation results in a lower ROI. For this reason, managers may be reluctant to replace worn out non-current assets.

10.6   Tripp and Hopp Limited
Both financial and non-financial performance indicators should relate to the company's strategic plans. The company's objective relates to the provision of a service, so its performance indicators should be service-oriented.

There are many possible ways of measuring the company's progress in meeting its objectives. The table below suggests some possible performance indicators, and ways of measuring them.

Aspect of service	Performance indicator	Measurement
Competitive	Price of service (e.g. commission charged)	Comparison with competitors' commission arrangements.
Competitive	Customer satisfaction	Could be measured using a questionnaire on the website, or a follow up survey.
Efficient	Number of complaints	Website link to a complaints form. Monitoring number of complaints and outcomes.
Efficient	Speed of transaction	Measure speed of each transaction on the website, and compare.
Efficient	Ease of use by customer	Could be measured using a questionnaire on the website, or a follow up survey.
Secure	Number of security breaches over a given period	Could be measured by analysing customer complaints.

10.7   Brookmaye

The issue of transfer pricing has arisen because of the change in the company's reward structure for its divisional managers. Presumably, the manager of Plastics was indifferent previously to the level of transfer price because it did not affect him directly. Under the new arrangements, however, profits are recorded in the Materials Assembly division and the manager of that division will benefit personally.

Cost-plus transfer prices are sometimes used in practice. Adoption of this method would result in Plastics division receiving a share of the profit, as represented by the 10% on cost. This method has the benefits of reliability and relative ease of administration. However, it is not without its problems. Under this method the manager of Plastics would have no incentive to control costs; in fact the reverse would be true as the 10% add-on would gain in value as costs rose. It could result in Plastics taking an unfairly large share of the available profit to the detriment of Materials Assembly, and could cause demotivation in the latter division's management.

10.8   Memo

To: Head of Department

Balanced scorecard

The Balanced Scorecard (BS) is a summary of management information that is used by managers to examine the performance of the business. The BS contains four dimensions relating to the fundamentals of a particular business. Any business that uses it has to ask the following questions:

How do customers see us? (The customer perspective.)

What must we excel at? (The internal perspective.)

Can we continue to improve and create value? (The innovation and learning perspective.)

How do we look to shareholders? (The financial perspective.)

The business needs to establish goals in respect of each of the four perspectives, and related performance measures that will help management in judging progress towards the goals. This may all seem fairly complicated, and it would certainly involve quite a lot of work up-front, but it results in a way of reporting useful and relevant performance measures concisely. Incidentally, some of the performance measures (although not necessarily all of them) would involve the use of figures.

Brian is quite right – the BS system has been adopted by very large numbers of US, European and Australian companies. The aeroplane analogy comes from the originators of the BS (two American academics: Robert Kaplan and David Norton). They compared running a business to flying an aeroplane: both pilots and managers need information about all sorts of measurements to be clearly set out in front of them.

I hope this explanation helps. There are several detailed sources of information on the subject of the BS – books, articles and websites. Let me know if you'd like any references.

Glossary

Absorption costing the costing of products and services to include both direct and indirect costs of production

Activity-based costing a costing system used in both service and manufacturing industries, and in both the private and public sectors, which identifies overhead costs as closely as possible with the drivers of cost, i.e. the different activities that take place in the organisation

Adverse variance an unfavourable difference between a budget figure and an actual figure (in terms of sales, an actual figure that is lower than budget; in terms of costs an actual figure that is higher than budget)

Agency theory in the organisational context, this theory proposes a relationship between a principal (the provider of funds) and the agent (the person who manages those funds)

Batch costing the accumulation of costs relating to a batch of identical products

Break-even chart a graph showing lines for costs and revenues, from which the break-even point can be estimated

Break-even point the point at which neither a profit nor a loss is made, i.e. where total costs equal total revenues

Budget a statement, prepared in advance, usually for a specific period (e.g. for one year) of a business's planned activities and financial outcomes

Budgetary slack an adverse effect observable in some businesses where managers deliberately set themselves easily achievable targets

Bureaucracy (in the sense used by Max Weber) a systematic approach to management involving a series of rules and procedures

Capital budgeting the process of decision-making in respect of selecting investment projects, and the amount of capital expenditure to be committed

Capital rationing where a shortage of capital available for investment requires prioritisation of investment projects

Cartel a price-fixing arrangement where a few major suppliers in a market agree between themselves to keep prices high

Contribution the amount which remains after deducting variable costs from sales revenue

Cost accounting the process of identifying and summarising the costs associated with an organisation's operations

Cost and management accounting accounting oriented towards the provision of information resources that managers can use to run the business

Cost centres functions or areas into which costs can be organised

Cost driver in activity-based costing, the various activities that take place in the organisation to which costs are attached

Cost object any product, activity or service that requires costing

Cost of capital the interest rate which is applicable to a particular business

Cost pools in activity-based costing, the accumulation of costs associated with particular activities in the organisation

Cost unit an item of production or a group of products or a service for which it is useful to have product cost information

Demand curve an economic model of the relationship between price and quantity demanded

Depreciation a measurement of the amount of non-current assets value which has been used up during the accounting period (the term usually relates to tangible non-current assets)

Direct costs those costs directly associated with the manufacturing process

Direct expenses direct costs other than direct materials and direct labour costs

Expenses the amounts incurred by the business in purchasing or manufacturing goods sold, and other expenditure on items like rent and telephone charges.

Favourable variance an advantageous difference between a budget figure and an actual figure (in terms of sales, an actual figure that is higher than budget; in terms of costs an actual figure that is lower than budget)

Financial reporting the regular reporting of financial information to interested parties external to the organisation

Finished goods inventory items which have been through a complete manufacturing process and which are now ready for sale

Fixed overhead costs those costs that do not tend to vary directly with increases and decreases in activity in a business

Goal congruence ensures that all divisions within an organisation work together to maximise returns for the organisation as a whole

Hawthorne effect describes the phenomenon, commonly noted in psychological research, where people's behaviour changes when they are under observation as part of a research project

Human relations school in organisation theory, those who emphasise the role of people in organisations, contrasted with the 'mechanical school' of theorists who treat the organisation as a machine

Incremental budgeting budget setting by taking a previous period's budget total and adding a standard percentage increase

Indirect costs those costs which are not directly identifiable with a unit of production

Intellectual capital the resources available to an organisation in the form of, for example, the technical know-how of employees and established relationships with other organisations

Inventory items bought by a business to sell on to somebody else, or to process or transform in some way to make saleable goods

Investment centre a method of divisional organisation where managers are able to control costs, pricing strategy and investment strategy

Job costing an accumulation of costs relating to one identifiable job or task

Joint-stock corporation the precursor to the modern limited liability company

Limiting factors constraints on the level of business activity

Loss leader a product or service which is used to attract customer attention to a range of goods or to a particular supplier

Management accountants specialists in the provision of financial information for use within the business

Management accounting accounting carried out within a business for its own internal uses, to assist management in controlling the business and in making business decisions

Marginal cost the cost of one additional unit

Marginal costing an approach to costing which excludes fixed costs

Margin of safety the excess of planned or actual sales above the breakeven point.

Mechanical school in organisation theory, those who treat the organisation as a machine. This contrasts with the 'human relations school' of theory

Monopoly a market condition where only one supplier supplies the market with a particular good or service

Net present value the aggregate of a set of cash inflows and outflows forecast to take place at future dates, discounted to present values

New Public Management (NPM) the adoption into the public sector of accounting and management techniques that originated in the private sector

Oligopoly a market condition where there are few suppliers (about three to five) of a particular good or service. Typically, the market shares between the suppliers are fairly evenly spread

Opportunity cost in decision-making, the potential benefit that is given up when a particular course of action is taken in preference to an alternative

Overhead absorption a method of allocating an appropriate portion of production overheads to cost units

Overhead absorption rate a rate used to estimate the amount of production overhead incurred in manufacturing

Perfect competition a hypothetical economic condition where no player in a market has the power to change prices

Period costs costs incurred during the accounting period

Present value the discounted value at the present time (i.e. now) of a cash flow expected to arise in the future

Price setter an influential supplier in a market with the power to influence the level of prices for a product or service

Price-skimming occurs where high prices are charged in the early stages of the life of a new product

Price taker a supplier in a market with little or no influence over the level of prices charged for a product or service

Prime cost the total of all direct costs associated with manufacture

Product costing the accumulation of costs relating to the production of a large number of identical units

Product costs those costs relating to the production of goods or services for sale by a business

Profit centre a method of divisional organisation where managers are able to determine pricing strategy and control costs, but do not determine investment strategy.

Raw materials materials which are bought in by a business and then put through a manufacturing process

Relevant range in decision-making, the range of activity within which certain assumptions about cost behaviour remain valid

Responsibility accounting accounting within the business which identifies the person or department responsible for particular outcomes

Return on Investment (ROI) a commonly used method of assessing divisional performance; it expresses divisional net profit as a percentage of the investment in divisional net assets

Revenue the amount of goods and/or services sold in an accounting period by a business, expressed in terms of monetary amounts

Rolling budget a budget which is updated on a regular basis as each period of time (usually one month) elapses

Scientific management a theory of management propounded by Frederick Taylor, sometimes nowadays referred to as 'Taylorism'

Semi-variable cost a cost which varies to some extent with the level of business activity; it has both fixed and variable elements

Stakeholders all those individuals and entities that have a interest in the activities of an organisation: the term includes, for example, shareholders, providers of finance, employees, the general public.

Standard costing a system of costing which attributes consistent costs to elements of production

Strategic management accounting the role played by management accountants and management accounting in strategic decision-making, involving, for example, analysis of markets and the business strategy of competitor organisations

Sunk cost a cost which is irrelevant to a decision, because it has already been incurred

Theory X and Theory Y two models of human behaviour proposed by McGregor. Theory X proposes that people actively dislike working and therefore must be controlled and directed in order to make them work. Theory Y proposes that people are self-motivated, will accept responsibility, and do not need to be threatened or punished to make them work

Transfer pricing the method of pricing sales of goods or services between divisions in an organisation

Utility in an economic context, a measurement of consumption of goods and services. Agency theory assumes that all individuals want to maximise their utility, that is, their ability to consume

Variable cost a cost which varies in proportion to the level of business activity

Zero-based budgeting (ZBB) a budget process that ignores any previous budgets and requires that budgetary allocations must be justified in full by managers

Index